Java

A Beginner's Tutorial

Fourth Edition

Budi Kurniawan

Java : A Beginner's Tutorial
Copyright © 2015 by Brainy Software Inc.
Fourth Edition: January 2015

ISBN: 978-0-9921330-4-7

Book and Cover Designer: Brainy Software Team

Technical Reviewer: Paul Deck
Indexer: Chris Mayle

Trademarks
Oracle and Java are registered trademarks of Oracle and/or its affiliates.
UNIX is a registered trademark of The Open Group.
Microsoft Internet Explorer is either a registered trademark or a trademark of Microsoft Corporation in The United States and/or other countries.
Apache is a trademark of The Apache Software Foundation.
Firefox is a registered trademark of the Mozilla Foundation.
Google is a trademark of Google, Inc.

Throughout this book the printing of trademarked names without the trademark symbol is for editorial purpose only. We have no intention of infringement of the trademark.

Warning and Disclaimer
Every effort has been made to make this book as accurate as possible. The author and the publisher shall have neither liability nor responsibility to any person or entity with respect to any loss or damages arising from the information in this book.

About the Author

Known for his clear writing style, Budi Kurniawan is a senior developer at Brainy Software and the author of *How Tomcat Works*, *Servlet and JSP: A Tutorial*, *Struts 2 Design and Programming*, and others. He has written software that is licensed by major corporations worldwide.

Table of Contents

Introduction

Welcome to *Java: A Beginner's Tutorial, Fourth Edition*.

This book covers the most important Java programming topics that you need to master in order to learn other technologies yourself. By fully understanding all the chapters and doing the exercises you'll be able to perform an intermediate Java programmer's daily tasks quite well.

This book offers all the three subjects that a professional Java programmer must be proficient in:

- Java programming language
- Object-oriented programming (OOP) with Java
- Java core libraries

What makes structuring an effective Java course difficult is the fact that the three subjects are interdependent. On the one hand, Java is an OOP language, so its syntax is easier to learn if you already know OOP. On the other hand, OOP features such as inheritance, polymorphism and data encapsulation are best taught when accompanied by real-world examples. Unfortunately, understanding real-world Java programs requires knowledge of the Java core libraries.

Because of such interdependence, the three main topics are not grouped into three isolated parts. Instead, chapters discussing a major topic and chapters teaching another are interwoven. For example, before explaining polymorphism, this book makes sure that you are familiar with certain Java classes so that real-world examples can be given. In addition, because a language feature such as generics cannot be explained effectively without the comprehension of a certain set of classes, it is covered after the discussion of the supporting classes.

There are also cases whereby a topic can be found in two or more places. For instance, the **for** statement is a basic language feature that should be discussed in an early chapter. However, **for** can also be used to iterate over an array or an object collection. Therefore, **for** is first presented in Chapter 3, "Statements" and then revisited in Chapter 6, "Arrays" and Chapter 14, "The Collections Framework."

The rest of this introduction presents a high-level overview of Java, an introduction to OOP and a brief description of each chapter.

Java, the Language and the Technology

Java is not only an object-oriented programming language, it is also a set of technologies that make software development more rapid and resulting applications more robust and secure. For years Java has been the technology of choice because of the benefits it offers:

- platform independence
- ease of use
- comprehensive libraries that speed up application development
- security
- scalability
- extensive industry support

Sun Microsystems introduced Java in 1995 and Java—even though it had been a general-purpose language right from the start—was soon well known as the language for writing applets, small programs that run inside web browsers and add interactivity to static websites. The growth of the Internet had much to contribute to the early success of Java.

Having said that, applets were not the only factor that made Java shine. The other most appealing feature of Java was its platform-independence promise, hence the slogan "Write Once, Run Anywhere." What this means is the very same program you write will run on Windows, Unix, Mac, Linux, and other operating systems. This was something no other programming language could do. At that time, C and C++ were the two most commonly used languages for developing serious applications. Java seemed to have stolen their thunder since its first birthday.

That was Java version 1.0.

In 1997, Java 1.1 was released, adding significant features such as a better event model, Java Beans, and internationalization to the original.

Java 1.2 was launched in December 1998. Three days after it was released, the version number was changed to 2, marking the beginning of a huge marketing campaign that started in 1999 to sell Java as the "next generation" technology. Java 2 was sold in four flavors: the Standard Edition (J2SE), the Enterprise Edition (J2EE), the Micro Edition (J2ME), and Java Card (that never adopted "2" in its brand name).

The next version released in 2000 was 1.3, hence J2SE 1.3. 1.4 came two years later to make J2SE 1.4. J2SE version 1.5 was released in 2004. However, the name Java 2 version 1.5 was then changed to Java 5.

On November 13, 2006, a month before the official release date of Java 6, Sun Microsystems announced that it had open-sourced Java. Java SE 6 was the first Java release for which Sun Microsystems had invited outside developers to contribute code and help fix bugs. True that the company had in the past accepted contributions from non-employees, like the work of Doug Lea on multithreading, but this was the first time Sun had posted an open invitation. The company admitted that they had limited resources, and outside contributors would help them cross the finish line sooner.

In May 2007 Sun released its Java source code to the OpenJDK community as free software. IBM, Oracle and Apple later joined OpenJDK.

In 2010 Oracle acquired Sun.

Java 7 was released in July 2011 and Java 8 in March 2014, both results of open-source collaboration through OpenJDK.

What Makes Java Platform Independent?

You must have heard of the terms "platform-independent" or "cross-platform," which means your program can run on multiple operating systems. It was a major feat that contributed to Java's popularity. But, what makes Java platform independent?

In traditional programming, source code is compiled to executable code. This executable code can run only on the platform it is intended to run. In other words, code written and compiled for Windows will only run on Windows, code written in Linux will only run on Linux, and so on. This is depicted in Figure I.1.

Figure I.1: Traditional programming paradigm

A Java program, on the other hand, is compiled to bytecode. You cannot run bytecode by itself because it is not native code. Bytecode can only run on a Java Virtual Machine (JVM). A JVM is a native application that interprets bytecode. By making the JVM available on many platforms, Sun transformed Java into a cross-platform language. As shown in Figure I.2, the very same bytecode can run on any operating system for which a JVM has been developed.

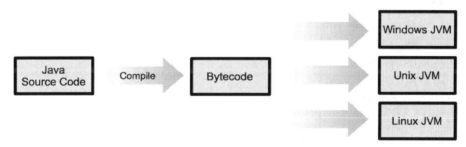

Figure I.2: Java programming model

Currently JVMs are available for Windows, Unix, Linux, Free BSD, and practically all other major operating systems in the world.

JDK, JRE, JVM, What's the Difference?

I mentioned that Java programs must be compiled. In fact, any programming language needs a compiler to be really useful. A compiler is a program that converts program source code to an executable format, either a bytecode, native code or something else. Before you can start programming Java, you need to download a Java compiler. The Java compiler is a program named **javac**, which is short for Java compiler.

While **javac** can compile Java sources to bytecode, to run bytecode you need a Java Virtual Machine. In addition, because you will invariably use classes in the Java core libraries, you also need to download these libraries. The Java Runtime Environment (JRE) contains both a JVM and class libraries. As you may suspect, the JRE for Windows is different from that for Linux, which is different from the one for yet another operating system.

The Java software is available in two distributions:

- The JRE, which includes a JVM and the core libraries. This is good for running

bytecode.
- The JDK, which includes the JRE plus a compiler and other tools. This is required software to compile Java programs as well as run the bytecode.

To summarize, a JVM is a native application that runs bytecode. The JRE is an environment that includes a JVM and Java class libraries. The JDK includes the JRE plus other tools including a Java compiler.

The first version of the JDK is 1.0. The versions after that are 1.1, 1.2, 1.3, 1.4, 1.5, 1.6, 1.7 and 1.8. For minor releases, add another number to the version number. For instance, 1.8.1 is the first minor upgrade to version 1.8.

JDK 1.8 is better known as JDK 8. The version of the JRE included in a JDK is the same as the JDK. Therefore, JDK 1.8 contains JRE 1.8. The JDK is also often called the SDK (Software Development Kit).

In addition to the JDK, a Java programmer needs to download Java documentation that explains classes, interfaces and enums in the core libraries. You can download the documentation from the same URL that provides the JRE and the JDK.

Java 2, J2SE, J2EE, J2ME, Java 8, What Are They?

Sun Microsystems has done a great deal promoting Java. Part of its marketing strategy was to coin the name Java 2, which was basically JDK 1.2. There were three editions of Java 2:

- Java 2 Platform, Standard Edition (J2SE). J2SE is basically the JDK. It also serves as the foundation for technologies defined in J2EE.
- Java 2 Platform, Enterprise Edition (J2EE). It defines the standard for developing component-based multi-tier enterprise applications. Features include web services support and development tools.
- Java 2 Platform, Micro Edition (J2ME). It provides an environment for applications that run on consumer devices, such as mobile phones and TV set-top boxes. J2ME includes a JVM and a limited set of class libraries.

Name changes occurred in version 5. J2SE became *Java Platform, Standard Edition 5* (Java SE 5). Also, the 2 in J2EE and J2ME was dropped. The current version of the enterprise edition is *Java Platform, Enterprise Edition 7* (Java EE 7). J2ME is now called *Java Platform, Micro Edition* (Java ME, without a version number). In this book, Java 8 is used to refer to Java SE 8.

Unlike the first versions of Java that were products of Sun, J2SE 1.4, Java SE 5 and later versions of Java are sets of specifications that define features that need to be implemented. The software itself is called a reference implementation. Oracle, IBM, and others work together through OpenJDK to provide the Java SE 8 reference implementation and reference implementations for the next versions of Java.

Java EE 6 and 7 are also sets of specifications that include technologies such as servlets, JavaServer Pages, JavaServer Faces, Java Messaging Service, etc. To develop and run Java EE applications, you need a Java EE application server. Anyone can implement a Java EE application server, which explains the availability of various application servers in the market, including many open source ones. Here are examples of Java EE 6 and 7 application servers:

- Oracle WebLogic

- IBM WebSphere
- GlassFish
- JBoss
- WildFly
- Apache Geronimo
- Apache TomEE

The complete list can be found here.

```
http://www.oracle.com/technetwork/java/javaee/overview/compatibility
-jsp-136984.html
```

JBoss, GlassFish, WildFly, Geronimo and TomEE are open source Java EE servers. They have different licenses, though, so make sure you read them before you decide to use the products.

The Java Community Process (JCP) Program

Java's continuous dominance as the technology of choice owes much to Sun's strategy to include other industry players in determining the future of Java. This way, many people feel that they also own Java. Many large corporations, such as IBM, Oracle, Nokia, Fujitsu, etc, invest heavily in Java because they too can propose a specification for a technology and put forward what they want to see in the next version of a Java technology. This collaborative effort takes the form of the JCP Program. The URL of its Web site is http://www.jcp.org.

Specifications produced by the JCP Program are known as Java Specification Requests (JSRs). For example, JSR 337 specifies Java SE 8.

An Overview of Object-Oriented Programming

Object-oriented programming (OOP) works by modeling applications on real-world objects. Three principles of OOP are encapsulation, inheritance and polymorphism.

The benefits of OOP are real. These are the reason why most modern programming languages, including Java, are object-oriented (OO). I can even cite two well-known examples of language transformation to support OOP: The C language evolved into C++ and Visual Basic was upgraded into Visual Basic.NET.

This section explains the benefits of OOP and provides an assessment of how easy or hard it is to learn OOP.

The Benefits of OOP

The benefits of OOP include easy code maintenance, code reuse, and extendibility. These benefits are presented in more detail below.

1. **Ease of maintenance**. Modern software applications tend to be very large. Once upon a time, a "large" system comprised a few thousand lines of code. Now, even those consisting of one million lines are not considered that large. When a system gets larger, it starts giving its developers problems. Bjarne Stroustrup, the father of

C++, once said this. A small program can be written in anything, anyhow. If you don't quit easily, you'll make it work, at the end. But a large program is a different story. If you don't use techniques of "good programming," new errors will emerge as fast as you fix the old ones.

The reason for this is there is interdependency among different parts of a large program. When you change something in some part of the program, you may not realize how the change might affect other parts. OOP makes it easy to make applications modular, and modularity makes maintenance less of a headache. Modularity is inherent in OOP because a class, which is a template for objects, is a module by itself. A good design should allow a class to contain similar functionality and related data. An important and related term that is used often in OOP is coupling, which means the degree of interaction between two modules. Loosely coupling among parts make code reuse—another benefit of OOP—easier to achieve.

2. **Reusability**. Reusability means that code that has previously been written can be reused by the code author and others who need the same functionality provided by the original code. It is not surprising, then, that an OOP language often comes with a set of ready-to-use libraries. In the case of Java, the language is accompanied by hundreds of class libraries or application programming interfaces (APIs) that have been carefully designed and tested. It is also easy to write and distribute your own library. Support for reusability in a programming platform is very attractive because it shortens development time.

   One of the main challenges to class reusability is creating good documentation for the class library. How fast can a programmer find a class that provides the functionality he or she is looking for? Is it faster to find such a class or write a new one from scratch? Fortunately, Java core and extended APIs come with extensive documentation.

   Reusability does not only apply to the coding phase through the reuse of classes and other types; when designing an application in an OO system, solutions to OO design problems can also be reused. These solutions are called design patterns. To make it easier to refer to each solution, each pattern is given a name. The early catalog of reusable design patterns can be found in the classic book *Design Patterns: Elements of Reusable Object-Oriented Software*, by Erich Gamma, Richard Helm, Ralph Johnson, and John Vlissides.

3. **Extendibility**. Every application is unique. It has its own requirements and specifications. In terms of reusability, sometimes you cannot find an existing class that provides the exact functionality that your application requires. However, you will probably find one or two that provide part of the functionality. Extendibility means that you can still use those classes by extending them to suit your need. You still save time, because you don't have to write code from scratch.

   In OOP, extendibility is achieved through inheritance. You can extend an existing class, add some methods or data to it, or change the behavior of methods you don't like. If you know the basic functionality that will be used in many cases, but you don't want your class to provide very specific functions, you can provide a generic class that can be extended later to provide functionality specific to an application.

Is OOP Hard?

Java programmers need to master OOP. As it happens, it does make a difference if you have programmed using a procedural language, such as C or Pascal. In the light of this, there is bad news and good news.

First the bad news.

Researchers have been debating the best way to teach OOP in school; some argue that it is best to teach procedural programming before OOP is introduced. In many curricula, an OOP course can be taken when a student is nearing the final year of his/her university term.

More recent studies, however, argue that someone with procedural programming skill thinks in a paradigm very different from how OO programmers view and try to solve problems. When this person needs to learn OOP, the greatest struggle he/she faces is having to go through a paradigm shift. It is said that it takes six to 18 months to switch your mindset from procedural to object-oriented paradigms. Another study shows that students who have not learned procedural programming do not find OOP that difficult.

Now the good news.

Java qualifies as one of the easiest OOP languages to learn. For example, you do not need to worry about pointers, don't have to spend precious time solving memory leaks caused by failing to destroy unused objects, etc. On top of that, Java comes with very comprehensive class libraries with relatively very few bugs in their early versions. Once you know the nuts and bolts of OOP, programming with Java is really easy.

About This Book

The following presents the overview of each chapter.

Chapter 1, "Getting Started" provides the instructions on how to download and install a JDK and aims at giving you the feel of working with Java. This includes writing a simple Java program, compiling it using the **javac** tool, and running it using the **java** program. In addition, some advice on code conventions and integrated development environments is given.

Chapter 2, "Language Fundamentals" teaches you the Java language syntax. You will be introduced to topics such as character sets, primitives, variables, operators, etc.

Chapter 3, "Statements" explains Java statements **for**, **while**, **do-while**, **if**, **if-else**, **switch**, **break**, and **continue**.

Chapter 4, "Objects and Classes," is the first OOP lesson in this book. It starts by explaining what a Java object is an how it is stored in memory. It then continues with a discussion of classes, class members, and two OOP concepts (abstraction and encapsulation).

Chapter 5, "Core Classes" covers important classes in the Java core libraries: **java.lang.Object**, **java.lang.String**, **java.lang.StringBuffer** and **java.lang.StringBuilder**, wrapper classes and **java.util.Scanner**. This is an important chapter because the classes explained in this chapter are some of the most commonly used classes in Java.

Chapter 6, "Arrays" discusses arrays, a special language feature of Java that is widely used. This chapter also covers a utility class for manipulating arrays.

Chapter 7, "Inheritance" discusses an OOP feature that enables code extendibility. This chapter teaches you how to extend a class, affect the visibility of a subclass, override a method and so forth.

Undoubtedly, error handling is an important feature of any programming language.

As a mature language, Java has a very robust error handling mechanism that can help prevent bugs from creeping in. Chapter 8, "Error Handling" is a detailed discussion of this mechanism.

Chapter 9, "Working with Numbers" deals with three issues when working with numbers: parsing, formatting, and manipulation. This chapter introduces Java classes that can help you with these tasks.

Chapter 10, "Interfaces and Abstract Classes" explains that an interface is more than a class without implementation. An interface defines a contract between a service provider and a client. This chapter explains how to work with interfaces and abstract classes.

Polymorphism is one of the main pillars of OOP. It is incredibly useful in situations whereby the type of an object in not known at compile time. Chapter 11, "Polymorphism" explains this feature and provides useful examples.

Chapter 12, "Enums" covers enum, a type added to Java since version 5.

Chapter 13, "Working with Dates and Times" explains how you can work with the new Date and Time API added to Java 8 as well as the old API used in the older versions of Java.

Chapter 14, "The Collections Framework" shows how you can use the members of the **java.util** package to group objects and manipulate them.

Generics are a very important feature in Java and Chapter 15, "Generics" adequately explains this feature.

Chapter 16, "Input/Output" introduces the concept of streams and explains how you can use the four stream types in the Java IO API to perform input-output operations. In addition, object serialization and deserialization are discussed.

Chapter 17, "Annotations" talks about annotations. It explains the standard annotations that come with the JDK, common annotations, meta-annotations and custom annotations.

Chapter 18, "Nested and Inner Classes" explains how you can write a class within another class and why this OOP feature can be very useful.

Chapter 19, "Lambda Expressions" covers lambda expressions, a feature added to Java 8. It explains the concept and provides useful examples.

Chapter 20, "Working with Streams" discusses streams, a new addition to Java 8. It shows you why streams play an important role in Java programming.

Accessing databases and manipulating data are some of the most important tasks in business applications. There are many flavors of database servers and accessing different databases requires different skills. Fortunately for Java programmers, Java Database Connectivity (JDBC) technology provides a uniform way of accessing databases. JDBC is discussed in Chapter 21, "Java Database Connectivity."

Chapter 22, "Swing Basics" is the first installment of the two chapters on Swing. It briefly discusses the AWT components and thoroughly explains some basic Swing components.

Chapter 23, "Swinging Higher" is the second chapter on Swing. It covers more advanced techniques such as layout management, event handling and the look and feel.

Applets are small programs that run on the Web browser. Chapter 24, "Applets" explains the lifecycle of an applet, security restrictions and **JApplet**.

Chapter 25, "Introduction to JavaFX" covers JavaFX, the latest Java technology for creating rich clients applications that can run on the desktop as well as in the browser.

Chapter 26, "JavaFX with FXML" discusses FXML, a markup language that can be used to separate the presentation layer and the business logic in JavaFX applications.

A thread is a basic processing unit to which an operating system allocates processor time, and more than one thread can be executing code inside a process. Chapter 27, "Java Threads," shows that in Java multithreaded programming is not only the domain of expert programmers.

Chapter 28, "The Concurrency Utilities" is the second chapter on multi-threaded programming. It discusses interfaces and classes that make writing multi-threaded programs easier.

Today it is common for software applications to be deployable to different countries and regions. Such applications need to be designed with internationalization in mind. Chapter 29, "Internationalization" explores techniques that Java programmers can use.

Chapter 30, "Java Networking" deals with classes that can be used in network programming. A simple Web server application is presented to illustrate how to use these classes.

Chapter 31, "Security" is a tutorial on how Java application users can restrict running Java applications and how you can use cryptography to secure your application and data.

Chapter 32, "Java Web Applications" explores Servlet technology and the Servlet API and presents several examples.

Chapter 33, "JavaServer Pages" explains another web development technology and shows how to write JSP pages.

Chapter 34, "JavaDoc" discusses the **javadoc** tool that Java programmers can use to generate documentation for their APIs.

Chapter 35, "Application Deployment," talks about Java Web Start and how to use it to deploy Java applications over the Internet, across a local network, and from a CD.

Appendix A, "javac", Appendix B, "java", and Appendix C, "jar" explain the **javac**, **java**, and **jar** tools, respectively.

Appendix D, "NetBeans" and Appendix E, "Eclipse" provide brief tutorials on NetBeans and Eclipse, respectively.

Downloading Program Examples and Answers

The program examples accompanying this book and answers to the questions in each chapter can be downloaded from the publisher's website:

```
http://books.brainysoftware.com
```

Extract the zip file to a working directory and you are good to go.

Chapter 1
Getting Started

To program in Java, you need the Java SE Development Kit (JDK). Therefore, the first section of this chapter provides instructions to download and install it.

Developing a Java program involves writing code, compiling it into bytecode, and running the bytecode. This is a process you will repeat again and again during your career as a Java programmer, and it is crucial that you feel comfortable with it. The main objective of this chapter therefore is to give you the opportunity to experience the process of software development in Java.

As it is important to write code that not only works but that is also easy to read and maintain, this chapter introduces you to Java code conventions. And, since the smart developer uses an integrated development environment (IDE), the last section of this chapter offers advice on Java IDEs.

Downloading and Installing Java

Before you can start compiling and running Java programs, you need to download and install the JDK as well as configure some system environment variables.

You can download the JRE and the JDK for Windows, Linux, and Mac OS X from this Oracle website:

http://www.oracle.com/technetwork/java/javase/downloads/index.html

If you click the Download link on the page, you'll be redirected to a page that lets you select an installation for your platform: Windows, Linux, Solaris or Mac OS X. The same link also provides the JRE. However, for development you need the JDK not only the JRE, which is only good for running compiled Java classes. The JDK includes the JRE.

After downloading the JDK, you need to install it. Installation varies from one operating system to another. These subsections detail the installation process.

Installing on Windows

Installing on Windows is easy. Simply double-click the executable file in you downloaded in Windows Explorer and follow the instructions. Figure 1.1 shows the first dialog of the installation wizard.

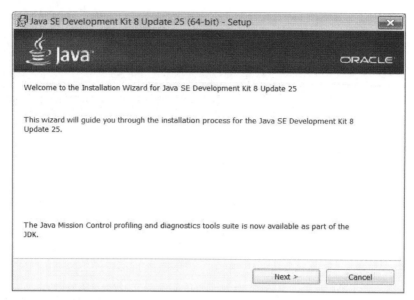

Figure 1.1: Installing the JDK 8 on Windows

Installing on Linux

On Linux platforms, the JDK is available in two installation formats.

- RPM, for Linux platforms that supports the RPM package management system, such as Red Hat and SuSE.
- Self-extracting package. A compressed file containing packages to be installed.

If you are using the RPM, follow these steps:

1. Become root by using the **su** command
2. Extract the downloaded file.
3. Change directory to where the downloaded file is located and type:

```
chmod a+x rpmFile
```

where *rpmFile* is the RPM file.
4. Run the RPM file:

```
./rpmFile
```

If you are using the self-extracting binary installation, follow these steps.

1. Extract the downloaded file.
2. Use **chmod** to give the file the execute permissions:

```
chmod a+x binFile
```

Here, *binFile* is the downloaded bin file for your platform.
3. Change directory to the location where you want the files to be installed.
4. Run the self-extracting binary. Execute the downloaded file with the path

prepended to it. For example, if the file is in the current directory, prepend it with "./":

```
./binFile
```

Installing on Mac OS X

To install the JDK 8 on Mac OS X, you need an Intel-based computer running OS X 10.8 (Mountain Lion) or later. You also need administrator privileges. Installation is straight-forward.

1. Double-click on the .dmg file you downloaded.
2. In the Finder window that appears, double-click the package icon.
3. On the first window that appears, click **Continue**.
4. The Installation Type window appears. Click **Install**.
5. A window appears that says "Installer is trying to install new software. Type your password to allow this." Enter your Admin password.
6. Click **Install Software** to start the installation.

Setting System Environment Variables

After you install the JDK, you can start compiling and running Java programs. However, you can only invoke the compiler and the JRE from the location of the **javac** and **java** programs or by including the installation path in your command. To make compiling and running programs easier, it is important that you set the **PATH** environment variable on your computer so that you can invoke **javac** and **java** from any directory.

Setting the Path Environment Variable on Windows

To set the **PATH** environment variable on Windows, do these steps:

1. Click **Start**, **Settings**, **Control Panel**.
2. Double-click **System**.
3. Select the **Advanced** tab and then click on **Environment Variables**.
4. Locate the **Path** environment variable in the **User Variables** or **System Variables** panes. The value of **Path** is a series of directories separated by semicolons. Now, add the full path to the **bin** directory of your Java installation directory to the end of the existing value of **Path**. The directory looks something like:

```
C:\Program Files\Java\jdk1.8.0_<version>\bin
```

5. Click **Set**, **OK**, or **Apply**.

Setting the Path Environment Variable on UNIX and Linux

Setting the path environment variable on these operating systems depends on the shell you use. For the C shell, add the following to the end of your ~/**.cshrc** file:

```
set path=(path/to/jdk/bin $path)
```

where *path/to/jdk/bin* is the bin directory under your JDK installation directory.

For the Bourne Again shell, add this line to the end of your ~/**.bashrc** or

~/.bash_profile file:

```
export PATH=/path/to/jdk/bin:$PATH
```

Here, *path/to/jdk/bin* is the **bin** directory under your JDK installation directory.

Testing the Installation

To confirm that you have installed the JDK correctly, type **javac** on the command line from any directory on your machine. If you see instructions on how to correctly run **javac**, then you have successfully installed it. On the other hand, if you can only run **javac** from the **bin** directory of the JDK installation directory, your **PATH** environment variable was not configured properly.

Downloading Java API Documentation

When programming Java, you will invariably use classes from the core libraries. Even seasoned programmers look up the documentation for those libraries when they are coding. Therefore, you should download the documentation from here.

```
http://www.oracle.com/technetwork/java/javase/downloads/index.html
```

(You need to scroll down until you see "Java SE 8 Documentation.")

The API is also available online here:

```
http://download.oracle.com/javase/8/docs/api
```

Your First Java Program

This section highlights steps in Java development: writing the program, compiling it into bytecode and running the bytecode.

Writing a Java Program

You can use any text editor to write a Java program. Open a text editor and write the code in Listing 1.1. Alternatively, if you have downloaded the program examples accompanying this book, you can simply copy it to your text editor.

> **Code Download**
> If you have not done so, now is a good time to download the examples from the publisher's website. The URL can be found in the last section of Introduction.

Listing 1.1: A simple Java program

```
class MyFirstProgram {
    public static void main(String[] args) {
        System.out.println("Java rocks.");
    }
}
```

For now, suffice it to say that Java code must reside in a class. Also, make sure you save the code in Listing 1.1 as a **MyFirstProgram.java** file. All Java source files must have **java** extension.

Compiling Your Java Program

You use the **javac** program in the **bin** directory of your JDK installation directory to compile Java programs. Assuming you have edited the **PATH** environment variable in your computer (if not, see the section "Downloading and Installing Java"), you should be able to invoke **javac** from any directory. To compile the **MyFirstProgram** class in Listing 1.1, do the following:

1. Open a terminal or a command prompt and change directory to the directory where the **MyFirstProgram.java** file was saved in.
2. Type the following command.

```
javac MyFirstProgram.java
```

If everything goes well, **javac** will create a file named **MyFirstProgram.class** in your working directory.

Note
The **javac** tool has more features that you can use by passing options. For example, you can tell it where you want the generated class file to be created. Appendix A, "javac" discusses **javac** in clear detail.

Running Your Java Program

To run your Java program, use the **java** program that is part of the JDK. Again, having added the **PATH** environment variable, you should be able to invoke **java** from any directory. From your working directory, type the following and press Enter.

```
java MyFirstProgram
```

Note that you do not include the **class** extension when running a Java program.

You will see the following on your console.

```
Java rocks.
```

Congratulations. You have successfully written your first Java program. Since the sole aim of this chapter is to familiarize yourself with the writing and compiling process, I will not explain how the program works.

You can also pass arguments to a Java program. For example, if you have a class named **Calculator** and you want to pass two arguments to it, you can do it like this:

```
java Calculator arg-1 arg-2
```

Here, *arg-1* is the first argument and *arg-2* the second. You can pass as many arguments as you want. The **java** program will then make these arguments available to your Java program as an array of strings. You'll learn to handle arguments in Chapter 6, "Arrays."

Note
The **java** tool is an advanced program that you can configure by passing options.
For instance, you can set the amount of memory allocated to it. Appendix B,
"java" explains these options.

Note
The **java** tool can also be used to run a Java class that is packaged in a jar file.
Check the section "Setting an Application's Entry Point" in Appendix C, "jar."

Java Code Conventions

It is important to write correct Java programs that run. However, it is also crucial to write
programs that are easy to read and maintain. It is believed that eighty percent of the
lifetime cost of a piece of software is spent on maintenance. Also, the turnover of
programmers is high, thus it is very likely that someone other than you will maintain your
code during its lifetime. Whoever inherits your code will appreciate clear and easy-to-read
program sources.

Using consistent code conventions is one way to make your code easier to read.
(Other ways include proper code organization and sufficient commenting.) Code
conventions include file names, file organization, indentation, comments, declaration,
statements, white space and naming conventions.

A class declaration starts with the keyword **class** followed by a class name and the
opening brace {. You can place the opening brace on the same line as the class name, as
shown in Listing 1.1, or you can write it on the next line, as demonstrated in Listing 1.2.

Listing 1.2: MyFirstProgram written using a different code convention
```
class MyFirstProgram
{
    public static void main(String[] args)
    {
        System.out.println("Java rocks.");
    }
}
```

The code in Listing 1.2 is as good as the one in Listing 1.1. It is just that the class has
been written using a different convention. You should adopt a consistent style for all your
program elements. It is up to you to define your own code conventions, however Sun
Microsystems has published a document that outlines standards that its employees should
follow. The document can be viewed here. (Of course, the document is now part of
Oracle.com)

http://www.oracle.com/technetwork/java/codeconvtoc-136057.html

Program samples in this book will follow the recommended conventions outlined in this
document. I'd also like to encourage you to develop the habit of following these
conventions since the first day of your programming career, so that writing clear code
comes naturally at a later stage.

Your first lesson on styles is about indentation. The unit of indentation must be four
spaces. If tabs are used in place of spaces, they must be set every eight spaces (not four).

Integrated Development Environments (IDEs)

It is true that you can write Java programs using a text editor. However, an IDE will help. Not only will it check the syntax of your code, an IDE can also auto complete code, debug, and trace your programs. In addition, compilation can happen automatically as you type, and running a Java program is simply a matter of clicking a button. As a result, you will develop in much shorter time.

There used to be dozens of Java IDEs out there, but today these three are the only major players left. Fortunately, the first two are completely free.

- NetBeans (free and open source)
- Eclipse (free and open source)
- IntelliJ IDEA (offers free and paid editions)

The two most popular Java IDEs are NetBeans and Eclipse and the past few years have seen a war between the two to become the number one. NetBeans and Eclipse are both open source projects with strong backers. Sun Microsystems launched NetBeans in 2000 after buying the Czech company Netbeans Ceska Republika. Eclipse was originated by IBM to compete with NetBeans.

Which one is better depends on who you ask, but their popularity has become the impetus that propelled other software makers to give away their IDEs too. Even Microsoft, whose .NET technology is Java's most fierce competitor, followed suit by no longer charging for the Express Editions of its Visual Studio.NET.

This book provides a brief tutorial of NetBeans and Eclipse in Appendix D and Appendix E, respectively. Do consider using an IDE because it helps a lot.

Summary

This chapter provided instructions on how to download and install the JDK and helped you write your first Java program. You used a text editor to write the program, used **javac** to compile it to a class file, and ran the class file with the **java** tool.

As programs grow in complexity and projects get larger, an IDE will help expedite application development.

Quiz

1. What is a compiler?
2. How is Java different from traditional programming?
3. What is bytecode?
4. What is the difference between the JRE and the JDK?
5. If you had saved the code in Listing 1.1 using a different name, such as **whatever.java**, would it have compiled?
6. If you had used a file extension other than java when saving the code in Listing 1.1, for example as **MyFirstProgram.txt**, would it have compiled?

7. Are these valid Java class names: **FirstJava, scientificCalculator, numberFormatter**?
8. How do you write to the console?
9. Write a Java class named **HelloWorld** that prints "Hello World".

Chapter 2
Language Fundamentals

Java is an object-oriented programming (OOP) language, therefore an understanding of OOP is of utmost importance. Chapter 4, "Objects and Classes" is the first lesson of OOP in this book. However, before you explore OOP features and techniques, you should first study Java language fundamentals.

ASCII and Unicode

Traditionally, computers in English speaking countries only used the ASCII (American Standard Code for Information Interchange) character set to represent alphanumeric characters. Each character in the ASCII is represented by 7 bits. There are therefore 128 characters in this character set. These include the lower case and upper case Latin letters, numbers, and punctuation marks.

The ASCII character set was later extended to include another 128 characters, such as the German characters ä, ö, ü and the British currency symbol £. This character set is called extended ASCII and each character is represented by 8 bits.

ASCII and the extended ASCII are only two of the many character sets available. Another popular one is the character set standardized by the ISO (International Standards Organization), ISO-8859-1, which is also known as Latin-1. Each character in ISO-8859-1 is represented by eight bits as well. This character set contains all the characters required for writing text in many of the western European languages, such as German, Danish, Dutch, French, Italian, Spanish, Portuguese and, of course, English. An eight-bit-per-character character set is convenient because a byte is also 8 bits long. As such, storing and transmitting text written in an 8-bit character set is most efficient.

However, not every language uses Latin letters. Chinese and Japanese are examples of languages that use different character sets. For example, each character in the Chinese language represents a word, not a letter. There are thousands of these characters and eight bits are not enough to represent all the characters in the character set. The Japanese use a different character set for their language too. In total, there are hundreds of different character sets for all the world languages. To unify all these characters sets, a computing standard called Unicode was created.

Unicode is a character set developed by a non-profit organization called the Unicode Consortium (www.unicode.org). This body attempts to include all characters in all languages in the world into one single character set. A unique number in Unicode represents exactly one character. Currently at version 7, Unicode is used in Java, XML, ECMAScript, LDAP, etc.

Initially, a Unicode character was represented by 16 bits, which were enough to represent more than 65,000 different characters. 65,000 characters are sufficient for encoding most of the characters in major languages in the world. However, the Unicode consortium planned to allow for encoding for as many as a million more characters. With this amount, you then need more than 16 bits to represent each character. In fact, a 32 bit system is considered a convenient way of storing Unicode characters.

Now, you see a problem already. While Unicode provides enough space for all the characters used in all languages, storing and transmitting Unicode text is not as efficient as storing and transmitting ASCII or Latin-1 characters. In the Internet world, this is a huge problem. Imagine having to transfer 4 times as much data as ASCII text!

Fortunately, character encoding can make it more efficient to store and transmit Unicode text. You can think of character encoding as analogous to data compression. And, there are many types of character encodings available today. The Unicode Consortium endorses three of them:

- UTF-8. This is popular for HTML and for protocols whereby Unicode characters are transformed into a variable length encoding of bytes. It has the advantages that the Unicode characters corresponding to the familiar ASCII set have the same byte values as ASCII, and that Unicode characters transformed into UTF-8 can be used with much existing software. Most browsers support the UTF-8 character encoding.
- UTF-16. In this character encoding, all the more commonly used characters fit into a single 16-bit code unit, and other less often used characters are accessible via pairs of 16-bit code units.
- UTF-32. This character encoding uses 32 bits for every single character. This is clearly not a choice for Internet applications. At least, not at present.

ASCII characters still play a dominant role in software programming. Java too uses ASCII for almost all input elements, except comments, identifiers, and the contents of characters and strings. For the latter, Java supports Unicode characters. This means, you can write comments, identifiers, and strings in languages other than English.

Separators

Java uses certain characters as separators. These special characters are presented in Table 2.1. It is important that you are familiar with the symbols and names, but don't worry if you don't understand the terms in the Description column for now.

Primitives

When writing an object-oriented (OO) application, you create an object model that resembles the real world. For example, a payroll application would have **Employee** objects, **Tax** objects, **Company** objects, etc. In Java, however, objects are not the only data type. There is another data type called *primitive*. There are eight primitive types in Java, each with a specific format and size. Table 2.2 lists Java primitives.

Symbol	Name	Description
( )	Parentheses	Used in: 1. method signatures to contain lists of arguments. 2. expressions to raise operator precedence. 3. narrowing conversions. 4. loops to contain expressions to be evaluated
{ }	Braces	Used in: 1. declaration of types. 2. blocks of statements 3. array initialization.
[ ]	Brackets	Used in: 1. array declaration. 2. array value dereferencing
< >	Angle brackets	Used to pass parameter to parameterized types.
;	Semicolon	Used to terminate statements and in the **for** statement to separate the initialization code, the expression, and the update code.
:	Colon	Used in the **for** statement that iterates over an array or a collection.
,	Comma	Used to separate arguments in method declarations.
.	Period	Used to separate package names from subpackages and type names, and to separate a field or method from a reference variable.

Table 2.1: Java separators

Primitive	Description	Range
byte	Byte-length integer (8 bits)	-128 (-2^7) to 127 (2^7-1)
short	Short integer (16 bits)	-32,768 (-2^{15}) to 32,767 (2^{15}-1)
int	Integer (32 bits)	-2,147,483,648 (-2^{31}) to 2,147,483,647 (-2^{31}-1)
long	Long integer (64 bits)	-9,223,372,036,854,775,808 (-2^{63}) to 9,223,372,036,854,775,807 (2^{63}-1)
float	Single-precision floating point (32-bits)	Smallest positive nonzero: $14e^{-45}$ Largest positive nonzero: 3.4028234^{e38}
double	Double-precision floating point (64-bits)	Smallest positive nonzero: $4.9e^{-324}$ Largest positive nonzero: $1.7976931348623157e^{308}$
char	A Unicode character	[See Unicode 6 specification]
boolean	A boolean value	true or false

Table 2.2: Java primitives

The first six primitives (**byte**, **short**, **int**, **long**, **float**, **double**) represent numbers. Each has a different size. For example, a **byte** can contain any whole number between -128 and 127. To understand how the smallest and largest numbers for an integer were obtained, look at its size in bits. A byte is 8 bits long so there are 2^8 or 256 possible values. The first 128 values are reserved for -128 to -1, then 0 takes one place, leaving 127 positive values. Therefore, the range for a byte is -128 to 127.

If you need a placeholder to store number 1000000, you need an **int**. A **long** is even larger, and you might ask, if a **long** can contain a larger set of numbers than a **byte** and an **int**, why not always use a **long**? It is because a **long** takes 64 bits and therefore consume more memory space than a **byte** or an **int**. Thus, to save space, you want to use a primitive with the smallest possible data size.

The primitives **byte**, **short**, **int**, and **long** can only hold integers or whole numbers, for numbers with decimal points you need either a **float** or a **double**. A float is a 32-bit value that conforms to the Institute of Electrical and Electronics Engineer (IEEE) Standard 754. A double is a 64-bit value that conforms to the same standard.

A **char** can contain a single Unicode character, such as 'a', '9' or '&'. The use of Unicode allows **char**s to also contain characters that do not exist in the English alphabet. A **boolean** can contain one of two possible states (**false** or **true**).

Note
The reason why not everything in Java is an object is speed. Objects are more expensive to create and operate on than primitives. In programming an operation is said to be expensive if it is resource intensive or consumes a lot of CPU cycles to complete.

Now that you know that there are two types of data in Java (primitives and objects), let's continue by studying how to use primitives. Let's start with variables.

Variables

Variables are data placeholders. Java is a strongly typed language, therefore every variable must have a declared type. There are two data types in Java:

- reference types. A variable of reference type provides a reference to an object.
- primitive types. A variable of primitive type holds a primitive.

In addition to the data type, a Java variable also has a name or an identifier. There are a few ground rules in choosing identifiers.

1. An identifier is an unlimited-length sequence of Java letters and Java digits. An identifier must begin with a Java letter.
2. An identifier must not be a Java keyword (given in Table 2.3), a **boolean** literal, or the **null** literal.
3. It must be unique within its scope. Scopes are discussed in Chapter 4, "Objects and Classes."

Java Letters and Java Digits
Java letters include uppercase and lowercase ASCII Latin letters A to Z (\u0041-\u005a—note that \u denotes a Unicode character) and a to z (\u0061-\u007a), and, for historical reasons, the ASCII underscore (_ or \u005f) and the dollar sign ($, or \u0024). The $ character should be used only in mechanically generated source code or, rarely, to access preexisting names on legacy systems.
Java digits include the ASCII digits 0-9 (\u0030-\u0039).

How Java Stores Integer Values

You must have heard that computers work with binary numbers, which are numbers that consists of only zeros and ones. This section provides an overview that may come in useful when you learn mathematical operators.

A byte takes eight bits, meaning there are eight bits allocated to store a byte. The leftmost bit is the sign bit. 0 indicates a positive number, and 1 denotes a negative number. 0000 0000 is the binary representation of 0, 0000 0001 of 1, 0000 0010 of 2, 0000 0011 of 3, and 0111 1111 of 127, which is the largest positive number that a byte can contain.

Now, how do you get the binary representation of a negative number? It's easy. Get the binary representation of its positive equivalent first, and reverse all the bits and add 1. For example, to get the binary representation of -3 you start with 3, which is 0000 0011. Reversing the bits results in

```
1111 1100
```

Adding 1 gives you

```
1111 1101
```

which is -3 in binary.

For **int**s, the rule is the same, i.e. the leftmost bit is the sign bit. The only difference is that an **int** takes 32 bits. To calculate the binary form of -1 in an **int**, we start from 1, which is

```
0000 0000 0000 0000 0000 0000 0000 0001
```

Reversing all the bits results in:

```
1111 1111 1111 1111 1111 1111 1111 1110
```

Adding 1 gives us the number we want (-1).

```
1111 1111 1111 1111 1111 1111 1111 1111
```

abstract	continue	for	new	switch
assert	default	if	package	synchronized
boolean	do	goto	private	this
break	double	implements	protected	throw
byte	else	import	public	throws
case	enum	instanceof	return	transient
catch	extends	int	short	try
char	final	interface	static	void
class	finally	long	strictfp	volatile
const	float	native	super	while

Table 2.3: Java keywords

Here are some legal identifiers:

```
salary
x2
_x3
row_count
```

Here are some invalid variables:

```
2x
java+variable
```

2x is invalid because it starts with a number. **java+variable** is invalid because it contains a plus sign.

Also note that names are case-sensitive. **x2** and **X2** are two different identifiers.

You declare a variable by writing the type first, followed by the name plus a semicolon. Here are some examples of variable declarations.

```
byte x;
int rowCount;
char c;
```

In the examples above you declare three variables:

- The variable **x** of type **byte**
- The variable **rowCount** of type **int**
- The variable **c** of type **char**

x, **rowCount** and **c** are variable names or identifiers.

It is also possible to declare multiple variables having the same type on the same line, separating two variables with a comma. For instance:

```
int a, b;
```

which is the same as

```
int a;
int b;
```

However, writing multiple declarations on the same line is not recommended as it reduces readability.

Finally, it is possible to assign a value to a variable at the same time the variable is declared:

```
byte x = 12;
int rowCount = 1000;
char c = 'x';
```

Naming Convention for Variables
Variable names should be short yet meaningful. They should be in mixed case with a lowercase first letter. Subsequent words start with capital letters. Variable names should not start with underscore _ or dollar sign $ characters. For example, here are some examples of variable names that are in compliance with Sun's code conventions: **userName**, **count**, **firstTimeLogin**.

Constants

In Java constants are variables whose values, once assigned, cannot be changed. You declare a constant by using the keyword **final**. By convention, constant names are all in upper case with words separated by underscores.

Here are examples of constants or final variables.

```
final int ROW_COUNT = 50;
final boolean ALLOW_USER_ACCESS = true;
```

Literals 直接量 在程序中通过源代码直接给出的值.

From time to time you need to assign values to variables in your program, such as number 2 to an **int** or the character 'c' to a **char**. For this, you need to write the value representation in a format that the Java compiler understands. This source code representation of a value is called *literal*. There are three types of literals: literals of primitive types, string literals, and the **null** literal. Only literals of primitive types are discussed in this chapter. The **null** literal is discussed in Chapter 4, "Objects and Classes" and string literals in Chapter 5, "Core Classes."

Literals of primitive types have four subtypes: integer literals, floating-point literals, character literals and boolean literals. Each of these subtypes is explained below.

Integer Literals

Integer literals may be written in decimal (base 10, something we are used to), hexadecimal (base 16) or octal (base 8). For example, one hundred can be expressed as **100**. The following are integer literals in decimal:

```
2
123456
```

As another example, the following code assigns 10 to variable **x** of type **int**.

```
int x = 10;
```

Hexadecimal integers are written by using the prefixes **0x** or **0X**. For example, the hexadecimal number 9E is written as 0X9E or 0x9E. Octal integers are written by prefixing the numbers with 0. For instance, the following is an octal number 567:

```
0567
```

Integer literals are used to assign values to variables of types **byte**, **short**, **int**, and **long**. Note, however, you must not assign a value that exceeds the capacity of a variable. For instance, the highest number for a **byte** is 127. Therefore, the following code generates a compile error because 200 is too big for a **byte**.

```
byte b = 200;
```

To assign a value to a **long**, suffix the number with the letter **L** or **l**. L is preferable because it is easily distinguishable from digit 1. A **long** can contain values between -9223372036854775808L and 9223372036854775807L (2^{63}).

Beginners of Java often ask why we need to use the suffix l or L, because even without it, such as in the following, the program still compiles.

```
long a = 123;
```

This is only partly true. An integer literal without a suffix L or l is regarded as an **int**. Therefore, the following will generate a compile error because 9876543210 is larger than the capacity for an **int**:

```
long a = 9876543210;
```

To rectify the problem, add an L or l at the end of the number like this:

```
long a = 9876543210L;
```

Longs, ints, shorts, and bytes can also be expressed in binaries by prefixing the numbers with **0B** or **0b**. For instance:

```
byte twelve = 0B1100; // = 12
```

If an integer literal is too long, readability suffers. For this reason, starting from Java 7 you can use underscores to separate digits in integer literals. For example, these two have the same meaning but the second one is obviously easier to read.

```
int million = 1000000;

int million = 1_000_000;
```

It does not matter where you put the underscores. You can use one every three digits, like the example above, or any number of digits. Here are some more examples:

```
short next = 12_345;

int twelve = 0B_1100;

long multiplier = 12_34_56_78_90_00L;
```

Floating-Point Literals

Numbers such as 0.4, 1.23, $0.5e^{10}$ are floating point numbers. A floating point number has the following parts:

- a whole number part
- a decimal point
- a fractional part
- an optional exponent

Take 1.23 as an example. For this floating point, the whole number part is 1, the fractional part is 23, and there is no optional exponent. In $0.5e^{10}$, 0 is the whole number part, 5 the fractional part, and 10 is the exponent.

In Java, there are two types of floating points:

- **float**. 32 bits in size. The largest positive float is 3.40282347e+38 and the smallest positive finite nonzero float is 1.40239846e-45.
- **double**. 64 bits in size. The largest positive double is 1.79769313486231570e+308 and the smallest positive finite nonzero double is 4.94065645841246544e-324.

In both **float**s and **double**s, a whole number part of 0 is optional. In other words, 0.5 can be written as .5. Also, the exponent can be represented by either e or E.

To express float literals, you use one of the following formats.

```
Digits . [Digits] [ExponentPart] f_or_F
. Digits [ExponentPart] f_or_F
Digits ExponentPart f_or_F
Digits [ExponentPart] f_or_F
```

Note that the part in brackets is optional.

The *f_or_F* part makes a floating point literal a **float**. The absence of this part makes a float literal a **double**. To explicitly express a double literal, you can suffix it with D or d.

To write double literals, use one of these formats.

```
Digits . [Digits] [ExponentPart] [d_or_D]
. Digits [ExponentPart] [d_or_D]
Digits ExponentPart [d_or_D]
Digits [ExponentPart] [d_or_D]
```

In both floats and doubles, *ExponentPart* is defined as follows.

```
ExponentIndicator SignedInteger
```

where *ExponentIndicator* is either **e** or **E** and *SignedInteger* is .

```
Sign_opt Digits
```

and *Sign* is either + or - and a plus sign is optional.

Examples of **float** literals include the following:

```
2e1f
8.f
.5f
0f
3.14f
9.0001e+12f
```

Here are examples of **double** literals:

```
2e1
8.
.5
0.0D
3.14
9e-9d
7e123D
```

Boolean Literals

The **boolean** type has two values, represented by literals **true** and **false**. For example, the following code declares a **boolean** variable **includeSign** and assigns it the value of **true**.

```
boolean includeSign = true;
```

Character Literals

A character literal is a Unicode character or an escape sequence enclosed in single quotes. An escape sequence is the representation of a Unicode character that cannot be entered using the keyboard or that has a special function in Java. For example, the carriage return and linefeed characters are used to terminate a line and do not have visual representation. To express a linefeed character, you need to escape it, i.e. write its character representation. Also, single quote characters need to be escaped because single quotes are used to enclosed characters.

Here are some examples of character literals:

```
'a'
'Z'
'0'
'ü'
```

Here are character literals that are escape sequences:

```
'\b'    the backspace character
'\t'    the tab character
'\\'    the backslash
'\''    single quote
'\"'    double quote
'\n'    linefeed
'\r'    carriage return
```

In addition, Java allows you to escape a Unicode character so that you can express a Unicode character using a sequence of ASCII characters. For example, the Unicode code for the character £ is 00A3. You can write the following character literal to express this character:

```
'£'
```

However, if you do not have the tool to produce that character using your keyboard, you can escape it this way:

```
'\u00A3'
```

Primitive Conversions

When dealing with different data types, you often need to perform conversions. For example, assigning the value of a variable to another variable involves a conversion. If both variables have the same type, the assignment will always succeed. Conversion from a type to the same type is called identity conversion. For example, the following operation is guaranteed to be successful:

```
int a = 90;
int b = a;
```

However, conversion to a different type is not guaranteed to be successful or even possible. There are two other kinds of primitive conversions, the widening conversion and the narrowing conversion.

The Widening Conversion

The widening primitive conversion occurs from a type to another type whose size is the same or larger than that of the first type, such as from **int** (32 bits) to **long** (64 bits). The widening conversion is permitted in the following cases:

- **byte** to **short**, **int**, **long**, **float**, or **double**
- **short** to **int**, **long**, **float**, or **double**
- **char** to **int**, **long**, **float**, or **double**
- **int** to **long**, **float**, or **double**
- **long** to **float** or **double**
- **float** to **double**

A widening conversion from an integer type to another integer type will not risk information loss. At the same token, a conversion from **float** to **double** preserves all the information. However, a conversion from an **int** or a **long** to a **float** may result in loss of precision.

The widening primitive conversion occurs implicitly. You do not need to do anything in your code. For example:

```
int a = 10;
long b = a; // widening conversion
```

The Narrowing Conversion

The narrowing conversion occurs from a type to a different type that has a smaller size, such as from a **long** (64 bits) to an **int** (32 bits). In general, the narrowing primitive conversion can occur in these cases:

- **short** to **byte** or **char**
- **char** to **byte** or **short**
- **int** to **byte**, **short**, or **char**
- **long** to **byte**, **short**, or **char**
- **float** to **byte**, **short**, **char**, **int**, or **long**
- **double** to **byte**, **short**, **char**, **int**, **long**, or **float**

Unlike the widening primitive conversion, the narrowing primitive conversion must be explicit. You need to specify the target type in parentheses. For example, here is a narrowing conversion from **long** to **int**.

```
long a = 10;
int b = (int) a; // narrowing conversion
```

The **(int)** on the second line tells the compiler that a narrowing conversion should occur.

The narrowing conversion may incur information loss, if the converted value is larger than the capacity of the target type. The preceding example did not cause information loss because 10 is small enough for an **int**. However, in the following conversion, there is some information loss because 9876543210L is too big for an **int**.

```
long a = 9876543210L;
```

```
int b = (int) a; // the value of b is now 1286608618
```

A narrowing conversion that results in information loss introduces a defect in your program.

Operators

A computer program is a collection of operations that together achieve a certain function. There are many types of operations, including addition, subtraction, multiplication, division, and bit shifting. In this section you will learn various Java operations.

An operator performs an operation on one, two or three operands. Operands are the targets of an operation and the operator is a symbol representing the action. For example, here is an additive operation:

```
x + 4
```

In this case, **x** and 4 are the operands and + is the operator.

An operator may or may not return a result.

Note
Any legal combination of operators and operands are called an expression. For example, **x + 4** is an expression. A boolean expression results in either **true** or **false**. An integer expression produces an integer. And, the result of a floating-point expression is a floating point number.

Operators that require only one operand are called unary operators. There are a few unary operators in Java. Binary operators, the most common type of Java operator, take two operands. There is also one ternary operator, the **? :** operator, that requires three operands.

Table 2.4 list Java operators.

```
=      >      <      !      ~      ? :    instanceof
==     <=     >=     !=     &&     ||     ++     --
+      -      *      /      &      |      ^      %      <<     >>     >>>
+=     -=     *=     /=     &=     |=     ^=     %=     <<=    >>=    >>>=
```
Table 2.4: Java operators

In Java, there are six categories of operators.

- Unary operators
- Arithmetic operators
- Relational and conditional operators
- Shift and logical operators
- Assignment operators
- Other operators

Each of these operators is discussed in the following sections.

Unary Operators

Unary operators operate on one operand. There are six unary operators, all discussed in this section.

Unary Minus Operator –

The unary minus operator returns the negative of its operand. The operand must be a numeric primitive or a variable of a numeric primitive type. For example, in the following code, the value of **y** is -4.5;

```
float x = 4.5f;
float y = -x;
```

Unary Plus Operator +

This operator returns the value of its operand. The operand must be a numeric primitive or a variable of a numeric primitive type. For example, in the following code, the value of **y** is 4.5.

```
float x = 4.5f;
float y = +x;
```

This operator does not have much significance since its absence makes no difference.

Increment Operator ++

This operator increments the value of its operand by one. The operand must be a variable of a numeric primitive type. The operator can appear before or after the operand. If the operator appears before the operand, it is called the prefix increment operator. If it is written after the operand, it becomes the postfix increment operator.

As an example, here is a prefix increment operator in action:

```
int x = 4;
++x;
```

After **++x**, the value of **x** is 5. The preceding code is the same as

```
int x = 4;
x++;
```

After **x++**, the value of **x** is 5.

However, if the result of an increment operator is assigned to another variable in the same expression, there is a difference between the prefix operator and its postfix twin. Consider this example.

```
int x = 4;
int y = ++x;
// y = 5, x = 5
```

The prefix increment operator is applied *before* the assignment. **x** is incremented to 5, and then its value is copied to **y**.

However, check the use of the postfix increment operator here.

```
int x = 4;
int y = x++;
// y = 4, x = 5
```

With the postfix increment operator, the value of the operand (**x**) is incremented *after* the value of the operand is assigned to another variable (**y**).

Note that the increment operator is most often applied to **int**s. However, it also works with other types of numeric primitives, such as **float** and **long**.

Decrement Operator --

This operator decrements the value of its operand by one. The operand must be a variable of a numeric primitive type. Like the increment operator, there are also the prefix decrement operator and the postfix decrement operator. For instance, the following code decrements **x** and assigns the value to **y**.

```
int x = 4;
int y = --x;
// x = 3; y = 3
```

In the following example, the postfix decrement operator is used:

```
int x = 4;
int y = x--;
// x = 3; y = 4
```

Logical Complement Operator !

This operator can only be applied to a **boolean** primitive or an instance of **java.lang.Boolean**. The value of this operator is **true** if the operand is **false**, and **false** if the operand is **true**. For example:

```
boolean x = false;
boolean y = !x;
// at this point, y is true and x is false
```

Bitwise Complement Operator ~

The operand of this operator must be an integer primitive or a variable of an integer primitive type. The result is the bitwise complement of the operand. For example:

```
int j = 2;
int k = ~j; // k = -3; j = 2
```

To understand how this operator works, you need to convert the operand to a binary number and reverse all the bits. The binary form of 2 in an integer is:

```
0000 0000 0000 0000 0000 0000 0000 0010
```

Its bitwise complement is

```
1111 1111 1111 1111 1111 1111 1111 1101
```

which is the representation of -3 in an integer.

Arithmetic Operators

There are four types of arithmetic operations: addition, subtraction, multiplication, division, and modulus. Each arithmetic operator is discussed here.

Addition Operator +

The addition operator adds two operands. The types of the operands must be convertible to a numeric primitive. For example:

```
byte x = 3;
int y = x + 5; // y = 8
```

Make sure the variable that accepts the addition result has a big enough capacity. For example, in the following code the value of **k** is -294967296 and not 4 billion.

```
int j = 2000000000; // 2 billion
int k = j + j; // not enough capacity. A bug!!!
```

On the other hand, the following works as expected:

```
long j = 2000000000; // 2 billion
long k = j + j; // the value of k is 4 billion
```

Subtraction Operator −

This operator performs subtraction between two operands. The types of the operands must be convertible to a numeric primitive type. As an example:

```
int x = 2;
int y = x - 1;     // y = 1
```

Multiplication Operator *

This operator perform multiplication between two operands. The type of the operands must be convertible to a numeric primitive type. As an example:

```
int x = 4;
int y = x * 4;     // y = 16
```

Division Operator /

This operator perform division between two operands. The left hand operand is the dividend and the right hand operand the divisor. Both the dividend and the divisor must be of a type convertible to a numeric primitive type. As an example:

```
int x = 4;
```

```
int y = x / 2;    // y = 2
```

Note that at runtime a division operation raises an error if the divisor is zero.

The result of a division using the / operator is always an integer. If the divisor does not divide the dividends equally, the remainder will be ignored. For example

```
int x = 4;
int y = x / 3;    // y = 1
```

The **java.lang.Math** class, explained in Chapter 5, "Core Classes," can perform more sophisticated division operations.

Modulus Operator %

The modulus operator perform division between two operands and returns the remainder. The left hand operand is the dividend and the right hand operand the divisor. Both the dividend and the divisor must be of a type that is convertible to a numeric primitive type. For example the result of the following operation is 2.

```
8 % 3
```

Equality Operators

There are two equality operators, == (equal to) and != (not equal to), both operating on two operands that can be integers, floating points, characters, or **boolean**. The outcome of equality operators is a **boolean**.

For example, the value of **c** is **true** after the comparison.

```
int a = 5;
int b = 5;
boolean c = a == b;
```

As another example,

```
boolean x = true;
boolean y = true;
boolean z = x != y;
```

The value of **z** is **false** after comparison because **x** is equal to **y**.

Relational Operators

There are five relational operators: <, >, <=, and >= and **instanceof**. The first four operators are explained in this section. **instanceof** is discussed in Chapter 7, "Inheritance."

The <, >, <=, and >= operators operate on two operands whose types must be convertible to a numeric primitive type. Relational operations return a **boolean**.

The < operator evaluates if the value of the left-hand operand is less than the value of the right-hand operand. For example, the following operation returns **false**:

```
9 < 6
```

The > operator evaluates if the value of the left-hand operand is greater than the value of the right-hand operand. For example, this operation returns **true**:

```
9 > 6
```

The <= operator tests if the value of the left-hand operand is less than or equal to the value of the right-hand operand. For example, the following operation evaluates to **false**:

```
9 <= 6
```

The >= operator tests if the value of the left-hand operand is greater than or equal to the value of the right-hand operand. For example, this operation returns **true**:

```
9 >= 9
```

Conditional Operators

There are three conditional operators: the AND operator **&&**, the OR operator **||**, and the **?** **:** operator. Each of these is detailed below.

The && operator

This operator takes two expressions as operands and both expressions must return a value that must be convertible to **boolean**. It returns **true** if both operands evaluate to **true**. Otherwise, it returns **false**. If the left-hand operand evaluates to **false**, the right-hand operand will not be evaluated. For example, the following returns **false**.

```
(5 < 3) && (6 < 9)
```

The || Operator

This operator takes two expressions as operands and both expressions must return a value that must be convertible to **boolean**. || returns **true** if one of the operands evaluates to **true**. If the left-hand operand evaluates to **true**, the right-hand operand will not be evaluated. For instance, the following returns **true**.

```
(5 < 3) || (6 < 9)
```

The ? : Operator

This operator operates on three operands. The syntax is

```
expression1 ? expression2 : expression3
```

Here, *expression1* must return a value convertible to **boolean**. If *expression1* evaluates to **true**, *expression2* is returned. Otherwise, *expression3* is returned.

For example, the following expression returns 4.

```
(8 < 4) ? 2 : 4
```

Shift Operators

A shift operator takes two operands whose type must be convertible to an integer primitive. The left-hand operand is the value to be shifted, the right-hand operand indicates the shift distance. There are three types of shift operators:

- the left shift operator <<
- the right shift operator >>
- the unsigned right shift operator >>>

The Left Shift Operator <<

The left shift operator bit-shifts a number to the left, padding the right bits with 0. The value of **n** << **s** is **n** left-shifted **s** bit positions. This is the same as multiplication by two to the power of s.

For example, left-shifting an **int** whose value is 1 with a shift distance of 3 (1 << 3) results in 8. Again, to figure this out, you convert the operand to a binary number.

```
0000 0000 0000 0000 0000 0000 0000 0001
```

Shifting to the left 3 shift units results in:

```
0000 0000 0000 0000 0000 0000 0000 1000
```

which is equivalent to 8 (the same as $1 * 2^3$).

Another rule is this. If the left-hand operand is an **int**, only the first five bits of the shift distance will be used. In other words, the shift distance must be within the range 0 and 31. If you pass an number greater than 31, only the first five bits will be used. This is to say, if **x** is an **int**, **x** << **32** is the same as **x** << **0**; **x** << **33** is the same as **x** << **1**.

If the left-hand operand is a **long**, only the first six bits of the shift distance will be used. In other words, the shift distance actually used is within the range 0 and 63.

The Right Shift Operator >>

The right shift operator >> bit-shifts the left-hand operand to the right. The value of **n** >> **s** is **n** right-shifted **s** bit positions. The resulting value is **n/2^s**.

As an example, **16 >> 1** is equal to 8. To prove this, write the binary representation of 16.

```
0000 0000 0000 0000 0000 0000 0001 0000
```

Then, shifting it to the right by 1 bit results in.

```
0000 0000 0000 0000 0000 0000 0000 1000
```

which is equal to 8.

The Unsigned Right Shift Operator >>>

The value of **n** >>> **s** depends on whether **n** is positive or negative. For a positive **n**, the value is the same as **n** >> **s**.

If **n** is negative, the value depends on the type of **n**. If **n** is an **int**, the value is **(n>>s) +(2<<~s)**. If **n** is a **long**, the value is **(n>>s)+(2L<<~s)**.

Assignment Operators

There are twelve assignment operators:

```
=   +=   -=   *=   /=   %=   <<=   >>=   >>>=   &=   ^=   |=
```

Assignment operators take two operands whose type must be of an integral primitive. The left-hand operand must be a variable. For instance:

```
int x = 5;
```

Except for the assignment operator =, the rest work the same way and you should see each of them as consisting of two operators. For example, += is actually + and =. The assignment operator <<= has two operators, << and =.

The two-part assignment operators work by applying the first operator to both operands and then assign the result to the left-hand operand. For example x += 5 is the same as x = x + 5.

x -= 5 is the same as x = x - 5.

x <<= 5 is equivalent to x = x << 5.

x &= 5 produces the same result as x = x &= 5.

Integer Bitwise Operators & | ^

The bitwise operators **& | ^** perform a bit to bit operation on two operands whose types must be convertible to **int**. **&** indicates an AND operation, **|** an OR operation, and **^** an exclusive OR operation. For example,

```
0xFFFF & 0x0000 = 0x0000
0xF0F0 & 0xFFFF = 0xF0F0
0xFFFF | 0x000F = 0xFFFF
0xFFF0 ^ 0x00FF = 0xFF0F
```

Logical Operators & | ^

The logical operators **& | ^** perform a logical operation on two operands that are convertible to **boolean**. **&** indicates an AND operation, **|** an OR operation, and **^** an exclusive OR operation. For example,

```
true & true  = true
true & false = false
true | false = true
false | false = false
```

```
true ^ true = false
false ^ false = false
false ^ true = true
```

Operator Precedence

In most programs, multiple operators often appear in an expression, such as.

```
int a = 1;
int b = 2;
int c = 3;
int d = a + b * c;
```

What is the value of **d** after the code is executed? If you say 9, you're wrong. It's actually 7.

Multiplication operator * takes precedence over addition operator +. As a result, multiplication will be performed before addition. However, if you want the addition to be executed first, you can use parentheses.

```
int d = (a + b) * c;
```

The latter will assign 9 to **d**.

Table 2.5 lists all the operators in the order of precedence. Operators in the same column have equal precedence.

Operator	
postfix operators	[ ] . (params) expr++ expr--
unary operators	++expr --expr +expr -expr ~ !
creation or cast	new (type)expr
multiplicative	* / %
additive	+ -
shift	<< >> >>>
relational	< > <= >= instanceof
equality	== !=
bitwise AND	&
bitwise exclusive OR	^
bitwise inclusive OR	|
logical AND	&&
logical OR	||
conditional	? :
assignment	= += -= *= /= %= &= ^= |= <<= >>= >>>=

Table 2.5: Operator precedence

Note that parentheses have the highest precedence. Parentheses can also make expressions clearer. For example, consider the following code:

```
int x = 5;
int y = 5;
boolean z = x * 5 == y + 20;
```

The value of **z** after comparison is **true**. However, the expression is far from clear.

You can rewrite the last line using parentheses.

```
boolean z = (x * 5) == (y + 20);
```

which does not change the result because * and + have higher precedence than ==, but this makes the expression much clearer.

Promotion

Some unary operators (such as +, -, and ~) and binary operators (such as +, -, *, /) cause automatic promotion, i.e. elevation to a wider type such as from **byte** to **int**. Consider the following code:

```
byte x = 5;
byte y = -x; // error
```

The second line surprisingly causes an error even though a byte can accommodate -5. The reason for this is the unary operator - causes the result of **-x** to be promoted to **int**. To rectify the problem, either change **y** to **int** or perform an explicit narrowing conversion like this.

```
byte x = 5;
byte y = (byte) -x;
```

For unary operators, if the type of the operand is **byte**, **short**, or **char**, the outcome is promoted to **int**.

For binary operators, the promotion rules are as follows.

- If any of the operands is of type **byte** or **short**, then both operands will be converted to **int** and the outcome will be an **int**.
- If any of the operands is of type **double**, then the other operand is converted to **double** and the outcome will be a **double**.
- If any of the operands is of type **float**, then the other operand is converted to **float** and the outcome will be a **float**.
- If any of the operands is of type **long**, then the other operand is converted to **long** and the outcome will be a **long**.

For example, the following code causes a compile error:

```
short x = 200;
short y = 400;
short z = x + y;
```

You can fix this by changing **z** to **int** or perform an explicit narrowing conversion of **x + y**, such as

```
short z = (short) (x + y);
```

Note that the parentheses around **x + y** is required, otherwise only **x** would be converted to **int** and the result of addition of a **short** and an **int** will be an **int**.

Comments

It is good practice to write comments throughout your code, sufficiently explaining what functionality a class provides, what a method does, what a field contains, and so forth.

There are two types of comments in Java, both with syntax similar to comments in C and C++.

- Traditional comments. Enclose a traditional comment in /* and */.
- End-of-line comments. Use double slashes (//) which causes the rest of the line after // to be ignored by the compiler.

For example, here is a comment that describes a method

```
/*
  toUpperCase capitalizes the characters of in a String object
*/
public void toUpperCase(String s) {
```

Here is an end-of-line comment:

```
public int rowCount; //the number of rows from the database
```

Traditional comments do not nest, which means

```
/*
  /* comment 1 */
  comment 2 */
```

is invalid because the first */ after the first /* will terminate the comment. As such, the comment above will have the extra **comment 2 */**, which will generate a compiler error.

On the other hand, end-of-line comments can contain anything, including the sequences of characters /* and */, such as this:

```
// /* this comment is okay */
```

Summary

This chapter presents Java language fundamentals, the basic concepts and topics that you should master before proceeding to more advanced subjects. Topics of discussion include character sets, variables, primitives, literals, operators, operator precedence, and comments.

Chapter 3 continues with statements, another important topic of the Java language.

Quiz

1. What does ASCII stand for?
2. Does Java use ASCII characters or Unicode characters?
3. What are reference type variables, and what are primitive type variables?
4. How are constants implemented in Java?
5. What is an expression?
6. You need to assign the British pound symbol to a **char** but you do not have the £ key on your keyboard. How do you do this if you know the Unicode code for it is 00A3?
7. Name at least ten operators in Java.
8. What is the ternary operator in Java?
9. What is operator precedence?
10. Consider the following code. What are the values of result1 and result2? Why the difference?

    ```
    int result1 = 1 + 2 * 3;
    int result2 = (1 + 2) * 3;
    ```

11. Name two types of Java comments.

Chapter 3
Statements

A computer program is a compilation of instructions called statements. There are many types of statements in Java and some—such as **if**, **while**, **for**, and **switch**—are conditional statements that determine the program flow. This chapter discusses Java statements, starting with an overview and then providing details of each of them. The **return** statement, which is the statement to exit a method, is discussed in Chapter 4, "Objects and Classes."

Overview

In programming, a statement is an instruction to do something. Statements control the sequence of program execution. Assigning a value to a variable is an example of a statement.

```
x = z + 5;
```

Even a variable declaration is a statement.

```
long secondsElapsed;
```

By contrast, an *expression* is a combination of operators and operands that gets evaluated. For example, **z + 5** is an expression.

In Java a statement is terminated with a semicolon and multiple statements can be written in a single line.

```
x = y + 1; z = y + 2;
```

However, writing multiple statements in a single line is not recommended as it obscures code readability.

Note
In Java, an empty statement is legal and does nothing:

```
;
```

Some expressions can be made statements by terminating them with a semicolon. For example, **x++** is an expression. However, this is a statement:

```
x++;
```

Statements can be grouped in a block. By definition, a block is a sequence of the following programming elements within braces:

- statements
- local class declarations
- local variable declaration statements

A statement and a statement block can be labeled. Label names follow the same rule as Java identifiers and are terminated with a colon. For example, the following statement is labeled **sectionA**.

```
sectionA: x = y + 1;
```

And, here is an example of labeling a block:

```
start: {
    // statements
}
```

The purpose of labeling a statement or a block is so that it can be referenced by the **break** and **continue** statements.

The if Statement

The **if** statement is a conditional branch statement. The syntax of the **if** statement is either one of these two:

```
if (booleanExpression) {
    statement(s)
}
```

```
if (booleanExpression) {
    statement(s)
} else {
    statement(s)
}
```

If *booleanExpression* evaluates to **true**, the statements in the block following the **if** statement are executed. If it evaluates to **false**, the statements in the **if** block are not executed. If *booleanExpression* evaluates to **false** and there is an **else** block, the statements in the **else** block are executed.

For example, in the following **if** statement, the **if** block will be executed if **x** is greater than 4.

```
if (x > 4) {
    // statements
}
```

In the following example, the **if** block will be executed if **a** is greater than 3. Otherwise, the **else** block will be executed.

```
if (a > 3) {
    // statements
} else {
    // statements
```

```
}
```

Note that the good coding style suggests that statements in a block be indented.

If you are evaluating a boolean in your if statement, it's not necessary to use the ==
operator like this:

```
boolean fileExist = ...
if (fileExist == true) {
```

Instead, you can simply write

```
if (fileExists) {
```

By the same token, instead of writing

```
if (fileExists == false) {
```

write

```
if (!fileExists) {
```

If the expression to be evaluated is too long to be written in a single line, it is
recommended that you use two units of indentation for subsequent lines. For example.

```
if (numberOfLoginAttempts < numberOfMaximumLoginAttempts
        || numberOfMinimumLoginAttempts > y) {
    y++;
}
```

If there is only one statement in an **if** or **else** block, the braces are optional.

```
if (a > 3)
    a++;
else
    a = 3;
```

However, this may pose what is called the dangling else problem. Consider the following
example:

```
if (a > 0 || b < 5)
    if (a > 2)
        System.out.println("a > 2");
    else
        System.out.println("a < 2");
```

The **else** statement is dangling because it is not clear which **if** statement the **else** statement
is associated with. An **else** statement is always associated with the immediately preceding
if. Using braces makes your code clearer.

```
if (a > 0 || b < 5) {
    if (a > 2) {
        System.out.println("a > 2");
    } else {
        System.out.println("a < 2");
    }
}
```

If there are multiple selections, you can also use **if** with a series of **else** statements.

```
if (booleanExpression1) {
    // statements
} else if (booleanExpression2) {
    // statements
}
...
else {
    // statements
}
```

For example

```
if (a == 1) {
    System.out.println("one");
} else if (a == 2) {
    System.out.println("two");
} else if (a == 3) {
    System.out.println("three");
} else {
    System.out.println("invalid");
}
```

In this case, the **else** statements that are immediately followed by an **if** do not use braces. See also the discussion of the **switch** statement in the section "The switch Statement" later in this chapter.

The while Statement

In many occasions, you may want to perform an action several times in a row. In other words, you have a block of code that you want executed repeatedly. Intuitively, this can be done by repeating the lines of code. For instance, a beep can be achieved using this line of code:

```
java.awt.Toolkit.getDefaultToolkit().beep();
```

And, to wait for half a second you use these lines of code.

```
try {
    Thread.currentThread().sleep(500);
} catch (Exception e) {
}
```

Therefore, to produce three beeps with a 500 milliseconds interval between two beeps, you can simply repeat the same code:

```
java.awt.Toolkit.getDefaultToolkit().beep();
try {
    Thread.currentThread().sleep(500);
} catch (Exception e) {
}
```

```
java.awt.Toolkit.getDefaultToolkit().beep();
try {
    Thread.currentThread().sleep(500);
} catch (Exception e) {
}
java.awt.Toolkit.getDefaultToolkit().beep();
```

However, there are circumstances where repeating code does not work. Here are some of those:

- The number of repetition is higher than 5, which means the number of lines of code increases five fold. If there is a line that you need to fix in the block, copies of the same line must also be modified.
- If the number of repetitions is not known in advance.

A much cleverer way is to put the repeated code in a loop. This way, you only write the code once but you can instruct Java to execute the code any number of times. One way to create a loop is by using the **while** statement, which is the topic of discussion of this section. Another way is to use the **for** statement, which is explained in the next section.

The **while** statement has the following syntax.

```
while (booleanExpression) {
    statement(s)
}
```

Here, *statement(s)* will be executed as long as *booleanExpression* evaluates to **true**. If there is only a single statement inside the braces, you may omit the braces. For clarity, however, you should always use braces even when there is only one statement.

As an example of the **while** statement, the following code prints integer numbers that are less than three.

```
int i = 0;
while (i < 3) {
    System.out.println(i);
    i++;
}
```

Note that the execution of the code in the loop is dependent on the value of **i**, which is incremented with each iteration until it reaches 3.

To produce three beeps with an interval of 500 milliseconds, use this code:

```
int j = 0;
while (j < 3) {
    java.awt.Toolkit.getDefaultToolkit().beep();
    try {
        Thread.currentThread().sleep(500);
    } catch (Exception e) {
    }
    j++;
}
```

Sometimes, you use an expression that always evaluates to **true** (such as the **boolean** literal **true**) but relies on the **break** statement to escape from the loop.

```
int k = 0;
while (true) {
    System.out.println(k);
    k++;
    if (k > 2) {
        break;
    }
}
```

You will learn about the **break** statement in the section, "The break Statement" later in this chapter.

The do-while Statement

The **do-while** statement is like the **while** statement, except that the associated block always gets executed at least once. Its syntax is as follows:

```
do {
    statement(s)
} while (booleanExpression);
```

With **do-while**, you put the statement(s) to be executed after the **do** keyword. Just like the **while** statement, you can omit the braces if there is only one statement within them. However, always use braces for the sake of clarity.

For example, here is an example of the **do-while** statement:

```
int i = 0;
do {
    System.out.println(i);
    i++;
} while (i < 3);
```

This prints the following to the console:

```
0
1
2
```

The following **do-while** demonstrates that at least the code in the **do** block will be executed once even though the initial value of **j** used to test the expression **j < 3** evaluates to **false**.

```
int j = 4;
do {
    System.out.println(j);
    j++;
} while (j < 3);
```

This prints the following on the console.

```
4
```

The for Statement

The **for** statement is like the **while** statement, i.e. you use it to enclose code that needs to be executed multiple times. However, **for** is more complex than **while**.

The **for** statement starts with an initialization, followed by an expression evaluation for each iteration and the execution of a statement block if the expression evaluates to **true**. An update statement will also be executed after the execution of the statement block for each iteration.

The **for** statement has following syntax:

```
for ( init ; booleanExpression ; update ) {
    statement(s)
}
```

Here, *init* is an initialization that will be performed before the first iteration, *booleanExpression* is a boolean expression which will cause the execution of *statement(s)* if it evaluates to **true**, and *update* is a statement that will be executed *after* the execution of the statement block. *init*, *expression*, and *update* are optional.

The **for** statement will stop only if one of the following conditions is met:

- *booleanEpression* evaluates to **false**
- A **break** or **continue** statement is executed
- A runtime error occurs.

It is common to declare a variable and assign a value to it in the initialization part. The variable declared will be visible to the *expression* and *update* parts as well as to the statement block.

For example, the following **for** statement loops three times and each time prints the value of **i**.

```
for (int i = 0; i < 3; i++) {
    System.out.println(i);
}
```

The **for** statement starts by declaring an **int** named **i** and assigning 0 to it:

```
int i = 0;
```

It then evaluates the expression **i < 3**, which evaluates to **true** since **i** equals 0. As a result, the statement block is executed, and the value of **i** is printed. It then performs the update statement **i++**, which increments **i** to 1. That concludes the first loop.

The **for** statement then evaluates the value of **i < 3** again. The result is again **true** because **i** equals 1. This causes the statement block to be executed and **1** is printed on the console. Afterwards, the update statement **i++** is executed, incrementing **i** to 2. That concludes the third loop.

Next, the expression **i < 3** is evaluated and the result is **true** because **i** equals 2. This causes the statement block to be run and 2 is printed on the console. Afterwards, the update statement **i++** is executed, causing **i** to be equal to 3. This concludes the second loop.

Next, the expression **i < 3** is evaluated again, and the result is **false**. This stops the **for** loop.

This is what you see on the console:

```
0
1
2
```

Note that the variable **i** is not visible anywhere else since it is declared within the **for** loop.

Note also that if the statement block within **for** only consists of one statement, you can remove the braces, so in this case the above **for** statement can be rewritten as:

```
for (int i = 0; i < 3; i++)
    System.out.println(i);
```

However, using braces even if there is only one statement makes your code clearer.

Here is another example of the **for** statement.

```
for (int i = 0; i < 3; i++) {
    if (i % 2 == 0) {
        System.out.println(i);
    }
}
```

This one loops three times. For each iteration the value of **i** is tested. If **i** is even, its value is printed. The result of the **for** loop is as follows:

```
0
2
```

The following **for** loop is similar to the previous case, but uses **i += 2** as the update statement. As a result, it only loops twice, when **i** equals 0 and when it is 2.

```
for (int i = 0; i < 3; i += 2) {
    System.out.println(i);
}
```

The result is

```
0
2
```

A statement that decrements a variable is often used too. Consider the following **for** loop:

```
for (int i = 3; i > 0; i--) {
    System.out.println(i);
}
```

which prints:

```
3
2
1
```

The initialization part of the **for** statement is optional. In the following **for** loop, the variable **j** is declared outside the loop, so potentially **j** can be used from other points in the code outside the **for** statement block.

```
int j = 0;
for ( ; j < 3; j++) {
    System.out.println(j);
}
// j is visible here
```

As mentioned previously, the update statement is optional. The following **for** statement moves the update statement to the end of the statement block. The result is the same.

```
int k = 0;
for ( ; k < 3; ) {
    System.out.println(k);
    k++;
}
```

In theory, you can even omit the *booleanExpression* part. For example, the following **for** statement does not have one, and the loop is only terminated with the **break** statement. See the section, "The break Statement" for more information.

```
int m = 0;
for ( ; ; ) {
    System.out.println(m);
    m++;
    if (m > 4) {
        break;
    }
}
```

If you compare **for** and **while**, you'll see that you can always replace the **while** statement with **for**. This is to say that

```
while (expression) {
    ...
}
```

can always be written as

```
for ( ; expression; ) {
    ...
}
```

> **Note**
> In addition, **for** can iterate over an array or a collection. See Chapters 6, "Arrays" and Chapter 14, "The Collections Framework" for discussions of the enhanced **for**.

The break Statement

The **break** statement is used to break from an enclosing **do**, **while**, **for**, or **switch** statement. It is a compile error to use **break** anywhere else.

For example, consider the following code

```java
int i = 0;
while (true) {
    System.out.println(i);
    i++;
    if (i > 3) {
        break;
    }
}
```

The result is

```
0
1
2
3
```

Note that **break** breaks the loop without executing the rest of the statements in the block.

Here is another example of break, this time in a **for** loop.

```java
int m = 0;
for ( ; ; ) {
    System.out.println(m);
    m++;
    if (m > 4) {
        break;
    }
}
```

The **break** statement can be followed by a label. The presence of a label will transfer control to the start of the code identified by the label. For example, consider this code.

```java
start:
for (int i = 0; i < 3; i++) {
    for (int j = 0; j < 4; j++) {
        if (j == 2) {
            break start;
        }
        System.out.println(i + ":" + j);
    }
}
```

The use of label start identifies the first **for** loop. The statement **break start;** therefore breaks from the first loop. The result of running the preceding code is as follows.

```
0:0
0:1
```

Java does not have a goto statement like in C or C++, and labels are meant as a form of goto. However, just as using goto in C/C++ may obscure your code, the use of labels in Java may make your code unstructured. The general advice is to avoid labels if possible and to always use them with caution.

The continue Statement

The **continue** statement is like **break** but it only stops the execution of the current iteration and causes control to begin with the next iteration.

For example, the following code prints the number 0 to 9, except 5.

```
for (int i = 0; i < 10; i++) {
    if (i == 5) {
        continue;
    }
    System.out.println(i);
}
```

When **i** is equals to 5, the expression of the **if** statement evaluates to **true** and causes the **continue** statement to be called. As a result, the statement below it that prints the value of **i** is not executed and control continues with the next loop, i.e. for **i** equal to 6.

As with **break, continue** may be followed by a label to identify which enclosing loop to continue to. As with labels with **break**, employ **continue label** with caution and avoid it if you can.

Here is an example of **continue** with a label.

```
start:
for (int i = 0; i < 3; i++) {
    for (int j = 0; j < 4; j++) {
        if (j == 2) {
            continue start;
        }
        System.out.println(i + ":" + j);
    }
}
```

The result of running this code is as follows:

```
0:0
0:1
1:0
1:1
2:0
2:1
```

The switch Statement

An alternative to a series of **else if**, as discussed in the last part of the section, "The if Statement," is the **switch** statement. **switch** allows you to choose a block of statements to run from a selection of code, based on the return value of an expression. The expression used in the **switch** statement must return an **int**, a **String**, or an enumerated value.

Note
The **String** class is discussed in Chapter 5, "Core Classes" and enumerated values in Chapter 12, "Enums."

The syntax of the **switch** statement is as follows.

```
switch(expression) {
case value_1 :
    statement(s);
    break;
case value_2 :
    statement(s);
    break;
    .
    .
    .
case value_n :
    statement(s);
    break;
default:
    statement(s);
}
```

Failure to add a **break** statement after a case will not generate a compile error but may have more serious consequences because the statements on the next case will be executed.

Here is an example of the **switch** statement. If the value of **i** is 1, "One player is playing this game." is printed. If the value is 2, "Two players are playing this game is printed." If the value is 3, "Three players are playing this game is printed. For any other value, "You did not enter a valid value." will be printed.

```
int i = ...;
switch (i) {
case 1 :
    System.out.println("One player is playing this game.");
    break;
case 2 :
    System.out.println("Two players are playing this game.");
    break;
case 3 :
    System.out.println("Three players are playing this game.");
    break;
default:
    System.out.println("You did not enter a valid value.");
}
```

For examples of switching on a String or an enumerated value, see Chapter 5, "Core Classes" and Chapter 10, "Enums," respectively.

Summary

The sequence of execution of a Java program is controlled by statements. In this chapter, you have learned the following Java control statements: **if**, **while**, **do-while**, **for**, **break**, **continue**, and **switch**. Understanding how to use these statements is crucial to writing correct programs.

Quiz

1. What is the difference between an expression and a statement?
2. How do you escape from the following while loop?

```
while (true) {
    // statements
}
```

3. Is there any difference between using the postfix increment operator and the prefix increment operator as the update statement of a **for** loop?

```
for (int x = 0; x < length; x++)
for (int x = 0; x < length; ++x)
```

4. What will be printed on the console if the code below is executed:

```
int i = 1;
switch (i) {
case 1 :
    System.out.println("One player is playing this game.");
case 2 :
    System.out.println("Two players are playing this game.");
    break;
default:
    System.out.println("You did not enter a valid value.");
}
```

Hint: no **break** after case 1.
5. Write a class that uses **for** to print all even numbers from 1 to 9.
6. Write a class that uses **for** to print all even numbers between two integers, *a* and *b*, including *b* if *b* is an even number.
7. Same as before, but print the numbers in descending order.

Chapter 4
Objects and Classes

Object-oriented programming (OOP) works by modeling applications on real-world objects. The benefits of OOP are real, which explains why OOP is the paradigm of choice today and why OOP languages like Java are popular. This chapter introduces you to objects and classes. If you are new to OOP, you may want to read this chapter carefully. A good understanding of OOP is key to writing quality programs.

This chapter starts by explaining what an object is and what constitutes a class. It then teaches you how to create an object with the **new** keyword, how objects are stored in memory, how classes can be organized into packages, how to use access control to achieve encapsulation, how the Java Virtual Machine (JVM) loads and links objects, and how Java manages unused objects. In addition, method overloading and static class members are explained.

What Is An Object?

When developing an application in an OOP language, you create a model that resembles a real-life situation to solve your problem. Take for example a payroll application, which calculates an employee's income tax and take home pay. An application like this would have a **Company** object to represent the company using the application, **Employee** objects that represent the employees in the company, **Tax** objects to represent the tax details of each employee, and so on. Before you can start programming such applications, however, you need to understand what Java objects are and how to create them.

Let's begin with a look at objects in life. Objects are everywhere, living (persons, pets, etc) and otherwise (cars, houses, streets, etc); concrete (books, televisions, etc) and abstract (love, knowledge, tax rate, regulations, and so forth). Every object has two features: the attributes and the actions the object can perform. For example, the following are some of a car's attributes:

- color
- number of doors
- plate number

Additionally, a car can perform these actions:

- run
- brake

As another example, a dog has the following attributes: color, age, type, weight, etc. And it can bark, run, urinate, sniff, etc.

A Java object also has attribute(s) and can perform action(s). In Java, attributes are called fields and actions are called methods. In other programming languages these may be known by other names. For example, methods are often called functions.

Both fields and methods are optional, meaning some Java objects may not have fields but have methods and some others may have fields but not methods. Some, of course, have both attributes and methods and some have neither.

How do you create Java objects? This is the same as asking, "How do you make cars?" Cars are expensive objects that need careful design that takes into account many things, such as safety and cost-effectiveness. You need a good blueprint to make good cars. To create Java objects, you need similar blueprints: classes.

Java Classes

A class is a blueprint or template to create objects of identical type. If you have an **Employee** class, you can create any number of **Employee** objects. To create **Street** objects, you need a **Street** class. A class determines what kind of object you get. For example, if you create an **Employee** class that has **age** and **position** fields, all **Employee** objects created out of this **Employee** class will have **age** and **position** fields as well. No more no less. The class determines the object.

In summary, classes are an OOP tool that enable programmers to create the abstraction of a problem. In OOP, abstraction is the act of using programming objects to represent real-world objects. As such, programming objects do not need to have the details of real-world objects. For instance, if an **Employee** object in a payroll application needs only be able to work and receive a salary, then the **Employee** class needs only two methods, **work** and **receiveSalary**. OOP abstraction ignores the fact that a real-world employee can do many other things including eat, run, kiss and kick.

Classes are the fundamental building blocks of a Java program. All program elements in Java must reside in a class, even if you are writing a simple program that does not require Java's object-oriented features. A Java beginner needs to consider three things when writing a class:

- the class name
- the fields
- the methods

There are other things that can be present in a class, but they will be discussed later.

A class declaration must use the keyword **class** followed by a class name. Also, a class has a body within braces. Here is a general syntax for a class:

```
class className {
    [class body]
}
```

For example, Listing 4.1 shows a Java class named **Employee**, where the lines in bold are the class body.

Listing 4.1: The Employee class

```
class Employee {
    int age;
    double salary;
}
```

Note

By convention, class names capitalize the initial of each word. For example, here are some names that follow the convention: **Employee**, **Boss**, **DateUtility**, **PostOffice**, **RegularRateCalculator**. This type of naming convention is known as Pascal naming convention. The other convention, the camel naming convention, capitalize the initial of each word, except the first word. Method and field names use the camel naming convention.

A public class definition must be saved in a file that has the same name as the class name, even though this restriction does not apply to non-public classes. The file name must have **java** extension.

Note

In UML class diagrams, a class is represented by a rectangle that consists of three parts: the topmost part is the class name, the middle part is the list of fields, and the bottom part is the list of methods. (See Figure 4.1) The fields and methods can be hidden if showing them is not important.

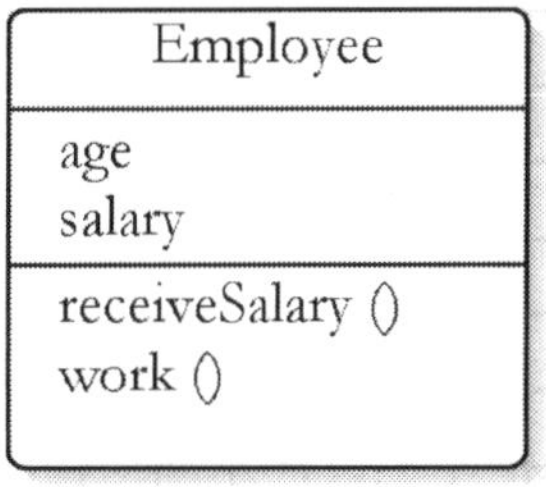

Figure 4.1: The Employee class in the UML class diagram

Fields

Fields are variables. They can be primitives or references to objects. For example, the **Employee** class in Listing 4.1 has two fields, **age** and **salary**. In Chapter 2, "Language Fundamentals" you learned how to declare and initialize variables of primitive types.

However, a field can also refer to another object. For instance, an **Empoyee** class may have an **address** field of type **Address**, which is a class that represents a street address:

```
Address address;
```

In other words, an object can contain other objects, that is if the class of the former contains variables that reference to the latter.

Field names should follow the camel naming convention. The initial of each word in the field, except for the first word, is written with a capital letter. For example, here are some "good" field names: **age**, **maxAge**, **address**, **validAddress**, **numberOfRows**.

Methods

A methods defines an action that a class's objects (or instances) can perform. A method has a declaration part and a body. The declaration part consists of a return value, the method name and a list of arguments. The body contains code that performs the action.

To declare a method, use the following syntax:

```
returnType methodName (listOfArguments)
```

The return type of a method can be a primitive, an object or void. The return type **void** means that the method returns nothing. The declaration part of a method is also called the signature of the method.

For example, here is a method named **getSalary** that returns a **double**.

```
double getSalary()
```

The **getSalary** method does not accept arguments.

As another example, here is a method that returns an **Address** object.

```
Address getAddress()
```

And, here is a method that accepts an argument:

```
int negate(int number)
```

If a method takes more than one argument, two arguments are separated by a comma. For example, the following **add** method takes two **int**s and return an **int**.

```
int add(int a, int b)
```

The Method main

A special method called **main** provides the entry point to an application. An application normally has many classes and only one of the classes needs to have a **main** method. This method allows the containing class to be invoked.

The signature of the **main** method is as follows.

```
public static void main(String[] args)
```

If you wonder why there is "public static void" before **main**, you will get the answer towards the end of this chapter.

You can pass arguments to **main** when using **java** to run a class. To pass arguments, type them after the class name. Two arguments are separated by a space.

```
java className arg1 arg2 arg3 ...
```

All arguments must be passed as strings. For instance, to pass two arguments, "1" and "safeMode" when running a **Test** class, type this:

```
java Test 1 safeMode
```

Strings are discussed in Chapter 5, "Core Classes."

Constructors

Every class must have at least one constructor. Otherwise, no objects could be created out of it and the class would be useless. As such, if your class does not explicitly define a constructor, the compiler adds one for you.

A constructor is used to construct an object. A constructor looks like a method and is sometimes called a constructor method. However, unlike a method, a constructor does not have a return value, not even **void**. Additionally, a constructor must have the same name as the class.

The syntax for a constructor is as follows.

```
constructorName (listOfArguments) {
    [constructor body]
}
```

A constructor may have zero argument, in which case it is called a no-argument (or no-arg, for short) constructor. Constructor arguments can be used to initialize the fields in the object.

If the Java compiler adds a no-arg constructor to a class because the class contains no constructor, the addition will be implicit, i.e. it will not be displayed in the source file. However, if there is a constructor in a class definition, regardless of the number of arguments it accepts, no constructor will be added to the class by the compiler.

As an example, Listing 4.2 adds two constructors to the **Employee** class in Listing 4.1.

Listing 4.2: The Employee class with constructors

```
public class Employee {
    public int age;
    public double salary;
    public Employee() {
    }
    public Employee(int ageValue, double salaryValue) {
        age = ageValue;
        salary = salaryValue;
    }
}
```

The second constructor is particularly useful. Without it, to assign values to age and position, you would need to write extra lines of code to initialize the fields:

```
employee.age = 20;
employee.salary = 90000.00;
```

With the second constructor, you can pass the values at the same time you create an object.

```
new Employee(20, 90000.00);
```

The **new** keyword is new to you, but you will learn how to use it later in this chapter.

Varargs

Varargs is a Java feature that allows methods to have a variable length of argument list. Here is an example of a method called **average** that accepts any number of **int**s and calculates their average.

```
public double average(int... args)
```

The ellipsis says that there is zero or more arguments of this type. For example, the following code calls **average** with two and three **int**s.

```
double avg1 = average(100, 1010);
double avg2 = average(10, 100, 1000);
```

If an argument list contains both fixed arguments (arguments that must exist) and variable arguments, the variable arguments must come last.

You should be able to implement methods that accept varargs after you read about arrays in Chapter 6, "Arrays." Basically, you receive a vararg as an array.

Class Members in UML Class Diagrams

Figure 4.1 depicts a class in a UML class diagram. The diagram provides a quick summary of all fields and methods. You could do more in UML. UML allows you to include field types and method signatures. For example, Figure 4.2 presents a **Book** class with five fields and one method.

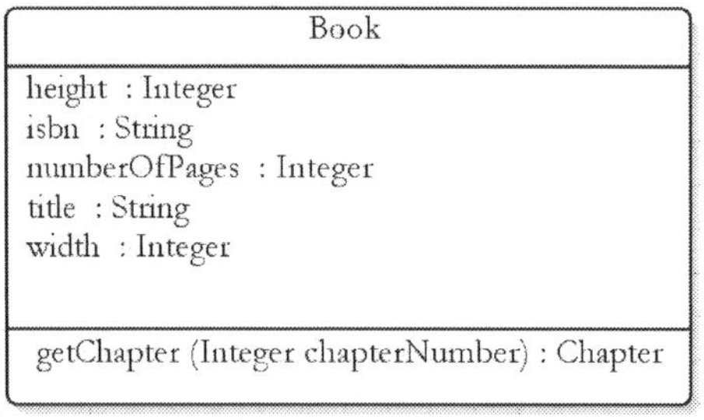

```
┌─────────────────────────────────────────────────┐
│                      Book                        │
├─────────────────────────────────────────────────┤
│ height  : Integer                                │
│ isbn  : String                                   │
│ numberOfPages  : Integer                         │
│ title  : String                                  │
│ width  : Integer                                 │
│                                                  │
├─────────────────────────────────────────────────┤
│ getChapter (Integer chapterNumber) : Chapter     │
└─────────────────────────────────────────────────┘
```

Figure 4.2: Including class member information in a class diagram

Note that in a UML class diagram a field and its type is separated by a colon. A method's argument list is presented in parentheses and its return type is written after a colon.

Creating An Object

Now that you know how to write a class, it is time to learn how to create an object from a class. An object is also called an instance. The word construct is often used in lieu of create, thus constructing an **Employee** object. Another term commonly used is *instantiate*. Instantiating the **Employee** class is the same as creating an instance of **Employee**.

There are a number of ways to create an object, but the most common one is by using the **new** keyword. **new** is always followed by the constructor of the class to be instantiated. For example, to create an **Employee** object, you write:

```
new Employee();
```

Most of the time, you will want to assign the created object to an object variable (or a reference variable), so that you can manipulate the object later. To achieve this, you need to declare an object reference with the same type as the object. For instance:

```
Employee employee = new Employee();
```

Here, **employee** is an object reference of type **Employee**.

Once you have an object, you can call its methods and access its fields, by using the object reference that was assigned the object. You use a period (.) to call a method or a field. For example:

```
objectReference.methodName
objectReference.fieldName
```

The following code, for instance, creates an **Employee** object and assigns values to its **age** and **salary** fields:

```
Employee employee = new Employee();
employee.age = 24;
employee.salary = 50000;
```

The null Keyword

A reference variable refers to an object. There are times, however, when a reference variable does not have a value (it is not referencing an object). Such a reference variable is said to have a null value. For example, the following class level reference variable is of type **Book** but has not been assigned a value;

```
Book book; // book is null
```

If you declare a local reference variable within a method but do not assign an object to it, you will need to assign null to it to satisfy the compiler:

```
Book book = null;
```

Class-level reference variables will be initialized when an instance is created, therefore you do not need to assign **null** to them.

Trying to access the field or method of a null variable reference raises an error, such as in the following code:

```
Book book = null;
System.out.println(book.title); // error because book is null
```

You can test if a reference variable is **null** by using the == operator. For instance.

```
if (book == null) {
    book = new Book();
}
```

```
System.out.println(book.title);
```

Memory Allocation for Objects

When you declare a variable in your class, either in the class level or in the method level, you allocate memory space for data that will be assigned to the variable. For primitives, it is easy to calculate the amount of memory taken. For example, declaring an **int** costs you four bytes and declaring a **long** sets you back eight bytes. However, calculation for reference variables is different.

When a program runs, some memory space is allocated for data. This data space is logically divided into two, the stack and the heap. Primitives are allocated in the stack and Java objects reside in the heap.

When you declare a primitive, several bytes are allocated in the stack. When you declare a reference variable, some bytes are also set aside in the stack, but the memory does not contain the object's data, it contains the address of the object in the heap. In other words, when you declare

```
Book book;
```

Some bytes are set aside for the reference variable **book**. The initial value of **book** is **null** because there is not yet an object assigned to it. When you write

```
Book book = new Book();
```

you create an instance of **Book**, which is stored in the heap, and assign the address of the instance to the reference variable **book**. A Java reference variable is like a C++ pointer except that you cannot manipulate a reference variable. In Java, a reference variable is used to access the member of the object it is referring to. Therefore, if the **Book** class has a public **review** method, you can call the method by using this syntax:

```
book.review();
```

An object can be referenced by more than one reference variable. For example,

```
Book myBook = new Book();
Book yourBook = myBook;
```

The second line copies the value of **myBook** to **yourBook**. As a result, **yourBook** is now referencing the same **Book** object as **myBook**.

Figure 4.3 illustrates memory allocation for a **Book** object referenced by **myBook** and **yourBook**.

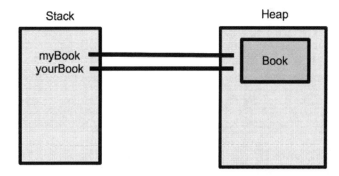

Figure 4.3: An object referenced by two variables

On the other hand, the following code creates two different **Book** objects:

```
Book myBook = new Book();
Book yourBook = new Book();
```

The memory allocation for this code is illustrated in Figure 4.4.

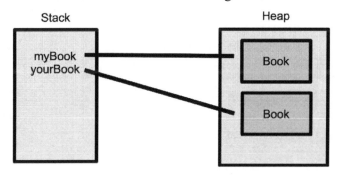

Figure 4.4: Two objects referenced by two variables

Now, how about an object that contains another object? For example, consider the code in Listing 4.3 that shows an **Employee** class that contains an **Address** class.

Listing 4.3: An Employee class that contains another class

```
public class Employee {
    Address address = new Address();
}
```

When you create an **Employee** object using the following code, an **Address** object is also created.

```
Employee employee = new Employee();
```

Figure 4.5 depicts the position of each object in the heap.

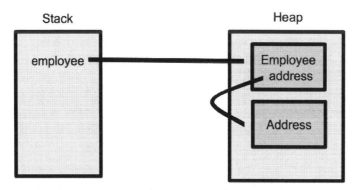

Figure 4.5: An object "within" another object

It turns out that the **Address** object is not really inside the **Employee** object. However, the **address** field within the **Employee** object has a reference to the **Address** object, thus allowing the **Employee** object to manipulate the **Address** object. Because in Java there is no way of accessing an object except through a reference variable assigned the object's address, no one else can access the **Address** object 'within' the **Employee** object.

Java Packages

If you are developing an application that consists of different parts, you may want to organize your classes to retain maintainability. With Java, you can group related classes or classes with similar functionality in packages. For example, standard Java classes come in packages. Java core classes are in the **java.lang** package. All classes for performing input and output operations are members of the **java.io** package, and so on. If a package needs to be organized in more detail, you can create packages that share part of the name of the former. For example, the Java class library comes with the **java.lang.annotation** and **java.lang.reflect** packages. However, mind you that sharing part of the name does not make two packages related. The **java.lang** package and the **java.lang.reflect** package are different packages.

Package names that start with **java** are reserved for the core libraries. Consequently, you cannot create a package that starts with the word **java**. You can compile classes that belong to such a package, but you cannot run them.

In addition, packages starting with **javax** are meant for extension libraries that accompany the core libraries. You should not create packages that start with **javax** either.

In addition to class organization, packaging can avoid naming conflict. For example, an application may use the **MathUtil** class from company A and an identically named class from another company if both classes belong to different packages. For this purpose, by convention your package names should be based on your domain name in reverse. Therefore, Sun's package names start with **com.sun**. My domain name is **brainysoftware.com**, so it's appropriate for me to start my package name with **com.brainysoftware**. For example, I would place all my applets in a **com.brainysoftware.applet** package and my servlets in **com.brainysoftware.servlet**.

A package is not a physical object, and therefore you do not need to create one. To group a class in a package, use the keyword **package** followed by the package name. For example, the following **MathUtil** class is part of the **com.brainysoftware.common** package:

```
package com.brainysoftware.common;
public class MathUtil {
    ...
}
```

Java also introduces the term *fully qualified name*, which refers to a class name that carries with it its package name. The fully qualified name of a class is its package name followed by a period and the class name. Therefore, the fully qualified name of a **Launcher** class that belongs to package **com.example** is **com.example.Launcher**.

A class that has no package declaration is said to belong to the default package. For example, the **Employee** class in Listing 4.1 belongs to the default package. You should always use a package because types in the default package cannot be used by other types outside the default package (except when using a technique called reflection). It is a bad idea for a class to not have a package.

Even though a package is not a physical object, package names have a bearing on the physical location of their class source files. A package name represents a directory structure in which a period in a package name indicates a subfolder. For example, all Java source files in the **com.brainysoftware.common** package must reside in the **common** directory that is a subdirectory of the **brainysoftware** directory. In turn, the latter must be a subdirectory of the **com** directory. Figure 4.6 depicts the folder structure for a **com.brainysoftware.common.MathUtil** class.

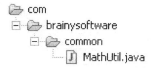

Figure 4.6: The physical location of a class in a package

Compiling a class in a non-default package presents a challenge for beginners. To compile such a class, you need to include the package name, replacing the dot (.) with /. For example, to compile the **com.brainysoftware.common.MathUtil** class, change directory to the working directory (the directory which is the parent directory of **com**) and type

```
javac com/brainysoftware/common/MathUtil.java
```

By default, **javac** will place the result in the same directory structure as the source. In this case, a **MathUtil.class** file will be created in the **com/brainysoftware/common** directory.

Running a class that belongs to a package follows a similar rule: you must include the package name, replacing . with /. For example, to run the **com.brainysoftware.common.MathUtil** class, type the following from your working directory.

```
java com/brainysoftware/common/MathUtil
```

The packaging of your classes also affects the visibility of your classes, as you will witness in the next section.

Encapsulation and Access Control

An OOP principle, encapsulation is a mechanism that protects parts of an object that need to be secure and exposes only parts that are safe to be exposed. A television is a good example of encapsulation. Inside it are thousands of electronic components that together form the parts that can receive signals and decode them into images and sound. These components are not to be accessible to the user, however, so Sony and other manufacturers wrap them in a strong metallic cover that does not break easily. For a television to be easy to use, it exposes buttons that the user can touch to turn on and off the set, adjust brightness, turn up and down the volume, and so on.

Back to encapsulation in OOP, let's take as an example a class that can encode and decode messages. The class exposes two methods called **encode** and **decode**, that users of the class can access. Internally, there are dozens of variables used to store temporary values and other methods that perform supporting tasks. The author of the class hides these variables and other methods because allowing access to them may compromise the security of the encoding/decoding algorithms. Besides, exposing too many things makes the class harder to use. As you can see later, encapsulation is a powerful feature.

Java supports encapsulation through access control. Access control is governed by access control modifiers. There are four access control modifiers in Java: **public**, **protected**, **private** and the default access level. Access control modifiers can be applied to classes or class members. They are explained in the following subsections.

Class Access Control Modifiers

In an application with many classes, a class may be instantiated and used from another class that is a member of the same package or a different package. You can control from which packages your class can be "seen" by employing an access control modifier at the beginning of the class declaration.

A class can have either the public or the default access control level. You make a class public by using the **public** access control modifier. A class whose declaration bears no access control modifier has default access. A public class is visible from anywhere. Listing 4.4 shows a public class named **Book**.

Listing 4.4: The public class Book

```
package app04;
public class Book {
    String isbn;
    String title;
    int width;
    int height;
    int numberOfPages;
}
```

The **Book** class is a member of the **app04** package and has five fields. Since **Book** is public, it can be instantiated from any other classes. In fact, the majority of the classes in the Java core libraries are public classes. For example, here is the declaration of the **java.lang.Runtime** class:

```
public class Runtime
```

A public class must be saved in a file that has the same name as the class, and the extension must be **java**. The **Book** class in Listing 4.4 must be saved in a **Book.java** file. Also, because **Book** belongs to package **app04**, the **Book.java** file must reside inside an **app04** directory.

Note
A Java source file can only contain one public class. However, it can contain multiple classes that are not public.

When there is no access control modifier preceding a class declaration, the class has the default access level. For example, Listing 4.5 presents the **Chapter** class that has the default access level.

Listing 4.5: The Chapter class, with the default access level

```
package app04;
class Chapter {
    String title;
    int numberOfPages;

    public void review() {
        Page page = new Page();
        int sentenceCount = page.numberOfSentences;
        int pageNumber = page.getPageNumber();
    }
}
```

Classes with the default access level can only be used by other classes that belong to the same package. For instance, the **Chapter** class can be instantiated from inside the **Book** class because **Book** belongs to the same package as **Chapter**. However, **Chapter** is not visible from other packages.

For example, you can add the following **getChapter** method inside the **Book** class:

```
Chapter getChapter() {
    return new Chapter();
}
```

On the other hand, if you try to add the same **getChapter** method to a class that does not belong to the **app04** package, a compile error will be raised.

Class Member Access Control Modifiers

Class members (methods, fields, constructors, etc) can have one of four access control levels: public, protected, private and default access. The access control modifier **public** is used to make a class member public, the **protected** modifier to make a class member protected, and the **private** modifier to make a class member private. Without an access control modifier, a class member will have the default access level.

Table 4.1 shows the visibility of each access level.

Access Level	From classes in other packages	From classes in the same package	From child classes	From the same class
public	yes	yes	yes	yes
protected	no	yes	yes	yes
default	no	yes	no	yes
private	no	no	no	yes

Table 4.1: Class member access levels

Note
The default access is sometimes called package private. To avoid confusion, this book will only use the term default access.

A public class member can be accessed by any other classes that can access the class containing the class member. For example, the **toString** method of the **java.lang.Object** class is public. Here is the method signature:

```
public String toString()
```

Once you construct an **Object** object, you can call its **toString** method because **toString** is public.

```
Object obj = new Object();
obj.toString();
```

Recall that you access a class member by using this syntax:

```
referenceVariable.memberName
```

In the preceding code, **obj** is a reference variable to an instance of **java.lang.Object** and **toString** is the method defined in the **java.lang.Object** class.

A protected class member has a more restricted access level. It can be accessed only from

- any class in the same package as the class containing the member
- a child class of the class containing the member

Note
A child class is a class that extends another class. Chapter 7, "Inheritance" explains this concept.

For instance, consider the public class **Page** in Listing 4.6.

Listing 4.6: The Page class
```
package app04;
public class Page {
    int numberOfSentences = 10;
    private int pageNumber = 5;
    protected int getPageNumber() {
        return pageNumber;
    }
}
```

Page has two fields (**numberOfSentences** and **pageNumber**) and one method (**getPageNumber**). First of all, because **Page** is public, it can be instantiated from any other class. However, even if you can instantiate it, there is no guarantee you can access its members. It depends on from which class you are accessing the **Page** class's members.

Its **getPageNumber** method is protected, so it can be accessed from any classes that belong to **app04**, the package that houses the **Page** class. For example, consider the **review** method in the **Chapter** class (given in Listing 4.5).

```
public void review() {
    Page page = new Page();
    int sentenceCount = page.numberOfSentences;
    int pageNumber = page.getPageNumber();
}
```

The **Chapter** class can access the **getPageNumber** method because **Chapter** belongs to the same package as the **Page** class. Therefore, **Chapter** can access all protected members of the **Page** class.

The default access allows classes in the same package access a class member. For instance, the **Chapter** class can access the **Page** class's **numberOfSentences** field because the **Page** and **Chapter** classes belong to the same package. However, **numberOfSentences** is not accessible from a subclass of **Page** if the subclass belongs to a different package. This differentiates the protected and default access levels and will be explained in detail in Chapter 7, "Inheritance."

The private members of a class can only be accessed from inside the same class. For example, there is no way you can access the **Page** class's private field **pageNumber** from anywhere other than the **Page** class itself. However, look at the following code from the **Page** class definition.

```
private int pageNumber = 5;
protected int getPageNumber() {
    return pageNumber;
}
```

The **pageNumber** field is private, so it can be accessed from the **getPageNumber** method, which is defined in the same class. The return value of **getPageNumber** is **pageNumber**, which is private. Beginners are often confused by this kind of code. If **pageNumber** is private, why use it as a return value of a protected method (**getPageNumber**)? Note that access to **pageNumber** is still private, so other classes cannot modify this field. However, using it as a return value of a non-private method is allowed.

How about constructors? Access levels to constructors are the same as those for fields and methods. Therefore, constructors can have public, protected, default, and private access levels. You may think that all constructors must be public because the intention of having a constructor is to make the class instantiable. However, to your surprise, this is not the case. Some constructors are made private so that their classes cannot be instantiated from other classes. Private constructors are normally used in singleton classes. If you are interested in this topic, there are articles on this that you can find easily on the Internet.

Note
In a UML class diagram, you can include information on the class member access level. Prefix a public member with a +, a protected member with a # and a private member with a -. Members with no prefix are regarded as having the default access level. Figure 4.7 shows the **Manager** class with members having various access levels.

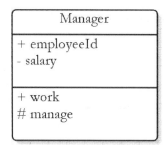

Figure 4.7: Including class member access level in a UML class diagram

The this Keyword

You use the **this** keyword from any method or constructor to refer to the current object. For example, if you have a class-level field with the same name as a local variable, you can use this syntax to refer to the former:

```
this.field
```

A common use is in the constructor that accepts values used to initialize fields. Consider the **Box** class in Listing 4.7.

Listing 4.7: The Box class
```
package app04;
public class Box {
    int length;
    int width;
    int height;
    public Box(int length, int width, int height) {
        this.length = length;
        this.width = width;
        this.height = height;
    }
}
```

The **Box** class has three fields, **length**, **width**, and **height**. Its constructor accepts three arguments used to initialize the fields. It is very convenient to use **length**, **width**, and **height** as the parameter names because they reflect what they are. Inside the constructor, **length** refers to the **length** argument, not the **length** field. **this.length** refers to the class-level **length** field.

It is of course possible to change the argument names, such as this.

```
public Box (int lengthArg, int widthArg, int heightArg) {
    length = lengthArg;
    width = widthArg;
    height = heightArg;
}
```

This way, the class-level fields are not shadowed by local variables and you do not need to use the **this** keyword to refer to the class-level fields However, using the **this** keyword spares you from having to think of different names for your method or constructor arguments.

Using Other Classes

It is common to use other classes from the class you are writing. Using classes in the same package as your current class is allowed by default. However, to use classes in other packages, you must first import the packages or the classes you want to use.

Java provides the keyword **import** to indicate that you want to use a package or a class from a package. For example, to use the **java.util.ArrayList** class from your code, you must have the following **import** statement:

```
package app04;
import java.util.ArrayList;

public class Demo {
    ...
}
```

Note that **import** statements must come after the **package** statement but before the class declaration. The **import** keyword can appear multiple times in a class.

```
package app04;
import java.time.Clock;
import java.util.ArrayList;

public class Demo {
    ...
}
```

Sometimes you need many classes in the same package. You can import all classes in the same package by using the wild character *. For example, the following code imports all members of the **java.util** package.

```
package app04;
import java.util.*;
public class Demo {
    ...
}
```

Now, not only can you use the **java.util.ArrayList** class, but you can use other members of the **java.util** package too. However, to make your code more readable, it is recommended that you import a package member one at a time. In other words, if you need to use both the **java.io.PrintWriter** class and the **java.io.FileReader** class, it is better to have two **import** statements like the following than to use the * character.

```
import java.io.PrintWriter;
import java.io.FileReader;
```

Note

Members of the **java.lang** package are imported automatically. Thus, to use the **java.lang.String** class, for example, you do not need to explicitly import the class.

The only way to use classes that belong to other packages without importing them is to use the fully qualified names of the classes in your code. For example, the following code declares the **java.io.File** class using its fully qualified name.

```
java.io.File file = new java.io.File(filename);
```

If you import identically-named classes from different packages, you must use the fully qualified names when declaring the classes. For example, the Java core libraries contain the classes **java.sql.Date** and **java.util.Date**. Importing both upsets the compiler. In this case, you must write the fully qualified names of **java.sql.Date** and **java.util.Date** in your class to use them.

Note

Java classes can be deployed in a jar file. Appendix A details how to compile a class that uses other classes in a jar file. Appendix B shows how to run a Java class in a jar file. Appendix C provides instructions on the **jar** tool, a program that comes with the JDK to package your Java classes and related resources.
A class that uses another class is said to "depend on" the latter. A UML diagram that depicts this dependency is shown in Figure 4.8.

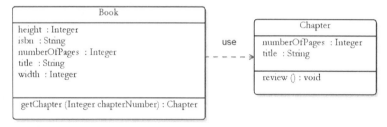

Figure 4.8: Dependency in the UML class diagram

A dependency relationship is represented by a dashed line with an arrow. In Figure 4.8 the **Book** class is dependent on **Chapter** because the **getChapter** method returns a **Chapter** object.

Final Variables

Java does not reserve the keyword constant to create constants. However, in Java you can prefix a variable declaration with the keyword **final** to make its value unchangeable. You can make both local variables and class fields final.

For example, the number of months in a year never changes, so you can write:

```
final int numberOfMonths = 12;
```

As another example, in a class that performs mathematical calculation, you can declare the variable **pi** whose value is equal to 22/7 (the circumference of a circle divided by its diameter, in math represented by the Greek letter π).

```
final float pi = (float) 22 / 7;
```

Once assigned a value, the value cannot change. Attempting to change it will result in a compile error.

Note that the casting **(float)** after **22 / 7** is needed to convert the value of division to **float**. Otherwise, an **int** will be returned and the **pi** variable will have a value of 3.0, instead of 3.1428.

Also note that since Java uses Unicode characters, you can simply define the variable **pi** as π if you don't think typing it is harder than typing **pi**.

```
final float π = (float) 22 / 7;
```

Note
You can also make a method final, thus prohibiting it from being overridden in a subclass. This will be discussed in Chapter 7, "Inheritance."

Static Members

You have learned that to access a public field or method of an object, you use a period after the object reference, such as:

```
// Create an instance of Book
Book book = new Book();
// access the review method
book.review();
```

This implies that you must create an object first before you can access its members. However, in previous chapters, there were examples that used **System.out.print** to print values to the console. You may have noticed that you could call the **out** field without first having to construct a **System** object. How come you did not have to do something like this?

```
System ref = new System();
ref.out;
```

Rather, you use a period after the class name:

```
System.out
```

Java (and many OOP languages) supports the notion of static members, which are class members that can be called without first instantiating the class. The **out** field in **java.lang.System** is static, which explains why you can write **System.out**.

Static members are not tied to class instances. Rather, they can be called without having an instance. In fact, the method **main**, which acts as the entry point to a class, is static because it must be called before any object is created.

To create a static member, you use the keyword **static** in front of a field or method declaration. If there is an access modifier, the **static** keyword may come before or after the access modifier. These two are correct:

```
public static int a;
static public int b;
```

However, the first form is more often used.

For example, Listing 4.8 shows the **MathUtil** class with a static method:

Listing 4.8: The MathUtil class

```
package app04;
public class MathUtil {
    public static int add(int a, int b) {
        return a + b;
    }
}
```

To use the **add** method, you can simply call it this way:

```
MathUtil.add(a, b)
```

The term instance methods/fields are used to refer to non-static methods and fields.

From inside a static method, you cannot call instance methods or instance fields because they only exist after you create an object. From a static method, you can access other static methods or static fields, however.

A common confusion that a beginner often encounters is when they cannot compile their class because they are calling instance members from the **main** method. Listing 4.9 shows such a class.

Listing 4.9: Calling non-static members from a static method

```
package app04;
public class StaticDemo {
    public int b = 8;
    public static void main(String[] args) {
        System.out.println(b);
    }
}
```

The line in bold causes a compile error because it attempts to access non-static field **b** from the **main** static method. There are two solutions to this.

1. Make **b** static
2. Create an instance of the class, then access **b** by using the object reference.

Which solution is appropriate depends on the situation. It often takes years of OOP experience to come up with a good decision that you're comfortable with.

Note
You can only declare a static variable in a class level. You cannot declare local static variables even if the method is static.

How about static reference variables? You can declare static reference variables. The variable will contain an address, but the object referenced is stored in the heap. For instance

```
static Book book = new Book();
```

Static reference variables provide a good way of exposing the same object that needs to be shared among other different objects.

Note
In UML class diagrams, static members are underlined. For example, Figure 4.9 shows the **MathUtil** class with the static method **add**.

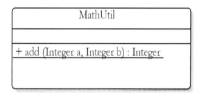

MathUtil
+ add (Integer a, Integer b) : Integer

Figure 4.9: Static members in UML class diagrams

Static Final Variables

In the section "Final Variables" earlier in this chapter, you learned that you could create a final variable by using the keyword **final**. However, final variables at a class level or local variables will always have the same value when the program is run. If you have multiple objects of the same class with final variables, the value of the final variables in those objects will have the same values. It is more common (and also more prudent) to make a final variable static too. This way, all objects share the same value.

The naming convention for static final variables is to have them in upper case and separate two words with an underscore. For example

```
static final int NUMBER_OF_MONTHS = 12;
static final float PI = (float) 22 / 7;
```

The positions of **static** and **final** are interchangeable, but it is more common to use "static final" than "final static."

If you want to make a static final variable accessible from outside the class, you can make it public too:

```
public static final int NUMBER_OF_MONTHS = 12;
public static final float PI = (float) 22 / 7;
```

To better organize your constants, sometimes you want to put all your static final variables in a class. This class most often does not have a method or other fields and is never instantiated.

For example, sometimes you want to represent a month as an **int**, therefore January is 1, February is 2, and so on. Then, you use the word January instead of number 1 because it's more descriptive. Listing 4.10 shows the **Months** class that contains the names of months and its representation.

Listing 4.10: The Months class
```
package app04;
public class Months {
    public static final int JANUARY = 1;
    public static final int FEBRUARY = 2;
    public static final int MARCH = 3;
    public static final int APRIL = 4;
```

```
    public static final int MAY = 5;
    public static final int JUNE = 6;
    public static final int JULY = 7;
    public static final int AUGUST = 8;
    public static final int SEPTEMBER = 9;
    public static final int OCTOBER = 10;
    public static final int NOVEMBER = 11;
    public static final int DECEMBER = 12;
}
```

In your code, you can get the representation of January by writing.

```
int thisMonth = Months.JANUARY;
```

Classes similar to **Months** are very common prior to Java 5. However, Java now offers the new type **enum** that can eliminate the need for public static final variables. **enum** is explain in Chapter 12, "Enums."

Static final reference variables are also possible. However, note that only the variable is final, which means once it is assigned an address to an instance, it cannot be assigned another object of the same type. The fields in the referenced object itself can be changed.

In the following line of code

```
public static final Book book = new Book();
```

book always refer to this particular instance of **Book**. Reassigning it to another **Book** object raises a compile error:

```
book = new Book(); // compile error
```

However, you can change the **Book** object's field value.

```
book.title = "No Excuses";  // assuming the title field is public
```

Static import

There are a number of classes in the Java core libraries that contain static final fields. One of them is the **java.util.Calendar** class, that has the static final fields representing days of the week (**MONDAY**, **TUESDAY**, etc). To use a static final field in the **Calendar** class, you must first import the **Calendar** class.

```
import java.util.Calendar;
```

Then, you can use it by using the notation *className.staticField*.

```
if (today == Calendar.SATURDAY)
```

However, you can also import static fields using the **import static** keywords. For example, you can do

```
import static java.util.Calendar.SATURDAY;
```

Then, to use the imported static field, you do not need the class name:

```
if (today == SATURDAY)
```

Variable Scope

You have seen that you can declare variables in several different places:

- In a class body as class fields. Variables declared here are referred to as class-level variables.
- As parameters of a method or constructor.
- In a method's body or a constructor's body.
- Within a statement block, such as inside a **while** or **for** block.

Now it's time to learn variable scope.

Variable scope refers to the accessibility of a variable. The rule is that variables defined in a block are only accessible from within the block. The scope of the variable is the block in which it is defined. For example, consider the following **for** statement.

```
for (int x = 0; x < 5; x++) {
    System.out.println(x);
}
```

The variable **x** is declared within the **for** statement. As a result, **x** is only available from within this **for** block. It is not accessible or visible from anywhere else. When the JVM executes the **for** statement, it creates **x**. When it is finished executing the **for** block, it destroys **x**. After **x** is destroyed, **x** is said to be out of scope.

Rule number 2 is a nested block can access variables declared in the outer block. Consider this code.

```
for (int x = 0; x < 5; x++) {
    for (int y = 0; y < 3; y++) {
        System.out.println(x);
        System.out.println(y);
    }
}
```

The preceding code is valid because the inner **for** block can access **x**, which is declared in the outer **for** block.

Following the rules, variables declared as method parameters can be accessed from within the method body. Also, class-level variables are accessible from anywhere in the class.

If a method declares a local variable that has the same name as a class-level variable, the former will 'shadow' the latter. To access the class-level variable from inside the method body, use the **this** keyword.

Method Overloading

Method names are very important and should reflect what the methods do. In many circumstances, you may want to use the same name for multiple methods because they have similar functionality. For instance, the method **printString** may take a **String** argument and prints the string. However, the same class may also provide a method that prints part of a **String** and accepts two arguments, the **String** to be printed and the character position to start printing from. You want to call the latter method **printString** too because it does print a **String**, but that would be the same as the first **printString** method.

Thankfully, it is okay in Java to have multiple methods having the same name, as long as each method accept different sets of argument types. In other words, in our example, it is legal to have these two methods in the same class.

```
public String printString(String string)
public String printString(String string, int offset)
```

This feature is called method overloading.

The return value of the method is not taken into consideration. As such, these two methods must not exist in the same class:

```
public int countRows(int number);
public String countRows(int number);
```

This is because a method can be called without assigning its return value to a variable. In such situations, having the above **countRows** methods would confuse the compiler as it would not know which method is being called when you write

```
System.out.println(countRows(3));.
```

A trickier situation is depicted in the following methods whose signatures are very similar.

```
public int printNumber(int i) {
    return i*2;
}

public long printNumber(long l) {
    return l*3;
}
```

It is legal to have these two methods in the same class. However, you might wonder, which method is being called if you write **printNumber(3)**?

The key is to recall from Chapter 2, "Language Fundamentals" that a numeric literal will be translated into an **int** unless it is suffixed **L** or **l**.. Therefore, **printNumber(3)** will invoke this method:

```
public int printNumber(int i)
```

To call the second, pass a **long**:

```
printNumber(3L);
```

System.out.print() (and **System.out.println()**) is an excellent example of method overloading. You can pass any primitive or object to the method because there are nine overloads of the method. There is an overload that accepts an **int**, one that accepts a **long**, one that accepts a **String**, and so on.

Note
Static methods can also be overloaded.

Static Factory Methods

You've learned to create an object using **new**. However, there are classes in Java class libraries that cannot be instantiated this way. For example, you cannot create an instance of **java.util.LocalDate** with **new** because its constructor is private. Instead, you would use one of its static methods, such as **now**:

```
LocalDate today = LocalDate.now();
```

Such methods are called static factory methods.

You can design your class to use static factory methods. Listing 4.11 shows a class named **Discount** with a private constructor. It is a simple class that contains an **int** that represents a discount rate. The value is either 10 (for small customers) or 12 (for bigger customers). It has a **getValue** method, which returns the value, and two static factory methods, **createSmallCustomerDiscount** and **createBigCustomerDiscount**. Note that the static factory methods can invoke the private constructor to create an object because they are in the same class. Recall that you can access a class private member from within the class. With this design, you restrict a **Discount** object to contain either 10 or 12. Other values are not possible.

Listing 4.11: The Discount classs
```
package app04;
import java.time.LocalDate;

public class Discount {
    private int value;
    private Discount(int value) {
        this.value = value;
    }

    public int getValue() {
        return this.value;
    }

    public static Discount createSmallCustomerDiscount() {
        return new Discount(10);
    }

    public static Discount createBigCustomerDiscount() {
        return new Discount(12);
    }
```

```
}
```

You can construct a **Discount** object by calling one of its static factory methods, for example

```
Discount discount = Discount.createBigCustomerDiscount();
System.out.println(discount.getValue());
```

There are also classes that allow you to create an instance through static factory methods and a constructor. In this case, the constructor must be public. Examples of such classes are **java.lang.Integer** and **java.lang.Boolean**.

With static factory methods, you can control what objects can be created out of your class, like you have seen in **Discount**. Also, you might cache an instance and return the same instance every time an instance is needed. Also, unlike constructors, you can name static factory methods to make clear what kind of object will be created.

By Value or By Reference?

You can pass primitive variables or reference variables to a method. Primitive variables are passed by value and reference variables are passed by reference. What this means is when you pass a primitive variable, the JVM will copy the value of the passed-in variable to a new local variable. If you change the value of the local variable, the change will not affect the passed in primitive variable.

If you pass a reference variable, the local variable will refer to the same object as the passed in reference variable. If you change the object referenced within your method, the change will also be reflected in the calling code. Listing 4.12 shows the **ReferencePassingTest** class that demonstrates this.

Listing 4.12: The ReferencePassingTest class

```
package app04;
class Point {
    public int x;
    public int y;
}
public class ReferencePassingTest {
    public static void increment(int x) {
        x++;
    }
    public static void reset(Point point) {
        point.x - 0;
        point.y = 0;
    }
    public static void main(String[] args) {
        int a = 9;
        increment(a);
        System.out.println(a); // prints 9
        Point p = new Point();
        p.x = 400;
        p.y = 600;
        reset(p);
```

```
        System.out.println(p.x); // prints 0
    }
}
```

There are two methods in **ReferencePassingTest**, **increment** and **reset**. The **increment** method takes an **int** and increments it. The **reset** method accepts a **Point** object and resets its **x** and **y** fields.

Now pay attention to the **main** method. We passed **a** (whose value is 9) to the **increment** method. After the method invocation, we printed the value of **a** and you get 9, which means that the value of **a** did not change.

Afterwards, you create a **Point** object and assign the reference to **p**. You then initialize its fields and pass it to the **reset** method. The changes in the **reset** method affects the **Point** object because objects are passed by reference. As a result, when you print the value of **p.x**, you get 0.

Loading, Linking, and Initialization

Now that you've learned how to create classes and objects, let's take a look at what happens when the JVM executes a class.

You run a Java program by using the **java** tool. For example, you use the following command to run the **DemoTest** class.

```
java DemoTest
```

After the JVM is loaded into memory, it starts its job by invoking the **DemoTest** class's **main** method. There are three things the JVM will do next in the specified order: loading, linking, and initialization.

Loading

The JVM loads the binary representation of the Java class (in this case, the **DemoTest** class) to memory and may cache it in memory, just in case the class is used again in the future. If the specified class is not found, an error will be thrown and the process stops here.

Linking

There are three things that need to be done in this phase: verification, preparation, and resolution (optional). Verification means the JVM checks that the binary representation complies with the semantic requirements of the Java programming language and the JVM. If, for example, you tamper with a class file created as a result of compilation, the class file may no longer work.

Preparation prepares the specified class for execution. This involves allocating memory space for static variables and other data structured for that class.

Resolution checks if the specified class references other classes/interfaces and if the other classes/interfaces can also be found and loaded. Checks will be done recursively to the referenced classes/interfaces.

For example, if the specified class contains the following code:

```
MathUtil.add(4, 3)
```

the JVM will load, link, and initialize the **MathUtil** class before calling the static **add** method.

Or, if the following code is found in the **DemoTest** class:

```
Book book = new Book();
```

the JVM will load, link, and initialize the **Book** class before an instance of **Book** is created.

Note that a JVM implementation may choose to perform resolution at a later stage, i.e. when the executing code actually requires the use of the referenced class/interface.

Initialization

In this last step, the JVM initializes static variables with assigned or default values and executes static initializers (code in **static** blocks). Initialization occurs just before the **main** method is executed. However, before the specified class can be initialized, its parent class will have to be initialized. If the parent class has not been loaded and linked, the JVM will first load and link the parent class. Again, when the parent class is about to be initialized, the parent's parent will be treated the same. This process occurs recursively until the initialized class is the topmost class in the hierarchy.

For example, if a class contains the following declaration

```
public static int z = 5;
```

the variable **z** will be assigned the value 5. If no initialization code is found, a static variable is given a default value. Table 4.2 lists default values for Java primitives and reference variables.

Type	Default Value
boolean	false
byte	0
short	0
int	0
long	0L
char	\u0000
float	0.0f
double	0.0d
object reference	null

Table 4.2: Default values for primitives and references

In addition, code in **static** blocks will be executed. For example, Listing 4.13 shows the **StaticCodeTest** class with static code that gets executed when the class is loaded. Like static members, you can only access static members from static code.

Listing 4.13: StaticCodeTest

```
package app04;
public class StaticInitializationTest {
    public static int a = 5;
```

```
    public static int b = a * 2;
    static {
        System.out.println("static");
        System.out.println(b);
    }
    public static void main(String[] args) {
        System.out.println("main method");
    }
}
```

If you run this class, you will see the following on your console:

```
static
10
main method
```

Object Creation Initialization

Initialization happens when a class is loaded, as described in the section "Linking, Loading, and Initialization" earlier in this chapter. However, you can also write code that performs initialization every time an instance of a class is created.

When the JVM encounters code that instantiates a class, the JVM does the following.

1. Allocates memory space for a new object, with room for the instance variables declared in the class plus room for instance variables declared in its parent classes.
2. Processes the invoked constructor. If the constructor has parameters, the JVM creates variables for these parameter and assigns them values passed to the constructor.
3. If the invoked constructor begins with a call to another constructor (using the **this** keyword), the JVM processes the called constructor.
4. Performs instance initialization and instance variable initialization for this class. Instance variables that are not assigned a value will be assigned default values (See Table 4.2). Instance initialization applies to code in braces:

   ```
   {
       // code
   }
   ```

5. Executes the rest of the body of the invoked constructor.
6. Returns a reference variable that refers to the new object.

Note that instance initialization is different from static initialization. The latter occurs when a class is loaded and has nothing to do with instantiation. Instance initialization, by contrast, is performed when an object is created. In addition, unlike static initializers, instance initialization may access instance variables.

For example, Listing 4.14 presents a class named **InitTest1** that has the initialization section. There is also some static initialization code to give you the idea of what is being run.

Listing 4.14: The InitTest1 class

```
package app04;

public class InitTest1 {
    int x = 3;
    int y;
    // instance initialization code
    {
        y = x * 2;
        System.out.println(y);
    }

    // static initialization code
    static {
        System.out.println("Static initialization");
    }
    public static void main(String[] args) {
        InitTest1 test = new InitTest1();
        InitTest1 moreTest = new InitTest1();
    }
}
```

When run, the **InitTest** class prints the following on the console:

```
Static initialization
6
6
```

The static initialization is performed first, before any instantiation takes place. This is where the JVM prints the "Static initialization" message. Afterward, the **InitTest1** class is instantiated twice, explaining why you see "6" twice.

The problem with having instance initialization code is this. As your class grows bigger it becomes harder to notice that there exists initialization code.

Another way to write initialization code is in the constructor. In fact, initialization code in a constructor is more noticeable and hence preferable. Listing 4.15 shows the **InitTest2** class that puts initialization code in the constructor.

Listing 4.15: The InitTest2 class

```
package app04;
public class InitTest2 {
    int x = 3;
    int y;
    // instance initialization code
    public InitTest2() {
        y = x * 2;
        System.out.println(y);
    }
    // static initialization code
    static {
        System.out.println("Static initialization");
    }
    public static void main(String[] args) {
```

```
        InitTest2 test = new InitTest2();
        InitTest2 moreTest = new InitTest2();
    }
}
```

The problem with this is when you have more than one constructor and each of them must call the same code. The solution is to wrap the initialization code in a method and let the constructors call them. Listing 4.16 shows this

Listing 4.16: The InitTest3 class

```
package app04;

public class InitTest3 {
    int x = 3;
    int y;
    // instance initialization code
    public InitTest3() {
        init();
    }
    public InitTest3(int x) {
        this.x = x;
        init();
    }
    private void init() {
        y = x * 2;
        System.out.println(y);
    }
    // static initialization code
    static {
        System.out.println("Static initialization");
    }
    public static void main(String[] args) {
        InitTest3 test = new InitTest3();
        InitTest3 moreTest = new InitTest3();
    }
}
```

Note that the **InitTest3** class is preferable because the calls to the **init** method from the constructors make the initialization code more obvious than if it is in an initialization block.

The Garbage Collector

In several examples so far, I have shown you how to create objects using the **new** keyword, but you have never seen code that explicitly destroys unused objects to release memory space. If you are a C++ programmer you may have wondered if I had shown flawed code, because in C++ you must destroy objects after use.

Java comes with a garbage collector, which destroys unused objects and frees memory. Unused objects are defined as objects that are no longer referenced or objects whose references are already out of scope.

With this feature, Java becomes much easier than C++ because Java programmers do not need to worry about reclaiming memory space. This, however, does not entail that you may create objects as many as you want because memory is (still) limited and it takes some time for the garbage collector to start. That's right, you can still run out of memory.

Summary

OOP models applications on real-world objects. Since Java is an OOP language, objects play a central role in Java programming. Objects are created based on a template called a class. In this chapter you've learned how to write a class and class members. There are many types of class members, including three that were discussed in this chapter: fields, methods, and constructors. There are other types of Java members such as enum and inner classes, which will be covered in other chapters.

In this chapter you have also learned two powerful OOP features, abstraction and encapsulation. Abstraction in OOP is the act of using programming objects to represent real-world objects. Encapsulation is a mechanism that protects parts of an object that need to be secure and exposes only parts that are safe to be exposed. Another feature discussed in this chapter is method overloading. Method overloading allows a class to have methods with the same name as long as their signatures are sufficiently different.

Java also comes with a garbage collector that eliminates to manually destroy unused objects. Objects are garbage collected when they are out of scope or no longer referenced.

Quiz

1. Name at least three element types that a class can contain.
2. What are the differences between a method and a constructor?
3. Does a class in a class diagram display its constructors?
4. What does **null** mean?
5. What do you use the **this** keyword for?
6. When you use the == operator to compare two object references, do you actually compare the contents of the objects? Why?
7. What is variable scope?
8. What does "out of scope" mean?
9. How does the garbage collector decide which objects to destroy?
10. What is method overloading?
11. Create a class whose fully-qualified name is **com.example.Tablet** to model an Android tablet. The class must have three private fields, **weight** (int), **screenSize** (float) and **wifiOnly** (boolean). Access to the fields must be through pairs of public get and set methods, i.e. **getWeight/setWeight**, **getScreenSize/setScreenSize** and **getWifiOnly/setWifiOnly**. The class must also have one constructor, a no-argument constructor.
12. Create a **TabletTest** class in the package **com.example.test** and instantiate the Tablet class. Print the value of the fields (by calling its get methods) right after instantiation. Then, set the field values and print them again.

Chapter 5
Core Classes

Before discussing other features of object-oriented programming (OOP), let's examine several important classes that are commonly used in Java. These classes are included in the Java core libraries that come with the JDK. Mastering them will help you understand the examples that accompany the next OOP lessons.

The most prominent class of all is definitely **java.lang.Object**. However, it is hard to talk about this class without first covering inheritance, which I will do in Chapter 7, "Inheritance." Therefore, **java.lang.Object** is only discussed briefly in this chapter. Right now I will concentrate on classes that you can use in your programs. I will start with **java.lang.String** and other types of strings: **java.lang.StringBuffer** and **java.lang.StringBuilder**. Then, I will discuss the **java.lang.System** class. The **java.util.Scanner** class is also included here because it provides a convenient way to take user input.

Note

When describing a method in a Java class, presenting the method signature always helps. A method often takes as parameters objects whose classes belong to different packages than the method's class. Or, it may return a type from a different package than its class. For clarity, fully qualified names will be used for classes from different packages. For example, here is the signature of the **toString** method of **java.lang.Object**:

```
public String toString()
```

A fully qualified name for the return type is not necessary because the return type **String** is part of the same package as **java.lang.Object**. On the other hand, the signature of the **toString** method in **java.util.Scanner** uses a fully qualified name because the **Scanner** class is part of a different package (**java.util**).

```
public java.lang.String toString()
```

---

java.lang.Object

The **java.lang.Object** class represents a Java object. In fact, all classes are direct or indirect descendants of this class. Since we have not learned inheritance (which is only given in Chapter 7, "Inheritance"), the word descendant probably makes no sense to you. Therefore, we will briefly discuss the method in this class and revisit this class in Chapter 7.

Table 5.1 shows the methods in the **Object** class.

Method	Description
clone	Creates and returns a copy of this object. A class implements this method to support object cloning.
equals	Compares this object with the passed-in object. A class must implement this method to provide a means to compare the contents of its instances.
finalize	Called by the garbage collector on an object that is about to be garbage-collected. In theory a subclass can override this method to dispose of system resources or to perform other cleanup. However, performing the aforesaid operations should be done somewhere else and you should not touch this method.
getClass	Returns a **java.lang.Class** object of this object. See the section "java.lang.Class" for more information on the **Class** class.
hashCode	Returns a hash code value for this object.
toString	Returns the description of this object.
wait, notify, notifyAll	Used in multithreaded programming in pre-5 Java. Should not be used directly in Java 5 or later. Instead, use the Java concurrency utilities.

Table 5.1: java.lang.Object methods

java.lang.String

I have not seen a serious Java program that does not use the **java.lang.String** class. It is one of the most often used classes and definitely one of the most important.

A **String** object represents a string, i.e. a piece of text. You can also think of a **String** as a sequence of Unicode characters. A **String** object can consists of any number of characters. A **String** that has zero character is called an empty **String**. **String** objects are constant. Once they are created, their values cannot be changed. Because of this, **String** instances are said to be immutable. And, because they are immutable, they can be safely shared.

You could construct a **String** object using the **new** keyword, but this is not a common way to create a **String**. Most often, you assign a string literal to a **String** reference variable. Here is an example:

```
String s = "Java is cool";
```

This produces a **String** object containing "Java is cool" and assigns a reference to it to **s**. It is the same as the following.

```
String message = new String("Java is cool");
```

However, assigning a string literal to a reference variable works differently from using the **new** keyword. If you use the **new** keyword, the JVM will always create a new instance of **String**. With a string literal, you get an identical **String** object, but the object is not always new. It may come from a pool if the string "Java is cool" has been created before.

Thus, using a string literal is better because the JVM can save some CPU cycles spent on constructing a new instance. Because of this, you seldom use the **new** keyword when creating a **String** object. The **String** class's constructors can be used if you have specific needs, such as converting a character array into a **String**.

Comparing Two Strings

String comparison is one of the most useful operations in Java programming. Consider the following code.

```
String s1 = "Java";
String s2 = "Java";
if (s1 == s2) {
    ...
}
```

Here, **(s1 == s2)** evaluates to **true** because **s1** and **s2** reference the same instance. On the other hand, in the following code **(s1 == s2)** evaluates to **false** because **s1** and **s2** reference different instances:

```
String s1 = new String("Java");
String s2 = new String("Java");
if (s1 == s2) {
    ...
}
```

This shows the difference between creating **String** objects by writing a string literal and by using the **new** keyword.

Comparing two **String** objects using the == operator is of little use because you are comparing the addresses referenced by two variables. Most of the time, when comparing two **String** objects, you want to know whether the values of the two objects are the same. In this case, you need to use the **String** class's **equals** method.

```
String s1 = "Java";
if (s1.equals("Java")) // returns true.
```

And, sometimes you see this style.

```
if ("Java".equals(s1))
```

In **(s1.equals("Java"))**, the **equals** method on **s1** is called. If **s1** is null, the expression will generate a runtime error. To be safe, you have to make sure that **s1** is not null, by first checking if the reference variable is null.

```
if (s1 != null && s1.equals("Java"))
```

If **s1** is null, the **if** statement will return **false** without evaluating the second expression because the AND operator **&&** will not try to evaluate the right hand operand if the left hand operand evaluates to **false**.

In **("Java".equals(s1))**, the JVM creates or takes from the pool a **String** object containing "Java" and calls its **equals** method. No nullity checking is required here because "Java" is obviously not null. If **s1** is null, the expression simply returns **false**. Therefore, these two lines of code have the same effect.

```
if (s1 != null && s1.equals("Java"))

if ("Java".equals(s1))
```

String Literals

Because you always work with **String** objects, it is important to understand the rules for working with string literals.

First of all, a string literal starts and ends with a double quote ("). Second, it is a compile error to change line before the closing double quote. For example, this code snippet will raise a compile error.

```
String s2 = "This is an important
        point to note";
```

You can compose long string literals by using the plus sign to concatenate two string literals.

```
String s1 = "Java strings " + "are important";
String s2 = "This is an important " +
        "point to note";
```

You can concatenate a String with a primitive or another object. For instance, this line of code concatenates a **String** and an integer.

```
String s3 = "String number " + 3;
```

If an object is concatenated with a String, the **toString** method of the former will be called and the result used in the concatenation.

Escaping Certain Characters

You sometimes need to use special characters in your strings such as carriage return (CR) and linefeed (LF). In other occasions, you may want to have a double quote character in your string. In the case of CR and LF, it is not possible to input these characters because pressing Enter changes lines. A way to include special characters is to escape them, i.e. use the character replacement for them.

Here are some escape sequences:

```
\u          /* a Unicode character
\b          /* \u0008: backspace BS */
\t          /* \u0009: horizontal tab HT */
\n          /* \u000a: linefeed LF */
\f          /* \u000c: form feed FF */
\r          /* \u000d: carriage return CR */
\"          /* \u0022: double quote " */
\'          /* \u0027: single quote ' */
\\          /* \u005c: backslash \ */
```

For example, the following code includes the Unicode character 0122 at the end of the string.

```
String s = "Please type this character \u0122";
```

To obtain a **String** object whose value is John "The Great" Monroe, you escape the double quotes:

```
String s = "John \"The Great\" Monroe";
```

Switching on A String

Starting from Java 7 you can use the **switch** statement with a String. Recall the syntax of the **switch** statement given in Chapter 3, "Statements."

```
switch(expression) {
case value_1 :
    statement(s);
    break;
case value_2 :
    statement(s);
    break;
    .
    .
    .
case value_n :
    statement(s);
    break;
default:
    statement(s);
}
```

Here is an example of using the **switch** statement on a String.

```
String input = ...;
switch (input) {
case "one" :
    System.out.println("You entered 1.");
    break;
case "two" :
    System.out.println("You entered 2.");
    break;
default:
    System.out.println("Invalid value.");
}
```

The String Class's Constructors

The **String** class provides a number of constructors. These constructors allow you to create an empty string, a copy of another string, and a **String** from an array of chars or bytes. Use the constructors with caution as they always create a new instance of **String**.

Note
Arrays are discussed in Chapter 6, "Arrays."

```
public String()
```
Creates an empty string.

```
public String(String original)
```
Creates a copy of the original string.

```
public String(char[] value)
```

Creates a **String** object from an array of chars.

```
public String(byte[] bytes)
```
Creates a **String** object by decoding the bytes in the array using the computer's default encoding.

```
public String(byte[] bytes, String encoding)
```
Creates a **String** object by decoding the bytes in the array using the specified encoding.

The String Class's Methods

The **String** class provides methods for manipulating the value of a **String**. However, since **String** objects are immutable, the result of the manipulation is always a new **String** object.

Here are some of the more useful methods.

```
public char charAt(int index)
```
Returns the char at the specified index. For example, the following code returns 'J'.

```
"Java is cool".charAt(0)
```

```
public String concat(String s)
```
Concatenates the specified string to the end of this **String** and return the result. For example, **"Java ".concat("is cool")** returns "Java is cool".

```
public boolean equals(String anotherString)
```
Compares the value of this **String** and *anotherString* and returns **true** if the values match.

```
public boolean endsWith(String suffix)
```
Tests if this **String** ends with the specified suffix.

```
public int indexOf(String substring)
```
Returns the index of the first occurrence of the specified substring. If no match is found, returns -1. For instance, the following code returns 8.

```
"Java is cool".indexOf("cool")
```

```
public int indexOf(String substring, int fromIndex)
```
Returns the index of the first occurrence of the specified substring starting from the specified index. If no match is found, returns -1.

```
public int lastIndexOf(String substring)
```
Returns the index of the last occurrence of the specified substring. If no match is found, returns -1.

```
public int lastIndexOf(String substring, int fromIndex)
```
Returns the index of the last occurrence of the specified substring starting from the specified index. If no match is found, returns -1. For example, the following expression returns 3.

```
"Java is cool".lastIndexOf("a")
```

```
public String substring(int beginIndex)
```
Returns a substring of the current string starting from the specified index. For instance, **"Java is cool".substring(8)** returns "cool".

```
public String substring(int beginIndex, int endIndex)
```
Returns a substring of the current string starting from *beginIndex* to *endIndex*. For example, the following code returns "is":

```
"Java is cool".substring(5, 7)
```

```
public String replace(char oldChar, char newChar)
```
Replaces every occurrence of *oldChar* with *newChar* in the current string and returns the new **String**. **"dingdong".replace('d', 'k')** returns "kingkong".

```
public int length()
```
Returns the number of characters in this **String**. For example, **"Java is cool".length()** returns 12. Prior to Java 6, this method was often used to test if a **String** was empty. However, the **isEmpty** method is preferred because it's more descriptive.

```
public boolean isEmpty()
```
Returns true is the string is empty (contains no characters).

```
public String[] split(String regEx)
```
Splits this **String** around matches of the specified regular expression. For example, **"Java is cool".split(" ")** returns an array of three **String**s. The first array element is "Java", the second "is", and the third "cool".

```
public boolean startsWith(String prefix)
```
Tests if the current string starts with the specified prefix.

```
public char[] toCharArray()
```
Converts this string to an array of chars.

```
public String toLowerCase()
```
Converts all the characters in the current string to lower case. For instance, **"Java is cool".toLowerCase()** returns "java is cool".

```
public String toUpperCase()
```
Converts all the characters in the current string to upper case. For instance, **"Java is cool".toUpperCase()** returns "JAVA IS COOL".

```
public String trim()
```
Trims the trailing and leading white spaces and returns a new string. For example, **" Java ".trim()** returns "Java".

In addition, there are static methods such as **valueOf** and **format**. The **valueOf** method converts a primitive, a char array, or an instance of **Object** into a string representation and there are nine overloads of this method.

```
public static String valueOf(boolean value)
public static String valueOf(char value)
public static String valueOf(char[] value)
public static String valueOf(char[] value, int offset, int length)
public static String valueOf(double value)
public static String valueOf(float value)
public static String valueOf(int value)
public static String valueOf(long value)
public static String valueOf(Object value)
```

For example, the following code returns the string "23"

```
String.valueOf(23);
```

The **format** method allows you to pass an arbitrary number of parameters. Here is its signature.

```
public static String format(String format, Object... args)
```

This method returns a **String** formatted using the specified format string and arguments. The format pattern must follow the rules specified in the **java.util.Formatter** class and you can read them in the JavaDoc for the **Formatter** class. A brief description of these rules are as follows.

To specify an argument, use the notation **%s**, which denotes the next argument in the array. For example, the following is a method call to the **printf** method.

```
String firstName = "John";
String lastName = "Adams";
System.out.format("First name: %s. Last name: %s",
        firstName, lastName);
```

This prints the following string to the console:

```
First name: John. Last name: Adams
```

Without varargs, you have to do it in a more cumbersome way.

```
String firstName = "John";
String lastName = "Adams";
System.out.println("First name: " + firstName +
        ". Last name: " + lastName);
```

Note
The **printf** method in **java.io.PrintStream** is an alias for **format**.

The formatting example described here is only the tip of the iceberg. The formatting feature is much more powerful than that and you are encouraged to explore it by reading the Javadoc for the **Formatter** class.

java.lang.StringBuffer and java.lang.StringBuilder

String objects are immutable and are not suitable to use if you need to append or insert characters into them because string operations on **String** always create a new **String** object. For append and insert, you'd be better off using the **java.lang.StringBuffer** or **java.lang.StringBuilder** class. Once you're finished manipulating the string, you can convert a **StringBuffer** or **StringBuilder** object to a **String**.

Until JDK 1.4, the **StringBuffer** class was solely used for mutable strings. Methods in **StringBuffer** are synchronized, making **StringBuffer** suitable for use in multithreaded environments. However, the price for synchronization is performance. JDK 5 added the **StringBuilder** class, which is the unsynchronized version of **StringBuffer**. **StringBuilder** should be chosen over **StringBuffer** if you do not need synchronization.

Note
Synchronization and thread safety are discussed in Chapter 22, "Java Threads."

The rest of this section will use **StringBuilder**. However, the discussion is also applicable to **StringBuffer** as both **StringBuilder** and **StringBuffer** shares similar constructors and methods.

StringBuilder Class's Constructors

The **StringBuilder** class has four constructors. You can pass a **java.lang.CharSequence**, a **String**, or an **int**.

```
public StringBuilder()
public StringBuilder(CharSequence seq)
public StringBuilder(int capacity)
public StringBuilder(String string)
```

If you create a **StringBuilder** object without specifying the capacity, the object will have a capacity of 16 characters. If its content exceeds 16 characters, it will grow automatically. If you know that your string will be longer than 16 characters, it is a good idea to allocate enough capacity as it takes time to increase a **StringBuilder**'s capacity.

StringBuilder Class's Methods

The **StringBuilder** class has several methods. The main ones are **capacity**, **length**, **append**, and **insert**.

```
public int capacity()
```
Returns the capacity of the **StringBuilder** object.

```
public int length()
```
Returns the length of the string the **StringBuilder** object stores. The value is less than or equal to the capacity of the **StringBuilder**.

```
public StringBuilder append(String string)
```
Appends the specified **String** to the end of the contained string. In addition, **append** has various overloads that allow you to pass a primitive, a char array, and an **java.lang.Object** instance.
For example, examine the following code.

```
StringBuilder sb = new StringBuilder(100);
sb.append("Matrix ");
sb.append(2);
```

After the last line, the content of **sb** is "Matrix 2".
An important point to note is that the **append** methods return the **StringBuilder** object itself, the same object on which **append** is invoked. As a result, you can chain calls to **append**.

```
sb.append("Matrix ").append(2);
```

```
public StringBuilder insert(int offset, String string)
```
Inserts the specified string at the position indicated by *offset*. In addition, **insert** has various overloads that allow you to pass primitives and a **java.lang.Object** instance. For example,

```
StringBuilder sb2 = new StringBuilder(100);
sb2.append("night");
```

```
sb2.insert(0, 'k'); // value = "knight"
```

Like **append**, **insert** also returns the current **StringBuilder** object, so chaining **insert** is also permitted.

```
public String toString()
```
Returns a **String** object representing the value of the **StringBuilder**.

Primitive Wrappers

For the sake of performance, not everything in Java is an object. There are also primitives, such as **int**, **long**, **float**, **double**, etc. When working with both primitives and objects, there are often circumstances that necessitate primitive to object conversions and vice versa. For example, a **java.util.Collection** object (discussed in Chapter 14, "The Collections Framework") can be used to store objects, not primitives. If you want to store primitive values in a **Collection**, they must be converted to objects first.

The **java.lang** package has several classes that function as primitive wrappers. They are **Boolean**, **Character**, **Byte**, **Double**, **Float**, **Integer**, **Long**, and **Short**. **Byte**, **Double**, **Float**, **Integer**, **Long**, and **Short** share similar methods, therefore only **Integer** will be discussed here. You should consult the Javadoc for information on the others.

The following sections discuss the wrapper classes in detail.

java.lang.Integer

The **java.lang.Integer** class wraps an **int**. The **Integer** class has two static final fields of type **int**: **MIN_VALUE** and **MAX_VALUE**. **MIN_VALUE** contains the minimum possible value for an **int** (-2^{31}) and **MAX_VALUE** the maximum possible value for an **int** (2^{31} - 1).

The **Integer** class has two constructors:

```
public Integer(int value)
public Integer(String value)
```

For example, this code constructs two **Integer** objects.

```
Integer i1 = new Integer(12);
Integer i2 = new Integer("123");
```

Integer has the no-arg **byteValue**, **doubleValue**, **floatValue**, **intValue**, **longValue**, and **shortValue** methods that convert the wrapped value to a **byte**, **double**, **float**, **int**, **long**, and **short**, respectively. In addition, the **toString** method converts the value to a **String**.

There are also static methods that you can use to parse a **String** to an **int** (**parseInt**) and convert an **int** to a **String** (**toString**). The signatures of the methods are as follows.

```
public static int parseInt(String string)
public static String toString(int i)
```

java.lang.Boolean

The **java.lang.Boolean** class wraps a **boolean**. Its static final fields **FALSE** and **TRUE** represents a **Boolean** object that wraps the primitive value **false** and a **Boolean** object wrapping the primitive value **true**, respectively.

You can construct a **Boolean** object from a **boolean** or a **String**, using one of these constructors.

```
public Boolean(boolean value)
public Boolean(String value)
```

For example:

```
Boolean b1 = new Boolean(false);
Boolean b2 = new Boolean("true");
```

To convert a **Boolean** to a **boolean**, use its **booleanValue** method:

```
public boolean booleanValue()
```

In addition, the static method **valueOf** parses a **String** to a **Boolean** object.

```
public static Boolean valueOf(String string)
```

And, the static method **toString** returns the string representation of a **boolean**.

```
public static String toString(boolean boolean)
```

java.lang.Character

The **Character** class wraps a **char**. There is only one constructor in this class:

```
public Character(char value)
```

To convert a **Character** object to a **char**, use its **charValue** method.

```
public char charValue()
```

There are also a number of static methods that can be used to manipulate characters.

```
public static boolean isDigit(char ch)
```
Determines if the specified argument is one of these: '1', '2', '3', '4', '5', '6', '7', '8', '9', '0'.

```
public static char toLowerCase(char ch)
```
Converts the specified char argument to its lower case.

```
public static char toUpperCase(char ch)
```
Converts the specified char argument to its upper case.

java.lang.Class

One of the members of the **java.lang** package is a class named **Class**. Every time the JVM creates an object, it also creates a **java.lang.Class** object that describes the type of the object. All instances of the same class share the same **Class** object. You can obtain the **Class** object by calling the **getClass** method of the object. This method is inherited from **java.lang.Object**.

For example, the following code creates a **String** object, invokes the **getClass** method on the **String** instance, and then invokes the **getName** method on the **Class** object.

```
String country = "Fiji";
Class myClass = country.getClass();
System.out.println(myClass.getName()); // prints java.lang.String
```

As it turns out, the **getName** method returns the fully qualified name of the class represented by a **Class** object.

The **Class** class also brings the possibility of creating an object without using the **new** keyword. You achieve this by using the two methods of the **Class** class, **forName** and **newInstance**.

```
public static Class forName(String className)
public Object newInstance()
```

The static **forName** method creates a **Class** object of the given class name. The **newInstance** method creates a new instance of a class.

The **ClassDemo** in Listing 5.1 uses **forName** to create a **Class** object of the **app05.Test** class and create an instance of the **Test** class. Since **newInstance** returns a **java.lang.Object** object, you need to downcast it to its original type.

Listing 5.1: The ClassDemo class

```
package app05;
public class ClassDemo {
    public static void main(String[] args) {
        String country = "Fiji";
        Class myClass = country.getClass();
        System.out.println(myClass.getName());
        Class klass = null;
        try {
            klass = Class.forName("app05.Test");
        } catch (ClassNotFoundException e) {
        }

        if (klass != null) {
            try {
                Test test = (Test) klass.newInstance();
                test.print();
            } catch (IllegalAccessException e) {
            } catch (InstantiationException e) {
            }
        }
```

```
        }
      }
    }
```

Do not worry about the **try ... catch** blocks as they will be explained in Chapter 8, "Error Handling."

You might want to ask this question, though. Why would you want to create an instance of a class using **forName** and **newInstance**, when using the **new** keyword is shorter and easier? The answer is because there are circumstances whereby the name of the class is not known when you are writing the program.

java.lang.System

The **System** class is a final class that exposes useful static fields and static methods that can help you with common tasks.

The three fields of the **System** class are **out**, **in**, and **err**:

```
public static final java.io.PrintStream out;
public static final java.io.InputStream in;
public static final java.io.PrintStream err;
```

The **out** field represents the standard output stream which by default is the same console used to run the running Java application. You will learn more about **PrintStream** in Chapter 16, "Input Output," but for now know that you can use the **out** field to write messages to the console. You will often write the following line of code:

```
System.out.print(message);
```

where *message* is a **String** object. However, **PrintStream** has many **print** method overloads that accept different types, so you can pass any primitive type to the **print** method:

```
System.out.print(12);
System.out.print('g');
```

In addition, there are **println** methods that are equivalent to **print**, except that **println** adds a line terminator at the end of the argument.

Note also that because **out** is static, you can access it by using this notation: **System.out**, which returns a **java.io.PrintStream** object. You can then access the many methods on the **PrintStream** object as you would methods of other objects: **System.out.print, System.out.format**, etc.

The **err** field also represents a **PrintStream** object, and by default the output is channeled to the console from where the current Java program was invoked. However, its purpose is to display error messages that should get immediate attention of the user.

For example, here is how you can use **err**:

```
System.err.println("You have a runtime error.");
```

The **in** field represents the standard input stream. You can use it to accept keyboard input. For example, the **getUserInput** method in Listing 5.2 accepts the user input and returns it as a String:

Listing 5.2: The InputDemo class

```
package app05;
import java.io.IOException;

public class InputDemo {
    public String getUserInput() {
        StringBuilder sb = new StringBuilder();
        try {
            char c = (char) System.in.read();
            while (c != '\r' && c != '\n') {
                sb.append(c);
                c = (char) System.in.read();
            }
        } catch (IOException e) {
        }
        return sb.toString();
    }

    public static void main(String[] args) {
        InputDemo demo = new InputDemo();
        String input = demo.getUserInput();
        System.out.println(input);
    }
}
```

However, an easier way to receive keyboard input is to use the **java.util.Scanner** class, discussed in the section "java.util.Scanner" later in this chapter.

The **System** class has many useful methods, all of which are static. Some of the more important ones are listed here.

```
public static void arraycopy(Object source, int sourcePos,
        Object destination, int destPos, int length)
```
This method copies the content of an array (*source*) to another array (*destination*), beginning at the specified position, to the specified position of the destination array. For example, the following code uses **arraycopy** to copy the contents of **array1** to **array2**.

```
int[] array1 = {1, 2, 3, 4};
int[] array2 = new int[array1.length];
System.arraycopy(array1, 0, array2, 0, array1.length);
```

```
public static void exit(int status)
```
Terminates the running program and the current JVM. You normally pass 0 to indicate that a normal exit and a nonzero to indicate there has been an error in the program prior to calling this method.

```
public static long currentTimeMillis()
```
Returns the computer time in milliseconds. The value represents the number of milliseconds that has elapsed since January 1, 1970 UTC.
Prior to Java 8, **currentTimeMillis** was used to time an operation. In Java 8 and

later, you can use the **java.time.Instant** class, instead. This class is discussed in Chapter 13, "Working with Dates and Times."

```
public static long nanoTime()
```
This method is similar to **currentTimeMillis**, but with nanosecond precision.

```
public static String getProperty(String key)
```
This method returns the value of the specified property. It returns **null** if the specified property does not exist. There are system properties and there are user-defined properties. When a Java program runs, the JVM provides values that may be used by the program as properties.

Each property comes as a key/value pair. For example, the **os.name** system property provides the name of the operating system running the JVM. Also, the directory name from which the application was invoked is provided by the JVM as a property named **user.dir**. To get the value of the **user.dir** property, you use:

```
System.getProperty("user.dir");
```
Table 5.2 lists the system properties.

System property	Description
java.version	Java Runtime Environment version
java.vendor	Java Runtime Environment vendor
java.vendor.url	Java vendor URL
java.home	Java installation directory
java.vm.specification.version	Java Virtual Machine specification version
java.vm.specification.vendor	Java Virtual Machine specification vendor
java.vm.specification.name	Java Virtual Machine specification name
java.vm.version	Java Virtual Machine implementation version
java.vm.vendor	Java Virtual Machine implementation vendor
java.vm.name	Java Virtual Machine implementation name
java.specification.version	Java Runtime Environment specification version
java.specification.vendor	Java Runtime Environment specification vendor
java.specification.name	Java Runtime Environment specification name
java.class.version	Java class format version number
java.class.path	Java class path
java.library.path	List of paths to search when loading libraries
java.io.tmpdir	Default temp file path
java.compiler	Name of JIT compiler to use
java.ext.dirs	Path of extension directory or directories
os.name	Operating system name
os.arch	Operating system architecture
os.version	Operating system version
file.separator	File separator ("/" on UNIX)
path.separator	Path separator (":" on UNIX)
line.separator	Line separator ("\n" on UNIX)
user.name	User's account name
user.home	User's home directory
user.dir	User's current working directory

Table 5.2: Java system properties

```
public static void setProperty(String property, String newValue)
```
You use **setProperty** to create a user-defined property or change the value of the current property. For instance, you can use this code to create a property named

password:

```
System.setProperty("password", "tarzan");
```

And, you can retrieve it by using **getProperty**:

```
System.getProperty("password")
```

For instance, here is how you change the **user.name** property.

```
System.setProperty("user.name", "tarzan");
```

```
public static String getProperty(String key, String default)
```
This method is similar to the single argument **getProperty** method, but returns a default value if the specified property does not exist.

```
public static java.util.Properties getProperties()
```
This method returns all system properties. The return value is a **java.util.Properties** object. The **Properties** class is a subclass of **java.util.Hashtable** (discussed in Chapter 11, "The Collections Framework"). For example, the following code uses the **list** method of the **Properties** class to iterate and display all system properties on the console.

```
java.util.Properties properties = System.getProperties();
properties.list(System.out);
```

java.util.Scanner

You use a **Scanner** object to scan a piece of text. In this chapter, we will only concentrate on its use to receive keyboard input.

Receiving keyboard input with **Scanner** is easy. All you need to do is instantiate the **Scanner** class by passing **System.in**. Then, to receive user input, call the **next** method on the instance. The **next** method buffers the characters the user input from the keyboard or other devices until the user presses Enter. It then returns a **String** containing the characters the user entered excluding the carriage-return character sequence. Listing 5.3 demonstrates the use of **Scanner** to receive user input.

Listing 5.3: Using Scanner to receive user input
```
package app05;
import java.util.Scanner;

public class ScannerDemo {
    public static void main(String[] args) {
        Scanner scanner = new Scanner(System.in);
        while (true) {
            System.out.print("What's your name? ");
            String input = scanner.nextLine();
            if (input.isEmpty()) {
                break;
            }
            System.out.println("Your name is " + input + ". ");
        }
        scanner.close();
```

```
        System.out.println("Good bye");
    }
}
```

Compared to the code in Listing 5.2, using **Scanner** is much simpler.

Summary

In this chapter you examined several important classes such as **java.lang.String**, arrays, **java.lang.System** and **java.util.Scanner**. You also learned about variable arguments. The last section covered the implementation of varargs in **java.lang.String** and **java.io.PrintStream**.

Quiz

1. What does it mean when people say that **Strings** are immutable objects?
2. How do you receive user input without **Scanner**? And, how do you do it with **Scanner**?
3. What is varargs?
4. Create a **com.example.Car** class that has these private fields: **year (int)**, **make (String)** and **model (String)**. Make **Car** immutable by providing only get methods. Fields are set by passing values to the constructor.
5. Create a **com.example.test.CarTest** class to instantiate **Car** and print its field values by calling the get methods.
6. Create a utility/helper class named **StringUtil** in **com.example.util**. This class should have two static methods, **getFileName** and **getFileExtension**. Both methods receive a file path and returns a file name or file extension, respectively. Create a **com.example.test.StringUtilTest** class to test the methods.
7. Show how you can use the **java.util.StringTokenizer** class to print the number of tokens in a **String** and each individual token.

Chapter 6
Arrays

In Java you can use an array to group primitives or objects of the same type. The entities belonging to an array is called the elements or components of the array. In this chapter you will learn how to create, initialize and iterate over an array as well as manipulate its elements. This chapter also features the **java.util.Arrays** class, a utility class for manipulating arrays.

Overview

In the background, every time you create an array, the compiler creates an object which allows you to:

- get the number of elements in the array through the **length** field. The length or size of an array is the number of elements in it.
- access each element by specifying an index. This indexing is zero-based. Index 0 refers to the first element, 1 to the second element, etc.

All the elements of an array have the same type, called the element type of the array. An array is not resizable and an array with zero element is called an empty array.

An array is a Java object. Therefore, an array variable behaves like other reference variables. For example, you can compare an array variable with **null**.

```
String[] names;
if (names == null)  // evaluates to true
```

If an array is a Java object, shouldn't there be a class that gets instantiated when you create an array? May be something like **java.lang.Array**? The truth is, no. Arrays are indeed special Java objects whose class is not documented and is not meant to be extended.

To use an array, first you need to declare one. You can use this syntax to declare an array:

```
type[] arrayName;
```

or

```
type arrayName[]
```

For example, the following declares an array of **long**s named **numbers**:

```
long[] numbers;
```

Declaring an array does not create an array or allocate space for its elements, the compiler simply creates an object reference. One way to create an array is by using the **new** keyword. You must specify the size of the array you are creating.

```
new type[size]
```

As an example, the following code creates an array of four **int**s:

```
new int[4]
```

Alternatively, you can declare and create an array in the same line.

```
int[] ints = new int[4];
```

After an array is created, its elements are either **null** (if the element type is a reference type) or the default value of the element type (if the array contains primitives). For example, an array of **int**s contain zeros by default.

To reference an array element, use an index. If the size of an array is *n*, then the valid indexes are all integers between 0 and *n*-1. For example, if an array has four elements, the valid indexes are 0, 1, 2 and 3. The following snippet creates an array of four **String** objects and assigns a value to its first element.

```
String[] names = new String[4];
names[0] = "Hello World";
```

Using a negative index or a positive integer equal to or greater than the array size will throw a **java.lang.ArrayIndexOutOfBoundsException**. See Chapter 8, "Error Handling" for information about exceptions.

Since an array is an object, you can call the **getClass** method on an array. The string representation of the **Class** object of an array has the following format:

```
[type
```

where *type* is the object type. Calling **getClass().getName()** on a **String** array returns **[Ljava.lang.String**. The class name of a primitive array, however, is harder to decipher. Calling **getClass().getName()** on an **int** array returns **[I** and on a long array returns **[J**.

You can create and initialize an array without using the **new** keyword. Java allows you to create an array by grouping values within a pair of braces. For example, the following code creates an array of three **String** objects.

```
String[] names = { "John", "Mary", "Paul" };
```

The following code creates an array of four **int**s and assign the array to the variable **matrix**.

```
int[] matrix = { 1, 2, 3, 10 };
```

Be careful when passing an array to a method because the following is illegal even though the method **average** takes an array of **int**s.

```
int avg = average( { 1, 2, 3, 10 } ); // illegal
```

Instead, you have to instantiate the array separately.

```
int[] numbers = { 1, 2, 3, 10 };
```

```
int avg = average(numbers);
```

or you can do this

```
int avg = average(new int[] { 1, 2, 3, 10 });
```

Iterating over an Array

Prior to Java 5, the only way to iterate the members of an array was to use a **for** loop and the array's indexes. For example, the following code iterates over a **String** array referenced by the variable **names**:

```
for (int i = 0; i < 3; i++) {
    System.out.println("\t- " + names[i]);
}
```

Java 5 enhanced the **for** statement. You can now use it to iterate over an array or a collection without the index. Use this syntax to iterate over an array:

```
for (elementType variable : arrayName)
```

Where *arrayName* is the reference to the array, *elementType* is the element type of the array, and *variable* is a variable that references each element of the array.

For example, the following code iterates over an array of **String**s.

```
String[] names = { "John", "Mary", "Paul" };
for (String name : names) {
    System.out.println(name);
}
```

The code prints this on the console.

```
John
Mary
Paul
```

The java.util.Arrays Class

The **Arrays** class provides static methods to manipulate arrays. Table 6.1 shows some of its methods.

Method	Description
asList	Returns a fixed-size **List** backed by the array. No other elements can be added to the **List**. **List** is discussed in Chapter 14, "The Collection Framework."
binarySearch	Searches an array for the specified key. If the key is found, returns the index of the element. If there is no match, returns the negative value of the insertion point minus one. See the section "Searching An Array" for details.
copyOf	Creates a new array having the specified length. The new array will have the same elements as the original array. If the new length is not the same as the length of the original array, it pads the new array with null or default values or truncates the original array.
copyOfRange	Creates a new array based on the specified range of the original array.
equals	Compares the contents of two arrays.
fill	Assigns the specified value to each element of the specified array.
sort	Sorts the elements of the specified array.
parallelSort	Parallel sorts the elements of the specified array.
toString	Returns the string representation of the specified array.

Table 6.1: More important methods of java.util.Arrays

Some of these methods are explained further in the next sections.

Changing an Array Size

Once an array is created, its size cannot be changed. If you want to change the size, you must create a new array and populates it using the values of the old array. For instance, the following code increases the size of **numbers**, an array of three **int**s, to 4.

```
int[] numbers = { 1, 2, 3 };
int[] temp = new int[4];
int length = numbers.length;
for (int j = 0; j < length; j++) {
    temp[j] = numbers[j];
}
numbers = temp;
```

A shorter way of doing this is by using the **copyOf** method of **java.util.Arrays**. For instance, this code creates a four-element array and copies the content of **numbers** to its first three elements.

```
int[] numbers = { 1, 2, 3 };
int[] newArray = Arrays.copyOf(numbers, 4);
```

Of course you can reassign the new array to the original variable:

```
numbers = Arrays.copyOf(numbers, 4);
```

The **copyOf** method comes with ten overloads, eight for each type of Java primitives and two for objects. Here are their signatures:

```
public static boolean[] copyOf(boolean[] original, int newLength)

public static byte[] copyOf(byte[] original, int newLength)

public static char[] copyOf(char[] original, int newLength)

public static double[] copyOf(double[] original, int newLength)

public static float[] copyOf(float[] original, int newLength)

public static int[] copyOf(int[] original, int newLength)

public static long[] copyOf(long[] original, int newLength)

public static short[] copyOf(short[] original, int newLength)

public static <T> T[] copyOf(T[] original, int newLength)

public static <T,U> T[] copyOf(U[] original, int newLength,
        java.lang.Class<? extends T[]> newType)
```

Each of these overloads may throw a **java.lang.NullPointerException** if *original* is null
and a **java.lang.NegativeArraySizeException** if *newLength* is negative.

The *newLength* argument can be smaller, equal to, or larger than the length of the
original array. If it is smaller, then only the first *newLength* elements will be included in
the copy. If it is larger, the last few elements will have default values, i.e. 0 if it is an array
of integers or **null** if it is an array of objects.

Another method similar to **copyOf** is **copyOfRange**. **copyOfRange** copies a range of
elements to a new array. Like **copyOf**, **copyOfRange** also provides overrides for each
Java data type. Here are their signatures:

```
public static boolean[] copyOfRange(boolean[] original,
        int from, int to)

public static byte[] copyOfRange(byte[] original,
        int from, int to)

public static char[] copyOfRange(char[] original,
        int from, int to)

public static double[] copyOfRange(double[] original,
        int from, int to)

public static float[] copyOfRange(float[] original,
        int from, int to)

public static int[] copyOfRange(int[] original, int from, int to)

public static long[] copyOfRange(long[] original, int from, int to)

public static short[] copyOfRange(short[] original, int from,
        int to)

public static <T> T[] copyOfRange(T[] original, int from, int to)

public static <T,U> T[] copyOfRange(U[] original, int from,
        int to, java.lang.Class<? extends T[]> newType)
```

You can also use **System.arraycopy()** to copy an array. However, **Arrays.copyOf()** is easier to use and internally it calls **System.arraycopy()**.

Searching An Array

You can use the **binarySearch** method of the **Arrays** class to search an array. This method comes with twenty overloads. Here are two of its overloads:

```
public static int binarySearch(int[] array, int key)

public static int binarySearch(java.lang.Object[] array,
        java.lang.Object key)
```

There are also overloads that restrict the search area.

```
public static int binarySearch(int[] array, int fromIndex,
        int toIndex, int key)

public static int binarySearch(java.lang.Object[] array,
        int fromIndex, int toIndex, java.lang.Object key)
```

The **binarySearch** method employs a binary search algorithm to do the search. Using this algorithm, the array is first sorted in ascending or descending order. It then compares the search key with the middle element of the array. If there is a match, the element index is returned. If there is no match, depending whether the search key is lower or higher than the index, the search continues in the first or second half of the array, repeating the same procedure until there is no or only one element left. If at the end of the search no match is found, the **binarySearch** method returns the negative value of the insertion point minus one. The example in Listing 6.1 will make this point clearer.

Listing 6.1: A binary search example
```
package app06;
import java.util.Arrays;

public class BinarySearchDemo {
    public static void main(String[] args) {
        int[] primes = { 2, 3, 5, 7, 11, 13, 17, 19 };
        int index = Arrays.binarySearch(primes, 13);
        System.out.println(index); // prints 5
        index = Arrays.binarySearch(primes, 4);
        System.out.println(index); // prints -3
    }
}
```

The **BinarySearchDemo** class in Listing 6.1 uses an **int** array containing the first eight prime numbers. Passing 13 as the search key returns 5 because 13 is the sixth element in the array, i.e. with index 5. Passing 4 does not find a match and the method returns -3, which is -2 minus one. If the key were to be inserted to the array, it would have the index 2.

Passing a String Array to main

The public static void method **main** that you use to invoke a Java class takes an array of **String**s. Here is the signature of **main**:

```
public static void main(String[] args)
```

You can pass arguments to **main** by typing them as arguments to the **java** program. The arguments should appear after the class name and two arguments are separated by a space. You use the following syntax:

```
java className arg1 arg2 arg3 ... arg-n
```

Listing 6.2 shows a class that iterates over the **main** method's **String** array argument.

Listing 6.2.: Accessing the main method's arguments
```
package app06;
public class MainMethodTest {
    public static void main(String[] args) {
        for (String arg : args) {
            System.out.println(arg);
        }
    }
}
```

The following command invokes the class and passes two arguments to the **main** method.

```
java app06/MainMethodTest john mary
```

The **main** method will then print the arguments to the console.

```
john
mary
```

If no argument is passed to **main**, the **String** array **args** will be empty and not null.

Multidimensional Arrays

In Java a multidimensional array is an array whose elements are also arrays. As such, the rows can have different lengths, unlike multidimensional arrays in C language.

To declare a two dimensional array, use two pairs of brackets after the type:

```
int[][] numbers;
```

To create an array, pass the sizes for both dimensions:

```
int[][] numbers = new int[3][2];
```

Listing 6.3 shows a multidimensional array of **int**s.

Listing 6.3: A multidimensional array.

```
package app06;
import java.util.Arrays;

public class MultidimensionalDemo1 {
    public static void main(String[] args) {
        int[][] matrix = new int[2][3];
        for (int i = 0; i < 2; i++) {
            for (int j = 0; j < 3; j++) {
                matrix[i][j] = j + i;
            }
        }

        for (int i = 0; i < 2; i++) {
            System.out.println(Arrays.toString(matrix[i]));
        }
    }
}
```

The following will be printed on the console if you run the class.

```
[0, 1, 2]

[1, 2, 3]
```

Summary

In this chapter you learned how to declare and initialize an array and work with this data structure. You also examined the **java.util.Arrays** class for manipulating arrays.

Quiz

1. What is an array?
2. How do you resize an array?
3. How do you create an array and pass it to a method without first assigning it to a variable?
4. Write a **com.example.app06.ArrayUtil** class that contains two static methods, **min** and **max**. Both methods receive an array of **int**s and returns the smallest largest element, respectively.

Chapter 7
Inheritance

Inheritance is a very important object-oriented programming (OOP) feature. It is what makes code extensible in an OOP language. Extending a class is also called inheriting or subclassing. In Java, by default all classes are extendible, but you can use the **final** keyword to prevent classes from being subclassed. This chapter explains inheritance in Java.

Overview

You extend a class by creating a new class. The former and the latter will then have a parent-child relationship. The original class is the parent class or the base class or the superclass. The new class is the child class or the subclass or the derived class of the parent. The process of extending a class in OOP is called inheritance. In a subclass you can add new methods and new fields as well as override existing methods to change their behaviors.

Figure 7.1 presents a UML class diagram that depicts a parent-child relationship between a class and a child class.

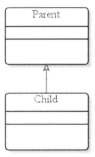

Figure 7.1: The UML class diagram for a parent class and a child class

Note that a line with an arrow is used to depict generalization, e.g. the parent-child relationship.

A child class in turn can be extended, unless you specifically make it inextensible by declaring it final. Final classes are discussed in the section "Final Classes" later in this chapter.

The benefits of inheritance are obvious. Inheritance gives you the opportunity to add some functionality that does not exist in the original class. It also gives you the chance to change the behaviors of the existing class to better suit your needs.

The extends Keyword

You extend a class by using the **extends** keyword in a class declaration, after the class name and before the parent class. Listing 7.1 presents a class named **Parent** and Listing 7.2 a class named **Child** that extends **Parent**.

Listing 7.1: The Parent class
```
public class Parent {
}
```

Listing 7.2: The Child class
```
public class Child extends Parent {
}
```

Extending a class is as simple as that.

Note
All Java classes that do not explicitly extend a parent class automatically extend the **java.lang.Object** class. **Object** is the ultimate superclass in Java. **Parent** in Listing 7.1 by default is a subclass of **Object**.

Note
In Java a class can only extend one class. This is unlike C++ where multiple inheritance is allowed. However, the notion of multiple inheritance can be achieved by using interfaces in Java, as discussed in Chapter 10, "Interfaces and Abstract Classes."

The Is-A Relationship

There is a special relationship that is formed when you create a new class by inheritance. The subclass and the superclass has an "is-a" relationship.

For example, **Animal** is a class that represents animals. There are many types of animals, including birds, fish and dogs, so you can create subclasses of **Animal** that model specific types of animals. Figure 7.2 features the **Animal** class with three subclasses, **Bird**, **Fish** and **Dog**.

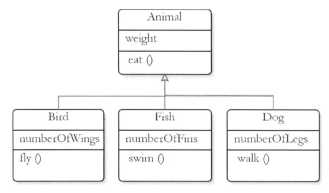

Figure 7.2: An example of inheritance

The is-a relationship between the subclasses and the superclass **Animal** is very apparent. A bird "is an" animal, a dog is an animal and a fish is an animal. A subclass is a special type of its superclass. For example, a bird is a special type of animal. The is-a relationship does not go the other way, however. An animal is not necessarily a bird or a dog.

Listing 7.3 presents the **Animal** class and its subclasses.

Listing 7.3: Animal and its subclasses

```
package app07;
class Animal {
    public float weight;
    public void eat() {
    }
}

class Bird extends Animal {
    public int numberOfWings = 2;
    public void fly() {
    }
}

class Fish extends Animal {
    public int numberOfFins = 2;
    public void swim() {
    }
}

class Dog extends Animal {
    public int numberOfLegs = 4;
    public void walk() {
    }
}
```

In this example, the **Animal** class defines a **weight** field that applies to all animals. It also declares an **eat** method because animals eat.

The **Bird** class is a special type of **Animal**, it inherits the **eat** method and the **weight** field. **Bird** also adds a **numberOfWings** field and a **fly** method. This shows that the more specific **Bird** class extends the functionality and behavior of the more generic **Animal** class.

A subclass inherits all public methods and fields of its superclass. For example, you can create a **Dog** object and call its **eat** method:

```
Dog dog = new Dog();
dog.eat();
```

The **eat** method is declared in the **Animal** class; the **Dog** class simply inherits it.

A consequence of the is-a relationship is that it is legal to assign an instance of a subclass to a reference variable of the parent type. For example, the following code is valid because **Bird** is a subclass of **Animal** and a **Bird** is always an **Animal**.

```
Animal animal = new Bird();
```

However, the following is illegal because there is no guarantee that an **Animal** is a **Dog**.:

```
Dog dog = new Animal();
```

Accessibility

From within a subclass you can access its superclass's public and protected methods and fields, but not the superclass's private methods. If the subclass and the superclass are in the same package, you can also access the superclass's default methods and fields.

Consider the **P** and **C** classes in Listing 7.4.

Listing 7.4: Showing accessibility

```
package app07;
public class P {
    public void publicMethod() {
    }
    protected void protectedMethod() {
    }
    void defaultMethod() {
    }
}
class C extends P {
    public void testMethods() {
        publicMethod();
        protectedMethod();
        defaultMethod();
    }
}
```

P has three methods, one public, one protected and one with the default access level. **C** is a subclass of **P**. As you can see in the **C** class's **testMethods** method, **C** can access its parent's public and protected methods. In addition, because **C** and **P** belong to the same package, **C** can also access **P**'s default method.

However, it does not mean you can expose **P**'s non-public methods through its subclass. For example, the following code will not compile:

```
package test;
import app07.C;
public class AccessibilityTest {
    public static void main(String[] args) {
        C c = new C();
        c.protectedMethod();
    }
}
```

protectedMethod is a protected method of **P**. It is not accessible from outside **P**, except from a subclass. Since **AccessibilityTest** is not a subclass of **P**, you cannot access **P**'s protected method through its subclass **C**.

Method Overriding

When you extends a class, you can change the behavior of a method in the parent class. This is called method overriding, and this happens when you write in a subclass a method that has the same signature as a method in the parent class. If only the name is the same but the list of arguments is not, then it is method overloading. (See Chapter 4, "Objects and Classes")

You override a method to change its behavior. To override a method, you simply have to write the new method in the subclass, without having to change anything in the parent class. You can override the superclass's public and protected methods. If the subclass and superclass are in the same package, you can also override methods with the default access level.

An example of method overriding is demonstrated by the **Box** class in Listing 7.5.

Listing 7.5: The Box class

```
package app07;
public class Box {
    public int length;
    public int width;
    public int height;

    public Box(int length, int width, int height) {
        this.length = length;
        this.width = width;
        this.height = height;
    }

    @Override
    public String toString() {
        return "I am a Box.";
    }

    @Override
    public Object clone() {
        return new Box(1, 1, 1);
    }
}
```

The **Box** class extends the **java.lang.Object** class. It is an implicit extension since the **extends** keyword is not used. **Box** overrides the public **toString** method and the protected **clone** method. Note that the **clone** method in **Box** is public whereas in **Object** it is protected. Increasing the visibility of a method defined in a superclass from protected to public is allowed. However, reducing visibility is illegal.

An overridden method is normally annotated with **@Override**. It is not required but it is good practice to do so. You will learn about annotations in Chapter 17, "Annotations."

What if you create a method that has the same signature as a private method in the superclass? It is not method overriding, since private methods are not visible from outside the class. It is just a method that happens to have the same signature as the private method.

Note
You cannot override a final method. To make a method final, use the **final** keyword in the method declaration. For example:

```
public final java.lang.String toUpperCase(java.lang.String s)
```

Calling the Constructors of the Superclass

A subclass is just like an ordinary class, you use the **new** keyword to create an instance of it. If you do not explicitly write a constructor in your subclass, the compiler will implicitly add a no-argument (no-arg) constructor.

When you instantiate a child class by invoking one of its constructors, the first thing the constructor does is call the no-argument constructor of the direct parent class. In the parent class, the constructor also calls the constructor of its direct parent class. This process repeats itself until it reaches the constructor of the **java.lang.Object** class. In other words, when you create a child object, all its parent classes are also instantiated.

This process is illustrated in the **Base** and **Sub** classes in Listing 7.6.

Listing 7.6: Calling a superclass's no-arg constructor
```
package app07;
class Base {
    public Base() {
        System.out.println("Base");
    }
    public Base(String s) {
        System.out.println("Base." + s);
    }
}
public class Sub extends Base {
    public Sub(String s) {
        System.out.println(s);
    }
    public static void main(String[] args) {
        Sub sub = new Sub("Start");
    }
}
```

If you run the **Sub** class, you'll see this on the console:

```
Base
Start
```

This proves that the first thing that the **Sub** class's constructor does is invoke the **Base** class's no-arg constructor. The Java compiler has quietly changed **Sub**'s constructor to the following without saving the modification to the source file.

```
public Sub(String s) {
    super();
    System.out.println(s);
}
```

The keyword **super** represents an instance of the direct superclass of the current object. Since **super** is called from an instance of **Sub**, **super** represents an instance of **Base**, its direct superclass.

You can explicitly call a parent's constructor from a subclass's constructor by using the **super** keyword, but **super** must be the first statement in the constructor. Using the **super** keyword is handy if you want another constructor in the superclass to be invoked. For example, you can modify the constructor in **Sub** to the following.

```
public Sub(String s) {
    super(s);
    System.out.println(s);
}
```

This constructor calls the single argument constructor of the parent class, by using **super(s)**. As a result, if you run the class you will see the following on the console.

```
Base.Start
Start
```

Now, what if the superclass does not have a no-arg constructor and you do not make an explicit call to another constructor from a subclass? This is illustrated in the **Parent** and **Child** classes in Listing 7.7.

Listing 7.7: Implicit calling to the parent's constructor that does not exist
```
package app07;
class Parent {
    public Parent(String s) {
        System.out.println("Parent(String)");
    }
}

public class Child extends Parent {
    public Child() {
    }
}
```

This will generate a compile error because the compiler adds an implicit call to the no-argument constructor in **Parent**, while the **Parent** class has only one constructor, the one that accepts a **String**. You can remedy this situation by explicitly calling the parent's constructor from the **Child** class's constructor:

```
public Child() {
    super(null);
}
```

Note
It actually makes sense for a child class to call its parent's constructor from its own constructor because an instance of a subclass must always be accompanied by an instance of each of its parents. This way, calls to a method that is not overridden in a child class can be passed to its parent until the first in the hierarchy is found.

Calling the Hidden Members of the Superclass

The **super** keyword has another purpose in life. It can be used to call a hidden member or an overridden method in a superclass. Since **super** represents an instance of the direct parent, super.*memberName* returns the specified member in the parent class. You can access any member in the superclass that is visible from the subclass. For example, Listing 7.8 shows two classes that have a parent-child relationship: **Tool** and **Pencil**.

Listing 7.8: Using super to access a hidden member

```
package app07;
class Tool {
    @Override
    public String toString() {
        return "Generic tool";
    }
}

public class Pencil extends Tool {
    @Override
    public String toString() {
        return "I am a Pencil";
    }

    public void write() {
        System.out.println(super.toString());
        System.out.println(toString());
    }

    public static void main(String[] args) {
        Pencil pencil = new Pencil();
        pencil.write();
    }
}
```

The **Pencil** class overrides the **toString** method in **Tool**. If you run the **Pencil** class, you will see the following on the console.

```
Generic tool
I am a Pencil
```

Unlike calling a parent's constructor, invoking a parent's method does not have to be the first statement in the caller method.

Type Casting

You can cast an object to another type. The rule is, you can only cast an instance of a subclass to its parent class. Casting an object to a parent class is called upcasting. Here is an example, assuming that **Child** is a subclass of **Parent**.

```
Child child = new Child();
```

```
Parent parent = child;
```

To upcast a **Child** object, all you need to do is assign the object to a reference variable of type **Parent**. Note that the **parent** reference variable cannot access members that are only available in **Child**.

Because **parent** in the snippet above references an object of type **Child**, you can cast it back to **Child**. This time, it is called downcasting because you are casting an object to a class down the inheritance hierarchy. Downcasting requires that you write the child type in brackets. For example:

```
Child child = new Child();
Parent parent = child;// parent pointing to an instance of Child
Child child2 = (Child) parent; // downcasting
```

Downcasting to a subclass is only allowed if the parent class reference is already pointing to an instance of the subclass. The following will generate a compile error.

```
Object parent = new Object();
Child child = (Child) parent; // illegal downcasting, compile error
```

Final Classes

You can prevent others from extending your class by making it final using the keyword **final** in the class declaration. **final** may appear after or before the access modifier. For example:

```
public final class Pencil
final public class Pen
```

The first form is more common.

Even though making a class final makes your code slightly faster, the difference is too insignificant to notice. Design consideration, and not speed, should be the reason you make a class final. For example, the **java.lang.String** class is final because the designer of the class did not want you to change the behavior of **String**.

The instanceof Operator

The **instanceof** operator can be used to test if an object is of a specified type. It is normally used in an **if** statement and its syntax is this.

```
if (objectReference instanceof type)
```

where *objectReference* references an object being investigated. For example, the following **if** statement returns **true**.

```
String s = "Hello";
if (s instanceof java.lang.String)
```

However, applying **instanceof** on a **null** reference variable returns **false**. For example, the following **if** statement returns **false**.

```
String s = null;
if (s instanceof java.lang.String)
```

Also, since a subclass "is a" type of its superclass, the following **if** statement, where **Child** is a subclass of **Parent**, returns **true**.

```
Child child = new Child();
if (child instanceof Parent)    // evaluates to true
```

Summary

Inheritance is one of the fundamental principles in object-oriented programming. Inheritance makes code extensible. In Java all classes by default extend the **java.lang.Object** class. To extend a class, use the **extends** keyword. Method overriding is another OOP feature directly related to inheritance. It enables you to change the behavior of a method in the parent class. You can prevent your class from being subclassed by making it final.

Quiz

1. Does a subclass inherit its superclass's constructors?
2. Why is it legal to assign an instance of a subclass to a superclass variable?
3. What is the difference between method overriding and method overloading?
4. Why is it necessary for an instance of a subclass to be accompanied by an instance of each parent?
5. Write a public **com.example.transport.Car** class that adds a public void method called **run** and overrides **toString()**. **run** prints the return value of **toString()**. Write another public class called **SUV** in the same package. **SUV** extends **Car** and overrides its **run** and **toString** methods. The **run** class of SUV should print the return value of the parent's **toString** method and its own **toString** method. Next, add a **main** method in **SUV** that creates an **SUV** object and calls its **run** method.

Chapter 8
Error Handling

Error handling is an important feature in any programming language. A good error handling mechanism makes it easier for programmers to write robust applications and to prevent bugs from creeping in. In some languages, programmers are forced to use multiple **if** statements to detect all possible conditions that might lead to an error. This could make code excessively complex. In a larger program, this could easily lead to spaghetti like code.

Java offers the **try** statement as a nice approach to error handling. With this strategy, part of the code that could potentially lead to an error is isolated in a block. Should an error occur, this error is caught and resolved locally. This chapter teaches you this.

Catching Exceptions

There are two types of errors, compile error and runtime error. Compile errors or compilation errors are due to errors in the source code. For example, if you forgot to terminate a statement with a semicolon, the compiler will tell you that and refuse to compile your code. Compile errors are caught by the compiler at compile time. Runtime errors, on the other hand, can only be caught when the program is running, i.e. at runtime, because the compiler could not have caught them. For example, running out of memory is a runtime error and a compiler could not have predicted this. Or, if a program tries to parse a user input to an integer, the input is only available when the program is running. If the user enters non-digits, then the parsing process will fail and a runtime error thrown. A runtime error, if not handled, will cause the program to quit abruptly.

In your program you can isolate code that may cause a runtime error using a **try** statement, which normally is accompanied by the **catch** and **finally** statements. Such isolation typically occurs in a method body. If an error is encountered, Java stops the processing of the **try** block and jump to the **catch** block. Here you can gracefully handle the error or notify the user by 'throwing' a **java.lang.Exception** object. Another scenario is to re-throw the exception or a new **Exception** object back to the code that called the method. It is then up to the client how he or she would handle the error. If a thrown exception is not caught, the application will crash.

This is the syntax of the **try** statement.

```
try {
    [code that may throw an exception]
} [catch (ExceptionType-1 e) {
    [code that is executed when ExceptionType-1 is thrown]
}] [catch (ExceptionType-2 e) {
    [code that is executed when ExceptionType-2 is thrown]
```

```
}]
    ...
} [catch (ExceptionType-n e) {
    [code that is executed when ExceptionType-n is thrown]
}]
[finally {
    [code that runs regardless of whether an exception was thrown]]
}]
```

The steps for error handling can be summarized as follows:

1. Isolate code that could lead to an error in the **try** block.
2. For each individual **catch** block, write code that is to be executed if an exception of that particular type occurs in the **try** block.
3. In the **finally** block, write code that will be run whether or not an error has occurred.

Note that the **catch** and **finally** blocks are optional, but one or both of them must exist. Therefore, you can have **try** with one or more **catch** blocks, **try** with **finally** or **try** with **catch** and **finally**.

The previous syntax shows that you can have more than one **catch** block. This is because some code may throw different types of exceptions. When an exception is thrown from a **try** block, control is passed to the first **catch** block. If the type of exception thrown matches the exception or is a subclass of the exception in the first **catch** block, the code in the **catch** block is executed and then control goes to the **finally** block, if one exists.

If the type of the exception thrown does not match the exception type in the first **catch** block, the JVM goes to the next **catch** block and does the same thing until it finds a match. If no match is found, the exception object will be thrown to the method caller. If the caller does not put the offending code that calls the method in a **try** block, the program will crash.

To illustrate the use of this error handling, consider the **NumberDoubler** class in Listing 8.1. When the class is run, it will prompt you for input. You can type anything, including non-digits. If your input is successfully converted to a number, it will double it and print the result. If your input is invalid, the program will print an "Invalid input" message.

Listing 8.1: The NumberDoubler class

```
package app08;
import java.util.Scanner;

public class NumberDoubler {
    public static void main(String[] args) {
        Scanner scanner = new Scanner(System.in);
        String input = scanner.next();
        try {
            double number = Double.parseDouble(input);
            System.out.printf("Result: %s", number);
        } catch (NumberFormatException e) {
            System.out.println("Invalid input.");
        }
        scanner.close();
    }
```

```
}
```

The **NumberDoubler** class uses the **java.util.Scanner** class to take user input (**Scanner** was discussed in Chapter 5, "Core Classes").

```
Scanner scanner = new Scanner(System.in);
String input = scanner.next();
```

It then uses the static **parseDouble** method of the **java.lang.Double** class to convert the string input to a **double**. Note that the code that calls **parseDouble** resides in a **try** block. This is necessary because **parseDouble** may throw a **java.lang.NumberFormatException**, as indicated by the signature of the **parseDouble** method:

```
public static double parseDouble(String s)
        throws NumberFormatExcpetion
```

The **throws** statement in the method signature tells you that it may throw a **NumberFormatException** and it is the responsibility of the method caller to catch it.

Without the **try** block, invalid input will give you this embarrassing error message before the system crashes:

```
Exception in thread "main" java.lang.NumberFormatException:
```

---

try without catch

A try statement can be used with **finally** without a catch block. You normally use this syntax to ensure that some code always gets executed whether or not an unexpected exception has been thrown in the **try** block. For example, after opening a database connection, you want to make sure the connection's **close** method is called after you're done with it. To illustrate this scenario, consider the following pseudocode that opens a database connection.

```
Connection connection = null;
try {

    // open connection
    // do something with the connection and perform other tasks

} finally {
    if (connection != null) {
        // close connection
    }
}
```

If something unexpected occurs in the **try** block, the **close** method will always be called to release the resource.

Catching Multiple Exceptions

Java 7 and later allow you to catch multiple exceptions in a single **catch** block if the caught exceptions are to be handled by the same code. The syntax of the **catch** block is as follows, two exceptions being separated by the pipe character |.

```
catch(exception-1 | exception-2 ... e) {

    // handle exceptions

}
```

For example, the **java.net.ServerSocket** class's **accept** method can throw four exceptions: **java.nio.channels.IllegalBlockingModeException**, **java.net.SocketTimeoutException**, **java.lang.SecurityException**, and **java.io.Exception**. If, say, the first three exceptions are to be handled by the same code, you can write your **try** block like this:

```
try {
    serverSocket.accept();
} catch (SocketTimeoutException | SecurityException |
        IllegalBlockingModeException e) {

    // handle exceptions

} catch (IOException e) {

    // handle IOException

}
```

The try-with-resources Statement

Many Java operations involve some kind of resource that has to be closed after use. Before JDK 7, you used **finally** to make sure a **close** method is guaranteed to be called:

```
try {

    // open resource

} catch (Exception e) {

} finally {
    // close resource
}
```

This syntax can be tedious especially if the **close** method can throw an exception and can be null. For example, here's a typical code fragment to open a database connection.

```
Connection connection = null;
try {

    // create connection and do something with it

} catch (SQLException e) {

} finally {
    if (connection != null) {
        try {
            connection.close();
        } catch (SQLException e) {
        }
    }
}
```

You see, you need quite a bit of code in the **finally** block just for one resource, and it's not uncommon to have to open multiple resources in a single **try** block. JDK 7 added a new feature, the try-with-resource statement, to make resource closing automatic. Its syntax is as follows.

```
try ( resources ) {

    // do something with the resources

} catch (Exception e) {
    // do something with e
}
```

For example, here is opening a database connection would look like in Java 7 and later.

```
Connection connection = null;
try (Connection connection = openConnection();
        // open other resources, if any) {

    // do something with connection

} catch (SQLException e) {

}
```

Not all resources can be automatically closed. Only resource classes that implement **java.lang.AutoCloseable** can be automatically closed. Fortunately, in JDK 7 many input/output and database resources have been modified to support this feature. You'll see more examples of try-with-resources in Chapter 16, "Input/Output" and Chapter 21, "Java Database Connectivity."

The java.lang.Exception Class

Erroneous code can throw any type of exception. For example, an invalid argument may throw a **java.lang.NumberFormatException**, and calling a method on a null reference variable throws a **java.lang.NullPointerException**. All Java exception classes derive from the **java.lang.Exception** class. It is therefore worthwhile to spend some time examining this class.

Among others, the **Exception** class overrides the **toString** method and adds a **printStackTrace** method. The **toString** method returns the description of the exception. The **printStackTrace** method has the following signature.

```
public void printStackTrace()
```

This method prints the description of the exception followed by a stack trace for the **Exception** object. By analyzing the stack trace, you can find out which line is causing the problem. Here is an example of what **printStackTrace** may print on the console.

```
java.lang.NullPointerException
    at MathUtil.doubleNumber(MathUtil.java:45)
    at MyClass.performMath(MyClass.java: 18)
    at MyClass.main(MyClass.java: 90)
```

This tells you that a **NullPointerException** has been thrown. The line that throws the exception is Line 45 of the **MathUtil.java** class, inside the **doubleNumber** method. The **doubleNumber** method was called by **MyClass.performMath**, which in turns was called by **MyClass.main**.

Most of the time a **try** block is accompanied by a **catch** block that catches the **java.lang.Exception** in addition to other **catch** blocks. The **catch** block that catches **Exception** must appear last. If other **catch** blocks fail to catch the exception, the last **catch** will do that. Here is an example.

```
try {
    // code
} catch (NumberFormatException e) {
    // handle NumberFormatException
} catch (Exception e) {
    // handle other exceptions
}
```

You may want to use multiple **catch** blocks in the code above because the statements in the **try** block may throw a **java.lang.NumberFormatException** or other type of exception. If the latter is thrown, it will be caught by the last **catch** block.

Be warned, though: The order of the **catch** blocks is important. You cannot, for example, put a **catch** block for handling **java.lang.Exception** before any other **catch** block. This is because the JVM tries to match the thrown exception with the argument of the **catch** blocks in the order of appearance. **java.lang.Exception** catches everything; therefore, the **catch** blocks after it would never be executed.

If you have several **catch** blocks and the exception type of one of the **catch** blocks is derived from the type of another **catch** block, make sure the more specific exception type appears first. For example, when trying to open a file, you need to catch the **java.io.FileNotFoundException** just in case the file cannot be found. However, you may want to make sure that you also catch **java.io.IOException** so that other I/O-related exceptions are caught. Since **FileNotFoundException** is a child class of **IOException**, the **catch** block that handles **FileNotFoundException** must appear before the **catch** block that handles **IOException**.

Throwing an Exception from a Method

When catching an exception in a method, you have two options to handle the error that occurs inside the method. You can either handle the error in the method, thus quietly catching the exception without notifying the caller (this has been demonstrated in the previous examples), or you can throw the exception back to the caller and let the caller handle it. If you choose the second option, the calling code must catch the exception that is thrown back by the method.

Listing 8.2 presents a **capitalize** method that changes the first letter of a **String** to upper case.

Listing 8.2: The capitalize method

```
public String capitalize(String s) throws NullPointerException {
    if (s == null) {
        throw new NullPointerException(
                "You passed a null argument");
    }
    Character firstChar = s.charAt(0);
    String theRest = s.substring(1);
    return firstChar.toString().toUpperCase() + theRest;
}
```

If you pass a null to **capitalize**, it will throw a new **NullPointerException**. Pay attention to the code that instantiates the **NullPointerException** class and throws the instance:

```
        throw new NullPointerException(
                "Your passed a null argument");
```

The **throw** keyword is used to throw an exception. Don't confuse it with the **throws** statement which is used at the end of a method signature to indicate that the method may throw an exception of the given type.

The following example shows code that calls **capitalize**.

```
String input = null;
try {
    String capitalized = util.capitalize(input);
    System.out.println(capitalized);
} catch (NullPointerException e) {
    System.out.println(e.toString());
}
```

Note
A constructor can also throw an exception.

User-Defined Exceptions

You can create a user-defined exception by subclassing **java.lang.Exception**. There are several reasons for having a user-defined exception. One of them is to create a customized error message.

For example, Listing 8.3 shows the **AlreadyCapitalizedException** class that derives from **java.lang.Exception**.

Listing 8.3: The AlreadyCapitalizedException class

```
package app08;
public class AlreadyCapitalizedException extends Exception {
    @Override
    public String toString() {
        return "Input has already been capitalized";
    }
}
```

You can throw an **AlreadyCapitalizedException** from the **capitalize** method in Listing 8.2. The modified **capitalize** method is given in Listing 8.4.

Listing 8.4: The modified capitalize method

```
public String capitalize(String s)
        throws NullPointerException, AlreadyCapitalizedException {
    if (s == null) {
        throw new NullPointerException(
                "Your passed a null argument");
    }
    Character firstChar = s.charAt(0);
    if (Character.isUpperCase(firstChar)) {
        throw new AlreadyCapitalizedException();
    }
    String theRest = s.substring(1);
    return firstChar.toString().toUpperCase() + theRest;
}
```

Now, **capitalize** may throw one of two exceptions. You comma-delimit multiple exceptions in a method signature.

Clients that call **capitalize** must now catch both exceptions. This code shows a call to **capitalize**.

```
StringUtil util = new StringUtil();
String input = "Capitalize";
try {
    String capitalized = util.capitalize(input);
    System.out.println(capitalized);
} catch (NullPointerException e) {
    System.out.println(e.toString());
} catch (AlreadyCapitalizedException e) {
    e.printStackTrace();
}
```

Since **NullPointerException** and **AlreadyCapitalizedException** do not have a parent-child relationship, the order of the **catch** blocks above is not important.

When a method throws multiple exceptions, rather than catch all the exceptions, you can simply write a **catch** block that handles **java.lang.Exception**. Rewriting the code above:

```
StringUtil util = new StringUtil();
String input = "Capitalize";
try {
    String capitalized = util.capitalize(input);
    System.out.println(capitalized);
} catch (Exception e) {
    System.out.println(e.toString());
}
```

While it's more concise, the latter lacks specifics and does not allow you to handle each exception separately.

Note on Exception Handling

The **try** statement imposes some performance penalty. Therefore, do not use it over-generously. If it is not hard to test for a condition, then you should do the testing rather than depending on the **try** statement. For example, calling a method on a null object throws a **NullPointerException**. Therefore, you could always surround a method call with a **try** block:

```
try {
    ref.method();
...
```

However, it is not hard at all to check if **ref** is null prior to calling **methodA**. Therefore, the following code is better because it eliminates the **try** block.

```
if (ref != null) {
    ref.methodA();
}
```

The **NullPointerException** is one of the most common exceptions a developer has to handle. Java 8 adds the **java.util.Optional** class that can reduce the amount of code for handling the **NullPointerException**. **Optional** is discussed in Chapter 19, "Lambda Expressions."

Summary

This chapter discussed the use of structured error handling and presented examples for each case. You have also been introduced to the **java.lang.Exception** class and its properties and methods. The chapter concluded with a discussion of user-defined exceptions.

Quiz

1. What is the advantage of the **try** statement?
2. Can a **try** statement be used with **finally** and without **catch**?
3. What is try-with-resources?
4. Write a utility class called **Util** (part of **com.example.app08**) that has a static method named **addArray** for adding two arrays of the same length. The signature of **addArray** is as follows.

```
public static long[] addArray(int[] array1, int[] array2)
        throws MismatchedArrayException,
        java.lang.NullPointerException
```

The method throws a **MismatchedArrayException** if the lengths of both arguments are not the same. The **toString** method of the exception class must return this value:

```
Mismatched array length. The first array's length is
length1. The second array's length is length2
```

where *length1* is the length of the first array and *length2* the length of the second array.

The method throws a **NullPointerException** if one of the arrays is null.

Chapter 9
Working with Numbers

In Java numbers are represented by the primitives **byte**, **short**, **int**, **long**, **float**, **double** and their wrapper classes, which were explained in Chapter 5, "Core Classes." Conversion from a primitive type to a wrapper object is called boxing and from a wrapper object to a primitive is called unboxing. Boxing and unboxing are the first topic in this chapter. Afterward, this chapter explain three issues you have to deal with when working with numbers, parsing, formatting and manipulation. Number parsing is the conversion of a string into a number and number formatting deals with presenting a number in a specific format. For instance, 1000000 may be displayed as 1,000,000.

To conclude, this chapter show how to perform monetary calculations and generate random numbers.

Boxing and Unboxing

Conversion from primitive types to corresponding wrapper objects and vice versa can happen automatically. Boxing refers to the conversion of a primitive to a wrapper instance, such as an **int** to a **java.lang.Integer**. Unboxing is the conversion of a wrapper instance to a primitive type, such as **Byte** to **byte**.

Here is an example of boxing.

```
Integer number = 3; // assign an int to Integer
```

Here is an example of unboxing.

```
Integer number = new Integer(100);
int simpleNumber = number;
```

When you can choose between a primitive type and its wrapper class, always favor the primitive over the wrapper, because primitives are faster than objects. There are cases where you need a wrapper class, however, such as when working with a collection. A collection, as discussed in Chapter 14, "The Collection Framework, accepts objects and does not accept primitives.

Number Parsing

A Java program may require that the user input a number that will be processed or become an argument to a method. For example, a currency converter program would need the user to type in a value to be converted. You can use the **java.util.Scanner** class to receive user input. However, the input will be a **String**, even though it represents a number. Before you can work with the number, you need to parse the string. The outcome of a successful parsing is a number.

Therefore, the purpose of number parsing is to convert a string into a numeric primitive type. If parsing fails, for example because the string is not a number or a number outside the specified range, your program can throw an exception.

The wrappers of primitives—the **Byte**, **Short**, **Integer**, **Long**, **Float**, and **Double** classes—provide static methods for parsing strings. For example, **Integer** has a **parseInteger** method with the following signature.

```
public static int parseInt(String s) throws NumberFormatException
```

This method parses a **String** and returns an **int**. If the **String** does not contain a valid integer representation, a **NumberFormatException** is thrown.

For example, the following snippet uses **parseInt** to parse the string "123" to 123.

```
int x = Integer.parseInt("123");
```

Similarly, **Byte** provides a **parseByte** method, **Long** a **parseLong** method, **Short** a **parseShort** method, **Float** a **parseFloat** method, and **Double** a **parseDouble** method.

For example, the **NumberTest** class in Listing 9.1 takes user input and parses it. If the user types in an invalid number, an error message will be displayed.

Listing 9.1: Parsing numbers (NumberTest.java)

```
package app09;
import java.util.Scanner;

public class NumberTest {
    public static void main(String[] args) {
        Scanner scanner = new Scanner(System.in);
        String userInput = scanner.next();
        try {
            int i = Integer.parseInt(userInput);
            System.out.println("The number entered: " + i);
        } catch (NumberFormatException e) {
            System.out.println("Invalid user input");
        }
    }
}
```

Chapter 9: Working with Numbers *137*

Number Formatting

Number formatting helps make numbers more readable. For example, 1000000 is more readable if printed as 1,000,000 (or 1.000.000 if your locale uses . to separate the thousands). For number formatting Java offers the **java.text.NumberFormat** class, which is an abstract class. Since it is abstract, you cannot create an instance using the **new** keyword. Instead, you instantiate its subclass **java.text.DecimalFormat**, which is a concrete implementation of **NumberFormat**.

```
NumberFormat nf = new DecimalFormat();
```

However, you should not call the **DecimalFormat** class's constructor directly. Instead, use the the **NumberFormat** class's **getInstance** static method. This method may return an instance of **DecimalFormat** but might also return an instance of a subclass other than **DecimalFormat**.

Now, how do you use **NumberFormat** to format numbers, such as 1234.56? Easy, simply pass the numbers to its **format** method and you'll get a **String**. However, should number 1234.56 be formatted as 1,234.56 or 1234,56? Well, it really depends in which side of the Atlantic you live. If you are in the US, you may want 1,234.56. If you live in Germany, however, 1234,56 makes more sense. Therefore, before you start using the **format** method, you want to make sure you get the correct instance of **NumberFormat** by telling it where you live, or, actually, in what locale you want it formatted. In Java, a locale is represented by the **java.util.Locale** class, which I'll explain in Chapter 19, "Internationalization." For now, remember that the **getInstance** method of the **NumberFormat** class also has an overload that accepts a **java.util.Locale**.

```
public NumberFormat getInstance(java.util.Locale locale)
```

If you pass **Locale.Germany** to the method, you'll get a **NumberFormat** object that formats numbers according to the German locale. If you pass **Locale.US**, you'll obtain one for the US number format. The no-argument **getInstance** method returns a **NumberFormat** object with the user's computer locale.

Listing 9.2 shows the **NumberFormatTest** class that demonstrates how to use the **NumberFormat** class to format a number.

Listing 9.2: The NumberFormatTest class

```
package app09;
import java.text.NumberFormat;
import java.util.Locale;

public class NumberFormatTest {
    public static void main(String[] args) {
        NumberFormat nf = NumberFormat.getInstance(Locale.US);
        System.out.println(nf.getClass().getName());
        System.out.println(nf.format(123445));
    }
}
```

When run, the output of the execution is

```
java.text.DecimalFormat
123,445
```

The first output line shows that a **java.text.DecimalFormat** object was produced upon calling **NumberFormat.getInstance**. The second shows how the **NumberFormat** formats the number 123445 into a more readable form.

Number Parsing with java.text.NumberFormat

You can use the **parse** method of **NumberFormat** to parse numbers. One of this method's overloads has the following signature:

```
public java.lang.Number parse(java.lang.String source)
        throws ParseException
```

parse returns an instance of **java.lang.Number**, the parent of such classes as **Integer**, **Long**, etc.

The java.lang.Math Class

The **Math** class is a utility class that provides static methods for mathematical operations. There are also two static final double fields: **E** and **PI**. **E** represents the base of natural logarithms (e). Its value is close to 2.718. **PI** is the ratio of the circumference of a circle to its diameter (pi). Its value is 22/7 or approximately 3.1428.

Some of the methods in **Math** are in Table 9.1.

Method	Description
abs	Returns the absolute value of the specified double.
acos	Returns the arc cosine of an angle, in the range of 0.0 through pi.
asin	Returns the arc sine of an angle, in the range of –pi/2 through pi/2.
atan	Returns the arc tangent of an angle, in the range of –pi/2 through pi/2.
cos	Returns the cosine of an angle.
exp	Returns Euler's number e raised to the power of the specified double.
log	Returns the natural logarithm (base e) of a double.
log10	Returns the base 10 logarithm of a double.
max	Returns the greater of two double values.
min	Returns the smaller of two double values.
random	Returns a pseudorandom double greater than or equal to 0.0 and less than 1.0.
round	Rounds a float to the nearest int.

Table 9.1: More important methods of java.lang.Math

Working with Money

Consider the following code that uses a **double** to represent a bank account balance. Suppose you have $10.00 in your account and you are charged a 10 cent account fee twice.

```
double balance = 10.00F;
balance -= 0.10F;
balance -= 0.10F;
```

What is the balance now? It should be $9.80, but no. The balance is 9.799999997019768, which is wrong.

Due to the way floats and doubles are represented as bits, these two primitives are not exact. If you are interested in knowing how a float or double is presented in bits, consult this Wikipedia page:

```
http://en.wikipedia.org/wiki/Single-precision_floating-point_format
```

The consequence is, floats and doubles are not suitable for monetary calculations. There are two ways to deal with money in Java. First, you can use an **int** or a **long** and calculate the cents (and not dollars) and convert the final result to the dollar. Second, you can use the **java.math.BigDecimal** class. The first approach is tedious so the second one is better even though operations involving a **BigDecimal** are slower than those involving an **int** or a **long**.

Listing 9.3 shows an example of using a **double** and **BigDecimal**.

Listing 9.3: Using BigDecimal

```
package app09;
import java.math.BigDecimal;

public class BigDecimalDemo {
    public static void main(String[] args) {
        double balance = 9.99;
        balance -= 0.10F;
        System.out.println(balance); // prints 9.889999769628048

        BigDecimal balance2 = BigDecimal.valueOf(9.99);
        BigDecimal accountFee = BigDecimal.valueOf(.1);
        BigDecimal r = balance2.subtract(accountFee);
        System.out.println(r.doubleValue()); // prints 9.89
    }
}
```

As you can see, **BigDecimal** gives you the exact result. You should use this for monetary calculations and any other calculations that require preciseness.

Generating Random Numbers

The **java.util.Random** class, which has been available since JDK 1.0, models a random number generator. However, the **random** method of the **java.lang.Math** class is much easier to use. This method returns a **double** between 0.0 to 1.0.

Listing 9.4 shows a **RandomNumberGenerator** class that generates an int between 0 and 9 (inclusive).

Lisitng 9.4: Random number generator

```
package app09;

public class RandomNumberGenerator {

    /*
     * Returns a random number between 0 and 9 (inclusive)
     */
    public int generate() {
        double random = Math.random();
        return (int) (random * 10);
    }

    public static void main(String[] args) {
        RandomNumberGenerator generator =
                new RandomNumberGenerator();
        for (int i = 0; i < 10; i++) {
            System.out.println(generator.generate());
        }

    }
}
```

Summary

In Java you use primitives and wrapper classes to model numbers. Conversion between a primitive and a wrapper class and the other way around happen automatically. There are three types of operations that you frequently perform when dealing with number and dates: parsing, formatting and manipulation. This chapter showed how to perform them.

In addition, this chapter explained the best way to perform monetary calculations and generate random numbers.

Quiz

1. What can you do with the **java.lang.Math** class's static methods?
2. Are wrapper classes still useful since boxing and unboxing happen automatically in Java?
3. Explain why you should not use doubles or floats to perform monetary calculations. What should you use instead?
4. Write a class called **RangeRandomGenerator** that can generate random numbers between two integers that you specify when instantiating the class.

Chapter 10
Interfaces and Abstract Classes

Java beginners often get the impression that an interface is simply a class without implementation. While this is not technically incorrect, it obscures the real purpose of having the interface in the first place. The interface is more than that. The interface should be regarded as a contract between a service provider and its clients. This chapter therefore focuses on the concepts before explaining how to write an interface.

The second topic in this chapter is the abstract class. Technically speaking, an abstract class is a class that cannot be instantiated and must be implemented by a subclass. However, the abstract class is important because in some situations it can take the role of the interface. You will learn how to use the abstract class too in this chapter.

The Concept of Interface

When learning about the interface for the first time, novices often focus on how to write one, rather than understanding the concept behind it. They would think an interface is something like a Java class declared with the **interface** keyword and whose methods have no body.

While the description is not inaccurate, treating an interface as an implementation-less class misses the big picture. A better definition of an interface is a contract. It is a contract between a service provider (server) and the user of such a service (client). Sometimes the server defines the contract, sometimes the client does.

Consider this real-world example. Microsoft Windows is the most popular operating system today, but Microsoft does not make printers. For printing, you still rely on those people at HP, Canon, Samsung, and the like. Each of these printer makers uses a proprietary technology. However, their products can all be used to print documents from any Windows application. How come?

This is because Microsoft said something to this effect to the printer manufacturers, "If you want your products useable on Windows (and we know you do), you must implement this **Printable** interface."

The interface is as simple as this:

```
interface Printable {
    void print(Document document);
}
```

where *document* is the document to be printed.

Implementing this interface, the printer makers then write printer drivers. Every printer has a different driver, but they all implement **Printable**. A printer driver is an implementation of **Printable**. In this case, these printer drivers are the service provider.

The client of the printing service is all Windows applications. It is easy to print on Windows because an application just needs to call the **print** method and pass a **Document** object. Because the interface is freely available, client applications can be compiled without waiting for an implementation to be available.

The point is, printing to different printers from different applications is possible thanks to the **Printable** interface. This interface is a contract between printing service providers and printing clients.

An interface can define both fields and methods. Prior to JDK 1.8 all methods in an interface were abstract, but starting from JDK 1.8 you can also write default and static methods in an interface. Unless specified otherwise, an interface method refers to an abstract method.

To be useful, an interface has to have an implementing class that actually performs the action.

Figure 10.1 illustrates the **Printable** interface and its implementation in an UML class diagram.

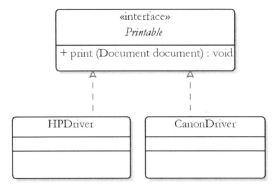

Figure 10.1: An interface and two implementation classes in a class diagram

In the class diagram, an interface has the same shape as a class, however the name is printed in italic and prefixed with <<interface>>. The **HPDriver** and **CanonDriver** classes are classes that implement the **Printable** interface. The implementations are of course different. In the **HPDriver** class, the **print** method contains code that enables printing to a HP printer. In **CanonDriver**, the code enables printing to a Canon driver. In a UML class diagram, a class and an interface are joined by a dash-line with an arrow. This type of relationship is often called realization because the class provides real implementation (code that actually works) of the abstraction provided by the interface.

Note
This case study is contrived but the problem and the solution are real. I hope this provides you with more understanding of what the interface really is. It is a contract.

The Interface, Technically Speaking

like a pure virtual class in C++

Now that you understand what the interface is, let's examine how you can create one. In Java, like the class, the interface is a type. Follow this format to write an interface:

```
accessModifier interface interfaceName {

}
```

Like a class, an interface has either the public or default access level. An interface can have fields and methods. All members of an interface are implicitly public. Listing 10.1 shows an interface named **Printable**.

Listing 10.1: The Printable interface

```
package app10;
public interface Printable {
    void print(Object o);
}
```

The **Printable** interface has a method, **print**. Note that **print** is public even though there is no **public** keyword in front of the method declaration. You are free to use the keyword **public** before the method signature, but it would be redundant.

Just like a class, an interface is a template for creating objects. Unlike an ordinary class, however, an interface cannot be instantiated. It simply defines a set of methods that Java classes can implement.

You compile an interface just you would a class. The compiler creates a .class file for each interface compiled successfully.

To implement an interface, you use the **implements** keyword after the class declaration. A class can implement multiple interfaces. For example, Listing 10.2 shows the **CanonDriver** class that implements **Printable**.

Listing 10.2: An implementation of the Printable interface

```
package app10;
public class CanonDriver implements Printable {
    @Override
    public void print(Object obj) {
        // code that does the printing
    }
}
```

Note that a method implementation should also be annotated with **@Override**.

Unless specified otherwise, all interface methods are abstract. An implementing class has to override all abstract methods in an interface. The relationship between an interface and its implementing class can be likened to a parent class and a subclass. An instance of the class is also an instance of the interface. For example, the following **if** statement evaluates to **true**.

```
CanonDriver driver = new CanonDriver();
if (driver instanceof Printable)    // evaluates to true
```

Some interfaces have neither fields nor methods, and are known as marker interfaces. Classes implement them as a marker. For example, the **java.io.Serializable** interface, has no fields nor methods. Classes implement it so that their instances can be serialized, i.e. saved to a file or to memory. You will learn more about Serializable in Chapter 16, "Input Output."

Fields in an Interface

Fields in an interface must be initialized and are implicitly public, static and final. However, you may redundantly use the modifiers **public**, **static**, and **final**. These lines of code have the same effect.

```
public int STATUS = 1;
int STATUS = 1;
public static final STATUS = 1;
```

Note that by convention field names in an interface are written in upper case.

It is a compile error to have two fields with the same name in an interface. However, an interface might inherit more than one field with the same name from its superinterfaces.

Abstract Methods

You declare abstract methods in an interface just as you would declare a method in a class. However, abstract methods in an interface do not have a body, they are immediately terminated by a semicolon. All abstract methods are implicitly public and abstract, even though it is legal to have the **public** and **abstract** modifiers in front of a method declaration.

The syntax of an abstract method in an interface is

```
[methodModifiers] ReturnType MethodName(listOfArgument)
        [ThrowClause];
```

where *methodModifiers* is **abstract** and **public**.

Extending An Interface

The interface supports inheritance. An interface can extend another interface. If interface **A** extends interface **B**, **A** is said to be a subinterface of **B**. **B** is the superinterface of **A**. Because **A** directly extends **B**, **B** is the direct superinterface of **A**. Any interfaces that extend **B** are indirect subinterfaces of **A**. Figure 10.2 shows an interface that extends another interface. Note that the type of the line connecting both interfaces is the same as the one used for extending a class.

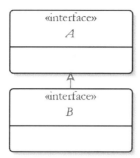

Figure 10.2: Extending an interface

What is the purpose of extending an interface? To safely add functionality to an interface without breaking existing code. This is so because you cannot add a new method to an interface once the interface has been published. Suppose an imaginary interface **XYZ** in JDK 1.7 was a popular interface with millions of implementation classes. Now, the designers of Java wanted to add a new method in **XYZ** in JDK 1.8. What would happen if a class that implemented the old **XYZ** and was compiled with a pre-JDK 1.8 compiler was deployed on JDK 1.8 (which would have shipped with the new version of **XYZ**)? It would break because the class had not provided the implementation for the new method.

The safe way would be to provide a new interface that extends **XYZ** so old software would still work and new applications can choose to implement the extension interface instead of **XYZ**.

Default Methods

Extending an interface is a safe way of adding functionality to the interface. However, you end up with two interfaces with similar functionality. This is acceptable if you only need to extend one or two interfaces. If you need to add features to hundred of interfaces, this has certainly become a serious issue.

This is exactly what the Java language designers faced when they were trying to add lambda expressions to Java 8 and add support for lambda in dozens of interfaces in the Collection Framework. Extending all the interfaces would double the number of interfaces and some would probably end up with ugly names such as **List2** or **ExtendedSet**.

Instead, they chose to add default methods. In other words, from JDK 1.8 onward, an interface can have default methods.

A default method in an interface is a method with implementation. A class implementing the interface does not have to implement the default method, which means you can add new methods to an interface without breaking backward compatibility.

To make a method in an interface a default method, add the keyword **default** in front of the method signature. Additionally, instead of terminating the signature with a semicolon, add a pair of brackets and write code in the brackets. Here is an example.

```
default java.lang.String getDescription() {
    return "This is a default method";
```

}

As you will learn later, a lot of Java interfaces in JDK 1.8 now have default methods.

When extending an interface with default methods, you have these options.

- Ignore the default methods, in effect inheriting them,
- Re-declare the default methods, which makes them abstract,
- Override the default methods.

Remember that the main reason Java now support default methods is for backward compatibility. By no means should you start writing programs without classes.

Static Methods

A static method in a class is shared by all instances of the class. In Java 8 and later you can have static methods in an interface so that all static methods associated with an interface can be written in the interface, rather than in a helper class.

The signature of a static method is similar to that of a default method. Instead of the keyword **default**, however, you use the keyword **static**. Static methods in an interface are public by default.

Static methods in an interface are rare. Of the close to 30 interfaces in the **java.util** package, only two contain static methods.

Base Classes

Some interfaces have many abstract methods, and implementing classes must override all the methods. This can be a tedious task if you only need some of the methods. For this reason, you can create a generic implementation class that overrides the abstract methods in an interface with default code. An implementing class can then extend the generic class and overrides only abstract methods it wants to change. This kind of generic class, often called a base class, is handy because it helps you code faster.

For example, the **javax.servlet.Servlet** interface is the interface that must be implemented by all servlet classes. This interface has five abstract methods: **init**, **service**, **destroy**, **getServletConfig**, **getServletInfo**. Of the five, only the **service** method is always implemented by servlet classes. The **init** method is implemented occasionally, but the rest are rarely used. Despite the fact, all implementing classes must provide implementation for all five methods. What a chore this would be for servlet programmers.

To make servlet programming easier and more fun, the Servlet API defines the **javax.servlet.GenericServlet** class, which provides default implementation for all methods in the **Servlet** interface. When you write a servlet, instead of writing a class that implements the **javax.servlet.Servlet** interface (and ending up implementing five methods), you extend the **javax.servlet.GenericServlet** and provide only implementation for methods you need to use (most probably, only the **service** method).

Compare the **TediousServlet** class in Listing 10.3, which implements **javax.servlet.Servlet**, and the one in Listing 10.4, which extends

javax.servlet.GenericServlet. Which one is simpler?

Listing 10.3: The TediousServlet class

```java
package test;
import java.io.IOException;
import javax.servlet.Servlet;
import javax.servlet.ServletConfig;
import javax.servlet.ServletException;
import javax.servlet.ServletRequest;
import javax.servlet.ServletResponse;

public class TediousServlet implements Servlet {
    @Override
    public void init(ServletConfig config)
            throws ServletException {
    }

    @Override
    public void service(ServletRequest request,
            ServletResponse response)
            throws ServletException, IOException {
        response.getWriter().print("Welcome");
    }

    @Override
    public void destroy() {
    }

    @Override
    public String getServletInfo() {
        return null;
    }

    @Override
    public ServletConfig getServletConfig() {
        return null;
    }
}
```

Listing 10.4: The FunServlet class

```java
package test;
import java.io.IOException;
import javax.servlet.GenericServlet;
import javax.servlet.ServletException;
import javax.servlet.ServletRequest;
import javax.servlet.ServletResponse;

public class FunServlet extends GenericServlet {
    @Override
    public void service(ServletRequest request,
            ServletResponse response)
            throws ServletException, IOException {
        response.getWriter().print("Welcome");
```

```
    }
}
```

Abstract Classes

With the interface, you have to write an implementation class that perform the actual action. If there are many abstract methods in the interface, you risk wasting time overriding methods that you don't use. An abstract class has a similar role to an interface, i.e. provide a contract between a service provider and its clients, but at the same time an abstract class can provide partial implementation. Methods that must be explicitly overridden can be declared abstract. You still need to create an implementation class because you cannot instantiate an abstract class, but you don't need to override methods you don't want to use or change.

You create an abstract class by using the **abstract** modifier in the class declaration. To make an abstract method, use the **abstract** modifier in front of the method declaration. Listing 10.5 shows an abstract **DefaultPrinter** class as an example.

Listing 10.5: The DefaultPrinter class

```
package app10;
public abstract class DefaultPrinter {
    @Override
    public String toString() {
        return "Use this to print documents.";
    }
    public abstract void print(Object document);
}
```

There are two methods in **DefaultPrinter**, **toString** and **print**. The **toString** method has an implementation, so you do not need to override this method in an implementation class, unless you want to change its return value. The **print** method is declared abstract and does not have a body. Listing 10.6 presents a **MyPrinterClass** class that is the implementation class of **DefaultPrinter**.

Listing 10.6: An implementation of DefaultPrinter

```
package app10;
public class MyPrinter extends DefaultPrinter {
    @Override
    public void print(Object document) {
        System.out.println("Printing document");
        // some code here
    }
}
```

A concrete implementation class such as **MyPrinter** must override all abstract methods. Otherwise, it itself must be declared abstract.

Declaring a class abstract is a way to tell the class user that you want them to extend the class. You can still declare a class abstract even if it does not have an abstract method.

In UML class diagrams, an abstract class looks similar to a concrete class, except that the name is italicized. Figure 10.3 shows an abstract class.

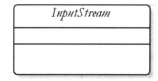

Figure 10.3: An abstract class

Summary

The interface plays an important role in Java because it defines a contract between a service provider and its clients. This chapter showed you how to use the interface. A base class provides a generic implementation of an interface and expedites program development by providing default implementation of code.

An abstract class is like an interface, but it may provide implementation of some of its methods.

Quiz

1. Why is it more appropriate to regard an interface as a contract than as a implementation-less class?
2. What is a base class?
3. What is an abstract class?
4. Is a base class the same as an abstract class?
5. Create an interface named **Calculator** in **com.example** with three methods, **add**, **subtract** and **multiply**. All methods take two **int** arguments and return a **long**.
6. Write an implementation of **Calculator** called **ScientificCalculator** and implement all the methods.

Chapter 11
Polymorphism

Polymorphism is the hardest concept to explain to those new to object-oriented programming (OOP). In fact, most of the time its definition does not make sense without an example or two. Well, try this. Here is a definition in many programming books: Polymorphism is an OOP feature that enables an object to determine which method implementation to invoke upon receiving a method call. If you find this hard to digest, you're not alone. Polymorphism is hard to explain in simple language, but it does not mean the concept is hard to understand.

This chapter starts with a simple example that should make polymorphism crystal clear. It then proceeds with another example that demonstrates the use of polymorphism with reflection.

Overview

In Java and other OOP languages, it is legal to assign to a reference variable an object whose type is different from the variable type, if certain conditions are met. In essence, if you have a reference variable **a** whose type is **A**, it is legal to assign an object of type **B**, like this

```
A a = new B();
```

provided one of the following conditions is met.

- **A** is a class and **B** is a subclass of **A**.
- **A** is an interface and **B** or one of its parents implements **A**.

As you have learned in Chapter 7, "Inheritance," this is called upcasting.

When you assign **a** an instance of **B** like in the code above, **a** is of type **A**. This means, you cannot call a method in **B** that is not defined in **A**. However, if you print the value of **a.getClass().getName()**, you'll get "B" and not "A." So, what does this mean? At compile time, the type of **a** is **A**, so the compiler will not allow you to call a method in **B** that is not defined in **A**. On the other hand, at runtime the type of **a** is **B**, as proven by the return value of **a.getClass().getName()**.

Now, here comes the essence of polymorphism. If **B** overrides a method (say, one named **play**) in **A**, calling **a.play()** will cause the implementation of **play** in **B** (and not in **A**) to be invoked. Polymorphism enables an object (in this example, the one referenced by **a**) to determine which method implementation to choose (either the one in **A** or the one in **B**) when a method is called. Polymorphism dictates that the implementation in the runtime object be invoked. But, polymorphism does not stop here.

What if you call another method in **a** (say, a method called **stop**) and the method is not implemented in **B**? The JVM will be smart enough to know this and look into the inheritance hierarchy of **B**. **B**, as it happens, must be a subclass of **A** or, if **A** is an interface, a subclass of another class that implements **A**. Otherwise, the code would not have compiled. Having figured this out, the JVM will climb up the class hierarchy and find the implementation of **stop** and run it.

Now, there is more sense in the definition of polymorphism: Polymorphism is an OOP feature that enables an object to determine which method implementation to invoke upon receiving a method call.

Technically, though, how does Java achieve this? The Java compiler, as it turns out, upon encountering a method call such as **a.play()**, checks if the class/interface represented by **a** defines such a method (a **play** method) and if the correct set of parameters are passed to the method. But, that is the farthest the compiler goes. With the exception of static and final methods, it does not connect (or bind) a method call with a method body. The JVM determines how to bind a method call with the method body at runtime. In other words, except for static and final methods, method binding in Java happens at runtime and not at compile time. Runtime binding is also called late binding or dynamic binding. The opposite is early binding, in which binding occurs at compile time or link time. Early binding occurs in other languages, such as C.

Therefore, polymorphism is made possible by the late binding mechanism in Java. Because of this, polymorphism is rather inaccurately also called late binding, dynamic binding or runtime binding in other languages.

Consider the Java code in Listing 11.1.

Listing 11.1: An example of polymorphism

```
package app11;
class Employee {
    public void work() {
        System.out.println("I am an employee.");
    }
}

class Manager extends Employee {
    public void work() {
        System.out.println("I am a manager.");
    }

    public void manage() {
        System.out.println("Managing ...");
    }
}

public class PolymorphismDemo1 {
    public static void main(String[] args) {
        Employee employee;
        employee = new Manager();
        System.out.println(employee.getClass().getName());
        employee.work();
        Manager manager = (Manager) employee;
        manager.manage();
    }
```

```
}
```

Listing 11.1 defines two non-public classes: **Employee** and **Manager**. **Employee** has a method called **work**, and **Manager** extends **Employee** and adds a new method called **manage**.

The **main** method in the **PolymorphismDemo1** class defines an object variable called **employee** of type **Employee**:

```
Employee employee;
```

However, **employee** is assigned an instance of **Manager**, as in:

```
employee = new Manager();
```

This is legal because **Manager** is a subclass of **Employee**, so a **Manager** "is an" **Employee**. Because **employee** is assigned an instance of **Manager**, what is the outcome of **employee.getClass().getName()**? You're right. It's "Manager," not "Employee."

Then, the **work** method is called.

```
employee.work();
```

Guess what is written on the console?

```
I am a manager.
```

This means that it is the **work** method in the **Manager** class that got called, which was polymorphism in action.

Note
Polymorphism does not work with static methods because they are early-bound. For example, if the **work** method in both the **Employee** and **Manager** classes were static, a call to **employee.work()** would print "I am an employee." Also, since you cannot extend final methods, polymorphism will not work with final methods either.

Now, because the runtime type of **a** is **Manager**, you can downcast **a** to **Manager**, as the code shows:

```
Manager manager = (Manager) employee;
manager.manage();
```

After seeing the code, you might ask, why would you declare **employee** as **Employee** in the first place? Why didn't you declare **employee** as type **Manager**, such as this?

```
Manager employee;
employee = new Manager();
```

You do this to ensure flexibility in cases where you don't know whether the object reference (**employee**) will be assigned an instance of **Manager** or something else.

The power of polymorphism will be more apparent in the example in the next section.

Polymorphism in Action

Suppose you have a **Greeting** interface that defines an abstract method named **greet**. This simple interface is given in Listing 11.2.

Listing 11.2: The Greeting interface

```
package app11;
public interface Greeting {
    public void greet();
}
```

The **Greeting** interface can be implemented to print a greeting in different languages. For example, the **EnglishGreeting** class in Listing 11.3 and the **FrenchGreeting** class in Listing 11.4 implement **Greeting** to greet the user in English and French, respectively.

Listing 11.3: The EnglishGreeting class

```
package app11;

public class EnglishGreeting implements Greeting {

    @Override
    public void greet() {
        System.out.println("Good Day!");
    }
}
```

Listing 11.4: The FrenchGreeting class

```
package app11;

public class FrenchGreeting implements Greeting {

    @Override
    public void greet() {
        System.out.println("Bonjour!");
    }
}
```

The **PolymorphismDemo2** class in Listing 11.5 shows polymorphism in action. It asks the user in what language they want to be greeted. If the user chooses English, then the **EnglishGreeting** class will be instantiated. If French is selected, **FrenchGreeting** will be instantiated. This is polymorphism because the class to be instantiated is only known at runtime, after the user types in a selection.

Listing 11.5: The PolymorphismDemo2 class

```
package app11;
import java.util.Scanner;

public class PolymorphismDemo2 {
```

```
    public static void main(String[] args) {
        String instruction = "What is your chosen language?" +
                "\nType 'English' or 'French'.";
        Greeting greeting = null;
        Scanner scanner = new Scanner(System.in);
        System.out.println(instruction);
        while (true) {
            String input = scanner.next();
            if (input.equalsIgnoreCase("english")) {
                greeting = new EnglishGreeting();
                break;
            } else if (input.equalsIgnoreCase("french")) {
                greeting = new FrenchGreeting();
                break;
            } else {
                System.out.println(instruction);
            }
        }

        scanner.close();
        greeting.greet();
    }
}
```

Polymorphism and Reflection

Polymorphism is often used along with reflection. Consider this scenario.

The Order Processing application is a business application for handling purchase orders. It can store orders in various databases (Oracle, MySQL, etc) and retrieve orders for display. The **Order** class represents purchase orders. Orders are stored in a database and an **OrderAccessObject** object handles the storing and retrieval of **Order** objects.

The **OrderAccessObject** class acts as an interface between the application and the database. All purchase order manipulations are done through an instance of this class. The **OrderAccessObject** interface is given in Listing 11.6.

Listing 11.6: The OrderAccessObject Interface
```
package app11;
public interface OrderAccessObject {
    public void addOrder(Order order);
    public void getOrder(int orderId);
}
```

The **OrderAccessObject** interface needs an implementation class that provides code for the two methods in it. The application may have many implementation classes for **OrderAccessObject**, each of which caters to a specific type of database. For example, the implementation class that connects to an Oracle database is called **OracleOrderAccessObject** class and the one for MySQL is **MySQLOrderAccessObject**. Figure 11.1 shows the UML diagram for **OrderAccessObject** and its implementing classes.

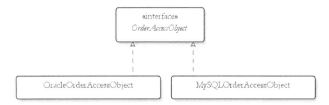

Figure 11.1: The OrderAccessObject interface and implementing classes

The need for multiple implementing classes arises from the fact that each database could have a specific command for performing certain function. For example, autonumbers are common in MySQL, but do not exist in Oracle.

The Order Processing application needs to be flexible enough that it can work with a different database without recompilation. It should also be possible to add support for a new database in the future without recompilation. In fact, you just need to specify the implementing class of **OrderAccessObject** when invoking the application. For example, to use an Oracle database you specify this

```
java OrderProcessing com.example.OracleOrderAccessObject
```

And to work with MySQL, you call it using this command:

```
java OrderProcessing com.example.MySqlOrderAccessObject
```

Now, here is the part of the code that instantiates an **OrderAccessObject** in the database:

```
public static void main (String[] args) {
    OrderAccessObject accessObject = null;
    Class klass = null;
    try {
        klass = Class.forName(args[0]);
        accessObject = (OrderAccessObject) klass.newInstance();
    } catch (ClassNotFoundException e) {
    } catch (Exception e) {
    }

    // continue here
}
```

This is polymorphism because the **accessObject** reference variable can be assigned a different object type each time.

Note
The **forName** and **newInstance** methods are explained in the section "java.lang.Class" in Chapter 5, "Core Classes."

Summary

Polymorphism is one of the main pillars in object-oriented programming. It is useful in circumstances where the type of an object is not known at compile time. This chapter has demonstrated polymorphism through several examples.

Quiz

1. In your own words, describe polymorphism.
2. In what situations is polymorphism most useful?

Chapter 12
Enums

In Chapter 2, "Language Fundamentals" you learned that you sometimes use static final fields as enumerated values. Java 5 added a new type, enum, for enumerating values. You will learn how to create and use enums in this chapter.

Overview

You use an enum to create a set of valid values for a field or a method. For example, in a typical application, the only possible values for the customer type are **Individual** or **Organization**. For a **State** field, valid values may be all the states in the US plus Canadian provinces, and probably some others. With an enum, you can easily restrict your program to take only one of the valid values.

The enum type can stand alone or can be part of a class. You make it stand alone if it needs to be referenced from multiple places in your application. If it is only used from inside a class, an enum is better made part of the class.

As an example, consider the **CustomerType** enum definition in Listing 12.1.

Listing 12.1: The CustomerType enum

```
package app12;
public enum CustomerType {
    INDIVIDUAL,
    ORGANIZATION
}
```

The **CustomerType** enum has two enumerated values: **INDIVIDUAL** and **ORGANIZATION**. Enum values are case sensitive and by convention are capitalized. Two enum values are separated by a comma and values can be written on a single line or multiple lines. The enum in Listing 12.1 is written in multiple lines to improve readability.

Internally, enum constants are given ordinal values that are integers starting with zero for the first constant. In case of the **CustomerType** enum, **INDIVIDUAL** is given the ordinal value 0 and **ORGANIZATION** the ordinal value 1. Enum ordinal values are rarely used.

Using an enum is like using a class or an interface. For example, the **Customer** class in Listing 12.2 uses the **CustomerType** enum as a field type.

Listing 12.2: The Customer class that uses CustomerType

```
package app12;
public class Customer {
    public String customerName;
    public CustomerType customerType;
    public String address;
}
```

You can use an enum constant just as you would a class's static member. For example, this code illustrates the use of **CustomerType**.

```
Customer customer = new Customer();
customer.customerType = CustomerType.INDIVIDUAL;
```

Notice how the **customerType** field of the **Customer** object is assigned the enumerated value **INDIVIDUAL** of the **CustomerType** enum? Because the **customerType** field is of type **CustomerType**, it can only be assigned a value of the **CustomerType** enum.

The use of an enum at first glance is no different than the use of static finals. However, there are some basic differences between an enum and a class incorporating static finals.

Static finals are not a perfect solution for something that should accept only predefined values. For example, consider the **CustomerTypeStaticFinals** class in Listing 12.3.

Listing 12.3: Using static finals

```
package app12;
public class CustomerTypeStaticFinals {
    public static final int INDIVIDUAL = 1;
    public static final int ORGANIZATION = 2;
}
```

Suppose you have a class named **OldFashionedCustomer** that resembles the **Customer** class in Listing 12.2, but uses an **int** for its **customerType** field.

The following code creates an instance of **OldFashionedCustomer** and assigns a value to its **customerType** field:

```
OldFashionedCustomer ofCustomer = new OldFashionedCustomer();
ofCustomer.customerType = 5;
```

Notice that there is nothing preventing you from assigning an invalid integer to **customerType**? In guaranteeing that a variable is assigned only a valid value, enums are better than static finals.

Another difference is that an enumerated value is an object. Therefore, it is compiled to a .class file and behaves like an object. For example, you can use it as a **Map** key. The section, "The Enum Class" discusses enums as objects in detail.

Enums in a Class

You can use enums as members of a class. You use this approach if the enum is only used internally inside the class. For example, the **Shape** class in Listing 12.4 defines a **ShapeType** enum.

Listing 12.4: Using an enum as a class member

```
package app12;
public class Shape {
    private enum ShapeType {
        RECTANGLE, TRIANGLE, OVAL
    };
    private ShapeType type = ShapeType.RECTANGLE;
    public String toString() {
        if (this.type == ShapeType.RECTANGLE) {
            return "Shape is rectangle";
        }
        if (this.type == ShapeType.TRIANGLE) {
            return "Shape is triangle";
        }
        return "Shape is oval";
    }
}
```

The java.lang.Enum Class

When you define an enum, the compiler creates a class definition that extends the **java.lang.Enum** class. This class is a direct descendant of **java.lang.Object**. Unlike ordinary classes, however, an enum has the following properties:

- There is no public constructor, making it impossible to instantiate.
- It is implicitly static
- There is only one instance for each enum constant.
- You can call the method **values** on an enum in order to iterate its enumerated values. This method returns an array of objects. If you call **getClass().getName()** on these objects, they will return the Java qualified name of the enum. See the next section "Iterating Enumerated Values" for more details on this.
- You can call the **name** and **ordinal** method on an object returned by **values** to get the name and ordinal value of the instance, respectively.

Iterating Enumerated Values

You can iterate the values in an enum using the **for** loop (discussed in Chapter 3, "Statements"). You first need to call the **values** method that returns an array-like object that contains all values in the specified enum. Using the **CustomerType** enum in Listing

12.1, you can use the following code to iterate over it.

```
for (CustomerType customerType : CustomerType.values() ) {
    System.out.println(customerType);
}
```

This prints all values in **CustomerType**, starting from the first value. Here is the result:

```
INDIVIDUAL
ORGANIZATION
```

Switching on Enum

The **switch** statement can also work on enumerated values of an enum. Here is an example using the **CustomerType** enum in Listing 12.1 and the **Customer** class in Listing 12.2:

```
Customer customer = new Customer();
customer.customerType = CustomerType.INDIVIDUAL;

switch (customer.customerType) {
case INDIVIDUAL:
    System.out.println("Customer Type: Individual");
    break;
case ORGANIZATION:
    System.out.println("Customer Type: Organization");
    break;
}
```

Note that you must *not* prefix each case with the enum type. The following would raise a compile error:

```
case CustomerType.INDIVIDUAL:
    //
case CustomerType.ORGANIZATION:
    //
```

Enum Members

Since an enum is technically a class, an enum can have constructors and methods. If it has constructors, their access levels must be either private or default. If an enum definition contains something other than constants, the constants must be defined before anything else and the last constant be terminated with a semicolon.

As an example, the Weekend enum in Listing 12.3 contains a private constructor, a **toString** method and a static **main** method for testing.

Listing 12.3: The Weekend enum

```
package app12;

public enum Weekend {
    SATURDAY,
    SUNDAY;

    private Weekend() {
    }

    @Override
    public String toString() {
        return "Fun day " + (this.ordinal() + 1);
    }

    public static void main(String[] args) {
        // print class name
        System.out.println(
                Weekend.SATURDAY.getClass().getName());
        for (Weekend w : Weekend.values()) {
            System.out.println(w.name() + ": " + w);
        }
    }
}
```

If you run this enum, it will print the following on the console.

```
app12.Weekend
SATURDAY: Fun day 1
SUNDAY: Fun day 2
```

You can pass values to a constructor, in which case the constants must be accompanied by arguments for the constructor. As another example, Listing 12.4 shows a **FuelEfficiency** enum with a constructor that takes two **int**s, the minimum MPG (miles per gallon) and the maximum MPG. These values are assigned to private fields **min** and **max**. Each of the three constants, **EFFICIENT**, **ACCEPTABLE** and **GAS_GUZZLER**, are accompanied by two **int**s to be passed to the constructor. The **getMin** and **getMax** methods return the minimum and maximum MPGs.

Listing 12.4: The FuelEfficiency enum

```
package com.example;

public enum FuelEfficiency {
    EFFICIENT(33, 55),
    ACCEPTABLE(20, 32),
    GAS_GUZZLER(1, 19);

    private int min;
    private int max;

    FuelEfficiency(int min, int max) {
        this.min = min;
        this.max = max;
```

```
    }

    public int getMin() {
        return this.min;
    }

    public int getMax() {
        return this.max;
    }
}
```

See the Quiz for an example of how to use the enum.

Summary

Java supports enum, a special class that is a subclass of **java.lang.Enum**. Enum is preferred over static finals because it is more secure. You can switch on an enum and iterate its values by using the **values** method in an enhanced **for** loop.

Quiz

1. How do you write an enum?
2. Why are enums safer than static final fields?
3. Write an abstract **Car** class that has two fields, name (of type **String**) and **fuelEfficiency** (of type FuelEfficiency given in Listing 12.4) and methods for calculating the minimum and maximum gas usage for a given distance (in miles). Next, write three child classes, **EfficientCar**, **AcceptableCar** and **GasGuzzler**. The constructor of each of this suclasses takes a name and sets the **fuelEfficiency** field. Finally, write a class to test it.

Chapter 13
Working with Dates and Times

Support for dates and times has been available since Java version 1.0, mainly through the **java.util.Date** class. However, **Date** was poorly designed. For examples, months in **Date** start at 1 but days start at 0. A lot of its methods were deprecated in JDK 1.1 at the same time the **java.util.Calendar** was brought in to take over some of the functionality in **Date**. The duo were the main classes for dealing with dates and times, right up to JDK 1.7, even though they had been considered inadequate and not easy to work with, causing many to resort to third party alternatives such as Joda Time (http://joda.org). The new Date and Time API in JDK 1.8 resolves many of the issues in the old API and is similar to the Joda Time API.

This chapter primarily covers the JDK 1.8 Date-Time API. However, since **Date** and **Calendar** have been used for decades in countless Java projects, they too will be discussed so that you will be ready to tackle dates and times in pre-JDK 1.8 projects.

Overview

The new Date and Time API makes it extremely easy to work with dates and times. The **java.time** package contains the core classes in the API. In addition, there are four other packages whose members are used less often: **java.time.chrono**, **java.time.format**, **java.time.temporal** and **java.time.zone**.

Within the **java.time** package, the **Instant** class represents a point on the time-line and is often used to time an operation. The **LocalDate** class models a date without the time component and time zone, suitable, for example, to represent a birthday.

If you need a date as well as a time, then **LocalDateTime** is for you. For instance, an order shipping date probably requires a time in addition to a date to make the order easier to track. If you need a time but do not care about the date, then you can use **LocalTime**.

On top of that, if a time zone is important, the Date and Time API provides the **ZonedDateTime** class. As the name implies, this class models a date-time with a time zone. For instance, you can use this class to calculate the flight time between two airports located in different time zones.

Then there are two classes for measuring an amount of time, **Duration** and **Period**. These two are similar except that **Duration** is time-based and **Period** is date-based. **Duration** provides a quantity of time to nanosecond precision. This class is good, for example, to model a flight time as it is often given in the number of hours and minutes. On the other hand, **Period** is suitable when you are only concerned with the number of days, months or years, such as when calculating your father's age.

The **java.time** package also comes with two enums, **DayOfWeek** and **Month**.

DayOfWeek represents the day of the week, from **MONDAY** to **SUNDAY**. The **Month** enum represents the twelve months of the year, from **JANUARY** to **DECEMBER**.

Working with dates and times frequently involves parsing and formatting. The Date and Time API addresses these two issues by providing **parse** and **format** methods in all its major classes. In addition, the **java.time.format** contains a **DateTimeFormatter** class for formatting dates and times.

The Instant Class

An **Instant** object represents a point on the time-line. The reference point is the standard Java epoch, which is 1970-01-01T00:00:00Z (January 1, 1970 00:00 GMT). The **EPOCH** field of the **Instant** class returns an **Instant** representing the Java epoch. Instants after the epoch have positive values and instants prior to that have negative values.

The static method **now** of **Instant** returns an **Instant** object that represents the current time:

```
Instant now = Instant.now();
```

The **getEpochSecond** method returns the number of seconds that have elapsed since the epoch. The **getNano** method returns the number of nanoseconds since the beginning of the last second.

A popular use of the **Instant** class is to time an operation, as demonstrated in Listing 13.1.

Listing 13.1: Using Instant to time an operation
```
package app13;
import java.time.Duration;
import java.time.Instant;

public class InstantDemo1 {
    public static void main(String[] args) {
        Instant start = Instant.now();
        // do something here
        Instant end = Instant.now();
        System.out.println(Duration.between(start, end).toMillis());
    }
}
```

As shown in Listing 13.1, the **Duration** class is used to return the difference between two **Instant**s. You will learn more about **Duration** later in this chapter.

LocalDate

The **LocalDate** class models a date without a time component. It also has no time zone. Table 13.1 shows some of the more important methods in **LocalDate**.

Method	Description
now	A static method that returns today's date.
of	A static method that creates a **LocalDate** from the specified year, month and date.
getDayOfMonth, getMonthValue, getYear	Returns the day, month or year part of this **LocalDate** as an **int**.
getMonth	Returns the month of this **LocalDate** as a **Month** enum constant.
plusDays, minusDays	Adds or subtracts the given number of days to or from this **LocalDate**.
plusWeeks, minusWeeks	Adds or subtracts the given number of weeks to or from this **LocalDate**.
plusMonths, minusMonths	Adds or subtracts the given number of months to or from this **LocalDate**.
plusYears, minusYears	Adds or subtracts the given number of years to or from this **LocalDate**.
isLeapYear	Checks if the year specified by this **LocalDate** is a leap year.
isAfter, isBefore	Checks if this **LocalDate** is after or before the given date.
lengthOfMonth	Returns the number of days in the month in this **LocalDate**.
withDayOfMonth	Returns a copy of this **LocalDate** with the day of month set to the given value.
withMonth	Returns a copy of this **LocalDate** with the month set to the given value.
withYear	Returns a copy of this **LocalDate** with the year set to the given value.

Table 13.1: More important methods of LocalDate

LocalDate offers various methods to create a date. For example, to create a **LocalDate** that represents today's date, use the static method **now**.

```
LocalDate today = LocalDate.now();
```

To create a **LocalDate** that represents a specific year, month and day, use its **of** method, which is also static. For instance, the following snippet creates a **LocalDate** that represents December 31, 2015.

```
LocalDate endOfYear = LocalDate.of(2015, 12, 31);
```

The method **of** has another override that accepts a constant of the **java.time.Month** enum as the second argument. For example, here is the code to construct the same date using the second method override.

```
LocalDate endOfYear = LocalDate.of(2015, Month.DECEMBER, 31);
```

There are also methods for obtaining the day, month or year of a **LocalDate**, such as **getDayOfMonth**, **getMonth**, **getMonthValue** and **getYear**. They all do not take any argument and either return an **int** or a **Month** enum constant. In addition, there is a **get** method that takes a **TemporalField** and returns a part of this **LocalDate**. For example, passing **ChronoField.YEAR** to **get** returns the year component of a **LocalDate**.

```
int year = localDate.get(ChronoField.YEAR));
```

ChronoField is an enum that implements the **TemporalField** interface, therefore you can pass a **ChronoField** constant to **get**. Both **TemporalField** and **ChronoField** are part of the **java.time.temporal** package. However, not all constants in **ChronoField** can be

passed to **get** as not all of them are supported. For example, passing
ChronoField.SECOND_OF_DAY to **get** throws an exception. As such, instead of **get**, it
is better to use **getMonth**, **getYear** or a similar method to obtain a component of a
LocalDate.

In addition, there are methods for copying a **LocalDate**, such as **plusDays**,
plusYears, **minusMonths**, and so on. For example, to get a **LocalDate** that represents
tomorrow, you can create a **LocalDate** that represents today and then calls its **plusDays**
method.

```
LocalDate tomorrow = LocalDate.now().plusDays(1);
```

To get a **LocalDate** that represents yesterday, you can use the **minusDays** method.

```
LocalDate yesterday = LocalDate.now().minusDays(1);
```

In addition, there are **plus** and **minus** methods to get a copy of a **LocalDate** in a more
generic way. Both accept an **int** and a **TemporalUnit**. The signatures of these methods
are as follows.

```
public LocalDate plus(long amountToAdd,
        java.time.temporal.TemporalUnit unit)
public LocalDate minus(long amountToSubtract,
        java.time.temporal.TemporalUnit unit)
```

As an example, to get a **LocalDate** that represents a past date exactly two decades ago
from today, you can use this code.

```
LocalDate pastDate = LocalDate.now().minus(2, ChronoUnit.DECADES);
```

ChronoUnit is an enum that implements **TemporalUnit**, so you can pass a **ChronoUnit**
constant to the **plus** or **minus** method.

A **LocalDate** is immutable and therefore cannot be changed. Any method that returns
a **LocalDate** returns a new instance of **LocalDate**.

Listing 13.2 shows an example of **LocalDate**.

Listing 13.2: LocalDate example

```
package app13;
import java.time.LocalDate;
import java.time.temporal.ChronoField;
import java.time.temporal.ChronoUnit;

public class LocalDateDemo1 {
    public static void main(String[] args) {
        LocalDate today = LocalDate.now();
        LocalDate tomorrow = today.plusDays(1);
        LocalDate oneDecadeAgo = today.minus(1,
                ChronoUnit.DECADES);
        System.out.println("Day of month: "
                + today.getDayOfMonth());
        System.out.println("Today is " + today);
        System.out.println("Tomorrow is " + tomorrow);
        System.out.println("A decade ago was " + oneDecadeAgo);
        System.out.println("Year : "
```

```
                    + today.get(ChronoField.YEAR));
        System.out.println("Day of year:" + today.getDayOfYear());
    }
}
```

Period

The **Period** class models a date-based amount of time, such as five days, a week or three years. Some of its more important methods are presented in Table 13.2.

Method	Description
between	Creates a **Period** between two **LocalDate**s.
ofDays, ofWeeks, ofMonths, ofYears	Creates a **Period** representing the given number of days/weeks/months/years.
of	Creates a **Period** from the given numbers of years, months and days.
getDays, getMonths, getYears	Returns the number of days/months/years of this period as an **int**.
isNegative	Returns **true** if any of the three components of this **Period** is negative. Returns **false** otherwise.
isZero	Returns **true** if all of the three components of this **Period** are zero. Otherwise, returns **false**.
plusDays, minusDays	Adds or subtracts the given number of days to or from this **Period**.
plusMonths, minusMonths	Adds or subtracts the given number of months to or from this **Period**.
plusYears, minusYears	Adds or subtracts the given number of years to or from this **Period**.
withDays	Returns a copy of this **Period** with the specified number of days.
withMonths	Returns a copy of this **Period** with the specified number of months.
withYears	Returns a copy of this **Period** with the specified number of years.

Table 13.2 More important methods of Period

Creating a **Period** is easy, thanks to the static factory methods **between**, **of**, and **ofDays/ofWeeks/ofMonths/ofYears**. For example, here is how you create a **Period** representing two weeks.

```
Period twoWeeks = Period.ofWeeks(2);
```

To create a **Period** representing one year, two months and three days, use the **of** method.

```
Period p = Period.of(1, 2, 3);
```

To obtain the year/month/day component of a **Period**, call its **getYears/getMonths/getDays** method. For instance, the **howManyDays** variable in the following code snippet will have a value of 14.

```
Period twoWeeks = Period.ofWeeks(2);
int howManyDays = twoWeeks.getDays();
```

Finally, you can create a copy of a **Period** using the **plusXXX** or **minusXXX** methods as well as one of the **withXXX** methods. A **Period** is immutable so these methods return new

Period instances.

As an example, the code in Listing 13.3 shows an age calculator that calculates a person's age. It creates a **Period** from two **LocalDate**s and calls its **getDays**, **getMonths**, and **getYears** methods.

Listing 13.3: Using Period

```
package app13;
import java.time.LocalDate;
import java.time.Period;

public class PeriodDemo1 {
    public static void main(String[] args) {
        LocalDate dateA = LocalDate.of(1978, 8, 26);
        LocalDate dateB = LocalDate.of(1988, 9, 28);
        Period period = Period.between(dateA, dateB);
        System.out.printf("Between %s and %s"
                + " there are %d years, %d months"
                + " and %d days%n", dateA, dateB,
                period.getYears(),
                period.getMonths(),
                period.getDays());
    }
}
```

When run, the **PeriodDemo1** class in Listing 13.3 will print this string.

```
Between 1978-08-26 and 1988-09-28 there are 10 years, 1 months and 2
days
```

LocalDateTime

The **LocalDateTime** class models a date-time without a time zone. Table 13.3 shows some of the more important methods in **LocalDateTime**. The methods are similar to those of **LocalDate** plus some other methods for modifying the time component, such as **plusHours**, **plusMinutes** and **plusSeconds**, that are not available in **LocalDate**.

LocalDateTime offers various static methods to create a date-time. The method **now** comes with three overrides and return the current date-time. The no-argument override is the easiest to use:

```
LocalDateTime now = LocalDateTime.now();
```

Method	Description
now	A static method that returns the current date and time.
of	A static method that creates a **LocalDateTime** from the specified year, month, date, hour, minute, second and millisecond.
getYear, getMonthValue, getDayOfMonth, getHour, getMinute, getSecond	Returns the year, month, day, hour, minute or second part of this **LocalDateTime** as an **int**.
plusDays, minusDays	Adds or subtracts the given number of days to or from the current **LocalDateTime**.
plusWeeks, minusWeeks	Adds or subtracts the given number of weeks to or from the current **LocalDateTime**.
plusMonths, minusMonths	Adds or subtracts the given number of months to or from the current **LocalDateTime**.
plusYears, minusYears	Adds or subtracts the given number of years to or from the current **LocalDateTime**.
plusHours, minusHours	Adds or subtracts the given number of hours to or from the current **LocalDateTime**.
plusMinutes, minusMinutes	Adds or subtracts the given number of minutes to or from the current **LocalDateTime**.
plusSeconds, minusSeconds	Add or subtracts the given number of seconds to or from the current **LocalDateTime**.
IsAfter, isBefore	Checks if this **LocalDateTime** is after or before the given date-time.
withDayOfMonth	Returns a copy of this **LocalDateTime** with the day of month set to the given value.
withMonth, withYear	Returns a copy of this **LocalDateTime** with the month or year set to the given value.
withHour, withMinute, withSecond	Returns a copy of this **LocalDateTime** with the hour/minute/second set to the given value.

Table 13.3: More important methods of LocalDateTime

To create a **LocalDateTime** with a specific date and time, use the **of** method. This method has a number of overrides and allows you to pass the individual component of a date-time or a **LocalDate** and a **LocalTime**. Here are the signatures of some of the **of** methods.

```
public static LocalDateTime of(int year, int month, int dayOfMonth,
        int hour, int minute)

public static LocalDateTime of(int year, int month, int dayOfMonth,
        int hour, int minute)

public static LocalDateTime of(int year, Month month,
        int dayOfMonth, int hour, int minute)

public static LocalDateTime of(int year, Month month,
        int dayOfMonth, int hour, int minute)

public static LocalDateTime of(LocalDate date, LocalTime time)
```

For instance, the following snippet creates a **LocalDateTime** that represents December 31, 2015 at eight o'clock in the morning.

```
LocalDateTime endOfYear = LocalDateTime.of(2015, 12, 31, 8, 0);
```

You can create a copy of a **LocalDateTime** using the **plus*XXX*** or **minus*XXX*** method. For example, this code creates a **LocalDateTime** that represents the same time tomorrow.

```
LocalDateTime now = LocalDateTime.now();
LocalDateTime sameTimeTomorrow = now.plusHours(24);
```

Time Zones

The Internet Assigned Numbers Authority (IANA) maintains a database of time zones that you can download from this web page:

```
http://www.iana.org/time-zones
```

For easy viewing, however, you can just visit this Wikipedia page:

```
http://en.wikipedia.org/wiki/List_of_tz_database_time_zones
```

The Java Date and Time API caters for time zones too. The abstract class **ZoneId** (in the **java.time** package) represents a zone identifier. It has a static method called **getAvailableZoneIds** that returns all zone identifiers. Listing 13.4 shows how you can print a sorted list of all time zones using this method.

Listing 13.4: Listing all zone identifiers

```java
package app13;
import java.time.ZoneId;
import java.util.ArrayList;
import java.util.Collections;
import java.util.List;
import java.util.Set;

public class TimeZoneDemo1 {
    public static void main(String[] args) {
        Set<String> allZoneIds = ZoneId.getAvailableZoneIds();
        List<String> zoneList = new ArrayList<>(allZoneIds);

        Collections.sort(zoneList);
        for (String zoneId : zoneList) {
            System.out.println(zoneId);
        }
        // alternatively, you can use this line of code to
        // print a sorted list of zone ids
        // ZoneId.getAvailableZoneIds().stream().sorted().
        //         forEach(System.out::println);
    }
}
```

getAvailableZoneIds returns a **Set** of **String**s. You can sort the **Set** using **Collections.sort()** or more elegantly by calling its **stream** method. You could have written this code to sort the zone identifiers.

```
ZoneId.getAvailableZoneIds().stream().sorted()
        .forEach(System.out::println);
```

Chapter 20, "Working with Streams" explains what streams are.

getAvailableZoneIds returns a **Set** of 586 zone identifiers. Here are some of the zone identifiers from the code above.

```
Africa/Cairo
Africa/Johannesburg
America/Chicago
America/Los_Angeles
America/Mexico_City
America/New_York
America/Toronto
Antarctica/South_Pole
Asia/Hong_Kong
Asia/Shanghai
Asia/Tokyo
Australia/Melbourne
Australia/Sydney
Canada/Atlantic
Europe/Amsterdam
Europe/London
Europe/Paris
US/Central
US/Eastern
US/Pacific
```

ZonedDateTime

The **ZonedDateTime** class models a date-time with a time zone. For example, the following is a zoned date-time:

```
2015-12-31T10:59:59+01:00 Europe/Paris
```

A **ZonedDateTime** is always immutable and the time component is stored to nanosecond precision.

Table 13.4 shows the more important methods in **ZonedDateTIme**.

Like **LocalDateTime**, the **ZonedDateTime** class offers the static methods **now** and **of** to construct a **ZonedDateTime**. **now** creates a **ZonedDateTime** representing the date and time of execution. The no-argument override of **now** creates a **ZonedDateTime** with the computer's default time zone.

```
ZonedDateTime now = ZonedDateTime.now();
```

Another override of **now** lets you pass a zone identifier:

```
ZonedDateTime parisTime =
        ZonedDateTime.now(ZoneId.of("Europe/Paris"));
```

Method	Description
now	A static method that returns the current date and time of the system's default zone.
of	A static method that creates a **ZonedDateTime** from the specified date-time and zone identifier.
getYear, getMonthValue, getDayOfMonth, getHour, getMinute, getSecond, getNano	Returns the year, month, day, hour, minute, second or nanosecond part of this **ZoneDateTime** as an **int**.
plusDays, minusDays	Adds or subtracts the given number of days to or from the current **ZonedDateTime**.
plusWeeks, minusWeeks	Adds or subtracts the given number of weeks to or from the current **ZonedDateTime**.
plusMonths, minusMonths	Adds or subtracts the given number of months to or from the current **ZonedDateTime**.
plusYears, minusYears	Adds or subtracts the given number of years to or from the current **ZonedDateTime**.
plusHours, minusHours	Adds or subtracts the given number of hours to or from the current **ZonedDateTime**.
plusMinutes, minusMinutes	Adds or subtracts the given number of minutes to or from the current **ZonedDateTime**.
plusSeconds, minusSeconds	Add or subtracts the given number of seconds to or from the current **ZonedDateTime**.
IsAfter, isBefore	Checks if this **ZonedDateTime** is after or before the given zoned date-time.
getZone	Returns the zone ID of this **ZonedDateTime**.
withYear, withMonth, withDayOfMonth	Returns a copy of this **ZonedDateTime** with the year/month/day of month set to the given value.
withHour, withMinute, withSecond	Returns a copy of this **ZonedDateTime** with the hour/minute/second set to the given value.
withNano	Returns a copy of this **ZonedDateTime** with the nanosecond set to the given value.

Table 13.4: More important methods of ZonedDateTime

The method **of** also comes with several overrides. In all cases, you need to pass a zone identifier. The first override allows you to pass each component of a zoned date-time, from the year to the nanosecond.

```
public static ZonedDateTime of(int year, int month, int dayOfMonth,
        int hour, int minute, int second, int nanosecond,
    ZoneId zone)
```

The second override of **of** takes a **LocalDate**, a **LocalTime** and a **ZoneId**:

```
public static ZonedDateTime of(LocalDate date, LocalTime time,
        ZoneId zone)
```

The last override of of takes a **LocalDateTime** and a **ZoneId**.

```
public static ZonedDateTime of(LocalDateTime datetime, ZoneId zone)
```

Like **LocalDate** and **LocalDateTime**, **ZonedDateTime** offers methods to create a copy of an instance using the **plusXXX**, **minusXXX** and **withXXX** methods.

For instance, these lines of code creates a **ZonedDateTime** with the default time zone and calls its **minusDays** method to create the same **ZonedDateTime** three days earlier.

```
ZonedDateTime now = ZonedDateTime.now();
ZonedDateTime threeDaysEarlier = now.minusDays(3);
```

Duration

The **Duration** class models a time-based duration. It is similar to **Period** except that a **Duration** has a time component to nanosecond precision and takes into account the time zones between **ZonedDateTime**s. Table 13.5 shows the more important methods in **Duration**.

Method	Description
between	Creates a **Duration** between two temporal objects, such as between two **LocalDateTime**s or two **LocalZonedDateTime**s.
ofYears, ofMonths, ofWeeks, ofDays, ofHours, ofMinutes, ofSeconds, ofNano	Creates a **Duration** representing the given number of years/months/weeks/days/hours/minutes/seconds/nanoseconds.
of	Creates a **Duration** from the given number of temporal units.
toDays, toHours, toMinutes	Returns the number of days/hours/minutes of this **Duration** as an int.
isNegative	Returns **true** if this **Duration** is negative. Returns **false** otherwise.
isZero	Returns **true** if this **Duration** is zero length. Otherwise, returns **false**.
plusDays, minusDays	Adds or subtracts the given number of days to or from this **Duration**.
plusMonths, minusMonths	Adds or subtracts the given number of months to or from this **Duration**.
plusYears, minusYears	Adds or subtracts the given number of years to or from this **Duration**.
withSeconds	Returns a copy of this **Duration** with the specified number of seconds.

Table 13.5: More important methods in Duration

You can create a **Duration** by calling its **between** or **of** static method. The code in Listing 13.5 creates a **Duration** between two **LocalDateTime**s, between January 26, 2015 11:10 and January 26, 2015 12:40.

Listing 13.5: Creating a Duration between two LocalDateTimes

```
package app13;
import java.time.Duration;
import java.time.LocalDateTime;

public class DurationDemo1 {
```

```
public static void main(String[] args) {
    LocalDateTime dateTimeA = LocalDateTime
            .of(2015, 1, 26, 8, 10, 0, 0);
    LocalDateTime dateTimeB = LocalDateTime
            .of(2015, 1, 26, 11, 40, 0, 0);
    Duration duration = Duration.between(
            dateTimeA, dateTimeB);
    System.out.printf("There are %d hours and %d minutes.%n",
            duration.toHours(),
            duration.toMinutes() % 60);
    }
}
```

The result of running the **DurationDemo1** class is this.

```
There are 3 hours and 30 minutes.
```

The code in Listing 13.6 creates a **Duration** between two **ZoneDateTime**s, with the same date-time but different timezones.

Listing 13.6: Creating a Duration between two ZonedDateTimes

```
package app13;
import java.time.Duration;
import java.time.LocalDateTime;
import java.time.Month;
import java.time.ZoneId;
import java.time.ZonedDateTime;

public class DurationDemo2 {

    public static void main(String[] args) {
        ZonedDateTime zdt1 = ZonedDateTime.of(
                LocalDateTime.of(2015, Month.JANUARY, 1,
                        8, 0),
                ZoneId.of("America/Denver"));
        ZonedDateTime zdt2 = ZonedDateTime.of(
                LocalDateTime.of(2015, Month.JANUARY, 1,
                        8, 0),
                ZoneId.of("America/Toronto"));
        Duration duration = Duration.between(zdt1, zdt2);
        System.out.printf("There are %d hours and %d minutes.%n",
                duration.toHours(),
                duration.toMinutes() % 60);
    }
}
```

Running the **DurationDemo2** class prints this on the console.

```
There are -2 hours and 0 minutes.
```

This is expected, because there are two hours difference between the time zones America/Denver and America/Toronto.

As a more complex example, the code in Listing 13.7 shows a bus travel time calculator. It has one method, **calculateTravelTime**, which takes a departure **ZonedDateTime** and an arrival **ZonedDateTime**. The code calls the **calculateTravelTime** method twice. Both times the bus departs from Denver, Colorado at 8 in the morning Denver time and arrives in Toronto at 8 in the next morning Toronto time. The first time the bus leaves on March 8, 2014 and the second time it leaves on March 18, 2014.

What are the travel time in both occasions?

Listing 13.7: Travel time calculator

```
package app13;
import java.time.Duration;
import java.time.LocalDateTime;
import java.time.Month;
import java.time.ZoneId;
import java.time.ZonedDateTime;

public class TravelTimeCalculator {
    public Duration calculateTravelTime(
            ZonedDateTime departure, ZonedDateTime arrival) {
        return Duration.between(departure, arrival);
    }

    public static void main(String[] args) {
        TravelTimeCalculator calculator =
                new TravelTimeCalculator();
        ZonedDateTime departure1 = ZonedDateTime.of(
                LocalDateTime.of(2014, Month.MARCH, 8,
                        8, 0),
                ZoneId.of("America/Denver"));
        ZonedDateTime arrival1 = ZonedDateTime.of(
                LocalDateTime.of(2014, Month.MARCH, 9,
                        8, 0),
                ZoneId.of("America/Toronto"));
        Duration travelTime1 = calculator
                .calculateTravelTime(departure1, arrival1);
        System.out.println("Travel time 1: "
                + travelTime1.toHours() + " hours");

        ZonedDateTime departure2 = ZonedDateTime.of(
                LocalDateTime.of(2014, Month.MARCH, 18,
                        8, 0),
                ZoneId.of("America/Denver"));
        ZonedDateTime arrival2 = ZonedDateTime.of(
                LocalDateTime.of(2014, Month.MARCH, 19,
                        8, 0),
                ZoneId.of("America/Toronto"));
        Duration travelTime2 = calculator
                .calculateTravelTime(departure2, arrival2);
        System.out.println("Travel time 2: "
                + travelTime2.toHours() + " hours");
    }
}
```

The result is this.

```
Travel time 1: 21 hours
Travel time 2: 22 hours
```

Why the difference? Because in 2014 daylight saving time began on Sunday, March 9 at 2AM. As such, you 'lost' one hour between March 8, 2014 and March 9, 2014.

Formatting A Date-Time

You use a **java.time.format.DateTimeFormatter** to format a local or zoned date-time. The **LocalDate**, **LocalDateTime**, **LocalTime** and **ZoneDateTime** classes offer a **format** method that has the following signature.

```
public java.lang.String format(java.time.format.DateTimeFormatter
        formatter)
```

It is clear that to format a date or time, you must first create an instance of **DateTimeFormatter**.

The code in Listing 13.8 formats the current date using two formatters.

Listing 13.8: Formatting dates

```
package app13;
import java.time.LocalDateTime;
import java.time.format.DateTimeFormatter;
import java.time.format.FormatStyle;

public class DateTimeFormatterDemo1 {
    public static void main(String[] args) {
        DateTimeFormatter formatter1 = DateTimeFormatter
                .ofLocalizedDateTime(FormatStyle.MEDIUM);
        LocalDateTime example = LocalDateTime.of(
                2000, 3, 19, 10, 56, 59);
        System.out.println("Format 1: " + example
                .format(formatter1));
        DateTimeFormatter formatter2 = DateTimeFormatter
                .ofPattern("MMMM dd, yyyy HH:mm:ss");
        System.out.println("Format 2: " +
                example.format(formatter2));
    }
}
```

The results are as follows (the first result depends on your locale).

```
Format 1: 19-Mar-2000 10:56:59 AM
Format 2: March 19, 2000 10:56:59
```

Parsing A Date-Time

There are two **parse** methods in many of the classes in the Java Date and Time API. The first requires a formatter, the second does not. The one that does not will parse the date-time based on the default pattern. To use your own pattern, use a **DateTimeFormatter**. The **parse** methods will throw a **DateTimeParseException** if the string passed cannot be parsed.

Listing 13.9 contains an age calculator to demonstrate date parsing.

Listing 13.9: An age calculator

```
package app13;
import java.time.LocalDate;
import java.time.Period;
import java.time.format.DateTimeFormatter;
import java.time.format.DateTimeParseException;
import java.util.Scanner;

public class AgeCalculator {
    DateTimeFormatter formatter = DateTimeFormatter.ofPattern("yyyy-M-
        d");
    public Period calculateAge(LocalDate birthday) {
        LocalDate today = LocalDate.now();
        return Period.between(birthday, today);
    }

    public LocalDate getBirthday() {
        Scanner scanner = new Scanner(System.in);
        LocalDate birthday;
        while (true) {
            System.out.println("Please enter your birthday "
                    + "in yyyy-MM-dd format (e.g. 1980-9-28): ");
            String input = scanner.nextLine();
            try {
                birthday = LocalDate.parse(input, formatter);
                return birthday;
            } catch(DateTimeParseException e) {
                System.out.println("Error! Please try again");
            }
        }
    }

    public static void main(String[] args) {
        AgeCalculator ageCalculator = new AgeCalculator();
        LocalDate birthday = ageCalculator.getBirthday();
        Period age = ageCalculator.calculateAge(birthday);
        System.out.printf("Today you are %d years, %d months"
                + " and %d days old%n",
                age.getYears(), age.getMonths(), age.getDays());
    }
```

```
}
```

The **AgeCalculator** class has two methods, **getBirthday** and **calculateAge**. The **getBirthday** method employs a **Scanner** to read user input and parses the input into a **LocalDate** using the class level **DateTimeFormatter**. The **getBirthday** method keeps begging for a date until the user types in a date in the correct format, in which case the method returns. The **calculateAge** method takes a birthday and creates a **Period** between the birthday and today.

If you run this example, you will see this on your console.

```
Please enter your birthday in yyyy-MM-dd format (e.g. 1980-9-28):
```

If you enter a date in the correct format, the program will print the calculated age, such as the following.

```
Today you are 79 years, 0 months and 15 days old
```

Using the Old Date and Time API

The old API centered around the **Date** and **Calendar** classes and is discussed here only because they were used extensively in pre-8 Java. Chances are you will still encounter them in many existing projects.

The java.util.Date Class

The **java.util.Date** class is normally used to represent dates and times. It has two constructors that you can safely use (the other constructors are deprecated):

```
public Date()
public Date(long time)
```

The no-arg constructor creates a **Date** representing the current date and time. The second constructor creates a **Date** that represents the specified number of milliseconds since January 1, 1970, 00:00:00 GMT.

The **Date** class features several useful methods, two of them are **after** and **before**.

```
public boolean after(Date when)
```

```
public boolean before(Date when)
```

The **after** method returns **true** if this date is a later time than the *when* argument. Otherwise, it returns **false**. The **before** method returns **true** if this date is before the specified date and returns **false** otherwise.

Many of the methods in **Date**, such as **getDate**, **getMonth**, **getYear**, are deprecated. You should not use these methods. Instead, use similar methods in the **java.util.Calendar** class.

The java.util.Calendar Class

The **java.util.Date** class has methods that allow you to construct a **Date** object from date components, such as the day, month, and year. However, these methods are deprecated. You should use **java.util.Calendar** instead.

To obtain a **Calendar** object, use one of the two static **getInstance** methods. Here are their signatures:

```
public static Calendar getInstance()

public static Calendar getInstance(Locale locale)
```

The first overload returns an instance that employs the computer's locale.

There's a lot you can do with a **Calendar**. For example, you can call its **getTime** method to obtain a **Date** object. Here is its signature:

```
public final Date getTime();
```

The resulting **Date** object, needless to say, contains components you initially passed to construct the **Calendar** object. In other words, if you construct a **Calendar** object that represents May 7, 2000 00:00:00, the **Date** object obtained from its **getTime** method will also represent May 7, 2000 00:00:00.

To obtain a date part, such as the hour, the month, or the year, use the **get** method. A first glance at its signature does not reveal much on how to use this method.

```
public int get(int field)
```

To use it, pass a valid field to the **get** method. A valid field is one of the following values: **Calendar.YEAR**, **Calendar.MONTH**, **Calendar.DATE**, **Calendar.HOUR**, **Calendar.MINUTE**, **Calendar.SECOND**, and **Calendar.MILLISECOND**.

get(Calendar.YEAR) returns an **int** representing the year. If it is year 2010, you get 2010. **get(Calendar.MONTH)** returns a zero-based index of the month, with 0 representing January and 11 representing December. The others (**get(Calendar.DATE)**, **get(Calendar.HOUR)**, and so on) return a number representing the date/time unit.

The last thing worth mentioning: if you already have a **Date** object and want to make use of the methods in **Calendar**, you can construct a **Calendar** object by using the **setTime** method:

```
public void setTime(Date date)
```

Here is an example:

```
// myDate is a Date
Calendar calendar = Calendar.getInstance();
calendar.setTime(myDate);
```

To change a date/time component, call its **set** method:

```
public void set(int field, int value)
```

For example, to change the month component of a **Calendar** object to **December**, write this.

```
calendar.set(Calendar.MONTH, Calendar.DECEMBER)
```

There are also **set** method overloads for changing multiple components at the same time:

```
public void set(int year, int month, int date)
```

```
public void set(int year, int month, int date,
        int hour, int minute, int second)
```

Parsing and Formatting with DateFormat

In the old API, Java's answer to date parsing and formatting is the **java.text.DateFormat** and **java.text.SimpleDateFormat** classes. **DateFormat** is an abstract class with static **getInstance** methods that allows you to obtain an instance of a subclass. **SimpleDateFormat** is a concrete implementation of **DateFormat** that is easier to use than its parent.

DateFormat

DateFormat supports styles and patterns. There are four styles for formatting a **Date**. Each style is represented by an **int** value. The four **int** fields that represent the styles are:

- **DateFormat.SHORT**. For example, 12/2/15
- **DateFormat.MEDIUM**. For example, Dec 2, 2015
- **DateFormat.LONG**. For example, December 2, 2015
- **DateFormat.FULL**. For example, Friday, December 2, 2015

When you create a **DateFormat**, you need to decide which style you will be using for parsing or formatting. You cannot change a **DateFormat**'s style once you create it, but you can definitely have multiple instances of **DateFormat** that support different styles.

To obtain a **DateFormat** instance, call this static method.

```
public static DateFormat getDateInstance(int style)
```

where *style* is one of **DateFormat.SHORT**, **DateFormat.MEDIUM**, **DateFormat.Long**, or **DateFormat.FULL**. For example, the following code creates a **DateFormat** instance having the **MEDIUM** style.

```
DateFormat df = DateFormat.getDateInstance(DateFormat.MEDIUM)
```

To format a **Date** object, call its **format** method:

```
public final java.lang.String format(java.util.Date date)
```

To parse a string representation of a date, use the **parse** method. Here is the signature of **parse**.

```
public java.util.Date parse(java.lang.String date)
        throws ParseException
```

Note that you must compose your string according to the style of the **DateFormat**.

Listing 13.10 shows a class that parses and formats a date.

Listing 13.10: The DateFormatDemo1 class

```java
package app13.oldapi;
import java.text.DateFormat;
import java.text.ParseException;
import java.util.Date;
public class DateFormatDemo1 {
    public static void main(String[] args) {
        DateFormat shortDf =
                DateFormat.getDateInstance(DateFormat.SHORT);
        DateFormat mediumDf =
                DateFormat.getDateInstance(DateFormat.MEDIUM);
        DateFormat longDf =
                DateFormat.getDateInstance(DateFormat.LONG);
        DateFormat fullDf =
                DateFormat.getDateInstance(DateFormat.FULL);
        System.out.println(shortDf.format(new Date()));
        System.out.println(mediumDf.format(new Date()));
        System.out.println(longDf.format(new Date()));
        System.out.println(fullDf.format(new Date()));

        // parsing
        try {
            Date date = shortDf.parse("12/12/2016");
        } catch (ParseException e) {
        }
    }
}
```

Another point to note when working with **DateFormat** (and **SimpleDateFormat**) is leniency. Leniency refers to whether or not a strict rule will be applied at parsing. For example, if a **DateFormat** is lenient, it will accept this **String**: Jan 32, 2016, despite the fact that such a date does not exist. In fact, it will take the liberty of converting it to Feb 1, 2016. If a **DateFormat** is not lenient, it will not accept dates that do not exist. By default, a **DateFormat** object is lenient. The **isLenient** method and **setLenient** method allow you to check a **DateFormat**'s leniency and change it.

```java
public boolean isLenient()
```

```java
public void setLenient(boolean value)
```

SimpleDateFormat

SimpleDateFormat is more powerful than **DateFormat** because you can use your own date patterns. For example, you can format and parse dates in dd/mm/yyyy, mm/dd/yyyy, yyyy-mm-dd, and so on. All you need to do is pass a pattern to a **SimpleDateFormat** constructor.

SimpleDateFormat is a better choice than **DateFormat** especially for parsing. Here is one of the constructors in **SimpleDateFormat**.

```java
public SimpleDateFormat(java.lang.String pattern)
        throws java.lang.NullPointerException,
        java.lang.IllegalArgumentException
```

The complete rules for a valid pattern can be read in the Javadoc for the
SimpleDateFormat class. The more commonly used patterns can be used by a
combination of y (representing a year digit), M (representing a month digit) and d
(representing a date digit). Examples of patterns are dd/MM/yyyy, dd-MM-yyyy,
MM/dd/yyyy, yyyy-MM-dd.

Listing 13.11 shows a class that uses **SimpleDateFormat** for parsing and formatting.

Listing 13.11: The SimpleDateFormatDemo1 class

```
package app13.oldapi;
import java.text.ParseException;
import java.text.SimpleDateFormat;
import java.util.Date;
public class SimpleDateFormatDemo1 {

    public static void main(String[] args) {
        String pattern = "MM/dd/yyyy";
        SimpleDateFormat format = new SimpleDateFormat(pattern);
        try {
            Date date = format.parse("12/31/2016");
        } catch (ParseException e) {
            e.printStackTrace();
        }
        // formatting
        System.out.println(format.format(new Date()));
    }
}
```

Summary

Java 8 brings with it a new Date-Time API to replace the old API that centered around the
java.util.Date class. In this chapter you have learned to use the core classes in the new
API, such as **Instant**, **LocalDate**, **LocalDateTime**, **ZonedDateTime**, **Period** and
Duration, as well as learned to format and parse a date-time.

Quiz

1. What were the two core classes in the old Date-Time API?
2. Why is the old Date-Time API being phased out?
3. What are the new packages for the new Date-Time API?
4. What are the main classes in the core package?
5. What are the two static methods for creating a **LocalDate**, **LocalDateTime** and **ZonedDateTime**?
6. What is the difference between **Period** and **Duration**?
7. What is the easiest way to time an operation?
8. How do you get a **Set** of all timezone identifiers?
9. What is the date-time formatter class in the new Date and Time API?

Chapter 14
The Collections Framework

When writing an object-oriented program, you often work with groups of objects. In Chapter 6, "Arrays" you learned that arrays can be used to group objects of the same type. Unfortunately, arrays lack the flexibility you need to rapidly develop applications. For example, arrays cannot be resized. Luckily, Java comes with a set of interfaces and classes that make working with groups of objects easier: the Collections Framework. This chapter deals with the most important types in the Collections Framework. Most of them are very easy to use and there's no need to provide extensive examples. More attention is paid to the last section of the chapter, "Making Your Objects Comparable and Sortable" where carefully designed examples are given because it is important for every Java programmer to know how to make objects comparable and sortable.

Note on Generics

Discussing the Collections Framework will be incomplete without generics. On the other hand, it is hard to explain generics without previous knowledge of the Collections Framework. Therefore, there needs to be a compromise: The Collections Framework will be explained first in this chapter and revisited in Chapter 15, "Generics." Since up to this point no knowledge of generics is assumed, the discussion of the Collections Framework in this chapter will have to use class and method signatures as they appear in pre-5 JDK's, instead of signatures used in Java 5 or later that imply the presence of generics. As long as you read both this chapter and Chapter 15, you will have up-to date knowledge of both the Collections Framework and generics.

An Overview of the Collections Framework

A collection is an object that groups other objects. Also referred to as a container, a collection provides methods to store, retrieve, and manipulate its elements. Collections help Java programmers manage objects easily.

A Java programmer should be familiar with the most important types in the Collections Framework, all of which are part of the **java.util** package. The relationships between these types are shown in Figure 14.1.

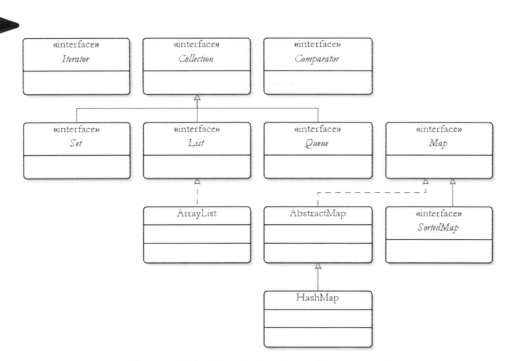

Figure 14.1: The Collections Framework

The main type in the Collections Framework is, unsurprisingly, the **Collection** interface. **List**, **Set**, and **Queue** are three main subinterfaces of **Collection**. In addition, there is a **Map** interface that can be used for storing key/value pairs. A subinterface of **Map**, **SortedMap**, guarantees that the keys are in ascending order. Other implementations of **Map** are **AbstractMap** and its concrete implementation **HashMap**. Other interfaces include **Iterator** and **Comparator**. The latter is used to make objects sortable and comparable.

Most of the interfaces in the Collections Frameworks come with implementation classes. Sometimes there are two versions of an implementation, the synchronized version and the unsynchronized version. For instance, the **java.util.Vector** class and the **ArrayList** class are implementations of the **List** interface. Both **Vector** and **ArrayList** provide similar functionality, however **Vector** is synchronized and **ArrayList** unsynchronized. Synchronized versions of an implementation were included in the first version of the JDK. Only later did Sun add the unsynchronized versions so that programmers could write better performing applications. The unsynchronized versions should thus be in preference to the synchronized ones. If you need to use an unsynchronized implementation in a multi-threaded environment, you can still synchronize it yourself.

Note
Working in a multi-threaded environment is discussed in Chapter 22, "Java Threads."

The Collection Interface

The **Collection** interface groups objects together. Unlike arrays that cannot be resized and can only group objects of the same type, collections allow you to add any type of object and do not force you to specify an initial size.

Collection comes with methods that are easy to use. To add an element, you use the **add** method. To add members of another **Collection**, use **addAll**. To remove all elements, use **clear**. To inquire about the number of elements in a **Collection**, call its **size** method. To test if a **Collection** contains an element, use **isEmpty**. And, to move its elements to an array, use **toArray**.

An important point to note is that **Collection** extends the **Iterable** interface, from which **Collection** inherits the **iterator** method. This method returns an **Iterator** object that you can use to iterate over the collection's elements. Check the section, "Iterable and Iterator" later in this chapter.

In addition, you'll learn how to use the **for** statement to iterate over a **Collection**'s elements.

List and ArrayList

List is the most popular subinterface of **Collection**, and **ArrayList** is the most commonly used implementation of **List**. Also known as a sequence, a **List** is an ordered collection. You can access its elements by using indices and you can insert an element into an exact location. Index 0 of a **List** references the first element, index 1 the second element, and so on.

The **add** method inherited from **Collection** appends the specified element to the end of the list. Here is its signature.

```
public boolean add(java.lang.Object element)
```

This method returns **true** if the addition is successful. Otherwise, it returns **false**. Some implementations of **List**, such as **ArrayList**, allow you to add null, some don't.

List adds another **add** method with the following signature:

```
public void add(int index, java.lang.Object element)
```

With this **add** method you can insert an element at any position.

In addition, you can replace and remove an element by using the **set** and **remove** methods, respectively.

```
public java.lang.Object set(int index, java.lang.Object element)
```

```
public java.lang.Object remove(int index)
```

The **set** method replaces the element at the position specified by *index* with *element* and returns the reference to the element inserted. The **remove** method removes the element at the specified position and returns a reference to the removed element.

To create a **List**, you normally assign an **ArrayList** object to a **List** reference variable.

```
List myList = new ArrayList();
```

The no-argument constructor of **ArrayList** creates an **ArrayList** object with an initial capacity of ten elements. The size will grow automatically as you add more elements than its capacity. If you know that the number of elements in your **ArrayList** will be more than its capacity, you can use the second constructor:

```
public ArrayList(int initialCapacity)
```

This will result in a slightly faster **ArrayList** because the instance does not have to grow in capacity.

List allows you to store duplicate elements in the sense that two or more references referencing the same object can be stored. Listing 14.1 demonstrates the use of **List** and some of its methods.

Listing 14.1: Using List

```
package app14;
import java.util.ArrayList;
import java.util.List;

public class ListDemo1 {
    public static void main(String[] args) {
        List myList = new ArrayList();
        String s1 = "Hello";
        String s2 = "Hello";
        myList.add(100);
        myList.add(s1);
        myList.add(s2);
        myList.add(s1);
        myList.add(1);
        myList.add(2, "World");
        myList.set(3, "Yes");
        myList.add(null);
        System.out.println("Size: " + myList.size());
        for (Object object : myList) {
            System.out.println(object);
        }
    }
}
```

When run, here is the result on the console.

```
Size: 7
100
Hello
World
Yes
Hello
1
null
```

The **java.util.Arrays** class provides an **asList** method that lets you add an array or any number of elements to a **List** in one go. For example, the following snippet adds multiple **String**s in a single call.

```
List members = Arrays.asList("Chuck", "Harry", "Larry", "Wang");
```

However, **Arrays.asList** returns a **List** with a fixed size, meaning you cannot add members to it.

List also adds methods to search the collection, **indexOf** and **lastIndexOf**:

```
public int indexOf(java.lang.Object obj)
public int lastIndexOf(java.lang.Object obj)
```

indexOf compares the *obj* argument with its elements by using the **equals** method starting from the first element, and returns the index of the first match. **lastIndexOf** does the same thing but comparison is done from the last element to the first. Both **indexOf** and **lastIndexOf** return -1 if no match was found.

Note
List allows duplicate elements. By contrast, **Set** does not.

the **java.util.Collections** class is a helper or utility class that provides static methods for manipulating **List**s and other **Collection**s. For example, you can sort a **List** easily using its **sort** method, as shown in Listing 14.2.

Listing 14.2: Sorting a List
```
package app14;
import java.util.Arrays;
import java.util.Collections;
import java.util.List;

public class ListDemo2 {
    public static void main(String[] args) {
        List numbers = Arrays.asList(9, 4, -9, 100);
        Collections.sort(numbers);
        for (Object i : numbers) {
            System.out.println(i);
        }
    }
}
```

If you run the **ListDemo2** class, you will see this on your console.

```
-9
4
9
100
```

Iterating Over a Collection with Iterator and for

Iterating over a **Collection** is one of the most common tasks around when working with collections. There are two ways to do this: by using **Iterator** and by using **for**.

Recall that **Collection** extends **Iterable**, which has one method: **iterator**. This method returns a **java.util.Iterator** that you can use to iterate over the **Collection**. The **Iterator** interface has the following methods:

- **hasNext**. **Iterator** employs an internal pointer that initially points to a place before the first element. **hasNext** returns **true** if there are more element(s) after the pointer. Calling **next** moves this pointer to the next element. Calling **next** for the first time on an **Iterator** causes its pointer to point to the first element.
- **next**. Moves the internal pointer to the next element and returns the element. Invoking **next** after the last element is returned throws a **java.util.NoSuchElementException**. Therefore, it is safest to call **hasNext** before invoking **next** to test if there is a next element.
- **remove**. Removes the element pointed to by the internal pointer.

A common way to iterate over a **Collection** using an **Iterator** is either by employing **while** or **for**. Suppose **myList** is an **ArrayList** that you want to iterate over. The following snippet uses a **while** statement to iterate over a collection and print each element in the collection.

```
Iterator iterator = myList.iterator();
while (iterator.hasNext()) {
    String element = (String) iterator.next();
    System.out.println(element);
}
```

This is identical to:

```
for (Iterator iterator = myList.iterator(); iterator.hasNext(); ) {
    String element = (String) iterator.next();
    System.out.println(element);
}
```

The **for** statement can iterate over a **Collection** without the need to call the **iterator** method. The syntax is

```
for (Type identifier : expression) {
    statement(s)
}
```

Here *expression* must be an **Iterable**. Since **Collection** extends **Iterable**, you can use enhanced **for** to iterate over any **Collection**. For example, this code shows how to use **for**.

```
for (Object object : myList) {
    System.out.println(object);
}
```

Using **for** to iterate over a collection is a shortcut for using **Iterator**. In fact, the code that uses **for** above is translated into the following by the compiler.

```
for (Iterator iterator = myList.iterator(); iterator.hasNext(); ) {
    String element = (String) iterator.next();
    System.out.println(element);
}
```

Set and HashSet

A **Set** represents a mathematical set. Unlike **List**, **Set** does not allow duplicates. There must not be two elements of a **Set**, say **e1** and **e2**, such that **e1.equals(e2)**. The **add** method of **Set** returns **false** if you try to add a duplicate element. For example, this code prints "addition failed."

```
Set set = new HashSet();
set.add("Hello");
if (set.add("Hello")) {
    System.out.println("addition successful");
} else {
    System.out.println("addition failed");
}
```

The first time you called **add**, the string "Hello" was added. The second time around it failed because adding another "Hello" would result in duplicates in the **Set**.

Some implementations of **Set** allow at most one null element. Some do not allow nulls. For instance, **HashSet**, the most popular implementation of **Set**, allows at most one null element. When using **HashSet**, be warned that there is no guarantee the order of elements will remain unchanged. **HashSet** should be your first choice of **Set** because it is faster than other implementations of **Set**, **TreeSet** and **LinkedHashSet**.

Queue and LinkedList

Queue extends **Collection** by adding methods that support the ordering of elements in a first-in-first-out (FIFO) basis. FIFO means that the element first added will be the first you get when retrieving elements. This is in contrast to a **List** in which you can choose which element to retrieve by passing an index to its **get** method.

Queue adds the following methods.

- **offer**. This method inserts an element just like the **add** method. However, **offer** should be used if adding an element may fail. This method returns **false** upon failing to add an element and does not throw an exception. On the other hand, a failed insertion with **add** throws an exception.
- **remove**. Removes and returns the element at the head of the **Queue**. If the **Queue** is empty, this method throws a **java.util.NoSuchElementException**.
- **poll**. This method is like the **remove** method. However, if the **Queue** is empty it returns null and does not throw an exception.
- **element**. Returns but does not remove the head of the **Queue**. If the **Queue** is empty, it throws a **java.util.NoSuchElementException**.
- **peek**. Also returns but does not remove the head of the **Queue**. However, **peek** returns null if the **Queue** is empty, instead of throwing an exception.

When you call the **add** or **offer** method on a **Queue**, the element is always added at the tail of the **Queue**. To retrieve an element, use the **remove** or **poll** method. **remove** and **poll** always remove and return the element at the head of the **Queue**.

For example, the following code creates a **LinkedList** (an implementation of **Queue**) to show the FIFO nature of **Queue**.

```
Queue queue = new LinkedList();
queue.add("one");
queue.add("two");
queue.add("three");
System.out.println(queue.remove());
System.out.println(queue.remove());
System.out.println(queue.remove());
```

The code produces this result:

```
one
two
three
```

This demonstrates that **remove** always removes the element at the head of the **Queue**. In other words, you cannot remove "three" (the third element added to the **Queue**) before removing "one" and "two."

> **Note**
> The **java.util.Stack** class is a **Collection** that behaves in a last-in-first-out (LIFO) manner.

Collection Conversion

Collection implementations normally have a constructor that accepts a **Collection** object. This enables you to convert a **Collection** to a different type of **Collection**. Here are the constructors of some implementations:

```
public ArrayList(Collection c)

public HashSet(Collection c)

public LinkedList(Collection c)
```

As an example, the following code converts a **Queue** to a **List**.

```
Queue queue = new LinkedList();
queue.add("Hello");
queue.add("World");
List list = new ArrayList(queue);
```

And this converts a **List** to a **Set**.

```
List myList = new ArrayList();
myList.add("Hello");
myList.add("World");
myList.add("World");
Set set = new HashSet(myList);
```

myList has three elements, two of which are duplicates. Since **Set** does not allow duplicate elements, only one of the duplicates will be accepted. The resulting **Set** in the above code only has two elements.

Map and HashMap

A **Map** holds key to value mappings. There cannot be duplicate keys in a **Map** and each key maps to at most one value.

To add a key/value pair to a **Map**, you use the **put** method. Its signature is as follows:

```
public void put(java.lang.Object key, java.lang.Object value)
```

Note that both the key and the value cannot be a primitive. However, the following code that passes primitives to both the key and the value is legal because boxing is performed before the **put** method is invoked.

```
map.put(1, 3000);
```

Alternatively, you can use **putAll** and pass a **Map**.

```
public void putAll(Map map)
```

You can remove a mapping by passing the key to the **remove** method.

```
public void remove(java.lang.Object key)
```

To remove all mappings, use **clear**. To find out the number of mappings, use the **size** method. In addition, **isEmpty** returns **true** if the size is zero.

To obtain a value, you can pass a key to the **get** method:

```
public java.lang.Object get(java.lang.Object key)
```

In addition to the methods discussed so far, there are three no-argument methods that provide a view to a **Map**.

- **keySet**. Returns a **Set** containing all keys in the **Map**.
- **values**. Returns a **Collection** containing all values in the **Map**.
- **entrySet**. Returns a **Set** containing **Map.Entry** objects, each of which represents a key/value pair. The **Map.Entry** interface provides the **getKey** method that returns the key part and the **getValue** method that returns the value.

There are several implementations of **Map** in the **java.util** package. The most commonly used are **HashMap** and **Hashtable**. **HashMap** is unsynchronized and **Hashtable** is synchronized. Therefore, **HashMap** is the faster one between the two.

The following code demonstrates the use of **Map** and **HashMap**.

```
Map map = new HashMap();
map.put("1", "one");
map.put("2", "two");

System.out.println(map.size()); //prints 2
System.out.println(map.get("1")); //prints "one"

Set keys = map.keySet();
// print the keys
for (Object object : keys) {
    System.out.println(object);
```

```
}
```

Making Objects Comparable and Sortable

In real life, when I say "My car is the same as your car" I mean my car is of the same type as yours, as new as your car, has the same color, etc.

In Java, you manipulate objects by using the variables that reference them. Bear in mind that reference variables do not contain objects but rather contain addresses to the objects in the memory. Therefore, when you compare two reference variables **a** and **b**, such as in this code

```
if (a == b)
```

you are actually asking if **a** and **b** are referencing the same object, and not whether or not the objects referenced by **a** and **b** are identical.

Consider this example.

```
Object a = new Object();
Object b = new Object();
```

The type of object that **a** references is identical to the type of object that **b** references. However, **a** and **b** reference two different instances and **a** and **b** contains different memory addresses. Therefore, **(a == b)** returns **false**.

Comparing object references this way is hardly useful because most of the time you are more concerned with the objects, not the addresses of the objects. If what you want is compare objects, you need to look for methods specifically provided by the class to compare objects. For example, to compare two **String** objects, you can call its **equals** method. Whether or not you can compare two objects depends on whether or not the objects' class supports it. A class can support object comparison by implementing the **equals** and **hashCode** methods it inherits from **java.lang.Object**.

In addition, you can make objects comparable by implementing the **java.lang.Comparable** and **java.util.Comparator** interfaces. You'll learn to use these interfaces in the following sections.

Using java.lang.Comparable

The **java.util.Arrays** class provides the static method **sort** that can sort an array of objects. Here is its signature.

```
public static void sort(java.lang.Object[] a)
```

Because all Java classes derive from **java.lang.Object**, all Java objects are a type of **java.lang.Object**. This means you can pass an array of any objects to the **sort** method.

Similar to Arrays, the **java.util.Collections** class has a **sort** method for sorting a **List**.

How do the **sort** methods know how to sort arbitrary objects? It's easy to sort numbers or strings, but how do you sort an array of **Elephant** objects, for example?

First, examine the **Elephant** class in Listing 14.3.

Listing 14.3: The Elephant class

```
public class Elephant {
    public float weight;
    public int age;
    public float tuskLength; // in centimeters
}
```

Since you are the author of the **Elephant** class, you get to decide how you want **Elephant** objects to be sorted. Let's say you want to sort them by their weights and ages. Now, how do you tell **Arrays.sort** or **Collections.sort** of your decision?

Both **sort** methods define a contract between themselves and objects that need sorting. The contract takes the form of the **java.lang.Comparable** interface. (See Listing 14.4)

Listing 14.4: The java.lang.Comparable method

```
package java.lang;
public interface Comparable {
    public int compareTo(Object obj);
}
```

Any class that needs to support sorting by **Arrays.sort** or **Collections.sort** must implement the **Comparable** interface. In Listing 14.4, the argument *obj* in the **compareTo** method refers to the object being compared with this object. The code implementation for this method in the implementing class must return a positive number if this object is greater than the argument object, zero if both are equal, and a negative number if this object is less than the argument object.

Listing 14.5 presents a modified **Elephant** class that implements **Comparable**.

Listing 14.5: The Elephant class implementing Comparable

```
package app14;
public class Elephant implements Comparable {
    public float weight;
    public int age;
    public float tuskLength;
    public int compareTo(Object obj) {
        Elephant anotherElephant = (Elephant) obj;
        if (this.weight > anotherElephant.weight) {
            return 1;
        } else if (this.weight < anotherElephant.weight) {
            return -1;
        } else {
            // both elephants have the same weight, now
            // compare their age
            return (this.age - anotherElephant.age);
        }
    }
}
```

Now that **Elephant** implements **Comparable**, you can use **Arrays.sort** or **Collections.sort** to sort an array or **List** of **Elephant** objects. The **sort** method will treat each **Elephant** object as a **Comparable** object (because **Elephant** implements **Comparable**, an **Elephant** object can be considered a type of **Comparable**) and call the

compareTo method on the object. The **sort** method does this repeatedly until the **Elephant** objects in the array have been organized correctly by their weights and ages. Listing 14.6 provides a class that tests the **sort** method on **Elephant** objects.

Listing 14.6: Sorting elephants

```
package app14;
import java.util.Arrays;

public class ElephantTest {
    public static void main(String[] args) {
        Elephant elephant1 = new Elephant();
        elephant1.weight = 100.12F;
        elephant1.age = 20;
        Elephant elephant2 = new Elephant();
        elephant2.weight = 120.12F;
        elephant2.age = 20;
        Elephant elephant3 = new Elephant();
        elephant3.weight = 100.12F;
        elephant3.age = 25;

        Elephant[] elephants = new Elephant[3];
        elephants[0] = elephant1;
        elephants[1] = elephant2;
        elephants[2] = elephant3;

        System.out.println("Before sorting");
        for (Elephant elephant : elephants) {
            System.out.println(elephant.weight + ":" +
                    elephant.age);
        }
        Arrays.sort(elephants);
        System.out.println("After sorting");
        for (Elephant elephant : elephants) {
            System.out.println(elephant.weight + ":" +
                    elephant.age);
        }
    }
}
```

If you run the **ElephantTest** class, you'll see this on your console.

```
Before sorting
100.12:20
120.12:20
100.12:25
After sorting
100.12:20
100.12:25
120.12:20
```

Classes such as **java.lang.String**, **java.util.Date**, and primitive wrapper classes all implement **java.lang.Comparable**. This explains why they can be sorted.

Using A Comparator

Implementing **java.lang.Comparable** enables you to define one way of comparing instances of your class. However, objects sometimes need to be comparable in more ways. For example, two **Person** objects may need to be compared by age or by last/first name. In cases like this, you need to create a **Comparator** that defines how two objects should be compared. To make objects comparable in two ways, you need two comparators. With a **Comparator**, you can compare objects even if their class does not implement **Comparable**.

To create a comparator, you write a class that implements the **Comparator** interface. You then provide the implementation for its **compare** method. This method has the following signature.

```
public int compare(java.lang.Object o1, java.lang.Object o2)
```

compare returns zero if *o1* and *o2* are equal, a negative integer if *o1* is less than *o2*, and a positive integer if *o1* is greater than *o2*.

As an example, the **Person** class in Listing 14.7 implements **Comparable**. Listings 14.8 and 14.9 present two comparators of **Person** objects (by last name and by first name), and Listing 14.10 offers the class that instantiates the **Person** class and the two comparators.

Listing 14.7: The Person class implementing Comparable.

```
package app14;

public class Person implements Comparable {
    private String firstName;
    private String lastName;
    private int age;
    public String getFirstName() {
        return firstName;
    }
    public void setFirstName(String firstName) {
        this.firstName = firstName;
    }
    public String getLastName() {
        return lastName;
    }
    public void setLastName(String lastName) {
        this.lastName = lastName;
    }
    public int getAge() {
        return age;
    }
    public void setAge(int age) {
        this.age = age;
    }
    public int compareTo(Object anotherPerson)
            throws ClassCastException {
        if (!(anotherPerson instanceof Person)) {
            throw new ClassCastException(
                    "A Person object expected.");
```

```
        }
        int anotherPersonAge = ((Person) anotherPerson).getAge();
        return this.age - anotherPersonAge;
    }
}
```

Listing 14.8: The LastNameComparator class

```java
package app14;
import java.util.Comparator;

public class LastNameComparator implements Comparator {
    public int compare(Object person, Object anotherPerson) {
        String lastName1 = ((Person)
                person).getLastName().toUpperCase();
        String firstName1 =
                ((Person) person).getFirstName().toUpperCase();
        String lastName2 = ((Person)
                anotherPerson).getLastName().toUpperCase();
        String firstName2 = ((Person) anotherPerson).getFirstName()
                .toUpperCase();
        if (lastName1.equals(lastName2)) {
            return firstName1.compareTo(firstName2);
        } else {
            return lastName1.compareTo(lastName2);
        }
    }
}
```

Listing 14.9: The FirstNameComparator class

```java
package app14;
import java.util.Comparator;

public class FirstNameComparator implements Comparator {
    public int compare(Object person, Object anotherPerson) {
        String lastName1 = ((Person)
                person).getLastName().toUpperCase();
        String firstName1 = ((Person)
                person).getFirstName().toUpperCase();
        String lastName2 = ((Person)
                anotherPerson).getLastName().toUpperCase();
        String firstName2 = ((Person) anotherPerson).getFirstName()
                .toUpperCase();
        if (firstName1.equals(firstName2)) {
            return lastName1.compareTo(lastName2);
        } else {
            return firstName1.compareTo(firstName2);
        }
    }
}
```

Listing 14.10: The PersonTest class

```
package app14;
import java.util.Arrays;

public class PersonTest {
    public static void main(String[] args) {
        Person[] persons = new Person[4];
        persons[0] = new Person();
        persons[0].setFirstName("Elvis");
        persons[0].setLastName("Goodyear");
        persons[0].setAge(56);

        persons[1] = new Person();
        persons[1].setFirstName("Stanley");
        persons[1].setLastName("Clark");
        persons[1].setAge(8);

        persons[2] = new Person();
        persons[2].setFirstName("Jane");
        persons[2].setLastName("Graff");
        persons[2].setAge(16);

        persons[3] = new Person();
        persons[3].setFirstName("Nancy");
        persons[3].setLastName("Goodyear");
        persons[3].setAge(69);

        System.out.println("Natural Order");
        for (int i = 0; i < 4; i++) {
            Person person = persons[i];
            String lastName = person.getLastName();
            String firstName = person.getFirstName();
            int age = person.getAge();
            System.out.println(lastName + ", " + firstName +
                    ". Age:" + age);
        }

        Arrays.sort(persons, new LastNameComparator());
        System.out.println();
        System.out.println("Sorted by last name");
        for (int i = 0; i < 4; i++) {
            Person person = persons[i];
            String lastName = person.getLastName();
            String firstName = person.getFirstName();
            int age = person.getAge();
            System.out.println(lastName + ", " + firstName +
                    ". Age:" + age);
        }

        Arrays.sort(persons, new FirstNameComparator());
        System.out.println();
        System.out.println("Sorted by first name");
```

```
            for (int i = 0; i < 4; i++) {
                Person person = persons[i];
                String lastName = person.getLastName();
                String firstName = person.getFirstName();
                int age = person.getAge();
                System.out.println(lastName + ", " + firstName +
                        ". Age:" + age);
            }

            Arrays.sort(persons);
            System.out.println();
            System.out.println("Sorted by age");
            for (int i = 0; i < 4; i++) {
                Person person = persons[i];
                String lastName = person.getLastName();
                String firstName = person.getFirstName();
                int age = person.getAge();
                System.out.println(lastName + ", " + firstName +
                        ". Age:" + age);
            }
        }
    }
}
```

If you run the **PersonTest** class, you will get the following result.

```
Natural Order
Goodyear, Elvis. Age:56
Clark, Stanley. Age:8
Graff, Jane. Age:16
Goodyear, Nancy. Age:69

Sorted by last name
Clark, Stanley. Age:8
Goodyear, Elvis. Age:56
Goodyear, Nancy. Age:69
Graff, Jane. Age:16

Sorted by first name
Goodyear, Elvis. Age:56
Graff, Jane. Age:16
Goodyear, Nancy. Age:69
Clark, Stanley. Age:8

Sorted by age
Clark, Stanley. Age:8
Graff, Jane. Age:16
Goodyear, Elvis. Age:56
Goodyear, Nancy. Age:69
```

Summary

In this chapter you have learned to use the core types in the Collections Framework. The main type is the **java.util.Collection** interface, which has three direct subinterfaces: **List**, **Set**, and **Queue**. Each subtype comes with several implementations. There are synchronized implementations and there are unsynchronized ones. The latter are usually preferable because they are faster.

There is also a **Map** interface for storing key/value pairs. Two main implementations of **Map** are **HashMap** and **Hashtable**. **HashMap** is faster than **Hashtable** because the former is unsynchronized and the latter is synchronized.

Finally, you have learned the **java.lang.Comparable** and **java.util.Comparator** interfaces. Both are important because they can make objects comparable and sortable.

Quiz

1. Name at least seven types in the Collections Framework.
2. What is the different between **ArrayList** and **Vector**?
3. Why is **Comparator** more powerful than **Comparable**?
4. Write a method to convert an array of **String**s to a resizable **List**.

Chapter 15
Generics

With generics you can write a parameterized type and create instances of the type by passing a reference type or reference types. The objects will then be restricted to the type(s). For example, the **java.util.List** interface is generic. If you create a **List** by passing **java.lang.String**, you'll get a **List** that will only accept **String**s; In addition to parameterized types, generics support parameterized methods too.

The first benefit of generics is stricter type checking at compile time. This is most apparent in the Collections Framework. In addition, generics eliminate most type castings you had to perform when working with the Collections Framework.

This chapter teaches you how to use and write generic types. It starts with the section "Life without Generics" to remind us what we missed in earlier versions of JDK's. Then, it presents some examples of generic types. After a discussion of the syntax, this chapter concludes with a section that explains how to write generic types.

Life without Generics

All Java classes derive from **java.lang.Object**, which means all Java objects can be cast to **Object**. Because of this, in pre-5 JDK's, many methods in the Collections Framework accept an **Object** argument. This way, collections become general-purpose utility types that can hold objects of any type. This imposes unpleasant consequences.

For example, the **add** method in **List** in pre-5 JDK's takes an **Object** argument:

```
public boolean add(java.lang.Object element)
```

As a result, you can pass an object of any type to **add**. The use of **Object** is by design. Otherwise, it could only work with a specific type of objects and there would then have to be different **List** types, e.g. **StringList**, **EmployeeList**, **AddressList**, etc.

The use of **Object** in **add** is fine, but consider the **get** method, which returns an element in a **List** instance. Here is its signature prior to Java 5.

```
public java.lang.Object get(int index)
        throws IndexOutOfBoundsException
```

get returns an **Object**. Here is where the unpleasant consequences start to kick in. Suppose you have stored two **String** objects in a **List**:

```
List stringList1 = new ArrayList();
stringList1.add("Java 5 and later");
stringList1.add("with generics");
```

When retrieving a member from **stringList1**, you get an instance of **java.lang.Object**. In order to work with the original type of the member element, you must first downcast it to **String**.

```
String s1 = (String) stringList1.get(0);
```

With generic types, you can forget about type casting when retrieving objects from a **List**. And, there is more. Using the generic **List** interface, you can create specialized **List**s, such as one that only takes **String**s.

Generic Types

A generic type can accept parameters. This is why a generic type is often called a parameterized type. Declaring a generic type is like declaring a non-generic one, except that you use angle brackets to enclose the list of type variables for the generic type.

```
MyType<typeVar1, typeVar2, ...>
```

For example, to declare a **java.util.List**, you would write

```
List<E> myList;
```

E is called a type variable, namely a variable that will be replaced by a type. The value substituting for a type variable will then be used as the argument type or the return type of a method in the generic type. For the **List** interface, when an instance is created, *E* will be used as the argument type of **add** and other methods. *E* will also be used as the return type of **get** and other methods. Here are the signatures of **add** and **get**.

```
public boolean add<E o>
```

```
public E get(int index)
```

> **Note**
> A generic type that uses a type variable *E* allows you to pass *E* when declaring or instantiating the generic type. Additionally, if *E* is a class, you may also pass a subclass of *E*; if *E* is an interface, you may also pass a class that implements *E*.

If you pass **String** to a declaration of **List**, as in

```
List<String> myList;
```

the **add** method of the **List** instance referenced by **myList** will expect a **String** as its argument and its **get** method will return a **String**. Because **get** returns a specific type of object, no downcasting is required.

> **Note**
> By convention, you use a single uppercase letter for type variable names.

To instantiate a generic type, you pass the same list of parameters as when declaring it. For instance, to create an **ArrayList** that works with **String**, you pass **String** in angle brackets.

```
List<String> myList = new ArrayList<String>();
```

The diamond language change in Java 7 allows explicit type arguments to constructors of parameterized classes, most notably collections, to be omitted in many situations. Therefore, the statement above can be written more concisely in Java 7 or later.

```
List<String> myList = new ArrayList<>();
```

In this case, the compiler will infer the arguments to the **ArrayList**.

As another example, **java.util.Map** is defined as

```
public interface Map<K, V>
```

K is used to denote the type of the map's keys and *V* the type of the map's values. The **put** and **values** methods have the following signatures:

```
V put(K key, V value)
Collection<V> values()
```

> **Note**
> A generic type must not be a direct or indirect child class of **java.lang.Throwable** because exceptions are thrown at runtime, and therefore it is not possible to check what type of exception that might be thrown at compile time.

As an example, Listing 15.1 compares **List** with and without generics.

Listing 15.1: Working with generic List

```
package app15;
import java.util.List;
import java.util.ArrayList;

public class GenericListDemo1 {
    public static void main(String[] args) {
        // without generics
        List stringList1 = new ArrayList();
        stringList1.add("Java");
        stringList1.add("without generics");
        // cast to java.lang.String
        String s1 = (String) stringList1.get(0);
        System.out.println(s1.toUpperCase());

        // with generics and diamond
        List<String> stringList2 = new ArrayList<>();
        stringList2.add("Java");
        stringList2.add("with generics");
        // no type casting is necessary
        String s2 = stringList2.get(0);
        System.out.println(s2.toUpperCase());
    }
}
```

In Listing 15.1, **stringList2** is a generic **List**. The declaration **List<String>** tells the compiler that this instance of **List** can only store **String**s. When retrieving member elements of the **List**, no downcasting is necessary because its **get** method returns the intended type, namely **String**.

> **Note**
> With generic types, type checking is done at compile time.

What's interesting here is the fact that a generic type is itself a type and can be used as a type variable. For example, if you want your **List** to store lists of strings, you can declare the **List** by passing **List\<String>** as its type variable, as in

```
List<List<String>> myListOfListsOfStrings;
```

To retrieve the first string from the first list in **myList**, you would write:

```
String s = myListOfListsOfStrings.get(0).get(0);
```

Listing 15.2 presents a class that uses a **List** that accepts a **List** of **String**s.

Listing 15.2: Working with List of Lists

```
package app15;
import java.util.ArrayList;
import java.util.List;
public class ListOfListsDemo1 {
    public static void main(String[] args) {
        List<String> listOfStrings = new ArrayList<>();
        listOfStrings.add("Hello again");
        List<List<String>> listOfLists =
                new ArrayList<>();
        listOfLists.add(listOfStrings);
        String s = listOfLists.get(0).get(0);
        System.out.println(s); // prints "Hello again"
    }
}
```

Additionally, a generic type can accept more than one type variables. For example, the **java.util.Map** interface has two type variables. The first defines the type of its keys and the second the type of its values. Listing 15.3 presents an example that uses a generic **Map**.

Listing 15.3: Using the generic Map

```
package app15;
import java.util.HashMap;
import java.util.Map;
public class MapDemo1 {
    public static void main(String[] args) {
        Map<String, String> map = new HashMap<>();
        map.put("key1", "value1");
        map.put("key2", "value2");
        String value1 = map.get("key1");
    }
}
```

In Listing 15.3, to retrieve a value indicated by **key1**, you do not need to perform type casting.

Using Generic Types without Type Parameters

Now that the collection types in Java have been made generic, what about legacy codes? Fortunately, they will still work in Java 5 or later because you can use generic types without type parameters. For example, you can still use **List** the old way, as demonstrated in Listing 15.1.

```
List stringList1 = new ArrayList();
stringList1.add("Java");
stringList1.add("without generics");
String s1 = (String) stringList1.get(0);
```

A generic type used without parameters is called a raw type. This means that code written for JDK 1.4 and earlier versions will continue to work in Java 5 or later.

One thing to note, though, starting from Java 5 the Java compiler expects you to use generic types with parameters. Otherwise, the compiler will issue warnings, thinking that you may have forgotten to define type variables with the generic type. For example, compiling the code in Listing 15.1 gave you the following warning because the first **List** was used as a raw type.

```
Note: app15/GenericListDemo1.java uses unchecked or unsafe operations.
Note: Recompile with -Xlint:unchecked for details.
```

You have these options at your disposal to get rid of the warnings when working with raw types:

- compile with the **–source 1.4** flag.
- use the **@SuppressWarnings("unchecked")** annotation (See Chapter 17, "Annotations")
- upgrade your code to use **List<Object>**. Instances of **List<Object>** can accept any type of object and behave like a raw type **List**. However, the compiler will not complain.

Warning
Raw types are available for backward compatibility. New development should shun them. It is possible that future versions of Java will not allow raw types.

Using the ? Wildcard

I mentioned that if you declare a **List<*aType*>**, the **List** works with instances of *aType* and you can store objects of one of these types:

- an instance of *aType*.
- an instance of a subclass of *aType*, if *aType* is a class
- an instance of a class implementing *aType* if *aType* is an interface.

However, note that a generic type is a Java type by itself, just like **java.lang.String** or **java.io.File**. Passing different lists of type variables to a generic type results in different types. For example, **list1** and **list2** below reference to different types of objects.

```
List<Object> list1 = new ArrayList<>();
List<String> list2 = new ArrayList<>();
```

list1 references a **List** of **java.lang.Object** instances and **list2** references a **List** of **String** objects. Even though **String** is a subclass of **Object**, **List<String>** has nothing to do with **List<Object>**. Therefore, passing a **List<String>** to a method that expects a **List<Object>** raises a compile time error. Listing 15.4 shows this.

Listing 15.4: The AllowedTypeDemo1 class

```
package app15;
import java.util.ArrayList;
import java.util.List;

public class AllowedTypeDemo1 {
    public static void doIt(List<Object> l) {
    }
    public static void main(String[] args) {
        List<String> myList = new ArrayList<>();
        // this will generate a compile error
        doIt(myList);
    }
}
```

Listing 15.4 will not compile because you are passing the wrong type to the **doIt** method. **doIt** expects an instance of **List<Object>** and you are passing an instance of **List<String>**.

The solution to this problem is the **?** wildcard. **List<?>** means a list of objects of any type. Therefore, the **doIt** method should be changed to:

```
public static void doIt(List<?> l) {
}
```

There are circumstances where you want to use the wildcard. For example, if you have a **printList** method that prints the members of a **List**, you may want to make it accept a **List** of any type. Otherwise, you would end up writing many overloads of **printList**. Listing 15.5 shows the **printList** method that uses the **?** wildcard.

Listing 15.5: Using the ? wildcard

```
package app15;
import java.util.ArrayList;
import java.util.List;

public class WildCardDemo1 {
    public static void printList(List<?> list) {
        for (Object element : list) {
            System.out.println(element);
        }
    }
    public static void main(String[] args) {
        List<String> list1 = new ArrayList<>();
        list1.add("Hello");
        list1.add("World");
```

```
            printList(list1);

            List<Integer> list2 = new ArrayList<>();
            list2.add(100);
            list2.add(200);
            printList(list2);
    }
}
```

The code in Listing 15.4 demonstrates that **List<?>** in the **printList** method means a **List** of any type.

Note, however, it is illegal to use the wildcard when declaring or creating a generic type, such as this.

```
List<?> myList = new ArrayList<?>(); // this is illegal
```

If you want to create a **List** that can accept any type of object, use **Object** as the type variable, as in the following line of code:

```
List<Object> myList = new ArrayList<>();
```

Using Bounded Wildcards in Methods

In the section "Using the ? Wildcard" above, you learned that passing different type variables to a generic type creates different Java types. In many cases, you might want a method that accepts a **List** of different types. For example, if you have a **getAverage** method that returns the average of numbers in a list, you may want the method to be able to work with a list of integers or a list of floats or a list of another number type. However, if you write **List<Number>** as the argument type to **getAverage**, you won't be able to pass a **List<Integer>** instance or a **List<Double>** instance because **List<Number>** is a different type from **List<Integer>** or **List<Double>**. You can use **List** as a raw type or use a wildcard, but this is depriving you of type safety checking at compile time because you could also pass a list of anything, such as an instance of **List<String>**. You could use **List<Number>**, but you must always pass a **List<Number>** to the method. This would make your method less useful because you work with **List<Integer>** or **List<Long>** probably more often than with **List<Number>**.

There is another rule to circumvent this restriction, i.e. by allowing you to define an upper bound of a type variable. This way, you can pass a type or its subtype. In the case of the **getAverage** method, you may be able to pass a **List<Number>** or a **List** of instances of a **Number** subclass, such as **List<Integer>** or **List<Float>**.

The syntax for using an upper bound is as follows:

```
GenericType<? extends upperBoundType>
```

For example, for the **getAverage** method, you would write:

```
List<? extends Number>
```

Listing 15.6 illustrates the use of such a bound.

Listing 15.6: Using a bounded wildcard

```
package app15;
import java.util.ArrayList;
import java.util.List;
public class BoundedWildcardDemo1 {
    public static double getAverage(
            List<? extends Number> numberList) {
        double total = 0.0;
        for (Number number : numberList) {
            total += number.doubleValue();
        }
        return total/numberList.size();
    }

    public static void main(String[] args) {
        List<Integer> integerList = new ArrayList<>();
        integerList.add(3);
        integerList.add(30);
        integerList.add(300);
        System.out.println(getAverage(integerList)); // 111.0
        List<Double> doubleList = new ArrayList<>();
        doubleList.add(3.0);
        doubleList.add(33.0);
        System.out.println(getAverage(doubleList)); // 18.0
    }
}
```

Thanks to the upper bound, the **getAverage** method in Listing 15.6 will allow you to pass a **List<Number>** or a **List** of instances of any subclass of **java.lang.Number**.

Lower Bounds

The **extends** keyword is used to define an upper bound of a type variable. It is also possible to define a lower bound of a type variable by using the **super** keyword. For example, using **List<? super Integer>** as the type to a method argument indicates that you can pass a **List<Integer>** or a **List** of objects whose class is a superclass of **java.lang.Integer**.

Generic Methods

A generic method is a method that declares their own type parameters. The type parameters of a generic method are declared in angle brackets and appear before the method's return value. The scope of a generic method's type parameters is limited to the method. Static and non-static generic methods are allowed, as well as generic constructors.

Generic methods can be declared within a generic type or a non-generic type.

For example, the **emptyList** method of the **java.util.Collections** class is a generic method. Look at the method signature:

```
public static final <T> List<T> emptyList()
```

emptyList has one type parameter, **T**, that appears after the keyword **final** and before the return value (**List<T>**).

Unlike a generic type where you have to explicitly specify the parameter types when instantiating the type, the parameter type(s) for a generic method are inferred from the method invocation and corresponding declaration. That is why you can simply write the following without specifying a parameter type for the generic method.

```
List<String> emptyList1 = Collections.emptyList();
```

```
List<Integer> emptyList2 = Collection.emptyList();
```

In both statements, the Java compiler infers the parameter type for **emptyList** from the reference variables that receive the return values.

NoteType inference is a language feature that enables the compiler to determine the type parameter(s) for a generic method from the corresponding declaration.

If you so wish, you can explicitly specify the type parameters of a generic method, in which case you pass the type parameters within angle brackets before the method name.

```
List<String> emptyList1 = Collections.<String>emptyList();
```

```
List<Integer> emptyList2 = Collection.<Integer>emptyList();
```

A type parameter of a generic method can have an upper or lower bound as well as use a wildcard. For example, the **binarySearch** method of **Collections** specifies both an upper bound and a lower bound:

```
public static <T> int binarySearch(List<? extends T> list, T key,
        Comparator<? super T> c)
```

Writing Generic Types

Writing a generic type is not much different from writing other types, except for the fact that you declare a list of type variables that you intend to use somewhere in your class. These type variables come in angle brackets after the type name. For example, the **Point** class in Listing 15.7 is a generic class. A **Point** object represents a point in a coordinate system and has an X component (abscissa) and a Y component (ordinate). By making **Point** generic, you can specify the degree of accuracy of a **Point** instance. For example, if a **Point** object needs to be very accurate, you can pass **Double** as the type variable. Otherwise, **Integer** would suffice.

Listing 15.7: The generic Point class
```
package app15;
public class Point<T> {
    T x;
    T y;
    public Point(T x, T y) {
        this.x = x;
        this.y = y;
    }
    public T getX() {
        return x;
```

```
    }
    public T getY() {
        return y;
    }
    public void setX(T x) {
        this.x = x;
    }
    public void setY(T y) {
        this.y = y;
    }
}
```

In Listing 15.7, **T** is the type variable for the **Point** class. **T** is used as the return value of both **getX** and **getY** and as the argument type for **setX** and **setY**. In addition, the constructor also accepts two **T** type variables.

Using **Point** is just like using other generic types. For example, the following code creates two **Point** objects, **point1** and **point2**. The former passes **Integer** as the type variable, the latter **Double**.

```
Point<Integer> point1 = new Point<>(4, 2);
point1.setX(7);
Point<Double> point2 = new Point<>(1.3, 2.6);
point2.setX(109.91);
```

Summary

Generics enable stricter type checking at compile time. Used especially in the Collections Framework, generics make two contributions. First, they add type checking to collection types at compile time, so that the type of objects that a collection can hold is restricted to the type passed to it. For example, you can now create an instance of **java.util.List** that hold strings and will not accept **Integer** or other types. Second, generics eliminate the need for type casting when retrieving an element from a collection.

Generic types can be used without type variables, i.e. as raw types. This provision makes it possible to run pre-Java 5 codes with JRE 5 or later. For new applications, you should not use raw types as future releases of Java may not support them.

In this chapter you have also learned that passing different type variables to a generic type results in different Java types. This is to say that **List<String>** is a different type from **List<Object>**. Even though **String** is a subclass of **java.lang.Object**, passing a **List<String>** to a method that expects a **List<Object>** generates a compile error. Methods that expect a **List** of anything can use the **?** wildcard. **List<?>** means a **List** of objects of any type.

Finally, you have seen that writing generic types is not that different from writing ordinary Java types. You just need to declare a list of type variables in angle brackets after the type name. You then use these type variables as the types of method return values or as the types of method arguments. By convention, a type variable name consists of a single uppercase letter.

Quiz

1. What are the main benefits of generics?
2. What is a parameterized type?
3. What is type inference?

Chapter 16
Input/Output

Input/output (I/O) is one of the most common operations performed by computer programs. Examples of I/O operations include

- creating and deleting files
- reading from and writing to a file or network socket
- serializing (or saving) objects to persistent storage and retrieving the saved objects

Java support for I/O has been available since JDK 1.0 in the form of the I/O API in the **java.io** package. JDK 1.4 added the New I/O (NIO) APIs that offer performance improvement in buffer management, scalable network and file I/O. Java NIO APIs are part of the **java.nio** package and its subpackages. JDK 7 introduced yet a new set of packages called NIO.2 to complement the existing technologies. There is no **java.nio2** package. Instead, new types can be found in the **java.nio.file** package and its subpackages. One of the features in NIO.2 is the **Path** interface, which was designed to displace the **java.io.File** class, now considered inferior. The old **File** class has often been a source of frustration because many of its methods fail to throw exceptions, its **delete** method often fails for inexplicable reasons and its **rename** method doesn't work consistently across different operating systems.

Another addition in JDK 7 that has big impacts on the I/O and NIO APIs is the **java.lang.AutoCloseable** interface. The majority of **java.io** classes in JDK 7 and later implement this interface to support try-with-resources.

This chapter presents topics based on functionality and select the most important members of **java.io** and **java.nio.file**. **java.io.File** is no longer discussed in favor of the new **Path** interface. However, **java.io.File** was widely used prior to JDK 7 and therefore can still be found in applications written in older versions of Java.

File systems and paths are the first topic in this chapter. Here you learn what a path is and how the file system is represented in Java.

The second section, "File and Directory Handling and Manipulation," discusses the powerful **java.nio.file.Files** class. You can use **Files** to create and delete files and directories, check the existence of a file, and read from and write to a file.

Note that support for reading from and writing to a file in **Files** is only suitable for small files. For larger files and for added functionality, you need a stream. Streams, which are discussed in the section "Input/Output Streams," act like water pipes that facilitate data transmission. There are four types of streams: **InputStream**, **OutputStream**, **Reader** and **Writer**. For better performance, there are also classes that wrap these streams and buffer the data being read or written.

Reading from and writing to a stream dictate that you do so sequentially, which means to read a second unit of data, you must read the first one first. For random access files—in other words, to access any part of a file randomly—you need a different Java type. The **java.io.RandomAccessFile** class used to be a good choice for non-sequential operations, however a better way now is to use **java.nio.channels.SeekableByteChannel**. The latter is discussed in the section "Random Access Files."

This chapter concludes with object serialization and deserialization.

File Systems and Paths

A file system can contain three types of objects: file, directory (a.k.a folder) and symbolic link. Not all operating systems support symbolic links, and early operating systems featured a flat-file system with no subdirectories. However most operating systems today support at least files and directories and allow directories to contain subdirectories. A directory on top of the directory tree is called a root. Linux/UNIX variants have one root: /. Windows can have multiple roots: **C:**, **D:** and so on.

An object in a file system can be uniquely identified by a path. For instance, you can refer to the **image1.png** file in your Mac's **/home/user** directory as **/home/user/image1.png**, which is a path. A **temp** directory under your Windows' **C:** drive is **C:\temp**, which is also a path. Paths must be unique throughout the file system. For example, you cannot create a **document.bak** directory in **/home/user** if there is already a file named **document.bak** in that directory.

A path can be absolute or relative. An absolute path has all the information to point to an object in the file system. For instance, **/home/kyleen** and **/home/alexis** are absolute paths. A relative path does not have all the information needed. For example, **home/jayden** is relative to the current directory. Only if the current directory is known, can **home/jayden** be resolved.

In Java a file or a directory was traditionally represented by a **java.io.File** object. However, the **File** class has many drawbacks and Java 7 brought with it a better replacement in its NIO.2 package, the **java.nio.file.Path** interface.

The aptly named **Path** interface represents a path, which can be a file, a directory, or a symbolic link. It can also represent a root. Before I explain **Path** in detail, let me introduce you to another member of the **java.nio.file** package, the **FileSystem** class.

As the name implies, **FileSystem** models a file system. It is an abstract class and its static method **getDefault** returns the current file system:

```
FileSystem fileSystem = FileSystems.getDefault();
```

FileSystems has other methods. The **getSeparator** method returns the name separator as **String**. In Windows this will be "\" and in UNIX/Linux it will be "/". Here is its signature.

```
public abstract java.lang.String getSeparator()
```

Another method of **FileSystem**, **getRootDirectories**, returns an **Iterable** for iterating root directories.

```
public abstract java.lang.Iterable<Path> getRootDirectories()
```

To create a **Path**, use **FileSystem**'s **getPath** method:

```
public abstract Path getPath(String first, String... more)
```

Only the *first* argument in **getPath** is required, the *more* argument is optional. If *more* is present, it will be appended to *first*. For example, to create a path that refers to **/home/user/images**, you would write either of these two statements.

```
Path path = FileSystems.getDefault().getPath("/home/user/images");
```

```
Path path = FileSystems.getDefault().getPath("/home", "user",
        "images");
```

The **java.nio.file.Paths** class provides a shortcut for creating a **Path** through its static **get** method:

```
Path path1 = Paths.get("/home/user/images");
Path path2 = Paths.get("/home", "user", "images");
Path path3 = Paths.get("C:\temp");
Path path4 = Paths.get("C:\", "temp");
```

Paths like **/home/user/images** or **C:\temp** can be broken into its elements. **/home/user/images** has three names, **home**, **user**, and **images**. **C:\temp** has only one name, **temp**, because the root does not count. The **getNameCount** method in **Path** returns the number of names in a path. Each individual name can be retrieved using **getName**:

```
Path getName(int index)
```

The *index* parameter is zero-based. Its value must be between 0 and the number of elements minus 1. The first element closest to the root has index 0. Consider this code snippet.

```
Path path = Paths.get("/home/user/images");
System.out.println(path.getNameCount()); // prints 3
System.out.println(path.getName(0)); // prints home
System.out.println(path.getName(1)); // prints user
System.out.println(path.getName(2)); // prints images
```

Other important methods of **Path** include **getFileName**, **getParent**, and **getRoot**.

```
Path getFileName()
```

```
Path getParent()
```

```
Path getRoot()
```

getFileName returns the file name of the current **Path**. Therefore, if **path1** denotes **/home/user1/Calculator.java**, **path1.getFileName()** will return a relative path referring to the **Calculator.java** file. Calling **path1.getParent()** would return **/home/user1** and calling **path1.getRoot()** would return **/**. Calling **getParent** on a root returns null.

A very important note: Creating a **Path** does not create a physical file or directory. Often **Path** instances reference non-existent physical objects. To create a file or directory, you need to use the **Files** class, which is discussed in the next section.

File and Directory Handling and Manipulation

java.nio.file.Files is a very powerful class that provides static methods for handling files and directories as well as reading from and writing to a file. With it you can create and delete a path, copy files, check if a path exists, and so on. In addition, **Files** comes with methods for creating stream objects that you'll find useful when working with input and output streams.

The following subsections elaborate what you can do with Files.

Creating and Deleting Files and Directories

To create a file you use the **createFile** method of **Files**. Here is its signature.

```
public static Path createFile(Path file,
        java.nio.file.attribute.FileAttribute<?>... attrs)
```

The *attrs* argument is optional, so you can ignore it if you don't need to set the file attributes. For example:

```
Path newFile = Paths.get("/home/jayden/newFile.txt");
Files.createFile(newFile);
```

createFile throws an **IOException** if the parent directory does not exist. It throws a **FileAlreadyExistsException** if there already exists a file, a directory, or a symbolic link by the name specified by *file*.

To create a directory, use the **createDirectory** method.

```
public static Path createDirectory(Path directory,
        java.nio.file.attribute.FileAttribute<?>... attrs)
```

Like **createFile**, **createDirectory** may throw an **IOException** or a **FileAlreadyExistsException**.

To delete a file, a directory or a symbolic link, use the **delete** method:

```
public static void delete(Path path)
```

If *path* is a directory, then the directory must be empty. If *path* is a symbolic link, only the link is deleted and not the link target. If *path* does not exist, a **NoSuchFileException** is thrown.

To avoid having to check if a path exists when deleting a path, use **deleteIfExists**:

```
public static void deleteIfExists(Path path)
```

If you're deleting a directory with **deleteIfExists**, the directory must be empty. If not, a **DirectoryNotEmptyException** will be thrown.

Retrieving A Directory's Objects

You can retrieve the files, subdirectories and symbolic links in a directory with the **newDirectoryStream** method of the **Files** class. This method returns a **DirectoryStream** to iterate over all objects in a directory. Here is the signature of **newDirectoryStream**.

```
public static DirectoryStream<Path> newDirectoryStream(Path path)
```

The returned **DirectoryStream** must be closed after use.

For example, the following snippet prints all the subdirectories and files in a directory.

```
Path parent = ...
try (DirectoryStream<Path> children =
        Files.newDirectoryStream(parent)) {
    for (Path child : children) {
        System.out.println(child);
    }
} catch (IOException e) {
    e.printStackTrace();
}
```

Copying and Moving Files

There are three **copy** methods for copying files and directories. The easiest one to use is this one.

```
public static Path copy(Path source, Path target,
        CopyOption... options) throws java.io.IOException
```

CopyOption is an interface in **java.nio.file**. The **StandardCopyOption** enum is one of its implementations and offers three copy options:

- **ATOMIC_MOVE**. Move the file as an atomic file system operation.
- **COPY_ATTRIBUTES**. Copy attributes to the new file.
- **REPLACE_EXISTING**. Replace an existing file if it exists.

As an example, the following code creates a copy of the **C:\temp\line1.bmp** file in the same directory and names it **backup.bmp**.

```
Path source = Paths.get("C:/temp/line1.bmp");
Path target = Paths.get("C:/temp/backup.bmp")
try {
    Files.copy(source, target,
            StandardCopyOption.REPLACE_EXISTING);
} catch (IOException e) {
    e.printStackTrace();
}
```

You use the **move** method to move a file.

```
public static Path move(Path source, Path target,
        CopyOption... options) throws java.io.IOException
```

For example, the following code moves **C:\temp\backup.bmp** to **C:\data**.

```
Path source = Paths.get("C:/temp/backup.bmp");
Path target = Paths.get("C:/data/backup.bmp")
try {
    Files.move(source, target,
            StandardCopyOption.REPLACE_EXISTING);
} catch (IOException e) {
    e.printStackTrace();
}
```

Reading from and Writing to A File

The **Files** class provides methods for reading from and writing to a small binary and text file. The **readAllBytes** and **readAllLines** methods are for reading from a binary and text file, respectively.

```
public static byte[] readAllBytes(Path path)
        throws java.io.IOException
```

```
public static List<String> readAllLines(Path path,
        java.nio.charset.Charset charset) throws java.io.IOException
```

These **write** methods are for writing to a binary and text file, respectively.

```
public static Path write(Path path, byte[] bytes,
        OpenOption... options) throws java.io.IOException
```

```
public static Path write(Path path, java.lang.Iterable<? extends
        CharSequence> lines, java.nio.charset.Charset charset,
        OpenOption... options) throws java.io.IOException
```

Both **write** method overloads take an optional **OpenOption** and the second overload also takes a **Charset**. The **OpenOption** interface defines options for opening a file for write access. The **StandardOpenOption** enum implements **OpenOption** and provides these values.

- **APPEND**. If the file is opened for write access, the data written will be appended to the end of the file.
- **CREATE**. Create a new file if it does not exist.
- **CREATE_NEW**. Create a new file and throws an exception if it already exists.
- **DELETE_ON_CLOSE**. Delete the file on close.
- **DSYNC**. Dictate that update to the file content be written synchronously.
- **READ**. Open for read access.
- **SPARSE**. Sparse file.
- **SYNC**. Dictate that update to the file content and metadata be written synchronously.
- **TRUNCATE_EXISTING**. Truncate the file's length to 0 if it is opened for write and it already exists.
- **WRITE**. Open for write access.

java.nio.charset.Charset is an abstract class that represents a character set. You need to specify the character set being used when encoding characters to bytes and decoding bytes to characters. See the discussion of ASCII and Unicode in Chapter 2, "Language Fundamentals," if you've forgotten about it.

The easiest way to create a **Charset** is by calling the static **Charset.forName** method, passing a character set name. For instance, to create a US ASCII **Charset**, you would write

```
Charset usAscii = Charset.forName("US-ASCII");
```

Now that you know a little bit about **OpenOption** and **Charset**, have a look at the following code snippet, which writes a few lines of text to **C:\temp\speech.txt** and read them back.

```
// write to and read from a text file
Path textFile = Paths.get("C:/temp/speech.txt");
Charset charset = Charset.forName("US-ASCII");
String line1 = "Easy read and write";
String line2 = "with java.nio.file.Files";
List<String> lines = Arrays.asList(line1, line2);
try {
    Files.write(textFile, lines, charset);
} catch (IOException ex) {
    ex.printStackTrace();
}

// read back
List<String> linesRead = null;
try {
    linesRead = Files.readAllLines(textFile, charset);
} catch (IOException ex) {
    ex.printStackTrace();
}

if (linesRead != null) {
    for (String line : linesRead) {
        System.out.println(line);
    }
}
```

Note that the **read** and **write** methods in **Files** are only good for small files. For medium-sized and large files, use streams instead.

Input/Output Streams

I/O streams can be likened to water pipes. Just like water pipes connect city houses to a water reservoir, a Java I/O stream connects Java code to a "data reservoir." In Java terminology, this "data reservoir" is called a sink and could be a file, a network socket or memory. The good thing about streams is you employ a uniform way to transport data from and to different sinks, hence simplifying your code. You just need to construct the correct stream.

Depending on the data direction, there are two types of streams, input stream and output stream. You use an input stream to read from a sink and an output stream to write to a sink. Because data can be classified into binary data and characters (human readable data), there are also two types of input streams and two types of output streams. These streams are represented by the following four abstract classes in the **java.io** package.

- **Reader**. A stream for reading characters from a sink.
- **Writer**. A stream for writing characters to a sink.
- **InputStream**. A stream for reading binary data from a sink.
- **OutputStream**. A stream for writing binary data to a sink.

The benefit of streams is they define methods for data reading and writing that can be used regardless of the data source or destination. To connect to a particular sink, you just need to construct the correct implementation class. The **java.nio.file.Files** class provides methods for constructing streams that connect to a file.

A typical sequence of operations when working with a stream is as follows:

1. Create a stream. The resulting object is already open, there is no **open** method to call.
2. Perform reading or writing operations.
3. Close the stream by calling its **close** method. Since most stream classes now implement **java.lang.AutoCloseable**, you can create a stream in a try-with-resources statement and get the streams automatically closed for you.

The stream classes will be discussed in clear detail in the following sections.

Reading Binary Data

You use an **InputStream** to read binary data from a sink. **InputStream** is an abstract class with a number of concrete subclasses, as shown in Figure 16.1.

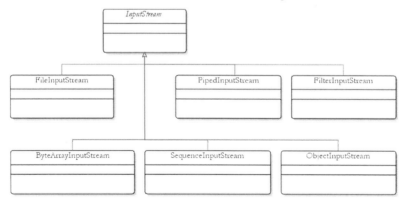

Figure 16.1: The hierarchy of InputStream

Prior to JDK 7 you used **FileInputStream** to read binary from a file. With the advent of NIO.2, you can call **Files.newInputStream** to obtain an **InputStream** with a file sink. Here is the signature of **newInputStream**:

```
public static java.io.InputStream newInputStream(Path path,
        OpenOption... options) throws java.io.IOException
```

InputStream implements **java.lang.AutoCloseable** so you can use it in a try-with-resources statement and don't need to explicitly close it. Here is some boilerplate code.

```
Path path = ...
try (InputStream inputStream = Files.newInputStream(path,
        StandardOpenOption.READ) {

    // manipulate inputStream

} catch (IOException e) {
    // do something with e
}
```

The **InputStream** returned by **Files.newInputStream** is not buffered so you should wrap it with a **BufferedInputStream** for better performance. As such, your boilerplate code would look like this.

```
Path path = ...
try (InputStream inputStream = Files.newInputStream(path,
        StandardOpenOption.READ;
        BufferedInputStream buffered =
                new BufferedInputStream(inputStream)) {

        // manipulate buffered, not inputStream

} catch (IOException e) {
    // do something with e
}
```

At the core of **InputStream** are three **read** method overloads.

```
public int read()
```

```
public int read(byte[] data)
```

```
public int read(byte[] data, int offset, int length)
```

InputStream employs an internal pointer that points to the starting position of the data to be read. Each of the **read** method overloads returns the number of bytes read or -1 if no data was read into the **InputStream**. It returns -1 when the internal pointer has reached the end of file.

The no-argument **read** method is the easiest to use. It reads the next single byte from this **InputStream** and returns an **int**, which you can then cast to **byte**. Using this method to read a file, you can employ a **while** block that keeps looping until the **read** method returns -1:

```
int i = inputStream.read();
while (i != -1) {
    byte b = (byte) I;
    // do something with b
}
```

For speedier reading, you should use the second or third **read** method overload, which requires you to pass a byte array. The data will then be stored in this array. The size of the array is a matter of compromise. If you assign a big number, the read operation will be faster because more bytes are read each time. However, this means allocating more memory space for the array. In practice, the array size should start from 1000 and up.

What if there are fewer bytes available than the size of the array? The **read** method overloads return the number of bytes read, so you always know which elements of your array contain valid data. For example, if you use an array of 1,000 bytes to read an **InputStream** and there are 1,500 bytes to read, you will need to invoke the **read** method twice. The first invocation will give you 1,000 bytes, the second 500 bytes.

You can choose to read fewer bytes than the array size using the three-argument **read** method overload:

```
public int read(byte[] data, int offset, int length)
```

This method overload reads *length* bytes into the byte array. The value of *offset* determines the position of the first byte read in the array.

In addition to the **read** methods, there are also these methods:

```
public int available() throws IOException
```
This method returns the number of bytes that can be read (or skipped over) without blocking.

```
public long skip(long n) throws IOException
```
Skips over the specified number of bytes from this **InputStream**. The actual number of bytes skipped is returned and this may be smaller than the prescribed number.

```
public void mark(int readLimit)
```
Remembers the current position of the internal pointer in this **InputStream**. Calling **reset** afterwards would return the pointer to the marked position. The *readLimit* argument specifies the number of bytes to be read before the mark position gets invalidated.

```
public void reset()
```
Repositions the internal pointer in this **InputStream** to the marked position.

```
public void close()
```
Closes this **InputStream**. Unless you created an **InputStream** in a try-with-resources statement, you should always call this method when you are done with the **InputStream** to release resources.

As an example, the code in Listing 16.1 shows an **InputStreamDemo1** class that contains a **compareFiles** method for comparing two files. You need to adjust the values of **path1** and **path2** and make sure the files exist before running this class.

Listing 16.1: The compareFiles method that uses InputStream

```
package app16;
import java.io.IOException;
import java.io.InputStream;
import java.nio.file.Files;
import java.nio.file.LinkOption;
import java.nio.file.NoSuchFileException;
import java.nio.file.Path;
import java.nio.file.Paths;
import java.nio.file.StandardOpenOption;

public class InputStreamDemo1 {
    public boolean compareFiles(Path path1, Path path2)
            throws NoSuchFileException {
```

```
        if (Files.notExists(path1)) {
            throw new NoSuchFileException(path1.toString());
        }
        if (Files.notExists(path2)) {
            throw new NoSuchFileException(path2.toString());
        }
        try {
            if (Files.size(path1) != Files.size(path2)) {
                return false;
            }
        } catch (IOException e) {
            e.printStackTrace();
        }
        try (InputStream inputStream1 = Files.newInputStream(
                    path1, StandardOpenOption.READ);
            InputStream inputStream2 = Files.newInputStream(
                    path2, StandardOpenOption.READ)) {

            int i1, i2;
            do {
                i1 = inputStream1.read();
                i2 = inputStream2.read();
                if (i1 != i2) {
                    return false;
                }
            } while (i1 != -1);
            return true;
        } catch (IOException e) {
            return false;
        }
    }

    public static void main(String[] args) {
        Path path1 = Paths.get("C:\\temp\\line1.bmp");
        Path path2 = Paths.get("C:\\temp\\line2.bmp");
        InputStreamDemo1 test = new InputStreamDemo1();
        try {
            if (test.compareFiles(path1, path2)) {
                System.out.println("Files are identical");
            } else {
                System.out.println("Files are not identical");
            }
        } catch (NoSuchFileException e) {
            e.printStackTrace();
        }

        // the compareFiles method is not the same as
        // Files.isSameFile
        try {
            System.out.println(Files.isSameFile(path1, path2));
        } catch (IOException e) {
            e.printStackTrace();
```

```
            }
        }
    }
```

compareFiles returns true if the two files compared are identical. The brain of the method is this block.

```
int i1, i2;
do {
    i1 = inputStream1.read();
    i2 = inputStream2.read();
    if (i1 != i2) {
        return false;
    }
} while (i1 != -1);
return true;
```

It reads the next byte from the first **InputStream** to **i1** and the second **InputStream** to **i2** and compares **i1** with **i2**. It will continue reading until **i1** and **i2** are different or the end of file is reached.

Writing Binary Data

The **OutputStream** abstract class represents a stream for writing binary data to a sink. Its child classes are shown in Figure 16.2.

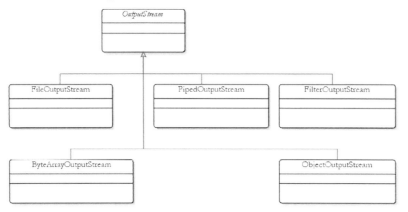

Figure 16.2: OutputStream implementation classes

In pre-7 JDKs you would use **java.io.FileOutputStream** to write binary to a file. Thanks to NIO.2, you can now call **Files.newOutputStream** to obtain an **OutputStream** with a file sink. Here's the signature of **newOutputStream**:

```
public static java.io.OutputStream newOutputStream(Path path,
        OpenOption... options) throws java.io.IOException
```

OutputStream implements **java.lang.AutoCloseable** so you can use it in a try-with-resources statement and don't need to explicitly close it. Here is how you can create an

OutputStream with a file sink:

```
Path path = ...
try (OutputStream outputStream = Files.newOutputStream(path,
        StandardOpenOption.CREATE, StandardOpenOption.APPEND) {

    // manipulate outputStream

} catch (IOException e) {
    // do something with e
}
```

The **OutputStream** returned from **Files.newOutputStream** is not buffered so you should wrap it with a **BufferedOutputStream** for better performance. Therefore, your boilerplate code would look like this.

```
Path path = ...
try (OutputStream outputStream = Files.newOututStream(path,
        StandardOpenOption.CREATE, StandardOpenOption.APPEND;
        BufferedOutputStream buffered =
                new BufferedOutputStream(outputStream)) {

    // manipulate buffered, not outputStream

} catch (IOException e) {
    // do something with e
}
```

OutputStream defines three **write** method overloads, which are mirrors of the **read** method overloads in **InputStream**:

```
public void write(int b)

public void write(byte[] data)

public void write(byte[] data, int offset, int length)
```

The first overload writes the lowest 8 bits of integer *b* to this **OutputStream**. The second writes the content of a byte array to this **OutputStream**. The third overload writes *length* bytes of the data starting at position *offset*.

In addition, there are also the no-argument **close** and **flush** methods. **close** closes the **OutputStream** and **flush** forces any buffered content to be written out to the sink. You don't need to call **close** if you created the OutputStream in a try-with-resources statement.

As an example, Listing 16.2 shows how to copy a file using **OutputStream**.

Listing 16.2: The OutputStreamDemo1 class

```
package app16;
import java.io.IOException;
import java.io.InputStream;
import java.io.OutputStream;
import java.nio.file.Files;
import java.nio.file.Path;
import java.nio.file.Paths;
import java.nio.file.StandardOpenOption;
```

```java
public class OutputStreamDemo1 {
    public void copyFiles(Path originPath, Path destinationPath)
            throws IOException {
        if (Files.notExists(originPath)
                || Files.exists(destinationPath)) {
            throw new IOException(
                    "Origin file must exist and " +
                    "Destination file must not exist");
        }
        byte[] readData = new byte[1024];
        try (InputStream inputStream =
                    Files.newInputStream(originPath,
                    StandardOpenOption.READ);
            OutputStream outputStream =
                    Files.newOutputStream(destinationPath,
                    StandardOpenOption.CREATE)) {
            int i = inputStream.read(readData);
            while (i != -1) {
                outputStream.write(readData, 0, i);
                i = inputStream.read(readData);
            }
        } catch (IOException e) {
            throw e;
        }
    }

    public static void main(String[] args) {
        OutputStreamDemo1 test = new OutputStreamDemo1();
        Path origin = Paths.get("C:\\temp\\line1.bmp");
        Path destination = Paths.get("C:\\temp\\line3.bmp");
        try {
            test.copyFiles(origin, destination);
            System.out.println("Copied Successfully");
        } catch (IOException e) {
            e.printStackTrace();
        }
    }
}
```

This part of the **copyFile** method does the work.

```java
byte[] readData = new byte[1024];
try (InputStream inputStream =
            Files.newInputStream(originPath,
            StandardOpenOption.READ);
    OutputStream outputStream =
            Files.newOutputStream(destinationPath,
            StandardOpenOption.CREATE)) {
    int i = inputStream.read(readData);
    while (i != -1) {
        outputStream.write(readData, 0, i);
        i = inputStream.read(readData);
```

```
    }
  } catch (IOException e) {
      throw e;
  }
```

The byte array **readData** is used to store the data read from the **InputStream**. The number of bytes read is assigned to **i**. The code then calls the **write** method on the **OutputStream**, passing the byte array and **i** as the third argument.

```
outputStream.write(readData, 0, i);
```

Writing Text (Characters)

The abstract class **Writer** defines a stream used for writing characters. Figure 16.3 shows the implementations of **Writer**.

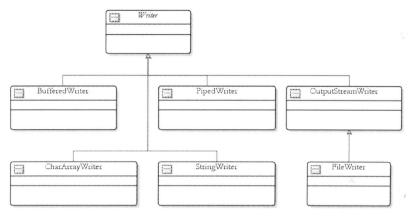

Figure 16.3: Writer subclasses

OutputStreamWriter facilitates the translation of characters into byte streams using a given character set. The character set guarantees that any Unicode characters you write to this **OutputStreamWriter** will be translated into the correct byte representation. **FileWriter** is a subclass of **OutputStreamWriter** that provides a convenient way to write characters to a file. However, **FileWriter** is not without flaws. When using **FileWriter** you are forced to output characters using the computer's encoding, which means characters outside the current character set will not be translated correctly into bytes. A better alternative to **FileWriter** is **PrintWriter**.

The following sections cover **Writer** and some of its descendants.

Writer

This class is similar to **OutputStream**, except that **Writer** deals with characters instead of bytes. Like **OutputStream**, **Writer** has three **write** method overloads:

```
public void write(int b)
```

```
public void write(char[] text)
```

```
public void write(char[] text, int offset, int length)
```

When working with text or characters, however, you ordinarily use strings. As such, there are two other overloads of the **write** method that accept a **String** object.

```
public void write(String text)
```

```
public void write(String text, int offset, int length)
```

The last **write** method overload allows you to pass a String and write part of the **String** to the **Writer**.

OutputStreamWriter

An **OutputStreamWriter** is a bridge from character streams to byte streams: Characters written to an **OutputStreamWriter** are encoded into bytes using a specified character set. The latter is an important element of **OutputStreamWriter** because it enables the correct translations of Unicode characters into byte representation.

The **OutputStreamWriter** class offers four constructors:

```
public OutputStreamWriter(OutputStream out)
```

```
public OutputStreamWriter(OutputStream out,
        java.nio.charset.Charset cs)
```

```
public OutputStreamWriter(OutputStream out,
        java.nio.charset.CharsetEncoder enc)
```

```
public OutputStreamWriter(OutputStream out, String encoding)
```

All the constructors accept an **OutputStream**, to which bytes resulting from the translation of characters written to this **OutputStreamWriter** will be written. Therefore, if you want to write to a file, you simply need to create an **OutputStream** with a file sink:

```
OutputStream os = Files.newOutputStream(path, openOption);
OutputStreamWriter writer = new OutputStreamWriter(os, charset);
```

Listing 16.3 shows an example of **OutputStreamWriter**.

Listing 16.3: Using OutputStreamWriter
```
package app16;
import java.io.IOException;
import java.io.OutputStream;
import java.io.OutputStreamWriter;
import java.nio.charset.Charset;
import java.nio.file.Files;
import java.nio.file.Path;
import java.nio.file.Paths;
import java.nio.file.StandardOpenOption;

public class OutputStreamWriterDemo1 {
    public static void main(String[] args) {
        char[] chars = new char[2];
        chars[0] = '\u4F60'; // representing 你
        chars[1] = '\u597D'; // representing 好 ;
```

```
    Path path = Paths.get("C:\\temp\\myFile.txt");
    Charset chineseSimplifiedCharset =
            Charset.forName("GB2312");

    try (OutputStream outputStream =
            Files.newOutputStream(path,
            StandardOpenOption.CREATE);
        OutputStreamWriter writer = new OutputStreamWriter(
                outputStream, chineseSimplifiedCharset)) {

        writer.write(chars);
    } catch (IOException e) {
        e.printStackTrace();
    }
    }
}
```

The code in Listing 16.3 creates an **OutputStreamWriter** based on a **OutputStream** that writes to **C:\temp\myFile.txt** on Windows. Therefore, if you are using Linux or Mac OS X, you need to change the value of **textFile**. The use of an absolute path is intentional since most readers find it easier to find if they want to open the file. The **OutputStreamWriter** uses the GB2312 character set (simplified Chinese).

The code in Listing 16.3 passes two Chinese characters: 你 (represented by the Unicode 4F60) and 好 (Unicode 597D). 你好 means 'How are you?' in Chinese.

When executed, the **OutputStreamWriterTest** class will create a **myFile.txt** file. It is 4 bytes long. You can open it and see the Chinese characters. For the characters to be displayed correctly, you need to have the Chinese font installed in your computer.

PrintWriter

PrintWriter is a better alternative to **OutputStreamWriter**. Like **OutputStreamWriter**, **PrintWriter** lets you choose an encoding by passing the encoding information to one of its constructors. Here are two of its constructors:

```
public PrintWriter(OutputStream out)
```

```
public PrintWriter(Writer out)
```

To create a **PrintWriter** that writes to a file, simply create an **OutputStream** with a file sink.

PrintWriter is more convenient to work with than **OutputStreamWriter** because the former adds nine **print** method overloads for printing any type of Java primitives and objects. Here are the method overloads:

```
public void print(boolean b)
```

```
public void print(char c)
```

```
public void print(char[] s)
```

```
public void print(double d)
```

```
public void print(float f)
```

```
public void print(int i)

public void print(long l)

public void print(Object object)

public void print(String string)
```

There are also nine **println** method overloads, which are the same as the **print** method overloads, except that they print a new line character after the argument.

In addition, there are two **format** method overloads that enable you to print according to a print format. This method was covered in Chapter 5, "Core Classes."

Always wrap your **Writer** with a **BufferedWriter** for better performance. **BufferedWriter** has the following constructors that allow you to pass a **Writer** object.

```
public BufferedWriter(Writer writer)

public BufferedWriter(Writer writer, in bufferSize)
```

The first constructor creates a **BufferedWriter** with the default buffer size (the documentation does not say how big). The second one lets you choose the buffer size.

With **PrintWriter**, however, you cannot wrap it like this

```
PrintWriter printWriter = ...;
BufferedWriter bw = new BufferedWriter(printWriter);
```

because then you would not be able to use the methods of the **PrintWriter**. Instead, wrap the **Writer** that is passed to a **PrintWriter**.

```
PrintWriter pw = new PrintWriter(new BufferedWriter(writer));
```

Listing 16.4 presents an example of **PrintWriter**.

Listing 16.4: Using PrintWriter

```
package app16;
import java.io.BufferedWriter;
import java.io.IOException;
import java.io.PrintWriter;
import java.nio.charset.Charset;
import java.nio.file.Files;
import java.nio.file.Path;
import java.nio.file.Paths;
import java.nio.file.StandardOpenOption;

public class PrintWriterDemo1 {
    public static void main(String[] args) {
        Path path = Paths.get("c:\\temp\\printWriterOutput.txt");
        Charset usAsciiCharset = Charset.forName("US-ASCII");
        try (BufferedWriter bufferedWriter =
                Files.newBufferedWriter(path, usAsciiCharset,
                StandardOpenOption.CREATE);
            PrintWriter printWriter =
                    new PrintWriter(bufferedWriter)) {
            printWriter.println("PrintWriter is easy to use.");
```

```
        printWriter.println(1234);
    } catch (IOException e) {
        e.printStackTrace();
    }
  }
}
```

The nice thing about writing with a **PrinterWriter** is when you open the resulting file, everything is human-readable. The file created by the preceding example says:

```
PrinterWriter is easy to use.
1234
```

Reading Text (Characters)

You use the **Reader** class to read text (characters, i.e. human readable data). The hierarchy of this class is shown in Figure 16.4.

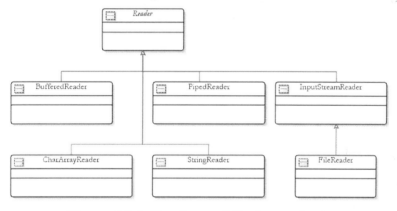

Figure 16.4: Reader and its descendants

The following sections discuss **Reader** and some of its descendants.

Reader

Reader is an abstract class that represents an input stream for reading characters. It is similar to **InputStream** except that **Reader** deals with characters and not bytes. **Reader** has three **read** method overloads that are similar to the **read** methods in **InputStream**:

```
public int read()
```

```
public int read(char[] data)
```

```
public int read(char[] data, int offset, int length)
```

These method overloads allow you to read a single character or multiple characters that will be stored in a char array. Additionally, there is a fourth **read** method for reading characters into a **java.nio.CharBuffer**.

```
public int read(java.nio.CharBuffer target)
```

Reader also provides the following methods that are similar to those in **InputStream**: **close**, **mark**, **reset**, and **skip**.

InputStreamReader

An **InputStreamReader** reads bytes and translates them into characters using the specified character set. Therefore, **InputStreamReader** is ideal for reading from the output of an **OutputStreamWriter** or a **PrintWriter**. The key is you must know the encoding used when writing the characters to correctly read them back.

The **InputStreamReader** class has four constructors, all of which require you to pass an **InputStream**.

```
public InputStreamReader(InputStream in)
```

```
public InputStreamReader(InputStream in,
        java.nio.charset.Charset charset)
```

```
public InputStreamReader(InputStream in,
        java.nio.charset.CharsetDecoder decoder)
```

```
public InputStreamReader(InputStream in, String charsetName)
```

For instance, to create an **InputStreamReader** that reads from a file, you can pass to its constructor an **InputStream** from **Files.newInputStream**.

```
Path path = ...
Charset charset = ...
InputStream inputStream = Files.newInputStream(path,
        StandardOpenOption.READ);
InputStreamReader reader = new InputStreamReader(
        inputStream, charset);
```

Listing 16.5 presents an example that uses a **PrintWriter** to write two Chinese characters and read them back.

Listing 16.5: Using InputStreamReader
```
package app16;
import java.io.BufferedWriter;
import java.io.FileInputStream;
import java.io.IOException;
import java.io.InputStream;
import java.io.InputStreamReader;
import java.nio.charset.Charset;
import java.nio.file.Files;
import java.nio.file.Path;
import java.nio.file.Paths;
import java.nio.file.StandardOpenOption;

public class InputStreamReaderDemo1 {
    public static void main(String[] args) {
        Path textFile = Paths.get("C:\\temp\\myFile.txt");
        Charset chineseSimplifiedCharset =
```

```
                Charset.forName("GB2312");
        char[] chars = new char[2];
        chars[0] = '\u4F60'; // representing 你
        chars[1] = '\u597D'; // representing 好

        // write text
        try (BufferedWriter writer =
                Files.newBufferedWriter(textFile,
                    chineseSimplifiedCharset,
                    StandardOpenOption.CREATE)) {
            writer.write(chars);
        } catch (IOException e) {
            System.out.println(e.toString());
        }

        // read back
        try (InputStream inputStream =
                Files.newInputStream(textFile,
                    StandardOpenOption.READ);

            InputStreamReader reader = new
                    InputStreamReader(inputStream,
                        chineseSimplifiedCharset)) {
            char[] chars2 = new char[2];
            reader.read(chars2);
            System.out.print(chars2[0]);
            System.out.print(chars2[1]);
        } catch (IOException e) {
            System.out.println(e.toString());
        }
    }
}
```

BufferedReader

BufferedReader is good for two things:

1. Wraps another **Reader** and provides a buffer that will generally improve performance.
2. Provides a **readLine** method to read a line of text.

The **readLine** method has the following signature:

```
public java.lang.String readLine() throws IOException
```

It returns a line of text from this **Reader** or null if the end of the stream has been reached.

The **java.nio.file.Files** class offers a **newBufferedReader** method that returns a **BufferedReader**. Here is the signature.

```
public static java.io.BufferedReader newBufferedReader(Path path,
        java.nio.charset.Charset charset)
```

As an example, this snippet reads a text file and prints all lines.

```
Path path = ...
BufferedReader br = Files.newBufferedReader(path, charset);
String line = br.readLine();
while (line != null) {
    System.out.println(line);
    line = br.readLine();
}
```

Also, prior to the addition of the **java.util.Scanner** class in Java 5, you had to use a **BufferedReader** to read user input to the console. Listing 16.6 shows a **getUserInput** method for taking user input on the console.

Listing 16.6: The getUserInput method

```
public static String getUserInput() {
    BufferedReader br = new BufferedReader(
            new InputStreamReader(System.in));
    try {
        return br.readLine();
    } catch (IOException ioe) {
    }
    return null;
}
```

You can do this because **System.in** is of type **java.io.InputStream**.

> **Note**
> java.util.Scanner was discused in Chapter 5, "Core Classes."

Logging with PrintStream

By now you must be familiar with the **print** method of **System.out**. You use it especially for displaying messages to help you debug your code. However, by default **System.out** sends the message to the console, and this is not always preferable. For instance, if the amount of data displayed exceeds a certain lines, previous messages are no longer visible. Also, you might want to process the messages further, such as sending the messages by email.

The **PrintStream** class is an indirect subclass of **OutpuStream**. Here are some of its constructors:

```
public PrintStream(OutputStream out)

public PrintStream(OutputStream out, boolean autoFlush)

public PrintStream(OutputStream out, boolean autoFlush,
        String encoding)
```

PrintStream is very similar to **PrintWriter**. For example, both have nine **print** method overloads. Also, **PrintStream** has a **format** method similar to the **format** method in the **String** class.

System.out is of type **java.io.PrintStream**. The **System** object lets you replace the default **PrintStream** by using the **setOut** method. Listing 16.7 presents an example that redirects **System.out** to a file.

Listing 16.7: Redirecting System.out to a file

```
package app16;
import java.io.IOException;
import java.io.OutputStream;
import java.io.PrintStream;
import java.nio.file.Files;
import java.nio.file.OpenOption;
import java.nio.filc.Path;
import java.nio.file.Paths;
import java.nio.file.StandardOpenOption;

public class PrintStreamDemo1 {
    public static void main(String[] args) {
        Path debugFile = Paths.get("C:\\temp\\debug.txt");
        try (OutputStream outputStream = Files.newOutputStream(
                debugFile, StandardOpenOption.CREATE,
                StandardOpenOption.APPEND);
            PrintStream printStream = new PrintStream(outputStream,
                    true)) {

            System.setOut(printStream);
            System.out.println("To file");

        } catch (IOException e) {
            e.printStackTrace();
        }
    }
}
```

Note
You can also replace the default **in** and **out** in the **System** object by using the **setIn** and **setErr** methods.

Random Access Files

Using a stream to access a file dictates that the file is accessed sequentially, e.g. the first character must be read before the second, etc. Streams are ideal when the data comes in a sequential fashion, for example if the medium is a tape (widely used long ago before the emergence of harddisk) or a network socket. Streams are good for most of your applications, however sometimes you need to access a file randomly and using a stream would not be fast enough. For example, you may want to change the 1000th byte of a file without having to read the first 999. For random access like this, there are a few Java types that offer a solution. The first is the **java.io.RandomAccessFile** class, which is easy to use but now out-dated. The second is the **java.nio.channels.SeekableByteChannel** interface, which should be used in new applications. A discussion of **RandomAccessFile** can be found in Chapter 13 of the second edition of this book. This edition, however, teaches random access files using **SeekableByteChannel**.

A **SeekableByteChannel** can perform both read and write operations. You can get an implementation of **SeekableByteChannel** using one of the **Files** class's **newByteChannel** methods:

```
public static java.nio.channels.SeekableByteChannel
        newByteChannel(Path path, OpenOption... options)
```

When using **Files.newByteChannel()** to open a file, you can choose an open option such as read-only or read-write or create-append. For instance

```
Path path1 = ...
SeekableByteChannel readOnlyByteChannel = Files.newByteChannel(path1,
        EnumSet.of(READ)));

Path path2 = ...
SeekableByteChannel writableByteChannel = Files.newByteChannel(path2,
        EnumSet.of(CREATE,APPEND));
```

SeekableByteChannel employs an internal pointer that points to the next byte to read or write. You can obtain the pointer position by calling the **position** method:

```
long position() throws java.io.IOException
```

When a **SeekableByteChannel** is created, initially it points to the first byte and **position()** would return 0L. You can change the pointer's position by invoking another **position** method whose signature is as follows.

```
SeekableByteChannel position(long newPosition)
        throws java.io.IOException
```

This pointer is zero-based, which means the first byte is indicated by index 0. You can pass a number greater than the file size without throwing an exception, but this will not change the size of the file. The **size** method returns the current size of the resource to which the **SeekableByteChannel** is connected:

```
long size() throws java.io.IOException
```

SeekableByteChannel is extremely simple. To read from or write to the underlying file, you call its **read** or **write** method, respectively.

```
int read(java.nio.ByteBuffer buffer) throws java.io.IOException

int write(java.nio.ByteBuffer buffer) throws java.io.IOException
```

Both **read** and **write** take a **java.nio.ByteBuffer**. This means to use **SeekableByteChannel** you need to be familiar with the **ByteBuffer** class. So, here is a crash course in **ByteBuffer**.

ByteBuffer is one of the many descendants of **java.nio.Buffer**, a data container for a specific primitive type. A **ByteBuffer** is of course a buffer for bytes. Other subclasses of **Buffer** include **CharBuffer**, **DoubleBuffer**, **FloatBuffer**, **IntBuffer**, **LongBuffer**, and **ShortBuffer**.

A buffer has a capacity, which is the number of elements it contains. It also employs an internal pointer to indicate the next element to read or write. An easy way to create a **ByteBuffer** is by calling the static allocate method of the **ByteBuffer** class:

```
public static ByteBuffer allocate(int capacity)
```

For example, to create a **ByteBuffer** with a capacity of 100, you would write

```
ByteBuffer byteBuffer = ByteBuffer.allocate(100);
```

As you may suspect, a **ByteBuffer** is backed by a byte array. To retrieve this array, call the **array** method of ByteBuffer:

```
public final byte[] array()
```

The length of the array is the same as the **ByteBuffer**'s capacity.

ByteBuffer provides two **put** methods for writing a byte:

```
public abstract ByteBuffer put(byte b)
```

```
public abstract ByteBuffer put(int index, byte b)
```

The first **put** method writes on the element pointed by the **ByteBuffer**'s internal pointer. The second allows you to put a byte anywhere by specifying an index.

There are also two **put** methods for writing a byte array. The first one allows the content of a byte array or a subset of it to be copied to the **ByteBuffer**. It has this signature:

```
public ByteBuffer put(byte[] src, int offset, int length)
```

The *src* argument is the source byte array, *offset* is the location of the first byte in *src*, and *length* is the number of bytes to be copied.

The second **put** method puts the whole source byte array to be copied from position 0:

```
public ByteBuffer put(byte[] src)
```

ByteBuffer also provides various **put*XXX*** methods for writing different data types to the buffer. The **putInt** method, for example, writes an **int** whereas **putShort** puts a **short**. There are two versions of **put*XXX***, one for putting a value at the next location pointed by the **ByteBuffer**'s internal pointer, one for putting a value at an absolute position. The signatures of the **putInt** methods are as follows.

```
public abstract ByteBuffer putInt(int value)
```

```
public abstract ByteBuffer putInt(int index, int value)
```

To read from a **ByteBuffer**, the **ByteBuffer** class provides a number of **get** and **get*XXX*** methods, which come in two flavors: one for reading from the relative position and one for reading from an absolute element. Here are the signatures of some of the **get** and **get*XXX*** methods:

```
public abstract byte get()
```

```
public abstract byte get(int index)
```

```
public abstract float getFloat()
```

```
public abstract float getFloat(int index)
```

Okay. That's all you need to know about **ByteBuffer**, and now you are ready for **SeekableByteChannel**. Listing 16.8 shows how to use **SeekableByteChannel**.

Listing 16.8: Random access file

```java
package app16;
import java.io.IOException;
import java.nio.ByteBuffer;
import java.nio.channels.SeekableByteChannel;
import java.nio.file.Files;
import java.nio.file.Path;
import java.nio.file.Paths;
import java.nio.file.StandardOpenOption;

public class SeekableByteChannelDemo1 {

    public static void main(String[] args) {
        ByteBuffer buffer = ByteBuffer.allocate(12);
        System.out.println(buffer.position()); // prints 0
        buffer.putInt(10);
        System.out.println(buffer.position()); // prints 8
        buffer.putLong(1234567890L);
        System.out.println(buffer.position()); // prints 16
        buffer.rewind(); // sets position to 0
        System.out.println(buffer.getInt()); // prints 10000
        System.out.println(buffer.getLong()); // prints 1234567890
        buffer.rewind();
        System.out.println(buffer.position()); // prints 0

        Path path = Paths.get("C:/temp/channel");
        System.out.println("------------------------");
        try (SeekableByteChannel byteChannel =
                Files.newByteChannel(path,
                    StandardOpenOption.CREATE,
                    StandardOpenOption.READ,
                    StandardOpenOption.WRITE);) {
            System.out.println(byteChannel.position()); // prints 0
            byteChannel.write(buffer);
            System.out.println(byteChannel.position()); //prints 20

            // read file
            ByteBuffer buffer3 = ByteBuffer.allocate(40);
            byteChannel.position(0);
            byteChannel.read(buffer3);
            buffer3.rewind();
            System.out.println("get int:" + buffer3.getInt());
            System.out.println("get long:" + buffer3.getLong());
            System.out.println(buffer3.getChar());
        } catch (IOException e) {
            e.printStackTrace();
        }
    }
}
```

The **SeekableByteChannelDemo1** class in Listing 16.8 starts by creating a **ByteBuffer** with a capacity of twelve and putting an **int** and a **long** in it. Remember that an **int** is four bytes long and a **long** takes 8 bytes.

```
ByteBuffer buffer = ByteBuffer.allocate(12);
buffer.putInt(10);
buffer.putLong(1234567890L);
```

After receiving an **int** and a **long**, the buffer's position is at 16.

```
System.out.println(buffer.position()); // prints 16
```

The class then creates a **SeekableByteChannel** and calls its **write** method, passing the **ByteBuffer**.

```
Path path = Paths.get("C:/temp/channel");
try (SeekableByteChannel byteChannel =
        Files.newByteChannel(path,
            StandardOpenOption.CREATE,
            StandardOpenOption.READ,
            StandardOpenOption.WRITE);) {
    byteChannel.write(buffer);
```

It then reads the file back and prints the results to the console.

```
// read file
ByteBuffer buffer3 = ByteBuffer.allocate(40);
byteChannel.position(0);
byteChannel.read(buffer3);
buffer3.rewind();
System.out.println("get int:" + buffer3.getInt());
System.out.println("get long:" + buffer3.getLong());
System.out.println(buffer3.getChar());
```

Object Serialization

Occasionally you need to persist objects into permanent storage so that the states of the objects can be retained and retrieved later. Java supports this through object serialization. To serialize an object, i.e. save it to permanent storage, you use an **ObjectOutputStream**. To deserialize an object, namely to retrieve the saved object, use **ObjectInputStream**. **ObjectOutputStream** is a subclass of **OutputStream** and **ObjectInputStream** is derived from **InputStream**.

The **ObjectOutputStream** class has one public constructor:

```
public ObjectOutputStream(OutputStream out)
```

After you create an **ObjectOutputStream**, you can serialize objects or primitives or the combination of both. The **ObjectOutputStream** class provides a **writeXXX** method for each individual type, where *XXX* denotes a type. Here is the list of the **writeXXX** methods.

```
public void writeBoolean(boolean value)
```

```
public void writeByte(int value)
```

```
public void writeBytes(String value)

public void writeChar(int value)

public void writeChars(String value)

public void writeDouble(double value)

public void writeFloat(float value)

public void writeInt(int value)

public void writeLong(long value)

public void writeShort(short value)

public void writeObject(java.lang.Object value)
```

For objects to be serializable their classes must implement **java.io.Serializable**. This interface has no method and is a marker interface. A marker interface is one that tells the JVM that an instance of an implementing class belongs to a certain type.

If a serialized object contains other objects, the contained objects' classes must also implement **Serializable** for the contained objects to be serializable.

The **ObjectInputStream** class has one public constructor:

```
public ObjectInputStream(InputStream in)
```

To deserialize from a file, you can pass a **InputStream** that is connected to a file sink. The **ObjectInputStream** class has methods that are the opposites of the **write***XXX* methods in **ObjectOutputStream**. They are as follows:

```
public boolean readBoolean()

public byte readByte()

public char readChar()

public double readDouble()

public float readFloat()

public int readInt()

public long readLong()

public short readShort()

public java.lang.Object readObject()
```

One important thing to note: object serialization is based on a last in first out method. When deserializing multiple primitives/objects, the objects that were serialized first must be deserialized last.

Listing 16.10 shows a class that serializes an **int** and a **Customer** object. Note that the **Customer** class, given in Listing 16.9, implements **Serializable**. The serialization runtime associates with each serializable class a version number called serialVersionUID. This number is used during deserialization to verify that the sender and receiver of a serialized object have loaded classes for that object that are compatible with respect to serialization. All classes implementing **Serializable** should declare a static final long **serialVersionUID** field. Otherwise, one will be calculated by the serialization runtime automatically.

Listing 16.9: The Customer class

```java
package app16;
import java.io.Serializable;

public class Customer implements Serializable {
    private static final long serialVersionUID = 1L;

    public int id;
    public String name;
    public String address;
    public Customer (int id, String name, String address) {
        this.id = id;
        this.name = name;
        this.address = address;
    }
}
```

Listing 16.10: Object serialization example

```java
package app16;
import java.io.IOException;
import java.io.InputStream;
import java.io.ObjectInputStream;
import java.io.ObjectOutputStream;
import java.io.OutputStream;
import java.nio.file.Files;
import java.nio.file.Path;
import java.nio.file.Paths;
import java.nio.file.StandardOpenOption;

public class ObjectSerializationDemo1 {

    public static void main(String[] args) {
        // Serialize
        Path path = Paths.get("C:\\temp\\objectOutput");
        Customer customer = new Customer(1, "Joe Blog",
                "12 West Cost");
        try (OutputStream outputStream =
                Files.newOutputStream(path,
                        StandardOpenOption.CREATE);
            ObjectOutputStream oos = new
                    ObjectOutputStream(outputStream)) {

            // write first object
            oos.writeObject(customer);
            // write second object
            oos.writeObject("Customer Info");
        } catch (IOException e) {
            System.out.print("IOException");
        }

        // Deserialize
```

```
        try (InputStream inputStream = Files.newInputStream(path,
                StandardOpenOption.READ);
            ObjectInputStream ois = new
                    ObjectInputStream(inputStream)) {
            // read first object
            Customer customer2 = (Customer) ois.readObject();
            System.out.println("First Object: ");
            System.out.println(customer2.id);
            System.out.println(customer2.name);
            System.out.println(customer2.address);

            // read second object
            System.out.println();
            System.out.println("Second object: ");
            String info = (String) ois.readObject();
            System.out.println(info);
        } catch (ClassNotFoundException ex) { // readObject still throws
    this exception
            System.out.print("ClassNotFound " + ex.getMessage());
        } catch (IOException ex2) {
            System.out.print("IOException " + ex2.getMessage());
        }
    }
}
```

Summary

Input/output operations are supported through the members of the **java.io** package. You can read and write data through streams and data is classified into binary data and text. In addition, Java support object serialization through the **Serializable** interface and the **ObjectInputStream** and **ObjectOutputStream** classes.

Quiz

1. What is an I/O stream?
2. Name four abstract classes that represent streams in the **java.io** package.
3. What is object serialization?
4. What is the requirement for a class to be serializable?

Chapter 17
Annotations

Annotations are notes in Java programs to instruct the Java compiler to do something. Java annotations were first defined in JSR 175, "A Metadata Facility for the Java Programming Language." Later JSR 250, "Common Annotations for the Java Platform" added annotations for common concepts. Both specifications can be downloaded from http://www.jcp.org.

This chapter starts with an overview of annotations, and then teaches you how to use the standard and common annotations. It concludes with a discussion of how to write your own custom annotation types.

Overview

overriding: in derived class. same method name, same parameter
overloading: in same class. same method name, different parameter

Annotations are notes for the Java compiler. When you annotate a program element in a source file, you add notes to the Java program elements in that source file. You can annotate Java packages, types (classes, interfaces, enumerated types), constructors, methods, fields, parameters and local variables. For example, you can annotate a Java class so that any warnings that the **javac** program would otherwise issue are suppressed. Or, you can annotate a method that you want to override to ask the compiler to verify that you are really <u>overriding</u> the method, not <u>overloading</u> it.

The Java compiler can be instructed to interpret annotations and discard them (so those annotations only live in source files) or include them in resulting Java classes. Those that are included in Java classes may be ignored by the Java virtual machine, or they may be loaded into the virtual machine. The latter type is called runtime-visible and you can use reflection to inquire about them.

Annotations and Annotation Types

When studying annotations, you will come across these two terms very frequently: annotations and annotation types. To understand their meanings, it is useful to first bear in mind that an annotation type is a special interface type. An annotation is an instance of an annotation type. Just like an interface, an annotation type has a name and members. The information contained in an annotation takes the form of key/value pairs. There can be zero or multiple pairs and each key has a specific type. It can be a **String**, **int** or other Java types. Annotation types with no key/value pairs are called marker annotation types. Those with one key/value pair are often referred to single-value annotation types.

Annotations were first added to Java 5, which brought with it three annotation types: **Deprecated**, **Override** and **SuppressWarnings**. They are part of the **java.lang** package and you will learn to use them in the section "Built-in Annotations." (Java 7 and 8 later added **SafeVarargs** and **FunctionalInterface** to **java.lang**) On top of that, there are six other annotation types that are part of the **java.lang.annotation** package, including **Documented**, **Inherited**, **Retention** and **Target**. These four annotation types are used to annotate annotations. Java 6 added common annotations, which are explained in the section "Common Annotations."

Annotation Syntax

You declare an annotation type using this syntax.

```
@AnnotationType
```

or

```
@AnnotationType(elementValuePairs)
```

The first syntax is for marker annotation types and the second for single-value and multi-value types. It is legal to put white spaces between the at sign (@) and annotation type, but this is not recommended.

For example, here is how you use the marker annotation type **Deprecated**:

```
@Deprecated
```

And, this is how you use the second syntax for multi-value annotation type **Author**:

```
@Author(firstName="Ted",lastName="Diong")
```

There is an exception to this rule. If an annotation type has a single key/value pair and the name of the key is **value**, then you can omit the key from the bracket. Therefore, if fictitious annotation type **Stage** has a single key named **value**, you can write

```
@Stage(value=1)
```

or

```
@Stage(1)
```

The Annotation Interface

An annotation type is a Java interface. All annotation types are subinterfaces of **java.lang.annotation.Annotation**. One of its methods, **annotationType**, returns a **java.lang.Class** object.

```
java.lang.Class<? extends Annotation> annotationType()
```

In addition, any implementation of **Annotation** will override the **equals**, **hashCode**, and **toString** methods from the **java.lang.Object** class. Here are their default implementations.

```
public boolean equals(Object object)
```
Returns **true** if *object* is an instance of the same annotation type as this one and all members of *object* are equal to the corresponding members of this annotation.

```
public int hashCode()
```
Returns the hash code of this annotation, which is the sum of the hash codes of its members

```
public String toString()
```
> Returns a string representation of this annotation, which typically lists all the key/value pairs of this annotation.

You will use this class when learning custom annotation types later in this chapter.

Standard Annotations

Annotations were a new feature in Java 5 and originally there were three standard annotations, all of which are in the **java.lang** package: **Override**, **Deprecated** and **SuppressWarnings**. They are discussed in this section.

Override

Override is a marker annotation type that can be applied to a method to indicate to the compiler that the method overrides a method in a superclass. This annotation type guards the programmer against making a mistake when overriding a method.

For example, consider this class **Parent**:

```
class Parent {
    public float calculate(float a, float b) {
        return a * b;
    }
}
```

Suppose, you want to extend **Parent** and override its **calculate** method. Here is a subclass of **Parent**:

```
public class Child extends Parent {
    public int calculate(int a, int b) {
        return (a + 1) * b;
    }
}
```

The **Child** class compiles. However, the **calculate** method in **Child** does not override the method in **Parent** because it has a different signature, namely it returns and accepts **int**s instead of **float**s. In this example, such a programming mistake is easy to spot because you can see both the **Parent** and **Child** classes. However, you won't be always this lucky. Sometimes the parent class is buried somewhere in another package. This seemingly trivial error could be fatal because when a client class calls the **calculate** method on a **Child** object and passes two floats, the method in the **Parent** class will be invoked and the wrong result returned.

Using the **Override** annotation type will prevent this kind of mistake. Whenever you want to override a method, declare the **Override** annotation type before the method:

```
public class Child extends Parent {
    @Override
    public int calculate(int a, int b) {
        return (a + 1) * b;
    }
```

```
}
```

This time, the compiler will generate a compile error and you'll be notified that the **calculate** method in **Child** is not overriding the method in the parent class.

It is clear that **@Override** is useful to make sure programmers override a method when they intend to override it, and not overload it.

Deprecated

Deprecated is a marker annotation type that can be applied to a method or a type to indicate that the method or type is deprecated. A deprecated method or type is marked so by the programmer to warn the users of his code that they should not use or override the method or use or extend the type. The reason why a method or a type is marked deprecated is usually because there is a better method or type and the deprecated method or type is retained in the current software version for backward compatibility.

For example, the **DeprecatedDemo1** class in Listing 17.1 uses the **Deprecated** annotation type.

Listing 17.1: Deprecating a method

```
package app17;
public class DeprecatedDemo1 {
    @Deprecated
    public void serve() {
    }
}
```

If you use or override a deprecated method, you will get a warning at compile time. For example, Listing 17.2 shows a **DeprecatedDemo2** class that uses the **serve** method in **DeprecatedDemo1**.

Listing 17.2: Using a deprecated method

```
package app17;
public class DeprecatedDemo2 {
    public static void main(String[] args) {
        DeprecatedDemo1 demo = new DeprecatedDemo1();
        demo.serve();
    }
}
```

Compiling **DeprecatedDemo2** generates this warning:

```
Note: app17/DeprecatedDemo2.java uses or overrides a deprecated
API.
Note: Recompile with -Xlint:deprecation for details.
```

On top of that, you can use **@Deprecated** to mark a class or an interface, as shown in Listing 17.3.

Listing 17.3: Marking a class deprecated

```
package app17;
@Deprecated
public class DeprecatedDemo3 {
```

```
    public void serve() {
    }
}
```

SuppressWarnings

SuppressWarnings is used, as you must have guessed, to suppress compiler warnings. You can apply **@SuppressWarnings** to types, constructors, methods, fields, parameters, and local variables.

You use it by passing a **String** array that contains warnings that need to be suppressed. Its syntax is as follows.

```
@SuppressWarnings(value={string-1, ..., string-n})
```

where *string-1* to *string-n* indicate the set of warnings to be suppressed. Duplicate and unrecognized warnings will be ignored.

The following are valid parameters to **@SuppressWarnings**:

- **unchecked**. Gives more detail for unchecked conversion warnings that are mandated by the Java Language Specification.
- **path**. Warns about nonexistent path (classpath, sourcepath, etc) directories.
- **serial**. Warns about missing serialVersionUID definitions on serializable classes.
- **finally**. Warns about finally clauses that cannot complete normally.
- **fallthrough**. Checks switch blocks for fall-through cases, namely cases, other than the last case in the block, whose code does not include a **break** statement, allowing code execution to "fall through" from that case to the next case. As an example, the code following the **case 2** label in this **switch** block does not contain a **break** statement:

```
switch (i) {
case 1:
    System.out.println("1");
    break;
case 2:
    System.out.println("2");
    //  falling through
case 3:
    System.out.println("3");
}
```

As an example, the **SuppressWarningsDemo1** class in Listing17.4 uses the **SuppressWarnings** annotation type to prevent the compiler from issuing unchecked and fallthrough warnings.

Listing 17.4 Using @SuppressWarnings

```
package app17;
import java.io.File;
import java.io.Serializable;
import java.util.ArrayList;

@SuppressWarnings(value={"unchecked","serial"})
public class SuppressWarningsDemo1 implements Serializable {
    public void openFile() {
```

```
        ArrayList a = new ArrayList();
        File file = new File("X:/java/doc.txt");
    }
}
```

Common Annotations

Java includes an implementation of JSR 250, "Common Annotations for the Java Platform," which specifies annotations for common concepts. The goal of this JSR is to avoid different Java technologies define similar annotations which would result in duplication.

The full list of common annotations can be found in the document that can be downloaded from http://jcp.org/en/jsr/detail?id=250.

Except for **Generated**, all of the annotations specified are, unfortunately, advanced materials or suitable for Java EE, and therefore beyond the scope of this book. As such, the only common annotation discussed is **@Generated**.

@Generated is used to mark computer generated source code, as opposed to hand-written code. It can be applied to classes, methods, and fields. The following are parameters to **@Generated**:

- **value**. The name of the code generator. The convention is to use the fully qualified name of the generator.
- **date**. The date the code was generated. It must be in a format compliant with ISO 8601.
- **comments**. Comments accompanying the generated code.

For example, in Listing 17.5 **@Generated** is used to annotate a generated class.

Listing 17.5: Using @Generated

```
package app17;
import javax.annotation.Generated;

@Generated(value="com.example.robot.CodeGenerator",
        date="2014-12-31", comments="Generated code")
public class GeneratedTest {

}
```

Standard Meta-Annotations

Meta annotations are annotations that annotate annotations. There are four meta-annotation types that can be used to annotate annotations: **Documented**, **Inherited**, **Retention** and **Target**. All the four are part of the **java.lang.annotation** package. This section discusses these annotation types.

Documented

Documented is a marker annotation type used to annotate the declaration of an annotation type so that instances of the annotation type will be included in the documentation generated using Javadoc or similar tools.

For example, the **Override** annotation type is not annotated using **Documented**. As a result, if you use Javadoc to generate a class whose method is annotated **@Override**, you will not see any trace of **@Override** in the resulting document.

For instance, Listing 17.6 shows a **OverrideDemo2** class that uses **@Override** to annotate the **toString** method.

Listing 17.6: The OverrideDemo2 class
```
package app17;
public class OverrideDemo2 {
    @Override
    public String toString() {
        return "OverrideDemo2";
    }
}
```

On the other hand, the **Deprecated** annotation type is annotated **@Documented**. Recall that the **serve** method in the **DeprecatedTest** class in Listing 17.2 is annotated **@Deprecated**. Now, if you use **Javadoc** to generate the documentation for **OverrideTest2**, the details of the **serve** method in the documentation will also include **@Deprecated**, like this:

```
serve
@Deprecated
public void serve()
```

Inherited

You use **Inherited** to annotate an annotation type so that any instance of the annotation type will be inherited. If you annotate a class using an inherited annotation type, the annotation will be inherited by any subclass of the annotated class. If the user queries the annotation type on a class declaration, and the class declaration has no annotation of this type, then the class's parent class will automatically be queried for the annotation type. This process will be repeated until an annotation of this type is found or the root class is reached.

Check the section "Custom Annotation Types" on how to query an annotation type.

Retention

@Retention indicates how long annotations whose annotated types are annotated **@Retention** are to be retained. The value of **@Retention** can be one of the members of the **java.lang.annotation.RetentionPolicy** enum:

- **SOURCE**. Annotations are to be discarded by the Java compiler.
- **CLASS**. Annotations are to be recorded in the class file but not retained by the

JVM. This is the default value.
- **RUNTIME**. Annotations are to be retained by the JVM so they can be queried using reflection.

For example, the declaration of the **SuppressWarnings** annotation type is annotated **@Retention** with the value of **SOURCE**.

```
@Retention(value=SOURCE)
public @interface SuppressWarnings
```

Target

Target indicates which program element(s) can be annotated using instances of the annotated annotation type. The value of **Target** is one of the members of the **java.lang.annotation.ElementType** enum:

- **ANNOTATION_TYPE**. The annotated annotation type can be used to annotate annotation type declaration.
- **CONSTRUCTOR**. The annotated annotation type can be used to annotate constructor declaration.
- **FIELD**. The annotated annotation type can be used to annotate field declaration.
- **LOCAL_VARIABLE**. The annotated annotation type can be used to annotate local variable declaration.
- **METHOD**. The annotated annotation type can be used to annotate method declaration.
- **PACKAGE**. The annotated annotation type can be used to annotate package declarations.
- **PARAMETER**. The annotated annotation type can be used to annotate parameter declarations.
- **TYPE**. The annotated annotation type can be used to annotate type declarations.

As an example, the **Override** annotation type declaration is annotated the following **Target** annotation, making **Override** only applicable to method declarations.

```
@Target(value=METHOD)
```

You can have multiple values in the **Target** annotation. For example, this is from the declaration of **SuppressWarnings**:

```
@Target(value={TYPE,FIELD, METHOD, PARAMETER,CONSTRUCTOR,
LOCAL_VARIABLE})
```

Custom Annotation Types

An annotation type is a Java interface, except that you must add an at sign before the **interface** keyword when declaring it.

```
public @interface CustomAnnotation {
}
```

By default, all annotation types implicitly or explicitly extend the **java.lang.annotation.Annotation** interface. In addition, even though you can extend an annotation type, its subtype is not treated as an annotation type.

Writing Your Own Custom Annotation Type

Listing 17.7 shows a custom annotation type called **Author**.

Listing 17.7: The Author annotation type

```
package app17.custom;
import java.lang.annotation.Documented;
import java.lang.annotation.Retention;
import java.lang.annotation.RetentionPolicy;

@Documented
@Retention(RetentionPolicy.RUNTIME)
public @interface Author {
    String firstName();
    String lastName();
    boolean internalEmployee();
}
```

Using Custom Annotation Types

The **Author** annotation type is like any other Java type. Once you import it into a class or an interface, you can use it simply by writing

```
@Author(firstName="firstName",lastName="lastName",
internalEmployee=true|false)
```

For example, the **Test1** class in Listing 17.8 is annotated **Author**.

Listing 17.8: A class annotated Author

```
package app17.custom;
@Author(firstName="John",lastName="Guddell",internalEmployee=true)
public class Test1 {
}
```

Is that it? Yes, that's it. Very simple, isn't it?

The next subsection "Using Reflection to Query Annotations" shows how the **Author** annotations can be of good use.

Using Reflection to Query Annotations

The **java.lang.Class** class has several methods related to annotations.

```
public <A extends java.lang.annotation.Annotation> A getAnnotation
        (Class<A> annotationClass)
```
Returns this element's annotation for the specified annotation type, if present. Otherwise, returns **null**.

```
public java.lang.annotation.Annotation[] getAnnotations()
```
Returns all annotations present on this class.

```
public boolean isAnnotation()
```
Returns **true** if this class is an annotation type.

```
public boolean isAnnotationPresent(Class<? extends
        java.lang.annotation.Annotation> annotationClass)
```
Indicates whether an annotation for the specified type is present on this class

The **app17.custom** package includes three test classes, **Test1**, **Test2**, and **Test3**, that are annotated **Author**. Listing 17.9 shows a test class that employs reflection to query the test classes.

Listing 17.9: Using reflection to query annotations

```java
package app17.custom;

public class CustomAnnotationDemo1 {
    public static void printClassInfo(Class c) {
        System.out.print(c.getName() + ". ");
        Author author = (Author) c.getAnnotation(Author.class);
        if (author != null) {
            System.out.println("Author:" + author.firstName()
                    + " " + author.lastName());
        } else {
            System.out.println("Author unknown");
        }
    }

    public static void main(String[] args) {
        CustomAnnotationDemo1.printClassInfo(Test1.class);
        CustomAnnotationDemo1.printClassInfo(Test2.class);
        CustomAnnotationDemo1.printClassInfo(Test3.class);
        CustomAnnotationDemo1.printClassInfo(
                CustomAnnotationDemo1.class);
    }
}
```

When run, you will see the following message in your console:

```
app17.custom.Test1. Author:John Guddell
app17.custom.Test2. Author:John Guddell
app17.custom.Test3. Author:Lesley Nielsen
app17.custom.CustomAnnotationDemo1. Author unknown
```

Summary

You use annotations to instruct the Java compiler to do something to an annotated program element. Any program element can be annotated, including Java packages, classes, constructors, fields, methods, parameters, and local variables. This chapter explained standard annotation types and taught how to create custom annotation types.

Quiz

1. What is an annotation type?
2. What is a meta-annotation?
3. What were the standard annotation types fist included in Java 5?

Chapter 18
Nested and Inner Classes

Nested and inner classes are often considered too confusing for beginners. However, they have some merits that make them a proper discussion topic in this book. To name a few, you can hide an implementation completely using a nested class and it provides a shorter way of writing an event-listener.

This chapter starts by defining what nested classes and inner classes are and continues by explaining types of nested classes.

An Overview of Nested Classes

Let's start by learning the correct definitions of nested and inner classes. A nested class is a class declared within the body of another class or interface. There are two types of nested classes: static and non-static. Non-static nested classes are called inner classes.

There are several types of inner classes:

- member inner classes
- local inner classes
- anonymous inner classes

The term "top level class" is used to refer to a class that is not defined within another class or interface. In other words, there is no class enclosing a top level class.

A nested class behaves pretty much like an ordinary (top level) class. A nested class can extend another class, implements interfaces, be the parent class of subclasses, etc. Here is an example of a simple nested class called **Nested** that is defined within a top level class named **Outer**.

```
package app18;
public class Outer {
    class Nested {
    }
}
```

And, though uncommon, it is not impossible to have a nested class inside another nested class, such as this:

```
package app18;
public class Outer {
    class Nested {
        class Nested2 {
        }
```

```
        }
    }
```

To a top-level class, a nested class is just like other class members, such as methods and fields. For example, a nested class can have one of the four access modifiers: private, protected, default (package) and public. This is unlike a top level class that can only have either public or default.

Because nested classes are members of an enclosing class, the behavior of static nested classes and the behavior of inner classes are not exactly the same. Here are some differences.

- Static nested classes can have static members, inner classes cannot.
- Just like instance methods, inner classes can access static and non-static members of the outer class, including its private members. Static nested classes can only access the static members of the outer class.
- You can create an instance of a static nested class without first creating an instance of its outer class. By contrast, you must first create an instance of the outer class enclosing an inner class before instantiating the inner class itself.

These are the benefits of inner classes:

1. Inner classes can have access to all (including private) members of the enclosing classes.
2. Inner classes help you hide the implementation of a class completely.
3. Inner classes provide a shorter way of writing listeners in Swing and other event-based applications.

Now, let's review each type of static class.

Static Nested Classes

A static nested class can be created without creating an instance of the outer class. Listing 18.1 shows this.

Listing 18.1: A Static Nested Class

```
package app18;
class Outer1 {
    private static int value = 9;
    static class Nested1 {
        int calculate() {
            return value;
        }
    }
}

public class StaticNestedDemo1 {
    public static void main(String[] args) {
        Outer1.Nested1 nested = new Outer1.Nested1();
        System.out.println(nested.calculate());
    }
}
```

There are a few things to note about static nested classes:

- You refer to a nested class by using this format:

  ```
  OuterClassName.InnerClassName
  ```

- You do not need to create an instance of the enclosing class to instantiate a static nested class.
- You have access to the outer class static members from inside your static nested class

In addition, if you declare a member in a nested class that has the same name as a member in the enclosing class, the former will shadow the latter. However, you can always reference the member in the enclosing class by using this format.

```
OuterClassName.memberName
```

Note that this will still work although *memberName* is private. Examine the example in Listing 18.2.

Listing 18.2: Shadowing an outer class's member.

```
package app18;
class Outer2 {
    private static int value = 9;
    static class Nested2 {
        int value = 10;
        int calculate() {
            return value;
        }
        int getOuterValue() {
            return Outer2.value;
        }
    }
}

public class StaticNestedDemo2 {
    public static void main(String[] args) {
        Outer2.Nested2 nested = new Outer2.Nested2();
        System.out.println(nested.calculate());      // returns 10
        System.out.println(nested.getOuterValue()); // returns 9
    }
}
```

Member Inner Classes

A member inner class is a class whose definition is *directly* enclosed by another class or interface declaration. An instance of a member inner class can be created only if you have a reference to an instance of its outer class. To create an instance of an inner class from within the enclosing class, you call the inner class's constructor, just as you would other ordinary classes. However, to create an instance of an inner class from outside the enclosing class, you use the following syntax:

```
EnclosingClassName.InnerClassName inner =
        enclosingClassObjectReference.new InnerClassName();
```

As usual, from within an inner class, you can use the keyword **this** to reference the current instance (the inner class's instance). To reference the enclosing class's instance you use this syntax.

```
EnclosingClassName.this
```

Listing 18.3 shows how you can create an instance of an inner class.

Listing 18.3: A member inner class

```java
package app18;
class TopLevel {
    private int value = 9;
    class Inner {
        int calculate() {
            return value;
        }
    }
}

public class MemberInnerDemo1 {
    public static void main(String[] args) {
        TopLevel topLevel = new TopLevel ();
        TopLevel.Inner inner = topLevel.new Inner();
        System.out.println(inner.calculate());
    }
}
```

Notice how you created an instance of the inner class in Listing 18.3?

A member inner class can be used to hide an implementation completely, something you cannot do without employing an inner class. The following example shows how you can use a member class to hide an implementation completely.

Listing 18.4: Hiding implementations completely

```java
package app18;
interface Printer {
    void print(String message);
}
class PrinterImpl implements Printer {
    public void print(String message) {
        System.out.println(message);
    }
}
class SecretPrinterImpl {
    private class Inner implements Printer {
        public void print(String message) {
            System.out.println("Inner:" + message);
        }
    }
    public Printer getPrinter() {
        return new Inner();
```

```
        }
    }
public class MemberInnerDemo2 {
    public static void main(String[] args) {
        Printer printer = new PrinterImpl();
        printer.print("oh");
        // downcast to PrinterImpl
        PrinterImpl impl = (PrinterImpl) printer;

        Printer hiddenPrinter =
                (new SecretPrinterImpl()).getPrinter();
        hiddenPrinter.print("oh");
        // cannot downcast hiddenPrinter to Outer.Inner
        // because Inner is private
    }
}
```

The **Printer** interface in Listing 18.4 has two implementations. The first is the **PrinterImpl** class, which is a normal class. It implements the **print** method as a public method. The second implementation can be found in **SecretPrinterImpl**. However, rather than implementing the **Printer** interface, the **SecretPrinterImpl** defines a private class called **Inner**, which implements **Printer**. The **getPrinter** method of **SecretPrinterImpl** returns an instance of **Inner**.

What is the difference between **PrinterImpl** and **SecretPrinterImpl**? You can see this from the main method in the test class:

```
Printer printer = new PrinterImpl();
printer.print("Hiding implementation");
// downcast to PrinterImpl
PrinterImpl impl = (PrinterImpl) printer;

Printer hiddenPrinter = (new SecretPrinterImpl()).getPrinter();
hiddenPrinter.print("Hiding implementation");
// cannot downcast hiddenPrinter to Outer.Inner
// because Inner is private
```

You assign **printer** an instance of **PrinterImpl**, and you can downcast **printer** back to **PrinterImpl**. In the second instance, you assign **Printer** with an instance of **Inner** by calling the **getPrinter** method on **SecretPrinterImpl**. However, there is no way you can downcast **hiddenPrinter** back to **SecretPrinterImpl.Inner** because **Inner** is private and therefore not visible.

Local Inner Classes

A local inner class, or local class for short, is an inner class that by definition is not a member class of any other class (because its declaration is not directly within the declaration of the outer class). Local classes have a name, as opposed to anonymous classes that do not.

A local class can be declared inside any block of code, and its scope is within the block. For example, you can declare a local class within a method, an **if** block, a **while** block, and so on. You want to write a local class if an instance of the class is only used within the scope. For example, Listing 18.5 shows an example of a local class.

Listing 18.5: Local inner class

```
package app18;
import java.time.LocalDateTime;
import java.time.format.DateTimeFormatter;
import java.time.format.FormatStyle;

interface Logger {
    public void log(String message);
}

public class LocalClassDemo1 {
    String appStartTime = LocalDateTime.now().format(
            DateTimeFormatter
            .ofLocalizedDateTime(FormatStyle.MEDIUM));

    public Logger getLogger() {
        class LoggerImpl implements Logger {
            public void log(String message) {
                System.out.println(appStartTime + " : " + message);
            }
        }
        return new LoggerImpl();
    }

    public static void main(String[] args) {
        LocalClassDemo1 test = new LocalClassDemo1();
        Logger logger = test.getLogger();
        logger.log("Local class example");
    }
}
```

The class in Listing 18.5 has a local class named **LoggerImpl** that resides inside a **getLogger** method. The **getLogger** method must return an implementation of the **Logger** interface and this implementation will not be used anywhere else. Therefore, it is a good idea to make an implementation that is local to **getLogger**. Note also that the **log** method within the local class has access to the instance field **appStartTime** of the outer class.

However, there is more. Not only does a local class have access to the members of its outer class, it also has access to the local variables. However, you can only access final local variables. The compiler will generate a compile error if you try to access a local variable that is not final.

Listing 18.6 modifies the code in Listing 18.5. The **getLogger** method in Listing 18.6 allows you to pass a **String** that will become the prefix of each line logged.

Listing 18.6: PrefixLogger test

```
package app18;
import java.util.Date;

interface PrefixLogger {
    public void log(String message);
```

```
    }

public class LocalClassDemo2 {
    public PrefixLogger getLogger(final String prefix) {
        class LoggerImpl implements PrefixLogger {
            public void log(String message) {
                System.out.println(prefix + " : " + message);
            }
        }
        return new LoggerImpl();
    }

    public static void main(String[] args) {
        LocalClassDemo2 test = new LocalClassDemo2();
        PrefixLogger logger = test.getLogger("DEBUG");
        logger.log("Local class example");
    }
}
```

Anonymous Inner Classes

An anonymous inner class does not have a name. A use of this type of nested class is for writing an interface implementation. For example, the **AnonymousInnerClassDemo1** class in Listing 18.7 creates an anonymous inner class which is an implementation of **Printable**.

Listing 18.7: Using an anonymous inner class

```
package app18;
interface Printable {
    void print(String message);
}

public class AnonymousInnerClassDemo1 {
    public static void main(String[] args) {

        Printable printer = new Printable() {
            public void print(String message) {
                System.out.println(message);
            }
        }; // this is a semicolon

        printer.print("Beach Music");
    }
}
```

The interesting thing here is that you create an anonymous inner class by using the **new** keyword followed by what looks like a class's constructor (in this case **Printable()**). However, note that **Printable** is an interface and does not have a constructor. **Printable()** is followed by the implementation of the **print** method. Also, note that after the closing brace, you use a semicolon to terminate the statement that instantiates the anonymous inner class.

In addition, you can also create an anonymous inner class by extending an abstract or concrete class, as demonstrated in the code in Listing 18.8.

Listing 18.8: Using an anonymous inner class with an abstract class

```
package app18;
abstract class Printable2 {
    void print(String message) {
    }
}

public class AnonymousInnerClassDemo2 {
    public static void main(String[] args) {
        Printable2 printer = new Printable2() {
            public void print(String message) {
                System.out.println(message);
            }
        }; // this is a semicolon

        printer.print("Beach Music");
    }
}
```

Behind Nested and Inner Classes

The JVM does not know the notion of nested classes. It is the compiler that works hard to compile an inner class into a top level class incorporating the outer class name and the inner class name as the name, both separated by a dollar sign. That is, the code that employs an inner class called **Inner** that resides inside **Outer** like this

```
public class Outer {
    class Inner {
    }
}
```

will be compiled into two classes: **Outer.class** and **Outer$Inner.class**.

What about anonymous inner classes? For anonymous classes, the compiler takes the liberty of generating a name for them, using numbers. Therefore, you'll see something like **Outer$1.class**, **Outer$2.class**, etc.

When a nested class is instantiated, the instance lives as a separate object in the heap. It does not actually live inside the outer class object.

However, with inner class objects, they have an automatic reference to the outer class object as shown. This reference does not exist in an instance of a static nested class, because a static nested class does not have access to its outer class's instance members.

How does an inner class object obtain a reference to its outer class object? Again, this happens because the compiler changes the constructor of the inner class a bit when the inner class is compiled, namely it adds an argument to every constructor. This argument is of type the outer class.

For example, a constructor like this:

```
public Inner()
```

is changed to this.

```
public Inner(Outer outer)
```

And, this

```
public Inner(int value)
```

to

```
public Inner(Outer outer, int value)
```

Note
Remember that the compiler has the discretion to change the code it compiles. For example, if a class (top level or nested) does not have a constructor, it adds a no-arg constructor to it.

The code that instantiates an inner class is also modified, with the compiler passing a reference to the outer class object to the inner class constructor. If you write:

```
Outer outer = new Outer();
Outer.Inner inner = outer.new Inner();
```

the compiler will change it to

```
Outer outer = new Outer();
Outer.Inner inner = outer.new Inner(outer);
```

When an inner class is instantiated inside the outer class, of course, the compiler passes the current instance of the outer class object using the keyword **this**.

```
// inside the Outer class
Inner inner = new Inner();
```

becomes

```
// inside the Outer class
Inner inner = new Inner(this);
```

Now, here is another piece of the puzzle. How does a nested class access its outer class's private members? No object is allowed to access another object's private members. Again, the compiler changes your code, creating a method that accesses the private member in the outer class definition. Therefore,

```
class TopLevel {
    private int value = 9;
    class Inner {
        int calculate() {
            return value;
        }
    }
}
```

is changed to two classes like this:

```
class TopLevel {
    private int value = 9;
    TopLevel() {
    }
    // added by the compiler
    static int access$0(TopLevel toplevel) {
        return toplevel.value;
    }
}
class TopLevel$Inner {
    final TopLevel this$0;
    TopLevel$Inner(TopLevel toplevel) {
        super();
        this$0 = toplevel;
    }
    int calculate() {
        // modified by the compiler
        return TopLevel.access$0(this$0);
    }
}
```

The addition happens in the background so you will not see it in your source. The compiler adds the **access$0** method that returns the private member value so that the inner class can access the private member.

Summary

A nested class is a class whose declaration is within another class. There are four types of nested classes:

- Static nested classes
- Member inner classes
- Local inner classes
- Anonymous inner classes

The benefits of using nested classes include hiding the implementation of a class completely and as a shorter way of writing a class whose instance will only live within a certain context.

Quiz

1. What is a nested class and what is an inner class?
2. What can you use nested classes for?
3. What is an anonymous class?

Chapter 19
Lambda Expressions

The lambda expression is the most important new feature in Java SE 8. Long considered a missing feature in Java, it has made the Java language complete. At least for now. In this chapter you will learn what lambda expressions are and why they are a nice addition to the language. You will also be introduced to new technical terms such as single abstract method (SAM) and functional interface as well as learn about method references.

Why Lambda Expressions?

Also known as closures, lambda expressions can make certain constructs shorter and more readable, especially when you are dealing with inner classes.

Consider the following code snippet that defines an anonymous inner class out of the **java.lang.Runnable** interface and instantiates the class.

```
Runnable runnable = new Runnable() {
    @Override
    public void run() {
        System.out.println("Running...");
    }
}
```

The code can be replaced with a lambda expression as short as this:

```
Runnable runnable = () -> System.out.println("Running...")
```

In other words, if you need to pass a **Runnable** to a **java.util.concurrent.Executor** like so

```
executor.execute(new Runnable() {
    @Override
    public void run() {
        System.out.println("Running...");
    }
});
```

you can use a lambda expression to produce code with the same effect:

```
executor.execute(() -> System.out.println("Running..."));
```

Short and sweet. And clearer and more expressive too.

Functional Interfaces

Before I explain the lambda expression further, I will introduce the functional interface. A functional interface is an interface that has exactly one abstract method that does not override a **java.lang.Object** method. A functional interface is also called a single abstract method (SAM) interface. For example, **java.lang.Runnable** is a functional interface because it has only one abstract method, **run**. A functional interface may have any number of default and static methods and methods that override public methods in **java.lang.Object** and still qualifies as a functional interface. For example, the **Calculator** interface in Listing 19.1 is a functional interface with a single abstract method called **calculate**. It is a functional interface even though it has two default methods and another abstract method overriding the **toString** method from **java.lang.Object**.

Listing 19.1: A functional interface

```
package app19;
public interface Calculator {

    double calculate(int a, int b);

    public default int subtract(int a, int b) {
        return a - b;
    }

    public default int add(int a, int b) {
        return a * b;
    }

    @Override
    public String toString();
}
```

Examples of functional interfaces in the core Java library include **java.lang.Runnable**, **java.lang.AutoCloseable**, **java.lang.Comparable** and **java.util.Comparator**. In addition, the new package **java.util.function** contains dozens of functional interfaces and is discussed in the section "Predefined Functional Interfaces" later in this chapter. Optionally, a functional interface can be annotated with **@FunctionalInterface**.

Why is the functional interface important? Because you can use a lambda expression to create the equivalent of an anonymous inner class from a functional interface. You cannot use an interface that is not a functional interface for this purpose.

So, let the fun begin.

Lambda Expression Syntax

The **Calculator** interface in Listing 19.1 has a **calculate** method that can be the basis of a lambda expression. The method allows you to define any mathematical operation that takes two integers and return a double. For instance, here are two lambda expressions based on **Calculator**.

```
Calculator addition = (int a, int b) -> (a + b);
System.out.println(addition.calculate(5, 20)); // prints 25.0

Calculator division  = (int a, int b) -> (double) a / b;
System.out.println(division.calculate(5, 2)); // prints 2.5
```

The lambda expression is such an elegant design. How many more lines of code would you need to implement the same program without lambda expressions?

Now that you have acquainted yourself with the lambda expression, I will show you its formal syntax.

```
(parameter list) -> expression
```

or

```
(parameter list) -> {
    statements
}
```

The parameter list is the same as the list of parameters of the abstract method in the underlying functional interface. However, the type for each parameter is optional. In other words, both of these expressions are valid.

```
Calculator addition = (int a, int b) -> (a + b);
```

```
Calculator addition = (a, b) -> (a + b);
```

To summarize, a lambda expression is a shortcut to defining an implementation of a functional interface. A lambda expression is equivalent to an instance of a functional interface implementation. Since it is possible to pass objects as parameters to a method, it is too possible to pass lambda expressions as parameters to a method.

Predefined Functional Interfaces

The **java.util.function** package is a new package in JDK 8. It contains more than forty predefined functional interfaces that can make it easier for you to write lambda expressions. Some of the predefined functional interfaces are shown in Table 19.1.

Function, BiFunction and Other Variants

The **Function** interface is used to create a one-argument function that returns a result. It is a parameterized type and here is its definition.

```
public interface Function<T, R>
```

Here, T represents the type of the argument and R the type of the result.

Function has one abstract method, **apply**, whose signature is as follows.

```
R apply(T argument)
```

This is the method you need to override when using **Function**. For example, the class in Listing 19.2 defines a **Function** for converting miles to kilometers. The **Function** takes an

Integer as an argument and returns a **Double**.

Functional Interface	Description
Function	Models a function that can take one parameter and return a result. The result can be of a different type than the parameter.
BiFunction	Models a function that can take two parameters and return a result. The result can be of a different type than any of the parameters.
UnaryOperator	Represents an operation on a single operand that returns a result whose type is the same as the type of the operand. A **UnaryOperator** can be thought of as a **Function** whose return value is of the same type as the parameter. In fact, **UnaryOperator** is a subinterface of **Function**.
BiOperator	Represents an operation on two operands. The result and the operands must be of the same type.
Predicate	A Function that takes a parameter and returns **true** or **false** based on the value of the parameter.
Supplier	Represents a supplier of results.
Consumer	An operation that takes a parameter and returns no result.

Table 19.1: Core functional interfaces

Listing 19.2: The FunctionDemo1 class

```
package app19.function;
import java.util.function.Function;

public class FunctionDemo1 {
    public static void main(String[] args) {
        Function<Integer, Double> milesToKms =
                (input) -> 1.6 * input;
        int miles = 3;
        double kms = milesToKms.apply(miles);
        System.out.printf("%d miles = %3.2f kilometers\n",
                miles, kms);
    }
}
```

If you run the **FunctionDemo1** class, you will see this on your console.

```
3 miles = 4.80 kilometers
```

A variant of **Function, BiFunction** takes two arguments and returns a result. Listing 19.3 shows an example of **BiFunction**. It uses **BiFunction** to create a function that calculates an area given a width and a length. Invoking the function is done by calling its **apply** method.

Listing 19.3: The BiFunctionDemo1 class

```
package app19.function;
import java.util.function.BiFunction;

public class BiFunctionDemo1 {
    public static void main(String[] args) {
        BiFunction<Float, Float, Float> area =
                (width, length) -> width * length;
        float width = 7.0F;
```

```
        float length = 10.0F;
        float result = area.apply(width, length);
        System.out.println(result);
    }
}
```

Running the **BiFunctionDemo1** class prints the following on the console.

```
70.0
```

In addition to **BiFunction**, there are also variants that are specializations of **Function**. For example, the **IntFunction** interface always takes an **Integer** and requires only one parameterized type for the result type. Its **apply** method returns an **int**.

```
R apply(int input)
```

The **LongFunction** and **DoubleFunction** interfaces are similar to **IntFunction**, except they take a long and a double as an argument, respectively.

Then, there are variants that do not require parameterized arguments at all, because they have been designed for a specific argument type and a specific return type. For instance, the **IntToDoubleFunction** interface can be used to create a function that accepts an int and returns a double. Instead of **apply**, the interface offers an **applyAsDouble** method. An example of **IntToDoubleFunction** interface is given in Listing 19.4. It is a function that converts a temperature on the Celcius scale to Fahrenheit.

Listing 19.4: The IntToDoubleFunctionDemo1 class

```
package app19.function;
import java.util.function.IntToDoubleFunction;

public class IntToDoubleFunctionDemo1 {
    public static void main(String[] args) {
        IntToDoubleFunction celciusToFahrenheit =
                (input) -> 1.8 * input + 32;
        int celcius = 100;
        double fahrenheit =
                celciusToFahrenheit.applyAsDouble(celcius);
        System.out.println(celcius + "\u2103" + " = "
                + fahrenheit + "\u2109\n");
    }
}
```

This is the output of **IntToDoubleFunctionDemo1**.

```
100℃ = 212.0℉
```

Similar to **IntToDoubleFunction** are **LongToDoubleFunction** and **LongToIntFunction**. I am sure you can guess what they do from their names.

The **UnaryOperator** interface is another specialization of **Function** whose operand type is the same as the return type. Its declaration is as follows.

public interfaceUnaryOperator<T> extends Function<T,T>**BinaryOperator** is a specialization of **BiFunction**. **BinaryOperator** represents an operation with two operands of the same type and returns a result that has the same type as the operands.

Predicate

A **Predicate** is a function that takes a parameter and returns **true** or **false** based on the value of the parameter. It has a single abstract method called **test**.

For example, the **PredicateDemo1** class in Listing 19.5 defines a **Predicate** that evaluates a string input and returns true if every character in the string is a number.

Listing 19.5: The PredicateDemo1 class

```java
package app19.function;
import java.util.function.Predicate;

public class PredicateDemo1 {
    public static void main(String[] args) {
        Predicate<String> numbersOnly = (input) -> {
            for (int i = 0; i < input.length(); i++) {
                char c = input.charAt(i);
                if ("0123456789".indexOf(c) == -1) {
                    return false;
                }
            }
            return true;
        };

        System.out.println(numbersOnly.test("12345"));// true
        System.out.println(numbersOnly.test("100a")); // false
    }
}
```

Supplier

A **Supplier** takes no parameter and returns a value. Implementations must override its **get** abstract method and returns an instance of the interface's type parameter.

Listing 19.6 shows an example of **Supplier**. It defines a **Supplier** that returns a one-digit random number and uses a **for** loop to print five random numbers.

Listing 19.6: The SupplierDemo1 class

```java
package app19.function;
import java.util.Random;
import java.util.function.Supplier;

public class SupplierDemo1 {
    public static void main(String[] args) {
        Supplier<Integer> oneDigitRandom = () -> {
            Random random = new Random();
            return random.nextInt(10);
        };
        for (int i = 0; i < 5; i++) {
            System.out.println(
                    oneDigitRandom.get());
        }
    }
}
```

```
}
```

There are also specialized variants of **Supplier**, such as **DoubleSupplier** (returns a **Double**), **IntSupplier** and **LongSupplier**.

Consumer

A **Consumer** is an operation that returns no result. It has one abstract method called **accept**.

Listing 19.7 shows an example of **Consumer** that takes a string and print it center-justified.

Listing 19.7: Consumer example

```java
package app19.function;
import java.util.function.Consumer;
import java.util.function.Function;

public class ConsumerDemo1 {
    public static void main(String[] args) {
        Function<Integer, String> spacer = (count) -> {
            StringBuilder sb = new StringBuilder(count);
            for (int i = 0; i < count; i++) {
                sb.append(" ");
            }
            return sb.toString();
        };

        int lineLength = 60; // characters
        Consumer<String> printCentered =
                (input) -> {
                    int length = input.length();
                    String spaces = spacer.apply(
                            (lineLength - length) / 2);
                    System.out.println(spaces + input);
                };

        printCentered.accept("A lambda expression a day");
        printCentered.accept("makes you");
        printCentered.accept("look smarter");
    }
}
```

The example in Listing 19.7 features a **Consumer** that takes a **String** and prints it after prefixing it with a certain number of spaces. The maximum number of characters in each line is 60 and the spaces are obtained by calling a **Function** named spacer. The implementation of the Consumer's **accept** method is given by this Lambda expression.

```java
            (input) -> {
                int length = input.length();
                String spaces = spacer.apply(
                        (lineLength - length) / 2);
                System.out.println(spaces + input);
```

```
        }
```

The function **spacer** returns the specified number of spaces and is defined as

```
Function<Integer, String> spacer = (count) -> {
    StringBuilder sb = new StringBuilder(count);
    for (int i = 0; i < count; i++) {
        sb.append(" ");
    }
    return sb.toString();
};
```

The function employs a **for** loop that appends a space to a **StringBuilder** *count* number of times, where *count* is the parameter to the function. When the loop exits, it returns the **String** representation of the **StringBuilder**.

If you run the **ConsumerDemo1** class, you will see this on your console.

```
A lambda expression a day
        makes you
      look smarter
```

Method References

A lot of Java methods take a functional interface as an argument. For instance, one of the **sort** methods in **java.util.Arrays** accepts an instance of **Comparator**, which is a functional interface. The signature of the **sort** method is as follows.

```
public static T[] sort(T[] array, Comparator<? super T> comparator)
```

Instead of passing an implementation of **Comparator** to the **sort** method, you can pass a lambda expression. You have seen how to do this in the previous sections.

Now, you can go one step further by passing a method reference in lieu of a lambda expression. A method reference is simply a class name or an object reference followed by the double colon operator (::) and a method name.

Why would you want to use a method reference? There are two reasons for this.

1. A method reference has shorter syntax than a lambda expression because a method reference does not contain a definition like a lambda expression. The method body is defined somewhere else.
2. You can use an existing method, thus promoting code reuse.

You can use a reference to a static method, an instance method or even a constructor. You use the double colon (::), a new operator in Java 8, to separate the class name/object reference and the method/constructor name. The class that encapsulates the referenced method does not have to implement the functional interface.

The syntax for method references is one of the following.

ClassName::*staticMethodName*

ContainingType::*instanceMethod*

objectReference::*methodName*

ClassName::new

Each of the kinds of method references are discussed in the following subsections.

Reference to A Static Method

A reference to a static method can be passed as an argument to a method that expects a functional interface if the method has a compatible return type and compatible argument types with the functional interface's abstract method.

As the first example in this topic, consider the **NoMethodRef** class in Listing 19.8, which illustrates the use of a functional interface without method references. The class defines a functional interface called **StringListFormatter** that takes a **List** of **String**s and formats the strings. The **format** method, the abstract method of the interface, takes a **delimiter** and a **List** of **String**s. There is also a **formatAndPrint** static method that takes an instance of **StringListFormatter**, a delimiter and a **List** of **String**s. This method in turn calls the **format** method on the **StringListFormatter** and prints the formatted list.

Listing 19.8: The NoMethodRef class

```
package app19.methodref;
import java.util.Arrays;
import java.util.List;

public class NoMethodRef {

    @FunctionalInterface
    interface StringListFormatter {
        String format(String delimiter, List<String> list);
    }

    public static void formatAndPrint(StringListFormatter formatter,
            String delimiter, List<String> list) {
        String formatted = formatter.format(delimiter, list);
        System.out.println(formatted);
    }

    public static void main(String[] args) {
        List<String> names = Arrays.asList("Don", "King", "Kong");

        StringListFormatter formatter =
                (delimiter, list) -> {
                    StringBuilder sb = new StringBuilder(100);
                    int size = list.size();
                    for (int i = 0; i < size; i++) {
                        sb.append(list.get(i));
                        if (i < size - 1) {
                            sb.append(delimiter);
                        }
                    }
                    return sb.toString();
                };
```

```
        formatAndPrint(formatter, ", ", names);
    }
}
```

The **main** method in **NoMethodRef** constructs a string list with three elements and creates an implementation of **StringListFormatter** with this lambda expression.

```
StringListFormatter formatter =
        (delimiter, list) -> {
            StringBuilder sb = new StringBuilder(100);
            int size = list.size();
            for (int i = 0; i < size; i++) {
                sb.append(list.get(i));
                if (i < size - 1) {
                    sb.append(delimiter);
                }
            }
            return sb.toString();
        };
```

Basically, it iterates over the **List** and adds a delimiter between two elements. No delimiter is appended after the last element.

The **main** method then calls the **formatAndPrint** method passing the lambda expression , a delimiter and the string list. If you run **NoMethodRef**, you will see the formatted list:

```
Don, King, Kong
```

After spending twenty minutes writing the code, you realized that the lambda expression does the same job as the **join** method of the **String** class. This is a static method added to **String** in JDK 1.8. One of its overrides has the following signature.

```
public static String join(CharSequence delimiter,
        Iterable<? extends CharSequence> elements)
```

Compare it with the **format** method in the functional interface in Listing 19.8.

```
public String format(java.langString delimiter,
        java.util.List<String> list);
```

Since **List** extends **Iterable** and **String** implements **CharSequence**, **join** is compatible with **format**.

A method reference allows you to reuse an existing implementation such as **String.join()**. As such, you can rewrite the **NoMethodRef** class to use a reference to **String.join()**. This is illustrated in the **MethodReferenceDemo1** class in Listing 19.9.

Listing 19.9: The MethodReferenceDemo1 class

```
package app19.methodref;
import java.util.Arrays;
import java.util.List;

public class MethodReferenceDemo1 {
```

```
@FunctionalInterface
interface StringListFormatter {
    String format(String delimiter, List<String> list);
}

public static void formatAndPrint(StringListFormatter formatter,
        String delimiter, List<String> list) {
    String formatted = formatter.format(delimiter, list);
    System.out.println(formatted);
}

public static void main(String[] args) {
    List<String> names = Arrays.asList("Don", "King", "Kong");
    formatAndPrint(String::join, ", ", names);
}
}
```

You still have the same **StringListFormatter** interface and the same **formatAndPrint**
method. However, the **main** method no longer contains a lambda expression
implementing **StringListFormatter**. Instead, you use **String.join** as an implementation
of **StringListFormatter**.

```
formatAndPrint(String::join, ", ", names);
```

As a side note, you notice that the abstract method in **StringListFormatter** takes two
parameters and returns a value. This is a good candidate for a **BiFunction**. The
WithBiFunction class in Listing 19.10 is a rewrite of the **MethodReferenceDemo1** class
that eliminates the **StringListFormatter** interface entirely. The **formatAndPrint** method
has also been modified to accept a **BiFunction** as its first parameter.

Listing 19.10: The WithBiFunction class

```
package app19.methodref;
import java.util.Arrays;
import java.util.List;
import java.util.function.BiFunction;

public class WithBiFunction {

    public static void formatAndPrint(
            BiFunction<String, List<String>, String> formatter,
            String delimiter, List<String> list) {
        String formatted = formatter.apply(delimiter, list);
        System.out.println(formatted);
    }

    public static void main(String[] args) {
        List<String> names = Arrays.asList("Don", "King", "Kong");
        formatAndPrint(String::join, ", ", names);
    }
}
```

Reference to An Instance Method where An Object Reference Is Available

The compatibility rule for this kind of method reference is the same as the method reference to a static method. The referenced method must have a compatible return value and compatible arguments as the abstract method of the functional interface the method replaces.

For example, in JDK 1.8 the **java.lang.Iterable** interface has a default method named **forEach** that accepts a **Consumer**:

```
default void forEach(java.util.function.Consumer<? super T> action)
```

forEach performs the given action for each element of the **Iterable**. Thanks to inheritance, this method is inherited by its subinterface **List**, which I will use in the example in Listing 19.11.

Listing 19.11: Referencing an instance method in an object

```
package app19.methodref;
import java.util.Arrays;
import java.util.List;

public class MethodReferenceDemo2 {
    public static void main(String[] args) {
        List<String> fruits = Arrays.asList("Apple", "Banana");
        // with lambda expression
        fruits.forEach((name) -> System.out.println(name));

        // with method reference
        fruits.forEach(System.out::println);
    }
}
```

The **MethodReferencDemo2** class has a list of fruits that needs to be printed. You can do this by calling the **forEach** method, passing a **Consumer** in the form of a lambda expression like so:

```
fruits.forEach((name) -> System.out.println(name));
```

Alternatively, since **System.out** is an existing object that the system has created for you, you can use a method reference to the **println** method on **System.out**.

```
fruits.forEach(System.out::println);
```

Reference to An Instance Method where No Object Reference Is Available

Hold on tight. This one is a bit tricky and requires your full concentration.

You can pass a reference to an instance method as a method argument to replace a functional interface. In this case, you do not have to explicitly create an instance of the containing class. The syntax for this kind of method reference is different from that of the first and second kinds of method references. With the first two kinds, the number of arguments must be the same as the number of arguments expected by the functional interface's abstract method. When using an instance method without an object reference, the referenced method must have one fewer argument than the number of arguments expected by the functional interface's abstract method. Therefore, if the functional interface's abstract method takes four arguments, the referenced instance method must take only three arguments, which must be compatible with the second, third and fourth arguments of the abstract method. In addition, the first argument of the abstract method must be of a type that is compatible as the class containing the instance method.

The compatibility rule for this kind of method reference is depicted below. The first line is a pseudo-signature of the functional interface's abstract method and the second line a pseudo-signature of the referenced instance method.

```
returnType abstractMethod(type-1, type-2, type-3, type-4)

returnType instanceMethod(type-2, type-3, type-4)
```

Here, *type-1* must be compatible with the class containing the instance method because the class will be instantiated and the instance passed as the first argument to the abstract method, along with the other arguments.

This will become clear after you have seen the example for this kind of method reference.

Listing 19.12: The MethodReferenceDemo3 class
```
package app19.methodref;
import java.util.Arrays;

public class MethodReferenceDemo3 {

    public static void main(String[] args) {
        String[] names = {"Alexis", "anna", "Kyleen"};

        Arrays.sort(names, String::compareToIgnoreCase);
        for (String name : names) {
            System.out.println(name);
        }
    }
}
```

The example in Listing 19.12 shows how to pass an instance method reference to **Arrays.sort** in lieu of a **Comparator**. The **MethodReferenceDemo3** class contains a string array with three names where case-sensitivity is not strictly adhered to. If you use an override of **Arrays.sort** that only takes one argument to sort this array, the names will be sorted as

```
Alexis, Kyleen, anna
```

This is not really what you really want. So, you need to use **Arrays.sort** that also takes a **Comparator**:

```
public static <T> void sort(T[] array, Comparator<? super T> c)
```

The example shows how you can use an instance method reference **String.compareIgnoreCase** to replace a **Comparator** (Recall that **Comparator** is a functional interface). Here is the signature of **String.compareToIgnoreCase**.

```
public int compareToIgnoreCase(String str)
```

It has one less argument than the signature of **Comparator.compare**.

```
int compare(String str1, String str2)
```

This is perfect for the second kind of method reference.

If you run the code, you will see that the names are sorted correctly. Here is the result.

```
Alexis
anna
Kyleen
```

Reference to A Constructor

The fourth kind of method reference uses a constructor. The syntax for a constructor reference is as follows.

```
ClassName::new
```

Suppose you need a method to convert an Integer array to a **Collection** and you need to be able to determine whether the resulting collection is a **List** or a **Set**. To this end, you can create the **arrayToCollection** method in Listing 19.13.

Listing 19.13: The MethodReferenceDemo4 class

```java
package app19.methodref;
import java.util.ArrayList;
import java.util.Collection;
import java.util.HashSet;
import java.util.function.Supplier;

public class MethodReferenceDemo4 {

    public static Collection<Integer> arrayToCollection(
            Supplier<Collection<Integer>> supplier, Integer[]
                numbers) {
        Collection<Integer> collection = supplier.get();
        for (int i : numbers) {
            collection.add(i);
        }
        return collection;
    }

    public static void main(String[] args) {
        Integer[] array = {1, 8, 5};
        Collection<Integer> col1
                = arrayToCollection(ArrayList<Integer>::new, array);
        System.out.println("Natural order");
        col1.forEach(System.out::println);
        System.out.println("========================");
        System.out.println("Ascending order");
        Collection<Integer> col2
                = arrayToCollection(HashSet<Integer>::new, array);
```

```
        col2.forEach(System.out::println);
    }
}
```

Instead of passing this lambda expression as the first argument to the method.

```
() -> new ArrayList<Integer>()
```

You can simply pass this reference to the **ArrayList** constructor.

```
ArrayList<Integer>::new
```

And, instead of this

```
() -> new HashSet<Integer>()
```

You can write

```
HashSet<Integer>::new
```

If you run the example, you will see this on the console.

```
Natural order
1
8
5
========================
Ascending order
1
5
8
```

More examples of constructor references can be found in Chapter 19, "Working with Streams."

Optional and Similar Classes

Java 8 adds the **Optional**, **OptionalInt**, **OptionalLong** and **OptionalDouble** classes to deal with **NullPointerException**s. Part of the **java.util** package, these classes are excellent examples of classes that heavily use lambda expressions and method references.

These four classes are similar and **Optional** is the most important of them as it can be used with any type whereas the other classes are only suitable for integers, longs or doubles. Consequently, **Optional** is the main focus of this section.

Optional is a container for a value that can potentially be null. As you should know by now, trying to call a method or a field on a null reference variable throws a **NullPointerException**. Handling null is not hard, but it can be tedious. Consider the code in Listing 19.14 that shows a Company class that can have an Office, which in turn can have an Address. To make things simple, here an Address only contains two fields, **street** and **city**. All these properties can be null. A **Company** may not have an **Office** and an **Address** may not have full data about the street and city.

Listing 19.14: Tedious way of checking for nullity

```
package app19.optional1;

class Company {
    private String name;
    private Office office;
    public Company(String name, Office office) {
        this.name = name;
        this.office = office;
    }

    public String getName() {
        return name;
    }

    public Office getOffice() {
        return office;
    }
}

class Office {
    private String id;
    private Address address;

    public Office(String id, Address address) {
        this.id = id;
        this.address = address;
    }

    public String getId() {
        return id;
    }

    public Address getAddress() {
        return address;
    }
}

class Address {
    private String street;
    private String city;

    public Address(String street, String city) {
        this.street = street;
        this.city = city;
    }

    public String getStreet() {
        return street;
    }

    public String getCity() {
```

```
        return city;
    }
}

public class OptionalDemo1 {

    public static void main(String[] args) {
        Address address1 = new Address(null, "New York");
        Office office1 = new Office("OF1", address1);
        Company company1 = new Company("Door Never Closed",
            office1);

        // What is the street address of company1?
        // In which city company1 is located?
        String streetAddress = null;
        String city = null;
        if (company1 != null) {
            Office office = company1.getOffice();
            if (office != null) {
                Address address = office.getAddress();
                if (address != null) {
                    streetAddress = address.getStreet();
                    city = address.getCity();
                }
            }
        }
        System.out.println("Street Name:" + streetAddress);
        System.out.println("City:" + city);
    }
}
```

The **OptionalDemo1** class in Listing 19.14 creates a **Company** for testing and tries to get the street address of the company. Realizing that any of the fields can be null, the programmer made a conscious attempt to test each single instance for nullity before calling a method on it, resulting in this code:

```
if (company1 != null) {
    Office office = company1.getOffice();

    if (office != null) {
        Address address = office.getAddress();
        if (address != null) {
            streetAddress = address.getStreet();
            city = address.getCity();
        }
    }
}
```

This is kind of tedious and readability suffers.

The **Optional** class can help. If you decide to use it, you wrap every field that can potentially be null in an **Optional**. For example, the **office** field in **Company** should now be:

```
private Optional<Office> office;
```

And the city field in Address should be

```
private Optional<String> city;
```

Before you learn how to rewrite the example in Listing 19.14 using **Optional**, look at the methods of **Optional** in Table 19.2.

Method	Description
empty	Returns an empty Optional
filter	If a value is present and matches the given predicate, return an **Optional** describing the value. Otherwise, returns an empty **Optional**.
flatMap	If a value is preset, apply the specified mapping function on the value and return and **Optional** describing the mapping result. If a value is not present, return an empty **Optional**.
get	If a value is present, returns the value. Otherwise, throw a **NoSuchElementException**.
ifPresent	If a value is present, invoked the given Consumer with the value.
isPresent	Returns true if a value is present. Otherwise, returns false.
map	If a value is present, apply the given mapping function to it. If the result is not null, return an **Optional** describing the result.
of	Returns an **Optional** describing the given non-null value.
ofNullable	If the given value is non-null, returns an **Optional** describing the value. If the value is null, returns an empty **Optional**.
orElse	If a value is present, returns the value. Otherwise, returns the specified value.

Table 19.2: More important methods of Optional

The methods are easy to use. To wrap a value in an **Optional**, call its static **of** or **ofNullable** method. You use **of** if you are certain the value you are wrapping is not null. If the value is potentially null, use **ofNullable** instead. Alternatively, the **empty** method is also static and returns an empty **Optional**, i.e. an **Optional** without a value.

The rest of the methods are for handling an **Optional**. If you simply want to retrieve the value in an **Optional**, you would first check if a value is present. You can do this by using **isPresent** followed by **get**:

```
if (optional.isPresent()) {
    value = optional.get();
}
```

However, this is similar to checking for nullity when not using **Optional**. There are better ways, though.

The **ifPresent** method accepts a **Consumer** that will be called if a value is present. So if you simply want to print the value, you can do this.

```
optional.ifPresent(System.out::println);
```

If no value is present, nothing will happen. So this is getting better, isn't it?

However, wait until you get to use **flatMap**. This method applies a mapping function and returns an **Optional** describing the value. Better still, it can be cascaded, like this to replace the series of null check in Listing 19.14:

```
company1.flatMap(Company::getOffice)
        .flatMap(Office::getAddress)
        .flatMap(Address::getCity)
        .ifPresent(System.out::println);
```

Now look at Listing 19.15 that contains a rewrite of the code in Listing 19.14. All fields that can potentially be null have been wrapped in **Optional**s.

Listing 19.15: Using Optional

```java
package app19.optional2;
import java.util.Optional;

class Company {
    private String name;
    private Optional<Office> office;

    public Company(String name, Optional<Office> office) {
        this.name = name;
        this.office = office;
    }

    public String getName() {
        return name;
    }

    public Optional<Office> getOffice() {
        return office;
    }
}

class Office {
    private String id;
    private Optional<Address> address;

    public Office(String id, Optional<Address> address) {
        this.id = id;
        this.address = address;
    }

    public String getId() {
        return id;
    }

    public Optional<Address> getAddress() {
        return address;
    }
}

class Address {
    private Optional<String> street;
    private Optional<String> city;
```

```java
    public Address(Optional<String> street, Optional<String> city) {
        this.street = street;
        this.city = city;
    }

    public Optional<String> getStreet() {
        return street;
    }

    public Optional<String> getCity() {
        return city;
    }
}

public class OptionalDemo2 {
    public static void main(String[] args) {
        Optional<Address> address1 = Optional.of(
                new Address(Optional.ofNullable(null),
                        Optional.of("New York")));
        Optional<Office> office1 = Optional.of(
                new Office("OF1", address1));

        Optional<Company> company1 = Optional.of(
                new Company("Door Never Closed", office1));

        // What is the street address of company1?
        // In which city company1 is located?
        Optional<Office> maybeOffice =
                company1.flatMap(Company::getOffice);
        Optional<Address> maybeAddress =
                maybeOffice.flatMap(Office::getAddress);
        Optional<String> maybeStreet =
                maybeAddress.flatMap(Address::getStreet);
        maybeStreet.ifPresent(System.out::println);
        if (maybeStreet.isPresent()) {
            System.out.println(maybeStreet.get());
        } else {
            System.out.println("Street not found");
        }

        // shorter way
        String city = company1.flatMap(Company::getOffice)
            .flatMap(Office::getAddress)
            .flatMap(Address::getCity)
            .orElse("City not found");
        System.out.println("City: " + city);

        // only print if city is not null
        company1.flatMap(Company::getOffice)
                .flatMap(Office::getAddress)
                .flatMap(Address::getCity)
                .ifPresent(System.out::println);
    }
```

}

The **OptionalDemo2** class shows how to get the street and city of a company, first by assigning the return value of each **flatMap** invocation to a variable and then by cascading it.

The **OptionalInt**, **OptionalLong** and **OptionalDouble** classes have a subset of the methods offered by **Optional**. For example, they have these methods: **empty**, **ifPresent**, **isPresent**, and **of**. of takes a primitive and since a primitive cannot be null, there is no **ofNullable** method. There is no get method either. Instead, **OptionalInt** has a **getAsInt** method, **OptionalLong** a **getAsLong** method and **OptionalDouble** a **getAsDouble** method. There are no **filter**, **flatMap** and **map** methods either.

Summary

A new feature in Java 8, lambda expressions can make certain constructs shorter and more readable, especially when you are dealing with inner classes. This chapter discussed lambda expressions, functional interfaces, the pre-defined functional interfaces and method references. The last section of this chapter explained how to deal with null pointer exceptions using **Optional**.

Quiz

1. Why add lambda expressions to Java?
2. What are lambda expressions also known as?
3. What is a function interface?
4. What is a method reference?
5. What is the operator used in the method reference?
6. What are the four classes in java.util for handling null pointer exceptions?

Chapter 20
Working with Streams

In this chapter you will learn about the Stream API, a new feature of JDK 8. To understand the topics in this chapter, you need to know how to use Lambda expressions and the predefined functional interfaces in **java.util.function**, both discussed in Chapter 19, "Lambda Expressions."

Overview

A stream is like a pipe, but instead of transporting water or oil, a stream transfers data from a source to a destination. Depending on the mode of transfer, a stream can be either sequential or parallel. A parallel stream is especially useful if the computer the program is running on has a multicore CPU.

At first glance, a stream may look like a collection. However, a stream is not a data structure for storing objects, it only moves them. As such, you cannot add an element to a stream as you would to a collection.

The main reason for using a stream is for its supports for sequential and parallel aggregate operations. For example, you can easily filter, sort or map the elements in a stream.

The Stream API consists of the types in the **java.util.stream** package. The **Stream** interface is the most frequently used stream type. A **Stream** can be used to transfer any type of objects. There are also specializations of **Stream**: **IntStream**, **LongStream** and **DoubleStream**. All the four stream types are derived from **BaseStream**.

Table 20.1 shows some of the methods defined in the **Stream** interface.

Some of the **Stream** methods perform intermediate operations and some perform terminal operations. An intermediate operation transforms a stream into another stream. Methods such as **filter**, **map** and **sorted** are examples of methods that perform intermediate operations. A terminal operation produces a result or side-effect. Methods such as **count** and **forEach** perform terminal operations.

It is worth noting that streams are lazy. Computation on the source is only performed when a terminal operation is started.

Stream's methods will be explained in detail in the sections to come.

Method	Description
concat	Lazily concatenates or links together two streams. It returns a new stream whose elements are all the elements of the first stream followed by all the elements of the second stream.
count	Returns the number of elements of the stream.
empty	Creates and returns an empty stream.
filter	Returns a new stream whose elements are all the elements of this stream that match the given predicate.
forEach	Performs an action on each element of the stream.
limit	Returns a new stream having the specified maximum number of elements from the current stream.
map	Returns a stream consisting of the results of applying the given function to the elements of this stream.
max	Returns the maximum element of this stream according to the given comparator.
min	Returns the minimum element of this stream according to the given comparator.
of	Returns a stream whose source is the given values.
reduce	Performs a reduction on this stream's elements using an identity and an accumulator.
sorted	Returns a new stream containing the elements of this stream in natural order
toArray	Returns an array containing the elements of this stream.

Table 20.1: More important methods of Stream

Creating and Obtaining a Stream

You can use the **of** static method in **Stream** to create a sequential stream. For example, the following code snippet creates a **Stream** of **Integer**s with three elements.

```
Stream<Integer> stream = Stream.of(100, 200, 300);
```

Or, you can pass an array to the **of** method:

```
String[] names = {"Bart", "Lisa", "Maggie"};
Stream<String> stream = Stream.of(names);
```

The **java.util.Arrays** utility class now has a **stream** method for converting an array to a sequential stream. For instance, you can rewrite the code above using **Arrays** to create a **Stream** from an array.

```
String[] names = {"Bart", "Lisa", "Maggie"};
Stream<String> stream = Arrays.stream(names);
```

In addition, the **java.util.Collection** interface also has default methods named **stream** and **parallelStream** that return a sequential or a parallel stream, respectively, with the collection as its source. Their signatures are as follows.

```
default java.util.stream.Stream<E> stream()

default java.util.stream.Stream<E> parallelStream()
```

Thanks to these methods in **Collection**, getting a **Stream** from a **List** or a **Set** is a breeze.

On top of that, the **java.nio.file.Files** class offers two methods that return a **Stream<Path>**, **list** and **walk**. **list** returns a **Stream** of **Path**s that point to the entries in the given path. On the other hand, **walk** walks through the entries in the given path and return them as a stream.

Files also contains a **lines** method that returns all lines in a text file as a **Stream<String>**.

For example, the **ObtainStreamDemo** class in Listing 20.1 shows how to obtain a stream from the **Files** class.

Listing 20.1: The ObtainStreamDemo class

```
package app20;
import java.io.IOException;
import java.nio.file.Files;
import java.nio.file.Path;
import java.nio.file.Paths;
import java.util.stream.Stream;

public class ObtainStreamDemo {

    public static void main(String[] args) {
        Path path = Paths.get(".");
        try {
            Stream<Path> list = Files.list(path);
            list.forEach(System.out::println);
        } catch (IOException ex) {
            ex.printStackTrace();
        }
    }
}
```

The code in Listing 20.1 constructs a **Path** that references the current directory (i.e. the directory from which the Java program was run) and passes it to **Files.list**. The method returns a **Stream** of **Path**s. The code then calls the **forEach** method on the **Stream** passing a **Consumer** that prints each entry. If you run the code, you will see all entries in the current path printed on the console.

Concatenating Streams

The **Stream** interface provides a **concat** method for lazily concatenating or linking two streams together. This method returns a new stream whose elements are all the elements of the first stream followed by all the elements of the second stream.

The code in Listing 20.2 shows how to concatenate two **Stream**s of **String**s and sort them.

Listing 20.2: Joining streams

```
package app20;
import java.util.stream.Stream;

public class StreamConcatDemo {
    public static void main(String[] args) {
        Stream<String> stream1 =
                Stream.of("January", "Christie");
        Stream<String> stream2 =
                Stream.of("Okanagan", "Sydney", "Alpha");
        Stream.concat(stream1, stream2).sorted().
                forEach(System.out::println);
    }
}
```

If you run the **StreamConcatDemo** class in Listing 20.2, you will see the following printed on the console.

```
Alpha
Christie
January
Okanagan
Sydney
```

Filtering

When you filter a stream you select the elements of the stream based on certain criteria and return a new **Stream** for the selected elements. You filter a stream by calling the **filter** method on a **Stream** object, passing a **Predicate**. The **Predicate** determines whether or not an element will be included in the new stream.

Here is the signature of the **filter** method.

```
Stream<T> filter(java.util.function.Predicate<? super T> predicate)
```

As an example, the code in Listing 20.3 reads the **example.txt** file in Listing 20.4 and let pass only lines that are not empty and not a comment. A comment line starts with a hash (#) after removing all trailing spaces.

Listing 20.3: The StreamFilterDemo1 class

```
package app20;
import java.io.BufferedReader;
import java.io.FileReader;
import java.io.IOException;
import java.util.function.Predicate;
import java.util.stream.Stream;

public class StreamFilterDemo1 {
    public static void main(String[] args) {
        Predicate<String> notCommentOrEmptyLine
                = (line) -> line.trim().length() > 0
```

```
                 && !line.trim().startsWith("#");
        try (FileReader fr = new FileReader("example.txt");
             BufferedReader br = new BufferedReader(fr)) {
            Stream<String> lines = br.lines();
            lines.filter(notCommentOrEmptyLine)
                    .forEach(System.out::println);
        } catch (IOException e) {
            e.printStackTrace();
        }
    }
}
```

Listing 20.4: The example.txt file

```
# Set path so it includes user's private bin if it exists
if [ -d "$HOME/bin" ] ; then
    PATH="$HOME/bin:$PATH"

fi
```

If you run the class in Listing 20.3, you will see these lines on the console. It prints three of five lines in the text file.

```
if [ -d "$HOME/bin" ] ; then
    PATH="$HOME/bin:$PATH"
fi
```

As a second example, the class in Listing 20.5 shows how you can use a stream to do a file search on your computer. To be more precise, the code displays all java files located in a given directory and any of its subdirectories.

Listing 20.5: The StreamFilterDemo2 class

```
package app20;
import java.io.IOException;
import java.nio.file.Files;
import java.nio.file.Path;
import java.nio.file.Paths;
import java.util.stream.Stream;

public class StreamFilterDemo2 {
    public static void main(String[] args) {
        // find all java files in the parent directory and
        // all its subdirectories
        Path parent = Paths.get("..");
        try {
            Stream<Path> list = Files.walk(parent);
            list.filter((Path p) -> p.toString().endsWith(".java"))
                    .forEach(System.out::println);
        } catch (IOException ex) {
            ex.printStackTrace();
        }
    }
}
```

The **StreamFilterDemo2** class starts by constructing a **Path** that points to the parent of the current directory. It then passes the **Path** to **Files.walk** to obtain a **Stream** of **Path**s and assign the result to a local variable named **list**. Next, it filters the stream with a **Predicate** that will include all **Path**s whose name ends with **.java** and calls the **forEach** method to print the path.

Mapping

The **Stream** interface's **map** method maps each element of a stream with the result of passing the element to a function. Here is the signature of **map**.

```
<R> Stream<R> map(java.util.function.Function<? super T,
        ? extends R> mapper)
```

As you can see from the signature, the **map** method returns a new **Stream** of elements whose type may be different from the type of the elements of the current stream.

Consider the code in Listing 20.6 that shows a more useful and realistic example of a **Stream** to calculate the average age of all employees in a company. It does this in two steps. First, it calls the **map** method to convert a **Stream** of **Employee** objects to a **Stream** of **Period** objects. Each **Period** element of the new stream contains the period between today and each employee's birthday. In other words, each **Period** element contains the age of an employee. In the second step, the code calls the **mapToLong** method to calculate the average age of all the employees.

Listing 20.6: The StreamMapDemo class

```
package app20;
import java.time.LocalDate;
import java.time.Month;
import java.time.Period;
import java.util.stream.Stream;

public class StreamMapDemo {
    class Employee {
        public String name;
        public LocalDate birthday;
        public Employee(String name, LocalDate birthday) {
            this.name = name;
            this.birthday = birthday;
        }
    }

    public Employee[] getEmployees() {
        Employee[] employees = {
            new Employee("Will Biteman",
                    LocalDate.of(1984, Month.JANUARY, 1)),
            new Employee("Sue Everyman",
                    LocalDate.of(1980, Month.DECEMBER, 25)),
            new Employee("Ann Wangi",
                    LocalDate.of(1976, Month.JULY, 4)),
            new Employee("Wong Kaching",
                    LocalDate.of(1980, Month.SEPTEMBER, 1))
```

```
        };
        return employees;
    }

    public double calculateAverageAge(Employee[] employees) {
        LocalDate today = LocalDate.now();
        Stream<Employee> stream = Stream.of(employees);
        Stream<Period> periods = stream.map(
                (employee)-> Period.between(
                        employee.birthday, today));
        double avgAge = periods.mapToLong(
                (period)->period.toTotalMonths())
                .average().getAsDouble() / 12;
        return avgAge;
    }


    public static void main(String[] args) {
        StreamMapDemo demo = new StreamMapDemo();
        Employee[] employees = demo.getEmployees();
        double avgAge = demo.calculateAverageAge(employees);
        System.out.printf("Average employee age : %2.2f\n",
                avgAge);
    }
}
```

If you run the **StreamMapDemo** class, you will see the average age of the employees. Of course, the result will depend on when you run the program. When I ran it on my computer at the time of writing this book, I got the following result.

```
Average employee age : 34.13
```

Reduction

One of the more useful methods in **Stream** is **reduce**, which can perform reduction operations. There are two overloads of this method:

```
java.util.Optional<T> reduce(java.util.function.BinaryOperator<T>
        accumulator)

T reduce(T identity,
        java.util.function.BinaryOperator<T> accumulator)
```

Looking at the two signatures, you probably notice that the **reduce** method reduces a **Stream** of type T to a single instance of type T, with the help of the specified **BinaryOperator**. Even though the description in the Java documentation is not that intuitive, in reality this method is not that hard to understand.

Figure 20.1 shows what happens behind the scene when a sequential stream of four elements is being reduced.

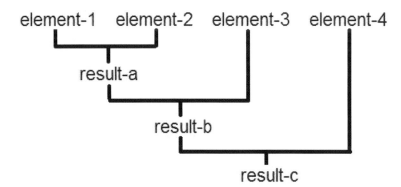

Figure 20.1: Reducing a stream

First, *element-1* and *element-2* are used as operands to the specified binary operator. The result of this operation is an object of the same type as the elements, which I call *result-a*. Next, *result-a* and *element-3* are passed to the binary operator, resulting *result-b*, which again has the same type as the elements. Finally, *result-b* and *element-4* are passed to the binary operator, returning *result-c*. Since there is no more element in the stream, *result-c* is returned as the result of the reduction.

For a parallel stream, operations can be done in parallel. This means, the operation on *element-1* and *element-2* may take place at the same time as the operation on *element-3* and *element-4*, and then the results of the first operation and the second operation are passed to the binary operator and its result returned.

Okay. Let's now look at an example.

The **StreamReductionDemo1** class in Listing 20.7 shows a **Stream** of four **Order** objects that is reduced to a single **Order** object, which is the **Order** placed most recently and having the largest value.

Listing 20.7: StreamReductionDemo1 class

```
package app20;
import java.time.LocalDate;
import java.time.Month;
import java.util.Optional;
import java.util.stream.Stream;

public class StreamReductionDemo1 {
    class Order {
        public int orderId;
        public double value;
        public LocalDate orderDate;
        public Order(int orderId, double value,
                LocalDate orderDate) {
            this.orderId = orderId;
            this.value = value;
            this.orderDate = orderDate;
        }
    }

    public Order[] getOrders() {
```

```
        Order[] orders = {
            new Order(1, 100.49,
                    LocalDate.of(2014, Month.DECEMBER, 11)),
            new Order(1, 88.09,
                    LocalDate.of(2014, Month.DECEMBER, 29)),
            new Order(1, 10.29,
                    LocalDate.of(2014, Month.DECEMBER, 30)),
            new Order(1, 100.49,
                    LocalDate.of(2014, Month.NOVEMBER, 22))
        };
        return orders;
    }

    public Optional<Order> getLatestLargestOrder(Order[] orders) {
        Stream<Order> stream = Stream.of(orders);
        Optional<Order> theOrder = stream.reduce((a, b) -> {
                if (a.value > b.value) {
                    return a;
                } else if (a.value < b.value) {
                    return b;
                } else {
                    if (a.orderDate.isAfter(b.orderDate)) {
                        return a;
                    } else {
                        return b;
                    }
                }
            });
        return theOrder;
    }

    public static void main(String[] args) {
        StreamReductionDemo1 demo = new StreamReductionDemo1();
        Order[] orders = demo.getOrders();
        Optional<Order> latestLargest = demo.getLatestLargestOrder(
                orders);
        if (latestLargest.isPresent()) {
            Order order = latestLargest.get();
            System.out.printf("Latest largest order value: $%2.2f,",
                    order.value);
            System.out.println(" date : " + order.orderDate);
        } else {
            System.out.println("No order found");
        }

    }
}
```

First, look at the **Order** class. The **Order** class models an order and has three fields, **orderId**, **value** and **orderDate**. The method **main** instantiates the **StreamReductionDemo1** class and calls its **getOrders** method, which returns an **Order** array containing four orders. **main** then calls the **getLatestLargestOrder** method, passing the **Order** array.

The **getLatestLargestOrder** method is of interest here. It first creates a **Stream<Order>** using **Stream**'s **of** static method.

```
Stream<Order> stream = Stream.of(orders);
```

It then calls the **reduce** method on the **Stream** passing a binary operator.

```
Optional<Order> theOrder = stream.reduce((a, b) -> {
        if (a.value > b.value) {
            return a;
        } else if (a.value < b.value) {
            return b;
        } else {
            if (a.orderDate.isAfter(b.orderDate)) {
                return a;
            } else {
                return b;
            }
        }
});
```

The binary operator compares the values of the two **Order** operands and returns the one with the larger value. If both values are equal, the order with the latest order date is returned.

main then checks if the returned **Optional** has an **Order**. If so, the **Order** is unwrapped and its value and date are printed. If not, an error message will be displayed.

If you run the class you will see this on the console.

```
Latest largest order value: $100.49, date : 2014-12-11
```

If the stream is empty, the **reduce** method will not throw an exception. It simply returns an empty **Optional**.

As a second example, consider the code in Listing 20.8. The demo class uses a **Stream** to calculate the total order value in a given month.

Listing 20.8: StreamReductionDemo2 class

```
package app20;
import java.time.LocalDate;
import java.time.Month;
import java.time.YearMonth;
import java.util.function.Predicate;
import java.util.stream.Stream;

public class StreamReductionDemo2 {
    class Order {
        public int orderId;
        public double value;
        public LocalDate orderDate;
        public Order(int orderId, double value,
                LocalDate orderDate) {
            this.orderId = orderId;
            this.value = value;
            this.orderDate = orderDate;
```

```
        }
    }

    public Order[] getOrders() {
        Order[] orders = {
            new Order(1, 100.49,
                    LocalDate.of(2014, Month.DECEMBER, 11)),
            new Order(1, 88.09,
                    LocalDate.of(2014, Month.DECEMBER, 29)),
            new Order(1, 10.29,
                    LocalDate.of(2014, Month.DECEMBER, 30)),
            new Order(1, 100.49,
                    LocalDate.of(2014, Month.NOVEMBER, 22))
        };
        return orders;
    }

    public double calculateSalesTotal(Order[] orders,
            YearMonth yearMonth) {
        Predicate<Order> orderInGivenMonth
                = (order) -> order.orderDate.getMonth()
                        == yearMonth.getMonth()
                && order.orderDate.getYear()
                        == yearMonth.getYear();

        Stream<Order> stream = Stream.of(orders);
        return stream.filter(orderInGivenMonth)
                .mapToDouble((order) -> order.value)
                .reduce(0, (a, b) -> a+b);
    }


    public static void main(String[] args) {
        StreamReductionDemo2 demo = new StreamReductionDemo2();
        Order[] orders = demo.getOrders();
        double totalSalesForMonth = demo.calculateSalesTotal(
                orders, YearMonth.of(2014, Month.NOVEMBER));
        System.out.printf("Sales for Nov 2014 : $%2.2f\n",
                totalSalesForMonth);

        totalSalesForMonth = demo.calculateSalesTotal(
                orders, YearMonth.of(2014, Month.DECEMBER));
        System.out.printf("Sales for Dec 2014 : $%2.2f\n",
                totalSalesForMonth);
    }
}
```

The **StreamReduceDemo2** class employs the same **Order** objects as those in **StreamReduceDemo1**. The **calculateSalesTotal** method creates a **Stream** from the **Order** array, filters the **Order**s to those having a given year/month and maps the elements to doubles before finally reducing them to a double.

If you run this demo class, you will see this on your console.

```
Sales for Nov 2014 : $100.49
Sales for Dec 2014 : $198.87
```

Mutable Reductions

A mutable reduction operation accumulates a **Stream**'s elements into a container and returns the container. The container is mutable, hence the term *mutable*.

You use the **Stream** interface's **collect** method to perform a mutable reduction operation. Its signature is as follows.

```
<R> R collect(java.util.function.Supplier<R> supplier,
        java.util.function.BiConsumer<R, ? super T> accumulator,
        java.util.function.BiConsumer<R, R> combiner);
```

The **collect** method does its job in three steps, each step processing one of the arguments to the method.

In the first step, the method handles its first argument, which is a **Supplier** that returns a container such as a **Collection** or a **StringBuilder**. In a sequential stream, the **Supplier** is only called once and there will only be one container. In a parallel stream, however, the **Supplier** may be called multiple times and there may be multiple containers.

In the second step, the method tackles the second argument, which is a **BiConsumer** that performs the collection. Recall that a **BiConsumer** accepts two arguments of different types and do not return any value. Practically, the **BiConsumer** adds each stream element to the container or containers that the **Supplier** produced. In the case of a sequential stream, all elements are added to the same container because there is only one container. In a parallel stream, each element is added to a different container.

In the last step, the method processes the third argument, which is also a **BiConsumer**. In a sequential stream, no processing takes place and the argument has no effect as it is never called. Nevertheless, you cannot pass a null as the third argument. In a parallel stream, the collectors are merged using the operation specified by the **BiConsumer**.

The first example of this kind of operation is given in Listing 20.9. It demonstrates how you can collect an array of strings into a **StringBuilder**. There are two streams involved, both doing the same thing. The first stream uses lambda expressions and the second uses method references.

Listing 20.9: StreamCollectDemo1 class

```
package app20;
import java.util.stream.Stream;

public class StreamCollectDemo1 {
    public static void main(String[] args) {
        String[] strings = { "a", "b", "c", "d" };
        Stream<String> stream1 = Stream.of(strings);
        StringBuilder sb1 = stream1.collect(
                () -> new StringBuilder(),
                (a1, b1) -> a1.append(b1),
                (a2, b2) -> a2.append(b2));
```

```
        System.out.println(sb1.toString());

        Stream<String> stream2 = Stream.of(strings);
        StringBuilder sb2 = stream2.collect(
                StringBuilder::new,
                StringBuilder::append,
                StringBuilder::append);
        System.out.println(sb2.toString());
    }
}
```

For each stream, the **collect** method starts by creating a **StringBuilder**. Since a sequential stream is involved, there is only one **StringBuilder**. Next, the method appends each stream element to the **StringBuilder**. Since there are four elements in the stream, the **append** method of the **StringBuilder** is called four times.

Since this is a sequential stream, the third argument is not processed. The **collect** method simply returns the **StringBuilder** that now contains "abcd".

Listing 20.10 shows a second example for the mutable reduction operation. This time I use a **List** as the container, in a sequential stream setting. Again, there are two streams involved, one using lambda expression one using a method reference. The **collect** method here returns a **List** that contains four elements.

Listing 20.10: StreamCollectDemo2 class

```
package app20;
import java.util.ArrayList;
import java.util.List;
import java.util.stream.Stream;

public class StreamCollectDemo2 {
    public static void main(String[] args) {
        String[] strings = { "a", "b", "c", "d" };
        Stream<String> stream1 = Stream.of(strings);
        List<String> list1 = stream1.collect(
                () -> new ArrayList<>(),
                (a1, b1) -> a1.add(b1),
                (a2, b2) -> a2.addAll(b2));
        for (String s: list1) {
            System.out.println(s);
        }

        Stream<String> stream2 = Stream.of(strings);
        List<String> list2 = stream2.collect(
                ArrayList::new,
                ArrayList::add,
                ArrayList::addAll);
        for (String s: list2) {
            System.out.println(s);
        }
    }
}
```

The last example in this category, the **StreamCollectDemo3** class in Listing 20.11, is a rewrite of **StreamCollectDemo1**. However, a parallel stream is used to show you how collection really works. The parallel stream is created by calling the **parallel** method on the initial stream. To show the exact moment each argument is processed, I have also created a custom **Supplier** by extending **ArrayList** and overriding its **add** and **addAll** methods. The new methods print a message and call a super method.

Listing 20.11: StreamCollectDemo3 class

```
package app20;
import java.util.ArrayList;
import java.util.Collection;
import java.util.List;
import java.util.concurrent.atomic.AtomicInteger;
import java.util.function.Supplier;
import java.util.stream.Stream;

public class StreamCollectDemo3 {

    public static void main(String[] args) {
        AtomicInteger counter = new AtomicInteger();
        Supplier<List<String>> supplier = () -> {
            System.out.println("supplier called");
            return new ArrayList<String>() {
                int id = counter.getAndIncrement();
                @Override
                public boolean add(String e) {
                    System.out.println(
                            "\"add\" called for " + e
                            + " on ArrayList " + id);
                    return super.add(e);
                }

                @Override
                public boolean addAll(
                        Collection<? extends String> c) {
                    System.out.println("\"addAll\" called"
                        + " on ArrayList " + id);
                    return super.addAll(c);
                }
            };
        };
        String[] strings = { "a", "b", "c", "d" };
        Stream<String> stream1 = Stream.of(strings).parallel();
        List<String> list1 = stream1.collect(
                supplier,
                (a1, b1) -> a1.add(b1),
                (a2, b2) -> a2.addAll(b2));
        for (String s: list1) {
            System.out.println(s);
        }
    }
}
```

If you run this example in a multi-core computer, you will see something similar to this on your console.

```
supplier called
supplier called
supplier called
supplier called
"add" called for d on ArrayList 0
"add" called for c on ArrayList 2
"add" called for a on ArrayList 1
"add" called for b on ArrayList 3
"addAll" called on ArrayList 2
"addAll" called on ArrayList 1
"addAll" called on ArrayList 1
a
b
c
d
```

You see that the **Supplier** was called four times since there were four elements in the stream, resulting in four brand new **ArrayList**s. Then, the **add** method on each **ArrayList** was called once for each element. Finally, the content of the four **ArrayList**s were merged into a single **ArrayList** and the **ArrayList** was returned.

Parallel Streams

Most computers today have a multi-core processor. This means, multiple threads can run concurrently in different cores, which makes using parallel streams make sense. However, a parallel stream is more expensive to construct than a sequential stream, which means using a parallel stream does not always make your program run faster.

The **ParallelStreamDemo** class in Listing 20.12 maps six integers with their fibonacci numbers. The objective of this example is to show how a parallel stream can run much faster in a multi-core processor machine.

Listing 20.12: The ParallelStreamDemo class

```
package app20;
import java.time.Duration;
import java.time.Instant;
import java.util.Arrays;
import java.util.List;

public class ParallelStreamDemo {

    public static long fibonacci(long i) {
        if (i == 1 || i == 2) {
            return 1;
        }
        return fibonacci(i - 1) + fibonacci(i - 2);
    }

    public static void main(String[] args) {
```

```
    List<Integer> numbers =
            Arrays.asList(10, 20, 30, 40, 41, 42);

    Instant start = Instant.now();
    numbers.parallelStream()
            .map((input) -> fibonacci(input))
            .forEach(System.out::println);
    Instant end = Instant.now();
    System.out.printf(
            "Processing time with parallel stream : %dms\n",
            Duration.between(start, end).toMillis());

    start = Instant.now();
    numbers.stream()
            .map((input) -> fibonacci(input))
            .forEach(System.out::println);
    end = Instant.now();
    System.out.printf(
            "Processing time with sequential stream : %dms\n",
            Duration.between(start, end).toMillis());
    }
}
```

If you run the code, you will see this on your console.

```
55
6765
832040
102334155
165580141
267914296
Processing time with parallel stream : 953ms
55
6765
832040
102334155
165580141
267914296
Processing time with sequential stream : 1764ms
```

As you can see, you can benefit from a parallel stream. However, for not so resource-intensive tasks, the advantage gets less and less and there is a point where the cost of setting up a parallel stream outweighs the cost of setting up a sequential stream plus the speed-up. For instance, if I replace the numbers with

```
    List<Integer> numbers =
            Arrays.asList(1, 2, 3, 4, 5, 6);
```

On my machine, the parallel stream actually takes more time to complete this.

So, before you decide to use a parallel stream, do some testing to see if a parallel stream is faster than a sequential stream for a particular task.

Summary

JDK 1.8 introduces a new Stream API that lets you work with streams. A stream is like a pipe. However, instead of transporting oil or water, a stream transfers data from a source to a destination. The main reason for using a stream is for its supports for sequential and parallel aggregate operations. You can easily filter, sort or map the elements of a stream.

Quiz

1. What is a Stream?
2. What are the four main types of streams?
3. What are reduction operations?
4. When do you use a parallel stream?

Chapter 21
Java Database Connectivity

Even though Java is an object-oriented programming language, data and object states are commonly stored in a relational database. Accessing a database and manipulating data are therefore a very important topic.

There are many brands of databases. To name a few: MySQL, Oracle, Sybase, Microsoft SQL Server, Microsoft Access, PostgreSQL, HSQLDB and Apache Derby. Derby is particularly interesting because it is included in the JDK. Every database engine allows access through a proprietary protocol. As such, accessing different databases requires different skills. Fortunately for Java programmers, Java Database Connectivity (JDBC) makes it easy to manipulate data in the database by providing a uniform way of accessing different relational databases.

Java 8 comes with JDBC version 4.2. The JDBC Application Programming Interface (API) is comprised of two parts: the JDBC Core API and the JDBC Optional Package API. The Core part is good for basic database programming, such as creating tables, retrieving data from a single table or multiple tables, storing data in a table and updating and deleting data. The classes and interfaces in the Core part are members of the **java.sql** package. The JDBC Optional Package API is specified in the **javax.sql** package and supports advanced features such as connection pooling, support for Java Naming and Directory Interface (JNDI), distributed transactions, etc. This chapter only deals with the Core part. Also, it is assumed you have basic knowledge of SQL.

Introduction to JDBC

JDBC enables Java programmers to use the same code to access different databases. This is achieved through the use of JDBC drivers that act as translators between Java code and relational databases.

Every database needs a different JDBC driver. Fortunately, there are JDBC drivers for virtually all database drivers on the market today. Because Java is so popular, database manufacturers make efforts to provide JDBC drivers for their products, even though JDBC drivers can also come from third parties. Popular databases even come with multiple JDBC drivers. Take Oracle as an example. There is an Oracle JDBC driver for server-side applications, there is one optimized for working with stored procedures, etc.

Technically, there are four types of JDBC drivers. They are simply called Type 1, Type 2, Type 3 and Type 4. Here are brief descriptions of each type.

- Type 1. Type 1 drivers implement the JDBC API as a mapping to another data access API, such as ODBC (Open Database Connectivity). The JDBC-ODBC bridge is the most prominent example of the Type 1 driver. It allows Java code to access any database that could be accessed via ODBC. This type of driver is slow and only appropriate for situations where no other JDBC driver is available. The JDBC-ODBC bridge was removed in JDK 8.

- Type 2. Type 2 drivers are written partly in native API and partly in Java. This type of driver uses the client API of the database to connect to the database.
- Type 3. This type of driver translates JDBC calls into the middleware vendor's protocol, which is then translated to the database access protocol by the middleware server.
- Type 4. This type of driver is written in Java and connects to the database directly.

You can find the architecture for each driver type here.

```
http://www.oracle.com/technetwork/java/javase/jdbc/index.html
```

> ### No More JDBC-ODBC
> When Java was first released, ODBC was the primary technology for connecting to the relational database. By providing a JDBC-ODBC bridge, Sun made it possible for developers to write Java code that could connect to virtually any database, without waiting for database vendors to provide JDBC drivers for their products. This proved a brilliant strategy to persuade businesses to start writing their business applications in Java.
> Today ODBC is less relevant and no longer included in the JDK starting Java 8. Good-bye ODBC.

Four Steps to Data Access

Database access and data manipulation through JDBC require four steps.

1. Loading the JDBC driver of the database to connect to. Java now does this automatically in JDBC 4.0 and later.
2. Obtaining a database connection.
3. Creating a **java.sql.Statement** or **java.sql.PreparedStatement** instance that represents an SQL statement.
4. Optionally creating a **java.sql.ResultSet** object to store data returned from the database.
5. Closing JDBC objects to free resources. Thanks to try-with-resources, you don't have to do this manually.

These steps are detailed in the following subsections.

Loading the JDBC Driver

You can skip this step if you are using JDBC 4.0 or later, that is if you are using Java 6 or later. Java 8, for example, comes with JDBC 4.2, so this step is optional in Java 8 because drivers are loaded automatically.

A JDBC driver is represented by the **java.sql.Driver** interface, which defines a contract between a JDBC driver and any Java class that needs to connect to the database. A JDBC driver is often deployed as a jar or zip file. You need to make sure that the driver file is included in the class path when running your Java application.

There are two ways of loading a JDBC driver, manual and dynamic loading.

You load a JDBC driver manually using **forName** static method of the **java.lang.Class** class:

```
class.forName(driverClass)
```

Here *driverClass* is the fully qualified name of the driver. For example, here is code for loading the MySQL driver and PostgreSQL driver:

```
Class.forName("com.mysql.jdbc.Driver");
```

```
Class.forName("org.postgresql.Driver");
```

The **forName** method may throw a **java.lang.ClassNotFoundException**, therefore you must enclose it in a **try** block like this:

```
try {
    Class.forName("org.postgresql.Driver");
} catch (ClassNotFoundException e) {
    // process the exception or re-throw it
}
```

When you load a JDBC driver, you automatically register it with the **java.sql.DriverManager** object so that the latter can find the driver to create connections.

With dynamic loading, there's no need to call **Class.forName** because the **DriverManager** searches for JDBC drivers in the class path and call the **forName** method in the background.

There is more advantage of dynamic loading than simply removing a few lines of code. Since you do not need to hard code the JDBC driver class name, upgrading a driver involves only replacing the old jar with a new one. The new class name does not need to match the old one.

Obtaining a Database Connection

A database connection facilitates communication between Java code and a relational database. The **java.sql.Connection** interface is the template for connection objects. You use the **java.sql.DriverManager** class's **getConnection** static method to obtain a **Connection**. This method searches the loaded JDBC drivers in memory and returns a **java.sql.Connection** object.

Here are the signatures of the most commonly used **getConnection** method overloads.

```
public static Connection getConnection(java.lang.String url)
        throws SQLException
```

```
public static Connection getConnection(java.lang.String url,
        java.lang.String userName, java.lang.String password)
        throws SQLException
```

The first overload is suitable for connecting to a database that requires no user authentication. The second is for connecting to one that requires user authentication. You can still use the first overload to pass user credentials. When using the second overload to connect to a database that requires no authentication, pass **null** to both the second and third arguments.

The *url* argument specifies the location of the database server and the name of the database to connect. The database server can reside in the same computer as the running Java code or in a computer in the network. In addition to the location, you must also pass your user name and password to prove to the database you are an authorized user. Most database servers require this before they grant you a connection. As such, the second **getConnection** method overload is easier to use. If you use the first overload, you can append the user name and password to the database URL. Here is the format of the *url* argument.

```
jdbc:subprotocol:subname
```

The *subprotocol* part specifies the database type. The JDBC driver documentation should tell you the value of the subprotocol. Here are some examples:

- **postgresql**: Connecting to a PostgreSQL database.
- **mysql**: Connecting to a My SQL database.
- **oracle:thin**. Connecting to an Oracle database using the thin driver (there are several types of Oracle JDBC drivers).
- **derby**. Specify this if you are connecting to an Apache Derby database.

The *subname* part specifies the name of the machine running the database server, the port the database is servicing connections and the database name. For example, the following is a URL for accessing a PostgreSQL database named **PurchasingDB** on **localhost**:

```
jdbc:postgresql://localhost/PurchasingDB
```

As another example, the following URL is used to connect to an Oracle database named **Customers** residing on a machine called **Production01**. Note that by default Oracle works on port 1521.

```
jdbc:oracle:thin:@Production01:1521:Customers
```

The following is a URL to connect to a MySQL database named **CustomerDB** on a computer named **PC2**.

```
jdbc:mysql://PC2/CustomerDB
```

The following is a URL to connect to a Derby database whose data source name is **Legacy** located in the **/home/db** directory on a Linux system.

```
jdbc:derby:/home/db/Legacy
```

And this is for connecting to a Derby database named **Marketing** on **C:\db** on a Windows machine.

```
jdbc:derby:c:/db/Marketing
```

The user name and password are best passed-in as separate arguments using the second **getConnection** overload. However, if you must use the first overload, use the following syntax:

```
url?user=username&password=password
```

Assuming that the user name is **Ray** and the password is **Pwd**, the previous three database URLs can be rewritten as follows.

```
jdbc:postgresql://localhost/PurchasingDB?user=Ray&password=Pwd

jdbc:oracle:thin:@Production01:1521:Customers?user=Ray&password=Pwd

jdbc:mysql://PC2/CustomerDB?user=Ray&password=Pwd

jdbc:derby:/home/db/Legacy?user=Ray&password=Pwd
```

The **Connection** interface has the **close** method to close the connection once you're finished with it.

Creating A Statement Object

A **java.sql.Statement** represents an SQL statement. You can get a **Statement** by calling the **createStatement** method on a **java.sql.Connection** object.

```
Statement statement = connection.createStatement();
```

Next, you need to call a method on the **Statement** object, passing an SQL statement. If your SQL statement retrieves data, you use the **executeQuery** method. Otherwise, use **executeUpdate**.

```
ResultSet executeQuery(java.lang.String sql) throws SQLException

int executeUpdate(java.lang.String sql) throws SQLException
```

Both **executeUpdate** and **executeQuery** methods accept a **String** containing an SQL statement. The SQL statement does not end with a database statement terminator, which can vary from one database to another. For example, Oracle uses a semicolon (;) to indicate the end of a statement, and Sybase uses the word **go**. The driver will automatically supply the appropriate statement terminator, and you will not need to include it in your JDBC code.

The **executeUpdate** method executes an SQL INSERT, UPDATE, or DELETE statement as well as data definition language (DDL) statements to create, drop, and alter tables. This method returns the row count for INSERT, UPDATE, or DELETE statements or returns 0 for SQL statements that return nothing.

The **executeQuery** method executes an SQL SELECT statement that returns data. This method returns a **java.sql.ResultSet** that contains the data produced by the given query. If there is no data returned, **executeQuery** returns an empty **ResultSet**. It never returns **null**.

Note that the SQL statement is executed on the server. Therefore, though not recommended, you could pass database-specific instructions.

PreparedStatement, which derives from **Statement**, is a popular alternative to **Statement**. **PreparedStatement** differs from **Statement** in that it pre-compiles and stores the SQL statement so that subsequent calls to the same SQL statement will be faster. You obtain a **PreparedStatement** by calling the **prepareStatement** method of **Connection**, passing an SQL statement.

```
PreparedStatement pStatement =
        connection.prepareStatement(java.lang.String sql);
```

You can then call the **executeQuery** or **executeUpdate** on the **PreparedStatement**.

```
ResultSet executeQuery() throws SQLException

int executeUpdate() throws SQLException
```

Note that the signatures for both methods are different from those in **Statement**. Because you pass an SQL statement when creating a **PreparedStatement**, you no longer need one when calling **executeQuery** or **executeUpdate**.

Creating a ResultSet Object

A **ResultSet** is the representation of a database table that is returned from a **Statement** or **PreparedStatement**. A **ResultSet** object maintains a cursor pointing to its current row of data. When the cursor is first returned, it is positioned before the first row. To access the first row of the **ResultSet**, you call the **next** method on the **ResultSet**.

The **next** method moves the cursor to the next row and returns either **true** or **false**. It returns **true** if the new current row is valid; it returns **false** if there are no more rows. Normally, you use this method in a **while** loop to iterate over the **ResultSet**.

To get data from a **ResultSet**, you can use one of the many **getXXX** methods of **ResultSet**, such as **getInt**, **getLong**, **getShort**, and so forth. You use **getInt** to obtain the value of the designated column in the current row as an **int**. **getLong** obtains the cell data as a **long**, etc. The most commonly used method is **getString**, which returns the cell data as a **String**. Using **getString** is preferable in many cases because you don't need to worry about the data type of the table field in the database.

The **getString** method, similar to other **getXXX** methods, has two overloads that allow you to retrieve a cell's data by passing either the column index or the column name. The signatures of the two overloads of **getString** are as follows:

```
public java.lang.String getString(int columnIndex)
        throws SQLException
```

```
public java.lang.String getString(java.lang.String columnName)
        throws SQLException
```

Closing JDBC Objects

If you're using a pre-7 JDK, you should always close all JDBC objects after use by calling their **close** methods. In an application that employs a connection pool, forgetting to close a **Connection** will cause it not to be returned to the pool for reuse. In addition, you should call **close** properly. Here is an unsafe way of calling **close**.

```
resultSet.close();
statement.close();
connection.close();
```

This method is not perfect because **resultSet.close()** and **statement.close()** might fail and throw an exception. Should this happen, **connection.close()** will never be executed.

The correct way is to enclose calls to **close** in a **finally** clause like this:

```
Connection connection = null;
PreparedStatement pStatement = null;
ResultSet resultSet = null;
try {
```

```
        connection = getConnection();
        pStatement = connection.prepareStatement(sql);
        resultSet = pStatement.executeQuery();
        while (resultSet.next()) {
            // manipulate the data here
        }
} catch (SQLException e) {
    throw newException;
} finally {
    if (resultSet != null) {
        try {
            resultSet.close();
        } catch (Exception e) {
        }
    }
    if (statement != null) {
        try {
            statement.close();
        } catch (Exception e) {
        }
    }
    if (connection != null) {
        try {
            connection.close();
        } catch (Exception e) {
        }
    }
}
}
```

In Java 7 and later, closing is done automatically when you use a try-with-resources statement to create JDBC objects. Here is what the previous code would look like in Java 7 and later.

```
try (Connection connection = getConnection();
    Prepared pStatement = connection.prepareStatement(sql);
    ResultSet resultSet = pStatement.executeQuery()) {
    while (resultSet.next()) {
        // manipulate the data here
    }
} catch (SQLException e) {
    throw newException;
}
```

Using Java DB

Java DB is Oracle's distribution of the Apache Derby database engine, an open source project written in Java. Java DB is included in the JDK and can be found in the **db** directory under the installation directory of the JDK. A JDBC driver is also included and can be found in the **lib** directory under the **db** directory. The driver comes in a jar file named **derby.jar**.

Apache Derby can run as a stand-alone server or embedded in a Java application. If run embedded, Derby runs on the same JVM as the Java application.

The example in Listing 21.1 shows how to create and run Derby in embedded mode. The code creates a new database named testdb in the current directory and creates a table called person. The table has two columns, person_id and name. It then inserts some data to the table and reads it back.

The URL used for connecting to the database is

```
jdbc:derby:testdb;create=true
```

The **create=true** part indicates that the database should be created if none exists.

Listing 21.1: Using Java DB

```
package app21;
import java.sql.Connection;
import java.sql.DriverManager;
import java.sql.PreparedStatement;
import java.sql.ResultSet;
import java.sql.SQLException;
import java.sql.Statement;

public class JavaDBDemo1 {
    private static String dbUrl = "jdbc:derby:testdb;create=true";

    private static final String CREATE_TABLE_SQL =
            "CREATE TABLE person "
            + "(person_id INT, name VARCHAR(100))";

    public void createTable() {
        try (Connection connection =
                DriverManager.getConnection(dbUrl);
                Statement statement =
                        connection.createStatement()) {
            statement.execute(CREATE_TABLE_SQL);
        } catch (SQLException e) {
            System.out.println(e.getMessage());
        }
    }

    private static final String INSERT_DATA_SQL =
            "INSERT INTO person (person_id, name) "
            + "VALUES (?, ?)";

    public void insertData(int id, String name) {
        try (Connection connection =
                DriverManager.getConnection(dbUrl);
                PreparedStatement pStatement =
                        connection.prepareStatement(
                                INSERT_DATA_SQL);) {
            pStatement.setInt(1, id);
            pStatement.setString(2, name);
            pStatement.executeUpdate();
```

```
        } catch (SQLException e) {
            e.printStackTrace();
        }
    }

    private static final String READ_DATA_SQL =
            "SELECT person_id, name FROM person";

    public void readData() {
        try (Connection connection =
                DriverManager.getConnection(dbUrl);
                PreparedStatement pStatement =
                        connection.prepareStatement(READ_DATA_SQL);
                ResultSet resultSet = pStatement.executeQuery()) {
            while (resultSet.next()) {
                System.out.println(resultSet.getString(2));
            }
        } catch (SQLException e) {
            e.printStackTrace();
        }
    }

    public static void main(String[] args) {
        // must add derby.jar to classpath
        JavaDBDemo1 demo = new JavaDBDemo1();
        demo.createTable();
        demo.insertData(2, "Alvin Average");
        demo.readData();
    }
}
```

The **JavaDBDemo1** class in Listing 21.1 provides methods for creating a table, insert a record and read the data back.

To compile the class, you do not need the JDBC driver. Just change directory to the parent directory of **app21** (the directory that contains the **JavaDBDemo1.java** file) and type

```
javac app21/JavaDBDemo1.java
```

To run it, however, you need to pass the JDBC driver in the classpath. From the same directory you compiled the Java file, and assuming the **derby.jar** file is located in **/usr/local/jdk1.8.0_25/db/lib** on a Linux or Mac OS X machine, type this to run the class.

```
java -cp ./:/usr/local/jdk1.8.0_25/db/lib/derby.jar app21/JavaDBDemo1
```

Note that you need to pass two paths to the **java** program, the current directory (./) and the path to the **derby.jar** file.

On a Windows machine, assuming the JDK is installed on C:\Program Files\Java, type this:

```
java -cp ./;"C:/Program Files/Java/jdk1.8.0_25/db/lib/derby.jar"
➡ app21/JavaDBDemo1
```

Using the DAO Pattern

Java is an object-oriented programming language and most of the time you deal with objects. The data you insert into and retrieve from a relational database is not structured as objects and is inconvenient to work with.

A good approach to accessing data in a database is by using a separate module for managing the complexity of obtaining a connection and building SQL statements. The DAO design pattern is a simple pattern that does this job very well. There are a few variants of this pattern, but one of the simplest is depicted in Figure 21.1.

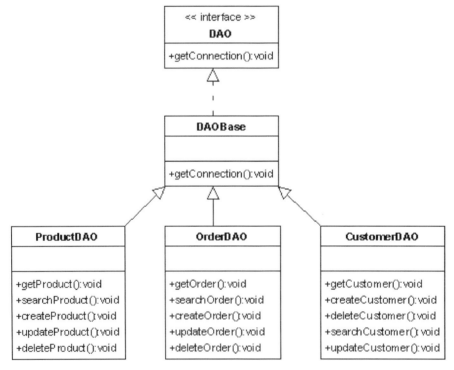

Figure 21.1: The DAO pattern

With this pattern, you write a class for each type of object you need to persist. For example, if your application needs to persist three types of objects—**Product**, **Customer**, and **Order**—you need three DAO classes, each of which takes care of an object type. Therefore, you would have the following classes: **ProductDAO**, **CustomerDAO**, and **OrderDAO**. The DAO suffix at the end of the class name indicates that the class is a DAO class. It is a convention that you should follow unless you have compelling reasons not to do so.

A typical DAO class takes care of the addition, deletion, modification and retrieval of objects as well as the searching for those objects. For example, a **ProductDAO** class might support the following methods:

```
void addProduct(Product product)

void updateProduct(Product product)
```

```
void deleteProduct(int productId)
```

```
Product getProduct(int productId)
```

```
List<Product> findProducts(SearchCriteria searchCriteria)
```

In your DAO implementation classes, you can either write SQL statements manually or use a Java Persistence API (JPA) implementation such as Hibernate to take care of database data. JPA is unfortunately outside the scope of this book, but you should know that it is a popular technology and many people would choose JPA for their data access needs. For now, I will use SQL statements.

For example, instances of the **Product** class in Listing 21.2 need to be persisted into a Derby database.

Listing 21.3: The Product class

```java
package app21.model;
import java.math.BigDecimal;

public class Product {
    private String name;
    private String description;
    private BigDecimal price;
    public String getName() {
        return name;
    }
    public void setName(String name) {
        this.name = name;
    }
    public String getDescription() {
        return description;
    }
    public void setDescription(String description) {
        this.description = description;
    }
    public BigDecimal getPrice() {
        return price;
    }
    public void setPrice(BigDecimal price) {
        this.price = price;
    }
    @Override
    public String toString() {
        return name + ", $" + price + ", " + description;
    }
}
```

Product is a simple class with three properties, **name**, **description** and **price**.

First, you need to create a database and a **products** table. Database creation in Derby may happen automatically so you do not have to worry about it. However, you still have to create the table using the SQL statement in Listing 21.3.

Listing 21.3: The SQL statement for creating the products table

```sql
CREATE TABLE products
```

```
(id INTEGER NOT NULL GENERATED ALWAYS AS IDENTITY,

name VARCHAR(255) NOT NULL,
description VARCHAR(1000) default NULL,
price DECIMAL(10,2) NOT NULL,
PRIMARY KEY  (id))
```

The DAO module consists of these interfaces and classes:

- The **DAO** interface in Listing 21.4, which all DAO interfaces are derived from.
- The **BaseDAO** class in Listing 21.5, which provides basic implementation for all DAO classes.
- The **DAOException** class in Listing 21.6 that a DAO method throws in the event of a runtime exception.
- **ProductDAO** interface in Listing 21.7 and **ProductDAOImpl** class in Listing 21.8. Both provide methods for persisting **Product** instances and retrieving them from the database.

Listing 21.4: The DAO interface

```
package app21.dao;
import java.sql.Connection;

public interface DAO {
    Connection getConnection() throws DAOException;
}
```

Listing 21.5: The BaseDAO class

```
package app21.dao;
import java.sql.Connection;
import java.sql.DriverManager;

public class BaseDAO implements DAO {
    public static final String dbUrl = "jdbc:derby:daotest";
    public Connection getConnection() throws DAOException {
        try {
            return DriverManager.getConnection(dbUrl);
        } catch (Exception e) {
            throw new DAOException();
        }
    }
}
```

For this example, the database URL is hardcoded in the **BaseDAO** class. However, it does not have to be so. It can come from a file or be passed to it so that you can change the URL without recompiling the classes.

Listing 21.6: The DAOException class

```
package app21.dao;

public class DAOException extends Exception {
    private static final long serialVersionUID = 19192L;

    public DAOException() {
```

```
    }
    public DAOException(String message) {
        this.message = message;
    }
    public String getMessage() {
        return message;
    }
    public void setMessage(String message) {
        this.message = message;
    }
    private String message;

    public String toString() {
        return message;
    }
}
```

Listing 21.7: The ProductDAO interface

```
package app21.dao;
import java.util.List;
import app21.model.Product;

public interface ProductDAO extends DAO {
    List<Product> getProducts() throws DAOException;
    void insert(Product product) throws DAOException;
}
```

For this example, the **ProductDAO** interface only contains two methods. In real-life applications, you may need methods for search, update and delete.

Listing 21.8: The ProductDAOImpl class

```
package app21.dao;
import java.sql.Connection;
import java.sql.PreparedStatement;
import java.sql.ResultSet;
import java.sql.SQLException;
import java.util.ArrayList;
import java.util.List;
import app21.model.Product;

public class ProductDAOImpl extends BaseDAO
        implements ProductDAO {

    private static final String GET_PRODUCTS_SQL =
            "SELECT name, description, price FROM products";

    public List<Product> getProducts() throws DAOException {
        List<Product> products = new ArrayList<Product>();
        try (Connection connection = getConnection();
                PreparedStatement pStatement = connection
                        .prepareStatement(GET_PRODUCTS_SQL);
                ResultSet resultSet = pStatement.executeQuery()) {
            while (resultSet.next()) {
```

```
                        Product product = new Product();
                        product.setName(resultSet.getString("name"));
                        product.setDescription(
                                resultSet.getString("description"));
                        product.setPrice(
                                resultSet.getBigDecimal("price"));
                        products.add(product);
                    }
            } catch (SQLException e) {
                throw new DAOException(
                        "Error getting products. " + e.getMessage());
            }
            return products;
        }

        private static final String INSERT_PRODUCT_SQL =
                "INSERT INTO products "
                + "(name, description, price) " + "VALUES (?, ?, ?)";

        public void insert(Product product) throws DAOException {
            try (Connection connection = getConnection();
                    PreparedStatement pStatement = connection
                            .prepareStatement(INSERT_PRODUCT_SQL);) {
                pStatement.setString(1, product.getName());
                pStatement.setString(2, product.getDescription());
                pStatement.setBigDecimal(3, product.getPrice());
                pStatement.execute();
            } catch (SQLException e) {
                throw new DAOException(
                        "Error adding product. " + e.getMessage());
            }
        }
    }
}
```

Finally, Listing 21.9 shows a class for testing the DAO module.

Listing 21.9: Testing the DAO module

```
package app21.test;

import java.math.BigDecimal;
import java.sql.Connection;
import java.sql.DriverManager;
import java.sql.SQLException;
import java.sql.Statement;
import java.util.List;
import app21.dao.DAOException;
import app21.dao.ProductDAO;
import app21.dao.ProductDAOImpl;
import app21.model.Product;

public class ProductDAOTest {
    private static final String CREATE_TABLE_SQL =
            "CREATE TABLE products ("
```

```
                + "id INTEGER NOT NULL GENERATED ALWAYS AS IDENTITY,"
                + "name VARCHAR(255) NOT NULL,"
                + "description VARCHAR(1000) default NULL,"
                + "price DECIMAL(10,2) NOT NULL,"
                + "PRIMARY KEY  (id))";
    private static void createDatabase() {
        String dbUrl = "jdbc:derby:daotest;create=true";
        try (Connection connection =
                DriverManager.getConnection(dbUrl);
                Statement statement =
                    connection.createStatement()) {
            statement.execute(CREATE_TABLE_SQL);
        } catch (SQLException e) {
            System.out.println(e.getMessage());
        }
    }

    public static void main(String[] args) {
        createDatabase();

        Product product = new Product();
        product.setName("Kiano tablet keyboard");
        product.setDescription("Low cost tablet keyboard, "
                + "compatible will all Android devices");
        product.setPrice(new BigDecimal(24.95));

        ProductDAO productDAO = new ProductDAOImpl();
        try {
            productDAO.insert(product);
        } catch (DAOException e) {
            e.printStackTrace();
        }

        List<Product> products = null;
        try {
            products = productDAO.getProducts();
        } catch (DAOException e) {
            e.printStackTrace();
        }

        products.stream().forEach(System.out::println);
    }
}
```

The test class starts by creating a database called daotest in the working directory, i.e. the directory you run **java**. It then creates a **Product** and a **ProductDAO** and inserts the product into the database by calling the **insert** method on the **ProductDAO**. Finally, it reads back the product from the database by calling the **getProducts** method on the **ProductDAO**.

Reading Metadata

In a few rare cases, you may want to read the metadata of a **ResultSet**. Metadata includes the number of columns in the **ResultSet**, the name and type of each individual column, and so on.

Metadata is encapsulated in a **java.sql.ResultSetMetaData** object, which you can by calling the **getMetaData** method on a **ResultSet**.

```
public ResultSetMetaData getMetaData() throws SQLException
```

Some of the methods in **ResultSetMetaData** are given below.

```
public int getColumnCount() throws SQLException
```
> Returns the number of columns in the **ResultSet**

```
public java.lang.String getColumnName(int columnIndex)
        throws SQLException
```
> Returns the name of the specified column. The index is 1-based, **getColumnName(1)** returns the first column name.

```
public int getColumnType(int columnIndex) throws SQLException
```
> Returns the type of the column. The value is one of the static final fields in the **java.sql.Types** class, such as **ARRAY, BIGINT, BINARY, BLOB, CHAR, DATE, DECIMAL, TINYINT, VARCHAR**, etc.

The following example shows how to deal with metadata. It presents an application that you can use to input an SQL statement and display the result. It uses the Derby database you created from the previous example, but can be modified to support other databases as well.

The SQLTool Class

Listing 21.10 shows the **SQLTool** class that you can use to pass SQL statements to the MySQL server running on the local machine.

Listing 21.10: The SQLTool class

```java
package app21;

import java.sql.Connection;
import java.sql.DriverManager;
import java.sql.ResultSet;
import java.sql.ResultSetMetaData;
import java.sql.SQLException;
import java.sql.Statement;
import javax.swing.JOptionPane;

public class SQLTool {
    private String dbUrl;
    private String dbUserName;
    private String dbPassword;
    private static final int COLUMN_WIDTH = 25;
```

```
public SQLTool(String dbUrl,
        String dbUserName, String dbPassword) {
    this.dbUrl = dbUrl;
    this.dbUserName = dbUserName;
    this.dbPassword = dbPassword;
}

public void executeSQL(String sql) {
    sql = sql.trim();
    try (Connection connection =
            DriverManager.getConnection(dbUrl,
                    dbUserName, dbPassword);
        Statement statement = connection.createStatement()) {
        if (sql.toUpperCase().startsWith("SELECT")) {
            try (ResultSet resultSet =
                    statement.executeQuery(sql)) {
                ResultSetMetaData metaData =
                        resultSet.getMetaData();
                int columnCount = metaData.getColumnCount();
                for (int i = 0; i < columnCount; i++) {
                    System.out.print(pad(
                            metaData.getColumnName(i + 1)));
                }
                // draw line
                int length = columnCount * COLUMN_WIDTH;
                StringBuilder sb = new StringBuilder(length);
                for (int i = 0; i < length; i++) {
                    sb.append('=');
                }
                System.out.println();
                System.out.println(sb.toString());

                while (resultSet.next()) {
                    String[] row = new String[columnCount];
                    for (int i = 0; i < columnCount; i++) {
                        row[i] = resultSet.getString(i + 1);
                        System.out.print(pad(row[i]));
                    }
                    System.out.println();
                }
            } catch (SQLException e) {
                e.printStackTrace();
            }
        } else {
            int recordsUpdated = statement.executeUpdate(sql);
            System.out.println(recordsUpdated
                    + " record(s) affected");
        }
    } catch (SQLException e) {
        System.err.println(e.getMessage());
    }
    System.out.println();
}
```

```java
// appends s with spaces so that the length is 25
private String pad(String s) {
    int padCount = COLUMN_WIDTH - s.length();
    StringBuilder sb = new StringBuilder(25);
    sb.append(s);
    for (int i = 0; i < padCount; i++) {
        sb.append(" ");
    }
    return sb.toString();
}

public static void main(String[] args) {
    String dbUrl = "jdbc:derby:testdb";
    String dbUserName = null;
    String dbPassword = null;

    SQLTool sqlTool = new SQLTool(dbUrl,
            dbUserName, dbPassword);
    String sql = null;
    do {
        sql = JOptionPane
                .showInputDialog("Enter an SQL Statement");
        if (sql != null && !sql.trim().isEmpty()) {
            sqlTool.executeSQL(sql);
        }
    } while (sql != null);
}
}
```

Note that the class takes a string input using a Swing class named **JOptionPane**. The code for this is only one statement long, so you do not have to know Swing well to use it.

Basically, the program uses a do-while loop to receive SQL statements and pass them to a JDBC driver. To quit, click the Cancel button on the **JOptionPane**.

```java
do {
    sql = JOptionPane
            .showInputDialog("Enter an SQL Statement");
    if (sql != null && !sql.trim().isEmpty()) {
        sqlTool.executeSQL(sql);
    }
} while (sql != null);
```

The **JOptionPane** is shown in Figure 21.2:

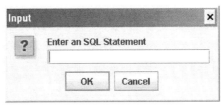

Figure 21.2: The JOptionPane for taking SQL statements

If you enter an SQL statement and click the OK button on the **JOptionPane**, the SQL statement will be passed to the **executeSQL** method:

```
sqlTool.executeSQL(sql);
```

For example, try this SQL statement:

```
SELECT name, price FROM products
```

The **executeSQL** method will create a connection to the database:

```
try (Connection connection =
        DriverManager.getConnection(dbUrl,
            dbUserName, dbPassword);
    Statement statement = connection.createStatement()) {
```

It then checks if the SQL statement is a SELECT statement or something else. If it is a SELECT statement, the **executeQuery** method of the **Statement** object is called and a **ResultSet** is returned. Opening a **ResultSet** is done in a try-with-resources statement.

```
if (sql.toUpperCase().startsWith("SELECT")) {
    try (ResultSet resultSet =
            statement.executeQuery(sql)) {
```

The **executeSQL** method will first display the **ResultSet**'s column names:

```
ResultSetMetaData metaData =
        resultSet.getMetaData();
int columnCount = metaData.getColumnCount();
for (int i = 0; i < columnCount; i++) {
    System.out.print(pad(metaData.getColumnName(i
            + 1)));
}
// draw line
int length = columnCount * COLUMN_WIDTH;
StringBuilder sb = new StringBuilder(length);
for (int i = 0; i < length; i++) {
    sb.append('=');
}
System.out.println();
System.out.println(sb.toString());
```

It then uses a **while** loop to iterate the **ResultSet** and prints the columns to the console.

```
while (resultSet.next()) {
    String[] row = new String[columnCount];
    for (int i = 0; i < columnCount; i++) {
        row[i] = resultSet.getString(i + 1);
        System.out.print(pad(row[i]));
    }
    System.out.println();
}
```

If the SQL statement passed is not a SELECT statement, the **executeSQL** method displays the number of records affected by the statement.

```
    } else {
        int recordsUpdated = statement.executeUpdate(sql);
        System.out.println(recordsUpdated +
                " record(s) updated");
    }
```

Passing the SQL statement "SELECT name, price FROM products" on my machine prints the following output on the console.

```
NAME                           PRICE
====================================================
Kiano tablet keyboard     24.94
```

Summary

Java has its own technology for database access and data manipulation called JDBC. Its functionality is wrapped in the types in the **java.sql** package. In this chapter, you have seen various members of this package and learned how to use them. You also have learned how to create a tool that takes any SQL statement and pass it to a Derby database.

Quiz

1. Name the five steps to accessing a database and manipulating the data in it.
2. Name the five most important types in the **java.sql** package.
3. What pattern can you use to hide the complexity of JDBC-related code?

Chapter 22
Swing Basics

There are three Java technologies you can use to develop desktop user-interface: Abstract Window Toolkit (AWT), Swing and JavaFX. AWT is an old technology—having been in existence since Java 1.0—that has been replaced by Swing. Swing has been the technology of choice for some time, but it will soon be superseded by JavaFX. JavaFX should be used for new projects. This chapter and the next cover Swing programming and they are only here because there are still a lot of Swing applications out there and you may be tasked with maintaining or extending some of them.

This chapter starts with AWT components, which will be only briefly discussed. Following it are sections on simple Swing components, such as **JFrame**, **JButton**, **JLabel**, **JTextArea**, **JOptionPane**, and **JDialog**. Chapter 23, "Swinging Higher" focuses on layout management and event handling. In addition, there is discussion of thread-related Swing classes in Chapter 27, "Java Threads" and Chapter 28, "The Concurrency Utilities."

Overview

Swing has a better collection of ready-to-use components than the AWT. Swing components are also much more powerful than their AWT counterparts. For one, some Swing components can render HTML tags, something AWT developers would not even dare to dream about. Nonetheless, the AWT is still relevant because Swing relies on the AWT event handling mechanism and layout managers as well as its various classes; therefore you still need to know about those classes. Moreover, when developing applets (See Chapter 24, "Applets"), your knowledge of AWT will come in handy too.

There are three things you need to learn to become an effective UI programmers:

- UI components. These include top-level containers (**JFrame**, **JDialog**, etc) and components that can be added to a container.
- Layout managers. How to lay out your components in a container.
- Event handling. How to write code that responds to an event, such as a button click, a mouse move, a window resize, etc.

The main difference between AWT and Swing lies in how they draw graphic components. AWT calls the native GUI functions of the operating system to do that. This means, programs that use AWT will look different on Windows than on Unix. The term 'peer' is often used when describing this approach. When you invoke an AWT method to draw a button, AWT will in turn delegate the task to a 'peer' native function. However, writing high-quality drawing methods that rely on native functions proves to be difficult because the native operating system does not always have a necessary function that can be used to perform certain functionality. As a result, Sun Microsystems invented Swing. Swing draws all its UI components itself, hence eliminating dependence on native peers. With Swing, a GUI program will look the same anywhere, be in on Linux, Mac OS X or Windows. (In practice, this is not really true.) In older machines, the side-effect of having to draw everything itself is that Swing programs look a little sluggish, because of course it takes more time than if the same graphics were displayed using native functions. However, with today's computers, it is no longer a problem.

AWT Components

AWT components are grouped into the **java.awt** package. At its core is the **Component** class, which is a direct subclass of **java.lang.Object**. This is described in Figure 22.1.

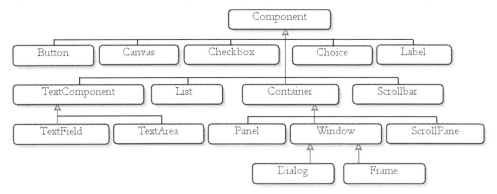

Figure 22.1: AWT components

The **Component** class has subclasses that represent components that you can draw on your UI program:

- **Button**. Represents a clickable button.
- **Canvas**. Represents a blank screen you can draw custom paintings on.
- **Checkbox**. Represents a check box.
- **Choice**. Represents a radio button.
- **Container**. Represents a component that can contain other components.
- **Label**. Represents a non-editable piece of text.
- **List**. Represents a list of options.
- **Scrollbar**. Represents horizontal and vertical scrollbars.
- **TextComponent**. A parent class of two concrete classes: **TextArea** and **TextField**. **TextField** can contain a single line of text and **TextArea** multiple lines of text.

Of special interest is the **Container** class. You can add components to a **Container** using one of its **add** methods. A concrete implementation of **Container** is **Window**, which is the parent of the **Frame** class. Even though you can instantiate **Window**, more often you will use a **Frame** or **Dialog** to contain other components because **Frame** and **Dialog** are easier to use and have more features than **Window**. **Frame** and **Dialog** are similar, except for the fact that **Dialog** is often used to take user input. Almost all AWT applications will have at least one **Frame**.

The **Frame** class offers the following methods:

- **setTitle**. Sets the frame's title.
- **add**. Adds an AWT component on to the frame.
- **remove**. Removes an AWT component from the frame.
- **show**. Displays this **Frame**.

In a typical AWT application, you normally start your program by constructing an instance of **Frame** and adding components to it. Listing 22.1 features the **AWTFrameDemo1** class that adds various AWT components to a **Frame**.

Listing 22.1: Using AWT components

```
package app22;
import java.awt.Button;
import java.awt.Checkbox;
import java.awt.FlowLayout;
import java.awt.Frame;
import java.awt.Label;
import java.awt.TextField;

public class AWTFrameDemo1 extends Frame {
    private static final long serialVersionUID = 1L;

    public static void main(String[] args) {
        AWTFrameDemo1 frame = new AWTFrameDemo1();
        frame.setTitle("My AWT Frame");
        frame.setSize(300, 100);
        frame.setLayout(new FlowLayout());
        // add components
        Label label = new Label("Name");
        frame.add(label);
        TextField textField = new TextField();
        frame.add(textField);
        Button button = new Button("Register");
        frame.add(button);
        Checkbox checkbox = new Checkbox();
        frame.add(checkbox);
        frame.setVisible(true);
    }
}
```

The **AWTFrameDemo1** class extends **java.awt.Frame**. After you create a **Frame**, you can call its **setTitle** method and pass a **String** for its title. You can also invoke the **setSize** method to set the frame's width and height in pixels.

The line in bold in Listing 22.1 is a call to the **setLayout** method. You pass a **LayoutManager** to this method and the object will determine how child components added to a frame are laid out. I discuss **LayoutManager** further in Chapter 16, "Swinging Higher."

You can add components to a frame by using the **add** method of the **Frame** class. In Listing 22.1, I added four components, a **Label**, a **TextField**, a **Checkbox** and a **Button**. Finally, the **setVisible** method is invoked to make the frame visible.

If you run the **AWTFrameTest** class, you will see something like Figure 22.2. Its actual appearance depends on the operating system the program is running on.

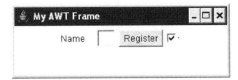

Figure 22.2: An AWT Frame and some components

The frame in Figure 22.2 has a size of 300 by 100 pixels. Its title says "My AWT Frame." There are four components added to it.

Note
The close button (indicated by X) does not close the frame. In fact, making an AWT frame closable by a single click is not straight-forward. This has been remedied in Swing, which is one of the reasons Swing is better and easier to program.

The GUI application in Figure 22.2 looks good enough for introduction, but you can do more with the AWT library. You can add menus and submenus, write code that responds to an event (such as a button click or window resize), use a layout manager to lay out components, and so on.

Useful AWT Classes

In addition to AWT classes that are parents to Swing components, there are other classes that are often used in Swing applications. These classes are discussed in this section.

java.awt.Color

A **Color** models a color. Creating a **Color** is supereasy because the **Color** class provides static fields that return specific **Color**s. The names of these fields are the same as the colors they represent. Here are some of the static final fields in **Color**: **BLACK**, **BLUE**, **GREEN**, **RED**, **CYAN**, **ORANGE**, **YELLOW**.

For example, here is how you obtain a green **Color**:

```
Color color = Color.GREEN;
```

You can also create a custom color by passing red-green-blue (RGB) values to the **Color** class's constructor. For example:

```
Color myColor = new Color(246, 27, 27);
```

To change a component's color, call the **setForeGround** and **setBackGround** methods of the component.

```
component.setForeGround(Color.YELLOW) ;
component.setBackGround(Color.RED);
```

java.awt.Font

A **Font** represents a font. Here is a constructor of the **Font** class.

```
public Font(java.lang.String name, int style, int size)
```

Here, *name* is the font name (such as "Verdana", "Arial", etc) and *size* is the point size of the font. The *style* argument takes an integer bitmask that may be **PLAIN** or a bitwise union of **BOLD** and/or **ITALIC**.

For example, the following code construct a **Font** object.

```
int style = Font.BOLD | Font.ITALIC;
Font font = new Font("Garamond", style , 11);
```

java.awt.Point

A **Point** represents a point in a coordinate system. It has two **int** fields, **x** and **y**. You can construct a **Point** object by using one of its constructors.

```
public Point()
```

```
public Point(int x, int y)
```

```
public Point(Point anotherPoint)
```

The **Point** class's **getX** and **getY** methods return the value of the **x** and **y** fields in **double**, respectively.

java.awt.Dimension

A **Dimension** represents a width and a height in **int**. It is meant to represent the dimension of an AWT or Swing component. There are two **int** fields, **width** and **height**. The **getWidth** and **getHeight** methods return a **double**, not an **int**. You can construct an instance of **Dimension** by using one of its constructors:

```
public Dimension()
```

```
public Dimension(Dimension d)
```

```
public Dimension(int width, int height)
```

The no-arg constructor creates a **Dimension** with a zero width and height.

java.awt.Rectangle

A **Rectange** specifies a rectangular area in the coordinate system. Its **x** and **y** fields specify the top-left corner coordinate. Its **width** and **height** fields specify the width and height of the rectangle, respectively.

Here are some of the constructors of **Rectangle**.

```
public Rectangle()
```

```
public Rectangle(Dimension d)
```

```
public Rectangle(int width, int height)
```

```
public Rectangle(int x, int y, int width, int height)
```

java.awt.Graphics

The **Graphics** class is an abstract class for rendering AWT and Swing components. You need to work with a **Graphics** if you want to change the appearance of a component, create a custom component, and so on. To do this, you override the component's **paint** method:

```
public void paint(Graphics graphics)
```

The overridden method takes a **Graphics** that you can use to paint your component. After you obtain a **Graphics**, you can call its various methods to draw on it. Here are some of the methods in **Graphics**: **drawArc, drawChars, drawImage, drawLine, drawOval, drawPolygon, drawPolyline, drawRect, drawString, fillArc, fillOval**, etc.

java.awt.Toolkit

The **Toolkit** abstract class has the following methods that make it interesting.

```
public static Toolkit getDefaultToolkit()
```
Returns the default implementation of the **Toolkit** class.

```
public abstract void beep()
```
Produces a beep sound.

```
public abstract Dimension getScreenSize()
```
Returns a **java.awt.Dimension** object containing the width and the height of the screen.

Basic Swing Components

Swing is the Java technology for developing desktop applications that need graphical user interface (GUI), replacing AWT but still using the AWT event model. As a technology, Swing is mature and complete, its rich set of classes and interfaces spanning across 17 packages. Swing components are contained in the **javax.swing** package. Figure 22.3 depicts the class hierarchy of Swing components. To save space, all classes with no package name belong to the **javax.swing** package.

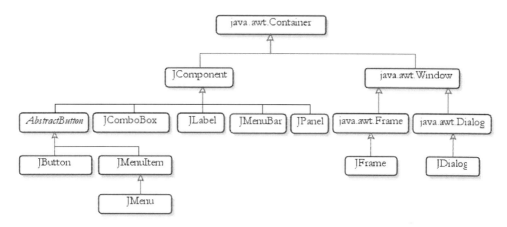

Figure 22.3: Swing components

Except for the three top-level containers **JFrame**, **JDialog**, and **JApplet**, all Swing components must reside in a container. You normally use **JFrame** as the main container of your Swing application. A **JDialog** represents a dialog, a window used to interact with the user. A **JDialog** is like a **JFrame**, but it normally lives within a **JFrame** or another **JDialog**. There are also other dialogs that are not made from **JDialog**, for example **JOptionPane** and **JColorChooser**. **JApplet** is a subclass of **java.applet.Applet**. It allows applet developers to use Swing components on applets. You will learn more about applets in Chapter 24, "Applets." To differentiate Swing components from AWT components, the names of Swing components are normally prefixed with **J**.

Note that the **javax.swing.JFrame** class is derived from **java.awt.Frame** and other Swing components from **javax.swing.JComponent**, which in turn extends **java.awt.Container**.

The following sections discuss the more important Swing components.

JFrame

A **JFrame** represents a frame container. **JFrame** is one of the three Swing top-level containers (the other two are **JDialog** and **JApplet**). Only top-level containers can appear onscreen without having to live in another container. Other Swing components must be child components of a container.

Just like **java.awt.Frame**, you can add components to a **JFrame** by calling one of its **add** methods. However, **JFrame** has only one child component, **JRootPane**, that manages a **java.awt.Container** called the content pane. The rule is you can only add non-menu components to this content pane, not to the **JFrame** itself. Therefore, you use this code to add a component:

```
jFrame.getContentPane().add(component)
```

However, Sun later added an **add** method as a shortcut to add a component directly to a **JFrame**.

```
jFrame.add(component)
```

The same holds true for the **remove** and **setLayout** methods.

A Swing component can only be added to one container. Adding a component that is already in a container to another container will automatically remove the component from the first container.

In addition, **JFrame** has the **setDefaultCloseOperation** method to control what the **JFrame**'s close button does. The **setDefaultCloseOperation** method can take one of these static finals defined in **JFrame**:

- **WindowConstants.DO_NOTHING_ON_CLOSE**. Do nothing.
- **WindowConstants.HIDE_ON_CLOSE** (the default). Hides the frame after invoking all registered **WindowListener** objects.
- **WindowConstants.DISPOSE_ON_CLOSE**. Hides and disposes the frame after invoking all registered **WindowListener** objects.
- **JFrame.EXIT_ON_CLOSE**. Exits the application by calling **System.exit()**.

Note that **JFrame** implements the **javax.swing.WindowConstants** interface, so you can use the static finals above directly from inside a **JFrame**.

As an example, to make a **JFrame** exit when the user clicks the close button, write this:

```
jFrame.setDefaultCloseOperation(JFrame.EXIT_ON_CLOSE)
```

JFrame has two methods to show a **JFrame** instance, **pack** and **setVisible**.

```
public void pack()
```

```
public void setVisible(boolean visible)
```

pack resizes the **JFrame** to fit the sizes and layouts of its child components. After calling **pack**, you would want to invoke **setVisible(true)** to display the **JFrame**. Two alternatives to **pack** are **setSize** and **setBounds**, which will be discussed in the subsection "Resizing and Positioning."

Listing 22.2 presents a class that creates a simple **JFrame**.

Listing 22.2: The JFrameDemo1 class

```
package app22;
import javax.swing.JFrame;
import javax.swing.JLabel;
import javax.swing.SwingUtilities;

public class JFrameDemo1 {
    private static void constructGUI() {
        JFrame.setDefaultLookAndFeelDecorated(true);
        JFrame frame = new JFrame();
        frame.setTitle("My First Swing Application");
        frame.setDefaultCloseOperation(JFrame.EXIT_ON_CLOSE);
        // add a JLabel that says Welcome
        JLabel label = new JLabel("Welcome");
        frame.add(label);
        frame.pack();
        frame.setVisible(true);
    }

    public static void main(String[] args) {
```

```
    SwingUtilities.invokeLater(new Runnable() {
        public void run() {
            constructGUI();
        }
    });
    }
}
```

The **JFrameTest1** class in Listing 22.2 displays a **JFrame** that looks like the one in Figure 22.4.

Figure 22.4: A JFrame

Notice that the window in the **JFrame** consists of two areas, the title bar and the content pane. The window has an icon on the left side of the title bar. There are also three buttons (minimize, restore, close) to the right of the title bar. The content pane is another object that gets created for each **JFrame**.

How does the code in Listing 22.2 work?

First, let's talk about the **main** method.

```
public static void main(String[] args) {
    SwingUtilities.invokeLater(new Runnable() {
        public void run() {
            constructGUI();
        }
    });
}
```

Sun recommends that you call the static **invokeLater** method of the **javax.swing.SwingUtilities** class to make sure that a special thread called the event-dispatching thread takes care of the creation of the GUI. The use of this method makes your code a bit more complex, but it ensures your Swing applications will be displayed correctly. If you do not understand this part, that's fine. Just make sure that the code in the **main** method becomes your standard way of creating Swing GUI. Read the Javadoc for the **SwingUtilities** class's **invokeLater** method for more information.

The **constructGUI** method constructs a **JFrame**, and you pass a **String** to its **setTitle** method. You then call the **JFrame**'s **setDefaultCloseOperation** method, passing **JFrame.EXIT_ON_CLOSE**. This line is useful because by default clicking the close button on a **JFrame** does not stop the JVM. Assigning **JFrame.EXIT_ON_CLOSE** to the **setDefaultCloseOperation** method allows you to exit the application when you click the close button.

```
    JFrame frame = new JFrame();
    frame.setTitle("My First Swing Application");
    frame.setDefaultCloseOperation(JFrame.EXIT_ON_CLOSE);
```

The **constructGUI** method then creates a **JLabel** control and adds it to the **JFrame**'s content pane.

```
JLabel label = new JLabel("Welcome");
frame.getContentPane().add(label);
```

Finally, it calls the **pack** method on the **JFrame** to size it to fit the preferred size and layout of its subcomponents. Lastly, it calls the **setVisible** method to make the **JFrame** visible.

```
frame.pack();
frame.setVisible(true);
```

The static **setDefaultLookAndFeelDecorated** method makes your **JFrame** decorated. Without this method, your **JFrame** would look like the frame in Figure 22.5.

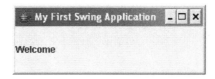

Figure 22.5: An undecorated JFrame

Resizing and Positioning

The **pack** method resizes a **JFrame** to a default width and height. Alternatively, you can resize a **JFrame** by calling the **setSize** and **setBounds** methods. If you choose to do this, **setSize** and **setBound** should be called just before the **setVisible** method. If you call **setSize**, you don't need to call **pack**.

JFrame inherits **setSize** from **java.awt.Component** and this method has two overloads:

```
public void setSize(int width, int height)
```

```
public void setSize(java.awt.Dimension d)
```

The **setBounds** method sets the size as well as the new top-left corner of the **JFrame**, relative to the screen's top-left corner. Here is its signature.

```
public void setBounds(int x, int y, int width, int height)
```

JFrame inherits **setBounds** from **java.awt.Window**.

In addition, the **setLocationRelativeTo** method sets a Swing component location relative to another component.

```
public void setLocationRelativeTo(java.awt.Component component)
```

If *component* is not visible or if you pass **null**, your **JFrame** will be centered on the screen.

Listing 22.3 presents another **JFrame** that is manually resized and positioned at the top-right corner of the screen.

Listing 22.3: Resizing and positioning a JFrame

```
package app22;
import java.awt.Dimension;
```

```
import java.awt.GridLayout;
import java.awt.Toolkit;
import javax.swing.JButton;
import javax.swing.JFrame;
import javax.swing.JLabel;
import javax.swing.JTextField;
import javax.swing.SwingUtilities;

public class JFrameDemo2 {
    private static void constructGUI() {
        JFrame.setDefaultLookAndFeelDecorated(true);
        JFrame frame = new JFrame();
        frame.setDefaultCloseOperation(JFrame.EXIT_ON_CLOSE);
        frame.setTitle("JFrame Test");
        frame.setLayout(new GridLayout(3, 2));
        frame.add(new JLabel("First Name:"));
        frame.add(new JTextField());
        frame.add(new JLabel("Last Name:"));
        frame.add(new JTextField());
        frame.add(new JButton("Register"));

        int frameWidth = 200;
        int frameHeight = 100;
        Dimension screenSize =
                Toolkit.getDefaultToolkit().getScreenSize();
        frame.setBounds((int) screenSize.getWidth() - frameWidth,
                0, frameWidth, frameHeight);
        frame.setVisible(true);
    }

    public static void main(String[] args) {
        SwingUtilities.invokeLater(new Runnable() {
            public void run() {
                constructGUI();
            }
        });
    }
}
```

The Running **JFrameDemo2** displays a **JFrame** like the one in Figure 22.6.

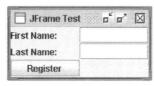

Figure 22.6: A JFrame that has been resized and repositioned

Extending JFrame

As your Swing applications grow more complex, it is often easier to extend **JFrame** and construct your GUI from inside a subclass than from within a static **constructGUI** method. Listing 22.4 rewrites the **JFrameTest2** class to extend **JFrame**. You still construct your GUI using the event-dispatching thread, however the complexity of constructing your GUI has been moved to a subclass.

Listing 22.4: Extending JFrame

```
package app22;
import java.awt.Dimension;
import java.awt.GridLayout;
import java.awt.Toolkit;
import javax.swing.JButton;
import javax.swing.JFrame;
import javax.swing.JLabel;
import javax.swing.JTextField;
import javax.swing.SwingUtilities;

class MyFrame extends JFrame {
    public MyFrame() {
        super();
        init();
    }

    public MyFrame(String title) {
        super(title);
        init();
    }

    private void init() {
        this.setDefaultCloseOperation(JFrame.EXIT_ON_CLOSE);
        this.setTitle("JFrame Test");
        this.setLayout(new GridLayout(3, 2));
        this.add(new JLabel("First Name:"));
        this.add(new JTextField());
        this.add(new JLabel("Last Name:"));
        this.add(new JTextField());
        this.add(new JButton("Register"));
        int frameWidth = 200;
        int frameHeight = 100;
        Dimension screenSize =
                Toolkit.getDefaultToolkit().getScreenSize();
        this.setBounds((int) screenSize.getWidth() - frameWidth, 0,
                frameWidth, frameHeight);
    }
}

public class JFrameDemo3 {
    private static void constructGUI() {
        JFrame.setDefaultLookAndFeelDecorated(true);
```

```
        MyFrame frame = new MyFrame();
        frame.setVisible(true);
    }

    public static void main(String[] args) {
        SwingUtilities.invokeLater(new Runnable() {
            public void run() {
                constructGUI();
            }
        });
    }
}
```

When run, the **JFrameDemo3** class produces the same result as the **JFrameDemo2** class in Listing 22.3.

JComponent

All Swing components derive from the abstract **javax.swing.JComponent** class. The following are the **JComponent** class's methods for manipulating the appearance of a component.

`public int getWidth()`
> Returns the current width of this component in pixel.

`public int getHeight()`
> Returns the current height of this component in pixel.

`public int getX()`
> Returns the current x coordinate of the component's top-left corner.

`public int getY()`
> Returns the current y coordinate of the component's top-left corner.

`public java.awt.Graphics getGraphics()`
> Returns this component's **Graphics** object you can draw on. This is useful if you want to change the appearance of a component.

`public void setBackground(java.awt.Color bg)`
> Sets this component's background color.

`public void setEnabled(boolean enabled)`
> Enables or disables this component.

`public void setFont(java.awt.Font font)`
> Set the font used to print text on this component.

`public void setForeground(java.awt.Color fg)`
> Set this component's foreground color.

`public void setToolTipText(java.lang.String text)`
> Sets the tool tip text.

`public void setVisible(boolean visible)`
> Makes this component visible or hides it.

I will discuss other methods later in this chapter.

Icon and ImageIcon

The **javax.swing.Icon** interface is a template for small images used to decorate Swing components. **Icon** is discussed before other Swing components because we often use icons to decorate Swing components. Components that can use an **Icon** object include **JLabel** and **JButton**. The **Icon** interface defines **getWidth** and **getHeight** methods that return the **Icon**'s width and height (in pixels), respectively.

```
public int getWidth()
```

```
public int getHeight()
```

The **javax.swing.ImageIcon** class is an implementation of **Icon**. The easiest constructor to use is the one that accepts a filename.

```
public ImageIcon(java.lang.String filename)
```

The *filename* argument can be a file name or the path to a file. Use a forward slash as a separator of a directory from a subdirectory. Formats supported include GIF, JPEG, and PNG.

Constructing an **Icon** by creating an instance of **ImageIcon** is as easy as this.

```
Icon icon = new ImageIcon("images/logo.gif");
```

You will see examples that create an **Icon** to decorate a Swing component in the sections "JLabel" and "JButton" later in this chapter.

JLabel

A **JLabel** represents a label, i.e. a display area for non-editable text. A **JLabel** can display both text and images. It can even render HTML tags so that you can create a **JLabel** that displays multicolors or multiline text. The **javax.swing.JLabel** class offers these constructors.

```
public JLabel()
```

```
public JLabel(java.lang.String text)
```

```
public JLabel(java.lang.String text, int horizontalAlignment)
```

```
public JLabel(Icon image)
```

```
public JLabel(Icon image, int horizontalAlignment)
```

```
public JLabel(java.lang.String text, Icon icon, int horizontalAlignment)
```

The value of *horizontalAlignment* is one of the following:

- **SwingConstants.LEFT**
- **SwingConstants.CENTER**
- **SwingConstants.RIGHT**
- **SwingConstants.LEADING**
- **SwingConstants.TRAILING**

JLabel has a **setText** method that takes a **String**. It also has a **setFont** method to set the font. Alternatively, if you want to use multifonts or multicolors in a **JLabel**, you can pass

HTML tags, as demonstrated in the example in Listing 22.5.

Listing 22.5: Using JLabel

```java
package app22;
import java.awt.Color;
import java.awt.FlowLayout;
import java.awt.Font;
import javax.swing.ImageIcon;
import javax.swing.JFrame;
import javax.swing.JLabel;
import javax.swing.SwingConstants;
import javax.swing.SwingUtilities;

public class JLabelDemo extends JFrame {
    private static void constructGUI() {
        JFrame.setDefaultLookAndFeelDecorated(true);
        JFrame frame = new JFrame();
        frame.setTitle("JLabel Test");
        frame.setLayout(new FlowLayout());
        frame.setDefaultCloseOperation(JFrame.EXIT_ON_CLOSE);
        JLabel label1 = new JLabel("First Name");
        label1.setFont(new Font("Courier New", Font.ITALIC, 12));
        label1.setForeground(Color.GRAY);

        JLabel label2 = new JLabel();
        label2.setText(
                "<html>Last Name<br><font face='courier new'"
                + " color=red>(mandatory)</font></html>");
        JLabel label3 = new JLabel();
        label3.setText("<html>Last Name<br><font face=garamond "
                + "color=red>(mandatory)</font></html>");
        ImageIcon imageIcon = new ImageIcon("triangle.jpg");
        JLabel label4 = new JLabel(imageIcon);
        JLabel label5 = new JLabel("Mixed", imageIcon,
                SwingConstants.RIGHT);
        frame.add(label1);
        frame.add(label2);
        frame.add(label3);
        frame.add(label4);
        frame.add(label5);
        frame.pack();
        frame.setVisible(true);
    }

    public static void main(String[] args) {
        SwingUtilities.invokeLater(new Runnable() {
            public void run() {
                constructGUI();
            }
        });
    }
}
```

If you pass HTML tags to the **setText** method on a **JLabel**, the tags must start with "<html>" and end with "</html>".

Figure 22.7 shows the result from running the code in Listing 22.5.

Figure 22.7: The JLabel example

JButton

A **JButton** represents a clickable button. In a typical Swing application, a **JButton** is connected to an event listener that provides code that gets executed when the **JButton** is clicked. Event listeners are discussed in Chapter 23, "Swinging Higher."

JButton has several constructors. Here are some of them.

```
public JButton()

public JButton(Icon icon)

public JButton(java.lang.String text)

public JButton(java.lang.String text, Icon icon)
```

You can create a **JButton** that has text on it or that has an **Icon** or text and an icon. The **setText** and **getText** methods allows you to assign text and retrieve a **JButton**'s text, respectively.

The code in Listing 22.6 shows a **JButton** example. The **JButton** contains both text and an icon.

Listing 22.6: Using JButton

```
package app22;
import javax.swing.ImageIcon;
import javax.swing.JFrame;
import javax.swing.JButton;
import javax.swing.SwingUtilities;

public class JButtonDemo extends JFrame {
    private static void constructGUI() {
        JFrame.setDefaultLookAndFeelDecorated(true);
        JFrame frame = new JFrame();
        frame.setDefaultCloseOperation(JFrame.EXIT_ON_CLOSE);
        frame.setTitle("JButton Test");
        ImageIcon imageIcon = new ImageIcon("triangle.jpg");
        JButton loginButton = new JButton("Login", imageIcon);
        frame.add(loginButton);
        frame.pack();
        frame.setVisible(true);
    }

    public static void main(String[] args) {
```

```
        SwingUtilities.invokeLater(new Runnable() {
            public void run() {
                constructGUI();
            }
        });
    }
}
```

Figure 22.8 shows how a **JButton** looks like when the code in Listing 22.6 is run. Note that in this example the **JButton** occupies the whole area of the **JFrame**'s content pane.

Figure 22.8: Using JButton

JTextField and JPasswordField

A **JTextField** represents a text field. The **JTextField** class derives from **JTextComponent**, which is also the direct parent of **JTextArea** and **JEditorPane**. **JFormattedTextField** and **JPasswordField** are some of **JTextField**'s subclasses.

A **JTextField** can only take a single line of text. By contrast, a **JTextArea** allows multiline text.

Here are two of the **JTextField** class's constructors.

```
public JTextField()
```

```
public JTextField(java.lang.String text)
```

The second constructor expects a **String** that will be used as the text of the constructed **JTextField**. If you use the first constructor, you can call the **setText** method to set the text:

```
public void setText(java.lang.String text)
```

To get the text, use the **getText** method.

```
public java.lang.String getText()
```

Both **setText** and **getText** are inherited from **JTextComponent**.

A descendant of **JTextField**, **JPasswordField** is similar to **JTextField**, except that each character of the text is displayed as an echo character, which by default is an asterisk. Here are two constructors of **JPasswordField**.

```
public void JPasswordField()
```

```
public void JPasswordField(java.lang.String initialPassword)
```

To set a password, use the **setText** method inherited from **JComponentText**. **JPasswordField** overrides the **getText** method which is now deprecated. To obtain the contents of a **JPasswordField**, use the **getPassword** method instead.

```
public char[] getPassword()
```

You can set the echo character using the **setEchoChar** method:

```
public void setEchoChar(char c)
```

Passing 0 to **setEchoChar** tells the **JPasswordField** to display the characters unmasked. The **getEchoChar** method allows you to obtain the echo character.

Listing 22.7 shows an example of **JTextField** and **JPasswordField**.

Listing 22.7: Using JTextField and JPasswordField

```
package app22;
import java.awt.GridLayout;
import javax.swing.JFrame;
import javax.swing.JLabel;
import javax.swing.JPasswordField;
import javax.swing.JTextField;
import javax.swing.SwingConstants;
import javax.swing.SwingUtilities;

public class JTextFieldDemo extends JFrame {
    private static void constructGUI() {
        JFrame.setDefaultLookAndFeelDecorated(true);
        JFrame frame = new JFrame();
        frame.setDefaultCloseOperation(JFrame.EXIT_ON_CLOSE);
        frame.setTitle("JTextField Test");
        frame.setLayout(new GridLayout(2, 2));
        JLabel label1 = new JLabel("User Name:",
                SwingConstants.RIGHT);
        JLabel label2 = new JLabel("Password:",
                SwingConstants.RIGHT);
        JTextField userNameField = new JTextField(20);
        JPasswordField passwordField = new JPasswordField();
        frame.add(label1);
        frame.add(userNameField);
        frame.add(label2);
        frame.add(passwordField);
        frame.setSize(200, 70);
        frame.setVisible(true);
    }

    public static void main(String[] args) {
        SwingUtilities.invokeLater(new Runnable() {
            public void run() {
                constructGUI();
            }
        });
    }
}
```

The result of running the code in Listing 22.7 is shown in Figure 22.9.

Figure 22.9: Using JTextField and JPasswordField

JTextArea

A **JTextArea** represents a multiline area for displaying text. You can change the number of lines that can be displayed as well as the number of columns. You can wrap lines and words too. You can also put a **JTextArea** in a **JScrollPane** to make it scrollable.

Here are some of the **JTextArea** class's constructors:

```
public JTextArea()

public JTextArea(int rows, int columns)

public JTextArea(java.lang.String text)

public JTextArea(java.lang.String text, int rows, int columns)
```

And, here are some of the more important methods in **JTextArea**.

```
public void append(java.lang.String str)
```
Appends a String to the end of the text.

```
public int getColumns()
```
Returns the number of columns in the **JTextArea**.

```
public int getRows()
```
Returns the number of rows in the **JTextArea**.

```
public void setColumns(int columns)
```
Sets the number of columns in the **JTextArea**.

```
public void setRows(int rows)
```
Sets the number of rows in the **JTextArea**.

The code in Listing 22.8 creates a **JFrame** with two **JTextArea** components. The second one is displayed in a **JScrollPane**.

Listing 22.8: Using JTextArea
```java
package app22;
import java.awt.Dimension;
import java.awt.FlowLayout;
import javax.swing.JFrame;
import javax.swing.JTextArea;
import javax.swing.JScrollPane;
import javax.swing.SwingUtilities;

public class JTextAreaDemo {

    private static void constructGUI() {
        JFrame.setDefaultLookAndFeelDecorated(true);
        JFrame frame = new JFrame("JTextArea Test");
        frame.setLayout(new FlowLayout());
```

```
        frame.setDefaultCloseOperation(JFrame.EXIT_ON_CLOSE);
        String text = "A JTextArea object represents" +
                "a multiline area for displaying text. " +
                "You can change the number of lines " +
                "that can be displayed at a time, " +
                "as well as the number of columns. " +
                "You can wrap lines and words too. " +
                "You can also put your JTextArea in a " +
                "JScrollPane to make it scrollable.";
        JTextArea textArea1 = new JTextArea(text, 5, 10);
        textArea1.setPreferredSize(new Dimension(100, 100));
        JTextArea textArea2 = new JTextArea(text, 5, 10);
        textArea2.setPreferredSize(new Dimension(100, 100));
        JScrollPane scrollPane = new JScrollPane(textArea2,
                JScrollPane.VERTICAL_SCROLLBAR_ALWAYS,
                JScrollPane.HORIZONTAL_SCROLLBAR_ALWAYS);
        textArea1.setLineWrap(true);
        textArea2.setLineWrap(true);
        frame.add(textArea1);
        frame.add(scrollPane);
        frame.pack();
        frame.setVisible(true);
    }

    public static void main(String[] args) {
        SwingUtilities.invokeLater(new Runnable() {
            public void run() {
                constructGUI();
            }
        });
    }
}
```

When run, the class will display something similar to Figure 22.10.

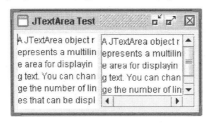

Figure 22.10: Using JTextArea

JCheckbox

A **JCheckBox** represents a check box. You construct a **JCheckBox** by passing a **String**, an icon, or a **String** and an icon to its constructor. Here are some of the constructors in the **JCheckBox** class.

```
public JCheckBox(java.lang.String text)
```

```
public JCheckBox(Icon icon)

public JCheckBox(java.lang.String text, Icon icon)
```

You can programmatically check a **JCheckBox** by passing **true** to its **setSelected** method. However, there is no **getSelected** method that you can use to check if a **JCheckBox** is checked. For this, you need to use an event listener. See Chapter 16, "Swinging Higher" for information about event listeners.

As an example, the code in Listing 22.9 demonstrates how to use **JCheckBox**. If you run it, you'll see something similar to Figure 22.11

Listing 22.9: Using JCheckBox

```java
package app22;
import javax.swing.JFrame;
import javax.swing.JCheckBox;
import java.awt.FlowLayout;
import javax.swing.JLabel;
import javax.swing.SwingUtilities;

public class JCheckBoxDemo {
    private static void constructGUI() {
        JFrame.setDefaultLookAndFeelDecorated(true);
        JFrame frame = new JFrame("JCheckBox Test");
        frame.setLayout(new FlowLayout());
        frame.setDefaultCloseOperation(JFrame.EXIT_ON_CLOSE);
        JCheckBox ac = new JCheckBox("A/C");
        ac.setSelected(true);
        JCheckBox cdPlayer = new JCheckBox("CD Player");
        JCheckBox cruiseControl = new JCheckBox("Cruise Control");
        JCheckBox keylessEntry = new JCheckBox("Keyless Entry");
        JCheckBox antiTheft = new JCheckBox("Anti-Theft Alarm");
        JCheckBox centralLock = new JCheckBox("Central Lock");

        frame.add(new JLabel("Car Features"));
        frame.add(ac);
        frame.add(cdPlayer);
        frame.add(cruiseControl);
        frame.add(keylessEntry);
        frame.add(antiTheft);
        frame.add(centralLock);
        frame.pack();
        frame.setVisible(true);
    }

    public static void main(String[] args) {
        SwingUtilities.invokeLater(new Runnable() {
            public void run() {
                constructGUI();
            }
        });
    }
}
```

Figure 22.11: Using JCheckBox

JRadioButton

A **JRadioButton** represents a radio button. You can use multiple **JRadioButtons** to represent a selection from which only one item can be selected. To indicate a logical grouping of radio buttons, you use a **javax.swing.ButtonGroup** object.

Like **JCheckBox**, you can pass a **String**, an icon, or a **String** and an icon to construct a **JRadioButton**. Here are some of its constructors.

```
public JRadioButton(java.lang.String text)

public JRadioButton (Icon icon)

public JRadioButton (java.lang.String text, Icon icon)
```

To programmatically select a **JRadioButton**, you pass **true** to its **setSelected** method. However, to detect which radio button in a button group is selected, you need to use a listener. Read Chapter 16, "Swinging Higher" to learn how to achieve this.

As an example, Listing 22.10 shows code that displays three radio buttons in a button group.

Listing 22.10: Using JRadioButton

```
package app22;
import java.awt.FlowLayout;
import javax.swing.ButtonGroup;
import javax.swing.JFrame;
import javax.swing.JLabel;
import javax.swing.JRadioButton;
import javax.swing.SwingUtilities;

public class JRadioButtonDemo {
    private static void constructGUI() {
        JFrame.setDefaultLookAndFeelDecorated(true);
        JFrame frame = new JFrame("JRadioButton Test");
        frame.setLayout(new FlowLayout());
        frame.setDefaultCloseOperation(JFrame.EXIT_ON_CLOSE);
        JRadioButton button1 = new JRadioButton("Red");
        JRadioButton button2 = new JRadioButton("Green");
        JRadioButton button3 = new JRadioButton("Blue");
        ButtonGroup colorButtonGroup = new ButtonGroup();
        colorButtonGroup.add(button1);
        colorButtonGroup.add(button2);
        colorButtonGroup.add(button3);
        button1.setSelected(true);
        frame.add(new JLabel("Color:"));
        frame.add(button1);
        frame.add(button2);
        frame.add(button3);
```

```
        frame.pack();
        frame.setVisible(true);
    }

    public static void main(String[] args) {
        SwingUtilities.invokeLater(new Runnable() {
            public void run() {
                constructGUI();
            }
        });
    }
}
```

Figure 22.12 shows the result of running the class in Listing 22.10.

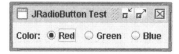

Figure 22.12: Using JRadioButton

JList

A **JList** displays a selection of objects from which the user can choose one or more options. The easiest way to construct a **JList** is to pass an array of **java.lang.Object** to its constructor:

```
public JList(java.lang.Object[] selections)
```

You can determine if the user can select a single item or multiple items from a **JList** by using the **setSelectionMode** method.

```
public void setSelectionMode(int selectionMode)
```

The valid value for *selectionMode* is one of the fields in the **ListSelectionModel** interface.

- **SINGLE_SELECTION**. Allows a single item selection.
- **SINGLE_INTERVAL_SELECTION**. Allows multiple item selection, but the selected items must be contiguous.
- **MULTIPLE_INTERVAL_SELECTION**. Allows multiple items and the selected items may or may not be contiguous.

You can set an initial selection(s) by using **setSelectedIndex** and **setSelectedIndices** methods (the indexing is zero-based, so index 0 refers to the first option in the **JList**).

```
public void setSelectedIndex(int index)
```

```
public void setSelectedIndices(int[] indices)
```

In addition, you can get the selected item(s) by using one of these methods:

```
public int getSelectedIndex()
```
        Returns the first selected index or -1 if there is no selected item.

```
public int[] getSelectedIndices()
```

Returns an array of the selected indices.

```
public java.lang.Object getSelectedValue()
```
Returns the first selected value, or null if no item is being selected.

```
public java.lang.Object[] getSelectedValues()
```
Returns all the selected items as an array of Objects.

Listing 22.11 shows code that uses **JList**.

Listing 22.11: Using JList

```java
package app22;
import java.awt.FlowLayout;
import javax.swing.JFrame;
import javax.swing.JList;
import javax.swing.SwingUtilities;

public class JListDemo {
    private static void constructGUI() {
        JFrame.setDefaultLookAndFeelDecorated(true);
        JFrame frame = new JFrame("JList Test");
        frame.setLayout(new FlowLayout());
        frame.setDefaultCloseOperation(JFrame.EXIT_ON_CLOSE);
        String[] selections = { "green", "red", "orange",
                "dark blue" };
        JList<String> list = new JList<String>(selections);
        list.setSelectedIndex(1);
        System.out.println(list.getSelectedValue());
        frame.add(list);
        frame.pack();
        frame.setVisible(true);
    }

    public static void main(String[] args) {
        SwingUtilities.invokeLater(new Runnable() {
            public void run() {
                constructGUI();
            }
        });
    }
}
```

When run, you should see something like Figure 22.13.

Figure 22.13: Using JList

JComboBox

JComboBox is very similar to **JList**, except that only one item can be selected. On top of that, **JComboBox** does not show all the options but only the selected item and an arrow that the user can click to see other options and select one of them.

Like **JList**, you can pass an array of selection objects to **JComboBox**:

```
public JComboBox(java.lang.Object[] selection)
```

Also, **JComboBox** has **getSelectedIndex**, **getSelectedItem**, and **getSelectedObjects** methods that return the selected item(s). Here are the signatures of these methods:

```
public int getSelectedIndex()
```
Returns the selected first item or -1 if there is no selected item.

```
public java.lang.Object getSelectedItem()
```
Returns the first value in the selection or null if no item is currently being selected.

```
public java.lang.Object[] getSelectedObjects()
```
Returns the selected item as an array of objects.

Note that **getSelectedObjects** returns an array that contains a maximum of one element because you cannot select multiple items with a **JComboBox**.

Listing 22.12 shows a **JFrame** that contains a **JComboBox**.

Listing 22.12: Using JComboBox
```
package app22;
import java.awt.FlowLayout;
import javax.swing.JComboBox;
import javax.swing.JFrame;
import javax.swing.SwingUtilities;

public class JComboBoxDemo {
    private static void constructGUI() {
        JFrame.setDefaultLookAndFeelDecorated(true);
        JFrame frame = new JFrame("JComboBox Test");
        frame.setLayout(new FlowLayout());
        frame.setDefaultCloseOperation(JFrame.EXIT_ON_CLOSE);
        String[] selections = { "green", "red", "orange",
                "dark blue" };
        JComboBox<String> comboBox =
                new JComboBox<String>(selections);
        comboBox.setSelectedIndex(1);
        System.out.println(comboBox.getSelectedItem());
        frame.add(comboBox);
        frame.pack();
        frame.setVisible(true);
    }

    public static void main(String[] args) {
        SwingUtilities.invokeLater(new Runnable() {
            public void run() {
```

```
                constructGUI();
            }
        });
    }
}
```

When run, you'll see a **JFrame** that looks like that in Figure 22.14.

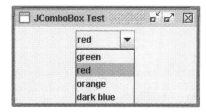

Figure 22.14: A JComboBox

JDialog

A **JDialog** represents a dialog, a top-level container that you can extend to create a window to interact with the user. You can use it to display messages, receive user input, etc. A dialog can be either modal or modeless. A modal dialog blocks user input to all other windows in the same application when it is visible. In other words, you have to close a modal dialog before other windows in the same application can get focus. A modeless one does not block user input. A dialog can belong to another dialog or a frame or stand alone like a **JFrame**. However, most of the time you would want to use a dialog that is part of a frame. For a stand alone top level container, you normally use a **JFrame**. When a dialog is part of another dialog or a frame, it will be destroyed when the owner is destroyed.

Note
The **JOptionPane** class, discussed in the section "JOptionPane," is handy for creating simple modal dialogs.

Like **JFrame**, **JDialog** has a **JRootPane** as its only child. This means, you only add components to its content pane. However, the **add**, **remove**, and **setLayout** methods have been overridden to call the appropriate methods in the content pane. In other words, like in **JFrame**, you can add a component to a **JDialog** just like this:

```
jDialog.add(component)
```

Here are some of the constructors of **JDialog**.

```
public JDialog()

public JDialog(java.awt.Dialog owner)

public JDialog(java.awt.Frame owner)

public JDialog(java.awt.Dialog owner, boolean modal)

public JDialog(java.awt.Frame owner, boolean modal)
```

You can use the last two constructors to create a modal **JDialog**.

As an example, Listing 22.13 shows an **AddressDialog** class for asking for the user's address.

Listing 22.13: AddressDialog

```
package app22;
import java.awt.Frame;
import java.awt.GridLayout;
import javax.swing.JDialog;
import javax.swing.JLabel;
import javax.swing.JTextField;

public class AddressDialog extends JDialog {
    JLabel label1 = new JLabel("Address");
    JLabel label2 = new JLabel("City");
    JLabel label3 = new JLabel("State");
    JLabel label4 = new JLabel("Zip Code");
    JTextField addressField = new JTextField();
    JTextField cityField = new JTextField();
    JTextField stateField = new JTextField();
    JTextField zipCodeField = new JTextField();
    String[] address = new String[4];

    public AddressDialog(Frame owner, boolean modal) {
        super(owner, modal);
        init();
    }

    private void init() {
        this.setTitle("Address Dialog");
        this.setLayout(new GridLayout(4, 2));
        this.add(label1);
        this.add(addressField);
        this.add(label2);
        this.add(cityField);
        this.add(label3);
        this.add(stateField);
        this.add(label4);
        this.add(zipCodeField);
    }

    public String[] getAddress() {
        address[0] = addressField.getText();
        address[1] = cityField.getText();
        address[2] = stateField.getText();
        address[3] = zipCodeField.getText();
        return address;
    }
}
```

Note that clients of **AddressDialog** can call its **getAddress** method to obtain the user's address information. When displayed, an **AddressDialog** looks like the one in Figure 22.15.

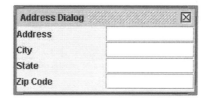

Figure 22.15: The AddressDialog

The **JDialogTest** class in Listing 22.14 uses the **AddressDialog** class.

Listing 22.14: The JDialogDemo class

```java
package app22;
import java.awt.FlowLayout;
import java.awt.event.ActionEvent;
import java.awt.event.ActionListener;
import javax.swing.JButton;
import javax.swing.JDialog;
import javax.swing.JFrame;
import javax.swing.SwingUtilities;

public class JDialogDemo extends JFrame {
    AddressDialog dialog = new AddressDialog(this, false);
    public JDialogDemo(String title) {
        super(title);
        init();
    }
    public JDialogDemo() {
        super();
        init();
    }
    private void init() {
        this.getContentPane().setLayout(new FlowLayout());
        this.setDefaultCloseOperation(JFrame.EXIT_ON_CLOSE);
        AddressDialog dialog = new AddressDialog(this, false);
        JButton button = new JButton("Show Dialog");
        button.addActionListener(new ActionListener() {
            public void actionPerformed(ActionEvent ae) {
                displayDialog();
            }
        });
        this.getContentPane().add(button);
    }

    private void displayDialog() {
        dialog.setSize(250, 120);
        dialog.setVisible(true);
    }
    private static void constructGUI() {
        JFrame.setDefaultLookAndFeelDecorated(true);
        JDialog.setDefaultLookAndFeelDecorated(true);
        JDialogDemo frame = new JDialogDemo();
        frame.pack();
```

```
        frame.setVisible(true);
    }

    public static void main(String[] args) {
        SwingUtilities.invokeLater(new Runnable() {
          public void run() {
            constructGUI();
          }
        });
    }
}
```

The **JDialogDemo** class displays a **JButton** you can click to display the **AddressDialog**. To achieve this **JDialogDemo** uses an **ActionListener**, a type discussed in Chapter 23, "Swinging Higher."

JOptionPane

A **JOptionPane** object represents a dialog box that you can use for several purposes:

- Display a message (through the use of the **showMessageDialog** method)
- Ask for user's confirmation (using the **showConfirmDialog** method)
- Obtain the user's input (using the **showInputDialog** method)
- Do all the three above (using the **showOptionDialog** method)

Most methods in **JOptionPane** are static, so you can create a dialog with a single line of code. You can use **JOptionPane** as a dialog of a frame or independently. You can pass a message, a visual component, or an icon to be displayed in the dialog. In addition, **JOptionPane** provides four default icons that are ready for use. You can even use **JOptionPane** in non-Swing applications as an easy way to interact with the user.

The following sections discuss the four main functions you can achieve using **JOptionPane**.

Using JOptionPane to Display a Message

You use the **JOptionPane** class's **showMessageDialog** method to display a message. There are three overloads of this method.

```
public static void showMessageDialog(java.awt.Component parent,
        java.lang.Object message)

public static void showMessageDialog(java.awt.Component parent,
        java.lang.Object message, java.lang.String title,
        int messageType)

public static void showMessageDialog(java.awt.Component parent,
        java.lang.Object message, java.lang.String title,
        int messageType, Icon icon)
```

The *parent* argument specifies a **java.awt.Component** in which the **JOptionPane** is to be displayed. If *component* is **null** or does not have a frame, the default frame will be used.

The *message* argument specifies the message to display. The *title* argument specifies the title for the dialog window. If the first overload is used, the title is "Message."

The *messageType* argument can be assigned one of these static finals:

- **JOptionPane.ERROR_MESSAGE**
- **JOptionPane.INFORMATION_MESSAGE**
- **JOptionPane.WARNING_MESSAGE**
- **JOptionPane.QUESTION_MESSAGE**
- **JOptionPane.PLAIN_MESSAGE** (no icon will be used)

Each value of **messageType** implies the use of a different default icon. No icon is used if *messageType* is assigned **JOptionPane.PLAIN_MESSAGE**.

For example, this code snippet displays four different **JOptionPane** dialogs.

```
JDialog.setDefaultLookAndFeelDecorated(true);
JOptionPane.showMessageDialog(null,
        "Thank you for visiting our store", "Thank You",
        JOptionPane.INFORMATION_MESSAGE);

JOptionPane.showMessageDialog(null,
        "You have not saved this document", "Warning",
        JOptionPane.WARNING_MESSAGE);

JOptionPane.showMessageDialog(null, "First Name must have a value",
        "Error", JOptionPane.ERROR_MESSAGE);
```

Figures 22.16, 22.17, and 22.18 show an information message dialog, a warning message dialog, and error message dialog, respectively.

Figure 22.16: An information message dialog

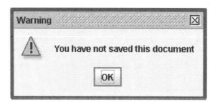

Figure 22.17: A warning message dialog

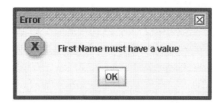

Figure 22.18: An error message dialog

Using JOptionPane to Prompt User Confirmation

You can use the **showConfirmDialog** static method to ask for user confirmation. This method displays a dialog with buttons on it, such as a Yes button, a No button, a Cancel button, or an OK button. You can select which buttons to appear or you can create your own buttons. Upon the user clicking a button, **JOptionPane** returns one of the following predefined **int**s:

- **JOptionPane.YES_OPTION**
- **JOptionPane.NO_OPTION**
- **JOptionPane.CANCEL_OPTION**
- **JOptionPane.OK_OPTION**

In addition, if the user closes a **JOptionPane** by clicking the close button at the top right hand corner of the dialog, the **JOptionPane.CLOSED_OPTION int** is returned.

The **showConfirmDialog** method has four overloads whose signatures are as follows.

```
public static int showConfirmDialog(java.awt.Component parent,
        java.lang.Object message)

public static int showConfirmDialog(java.awt.Component parent,
        java.lang.Object message, java.lang.String title,
        int optionType)

public static int showConfirmDialog(java.awt.Component parent,
        java.lang.Object message, java.lang.String title,
        int optionType, int messageType)

public static int showConfirmDialog(java.awt.Component parent,
        java.lang.Object message, java.lang.String title,
        int optionType, int messageType, Icon icon)
```

The *parent* argument specifies the **java.awt.Frame** in which this **JOptionPane** will be displayed. If **null** is passed to this argument or if the parent component does not have a frame, the default frame will be used.

The *message* argument specifies the message to be displayed. The title argument specifies the title that will be printed on the dialog title bar.

The *optionType* argument specifies the buttons that will be displayed. The possible values are as follows:

- **JOptionPanel.YES_NO_OPTION**, which causes the Yes and No button to be displayed.
- **JOptionPane.YES_NO_CANCEL_OPTION**, which causes the Yes, No, and

Cancel buttons to be displayed.

If the first overload is used where there is no argument *optionType* is required, **JOptionPane.YES_NO_CANCEL_OPTION** is assumed.

For example, the **JOptionPaneTest2** class in Listing 22.15 shows how you can use the **JOptionPane** class to prompt user confirmation.

Listing 22.15: Using JOptionPane to prompt user confirmation

```
package app22;
import javax.swing.JDialog;
import javax.swing.JOptionPane;

public class JOptionPaneDemo2 {
    public static void main(String[] args) {
        JDialog.setDefaultLookAndFeelDecorated(true);
        int response = JOptionPane.showConfirmDialog(null,
                "Do you want to continue?", "Confirm",
                JOptionPane.YES_NO_OPTION,
                JOptionPane.QUESTION_MESSAGE);
        if (response == JOptionPane.NO_OPTION) {
            System.out.println("No button clicked");
        } else if (response == JOptionPane.YES_OPTION) {
            System.out.println("Yes button clicked");
        } else if (response == JOptionPane.CLOSED_OPTION) {
            System.out.println("JOptionPane closed");
        }
    }
}
```

If you run the program, you'll see a **JOptionPane** dialog like the one shown in Figure 22.19.

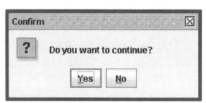

Figure 22.19: Asking user confirmation

Using JOptionPane to Obtain User Input

The third use of **JOptionPane** is to obtain user input, by using the **showInputDialog** method. This method displays a **JOptionPane** with a box for the user to type in a value. **showInputDialog** can return one of these:

- the string entered by the user, if the OK button is clicked after the user types in a value.
- an empty string, if the user clicks the OK button without entering a value and there is no initial value displayed.
- null, if the **JOptionPane** is closed by clicking the close button or the Cancel

button.
- a **java.lang.Object**, if the user selects one of the predefined options displayed by the **JOptionPane**.

The **showInputDialog** method has six overloads whose signatures are as follows.

```
public static java.lang.String showInputDialog(
        java.awt.Component parent, java.lang.Object message)
```

```
public static java.lang.String showInputDialog(
        java.awt.Component parent, java.lang.Object message,
        java.lang.Object initialSelectionValue)
```

```
public static java.lang.String showInputDialog(
        java.awt.Component parent, java.lang.Object message,
        java.lang.String title, int messageType)
```

```
public static java.lang.String showInputDialog(
        java.awt.Component parent, java.lang.Object message,
        java.lang.String title, int messageType, Icon icon,
        java.lang.Object[] selectionValues,
        java.lang.Object initialSelectionValue)
```

```
public static java.lang.String showInputDialog(
        java.lang.Object message)
```

```
public static java.lang.Object showInputDialog(
        java.lang.Object message,
        java.lang.Object intialSelectionValue)
```

The *parent* argument specifies the **java.awt.Frame** in which this **JOptionPane** will be displayed. If **null** is passed to this argument or if the parent component does not have a frame, the default frame is used.

The *message* argument specifies the message to be displayed.

The *title* argument specifies the title that will be printed on the dialog title bar. If no title argument is present, the string "Input" is displayed on the title bar.

The *messageType* argument specifies the type of the message, and its values is one of the following:

- **JOptionPane.INFORMATION_MESSAGE**
- **JOptionPane.ERROR_MESSAGE**
- **JOptionPane.WARNING_MESSAGE**
- **JOptionPane.QUESTION_MESSAGE**
- **JOptionPane.PLAIN_MESSAGE**

The **JOptionPane.QUESTION_MESSAGE** value is assumed if no *messageType* argument is present.

The *selectionValues* argument specifies an array of objects that provides possible selections and the *initialSelectionValue* argument specifies the initial value in the input field.

For example, the following lines of code display an input data shown in Figure 22.20.

```
String input = JOptionPane.showInputDialog(null,
```

```
"Enter Your Name", "John Average");
```

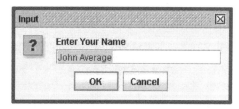

Figure 22.20: The Input data

As another example, consider the **JOptionPaneTest3** class in Listing 22.16.

Listing 22.16: Using JOptionPane with a predefined selections

```
package app22;
import javax.swing.JDialog;
import javax.swing.JOptionPane;

public class JOptionPaneDemo3 {
    public static void main(String[] args) {
        JDialog.setDefaultLookAndFeelDecorated(true);
        Object[] selectionValues = { "Pandas", "Dogs", "Horses" };
        String initialSelection = "Dogs";
        Object selection = JOptionPane.showInputDialog(null,
                "What are your favorite animals?", "Zoo Quiz",
                JOptionPane.QUESTION_MESSAGE, null,
                selectionValues, initialSelection);
        System.out.println(selection);
    }
}
```

The **JOptionPaneDemo3** class displays a predefined selections. Here there are three values predefined, "Pandas", "Dogs", and "Horses." The value for the *initialSelection* argument is "Dogs," so this is the initial selected value. When run, the **JOptionPaneDemo3** class displays something that looks like Figure 22.21

Figure 22.21: Using JOptionPane with predefined values

JFileChooser

A **JFileChooser** is a dialog specifically designed to enable users to easily select a file or files. You can create a **JFileChooser** that allows multiple selection by passing **true** to its **setMultiSelectionEnabled** method.

After you create an instance of **JFileChooser**, you can call its **showXXX** method to make it visible. There are three methods you can use for this purpose.

```
public int showDialog(java.awt.Component parent,
        java.lang.String approveButtonText)
```
Displays the **JFileChooser** with a custom Approve button.

```
public int showOpenDialog(java.awt.Component parent)
```
Displays the **JFileChooser** in the "Open File" mode.

```
public int showSaveDialog(java.awt.Component parent)
```
Displays the **JFileChooser** in the "Save File" mode.

The return value of the three methods is one of the following:

- **JFileChooser.CANCEL_OPTION**, if the user clicks Cancel.
- **JFileChooser.APPROVE_OPTION**, if the user clicks an OK/Open/Save button.
- **JFileCHooser.ERROR_OPTION**, if the user closes the dialog

A return value of **JFileChooser.APPROVE_OPTION** indicates that you can call its **getSelectedFile** or **getSelectedFiles** methods. Here are the signatures of the methods.

```
public java.io.File getSelectedFile()
```

```
public java.io.File[] getSelectedFiles()
```

The **JFileChooserTest** class in Listing 22.17 presents a **JFrame** with a button. Clicking the button brings up a **JFileChooser** dialog. The name of the selected file will be displayed after you click the Open button.

Listing 22.17: Using JFileChooser

```
package app22;
import java.awt.FlowLayout;
import java.awt.event.ActionEvent;
import java.awt.event.ActionListener;
import java.io.File;
import javax.swing.JButton;
import javax.swing.JDialog;
import javax.swing.JFileChooser;
import javax.swing.JFrame;
import javax.swing.SwingUtilities;

public class JFileChooserDemo extends JFrame {
    private static void constructGUI() {
        JFrame.setDefaultLookAndFeelDecorated(true);
        JDialog.setDefaultLookAndFeelDecorated(true);
        JFrame frame = new JFrame("JComboBox Test");
        frame.setLayout(new FlowLayout());
        frame.setDefaultCloseOperation(JFrame.EXIT_ON_CLOSE);
        JButton button = new JButton("Select File");
        button.addActionListener(new ActionListener() {
            public void actionPerformed(ActionEvent ae) {
                JFileChooser fileChooser = new JFileChooser();
                int returnValue = fileChooser.showOpenDialog(null);
                if (returnValue == JFileChooser.APPROVE_OPTION) {
                    File selectedFile =
                            fileChooser.getSelectedFile();
```

```
                    System.out.println(selectedFile.getName());
                }
            }
        });
        frame.add(button);
        frame.pack();
        frame.setVisible(true);
    }

    public static void main(String[] args) {
        SwingUtilities.invokeLater(new Runnable() {
            public void run() {
                constructGUI();
            }
        });
    }
}
```

Figure 22.22 displays a **JFileChooser**.

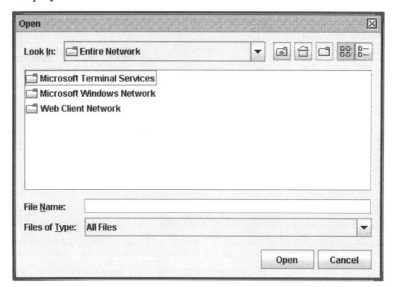

Figure 22.22: A JFileChooser

Summary

This chapter is the first of two installments on Swing. In this chapter you learned the AWT basic components as well as some in the Swing collection. This chapter covered **JFrame**, **JButton**, **JLabel**, **JList**, **JComboBox**, **JDialog**, **JOptionPane**, and **JFileChooser**.

Quiz

1. Why is studying AWT still relevant today?
2. What is the AWT class that represents a component?
3. What is the easiest way to construct a **Color** object?
4. What is the only non-menu child component that can be added to a **JFrame**?
5. What is the significance of using **SwingUtilities.invokeLater** to construct Swing GUI?
6. What are the three top-level Swing containers?

Chapter 23
Swinging Higher

In Chapter 22, "Swing Basics" you learned about AWT and Swing components. This chapter is the second installment of Swing and discusses techniques that you invariably use in Swing programming: layout management and event handling. In addition, there is discussion about menus, the look and feel, fast splash screens, the system tray and Java Desktop.

Layout Managers

A container, such as a **JFrame** and a **JDialog**, needs a **java.awt.LayoutManager** to lay out child components. A **LayoutManager** resizes and positions all child components, as well as rearranges the components when the container is resized. The **java.awt.Container** class has a **setLayout** method for adding a layout manager. Since **javax.swing.JComponent** extends **Container**, you can add a **LayoutManager** to a Swing component as well. For example, it is not uncommon to add a **LayoutManager** to a **JLabel** if the latter has components added to it.

With some components, you can pass a **LayoutManager** to the component class. This is the case for **JPanel**.

```
JPanel panel = new JPanel(layoutManager);
```

As for **JFrame**, you add a **LayoutManager** to its content pane:

```
jFrame.getContentPane().setLayoutManager(layoutManager)
```

There is also a **setLayoutManager** method in **JFrame** to add a **LayoutManager** to its content pane:

```
jFrame.setLayoutManager(layoutManager)
```

To tell the layout manager the preferred size of a component, pass a **java.awt.Dimension** object to the **setPreferredSize** method on the component. For example:

```
button.setPreferredSize(new Dimension(300, 300));
```

The **LayoutManager** interface defines the methods that a layout manager has to implement. There are a few default implementations of this interface in both **java.awt** and **javax.swing** packages. Unless you are writing a **LayoutManager** implementation, you seldom have to call the **LayoutManager** interface's methods. In most scenarios, these default implementations are sufficient.

Figure 23.1 shows the **LayoutManager** interface and some of its implementations.

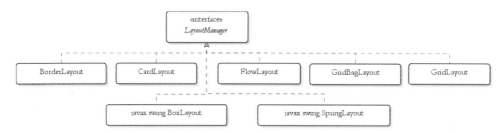

Figure 23.1: The LayoutManager interface and its implementations

To save space, members of **java.awt** are drawn without package information in Figure 23.1. Two implementations in Figure 23.1, **BoxLayout** and **SpringLayout**, belong to the **javax.swing** package.

Some of the **LayoutManager** implementations are discussed in the following sections.

BorderLayout

A **BorderLayout** arranges components to fit in five regions: north, south, east, west, and center. There are five static final fields of type **java.lang.String** in **BorderLayout** that indicate these regions: **NORTH**, **SOUTH**, **EAST**, **WEST**, and **CENTER**. Each region may not contain more than one component. If you add multiple components to a region, only the last one will be displayed.

To add a component to a container employing a **BorderLayout**, you call the container's **add** method, passing the component and the region field. For example, the following code adds a **JButton** to a **JFrame**.

```
jFrame.add(new JButton("Register"), BorderLayout.NORTH);
```

The absence of a region field will place the component at the center.

BorderLayout is the default layout manager. If you do not specifically add a **LayoutManager** to a container, a **BorderLayout** will be used to lay out child components in the container.

Listing 23.1 presents an example to show how to use **BorderLayout**.

Listing 23.1: Using BorderLayout
```
package app23;
import java.awt.BorderLayout;
import javax.swing.JButton;
import javax.swing.JFrame;
import javax.swing.JTextField;
import javax.swing.SwingUtilities;

public class BorderLayoutDemo1 extends JFrame {
    private static void constructGUI() {
        JFrame.setDefaultLookAndFeelDecorated(true);
```

```
            JFrame frame = new JFrame("BorderLayout Test");
            frame.setDefaultCloseOperation(JFrame.EXIT_ON_CLOSE);
            frame.setLayout(new BorderLayout());
            JTextField textField = new JTextField("<your name>");
            frame.add(textField, BorderLayout.WEST);
            JButton button =
                    new JButton("<html>R<b>e</b>gister</html>");
            frame.add(button, BorderLayout.EAST);
            frame.pack();
            frame.setVisible(true);
        }

    public static void main(String[] args) {
        SwingUtilities.invokeLater(new Runnable() {
            public void run() {
                constructGUI();
            }
        });
    }
}
```

The result of running the **BorderLayoutTest1** class is shown in Figure 23.2.

Figure 23.2: A JFrame that uses a BorderLayout (left) and the same JFrame resized (right)

Note that the **JTextField** and the **JButton** are placed in the west and east regions of the **JFrame**. If you resize the **JFrame**, the components will maintain their positions. The size of each component adjusts accordingly, and setting the size of the components (by using **setSize**) does not have effect. It is clear the **BorderLayout** has the final say with regard to the components' sizes and positions.

Listing 23.2 shows another example of **BorderLayout**.

Listing 23.2: Another example of BorderLayout

```
package app23;
import java.awt.BorderLayout;
import javax.swing.JButton;
import javax.swing.JFrame;
import javax.swing.JLabel;
import javax.swing.JTextField;
import javax.swing.SwingUtilities;

public class BorderLayoutDemo2 extends JFrame {
    private static void constructGUI() {
        JFrame.setDefaultLookAndFeelDecorated(true);
        JFrame frame = new JFrame("BorderLayout Test");
        frame.setDefaultCloseOperation(JFrame.EXIT_ON_CLOSE);
```

```
        frame.setLayout(new BorderLayout());
        JLabel label1 = new JLabel("Registration Form");
        label1.setHorizontalAlignment(JLabel.CENTER);
        frame.add(label1, BorderLayout.NORTH);
        JLabel label2 = new JLabel("Name:");
        frame.add(label2, BorderLayout.WEST);
        JTextField textField = new JTextField("<your name>");
        frame.add(textField, BorderLayout.CENTER);
        JButton button1 = new JButton("Register");
        frame.add(button1, BorderLayout.EAST);
        JButton button2 = new JButton("Clear Form");
        frame.add(button2, BorderLayout.SOUTH);
        frame.setSize(300, 150);
        frame.setVisible(true);
    }

    public static void main(String[] args) {
        SwingUtilities.invokeLater(new Runnable() {
            public void run() {
                constructGUI();
            }
        });
    }
}
```

Figure 23.3 shows the result of running the code in Listing 23.2.

Figure 23.3: Another example of BorderLayout

BorderLayout is also appropriate for containers with a single component. In this case, you add the component to the center region to make it occupy the whole area of the container.

FlowLayout

The **FlowLayout** arranges components in a horizontal line. By default, the flow goes from left to right, which means components added first will be on the left side of components added later. Components will be added to the same line until there is no more room for a component, then the next line will be used. You can change the direction of the flow by changing the **componentOrientation** property of the container:

```
frame.setComponentOrientation(java.awt.ComponentOrientation.LEFT)
```

There are three constructors in the **FlowLayout** class.

```
public FlowLayout()

public FlowLayout(int align)

public FlowLayout(int align, int horizontalGap, int verticalGap)
```

The *align* argument indicates the alignment of each component row. The possible values are these.

- **FlowLayout.LEFT**. Left-justifies component rows.
- **FlowLayout.RIGHT**. Right-justifies component rows.
- **FlowLayout.CENTER**. Centers component rows.
- **FlowLayout.LEADING**. Justifies component rows to the leading edge of the container's orientation, e.g. to the left in the left-to-right orientation.
- **FlowLayout.TRAILING**. Justifies component rows to the trailing edge of the container's orientation, e.g. to the right in the left-to-right orientation.

In the absence of the *align* argument, the default **FlowLayout.LEFT** will be used.

The *horizontalGap* argument determines the distance between two components in the same row and between the components and the container border. The *verticalGap* argument determines the distance between components in adjacent rows and the components and the container border. The default for both *horizontalGap* and *verticalGap* is 5 units.

Listing 23.3 shows a **JFrame** that uses a **FlowLayout**.

Listing 23.3: Using FlowLayout

```
package app23;
import java.awt.Dimension;
import java.awt.FlowLayout;
import javax.swing.JFrame;
import javax.swing.JScrollPane;
import javax.swing.JTextArea;
import javax.swing.SwingUtilities;

public class FlowLayoutDemo {
    private static void constructGUI() {
        JFrame.setDefaultLookAndFeelDecorated(true);
        JFrame frame = new JFrame("FlowLayout Test");
        frame.setLayout(new FlowLayout());
        frame.setDefaultCloseOperation(JFrame.EXIT_ON_CLOSE);
        String text = "A JTextArea object represents "
                + "a multiline area for displaying text. "
                + "You can change the number of lines "
                + "that can be displayed at a time. ";
        JTextArea textArea1 = new JTextArea(text, 5, 10);
        textArea1.setPreferredSize(new Dimension(100, 100));
        JTextArea textArea2 = new JTextArea(text, 5, 10);
        textArea2.setPreferredSize(new Dimension(100, 100));
        JScrollPane scrollPane = new JScrollPane(textArea2,
                JScrollPane.VERTICAL_SCROLLBAR_ALWAYS,
                JScrollPane.HORIZONTAL_SCROLLBAR_ALWAYS);
        textArea1.setLineWrap(true);
```

```
        textArea2.setLineWrap(true);
        frame.add(textArea1);
        frame.add(scrollPane);
        frame.pack();
        frame.setVisible(true);
    }

    public static void main(String[] args) {
        SwingUtilities.invokeLater(new Runnable() {
            public void run() {
                constructGUI();
            }
        });
    }
}
```

If you run this program, you'll see something similar to Figure 23.4.

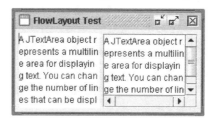

Figure 23.4: Using FlowLayout

BoxLayout

If you've been using **FlowLayout** for a while, you might be wondering if it is possible to change the direction of the flow from top to bottom or bottom to top. While you cannot do it with **FlowLayout**, **javax.swing.BoxLayout** is there to take up the challenge.

The **BoxLayout** class has only one constructor:

```
public BoxLayout(java.awt.Container target, int axis)
```

The *target* argument specifies the container that needs to be laid out and *axis* specifies the axis to lay out components along. The value of *axis* can be one of the following:

- **BoxLayout.X_AXIS**
- **BoxLayout.Y_AXIS**
- **BoxLayout.LINE_AXIS**
- **BoxLayout.PAGE_AXIS**

As an example, examine the code in Listing 23.4.

Listing 23.4: Using BoxLayout

```
package app23;
import javax.swing.BoxLayout;
import javax.swing.JButton;
import javax.swing.JFrame;
import javax.swing.SwingUtilities;
```

```
public class BoxLayoutDemo {
    private static void constructGUI() {
        JFrame.setDefaultLookAndFeelDecorated(true);
        JFrame frame = new JFrame("BoxLayout Test");
        frame.setDefaultCloseOperation(JFrame.EXIT_ON_CLOSE);
        BoxLayout boxLayout = new BoxLayout(frame.getContentPane(),
                BoxLayout.Y_AXIS); // top to bottom
        frame.setLayout(boxLayout);
        frame.add(new JButton("Button 1"));
        frame.add(new JButton("Button 2"));
        frame.add(new JButton("Button 3"));
        frame.pack();
        frame.setVisible(true);
    }

    public static void main(String[] args) {
        SwingUtilities.invokeLater(new Runnable() {
            public void run() {
                constructGUI();
            }
        });
    }
}
```

When you run it, you'll get a **JFrame** like the one in Figure 23.5.

Figure 23.5: Using BoxLayout

GridLayout

As the name implies, the **GridLayout** arranges components in a grid of cells. You decide the number of cells per row and how many cells per column when you call the **GridLayout** class's constructor. Here are two of its three constructors:

```
public GridLayout(int rows, int columns)
```

```
public GridLayout(int rows, int columns,
        int horizontalGap, int verticalGap)
```

At least one of the rows and columns arguments must be nonzero.

Listing 23.5 shows an example of **GridLayout**.

Listing 23.5: Using GridLayout
```
package app23;
import java.awt.GridLayout;
import javax.swing.JButton;
```

```
import javax.swing.JFrame;
import javax.swing.SwingUtilities;

public class GridLayoutDemo {
    private static void constructGUI() {
        JFrame.setDefaultLookAndFeelDecorated(true);
        JFrame frame = new JFrame("GridLayout Test");
        frame.setDefaultCloseOperation(JFrame.EXIT_ON_CLOSE);
        frame.setLayout(new GridLayout(3, 2));
        frame.add(new JButton("Button 1"));
        frame.add(new JButton("Button 2"));
        frame.add(new JButton("Button 3"));
        frame.add(new JButton("Button 4"));
        frame.add(new JButton("Button 5"));
        frame.add(new JButton("Button 6"));
        frame.add(new JButton("Button 7"));
        frame.add(new JButton("Button 8"));
        frame.pack();
        frame.setVisible(true);
    }

    public static void main(String[] args) {
        SwingUtilities.invokeLater(new Runnable() {
            public void run() {
                constructGUI();
            }
        });
    }
}
```

The **GridLayoutTest** class in Listing 23.5 produces something like Figure 23.6.

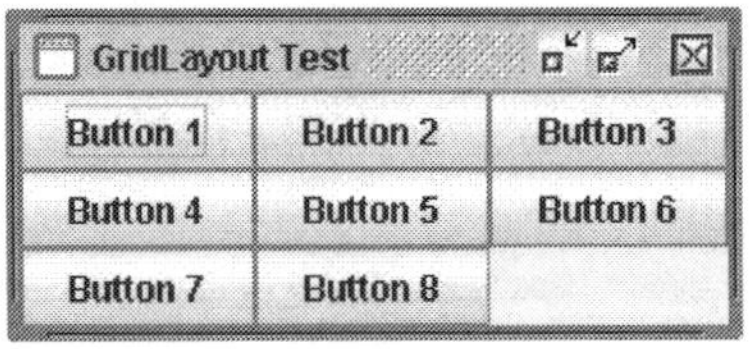

Figure 23.6: Using GridLayout

No LayoutManager

If none of the default layout manager suits your need, you can try absolute positioning by passing **null** to the **setLayout** method of a container. This is the most flexible layout manager out there, but use it with care because you have to rearrange your components when your container is resized.

For each component added to a container with no layout manager, you specify its size and its position in the container. The **setBounds** method of a component can help you achieve both with a single line. As an example, Listing 23.6 features a **JFrame** that utilizes no layout manager.

Listing 23.6: Absolute positioning

```
package app23;
import javax.swing.JFrame;
import javax.swing.JLabel;
import javax.swing.JTextField;
import javax.swing.SwingUtilities;

public class NoLayoutDemo extends JFrame {
    private static void constructGUI() {
        JFrame.setDefaultLookAndFeelDecorated(true);
        JFrame frame = new JFrame("NoLayout Test");
        frame.setDefaultCloseOperation(JFrame.EXIT_ON_CLOSE);
        frame.setLayout(null);
        JLabel label = new JLabel("First Name:");
        label.setBounds(20, 20, 100, 20);
        JTextField textField = new JTextField();
        textField.setBounds(124, 25, 100, 20);
        frame.add(label);
        frame.add(textField);
        frame.setSize(300, 100);
        frame.setVisible(true);
    }

    public static void main(String[] args) {
        SwingUtilities.invokeLater(new Runnable() {
            public void run() {
                constructGUI();
            }
        });
    }
}
```

If you run this class, you'll see something similar to Figure 23.7.

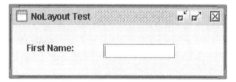

Figure 23.7: Absolute positioning

Event Handling

Swing is event-driven. A component can raise an event or events and you can write code to handle the events. This event-driven-ness is the foundation of user interactivity in Swing applications. Before you jump straight to handling events in Swing, you should first get yourself familiar with the Java event model because Swing follows this model.

The Java Event Model

In the Java event model any object can notify other objects about a change in its state. In event-driven programming, such change in state is called an event. The information about the event is encapsulated in an event object. In this model, there are three participants involved:

- The event source, which is the object whose state changes
- The event object, which encapsulates the state changes in the event source
- The event listener, which is the object that wants to be notified of the state changes in the event source.

To put it more briefly: When an event occurs, the event source generates an event object and sends it to the event listener.

Let's take a look at each participant in the Java event model.

The Event Source

Any object can be an event source. However, an event source class must provide methods for event listeners to register and de-register their interest in receiving events. Also, an event source must maintain a list of interested event listeners. For example, a **JButton** emits a **java.awt.event.ActionEvent** object when clicked. Therefore, the **JButton** is an event source. The **JButton** class has an **addActionListener** and a **removeActionListener** methods for action event listeners to register and deregister their interests. In addition, **JButton** has a protected field called **listenerList** (inherited from **JComponent**) that helps maintain registered event listeners internally.

Note
An object can be the source of more than one event. For example, **JButton** can raise a **java.awt.event.ActionEvent** as well as a **javax.swing.event.Change** events.

The Event Object

An event object encapsulates information about a particular type of event, such as the old and new values of the state that changed. The class for an event object must extends the **java.util.EventObject** class. **EventObject** has a **getSource** method that returns the event source.

```
public java.lang.Object getSource()
```

For example, when a **JButton** is clicked, it emits the action event. Information about the event is encapsulated in a **java.awt.event.ActionEvent** object. The **ActionEvent** class extends **java.awt.AWTEvent**, which in turns extends **java.util.EventObject**.

Event Listeners

An event listener can receive a particular type of event by implementing the appropriate listener interface. All listener interfaces are subinterfaces of **java.util.EventListener**. This interface has no methods and acts as a marker interface. Your event listener interface must then define a method for receiving the appropriate event object.

For example, to receive a notification from a **JButton** when it is clicked, you can create a class that implements **java.awt.event.ActionListener**, a subinterface of **java.util.EventListener**. **ActionListener** has one method, **actionPerformed**.

```
public void actionPerformed(ActionEvent event)
```

There are two things to note about the listener. First, you do not call its methods directly. Instead, they are called by the JVM when the event in question occurs. Second, the method being called receives an event object. For instance, when an action event occurs, the **actionPerformed** method of any registered action listener gets called and passed an **ActionEvent** object.

Note
To handle a Swing event, you write an event listener. You do not have to worry about event sources and event objects because Swing's support for event handling is very thorough.

Swing Event Handling

Different Swing components raise different events. Events can be raised by a user action (such as a user clicking a button) or by the application itself (such as when you programmatically add items to a **JList**). In either case, you need to write an event listener if you want some code to be executed when an event occurs.

The API for event handling does not come with Swing. Instead, it is available in the **java.awt.event** package. Therefore, Swing's event handling is based on the AWT. The good thing about the AWT (and Swing) event handling is the availability of adapters, which are base classes that provide default implementations for event listener interfaces. For example, the **java.awt.event.MouseListener** interface has five methods. If you write a listener class by implementing **MouseListener**, you have to write the implementations for all these five methods, even if you are only interested in one. The **MyMouseListener** class in Listing 23.7 should make this clear.

Listing 23.7: Writing a listener by implementing an interface

```
package app23;
import java.awt.event.MouseEvent;
import java.awt.event.MouseListener;
public class MyMouseListener implements MouseListener {
    public void mouseClicked(MouseEvent e) {
        System.out.println("Mouse clicked");
    }
    public void mouseEntered(MouseEvent e) {
    }
    public void mouseExited(MouseEvent e) {
    }
    public void mousePressed(MouseEvent e) {
    }
    public void mouseReleased(MouseEvent e) {
    }
}
```

Fortunately, the **java.awt.event** package also provides the **java.awt.event.MouseAdapter** class. This class implements **java.awt.event.MouseListener** and provides default implementations of its five methods.

Instead of implementing **MouseListener**, you can extend **MouseAdapter** and override only the methods you want to change. The **MyShorterMouseListener** class in Listing 23.8 has the same functionality as the **MyMouseListener** class in Listing 23.7, but is shorter.

Listing 23.8: Writing listener by extending an adapter

```
package app23;
import java.awt.event.MouseAdapter;
import java.awt.event.MouseEvent;
public class MyShorterMouseListener extends MouseAdapter {
    // override methods here
    public void mouseClicked(MouseEvent e) {
        System.out.println("Mouse clicked");
    }
}
```

In addition to **ActionEvent** and **MouseEvent** described earlier, there are also other types of events you can capture in your Swing applications. Some of these events are listed in Table 23.1.

Event	Listener/Adapter	Component
ActionEvent	ActionListener	JButton, JCheckBox, JRadioButton, JMenuItem, etc
MouseEvent	MouseListener	JFrame, JDialog, all Swing components
KeyEvent	KeyListener	JFrame, JDialog, all Swing components
WindowEvent	WindowListener	JFrame, JDialog

Table 23.1: Swing events

What events a **JComponent** can trigger are indicated by what listeners you can register. For example, the **JButton** class has an **addActionListener** method. This indicates that a **JButton** can raise an action event.

JButton, **JCheckBox**, and some other components can raise both **ActionEvent** and **MouseEvent**. The difference between the two events are sometimes unclear. However, as a rule, you should use **ActionEvent** if you want to be notified when it is clicked. This is because a **JButton** can be 'pushed' or a **JCheckBox** can be checked by using a keyboard shortcut. Pushing a **JButton** like this will still trigger an action event, but not a mouse event. **MouseEvent**, on the other hand, is captured if you want to know the coordinate of where the mouse pointer is clicked, etc.

The AWT Event API

Before I present some event-handling examples, let's review several types in the **java.awt.event** package commonly used in Swing applications.

The java.awt.event.ActionEvent Class

An **ActionEvent** object encapsulates information about an action event. This event is raised by several components to signal that a **JButton** is pushed or a **JCheckBox** is checked/unchecked, either by clicking the mouse or by pressing the keyboard. Here are the methods defined in **ActionEvent**.

```
public java.lang.String getActionCommand()
```
Returns the command string associated with this action. This is normally the text on a **JButton** or **JCheckBox** that raised the event.

```
public long getWhen()
```
Returns a long that represents the time the action occurred.

```
public int getModifiers()
```
Returns the modifier keys held down when this event was raised.

```
public java.lang.String paramString()
```
Returns a parameter identifying the event.

The java.awt.event.ActionListener Interface

You implement this interface to capture an action event. There is only one method defined in this interface, **actionPerformed**.

```
public void actionPerformed(ActionEvent e)
```

The **actionPerformed** method of a registered action listener is invoked when an action event occurred.

The java.awt.event.MouseEvent Class

A **MouseEvent** encapsulates information about a mouse event. There are several actions that can raise a mouse event, including clicking a mouse button, pressing and releasing a mouse button, moving the mouse cursor to enter a component area, and moving the mouse cursor to exit a component area.

Here are some of the methods in **MouseEvent**.

```
public int getButton()
```
Returns an **int** that indicates which button has changed state. The value can be one of the following static final fields: **NOBUTTON**, **BUTTON1**, **BUTTON2**, and **BUTTON3**.

```
public int getClickCount()
```
Returns the number of times the mouse was clicked.

```
public java.awt.Point getPoint()
```
Returns the coordinate relative to the top-left corner of the component at which the mouse event occurred.

```
public int getX()
```
Returns the horizontal position relative to the left edge of the component at which the mouse event occurred.

```
public int getY()
```
Returns the vertical position relative to the top edge of the component at which the mouse event occurred.

The java.awt.event.MouseListener Interface

You implement this interface to capture a mouse event. There are five methods, all self-explanatory, defined in this interface.

```
public void mouseClicked(MouseEvent e)

public void mousePressed(MouseEvent e)

public void mouseReleased(MouseEvent e)

public void mouseEntered(MouseEvent e)

public void mouseExited(MouseEvent e)
```

The java.awt.event.KeyEvent Class

This class represents a key event as a result of a keystroke on the keyboard. There are a good number of static final **int** fields that each represent a keyboard key, such as **VK_A** (representing the A key), **VK_Z** (representing the Z key), **VK_SHIFT**, **VK_SPACE**, **VK_F1**, **VK_ALT**, **VK_AMPERSAND**, etc.

In addition, here are methods you often invoke on a **KeyEvent** object.

```
public int getKeyCode()
```
        Returns an integer key code associated with the key in the event. For example, if the A key was pressed this method returns **KeyEvent.VK_A**.

```
public char getKeyChar()
```
        Returns the char associated with the key in this event.

The java.awt.event.KeyListener Interface

You implement this interface to handle a key event. This interface defines the following methods.

```
public void keyPressed(KeyEvent e)

public void keyReleased(KeyEvent e)

public void keyTyped(KeyEvent e)
```

The java.awt.event.WindowEvent Class

A **WindowEvent** encapsulates information on a window event. A window event is triggered when a source object is opened, closed, activated, deactivated, iconified, deiconified, or when it gets focus. The following methods are defined in **WindowEvent**.

```
public int getNewState()
```
        Returns the new state of the window. The return value is a bitwise mask of the following static final fields: **NORMAL**, **ICONIFIED**, **MAZIMIZED_HORIZ**, **MAXIMIZED_VERT** and **MAXIMIZED_BOTH**.

```
public int getOldState()
```
   Returns the old state of the window. The return value is a bitwise mask of the final
   fields described under the **getNewState** method.

```
public java.awt.Window getWindow()
```
   Returns the source object.

The java.awt.event.WindowListener Interface

You implement this interface to handle a window event. This interface defines the following
methods.

```
public void windowActivated(WindowEvent e)

public void windowClosed(WindowEvent e)

public void windowClosing(WindowEvent e)

public void windowDeactivated(WindowEvent e)

public void windowDeiconified(WindowEvent e)

public void windowIconified(WindowEvent e)

public void windowOpened(WindowEvent e)
```

Handling ActionEvent

Let's now learn how to handle an action event that originates from a **JButton**. Please read the
MyActionListener class and the **ActionListenerTest1** class in Listing 23.9.

Listing 23.9: Handling an action listener

```
package app23;
import java.awt.event.ActionEvent;
import java.awt.event.ActionListener;
import javax.swing.JButton;
import javax.swing.JDialog;
import javax.swing.JFrame;
import javax.swing.JOptionPane;
import javax.swing.SwingUtilities;

class MyActionListener implements ActionListener {
    public void actionPerformed(ActionEvent e) {
        JButton source = (JButton) e.getSource();
        String buttonText = source.getText();
        JOptionPane.showMessageDialog(null,
                "You clicked " + buttonText);
    }
}

public class ActionListenerDemo1 {
    private static void constructGUI() {
        JFrame.setDefaultLookAndFeelDecorated(true);
        JDialog.setDefaultLookAndFeelDecorated(true);
        JFrame frame = new JFrame("ActionListener Test 1");
```

```
        frame.setDefaultCloseOperation(JFrame.EXIT_ON_CLOSE);
        JButton button = new JButton("Register");
        button.addActionListener(new MyActionListener());
        frame.getContentPane().add(button);
        frame.pack();
        frame.setVisible(true);
    }

    public static void main(String[] args) {
        SwingUtilities.invokeLater(new Runnable() {
            public void run() {
                constructGUI();
            }
        });
    }
}
```

The **MyActionListener** class is an action listener that captures an action event of a
JButton. Here is its **actionPerformed** method.

```
        public void actionPerformed(ActionEvent e) {
            JButton source = (JButton) e.getSource();
            String buttonText = source.getText();
            JOptionPane.showMessageDialog(null,
                    "You clicked " + buttonText);
        }
```

It downcasts the source object to a **JButton** and displays its text in a **JOptionPane**.

The **ActionListenerTest1** class constructs a **JFrame** with a **JButton**. Pay attention to
the code in bold in the **constructGUI** method:

```
button.addActionListener(new MyActionListener());
```

This line of code creates an instance of **MyActionListener** and passes it to the
addActionListener method. This in effect registers the **MyActionListener** object as an
interested party for the **JButton**'s action event.

To test this example, run the **ActionListenerTest1** class. You'll see a **JFrame** like
the one in Figure 23.8:

Figure 23.8: The result of running the ActionListenerTest1 class

Now, click the Register button. You will see a **JOptionPane** like that in Figure 23.9.

Figure 23.9: A JOptionPane that is displayed when a Jbutton is clicked

Handling MouseEvent

This example shows how you can handle a mouse event. There are two classes in this example, **MouseClickListener** and **MouseListenerTest1**. The **MouseClickListener** class is a mouse listener that extends the **java.awt.event.MouseAdapter**. The **MouseListenerTest1** displays an area you can click on. Both classes are shown in Listing 23.10.

Listing 23.10: Handling a mouse event

```
package app23;
import java.awt.event.MouseAdapter;
import java.awt.event.MouseEvent;
import javax.swing.JFrame;
import javax.swing.SwingUtilities;

class MouseClickListener extends MouseAdapter {
    public void mouseClicked(MouseEvent e) {
        if (SwingUtilities.isLeftMouseButton(e)) {
            System.out.print("The mouse left button was clicked ");
        } else if (SwingUtilities.isRightMouseButton(e)) {
            System.out.print(
                    "The mouse right button was clicked ");
        } else if (SwingUtilities.isMiddleMouseButton(e)) {
            System.out.print(
                    "The mouse middle button was clicked ");
        }
        System.out.print(e.getClickCount() + " time(s)");
        int x = e.getX();
        int y = e.getY();
        System.out.println(" at  (" + x + "," + y + ")");
    }
}

public class MouseListenerDemo1 {
    private static void constructGUI() {
        JFrame.setDefaultLookAndFeelDecorated(true);
        JFrame frame = new JFrame("MouseListener Test 1");
        frame.setDefaultCloseOperation(JFrame.EXIT_ON_CLOSE);
        frame.addMouseListener(new MouseClickListener());
        frame.setSize(200, 200);
        frame.setVisible(true);
    }
```

```
    public static void main(String[] args) {
        SwingUtilities.invokeLater(new Runnable() {
            public void run() {
                constructGUI();
            }
        });
    }
}
```

If you run the **MouseListenerDemo1** class, you will see a **JFrame** like the one shown in Figure 23.10.

Figure 23.10: Handling mouse events

Now click on the area, you will see a message printed on your console. For example:

```
The mouse right button was clicked 1 time(s) at (110,165)
```

Writing a Listener as an Anonymous Class

In the last two examples, you created a different class for each listener. While this works well, you can reduce the number of classes in your Swing application by using anonymous classes. (Anonymous classes were explained in Chapter 14, "Nested and Inner Classes.")

First, let's review the code in Listing 23.11, which features an action listener written as a nested class.

Listing 23.11: Writing a listener as a nested class

```
package app23;
import java.awt.event.ActionEvent;
import java.awt.event.ActionListener;
import javax.swing.JButton;
import javax.swing.JFileChooser;
import javax.swing.JFrame;
import javax.swing.SwingUtilities;

public class ActionListenerDemo2 extends JFrame {
    String fileSelected;
    public ActionListenerDemo2(String title) {
        super(title);
    }
```

```
    public void init() {
        JButton button = new JButton("Select File");
        button.addActionListener(new MyActionListener());
        this.getContentPane().add(button);
    }

    private static void constructGUI() {
        JFrame.setDefaultLookAndFeelDecorated(true);
        ActionListenerDemo2 frame = new ActionListenerDemo2(
                "ActionListener Demo 2");
        frame.setDefaultCloseOperation(JFrame.EXIT_ON_CLOSE);
        frame.init();
        frame.pack();
        frame.setVisible(true);
    }

    public static void main(String[] args) {
        SwingUtilities.invokeLater(new Runnable() {
            public void run() {
                constructGUI();
            }
        });
    }

    class MyActionListener implements ActionListener {
        public void actionPerformed(ActionEvent e) {
            JFileChooser fileChooser = new JFileChooser();
            int returnVal = fileChooser.showOpenDialog(null);
            if (returnVal == JFileChooser.APPROVE_OPTION) {
                fileSelected =
                        fileChooser.getSelectedFile().getName();
                System.out.print(fileSelected);
            }
        }
    }
}
```

The **MyActionListener** nested class is an action listener that listens on a **JButton**. If the source object is clicked, it will display a **JFileChooser** and print the name of the file the user selected.

Running the **ActionListenerTest2** class gives you the **JFrame** in Figure 23.11.

Figure 23.11: A listener as a nested class

When you click the **JButton**, a **JFileChooser** like the one in Figure 23.12 will be displayed.

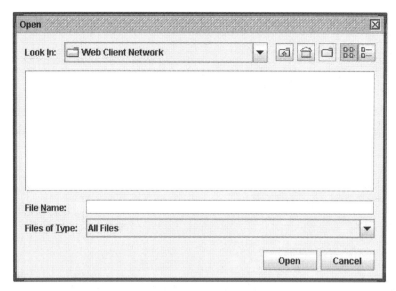

Figure 23.12: A JFileChooser that is displayed when a Jbutton is clicked

Now, examine the code in Listing 23.12.

Listing 23.12: An anonymous listener class

```
package app23;
import java.awt.event.ActionEvent;
import java.awt.event.ActionListener;
import javax.swing.JButton;
import javax.swing.JFileChooser;
import javax.swing.JFrame;
import javax.swing.SwingUtilities;

public class ActionListenerDemo3 extends JFrame {
    String fileSelected;

    public ActionListenerDemo3(String title) {
        super(title);
    }

    public void init() {
        JButton button = new JButton("Select File");
        button.addActionListener(new ActionListener() {
            public void actionPerformed(ActionEvent e) {
                JFileChooser fileChooser = new JFileChooser();
                int returnVal = fileChooser.showOpenDialog(null);
                if (returnVal == JFileChooser.APPROVE_OPTION) {
                    fileSelected =
                            fileChooser.getSelectedFile().getName();
                    System.out.print(fileSelected);
                }
            }
        });
```

```
            this.getContentPane().add(button);
    }

    private static void constructGUI() {
        JFrame.setDefaultLookAndFeelDecorated(true);
        ActionListenerDemo3 frame = new ActionListenerDemo3(
                "ActionListener Demo 3");
        frame.setDefaultCloseOperation(JFrame.EXIT_ON_CLOSE);
        frame.init();
        frame.pack();
        frame.setVisible(true);
    }

    public static void main(String[] args) {
        SwingUtilities.invokeLater(new Runnable() {
            public void run() {
                constructGUI();
            }
        });
    }
}
```

The code in bold shows the anonymous class. If a listener is only used to listen on a single component, then it may be a good candidate for an anonymous class.

Handling ActionEvent of JRadioButton

As another example, let's see how we can handle action events raised by a **JRadioButton**. There are three **JRadioButton**s used in this example and they share the same listener. As such, you cannot write your listener as an anonymous class. This example writes it as a nested class.

The code is given in Listing 23.13.

Listing 23.13: Handling JRadioButtons' action event

```
package app23;
import java.awt.FlowLayout;
import java.awt.event.ActionEvent;
import java.awt.event.ActionListener;
import javax.swing.ButtonGroup;
import javax.swing.JFrame;
import javax.swing.JLabel;
import javax.swing.JRadioButton;
import javax.swing.SwingUtilities;

public class ActionListenerDemo4 extends JFrame {
    class RadioClickListener implements ActionListener {
        public void actionPerformed(ActionEvent e) {
            String command = e.getActionCommand();
            ActionListenerDemo4.this.setTitle(command);
        }
    }
```

```
public ActionListenerDemo4(String title) {
    super(title);
    init();
}

private void init() {
    this.setLayout(new FlowLayout());
    this.setDefaultCloseOperation(JFrame.EXIT_ON_CLOSE);
    JRadioButton button1 = new JRadioButton("Red");
    JRadioButton button2 = new JRadioButton("Green");
    JRadioButton button3 = new JRadioButton("Blue");
    RadioClickListener listener = new RadioClickListener();
    button1.addActionListener(listener);
    button2.addActionListener(listener);
    button3.addActionListener(listener);
    ButtonGroup colorButtonGroup = new ButtonGroup();
    colorButtonGroup.add(button1);
    colorButtonGroup.add(button2);
    colorButtonGroup.add(button3);
    button1.setSelected(true);
    this.add(new JLabel("Color:"));
    this.add(button1);
    this.add(button2);
    this.add(button3);
}

private static void constructGUI() {
    JFrame.setDefaultLookAndFeelDecorated(true);
    ActionListenerDemo4 frame = new ActionListenerDemo4(
            "ActionListener Demo 4");
    frame.pack();
    frame.setVisible(true);
}

public static void main(String[] args) {
    SwingUtilities.invokeLater(new Runnable() {
        public void run() {
            constructGUI();
        }
    });
}
}
```

If you run the **ActionListenerTest4** class, you'll see a **JFrame** like the one in Figure 23.13.

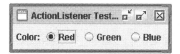

Figure 23.13: Capturing JRadioButtons' action event

The **actionPerformed** method in the **RadioClickListener** class reads the return value of the **getActionCommand** method and assigns it as the **JFrame**'s title.

Handling KeyEvent

The following example shows how you can handle a key event. The listener captures the user's keyboard input and capitalizes it. The code is shown in Listing 23.14.

Listing 23.14: Key event listener

```
package app23;
import java.awt.BorderLayout;
import java.awt.event.KeyEvent;
import java.awt.event.KeyListener;
import javax.swing.JFrame;
import javax.swing.JTextField;

public class KeyListenerDemo1 extends JFrame
        implements KeyListener {
    public KeyListenerDemo1(String title) {
        super(title);
        this.getContentPane().setLayout(new BorderLayout());
        JTextField textField = new JTextField(20);
        textField.addKeyListener(this);
        this.getContentPane().add(textField);
    }

    public void keyTyped(KeyEvent e) {
        e.setKeyChar(Character.toUpperCase(e.getKeyChar()));
    }

    public void keyPressed(KeyEvent e) {
    }

    public void keyReleased(KeyEvent e) {
    }

    private static void constructGUI() {
        // Make sure we have nice window decorations.
        JFrame.setDefaultLookAndFeelDecorated(true);
        KeyListenerDemo1 frame =
                new KeyListenerDemo1("KeyListener Demo 1");
        frame.setDefaultCloseOperation(JFrame.EXIT_ON_CLOSE);
        frame.pack();
        frame.setVisible(true);
    }

    public static void main(String[] args) {
        javax.swing.SwingUtilities.invokeLater(new Runnable() {
            public void run() {
                constructGUI();
            }
        });
```

```
    }
}
```

What's special in this example is that the listener interface is implemented by the main class itself. As a result, you override the **KeyListener** interface methods within the class itself.

If you run the **KeyListenerTest1** class, you will see a **JFrame** with a **JTextField** control like the one in Figure 23.14.

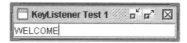

Figure 23.14: Using KeyListener

Handling WindowListener

This example demonstrates how you can write a window listener. The listener is implemented as an anonymous class that overrides the **windowIconified** method and sets the window state to normal. As a result, you cannot minimize the window.

The code is given in Listing 23.15.

Listing 23.15: A window listener

```
package app23;
import java.awt.Frame;
import java.awt.event.WindowAdapter;
import java.awt.event.WindowEvent;
import javax.swing.JFrame;

public class WindowListenerDemo1 extends JFrame {
    public WindowListenerDemo1(String title) {
        super(title);
        this.addWindowListener(new WindowAdapter() {
            public void windowIconified(WindowEvent e) {
                WindowListenerDemo1.this.setState(Frame.NORMAL);
            }
        });
    }

    private static void constructGUI() {
        JFrame.setDefaultLookAndFeelDecorated(true);
        WindowListenerDemo1 frame =
                new WindowListenerDemo1("WindowEventDemo");
        frame.setDefaultCloseOperation(JFrame.EXIT_ON_CLOSE);
        frame.setSize(100, 100);
        frame.setVisible(true);
    }

    public static void main(String[] args) {
        javax.swing.SwingUtilities.invokeLater(new Runnable() {
            public void run() {
                constructGUI();
```

```
            }
        });
    }
}
```

Working with Menus

A serious Swing application rarely goes by without menus. Menus are handy because they only take little space out of the screen real estate. Also, only a menu bar needs to appear at all times. Most menu items are hidden and do not take space at all. To use menus, first add a menu bar to the container and add menus to the menu bar. Then, add menu items to a menu. To support hierarchical menus, you can add menu items to a menu item.

In Swing, a menu bar is represented by the **javax.swing.JMenuBar** class, a menu by **javax.swing.JMenu**, and a menu item by **javax.swing.JMenuItem**, which is a child class of **JAbstractButton**. **JMenuItem** has the following subclasses: **JMenu**, **JCheckboxMenuItem**, and **JRadioButtonMenuItem**

Clicking a menu on the menu bar displays the menu. This happens automatically without you having to write a listener. A menu item acts more like a **JButton**, you can add an action listener to handle a mouse click.

The **JMenuTest1** class in Listing 23.16 displays a **JFrame** with menus.

Listing 23.16: Using JMenu

```
package app23;
import java.awt.event.ActionEvent;
import java.awt.event.ActionListener;
import javax.swing.JFrame;
import javax.swing.JMenu;
import javax.swing.JMenuBar;
import javax.swing.JMenuItem;
import javax.swing.SwingUtilities;

class MyMenuActionListener implements ActionListener {
    public void actionPerformed(ActionEvent e) {
        System.out.println(e.getActionCommand());
    }
}

public class JMenuDemo1 {
    private static void constructGUI() {
        JFrame.setDefaultLookAndFeelDecorated(true);
        JFrame frame = new JFrame("JMenu Demo 1");
        frame.setDefaultCloseOperation(JFrame.EXIT_ON_CLOSE);
        MyMenuActionListener actionListener =
                new MyMenuActionListener();
        JMenuBar menuBar = new JMenuBar();
        JMenu fileMenu = new JMenu("File");
        JMenu editMenu = new JMenu("Edit");
        JMenu helpMenu = new JMenu("Help");
        menuBar.add(fileMenu);
```

```
        menuBar.add(editMenu);
        menuBar.add(helpMenu);
        JMenuItem fileNewMI = new JMenuItem("New");
        JMenuItem fileOpenMI = new JMenuItem("Open");
        JMenuItem fileSaveMI = new JMenuItem("Save");
        JMenuItem fileExitMI = new JMenuItem("Exit");
        fileMenu.add(fileNewMI);
        fileNewMI.addActionListener(actionListener);
        fileMenu.add(fileOpenMI);
        fileOpenMI.addActionListener(actionListener);
        fileMenu.add(fileSaveMI);
        fileSaveMI.addActionListener(actionListener);
        fileMenu.addSeparator();
        fileMenu.add(fileExitMI);
        fileExitMI.addActionListener(actionListener);

        JMenuItem editCopyMI = new JMenuItem("Copy");
        JMenuItem editPasteMI = new JMenuItem("Paste");
        editMenu.add(editCopyMI);
        editMenu.add(editPasteMI);

        JMenuItem helpAboutMI = new JMenuItem("About");
        helpMenu.add(helpAboutMI);

        frame.setJMenuBar(menuBar);
        frame.setSize(200, 100);
        frame.setVisible(true);
    }

    public static void main(String[] args) {
        SwingUtilities.invokeLater(new Runnable() {
            public void run() {
                constructGUI();
            }
        });
    }
}
```

Running the **JMenuDemo1** class produces a **JFrame** like that in Figure 23.15.

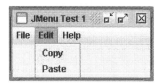

Figure 23.15: Using JMenu

The Look and Feel

The look and feel of a GUI application is very important. Swing is a GUI technology where you can expect uniformity of the look and feel of your GUI, regardless the operating system the application is running on. This is in contrast to the AWT or the Eclipse SWT (the GUI technology used and developed by the Eclipse community) whereby the look and feel of your application depends on the platform. However, it does not mean Swing only supports one type of look and feel. In fact, there are several. Once you choose a look and feel, your application looks the same everywhere. Figures 23.16 to 23.18 show some of the look and feels available in Swing.

Figure 23.16: Swing on GTK

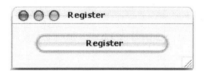

Figure 23.17: Swing on Macintosh

Figure 23.18: Swing on Windows

Changing the look and feel is easy because each look and feel is governed by a **javax.swing.LookAndFeel** object. Changing the **LookAndFeel** class of an application results in a different look and feel.

Choosing the Look and Feel

Unless instructed otherwise, Java uses the default look and feel. To change the look and feel, you use the **javax.swing.UIManager** class's **setLookAndFeel** method to select a look and feel. Here is its signature:

```
public static void setLookAndFeel(java.lang.String className)
        throws java.lang.ClassNotFoundException,
        java.lang.InstantiationException,
        java.lang.IllegalAccessException,
        UnsupportedLookAndFeelException
```

The default JDK has provided a few subclass of LookAndFeel that you can use as the argument to **setLookAndFeel**. They are as follows:

- **com.sun.java.swing.plaf.gtk.GTKLookAndFeel**
- **javax.swing.plaf.metal.MetalLookAndFeel**
- **com.sun.java.swing.plaf.windows.WindowsLookAndFeel**
- **com.sun.java.swing.plaf.motif.MotifLookAndFeel**
- **com.sun.java.swing.plaf.nimbus.NimbusLookAndFeel**

For instance, the following code forces the application to use the Nimbus look and feel.

```
UIManager.setLookAndFeel(
        "com.sun.java.swing.plaf.nimbus.NimbusLookAndFeel");
```

In addition, you can pass the return value of the following methods as an argument to **setLookAndFeel**:

```
UIManager.getCrossPlatformLookAndFeelClassName()
```
Returns the look and feel tat works on all platforms (the Java look and feel).

```
UIManager.getSystemLookAndFeelClassName()
```
Returns the look and feel for the current platform, that is, if the application is running on Windows the Windows look and feel will be used, etc.

You must call the **setLookAndFeel** method before constructing your GUI. Normally, you do this before calling the **constructGUI** method in your application. Here is an example of using the current system's look and feel:

```
public static void main(String[] args) {
    try {
        UIManager.setLookAndFeel(
                UIManager.getSystemLookAndFeelClassName());
    } catch (Exception e) {
        e.printStackTrace();
    }
    SwingUtilities.invokeLater(new Runnable() {
        public void run() {
            constructGUI();
        }
    });
}
```

Alternatively, you can select a look and feel by using the –D flag when invoking the application. This way, you do not have to hardcode it in your class. For example, the following command invokes the **MySwingApp** application and tells the JVM to use the **com.sun.java.swing.plaf.gtk.GTKLookAndFeel** class:

```
java –Dswing.defaultlaf=com.sun.java.swing.plaf.gtk.GTKLookAndFeel
```

Fast Splash Screens

The **java.awt.SplashScreen** class can be used to display a splash screen before the JVM starts. The splash screen is a window that contains an image and is centered in the screen. The GIF, PNG, and JPG formats are supported, and so are transparency in GIF and PNG and animation in GIF. The splash screen is shown until the first Swing/AWT window is displayed.

To use a splash screen, include the new **splash** option in **java** when you invoke your application. For example, the following uses the **myImage.jpg** file as the splash screen.

```
java -splash:myImage.jpg MyClass
```

To use a splash screen in an application packaged in a JAR file, you must use the **SplashScreenImage** option in a manifest file and include the image file in the JAR. You must also specify the path to the image without a leading slash. For instance, the following **manifest.mf** file indicates that the **myImage.jpg** file should be used as the splash screen.

```
Manifest-Version: 1.0
Main-Class: MyClass
SplashScreen-Image: myImage.jpg
```

The **SplashScreen** class is a singleton whose instance can be obtained by calling the static **getSplashScreen** method. The **createGraphics** method returns a **Graphics2D** object that allows you to draw over the splash screen. Here is the complete list of methods in **SplashScreen**.

```
public void close() throws IllegalStateException
```
  Closes the splash screen and releases all related resources.

```
public Graphics2D createGraphics()
```
  Returns a **Graphics2D** object as a context for drawing on the splash screen.

```
public Rectangle getBounds()
```
  Returns the bounds of the splash screen window.

```
public java.net.URL getImageURL()
```
  Returns the URL of the current splash screen.

```
public Dimension getSize()
```
  Returns the size of the splash screen.

```
public static SplashScreen getSplashScreen()
```
  Returns the **SplashScreen** Instance.

```
public boolean isVisible()
```
  Indicates whether the splash screen is visible

```
public void setImageURL(java.net.URL imageURL)
```
  Specifies a new image for the splash screen.

```
public void update()
```
  Updates the splash screen with current contents of the overlay image.

The **SplashScreenDemo** class in Listing 23.17 demonstrates the power of **SplashScreen**.

Listing 23.17: The splash screen

```
package app23;
import java.awt.AlphaComposite;
import java.awt.Color;
import java.awt.Graphics2D;
import java.awt.SplashScreen;
```

```
import javax.swing.JFrame;
import javax.swing.SwingUtilities;

public class SplashScreenDemo {
    private static void constructGUI() {
        SplashScreen splash = SplashScreen.getSplashScreen();
        if (splash != null) {
            Graphics2D g = (Graphics2D) splash.createGraphics();

            // Simulate lengthy loading
            for (int i = 0; i < 10; i++) {
                String message = "Process " + i + " of 10 ...";
                g.setComposite(AlphaComposite.Clear);
                g.fillRect(130, 350, 280, 40);
                g.setPaintMode();
                g.setColor(Color.RED);
                g.drawString(message, 130, 360);
                g.fillRect(130, 370, i * 30, 20);

                splash.update();
                try {
                    Thread.sleep(500);
                } catch (InterruptedException e) {
                    e.printStackTrace();
                }
            }
        }

        JFrame frame = new JFrame("Splash Screen Demo");
        frame.setDefaultCloseOperation(JFrame.EXIT_ON_CLOSE);
        frame.setSize(300, 200);
        frame.setLocationRelativeTo(null);
        frame.setVisible(true);
    }

    public static void main(String[] args) {
        SwingUtilities.invokeLater(new Runnable() {
            public void run() {
                constructGUI();
            }
        });
    }
}
```

You need to run the class from the location of the **SplashScreenDemo.class** file and make sure the **splash.jpg** is in the same directory. To run the application, type this:

```
java -splash:splash.jpg app23/SplashScreenDemo
```

The code itself is nothing more than a blank frame. However, before it is uploaded, the user will see a splash screen like that in Figure 23.19.

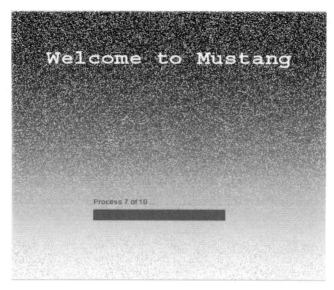

Figure 23.19: Splash screen

System Tray Support

Thinking about learning C++ so you can create GUI applications that can be added to the system tray? Maybe it's no longer necessary because Java can now access the operating system's system tray through the **SystemTray** class.

Like **SplashScreen**, **SystemTray** is a singleton, so there is only one instance per application. You can get the instance by calling the **SystemTray** class's **getSystemTray** method:

```
public static SystemTray getSystemTray()
```

Because you normally use Java to write programs that run in various operating systems, a word of caution here. **SystemTray** works on many platforms, including Windows, KDE, and Gnome, but some systems may not be supported. Therefore, you may want to check if **SystemTray** is supported using the **isSupported** method:

```
public static boolean isSupported()
```

The **SystemTray** class represents the tray bar, each icon on it is represented by the **TrayIcon** class. You can add a **TrayIcon** to the **SystemTray** by invoking the **add** method.

```
public void add(TrayIcon trayIcon) throws AWTException
```

To remove a **TrayIcon**, use its **remove** method:

```
public void remove(TrayIcon trayIcon)
```

In addition, all the **TrayIcon**s in the **SystemTray** can be retrieved by using **getTrayIcons**.

```
public TrayIcon[] getTrayIcons()
```

Now, let's take a look at the **TrayIcon** class. An instance of this class resembles a tray icon in a native application. It can have a tooltip, an image, and a popup menu. You can create a **TrayIcon** using one of its three constructors:

```
public TrayIcon(Image image)

public TrayIcon(Image image, java.lang.String tooltip)

public TrayIcon(Image image, java.lang.String tooltip,
        PopupMenu popup)
```

The **SystemTrayDemo** class in Listing 23.18 uses **SystemTray** and **TrayIcon**. The application adds a **TrayIcon** with an image, a tooltip, and a **PopupMenu**.

Listing 23.18: Using system tray

```
package app23;
import java.awt.AWTException;
import java.awt.Image;
import java.awt.MenuItem;
import java.awt.PopupMenu;
import java.awt.SystemTray;
import java.awt.Toolkit;
import java.awt.TrayIcon;
import java.awt.event.ActionEvent;
import java.awt.event.ActionListener;
import javax.swing.JOptionPane;
import javax.swing.SwingUtilities;

public class SystemTrayDemo {
    private static void constructGUI() {
        if (! SystemTray.isSupported()) {
            System.out.println("SystemTray is not supported");
            return;
        }

        SystemTray tray = SystemTray.getSystemTray();
        Toolkit toolkit = Toolkit.getDefaultToolkit();
        Image image = toolkit.getImage("trayIcon.jpg");

        PopupMenu menu = new PopupMenu();
        // Menu item to show the message
        MenuItem messageItem = new MenuItem("Show Message");
        messageItem.addActionListener(new ActionListener() {
            public void actionPerformed(ActionEvent e) {
                JOptionPane.showMessageDialog(null,
                        "Java 6 - Mustang");
            }
        });
        menu.add(messageItem);

        // create menu item to close the application
        MenuItem closeItem = new MenuItem("Close");
```

```
        closeItem.addActionListener(new ActionListener() {
            public void actionPerformed(ActionEvent e) {
                System.exit(0);
            }
        });
        menu.add(closeItem);
        TrayIcon icon = new TrayIcon(image, "SystemTray Demo",
                menu);
        icon.setImageAutoSize(true);

        try {
            tray.add(icon);
        } catch (AWTException e) {
            System.err.println(
                    "Could not add tray icon to system tray");
        }
    }

    public static void main(String[] args) {
        SwingUtilities.invokeLater(new Runnable() {
            public void run() {
                constructGUI();
            }
        });
    }
}
```

Upon running the class, an icon will be added to the system tray. If you right-click on it, the menu will be shown. (See Figure 23.20)

Figure 23.20: Java system tray

Desktop Help Applications

If you are a Windows user, you must know how handy Windows Explorer could be. Not only does it allow you to navigate through the file system, it also lets you double-click on a document file to open the file with the default application and right-click on it to print it. You can do the same in Java thanks to the **java.awt.Desktop** class. In addition to launching the default application to open, edit, or print, **Desktop** also allows you to open the default browser and direct it to a URL as well as launch the user's default email client.

  Desktop is a singleton class and you get the instance by using the static **getDesktop** method:

```
public static Desktop getDesktop()
```

After you obtain the instance, you should check if **Desktop** is supported on the running platform using the **isDesktopSupported** method, before calling other methods of **Desktop**. Here is the signature of **isDesktopSupported**.

```
public static boolean isDesktopSupported()
```

The **open**, **edit**, and **print** methods allow you to pass a **java.io.File** to open, edit, or print the file.

```
public void open(java.io.File file) throws java.io.IOException

public void edit(java.io.File file) throws java.io.IOException

public void print(java.io.File file) throws java.io.IOException
```

Each of these methods can throw an **IOException** if the extension of the specified file has no associated application that can handle it. For example, an **IOException** will be thrown if you try to open a PDF file and your computer does not have a PDF reader registered.

The **browse** method launches the default browser and direct the browser to the specified URL. Here is its signature.

```
public void browse(java.net.URI uri) throws java.io.IOException
```

browse throws an **IOException** if the default browser cannot be found or fails to launch.

Also, the **mail** methods launches the Compose window of the default email client application.

```
public void mail() throws java.io.IOException
public void mail(java.netURI mailtoURI) throws java.io.IOException
```

The mail methods throw an **IOException** if the user's default mail client is not found or if it fails to launch.

Now, how do you prevent an embarrassing **IOException** when trying to perform a **Desktop** action? By using **isSupported** method:

```
public void boolean isSupported(Desktop.Action action)
```

The **Desktop.Action** enum has these values: **BROWSE**, **EDIT**, **MAIL**, **OPEN**, and **PRINT**. You should always test if an action is supported before calling the action.

The **DesktopDemo** class in Listing 23.19 shows how convenient and powerful the **Desktop** class can be.

Listing 23.19: Using the Desktop class

```
package app23;
import java.awt.Desktop;
import java.awt.event.ActionEvent;
import java.awt.event.ActionListener;
import java.io.File;
import java.net.URI;
import java.net.URISyntaxException;
import java.net.URL;
import javax.swing.JFileChooser;
import javax.swing.JFrame;
import javax.swing.JMenu;
import javax.swing.JMenuBar;
```

```java
import javax.swing.JMenuItem;
import javax.swing.SwingUtilities;

public class DesktopDemo {
    private static Desktop desktop;

    private static void constructGUI() {
        JMenuItem openItem;
        JMenuItem editItem;
        JMenuItem printItem;
        JMenuItem browseToItem;
        JMenuItem mailToItem;
        JMenu fileMenu = new JMenu("File");
        JMenu mailMenu = new JMenu("Email");
        JMenu browseMenu = new JMenu("Browser");

        openItem = new JMenuItem("Open");
        openItem.addActionListener(new ActionListener() {
            public void actionPerformed(ActionEvent e) {
                JFileChooser chooser = new JFileChooser();
                if(chooser.showOpenDialog(null) ==
                        JFileChooser.APPROVE_OPTION) {
                    try {
                        desktop.open(chooser.getSelectedFile().
                                getAbsoluteFile());
                    } catch (Exception ex) {
                        ex.printStackTrace();
                    }
                }
            }
        });
        fileMenu.add(openItem);

        editItem = new JMenuItem("Edit");
        editItem.addActionListener(new ActionListener() {
            public void actionPerformed(ActionEvent e) {
                JFileChooser chooser = new JFileChooser();
                if(chooser.showOpenDialog(null) ==
                        JFileChooser.APPROVE_OPTION) {
                    try {

                        desktop.edit(chooser.getSelectedFile()
                                .getAbsoluteFile());
                    } catch (Exception ex) {
                        ex.printStackTrace();
                    }
                }
            }
        });
        fileMenu.add(editItem);

        printItem = new JMenuItem("Print");
        printItem.addActionListener(new ActionListener() {
```

```java
        public void actionPerformed(ActionEvent e) {
            JFileChooser chooser = new JFileChooser();
            if(chooser.showOpenDialog(null) ==
                    JFileChooser.APPROVE_OPTION) {
                try {
                    desktop.print(chooser.getSelectedFile().
                        getAbsoluteFile());
                } catch (Exception ex) {
                    ex.printStackTrace();
                }
            }
        }
    });
    fileMenu.add(printItem);

    browseToItem = new JMenuItem("Go to www.yahoo.com");
    browseToItem.addActionListener(new ActionListener() {
        public void actionPerformed(ActionEvent e) {
            try {
                URI browseURI = new URI("www.yahoo.com");
                desktop.browse(browseURI);
            } catch (Exception ex) {
                System.out.println(ex.getMessage());
            }
        }
    });
    browseMenu.add(browseToItem);

    mailToItem = new JMenuItem("Email to sun@sun.com");
    mailToItem.addActionListener(new ActionListener() {
        public void actionPerformed(ActionEvent e) {
            try {
                URI mailURI = new
                        URI("mailto:support@mycompany.com");
                desktop.mail(mailURI);
            } catch (Exception ex) {
                System.out.println(ex.getMessage());
            }
        }
    });
    mailMenu.add(mailToItem);

    JMenuBar jMenuBar = new JMenuBar();
    jMenuBar.add(fileMenu);
    jMenuBar.add(browseMenu);
    jMenuBar.add(mailMenu);

    JFrame frame = new JFrame();
    frame.setTitle("Desktop Helper Applications");
    frame.setSize(300, 100);
    frame.setDefaultCloseOperation(JFrame.EXIT_ON_CLOSE);
    frame.setJMenuBar(jMenuBar);
    frame.setVisible(true);
```

```
        }

    public static void main(String[] args) {
        if (Desktop.isDesktopSupported()) {
            desktop = Desktop.getDesktop();
        } else {
            System.out.println("Desktop class is not supported");
            System.exit(1);
        }
        SwingUtilities.invokeLater(new Runnable() {
            public void run() {
                constructGUI();
            }
        });
    }
}
```

If you run the class in Listing 23.19, you'll see something similar to Figure 23.21. You can select a file from the File menu and open, edit, and print the file. Alternatively, you can go to Yahoo.com or send an email.

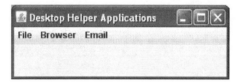

Figure 23.21: Java Desktop

Summary

Chapter 22, "Swing Basics" discussed simple Swing components. This chapter covered more advanced topics such as layout management, event handling, working with menus, the look and feel, splash screen, the system tray, and Java Desktop.

Quiz

1. What is a layout manager?
2. Name at least four types of layout managers.
3. What is a source object in event-handling?
4. Name at least four Swing events.
5. What is the advantage of writing your listener as an anonymous class?

Chapter 24
Applets

An applet is small a Java program that runs inside another application, usually a web browser or an applet viewer. The JDK includes an applet viewer to help you test your applets. However, most of the time applets will run inside a web browser.

This chapter starts with a brief history of applets and by introducing the **java.applet.Applet** class. However, don't use **Applet** directly. Instead, use **javax.swing.JApplet**, a subclass of **Applet** that is more powerful than its parent.

A Brief History of Applets

A couple of years after Java 1.0 was launched in 1995, applets dominated the World Wide Web's dynamic content arena. People used applets to achieve what server technologies are good for today as well as to improve interactivity on the client-side. Applets used to be the only widely accepted technology that could read and write to the server, access and manipulate data in the database, take user input, perform interactive animation, play sound files on the browser, and so on.

Then, we saw server-side technologies such as Servlet/JSP, Microsoft's ASP and ASP.NET, PHP, etc, mature and get accepted as the technologies for developing server applications. They can do many things that applets can plus more. The role of applets started to diminish and applets started to become less and less appealing. Several factors attributed to the near-demise of applets.

1. The emergence of scripting languages such as JavaScript and VBScript. These scripts are easier to write and do not need to be compiled.
2. The emergence of competing technologies that can add interactivity to the client side, such as Microsoft's ActiveX components, Adobe Flash and HTML 5.
3. The lawsuit between Sun Microsystems and Microsoft that resulted in Microsoft's unplugging its Microsoft Java Virtual Machine from Internet Explorer 6. Even though users can download a JVM from Sun's website to run applets, application developers realized applets would not run automatically in IE 6 (the most commonly used browser then) and many started to shy away from applets. Apart from this, Microsoft's winning the browser war certainly did not help applets. Microsoft JVM in Internet Explorer was only compliant with JDK 1.1, making it impractical to write **JApplets** because they would not run automatically in IE. If **JApplet**, which allows you to use the richer Swing components (rather than AWT components) in your applets, had been given all possible supports, it's not impossible that applets would have continued to be the main technology for writing active contents on the browser.
   Later on, top computer makers such as Dell, HP, and Lenovo took the initiative of

installing a JVM in all boxes they sell, but this did not help applets make a comeback.

The Applet API

The API for writing applets is packaged into the **java.applet** package. There is only one class, **Applet**, in this package and three interfaces: **AppletContext**, **AudioClip**, and **AppletStub**. These members of **java.applet** are discussed in the next sections.

The Applet Class

The **java.applet.Applet** class is a template for all applets. This class is a subclass of **java.awt.Panel**, so to write effective applets, you also need some knowledge of the Abstract Window Toolkit (AWT) discussed in Chapter 22, "Swing Basics."

Because an **Applet** is a **Panel**, you can add AWT components to it. As such, writing applets is like writing AWT applications. You use AWT components or draw on its **java.awt.Graphics** object. You can also use AWT layout managers and event listeners described in Chapter 23, "Swinging Higher."

The class diagram in Figure 24.1 shows the **Applet** class with its parent and child.

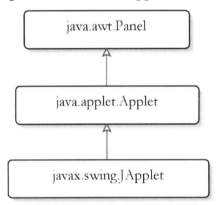

Figure 24.1: Applet class hierarchy

What makes **Applet** different from other AWT controls are its four lifecycle methods.

```
public void init()
```
Called by the web browser or applet viewer right after the applet class is loaded. It is called before the first invocation of the **start** method.

```
public void start()
```
Called by the Web browser or applet viewer to tell this applet that it can start execution. The **start** method is called each time the applet is revisited in the web page.

```
public void stop()
```
Called by the web browser or applet viewer before the current Web page containing the applet is unloaded, for example when the user navigates to another

page. The **stop** method is called before the **destroy** method is called.

```
public void destroy()
```
Called by the web browser or applet viewer to tell this applet that it is being reclaimed and it should release all resources it has allocated.

In addition, there are also the following methods in the **Applet** class.

```
public boolean isActive()
```
Indicates if the current applet is active. An applet is made active just before the **start** method is called and made inactive just before the **stop** method is invoked.

```
public void paint(java.awt.Graphics g)
```
This method is inherited from **java.awt.Container** to draw on an applet user interface. The **paint** method is called to draw the content of an applet.

```
public void showStatus(java.lang.String message)
```
This method displays a method in the status bar of the applet viewer or the Web browser running this applet.

```
public String getParameter(java.lang.String parameterName)
```
Returns a parameter passed by using the **param** tag in the HTML file. If the specified parameter name is not found, **getParameter** returns **null**.

```
public java.net.URL getCodeBase()
```
Returns the URL of the directory from which this applet was downloaded. **getCodeBase** is different from **getDocumentBase** because the latter returns the URL of the Web page that contains this applet. If the applet and its containing Web page come from the same directory, the **getCodeBase** method and the **getDocumentBase** method return identical URL objects.

```
public java.net.URL getDocumentBase()
```
Returns the URL of the directory of the web page containing this applet. The **getDocumentBase** method is different from the **getCodeBase** method. See the description of the **getCodeBase** method.

```
public AudioClip getAudioClip(java.net.URL url)
```
Returns the **AudioClip** object specified by the URL.

```
public AudioClip getAudioClip(java.net.URL url,
        java.lang.String filename)
```
Returns the **AudioClip** object specified by the URL and the *filename* argument.

```
public void play(java.net.URL url)
```
Plays the audio clip specified by the URL.

```
public void play(java.net.URL url, java.lang.String filename)
```
Plays the audio clip specified by the URL and *filename*.

```
public static final AudioClip newAudioClip(java.net.URL url)
```
A convenience method that returns an **AudioClip** object specified by the URL. This method can be used in non-applet applications.

```
public java.awt.Image getImage(java.net.URL url)
```
Returns an Image object from the specified URL.

```
public java.awt.Image getImage(java.net.URL url,
        java.lang.String filename)
```
Returns an **Image** object from the specified URL and filename.

```
public AppletContext getAppletContext()
```
Returns the **AppletContext** object. Read the description of the **AppletContext** interface.

The AppletContext Interface

An **AppletContext** is created by the web browser or applet viewer and represents the environment in which an applet is running. An applet can obtain the reference to its **AppletContext** object by calling the **getAppletContext** method. Most methods in **AppletContext** are duplicated in **Applet**, except the **showDocument** methods, that you can use to navigate to a different web page than the current one. Here are the two overloads of **showDocument**.

```
public void showDocument(java.net.URL url)
```
Navigates to the specified URL

```
public void showDocument(java.net.URL url,
        java.lang.String filename)
```
Navigates to the specified URL and filename.

See the **NewsTickerApplet** applet for an example.

The AudioClip Interface

An **AudioClip** object represents an audio clip. The following audio formats can be played by the **AudioClip** interface's **play** and **loop** methods: .au, .wav, mid, rmf, aif.

The **AudioClip** interface has three methods:

```
public void play()
```
Plays the audio clip.

```
public void loop()
```
Plays the audio clip and keeps repeating indefinitely, until the stop method is called..

```
public void stop()
```
Stops playing this audio clip.

The AppletStub Interface

When a web browser or an applet viewer creates an applet, it also creates an **AppletStub** object that it passes to the applet by calling the **setStub** method on the **Applet** object. **AppletStub** acts as an interface between an applet and the browser environment or applet viewer environment in which the applet is running. Unless you are writing an applet viewer, you will rarely need to worry about creating an **AppletStub**.

Security Restrictions

For security reasons, applets downloaded from the Internet are restricted. They cannot do the following operations:

- read from and write to files in the client computer
- make network connections other than the originating host.
- define native calls.
- read system properties other than those listed in Table 24.1.

Property	Description
file.separator	File separator (for example, "/")
java.class.version	Java class version number
java.vendor	Java vendor-specific string
java.vendor.url	Java vendor URL
java.version	Java version number
line.separator	Line separator
os.arch	Operating system architecture
os.name	Operating system name
path.separator	Path separator (for example, ":")

Table 24.1: System properties accessible to applets

To read a system property from within an applet, use the **getProperty** method of the **java.lang.System** class. For example:

```
String newline = System.getProperty("line.separator");
```

To give an applet greater access, you need to digitally sign it.

Writing and Deploying Applets

As an example, the code in Listing 24.1 presents an applet class.

Listing 24.1: LifeCycleApplet

```
package app24;
import java.applet.Applet;
import java.awt.Graphics;

public class LifeCycleApplet extends Applet {
    StringBuilder stringBuilder = new StringBuilder();
    public void init() {
        stringBuilder.append("init()... ");
    }
    public void start() {
        stringBuilder.append("start()... ");
    }
    public void stop() {
```

```
            stringBuilder.append("stop()... ");
    }
    public void destroy() {
            stringBuilder.append("destroy()... ");
    }
    public void paint(Graphics g) {
            stringBuilder.append("paint(g)... ");
            g.drawString(stringBuilder.toString(), 4, 10);
    }
}
```

You can compile the applet as you would other Java classes. To run the applet, you first have to write an HTML page that references the applet's class. Listing 24.2 shows the content of **runApplet.html**, an HTML file that references the **LifeCycleApplet** applet.

Listing 24.2: The runApplet.html page
```
<html>
<head>
<title>Testing LifeCycleApplet</title>
</head>
<body>
<applet code="app24.LifeCycleApplet.class"
        width="400" height="300">
</applet>
</body>
</html>
```

The HTML file must reside in the same directory as the class's root directory. Figure 24.2 shows the directory structure of the applet and the HTML file (**runApplet.html** file).

▼ 📂 app24
    📄 LifeCycleApplet.class
    🌐 runApplet.html

Figure 24.2: The directory structure of the HTML file and the applet class

You can either run the HTML file using a web browser or by using the **AppletViewer** application that comes with the JDK. The **appletviewer.exe** file can be found in the same directory as the **java.exe** and **javac.exe** programs.

To run your applet using **AppletViewer**, from the directory on which the **runApplet.html** file resides, type

```
appletviewer runApplet.html
```

Figure 24.3 displays the applet in **AppletViewer** and Figure 24.4 in a web browser.

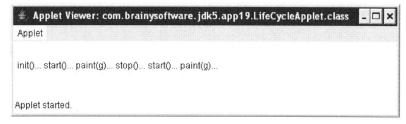

Figure 24.3: Running LifeCycleApplet in AppletViewer

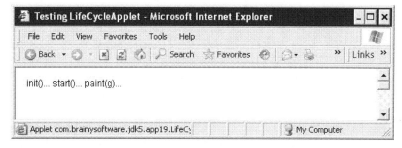

Figure 24.4: Running LifeCycleApplet in a web browser

There is a difference between running in the applet viewer and the browser. When you minimize the applet viewer, it invokes the **stop** method of the applet. When you restore the applet viewer, it invokes the **start** method and **paint** method again. When you minimize your browser, the applet's **stop** method is not invoked.

How AppletViewer Works

It is not hard to understand how an applet viewer, such as the **AppletViewer** program, works. These are the things you need to bear in mind. An applet is an AWT component that can be added to a container, and an applet viewer needs to call the **init** and **start** methods of the applet it's running.

Listing 24.3 presents a **JFrame** that acts as an applet viewer.

Listing 24.3: A custom applet viewer called AppletRunner

```
package app24;
import java.applet.Applet;
import java.awt.BorderLayout;
import javax.swing.JFrame;

public class AppletRunner extends JFrame {
    private static final long serialVersionUID =
            -4158064205501217649L;

    public void run(String appletClassName) {
        this.setDefaultCloseOperation(JFrame.EXIT_ON_CLOSE);
        this.setLayout(new BorderLayout());
        this.setTitle("Applet Runner");
```

```
        Applet applet = null;
        try {
            // use reflection to instantiate the applet
            Class appletClass = Class.forName(appletClassName);
            applet = (Applet) appletClass.newInstance();
        }
        catch (Exception e) {
            e.printStackTrace();
        }
        if (applet!=null) {
            this.add(applet);
            this.pack();
            this.setVisible(true);
            // call the applet's lifecycle methods
            applet.init();
            applet.start();
        }
        else {
            System.exit(-1);
        }
    }

    public static void main(String[] args) {
        if (args.length!=1) {
            System.out.println(
                    "Usage: AppletRunner appletClassName");
            System.exit(0);
        }
        // args[0] should be the fully qualified class name of the
        // applet to be run
        (new AppletRunner()).run(args[0]);
    }
}
```

To use the program, you pass an applet's fully qualified class name as the argument to the **AppletRunner** class:

```
java AppletRunner appletClassName
```

For example, to run the **LifeCycleApplet**, type

```
java AppletRunner app24.LifeCycleApplet
```

Figure 24.5 shows the **LifeCycleApplet** in **AppletRunner**.

Figure 24.5: A home-made applet viewer

Passing Parameters to an Applet

To pass parameters to an applet, you use the **param** tag inside the **applet** tag in your HTML file. The **param** tag can have two attributes:

- **name**. Represents the parameter name.
- **value**. Represents the parameter value.

For example:

```
<param name="customer" value="Jane Goddall"/>
```

From inside an applet, you can retrieve a parameter by using the **Applet** class's **getParameter** method:

```
public java.lang.String getParameter(java.lang.String paramName)
```

Let's now examine the **NewsTickerApplet** class in Listing 24.4. The applet can be used to display headlines that you pass as parameters in **param** tags. A headline can be associated with a URL. If a headline is clicked, the applet redirects you the corresponding URL.

Listing 24.4: The NewsTickerApplet class

```
package app24;
import java.applet.Applet;
import java.awt.BorderLayout;
import java.awt.Color;
import java.awt.Label;
import java.awt.event.MouseAdapter;
import java.awt.event.MouseEvent;
import java.net.MalformedURLException;
import java.net.URL;
import java.util.ArrayList;
import java.util.List;

public class NewsTickerApplet extends Applet implements Runnable {
    Label label = new Label();
    String[] headlines;
    String[] urls;
    boolean running = true;
```

```java
Thread thread;
int counter = 0;

public void run() {
    while (running) {
        label.setText(headlines[counter]);
        try {
            Thread.sleep(1500);
        } catch (InterruptedException e) {
        }
        counter++;
        if (counter == headlines.length)
            counter = 0;
    }
}

public void init() {
    this.setLayout(new BorderLayout());
    this.add(label);
    label.setBackground(Color.LIGHT_GRAY);
    label.addMouseListener(new MouseAdapter() {
        public void mouseClicked(MouseEvent me) {
            try {
                URL url = new URL(urls[counter]);
                getAppletContext().showDocument(url);
            } catch (MalformedURLException e) {
            } catch (Exception e) {
            }
        }
    });
}

public void start() {
    List<String> list = new ArrayList<>();
    for (int i = 1;; i++) {
        String headline = this.getParameter("headline"
                + Integer.toString(i));
        if (headline != null) {
            list.add(headline);
        } else {
            headlines = new String[list.size()];
            list.toArray(headlines);
            break;
        }
    }
    list.clear();
    for (int i = 1;; i++) {
        String url = this.getParameter("url" +
                Integer.toString(i));
        if (url != null) {
            list.add(url);
        } else {
            urls = new String[list.size()];
```

```
                list.toArray(urls);
                break;
            }
        }
    }
    if (thread == null) {
        thread = new Thread(this);
        thread.start();
    }
}

public void stop() {
    running = false;
}
}
```

The **NewsTickerApplet** class uses a **java.awt.Label** to display headlines. It also employs two class-level **String** arrays to store headlines and corresponding URLs.

```
Label label = new Label();
String[] headlines;
String[] urls;
```

The **init** method, which is called when the applet is initialized, adds the label to the applet and adds a mouse listener to the label. This listener will redirects the user to the URL corresponding to the headline clicked.

```
public void init() {
    this.setLayout(new BorderLayout());
    this.add(label);
    label.setBackground(Color.LIGHT_GRAY);
    label.addMouseListener(new MouseAdapter() {
        public void mouseClicked(MouseEvent me) {
            try {
                URL url = new URL(urls[counter]);
                getAppletContext().showDocument(url);
            } catch (MalformedURLException e) {
            } catch (Exception e) {
            }
        }
    });
}
```

The listener is implemented as an anonymous class (discussed in Chapter 18, "Nested and Inner Classes").

The **start** method reads parameters from the **param** tags. The first headline is stored in the parameter named **headline1** and the first URL by **url1**. Similarly, the second headline is stored in the **headline2** parameter, and so on.

To display the headlines, you use a thread. Java threads are explained in Chapter 27, for now know that the **run** method in the applet displays the headlines one at a time.

Listing 24.5 shows the HTML file that contains the **NewsTickerApplet** applet.

Listing 24.5: The HTML file that contains NewsTickerApplet

```
<html>
<head>
<title>Testing NewsTickerApplet</title>
</head>
<body>
<applet code="app24.NewsTickerApplet.class"
    width="200" height="20">
<param name="headline1" value="Economic Survey"/>
<param name="url1" value="http://www.economist.com"/>
<param name="headline2" value="Business Today"/>
<param name="url2" value="http://news.yahoo.com"/>
<param name="headline3" value="World Live"/>
<param name="url3" value="http://www.cnn.com"/>
</applet>
</body>
</html>
```

Load the HTML file in Listing 24.5 to a web browser, and you should be able to see the applet in the browser, like the one shown in Figure 24.6.

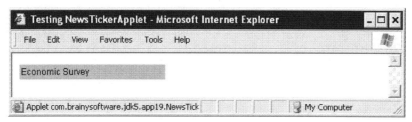

Figure 24.6: Passing parameters to the NewsTickerApplet

SoundPlayerApplet

The following example shows an important feature of the **Applet** class: play audio clips. Playing an audio clip is as easy as composing a URL that points to the location of an audio file. Most of the time, you can simply call the **getCodeBase** and **getDocumentBase** methods to get a URL object.

Listing 24.6 shows the **SoundPlayerApplet** class that play the **quick.au** sound file.

Listing 24.6: The SoundPlayerApplet class

```
package app24;
import java.applet.Applet;
import java.applct.AudioClip;

public class SoundPlayerApplet extends Applet {
    private static final long serialVersionUID = 1L;

    public void start() {
        AudioClip audioClip = this.getAudioClip(getCodeBase(),
                "quack.au");
        // audioClip.play();
```

```
        audioClip.loop();
    }
}
```

Note that calling **play** before **loop** causes the audio clip to be played once only.

JApplet

The Swing API (discussed in Chapter 22, "Swing Basics") includes the **javax.swing.JApplet** class. This class is a direct child of **java.applet.Applet** and allows you to add Swing components on it. When Swing was first released, people shunned **JApplet** because most browsers did not yet support Java 1.2. As such, applets that subclass **JApplet** would not run in many web browsers. Those awful years have passed, though, because now most browsers that support Java use JDK 1.2 or later. Therefore, **JApplet** is the preferred choice when writing applets today.

JApplet is a Swing component, but it is also a subclass of **java.applet.Applet**. As such, a **JApplet** is still an applet that needs to run on an applet viewer or a Web browser. On the other hand, it behaves much like a **JFrame**. For example, you can add Swing components, respond to events, and use Swing layout management.

Listing 24.7 presents an example of **JApplet**.

Listing 24.7: A JApplet
```
package app24;
import java.awt.BorderLayout;
import javax.swing.JApplet;
import javax.swing.JButton;
import javax.swing.JLabel;
import javax.swing.JTextField;

public class MyJApplet extends JApplet {
    private static final long serialVersionUID = 1L;

    public void start() {
        this.setLayout(new BorderLayout());
        JLabel label1 = new JLabel("Registration Form");
        label1.setHorizontalAlignment(JLabel.CENTER);
        this.add(label1, BorderLayout.NORTH);
        JLabel label2 = new JLabel("Name:");
        this.add(label2, BorderLayout.WEST);
        JTextField textField = new JTextField("<your name>");
        this.add(textField, BorderLayout.CENTER);
        JButton button1 = new JButton("Register");
        this.add(button1, BorderLayout.EAST);
        JButton button2 = new JButton("Clear Form");
        this.add(button2, BorderLayout.SOUTH);
    }
}
```

When run, the **JApplet** looks like a **JFrame**, but it runs on an applet viewer or a Web browser. Figure 24.7 shows this.

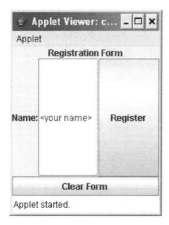

Figure 24.7: A JApplet

Applet Deployment in a JAR File

Applets can be packaged into a jar file and deployed. The advantage is you can deploy your applet and its resources in one single file. In addition, if your applet needs to access restricted resources, you can digitally sign it. Signing a jar file is discussed in Chapter 25, "Security."

To package Java classes and related resources into a jar file, you use the **jar** tool included in the JDK. To create a jar file, use this command.

```
jar cf jarfile inputfiles
```

where *jarfile* is the name of the JAR file to be created and *inputfiles* is a list of files to be included in the JAR file.

For example, to jar all Java classes that belong to the package **app24** and all audio files in the working directory into the **MyJar.jar** file, change directory to the working directory of this chapter's application and type this.

```
jar cf MyJar.jar app24/*.class *.au
```

Note
A jar file has the same format as a zip file. If you have a zip file viewer, you can change the extension of the jar file to .zip and use the viewer to view the content of the jar file.

The **jar** tool can also be used with options and to update and extract a jar file. For details see Appendix C, "The Jar Tool."

If you deploy your applet in a jar file, you need to use the **archive** attribute in your **applet** tag to tell Web browsers how to find the jar file. Because a jar file can house more than one Java class, you still need the **code** attribute to tell Web browsers which class to invoke. The following is an **applet** tag that downloads an applet from a jar file (**MyJar.jar**) and invoke the **MyApplet.class** in the jar file.

```
<applet code="MyApplet.class" archive="MyJar.jar" width="600"
    height="50">
</applet>
```

If you have dependencies, you can specify the dependencies in the **archive** attribute separated by commas. For instance, this **applet** tag has two dependencies, one in the parent directory and one in the **lib** directory.

```
<applet code="MyApplet.class"
    archive="MyJar.jar,../dependencies1.jar,lib/dependencies2.jar"
    width="600"
    height="50">
</applet>
```

Faster Loading

An **applet** tag will start the class specified in its **code** attribute. If an **archive** attribute is present, the first jar file will be downloaded. However, it will not download other dependencies until one of the classes in the dependencies is needed. Therefore, it's a good idea to divide a big applet in different jar files for faster loading.

Summary

Applets are small Java programs that run on an applet viewer or a web browser. The Applet API is deployed in the **java.applet** package. The **Applet** class represents an applet. The **init**, **start**, and **destroy** methods are life cycle methods of an applet. They get called by the applet viewer.

When Swing was released, it included **javax.swing.JApplet** that is a child class of **java.applet.Applet**. **JApplet** is a Swing component and allows you to add Swing components on it.

Applets are normally downloaded from the Internet. As such, it must be defined using the **applet** tag in the HTML file.

Quiz

1. What are the life cycle methods of an applet?
2. How do you pass parameters to an applet?
3. Is **JApplet** an applet or a **JFrame**?

Chapter 25
Introduction to JavaFX

JavaFX is a technology for creating rich client applications that can run on the desktop and in the browser. It is similar to Swing but with a better and simpler object model and will replace Swing and AWT.

This chapter provides an introduction to JavaFX and Chapter 26, "JavaFX with FXML" explains how to separate the presentation layer and business logic using a special markup language called FXML.

Overview

JavaFX is a technology for building rich applications that can be deployed as desktop applications as well as run in the browser as applets. JavaFX will eventually replace Swing, and to ease transition from Swing to JavaFX, there is support for interoperability between the two. You can easily use Swing components from within your JavaFX application.

As a desktop technology, JavaFX is an excellent choice for any Java developer or anyone aspiring to be a GUI developer, thanks to its features and ease of use. In addition, JavaFX enjoys the full support from Oracle and the Java community at large, so getting help is easy.

As a technology for building in-browser applications, JavaFX must compete with other technologies, notably HTML 5, Flash, and Microsoft Silverlight. HTML 5 has the advantage of being natively supported by modern browsers, which means everything built in HTML 5 is guaranteed to work seamlessly in those browsers, despite the fact thatHTML 5 is not as feature-rich as JavaFX, Flash, and Silverlight. JavaFX, Flash, and Silverlight applications require plug-ins to run in a browser and browsers do not necessarily ship with these plug-ins so JavaFX applet users, for example, may have to install a Java browser plug-in before being able to run a JavaFX applet. Installing a plug-in may or may not discourage people from liking JavaFX applets. You can judge yourself whether it is easy enough to install the plug-in by reading the instructions on this web page.

```
http://java.com/en/download/help/enable_browser.xml
```

Setting up

JavaFX started as an independent technology that had to be downloaded separately from the JDK. Starting from JDK 1.7 update 6 (JDK7u6), however, the JDK ships with the latest version of JavaFX. JDK 1.7 includes JavaFX 2.2 and Java 8 comes with JavaFX 8, the release after version 2.2.

At the time of writing, the easiest way to develop JavaFX applications is by using NetBeans 8 or later. Simply click **File** → **New Project** → **JavaFX** to create a new JavaFX project.

If you are not using NetBeans, you need to include the **jfxrt.jar** file in your class path when compiling and running your application. In JDK 1.8, the file is located in **$JAVA_HOME/jre/lib/ext/** where **$JAVA_HOME** is the installation directory of your JDK. In JDK 1.7 update 6 and later, the file can be found in **$JAVA_HOME/jre/lib/**.

If you're using Eclipse, right-click the project icon and click on **Properties**. On the left hand side of the window that appears, click **Java Build Path**, then select the **Libraries** tab on the right. Next, click the **Add External JARs** button and navigate to the location of the jar file and select it.

There is an Eclipse plug-in called e(fx)clipse that you can add to Eclipse 4.4 and later to help you develop JavaFX applications. The instruction can be found here.

```
http://www.eclipse.org/efxclipse/install.html
```

You can also compile and run a JavaFX application from outside an IDE. To compile a JavaFX class named **MyFXApp** in package **mypackage** using the **javac** program on the command line, go to the source directory of your project and type

```
javac -cp ${JAVA_HOME}/jre/lib/ext/jfxrt.jar mypackage/MyFXApp.java
```

replacing *${JAVA_HOME}* with the path to Java installation. For example, if your Java installation is in **/opt/jdk1.8.0_25**, use this command.

```
javac -cp /opt/jdk1.8.0_25/jre/lib/ext/jfxrt.jar mypackage/MyFXApp.java
```

To run the application (on Linux and Mac OS X), include the current directory in the class path:

```
java -cp /opt/jdk1.8.0_25/jre/lib/ext/jfxrt.jar:. mypackage.MyFXApp
```

On Windows, replace the colon with a semicolon.

```
java -cp /opt/jdk1.8.0_25/jre/lib/ext/jfxrt.jar;. mypackage.MyFXApp
```

Your First JavaFX Application

This section shows how easy it is to develop a JavaFX application. The example consists of only one class, which is called **FirstApp** and shown in Listing 25.1.

Listing 25.1: The FirstApp class

```
package app25;
import javafx.application.Application;
import javafx.scene.Scene;
import javafx.scene.control.Label;
import javafx.scene.layout.StackPane;
import javafx.scene.paint.Color;
import javafx.stage.Stage;

public class FirstApp extends Application {

    @Override
    public void start(Stage stage) {
        Label label = new Label("Welcome");
        StackPane root = new StackPane();
        root.getChildren().add(label);

        Scene scene = new Scene(root, 400, 100);
        scene.setFill(Color.BEIGE);

        stage.setTitle("First FX");
        stage.setScene(scene);
        stage.show();
    }

    public static void main(String[] args) {
        launch(args);
    }
}
```

Run it just as you would any Java application and you'll see a window like the one in Figure 25.1.

Figure 25.1: A simple JavaFX application (on Ubuntu)

The JavaFX API is explained in the next section.

Application, Stage, and Scene

The JavaFX API takes the form of the types in the **javafx** package and its subpackages. One of its most important types is the **javafx.application.Application** class, which represents a JavaFX application. A JavaFX application consists of one or more windows and other resources.

In JavaFX a window is represented by the **javafx.stage.Window** class, which has two subclasses, **Stage** and **PopupWindow**. A **Stage** (an instance of **javafx.stage.Stage**) is a top-level container to which you add a second-level container called **Scene**, which in turn contains the UI components for that window. The primary **Stage** is created for you by the JavaFX runtime, but you can create additional **Stage**s and **PopupWindow**s if needed.

The **javafx.scene.Scene** class is a container for UI components. In JavaFX a UI component is called a graph scene node (or a node, for short). To create a **Scene** you must pass a parent node (an instance of **javafx.scene.Parent**) responsible for laying out child UI components.

Now let's take a look at the three main classes, **Application**, **Stage**, and **Scene**. Details on other JavaFX types can be viewed here.

```
http://docs.oracle.com/javase/8/javafx/api/toc.htm
```

The Application Class

You extend the **Application** class to create a JavaFX application. To run it as a stand-alone program, you call one of its **launch** methods.

```
public static void launch(java.lang.String... args)
```

```
public static void launch(java.lang.Class<? extends Application>
        appClass, java.lang.String... args)
```

Any parameter you pass to the **launch** methods can be retrieved from inside an **Application** using the **getParameters** method.

```
public final Application.Parameters getParameters()
```

The **Application** class has the following life-cycle methods that will be called when an instance is launched.

```
public void init() throws java.lang.Exception
```
    This method is called after the application is constructed. It should be overriden if the application needs to perform initialization.

```
public abstract void start(Stage stage) throws
        java.lang.Exception
```
    This method is called after **init()** returns and you should construct your UI in this method implementation. The JavaFX runtime creates a **Stage** object that is passed as a method argument.

```
public void stop() throws java.lang.Exception
```
This method is called when the application should stop. You should release any held resources here.

Of the life-cycle methods, only **start** must be overriden.

The Stage Class

The **Stage** class represents a top-level container for your UI components. An instance is created and passed to you when the application's **start** method is called. The **Stage** that the application created is the primary window of the application. You can create your own **Stage** if necessary.

A **Stage**, just like any other UI window, can have a title that you can populate using the **Stage** class's **title** property. On top of that, you can add a **Scene** to a **Stage** by calling the **setScene** method on the **Stage**. Then, to show a **Stage** you call its **show** method.

The Scene Class

A **Scene** is a container that can be added to a **Stage**. A **Scene** must contain a parent node that is the root of all components added to the **Scene**. A parent node is represented by the **javafx.scene.Parent** class. The simplest constructor in **Scene** takes one argument, an instance of **Parent**.

```
public Scene(Parent root)
```

There are other constructors that let you specify the dimension of the **Scene** as well as its fill.

```
public Scene(Parent root, double width, double height)
```

```
public Scene(Parent root, javafx.scene.paint.Paint fill)
```

```
public Scene(Parent root, double width, double height,
        javafx.scene.paint.Paint fill)
```

UI Components

Built-in UI components make writing JavaFX applications so easy and fun. A UI component is called a scene graph node (or simply a node) in the parlance of JavaFX developers. The **javafx.scene.Node** class is the base class for all nodes. It has five subclasses that distinguish the types of nodes in JavaFX:

- **Canvas**. A rectangular area you can draw on.
- **Parent**. A container to which you can add other UI components.
- **Shape**. Represents a shape, such as a rectangle, a circle, or an arc.
- **ImageView**. A view area for showing an image.
- **MediaView**. Provides a view of media being played by a MediaPlayer.

Canvas, **ImageView**, and **MediaView** do not have subclasses. **Parent** and **Shape** do.

The **Parent** class has the following subclasses.

- **Control**. This class is a base class for all UI controls, from simple controls like **Button** and **Label** to more complex ones such as **ProgressBar**, **TreeView**, and **TableView**.
- **Region**. Represents a screen area that can contain other nodes and be styled using CSS. Subclasses include **Chart** and various **Pane**s, including **BorderPane**, **StackPane**, **FlowPane**, **GridPane**, **HBox**, **VBox**, **AnchorPane**, etc.
- **Group**. An area that contains an **ObservableList** of children and is the best **Parent** for working with **Shape** objects.
- **WebView**. A **WebView** is used to manage a **WebEngine** and display its content. As the name implies, a **WebEngine** can load web pages, create document models, and run JavaScript on pages.

The **Control** and **Region** classes are discussed further in the next sections.

The **javafx.scene.shape.Shape** class is a base class for various geometric shapes, including **Arc**, **Circle**, **Ellipse**, **Line**, **Path**, and **Rectangle**.

Controls

UI controls are nodes that the user can interact with. The **javafx.scene.control.Control** class is the base class for all UI controls. Figure 25.2 shows direct and indirect subclasses of **Control**.

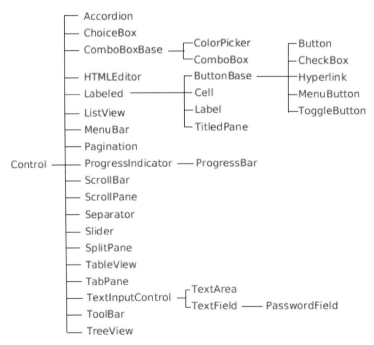

Figure 25.2: Control implementations

Figure 25.3 shows a **Scene** that contains some JavaFX controls and Listing 25.2 presents the code that produces the **Scene**.

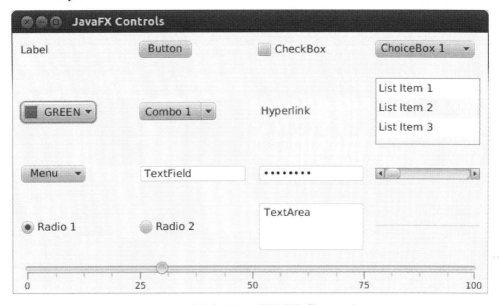

Figure 25.3: JavaFX UI Controls

Listing 25.2: The ControlsDemo class

```
package app25;
import javafx.application.Application;
import javafx.geometry.Insets;
import javafx.scene.Scene;
import javafx.scene.control.Button;
import javafx.scene.control.CheckBox;
import javafx.scene.control.ChoiceBox;
import javafx.scene.control.ColorPicker;
import javafx.scene.control.ComboBox;
import javafx.scene.control.Hyperlink;
import javafx.scene.control.Label;
import javafx.scene.control.ListView;
import javafx.scene.control.MenuButton;
import javafx.scene.control.MenuItem;
import javafx.scene.control.PasswordField;
import javafx.scene.control.RadioButton;
import javafx.scene.control.ScrollBar;
import javafx.scene.control.Separator;
import javafx.scene.control.Slider;
import javafx.scene.control.TextArea;
import javafx.scene.control.TextField;
import javafx.scene.control.ToggleGroup;
import javafx.scene.layout.ColumnConstraints;
import javafx.scene.layout.GridPane;
import javafx.scene.paint.Color;
import javafx.stage.Stage;
```

```
public class ControlsDemo extends Application {

    @Override
    public void start(Stage stage) {
        GridPane grid = new GridPane();
        grid.setHgap(15);
        grid.setVgap(25);
        ColumnConstraints constraint = new ColumnConstraints();
        constraint.setPercentWidth(25);
        grid.getColumnConstraints().addAll(constraint,
                constraint, constraint, constraint);
        grid.setPadding(new Insets(10));

        grid.add(new Label("Label"), 0, 0);
        grid.add(new Button("Button"), 1, 0);
        grid.add(new CheckBox("CheckBox"), 2, 0);

        ChoiceBox<String> choiceBox = new ChoiceBox<String>();

        choiceBox.getItems().addAll("ChoiceBox 1", "ChoiceBox 2");
        choiceBox.setValue("ChoiceBox 1");
        grid.add(choiceBox, 3, 0);

        grid.add(new ColorPicker(Color.GREEN), 0, 1);

        ComboBox<String> comboBox = new ComboBox<String>();
        comboBox.getItems().addAll("Combo 1", "Combo 2");
        comboBox.setValue("Combo 1");
        grid.add(comboBox, 1, 1);

        grid.add(new Hyperlink("Hyperlink"), 2, 1);

        ListView<String> listView = new ListView<String>();
        listView.getItems().addAll("List Item 1",
                "List Item 2", "List Item 3");
        grid.add(listView, 3, 1);

        MenuButton menuButton = new MenuButton("Menu");
        menuButton.getItems().addAll(new MenuItem("Menu 1"),
                new MenuItem("Menu 1"));
        grid.add(menuButton, 0, 2);

        grid.add(new TextField("TextField"), 1, 2);

        PasswordField passwordField = new PasswordField();
        passwordField.setText("Password");
        grid.add(passwordField, 2, 2);

        grid.add(new ScrollBar(), 3, 2);

        ToggleGroup group = new ToggleGroup();
        RadioButton radioButton1 = new RadioButton("Radio 1");
        radioButton1.setToggleGroup(group);
```

```
            radioButton1.setSelected(true);
            RadioButton radioButton2 = new RadioButton("Radio 2");
            radioButton2.setToggleGroup(group);
            grid.add(radioButton1, 0, 3);
            grid.add(radioButton2, 1, 3);

            TextArea textArea = new TextArea("TextArea");
            textArea.setMinHeight(60.00);
            grid.add(textArea, 2, 3);

            grid.add(new Separator(), 3, 3);

            Slider slider2 = new Slider(0, 100, 30);
            slider2.setShowTickMarks(true);
            slider2.setShowTickLabels(true);
            grid.add(slider2, 0, 4, 4, 1);

            Scene scene = new Scene(grid, 600, 320);
            scene.setFill(Color.BEIGE);

            stage.setTitle("JavaFX Controls");
            stage.setScene(scene);
            stage.show();
    }

    public static void main(String[] args) {
        launch(args);
    }
}
```

Regions

A **Region** is a screen area that can contain other nodes and be styled using CSS. All Regions are subclasses of the **javafx.scene.layout.Region** class. There are three direct descendents of **Region**: **Axis**, **Chart**, and **Pane**. An **Axis** is used to render an axis on a chart area and a **Chart** models a chart. A **Pane** is a region that is normally used for laying out UI controls.

This section only discusses **Pane**.

Subclasses of **Pane** include **BorderPane**, **StackPane**, **GridPane**, **FlowPane**, **AnchorPane**, **HBox**, and **VBox**.

BorderPane divides a **Parent** into five areas, top, bottom, left, right, and center. The diagram in Figure 25.4 shows the different areas in a **BorderPane**.

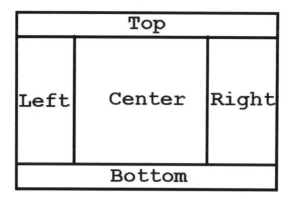

Figure 25.4: The five areas of BorderPane

HBox lays out its children in a single horizontal row and **VBox** does it in a single vertical row. **GridPane**, on the other hand, arranges children in a grid and is often used to layout the controls of a form.

The **BorderPaneDemo** class Listing 25.3 uses **BorderPane** to lay out controls. Only the top, left and center areas are used. The top section contains an **HBox** with two buttons and the left section contains a **Label** and a **ColorPicker**. The center section has an **ImageView** with an **Image**.

Listing 25.3: The BorderPaneDemo class

```
package app25;

import javafx.application.Application;
import javafx.geometry.Insets;
import javafx.scene.Scene;
import javafx.scene.control.Button;
import javafx.scene.control.ColorPicker;
import javafx.scene.control.Label;
import javafx.scene.image.ImageView;
import javafx.scene.layout.BorderPane;
import javafx.scene.layout.HBox;
import javafx.scene.layout.VBox;
import javafx.stage.Stage;

public class BorderPaneDemo extends Application {

    @Override
    public void start(Stage stage) {
        Button okButton = new Button("OK");
        okButton.setDefaultButton(true);

        Button cancelButton = new Button("Cancel");
        HBox hBox = new HBox();
        hBox.setPadding(new Insets(15, 12, 15, 12));
        hBox.setSpacing(10);
        hBox.setStyle("-fx-background-color: #886699;");
        hBox.getChildren().addAll(okButton, cancelButton);
        BorderPane root = new BorderPane();
```

```
        root.setTop(hBox);

        ImageView imageView = new ImageView("image/1.jpg");
        root.setCenter(imageView);

        VBox vBox = new VBox();
        vBox.setStyle("-fx-background-color: " +
                "#ddeeff;-fx-padding:10px");
        vBox.getChildren().addAll(
            new Label("Select Color:"),
            new ColorPicker());
        root.setLeft(vBox);

        root.setStyle("-fx-background-color: #6680e6;");
        Scene scene = new Scene(root, 740, 530);

        stage.setTitle("HBox, VBox, BorderPane Demo");
        stage.setScene(scene);
        stage.show();
    }

    public static void main(String[] args) {
        launch(args);
    }
}
```

Figure 25.5 shows the **BorderPaneDemo** application on Windows.

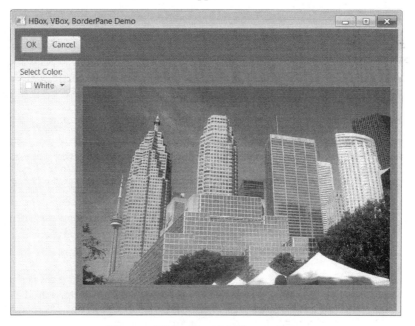

Figure 25.5: BorderPane demo

Event Handling

JavaFX is event-driven. A UI component can raise events and you can write code to handle the events. This event-driven-ness enables user interactivity in JavaFX applications.

There are many types of events, all derive from the **javafx.event.Event** class. Subclasses of **Event** include **ActionEvent**, **InputMethodEvent**, **MouseEvent**, **MouseDragEvent**, **ScrollEvent**, **SwipeEvent**, and so on.

Different components may raise different events. For example, clicking a button raises an **ActionEvent** and changing the text in a **TextField** triggers an **InputMethodEvent**. You can write and register an event handler that will be called when the corresponding event occurs. For instance, you can write a handler for the **InputMethodEvent** of a **TextField** to change entered text to upper case. Or, you can write a handler that will open another **Stage** if a button is clicked.

The easiest way to write and register an event handler in JavaFX is by using one of the convenience methods provided by the **Node** class. The method names have the pattern set**On**_XXX_ and the methods are inherited by all descendents of **Node**. Examples of the convenience methods are **setOnDragEntered**, **setOnDragExited**, **setOnInputMethodTextChanged**, **setOnKeyTyped**, **setOnMouseClicked**, and many, many others. Subclasses of **Node** may add more convenience methods to accommodate events specific to them.

These convenience methods take an **EventHandler** object as an argument. **javafx.event.EventHandler** is a parameterized interface with a method, **handle**. Here is the definition of **EventHandler**.

```
package javafx.event;
public interface EventHandler<T extends Event> extends
        java.util.EventListener {

    void handle(T event)

}
```

When constructing an **EventHandler**, you must pass an appropriate event type. For example, the following code construct an **EventHandler** for the **ActionEvent**.

```
EventHandler handler = new EventHandler<ActionEvent>() {

    @Override
    public void handle(ActionEvent event) {
        // do something
    }
};
```

The **RotateTest** class in Listing 25.4 shows JavaFX event processing. The class has a **Rectangle** and a **Button** and captures the **ActionEvent** of the Button. Whenever the button is clicked, the **Rectangle** is rotated 10 degrees clock-wise.

Listing 25.4: The RotateTest class

```
package app25;

import javafx.application.Application;
import javafx.collections.ObservableList;
import javafx.event.ActionEvent;
import javafx.event.EventHandler;
import javafx.scene.Node;
import javafx.scene.Scene;
import javafx.scene.control.Button;
import javafx.scene.layout.VBox;
import javafx.scene.paint.Color;
import javafx.scene.shape.Rectangle;
import javafx.stage.Stage;

public class RotateDemo extends Application {

    @Override
    public void start(Stage stage) {
        VBox root = new VBox(40);
        ObservableList<Node> children = root.getChildren();
        final Rectangle rect = new Rectangle(80, 50);
        rect.setFill(Color.AQUAMARINE);
        children.add(rect);

        Button button = new Button("Rotate");
        button.setOnAction(new EventHandler<ActionEvent>() {
            @Override
            public void handle(ActionEvent event) {
                rect.setRotate(rect.getRotate() + 10);
            }
        });
        children.add(button);

        Scene scene = new Scene(root, 120, 130);
        scene.setFill(Color.BEIGE);

        stage.setTitle("Rotate Test");
        stage.setScene(scene);
        stage.show();
    }

    public static void main(String[] args) {
        launch(args);
    }
}
```

In the **start** method of the application, a **Button** is created and its **setOnAction** method called.

```
        Button button = new Button("Rotate");
        button.setOnAction(new EventHandler<ActionEvent>() {
```

```
        @Override
        public void handle(ActionEvent event) {
            rect.setRotate(rect.getRotate() + 10);
        }
    });
```

Note how the **EventHandler** was created and passed to the button's **setOnAction** convenience method.

Figure 25.6 shows the application. Try clicking the button and watch the effect.

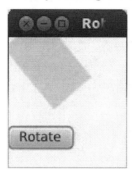

Figure 25.6: Event handling in JavaFX

Styling with CSS

Some of the controls offer methods to change their look and feel. For example, the **setFont** method of the **Label** class allows you to set the font to display the label text. While these methods are easy to use, they have to be called from within the code and this implies tight-coupling between the presentation layer and the business logic. A better way is to style the UI components using CSS (Cascading Style Sheet). JavaFX CSS is not exactly the same as that used in web design. In this chapter CSS refers to the CSS used in JavaFX applications.

A CSS file contains styles that can be referred to by id or by class. Each of the JavaFX controls is already assigned a default CSS class that is similar to the Java class name of the control. For example, the default style for **Button** is **button** and the default style for **Label** is **label**. This means, to provide a style that affects all buttons, you simply need a style named **button** in your CSS file. For example,

```
.button {
    -fx-border-width: 3px;
    -fx-background-color:#dd8818;
}
```

The default style for a control with a multiword name is the combination of the words separated by a hyphen. For instance, the default style for **CheckBox** is **check-box** and the default style for **ProgressBar** is **progress-bar**.

Non-control nodes do not have a default style. If you want to style a **VBox**, for example, you first need to add a CSS class to the instance. For example, the following code adds a style named **vbox** to a **Vbox**.

```
VBox vBox = new VBox();
vBox.getStyleClass().add("vbox");
```

The **VBox** will then react to a **vbox** style in any CSS file referred to by the application.

In addition to using style classes, you can also create a style that will be referred by the component identifier. You do this if you want a style that will only affect a certain instance of a type, and not all instances of that particular type. For example, the **.button** style affects all **Button** controls in an application. If you want a style to affect a certain **Button** and not all **Button**s, you can either add a new class to the **Button** or add an identifier to it. Here is an example of a **Button** that is assigned the id **nextBtn**.

```
Button nextButton = new Button("Next");
nextButton.setId("nextBtn");
```

You can then create this style in your CSS file that will only affect that **Button**.

```
#nextBtn {
    -fx-font-weight: bold;
}
```

Note that each node has a **setStyle** method that you can call to assign a CSS style. However, this practice is not recommended as you are mixing presentation and business logic. Here is an example of how you can use **setStyle**.

```
Button button = new Button();
button.setStyle("-fx-background-color:green");
```

It's better to write all your styles in a CSS file. Once your CSS file is ready, you can load it from the application's **start** method, like this.

```
@Override
public void start(Stage stage) {
    ...
    Scene scene = ...;
    scene.getStylesheets().add("style.css");
    ...
}
```

Here, **style.css** is the CSS file located in the same location as the class file.

The following are some of the styles used in this chapter.

- -fx-fill
- -fx-font-family
- -fx-font-size
- -fx-font-style
- -fx-font-weight
- -fx-background-color
- -fx-text-fill

As an example, consider the **CSSDemo** class in Listing 25.5 that uses the **style.css** file in Listing 25.6.

Listing 25.5: The CSSDemo class

```
package app25;
import javafx.application.Application;
import javafx.scene.Scene;
import javafx.scene.control.Button;
import javafx.scene.control.Label;
import javafx.scene.layout.BorderPane;
import javafx.scene.layout.HBox;
import javafx.stage.Stage;

public class CSSDemo extends Application {

    @Override
    public void start(Stage stage) {
        BorderPane root = new BorderPane();

        root.setCenter(new Label("Welcome"));

        HBox hBox = new HBox();
        hBox.getStyleClass().add("hbox");

        Button backButton = new Button("Back");
        hBox.getChildren().add(backButton);
        Button nextButton = new Button("Next");
        nextButton.setId("nextBtn");
        hBox.getChildren().add(nextButton);
        root.setBottom(hBox);

        Scene scene = new Scene(root, 400, 300);
        scene.getStylesheets().add("style.css");

        stage.setTitle("CSS Demo");
        stage.setScene(scene);
        stage.show();
    }

    public static void main(String[] args) {
        launch(args);
    }
}
```

Listing 25.6: The style.css file

```
.label {
    -fx-background-color: #778855;
    -fx-font-family: helvetica;
    -fx-font-size: 450%;
    -fx-text-fill: yellow;
}
.hbox {
    -fx-background-color: #2f4f4f;
    -fx-padding: 15;
    -fx-spacing: 10;
    -fx-alignment: center-right;
```

```
}

.button {
    -fx-border-width: 2px;
    -fx-background-color:#ff8800;
    -fx-cursor: hand;
}

#nextBtn {
    -fx-font-weight: bold;
}
```

If you run the application, you'll see a **Stage** just like that in Figure 25.7.

Figure 25.7: CSS Demo

As a side note, the **jfxrt.jar** file, the JavaFX runtime file, includes a **modena.css** file. This is the default style sheet for the root node and UI controls. I recommend that you look at the content of this file to learn all the styles defined. To view this file, go to the directory the jar file is located and run this command.

```
jar xf jfxrt.jar com/sun/javafx/scene/control/skin/modena/modena.css
```

Summary

JavaFX is a Java technology for creating desktop and in-browser applications. It is a better solution than both AWT and Swing and is therefore destined to replace its predecessors.

This chapter introduced JavaFX and provided a couple of examples. The next chapter, "JavaFX with FXML" explains how to separate the presentation layer and the business logic using a special markup language called FXML.

Quiz

1. What is the class that is a template for all JavaFX applications?
2. What is the top-level container window in JavaFX?
3. What is a node?
4. What is the best way to style JavaFX UI components?

Chapter 26
JavaFX with FXML

FXML is an XML-based markup language for constructing JavaFX user interface (UI).
Using FXML in JavaFX applications is a great way of separating the presentation layer
and the application logic. This chapter discusses FXML and shows how to use it in
JavaFX application development.

Overview

A new feature of JavaFX 2, FXML greatly reduces the complexity of your JavaFX classes
by moving user interface component construction to an XML-based document. In
addition, FXML visualizes the UI component hierarchy much better than Java classes.
The root of an FXML document represents a **javafx.scene.Parent** that can be loaded to
JavaFX using a special loader called **FXMLLoader**. Here is the **start** method of an
Application subclass that uses FXML.

```
@Override
public void start(Stage stage) throws Exception {
    stage.setTitle("FXML Example");
    Parent root = (Parent) FXMLLoader.load(
            getClass().getResource("example1.fxml"));
    Scene scene = new Scene(root, 740, 530);
    stage.setScene(scene);
    stage.show();
}
```

The code above calls the **load** method of **FXMLLoader** to read an FXML file and
convert its content to a **Parent** object. The **Parent** object is then used to construct a
Scene.

Writing an FXML file is easy. You start by creating a text file and saving it in the
same directory as your class file. You can store it somewhere else, but it is easiest to load
it if it is in the same directory as the class that will load it.

As an FXML file is an XML document, all FXML documents start with this
declaration.

```
<?xml version="1.0" encoding="UTF-8"?>
```

Next come the **import** directives to import types you will reference in the FXML file.
You can import a package or a type.

```
<?import javafx.scene.*?>
<?import javafx.scene.control.*?>
<?import javafx.scene.layout.*?>
<?import javafx.geometry.Insets?>
```

The root element comes next. It can be any subclass of **Parent**. Here is an example.

```
<GridPane xmlns:fx="http://javafx.com/fxml"
        hgap="5" vgap="12" layoutY="30">

</GridPane>
```

The **fx** prefix is a special prefix in FXML. You will learn its use later in this chapter.

To set a property in an object, use a nested element or an attribute. For example, the **hgap** attribute in the **GridPane** element above populates the **GridPane**'s **hgap** property.

Inside the root element, construct your UI. Listing 26.1 shows an example FXML file.

Listing 26.1: An example FXML file

```
<?xml version="1.0" encoding="UTF-8"?>
<?import javafx.scene.*?>
<?import javafx.scene.control.*?>
<?import javafx.scene.layout.*?>
<?import javafx.geometry.Insets?>
<?import javafx.scene.image.Image?>
<?import javafx.scene.image.ImageView?>


<BorderPane>
    <top>
        <HBox spacing="10.0" style="-fx-background-color:#886699;">
            <padding>
                <Insets top="15" bottom="15" left="12" right="12"/>
            </padding>
            <Button id="okButton" text="OK" defaultButton="true"/>
            <Button text="Cancel"/>
        </HBox>
    </top>
</BorderPane>
```

An element may contain a class to be instantiated or a property to be populated. The FXML file in Listing 26.1 contains a root of type **BorderPane**. The **BorderPane** has its **top** property populated with an **HBox**. The **HBox** in turn contains two **Button**s and has its **padding** property populated with an **Insets**.

More details on FXML can be found here.

```
http://docs.oracle.com/javafx/2/api/javafx/fxml/doc-files/
introduction_to_fxml.html
```

Note

It is recommended that you use an IDE that supports JavaFX when writing an FXML and take advantage of its code completion feature to make writing FXML easier. NetBeans and IntelliJ support JavaFX, and Eclipse supports JavaFX through a plug-in.

The next sections present examples of using FXML in JavaFX applications.

A Simple FXML-Based Application

This example is a rewrite of the **BorderPaneDemo** application created in the previous chapter. This time an FXML document is used to construct and organize the UI components. For your reading convenience, the **BorderPaneDemo** class is reprinted here.

```java
package app26;
import javafx.application.Application;
import javafx.geometry.Insets;
import javafx.scene.Scene;
import javafx.scene.control.Button;
import javafx.scene.control.ColorPicker;
import javafx.scene.control.Label;
import javafx.scene.image.ImageView;
import javafx.scene.layout.BorderPane;
import javafx.scene.layout.HBox;
import javafx.scene.layout.VBox;
import javafx.stage.Stage;

public class BorderPaneDemo extends Application {

    @Override
    public void start(Stage stage) {
        Button okButton = new Button("OK");
        okButton.setDefaultButton(true);

        Button cancelButton = new Button("Cancel");
        HBox hBox = new HBox();
        hBox.setPadding(new Insets(15, 12, 15, 12));
        hBox.setSpacing(10);
        hBox.setStyle("-fx-background-color: #886699;");
        hBox.getChildren().addAll(okButton, cancelButton);
        BorderPane root = new BorderPane();
        root.setTop(hBox);

        ImageView imageView = new ImageView("image/1.jpg");
        root.setCenter(imageView);

        VBox vBox = new VBox();
        vBox.setStyle("-fx-background-color: " +
                "#ddeeff;-fx-padding:10px");
        vBox.getChildren().addAll(
                new Label("Select Color:"),
                new ColorPicker());
        root.setLeft(vBox);

        root.setStyle("-fx-background-color: #6680e6;");
        Scene scene = new Scene(root, 740, 530);
```

```
        stage.setTitle("HBox, VBox, BorderPane Demo");
        stage.setScene(scene);
        stage.show();
    }

    public static void main(String[] args) {
        launch(args);
    }
}
```

The UI construction part of the **BorderPaneDemo** class can be replaced with the markup in the **example1.fxml** file shown in Listing 26.2.

Listing 26.2: The example1.fxml file

```xml
<?xml version="1.0" encoding="UTF-8"?>
<?import javafx.scene.*?>
<?import javafx.scene.control.*?>
<?import javafx.scene.layout.*?>
<?import javafx.geometry.Insets?>
<?import javafx.scene.image.Image?>
<?import javafx.scene.image.ImageView?>

<BorderPane>
    <top>
        <HBox spacing="10.0" style="-fx-background-color:#886699;">
            <padding>
                <Insets top="15" bottom="15" left="12" right="12"/>
            </padding>
            <Button id="okButton" text="OK" defaultButton="true"/>
            <Button text="Cancel"/>
        </HBox>
    </top>
    <left>
        <VBox style="-fx-background-color:#ddeeff;-fx-padding:10px">
            <Label text="Select Color:"/>
            <ColorPicker />
        </VBox>
    </left>
    <center>
        <ImageView>
            <Image url="/image/1.jpg"></Image>
        </ImageView>
    </center>
</BorderPane>
```

The main Java class, called **Example1**, is given in Listing 26.3. It extends **Application** and provides an implementation of the **start** method.

Listing 26.3: The Example1 class

```
package app26;

import javafx.application.Application;
import javafx.fxml.FXMLLoader;
import javafx.scene.Parent;
import javafx.scene.Scene;
import javafx.stage.Stage;

public class Example1 extends Application {

    @Override
    public void start(Stage stage) throws Exception {
        // Example1.fxml must be located in the same directory
        // as Example1.class
        Parent root = FXMLLoader.load(
                getClass().getResource("example1.fxml"));
        root.setStyle("-fx-background-color: #6680e6;");
        Scene scene = new Scene(root, 740, 530);
        stage.setTitle("JavaFX with FXML (Example 1)");
        stage.setScene(scene);
        stage.show();
    }

    public static void main(String[] args) {
        launch(args);
    }
}
```

The **start** method uses **FXMLLoader** to load the FXML document and return a **Parent** object that contains the components declared in the document. The method then creates a **Scene** and passes the **Scene** to the **Stage** before calling the **show** method on the **Stage**.

Figure 26.1 shows the result of running the application.

Figure 26.1: Using FXML

Event Handling with FXML

FXML is a powerful language. Among its features is the ability to bind a UI component with an event-processing method (event handler) in a controller, so that the method will be called when the event occurs. A controller is a Java class that implements **javafx.fxml.Initializable**. To take advantage of this feature, you must use the **fx:controller** attribute in your root element, like this.

```
<Group fx:controller="app26.Example2Controller"
```

Recall that **fx** is a special prefix in FXML.

To bind a component to an event handler, use the relevant **onXXX** attribute of the element. For example, to bind the **ActionEvent** with a method called **handleAction** in the controller, write this.

```
onAction="#handleAction"
```

For example, consider the following application that features a Login form that takes a user name and password. The primary stage of the application is shown in Figure 26.2.

Figure 26.2: The Login form in Example 2

The user may enter a user name and password. Clicking Reset clears the User Name and Password fields. Clicking Login authenticates the user. The authentication result will be written on the **Label** above the fields.

The application consists of an FXML document (**example2.fxml** in Listing 26.4), a controller class (**Example2Controller** in Listing 26.5), and the main class (**Example2** in Listing 26.6).

Listing 26.4: The example2.fxml file

```xml
<?xml version="1.0" encoding="UTF-8"?>

<?import javafx.scene.*?>
<?import javafx.scene.control.*?>
<?import javafx.scene.layout.*?>
<?import javafx.geometry.Insets?>

<GridPane xmlns:fx="http://javafx.com/fxml"
        fx:controller="app26.Example2Controller"
        hgap="5" vgap="12" layoutY="30"  >
    <columnConstraints>
        <ColumnConstraints percentWidth="15"/>
        <ColumnConstraints percentWidth="35"
                halignment="RIGHT"/>
        <ColumnConstraints percentWidth="35"/>
        <ColumnConstraints percentWidth="10"/>
    </columnConstraints>

    <children>
        <Label fx:id="statusLabel" >
            <GridPane.columnIndex>1</GridPane.columnIndex>
            <GridPane.rowIndex>0</GridPane.rowIndex>
            <GridPane.columnSpan>2</GridPane.columnSpan>
        </Label>

        <Label text="User Name:">
```

```
            <GridPane.columnIndex>1</GridPane.columnIndex>
            <GridPane.rowIndex>1</GridPane.rowIndex>
        </Label>
        <TextField fx:id="userNameField">
            <GridPane.columnIndex>2</GridPane.columnIndex>
            <GridPane.rowIndex>1</GridPane.rowIndex>
        </TextField>

        <Label text="Password:">
            <GridPane.columnIndex>1</GridPane.columnIndex>
            <GridPane.rowIndex>2</GridPane.rowIndex>
        </Label>
        <PasswordField fx:id="passwordField">
            <GridPane.columnIndex>2</GridPane.columnIndex>
            <GridPane.rowIndex>2</GridPane.rowIndex>
        </PasswordField>
        <Button fx:id="resetButton" text="Reset"
                onAction="#handleReset">
            <GridPane.columnIndex>1</GridPane.columnIndex>
            <GridPane.rowIndex>3</GridPane.rowIndex>
        </Button>
        <Button fx:id="loginButton" text="Login"
                defaultButton="true" onAction="#handleLogin">
            <GridPane.columnIndex>2</GridPane.columnIndex>
            <GridPane.rowIndex>3</GridPane.rowIndex>
        </Button>
    </children>
</GridPane>
```

The FXML document in Listing 26.2 uses a **GridPane** as the root element. The markup also populates the **columnConstraints** and **children** properties of the **GridPane**. The **columnContraints** contains **ColumnConstraints** elements that specify the width for each of its columns. The **children** property specifies the UI components to be rendered inside the **GridPane**.

Pay special attention to the **onAction** attributes of the **Button** elements. They are used to bind the **ActionEvent** with the **handleLogin** and **handleReset** methods, respectively.

Listing 26.5: The Example2Controller class

```
package app26;
import java.net.URL;
import java.util.ResourceBundle;
import javafx.event.ActionEvent;
import javafx.fxml.FXML;
import javafx.fxml.Initializable;
import javafx.scene.control.Label;
import javafx.scene.control.PasswordField;
import javafx.scene.control.TextField;

public class Example2Controller implements Initializable {

    @FXML
    private TextField userNameField;
```

```
    @FXML
    private PasswordField passwordField;
    @FXML
    private Label statusLabel;

    @FXML
    private void handleReset(ActionEvent event) {
        userNameField.setText("");
        passwordField.setText("");
        statusLabel.setText("");
    }

    @FXML
    private void handleLogin(ActionEvent event) {
        String userName = userNameField.getText();
        String password = passwordField.getText();
        if ("john".equals(userName)
                && "secret".equals(password)) {
            statusLabel.setText("Login successul");
        } else {
            statusLabel.setText("Login failed");
        }
    }

    @Override
    public void initialize(URL url, ResourceBundle rb) {
    }
}
```

A controller provides event-handlers for the FXML document it is bound with. An event-handler must be annotated with **@FXML**. In addition, to allow access to a UI component, you can annotate a field with **@FXML**. The annotated field must have the same name as the **fx:id** attribute of the component it is bound to.

In the controller class in Listing 26.5, three fields are declared and annotated with **@FXML**: **userNameField**, **passwordField**, and **statusLabel**.

Listing 26.6: The Example2 class

```
package app26;
import javafx.application.Application;
import javafx.fxml.FXMLLoader;
import javafx.scene.Parent;
import javafx.scene.Scene;
import javafx.stage.Stage;

public class Example2 extends Application {

    @Override
    public void start(Stage stage) throws Exception {
        Parent root = FXMLLoader.load(
                getClass().getResource("example2.fxml"));
        Scene scene = new Scene(root, 300, 200);
```

```
        stage.setTitle("Login Form");
        stage.setScene(scene);
        stage.show();
    }

    public static void main(String[] args) {
        launch(args);
    }
}
```

Finally, the **Example2** class in Listing 26.6 loads the FXML document and creates and shows the primary stage.

Summary

FXML is a markup language for constructing the UI component graph of a JavaFX application. Using FXML makes writing the UI easier. In this chapter you learned the basics of FXML and how to use it.

Quiz

1. What is FXML?
2. What is a controller class?

Chapter 27
Java Threads

One of the most appealing features in Java is the support for easy thread programming. Prior to 1995, the year Java was released, threads were the domain of programming experts only. With Java, even beginners can write multi-threaded applications.

This chapter explains what threads are and why they are important. It also talks about related topics such as synchronization and the visibility problem.

Introduction to Java Threads

The next time you play a computer game, ask yourself this question: I am not using a multi-processor computer, how come there seems to be two processors running at the same time, one moving the asteroids and one moving the spaceships? Well, the simultaneous movements are possible thanks to multi-threaded programming.

A program can allocate processor time to units in its body. Each unit is then given a portion of the processor time. Even if your computer only has one processor, it can have multiple units that work at the same time. The trick for single-processor computers is to slice processor time and give each slice to each processing unit. The smallest unit that can take processor time is called a thread. A program that has multiple threads is referred to as a multi-threaded application. Therefore, a computer game is often multi-threaded.

The formal definition of thread is this. A thread is a basic processing unit to which an operating system allocates processor time, and more than one thread can be executing code inside a process. A thread is sometimes called an lightweight process or an execution context.

Threads do consume resources, so you should not create more threads than necessary. In addition, keeping track of many threads is a complex programming task.

Every Java program has at least one thread, the thread that executes the Java program. It is created when you invoke the static **main** method of your Java class. Many Java programs have more than one thread without you realizing it. For example, a Swing application has a thread for processing events in addition to the main thread.

Multi-threaded programming is not only for games. Non-game applications can use multithreads to improve user responsiveness. For example, with only one single thread executing, an application may seem to be 'hanging' when writing a large file to the hard disk, with the mouse cursor unable to move and buttons refusing to be clicked. By dedicating a thread to save a file and another to receive user input, your application can be more responsive.

Creating a Thread

There are two ways to create a thread.

1. Extend the **java.lang.Thread** class.
2. Implement the **java.lang.Runnable** interface.

If you choose the first, you need to override its **run** method and write in it code that you want executed by the thread. Once you have a **Thread** object, you call its **start** method to start the thread. When a thread is started, its **run** method is executed. Once the **run** method returns or throws an exception, the thread dies and will be garbage-collected.

Note
The Concurrency Utilities, discussed in Chapter 24, provides a better way of creating and executing a thread. In most cases, you should not work with the **Thread** class directly.

In Java you can give a **Thread** object a name, which is a common practice when working with multiple threads. In addition, every **Thread** has a state and can be in one of these six states.

- new. A state in which a thread has not been started.
- runnable. A state in which a thread is executing.
- blocked. A state in which a thread is waiting for a lock to access an object.
- waiting. A state in which a thread is waiting indefinitely for another thread to perform an action.
- timed_waiting. A state in which a thread is waiting for up to a specified period of time for another thread to perform an action.
- terminated. A state in which a thread has exited.

The values that represent these states are encapsulated in the **java.lang.Thread.State** enum. The members of this enum are **NEW, RUNNABLE, BLOCKED, WAITING, TIMED_WAITING**, and **TERMINATED**.

The **Thread** class provides public constructors you can use to create **Thread** objects. Here are some of them.

```
public Thread()

public Thread(String name)

public Thread(Runnable target)

public Thread(Runnable target, String name)
```

Note
I will explain the third and fourth constructors later after the discussion of the **Runnable** interface.

Here are some useful methods in the **Thread** class.

```
public String getName()
```
Returns the thread's name.

```
public Thread.State getState()
```

Returns the state the thread is currently in.

```
public void interrupt()
```
Interrupts this thread.

```
public void start()
```
Starts this thread.

```
public static void sleep(long millis)
```
Stops the current thread for the specified number of milliseconds.

In addition, the **Thread** class provides the static **currentThread** method that returns the current working thread.

```
public static Thread currentThread()
```

Extending Thread

The code in Listing 27.1 shows how you can create a thread by extending **java.lang.Thread**.

Listing 27.1: A simple multi-threaded program

```
package app27;
public class ThreadDemo1 extends Thread {
    public void run() {
        for (int i = 1; i <= 10; i++) {
            System.out.println(i);
            try {
                sleep(1000);
            } catch (InterruptedException e) {
            }
        }
    }
    public static void main(String[] args) {
        (new ThreadDemo1()).start();
    }
}
```

The **ThreadDemo1** class extends the **Thread** class and overrides its **run** method. The **ThreadDemo1** class begins by instantiating itself. A newly created **Thread** will be in the NEW state. Calling the **start** method will make the thread move from NEW to RUNNABLE, which causes the **run** method to be called. This method prints number 1 to 10 and between two numbers the thread sleeps for a second. When the **run** method returns the thread dies and will be garbage collected. There is nothing fancy about this class, but it gives you a general idea of how to work with **Thread**.

Of course, you do not always have the luxury of extending **Thread** from the main class. For example, if your class extends **javax.swing.JFrame**, then you cannot extend **Thread** because Java does not support multiple inheritance. However, you can always create a second class that extends **Thread**, as shown in the code in Listing 27.2. Or, if you need to access members of the main class, you can write a nested class that extends **Thread**.

Listing 27.2: Using a separate class that extends Thread

```
package app27;
class MyThread extends Thread {
    public void run() {
        for (int i = 1; i <= 10; i++) {
            System.out.println(i);
            try {
                sleep(1000);
            } catch (InterruptedException e) {
            }
        }
    }
}

public class ThreadDemo2 {
    public static void main(String[] args) {
        MyThread thread = new MyThread();
        thread.start();
    }
}
```

The **ThreadDemo2** class in Listing 27.2 does exactly the same thing as **ThreadDemo1** in Listing 27.1. The difference is the **ThreadDemo2** class is free to extend another class.

Implementing Runnable

Another way to create a thread is by implementing **java.lang.Runnable**. This interface has a **run** method that you need to implement. The **run** method in **Runnable** is the same as the **run** method in the **Thread** class. In fact, **Thread** itself implements **Runnable**.

If you use **Runnable**, you have to instantiate the **Thread** class and pass the **Runnable**. Listing 27.3 shows how to work with **Runnable**. It does the same thing as the classes in Listings 27.1 and 27.2.

Listing 27.3: Using Runnable

```
package app27;
public class RunnableDemo1 implements Runnable {
    public void run() {
        for (int i = 1; i <= 10; i++) {
            System.out.println(i);
            try {
                Thread.sleep(1000);
            } catch (InterruptedException e) {
            }
        }
    }

    public static void main(String[] args) {
        RunnableDemo1 demo = new RunnableDemo1();
        Thread thread = new Thread(demo);
        thread.start();
    }
```

```
        }
```

Working with Multiple Threads

You can work with multiple threads. The following example is a Swing application that creates two **Thread** objects. The first is responsible for incrementing a counter and the second for decrementing another counter. Listing 27.4 shows it.

Listing 27.4: Using two threads

```java
package app27;
import java.awt.FlowLayout;
import javax.swing.JFrame;
import javax.swing.JLabel;

public class ThreadDemo3 extends JFrame {
    JLabel countUpLabel = new JLabel("Count Up");
    JLabel countDownLabel = new JLabel("Count Down");

    class CountUpThread extends Thread {
        public void run() {
            int count = 1000;
            while (true) {
                try {
                    sleep(100);
                } catch (InterruptedException e) {
                }
                if (count == 0)
                    count = 1000;
                countUpLabel.setText(Integer.toString(count--));
            }
        }
    }

    class CountDownThread extends Thread {
        public void run() {
            int count = 0;
            while (true) {
                try {
                    sleep(50);
                } catch (InterruptedException e) {
                }
                if (count == 1000)
                    count = 0;
                countDownLabel.setText(Integer.toString(count++));
            }
        }
    }
    public ThreadDemo3(String title) {
        super(title);
        init();
```

```
    }

    private void init() {
        this.setDefaultCloseOperation(JFrame.EXIT_ON_CLOSE);
        this.getContentPane().setLayout(new FlowLayout());
        this.add(countUpLabel);
        this.add(countDownLabel);
        this.pack();
        this.setVisible(true);
        new CountUpThread().start();
        new CountDownThread().start();
    }

    private static void constructGUI() {
        JFrame.setDefaultLookAndFeelDecorated(true);
        ThreadDemo3 frame = new ThreadDemo3("Thread Demo 3");
    }

    public static void main(String[] args) {
        javax.swing.SwingUtilities.invokeLater(new Runnable() {
            public void run() {
                constructGUI();
            }
        });
    }
}
```

The **ThreadTest3** class defines two nested classes, **CountUpThread** and
CountDownThread, that extend **Thread**. Both are nested in the main class so that they
can access the **JLabel** controls and change their labels. Running the code, you will see
something similar to Figure 27.1.

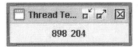

Figure 27.1: Using two threads

Thread Priority

When dealing with multiple threads, you sometimes have to think about thread
scheduling. In other words, you need to make sure each thread gets a fair chance to run.
This is achieved by calling **sleep** from a thread's **run** method. A long processing thread
should always calls the **sleep** method to give other threads a slice of the CPU processing
time. A thread that calls **sleep** is said to yield.

Now, if there are more than one thread waiting, which one gets to run when the
running thread yields? The thread with the highest priority. To set a thread priority, call its
setPriority method. Its signature is as follows.

```
public final void setPriority(int priority)
```

The following example is a Swing application that has two counters. The counter on the left is powered by a thread that has a priority of 10 and another by a thread whose priority is 1. Run the code and see how the thread with the higher priority runs faster.

Listing 27.5: Testing thread priority

```
package app27;
import java.awt.FlowLayout;
import javax.swing.JFrame;
import javax.swing.JLabel;

public class ThreadPriorityDemo extends JFrame {
    JLabel counter1Label = new JLabel("Priority 10");
    JLabel counter2Label = new JLabel("Priority 1");

    class CounterThread extends Thread {
        JLabel counterLabel;
        public CounterThread(JLabel counterLabel) {
            super();
            this.counterLabel = counterLabel;
        }

        public void run() {
            int count = 0;
            while (true) {
                try {
                    sleep(1);
                } catch (InterruptedException e) {
                }
                if (count == 50000)
                    count = 0;
                counterLabel.setText(Integer.toString(count++));
            }
        }
    }

    public ThreadPriorityDemo(String title) {
        super(title);
        init();
    }

    private void init() {
        this.setDefaultCloseOperation(JFrame.EXIT_ON_CLOSE);
        this.setLayout(new FlowLayout());
        this.add(counter1Label);
        this.add(counter2Label);
        this.pack();
        this.setVisible(true);
        CounterThread thread1 = new CounterThread(counter1Label);
        thread1.setPriority(10);
        CounterThread thread2 = new CounterThread(counter2Label);
        thread2.setPriority(1);
        thread2.start();
        thread1.start();
```

```
    }

    private static void constructGUI() {
        JFrame.setDefaultLookAndFeelDecorated(true);
        ThreadPriorityDemo frame = new ThreadPriorityDemo(
                "Thread Priority Demo");
    }

    public static void main(String[] args) {
        javax.swing.SwingUtilities.invokeLater(new Runnable() {
            public void run() {
                constructGUI();
            }
        });
    }
}
```

The two threads running are instances of the same class (**CounterThread**). The first thread has a priority of 10, and the second 1. Figure 27.2 shows that even though the second thread starts first, the first thread runs faster.

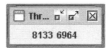

Figure 27.2: Threads with different priorities

Stopping a Thread

The **Thread** class has a **stop** method to stop a thread. However, you should not use this method because it is unsafe. Instead, you should arrange so that the **run** method exits naturally when you want to stop a thread. A common technique used is to employ a **while** loop with a condition. When you want to stop the thread, simply make the condition evaluates to false. For example:

```
boolean condition = true;
public void run {
    while (condition) {
        // do something here
    }
}
```

In your class, you also need to provide a method to change the value of **condition**.

```
public synchronized void stopThread() {
    condition = false;
}
```

Note
The keyword **synchronized** is explained in the section, "Synchronizing Threads."

Stopping a thread is illustrated in the example in Listing 27.6.

Listing 27.6: Stopping a thread

```java
package app27;
import java.awt.FlowLayout;
import java.awt.event.ActionEvent;
import java.awt.event.ActionListener;
import javax.swing.JButton;
import javax.swing.JFrame;
import javax.swing.JLabel;

public class StopThreadDemo extends JFrame {
    JLabel counterLabel = new JLabel("Counter");
    JButton startButton = new JButton("Start");
    JButton stopButton = new JButton("Stop");
    CounterThread thread = null;
    boolean stopped = false;
    int count = 1;

    class CounterThread extends Thread {
        public void run() {
            while (!stopped) {
                try {
                    sleep(10);
                } catch (InterruptedException e) {
                }
                if (count == 1000) {
                    count = 1;
                }
                counterLabel.setText(Integer.toString(count++));
            }
        }
    }

    public StopThreadDemo(String title) {
        super(title);
        init();
    }

    private void init() {
        this.setDefaultCloseOperation(JFrame.EXIT_ON_CLOSE);
        this.getContentPane().setLayout(new FlowLayout());
        this.stopButton.setEnabled(false);
        startButton.addActionListener(new ActionListener() {
            public void actionPerformed(ActionEvent e) {
                StopThreadDemo.this.startButton.setEnabled(false);
                StopThreadDemo.this.stopButton.setEnabled(true);
                startThread();
            }
        });
        stopButton.addActionListener(new ActionListener() {
            public void actionPerformed(ActionEvent e) {
                StopThreadDemo.this.startButton.setEnabled(true);
                StopThreadDemo.this.stopButton.setEnabled(false);
```

```
                    stopThread();
            }
        });
        this.getContentPane().add(counterLabel);
        this.getContentPane().add(startButton);
        this.getContentPane().add(stopButton);
        this.pack();
        this.setVisible(true);
    }

    public synchronized void startThread() {
        stopped = false;
        thread = new CounterThread();
        thread.start();
    }

    public synchronized void stopThread() {
        stopped = true;
    }

    private static void constructGUI() {
        JFrame.setDefaultLookAndFeelDecorated(true);
        StopThreadDemo frame = new StopThreadDemo(
                "Stop Thread Demo");
    }

    public static void main(String[] args) {
        javax.swing.SwingUtilities.invokeLater(new Runnable() {
            public void run() {
                constructGUI();
            }
        });
    }
}
```

The **StopThreadDemo** class uses a **JLabel** to display a counter and two **JButton**s to start and stop the counter, respectively. An action listener is added to each **JButton**. The action listener in the Start button calls the **startThread** method and the one in the Stop button invokes the **stopThread** method.

```
    public synchronized void startThread() {
        stopped = false;
        thread = new CounterThread();
        thread.start();
    }
    public synchronized void stopThread() {
        stopped = true;
    }
```

To stop the counter, simply change the **stopped** variable to **true**. This will cause the **while** loop in the **run** method to exit. To start or restart the counter, you must create a new **Thread**. Once the **run** method of a thread exits, the thread is dead and you cannot re-call the thread's **start** method.

Figure 27.3 shows the counter from the **StopThreadTest** class. It can be stopped and restarted.

Figure 27.3: Stopping and restarting a thread

Synchronization

You've seen threads that run independently from each other. In real life, however, there are often situations whereby multiple threads need access to the same resource or data. Thread interference problems might arise if you cannot guarantee that no two threads will simultaneously have access to the same object.

This section explains the topic of thread interference and the language built-in locking mechanism for securing exclusive access to an object through the **synchronized** modifier.

Note
Java offers the Concurrency Utilities, which include better locks. When possible you should use these locks instead of **synchronized**. The Concurrency Utilities are explained in Chapter 24.

Thread Interference

To better appreciate the issues associated with multiple threads attempting to access the same resource, consider the code in Listing 27.7.

Listing 27.7: The UserStat class

```
package app27;
public class UserStat {
    int userCount;

    public int getUserCount() {
        return userCount;
    }

    public void increment() {
        userCount++;
    }

    public void decrement() {
        userCount--;
    }
}
```

What happens if a thread attempts to read the **userCount** variable by calling **getUserCount** while another thread is incrementing it? Bear in mind that the statement **userCount++** is actually composed of three consecutive steps:

- Read the value of **userCount** and store it in some temporary storage;
- Increment the value
- Write the incremented value back to **userCount**

Suppose a thread reads and increments the value of **userCount**. Before it has the opportunity to store the incremented value back, another thread reads it and gets the old value. When the second thread finally gets a chance to write to **userCount**, it replaces the incremented value of the first thread. As a result, **userCount** does not reflect the number of users correctly. An event whereby two *non*-atomic operations running in different threads, but acting on the same data, interleave is called thread interference.

Atomic Operations

An atomic operation is a set of operations that can be combined to appear to the rest of the system as a single operation. It cannot cause thread interference. As you have witnessed, incrementing an integer is not an atomic operation.

In Java, all primitives except **long** and **double** are atomically readable and writable.Thread Safety

Thread safe code functions correctly when accessed by multiple threads. The **UserStat** class in Listing 27.7 is not thread-safe.

Thread interference can lead to a race condition. It is one in which multiple threads are reading or writing some shared data simultaneously and the result is unpredictable. Race conditions can lead to subtle or severe bugs that are hard to find.

The next sections, "Method Synchronization" and "Block Synchronization" explain how to use **synchronized** to write thread-safe code.

Method Synchronization

Every Java object has an intrinsic lock, which is sometimes called a monitor lock. Acquiring an object's intrinsic lock is a way of having exclusive access to the object. To acquire an object's intrinsic lock is the same as locking the object. Threads attempting to access a locked object will block until the thread holding the lock releases the lock.Mutual Exclusion and Visibility

Because a locked object can be accessed only by one thread, locks are said to offer a mutual exclusion feature. Another feature offered by locks is visibility, which is discussed in the next section.

The **synchronized** modifier can be used to lock an object. When a thread calls a non-static synchronized method, it will automatically attempt to acquire the intrinsic lock of the method's object before the method can execute. The thread holds the lock until the method returns. Once a thread locks an object, other threads cannot call the same method or other synchronized methods on the same object. The other threads will have to wait until the lock becomes available again. The lock is reentrant, which means the thread holding the lock can invoke other synchronized methods in the same object. The intrinsic lock is released when the method returns.

Note

You can also synchronize a static method, in which case the lock of the **Class** object associated with the method's class will be used.

The **SafeUserStat** class in Listing 27.8 is a rewrite of the **UserStat** class. Unlike **UserStat**, **SafeUserStat** is thread-safe.

Listing 27.8: The SafeUserStat class

```
package app27;
public class SafeUserStat {
    int userCount;

    public synchronized int getUserCount() {
        return userCount;
    }

    public synchronized void increment() {
        userCount++;
    }

    public synchronized void decrement() {
        userCount--;
    }
}
```

Within a program, the code segments that guarantee only one thread at a time has access to a shared resource are called critical sections. In Java critical sections are achieved using the **synchronized** keyword. In the **SafeUserStat** class, the **increment**, **decrement**, and **getUserCount** methods are critical sections. Access to **userCount** is only permitted through a synchronized method. This ensures race conditions will not happen.

Block Synchronization

Synchronizing a method is not always possible. Imagine writing a multi-threaded application with multiple threads accessing a shared object, but the object class was not written with thread safety in mind. Worse still, you do not have access to the source code of the shared object. Just say, you have to work with a thread-unsafe **UserStat** class and its source code is not available.

Fortunately, Java allows you to lock any object through block synchronization. Its syntax is this.

```
synchronized(object) {
    // do something while locking object
}
```

A synchronized block gives you the intrinsic lock of an object. The lock is released after the code in the block is executed.

For instance, the following code uses the thread-unsafe **UserStat** class in Listing 27.7 as a counter. To lock the counter when incrementing it, the **incrementCounter** method locks the **UserStat** instance.

```
UserStat userStat = new UserStat();
...
public void incrementCounter() {
    synchronized(userStat) {
        // statements to be synchronized, such as calls to
        // the increment, decrement, and getUserCount methods
        // on userStat
```

```
            userStat.increment();
    }
}
```

As an aside note, method synchronization is the same as block synchronization that locks the current object:

```
synchronized(this) {
    ...
}
```

Visibility

In the section "Synchronization" you learned to synchronize non-atomic operations that could be accessed by multiple threads. At this point you probably got the impression that if you don't have non-atomic operations, then you don't have to bother synchronizing resources that are accessed by multiple threads.

This is not true.

In a single-threaded program, reading the value of a variable always gives you the value last written to the variable. However, due to the memory model in Java, it's not always so in a multithreaded application. A thread may not see changes made by another thread unless the operations that act on the data are synchronized.

For example, the **Inconsistent** class in Listing 27.9 creates a background thread that is supposed to wait three seconds before changing the value of **started**, a boolean. The **while** loop in the **main** method should continuously check the value of **started** and continue once **started** is set to **true**.

Listing 27.9: The Inconsistent class

```
package app27;
public class Inconsistent {
    static boolean started = false;
    public static void main(String[] args) {
        Thread thread1 = new Thread(new Runnable() {
            public void run() {
                try {
                    Thread.sleep(3000);
                } catch (InterruptedException e) {
                }
                started = true;
                System.out.println("started set to true");
            }
        });
        thread1.start();

        while (!started) {
            // wait until started
        }

        System.out.println("Wait 3 seconds and exit");
```

```
        }

}
```

However, when I ran it in my computer, it never printed the string and exited. What happened? It looks like the **while** loop (running in the **main** method) never saw the value of **started** change.

You can remedy this by synchronizing access to **started**, as illustrated in the **Consistent** class in Listing 27.10.

Listing 27.10: The Consistent class

```
package app27;
public class Consistent {
    static boolean started = false;

    public synchronized static void setStarted() {
        started = true;
    }

    public synchronized static boolean getStarted() {
        return started;
    }

    public static void main(String[] args) {
        Thread thread1 = new Thread(new Runnable() {
            public void run() {
                try {
                    Thread.sleep(3000);
                } catch (InterruptedException e) {
                }
                setStarted();
                System.out.println("started set to true");
            }
        });
        thread1.start();

        while (!getStarted()) {
            // wait until started
        }

        System.out.println("Wait 3 seconds and exit");
    }

}
```

Note that both **setStarted** and **getStarted** are synchronized to have the desire effect. It won't work if only **setStarted** is synchronized.

However, synchronization comes at a price. Locking an object incurs runtime overhead. If what you're after is visibility and you don't need mutual exclusion, you can use the **volatile** keyword instead of **synchronized**.

Declaring a variable volatile guarantees visibility by all threads accessing the variable.

Here is an example.

```
static volatile boolean started = false;
```

You can therefore rewrite the **Consistent** class to use **volatile** to reduce overhead.

Listing 27.11: Solving visibility problem with volatile
```
package app27;
public class LightAndConsistent {
    static volatile boolean started = false;

    public static void main(String[] args) {
        Thread thread1 = new Thread(new Runnable() {
            public void run() {
                try {
                    Thread.sleep(3000);
                } catch (InterruptedException e) {
                }
                started = true;
                System.out.println("started set to true");
            }
        });
        thread1.start();

        while (!started) {
            // wait until started
        }
        System.out.println("Wait 3 seconds and exit");
    }
}
```

Note that while **volatile** solves the visibility problem, it cannot be used to address a mutual exclusion issue.

Thread Coordination

There are even more delicate situations where the timing of a thread accessing an object affects other threads that need to access the same object. Such situations compel you to coordinate the threads. The following example illustrates this situation and presents a solution.

You own a courier service company that picks up and delivers goods. You employ a dispatcher and several truck drivers. The dispatcher's job is to prepare delivery notes and place them in a delivery note holder. Any free driver checks the note holder. If a delivery note is found, the driver should perform a pick up and delivery service. If no delivery note is found, he/she should wait until there is one. In addition, to guarantee fairness you want the delivery notes to be executed in a first-in-first-out fashion. To facilitate this, you only allow one delivery note to be in the holder at a time. The dispatcher will notify any waiting driver if a new note is available in the holder.

The **java.lang.Object** class provides several methods that are useful in thread coordination:

```
public final void wait() throws InterruptedException
```
Causes the current thread to wait until another thread invokes the **notify** or **notifyAll** method. **wait** normally occurs in a synchronized method and causes the calling thread that is accessing the synchronized method to place itself in the wait state and relinquish the object lock.

```
public final void wait(long timeout) throws InterruptedException
```
Causes the current thread to wait until another thread invokes the **notify** or **notifyAll** method for this object, or the specified amount of time has elapsed. **wait** normally occurs in a synchronized method and causes the calling thread that is accessing the synchronized method to place itself in the wait state and relinquish the object lock.

```
public final void notify()
```
Notifies a single thread that is waiting on this object's lock. If there are multiple threads waiting, one of them is chosen to be notified and the choice is arbitrary.

```
pubic final void notifyAll()
```
Notifies all the threads waiting on this object's lock.

Let's see how we can implement the delivery service business model in Java using **wait**, **notify**, and **notifyAll**. There are three types of objects involved:

- **DeliveryNoteHolder**. Represents the note holder and is given in Listing 27.12. It is accessed by the **DispatcherThread** and **DriverThread**.
- **DispatcherThread**. Represents the dispatcher and is presented in Listing 27.13.
- **DriverThread**. Represents a driver, shown in Listing 27.14.

Listing 27.12: The DeliveryNoteHolder class

```
package app27;
public class DeliveryNoteHolder {
    private String deliveryNote;
    private boolean available = false;

    public synchronized String get() {
        while (available == false) {
            try {
                wait();
            } catch (InterruptedException e) { }
        }
        available = false;
        System.out.println(System.currentTimeMillis()
                + ": got " + deliveryNote);
        notifyAll();
        return deliveryNote;
    }

    public synchronized void put(String deliveryNote) {
        while (available == true) {
            try {
                wait();
            } catch (InterruptedException e) { }
        }
        this.deliveryNote = deliveryNote;
        available = true;
```

```
        System.out.println(System.currentTimeMillis() +
                ": Put " + deliveryNote);
        notifyAll();
    }
}
```

There are two synchronized methods in the **DeliveryNoteHolder** class, **get** and **put**. The **DispatcherThread** object calls the **put** method and the **DriverThread** object calls the **get** method. A delivery note is simply a **String (deliveryNote)** that contains delivery information. The **available** variable indicates if a delivery note is available in this holder. The initial value of **available** is **false**, denoting that the **DeliveryNoteHolder** object is empty. Note that only one thread at a time can call any of the synchronized methods.

If the **DriverThread** is the first thread that accesses **DeliveryNoteHolder**, it will encounter the following **while** loop in the **get** method:

```
while (available == false) {
    try {
        wait();
    } catch (InterruptedException e) {
    }
}
```

Since **available** is **false**, the thread will invoke **wait** that causes the thread to lie dormant and relinquish the lock. Now, other threads can access the **DeliveryNoteHolder** object.

If the **DispatcherThread** is the first thread that accesses **DeliveryNoteHolder**, it will see the following code:

```
while (available == true) {
    try {
        wait();
    } catch (InterruptedException e) {
    }
}
this.deliveryNote = deliveryNote;
available = true;
notifyAll();
```

Because the value of **available** is **false**, it will skip the **while** loop and causes the **DeliveryNoteHolder** object's **deliveryNote** to be assigned a value. The thread will also set **available** to **true** and notify all waiting threads.

On the invocation of **notifyAll**, if the **DriverThread** is waiting on the **DeliveryNoteHolder** object, it will awaken, reacquire the **DeliveryNoteHolder** object's lock, escape from the **while** loop, and execute the rest of the **get** method:

```
available = false;
notifyAll();
return deliveryNote;
```

The **available boolean** will be switched back to **false**, the **notifyAll** method called, and the **deliveryNote** returned.

Now, let's examine the **DispatcherThread** class in Listing 27.13.

Listing 27.13: The DispatcherThread class

```
package app27;

public class DispatcherThread extends Thread {
    private DeliveryNoteHolder deliveryNoteHolder;

    String[] deliveryNotes = { "XY23. 1234 Arnie Rd.",
            "XY24. 3330 Quebec St.",
            "XY25. 909 Swenson Ave.",
            "XY26. 4830 Davidson Blvd.",
            "XY27. 9900 Old York Dr." };

    public DispatcherThread(DeliveryNoteHolder holder) {
        deliveryNoteHolder = holder;
    }

    public void run() {
        for (int i = 0; i < deliveryNotes.length; i++) {
            String deliveryNote = deliveryNotes[i];
            deliveryNoteHolder.put(deliveryNote);
            try {
                sleep(100);
            } catch (InterruptedException e) {
            }
        }
    }
}
```

The **DispatcherThread** class extends **java.lang.Thread** and declares a **String** array that contain delivery notes to be put in the **DeliveryNoteHolder** object. It gets access to the **DeliveryNoteHolder** object from its constructor. Its **run** method contains a **for** loop that attempts to call the **put** method on the **DeliveryNoteHolder** object.

The **DriverThread** class also extends **java.lang.Thread** and is given in Listing 27.14.

Listing 27.14: The DriverThread class

```
package app27;
public class DriverThread extends Thread {
    DeliveryNoteHolder deliveryNoteHolder;
    boolean stopped = false;
    String driverName;

    public DriverThread(DeliveryNoteHolder holder, String
                driverName) {
        deliveryNoteHolder = holder;
        this.driverName = driverName;
    }

    public void run() {
        while (!stopped) {
            String deliveryNote = deliveryNoteHolder.get();
            try {
```

```
            sleep(300);
        } catch (InterruptedException e) {
        }
    }
    }
  }
}
```

The **DriverThread** method attempts to obtain delivery notes by calling the **get** method on the **DeliveryNoteHolder** object. The **run** method employs a **while** loop controlled by the **stopped** variable. A method to change **stopped** is not given here to keep this example simple.

Finally, the **ThreadCoordinationDemo** class in Listing 27.15 puts everything together.

Listing 27.15: ThreadCoordinationDemo class

```
package app27;
public class ThreadCoordinationDemo {
    public static void main(String[] args) {
        DeliveryNoteHolder c = new DeliveryNoteHolder();
        DispatcherThread dispatcherThread =
                new DispatcherThread(c);
        DriverThread driverThread1 = new DriverThread(c, "Eddie");
        dispatcherThread.start();
        driverThread1.start();
    }
}
```

Here is the output from running **ThreadCoordinationDemo** class.:

```
1135212236001: Put XY23. 1234 Arnie Rd.
1135212236001: got XY23. 1234 Arnie Rd.
1135212236102: Put XY24. 3330 Quebec St.
1135212236302: got XY24. 3330 Quebec St.
1135212236302: Put XY25. 909 Swenson Ave.
1135212236602: got XY25. 909 Swenson Ave.
1135212236602: Put XY26. 4830 Davidson Blvd.
1135212236903: got XY26. 4830 Davidson Blvd.
1135212236903: Put XY27. 9900 Old York Dr.
1135212237203: got XY27. 9900 Old York Dr.
```

Using Timers

The **java.util.Timer** class provides an alternative approach to performing scheduled or recurrent tasks. It is easy to use too. After you create a **Timer**, call its **schedule** method, passing a **java.util.TimerTask** object. The latter contains code that needs to be executed by the **Timer**.

The easiest constructor to use is the no-argument one.

```
public Timer()
```

The **Timer** class's **schedule** method has several overloads:

```
public void schedule(TimerTask task, Date time)
```
Schedules the specified task to be executed once at the specified time.

```
public void schedule(TimerTask task, Date firstTime, long period)
```
Schedules the specified task to be executed for the first time at the specified time and then recurrently at an interval specified by the period argument (in milliseconds)

```
public void schedule(TimerTask task, long delay, long period)
```
Schedules the specified task to be executed for the first time after the specified delay and then recurrently at an interval specified by the period argument (in milliseconds).

To cancel a scheduled task, call the **Timer** class's **cancel** method:

```
public void cancel()
```

The **TimerTask** class has a **run** method that you need to override in your task class. Unlike the **run** method in **java.lang.Runnable**, you do not need to enclose the scheduled or recurrent task code in a loop.

The **TimerDemo** class in Listing 27.16 shows a Swing application that uses **Timer** and **TimerTask** to conduct a quiz. There are five questions in the quiz and each question is displayed in a **JLabel** for ten seconds, giving the user enough time to answer. Any answer will be inserted into a **JComboBox** control.

Listing 27.16: Using Timer

```java
package app27;
import java.awt.BorderLayout;
import java.awt.Dimension;
import java.awt.Toolkit;
import java.awt.event.ActionEvent;
import java.awt.event.ActionListener;
import java.util.Timer;
import java.util.TimerTask;
import javax.swing.JButton;
import javax.swing.JComboBox;
import javax.swing.JFrame;
import javax.swing.JLabel;
import javax.swing.JTextField;

public class TimerDemo extends JFrame {
    String[] questions = { "What is the largest mammal?",
            "Who is the current prime minister of Japan?",
            "Who invented the Internet?",
            "What is the smallest country in the world?",
            "What is the biggest city in America?",
            "Finished. Please remain seated" };

    JLabel questionLabel = new JLabel("Click Start to begin");
    JTextField answer = new JTextField();
    JButton startButton = new JButton("Start");
    JComboBox answerBox = new JComboBox();
```

```java
int counter = 0;
Timer timer = new Timer();

public TimerDemo(String title) {
    super(title);
    init();
}

private void init() {
    this.setDefaultCloseOperation(JFrame.EXIT_ON_CLOSE);
    this.getContentPane().setLayout(new BorderLayout());
    this.getContentPane().add(questionLabel, BorderLayout.WEST);
    questionLabel.setPreferredSize(new Dimension(300, 15));
    answer.setPreferredSize(new Dimension(100, 15));
    this.getContentPane().add(answer, BorderLayout.CENTER);
    this.getContentPane().add(startButton, BorderLayout.EAST);
    startButton.addActionListener(new ActionListener() {
        public void actionPerformed(ActionEvent e) {
            ((JButton) e.getSource()).setEnabled(false);
            timer.schedule(
                    new DisplayQuestionTask(), 0, 10 * 1000);
        }
    });
    this.getContentPane().add(answerBox, BorderLayout.SOUTH);
    this.startButton.setFocusable(true);
    this.pack();
    this.setVisible(true);
}

private String getNextQuestion() {
    return questions[counter++];
}

private static void constructGUI() {
    JFrame.setDefaultLookAndFeelDecorated(true);
    TimerDemo frame = new TimerDemo("Timer Demo");
}

public static void main(String[] args) {
    javax.swing.SwingUtilities.invokeLater(new Runnable() {
        public void run() {
            constructGUI();
        }
    });
}

class DisplayQuestionTask extends TimerTask {
    public void run() {
        Toolkit.getDefaultToolkit().beep();
        if (counter > 0) {
            answerBox.addItem(answer.getText());
            answer.setText("");
        }
```

```
        String nextQuestion = getNextQuestion();
        questionLabel.setText(nextQuestion);
        if (counter == questions.length) {
            timer.cancel();
        }
      }
    }
}
```

The questions are stored in the **String** array **questions**. It contains six members, the first five being questions and the last one being an instruction for the user to remain seated.

The **DisplayQuestionTimerTask** nested class extends **java.util.TimerTask** and provides the code to be executed. Each task begins with a beep and continues with displaying the next question in the array. When all the array members have been displayed, the **cancel** method of the **Timer** object is called.

Figure 27.4 shows the application.

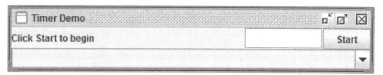

Figure 27.4: A Timer application

Swing Timers

Similar to the **java.util.Timer** class, the **javax.swing.Timer** class can only be used in Swing applications. **javax.swing.Timer** is not as powerful as **java.util.Timer** but gives you the familiar feeling of working with Swing and is a more appropriate choice than **java.util.Timer** for Swing applications because **javax.swing.Timer** handles thread sharing. Instead of putting scheduled tasks in the **run** method of a **TimerTask** subclass, you implement the **java.awt.event.ActionListener** interface and write your task code in its **actionPerformed** method. In addition, to cancel a task, you use the **javax.swing.Timer** class's **stop** method.

The **javax.swing.Timer** class only has one constructor:

```
public Timer(int delay, java.awt.event.ActionListener listener)
```

where *delay* specifies the number of milliseconds from the time the **start** method is invoked to the first invocation of the task and *listener* is an **ActionListener** instance that contains code to be called.

The quiz application in Listing 27.16 is rewritten in Listing 27.17 to use **javax.swing.Timer**.

Listing 27.17: Using Swing Timer.

```
package app27;
import java.awt.BorderLayout;
import java.awt.Dimension;
import java.awt.Toolkit;
```

```java
import java.awt.event.ActionEvent;
import java.awt.event.ActionListener;
import javax.swing.JButton;
import javax.swing.JComboBox;
import javax.swing.JFrame;
import javax.swing.JLabel;
import javax.swing.JTextField;
import javax.swing.Timer;

public class SwingTimerDemo extends JFrame {
    String[] questions = { "What is the largest mammal?",
            "Who is the current prime minister of Japan?",
            "Who invented the Internet?",
            "What is the smallest country in the world?",
            "What is the biggest city in America?",
            "Finished. Please remain seated" };

    JLabel questionLabel = new JLabel("Click Start to begin");
    JTextField answer = new JTextField();
    JButton startButton = new JButton("Start");
    JComboBox answerBox = new JComboBox();
    int counter = 0;
    Timer timer = new Timer(10000, new MyTimerActionListener());

    public SwingTimerDemo(String title) {
        super(title);
        init();
    }

    private void init() {
        this.setDefaultCloseOperation(JFrame.EXIT_ON_CLOSE);
        this.getContentPane().setLayout(new BorderLayout());
        this.getContentPane().add(questionLabel, BorderLayout.WEST);
        questionLabel.setPreferredSize(new Dimension(300, 15));
        answer.setPreferredSize(new Dimension(100, 15));
        this.getContentPane().add(answer, BorderLayout.CENTER);
        this.getContentPane().add(startButton, BorderLayout.EAST);
        startButton.addActionListener(new ActionListener() {
            public void actionPerformed(ActionEvent e) {
                ((JButton) e.getSource()).setEnabled(false);
                timer.start();
            }
        });
        this.getContentPane().add(answerBox, BorderLayout.SOUTH);
        this.startButton.setFocusable(true);
        this.pack();
        this.setVisible(true);
    }

    private String getNextQuestion() {
        return questions[counter++];
    }
}
```

```
    private static void constructGUI() {
        JFrame.setDefaultLookAndFeelDecorated(true);
        SwingTimerTest frame = new SwingTimerTest(
                "Swing Timer Demo");
    }

    public static void main(String[] args) {
        javax.swing.SwingUtilities.invokeLater(new Runnable() {
            public void run() {
                constructGUI();
            }
        });
    }

    class MyTimerActionListener implements ActionListener {
        public void actionPerformed(ActionEvent e) {
            Toolkit.getDefaultToolkit().beep();
            if (counter > 0) {
                answerBox.addItem(answer.getText());
                answer.setText("");
            }
            String nextQuestion = getNextQuestion();
            questionLabel.setText(nextQuestion);
            if (counter == questions.length) {
                timer.stop();
            }
        }
    }
}
```

Summary

Multi-threaded application development in Java is easy, thanks to Java support for threads. To create a thread, you can extend the **java.lang.Thread** class or implement the **java.lang.Runnable** interface. In this chapter you have learned how to write programs that manipulate threads and synchronize threads. You have also learned how to write thread-safe code. In the last two sections of this chapter, you have learned how to use the **java.util.Timer** and **javax.swing.Timer** classes to run scheduled tasks.

Quiz

1. What is a thread?
2. What does the **synchronized** modifier do?
3. What is a critical section?
4. Where do you write a scheduled task for a **java.util.Timer**?
5. What is the difference between **java.util.Timer** and **javax.swing.Timer**.

Chapter 28
Concurrency Utilities

Java's built-in support for writing multi-threaded applications, such as the **Thread** class and the **synchronized** keyword, are hard to use correctly because they are too low level. Java 5 added the Concurrency Utilities in the **java.util.concurrent** package and subpackages. The types in these packages have been designed to provide better alternatives to Java's built-in thread and synchronization features. This chapter discusses the more important types in the Concurrency Utilities, starting from atomic variables and followed by executors, **Callable**, and **Future**. Also included is a discussion of **SwingWorker**, which is a utility for writing asynchronous tasks in Swing.

Atomic Variables

The **java.util.concurrent.atomic** package provides classes such as **AtomicBoolean**, **AtomicInteger**, **AtomicLong**, and **AtomicReference**. These classes can perform various operations atomically. For example, an **AtomicInteger** stores an integer internally and offers method to atomically manipulate the integer, such as **addAndGet**, **decrementAndGet**, **getAndIncrement**, **incrementAndGet**, and so on.

The **getAndIncrement** and **incrementAndGet** methods return different results. **getAndIncrement** returns the current value of the atomic variable and then increments the value. Therefore, after executing these lines of code, the value of **a** is 0 and the value of **b** is 1.

```
AtomicInteger counter = new AtomicInteger(0);
int a = counter.getAndIncrement(); // a = 0
int b = counter.get();             // b = 1
```

The **incrementAndGet** method, on the other hand, increments the atomic variable first and returns the result. For instance, after running this snippet both **a** and **b** will have a value of 1.

```
AtomicInteger counter = new AtomicInteger(0);
int a = counter.incrementAndGet(); // a = 1
int b = counter.get();             // b = 1
```

Listing 28.1 presents a thread safe counter that utilizes **AtomicInteger**. Compare this with the thread-unsafe **UserStat** class in Chapter 27.

Listing 28.1: A counter with an AtomicInteger
```
package app28;
import java.util.concurrent.atomic.AtomicInteger;
```

```
public class AtomicCounter {
    AtomicInteger userCount = new AtomicInteger(0);

    public int getUserCount() {
        return userCount.get();
    }

    public void increment() {
        userCount.getAndIncrement();
    }

    public void decrement() {
        userCount.getAndDecrement();
    }
}
```

Executor and ExecutorService

Whenever possible, do not use **java.lang.Thread** to execute a **Runnable** task. Instead, use an implementation of **java.util.concurrent.Executor** or its subinterface **ExecutorService**.

Executor has only one method, **execute**.

```
void execute(java.lang.Runnable task)
```

ExecutorService, an extension to **Executor**, adds termination methods and methods for executing **Callable**. **Callable** is akin to **Runnable** except that it can return a value and facilitate cancellation through the **Future** interface. **Callable** and **Future** are explained in the next section "Callable and Future."

You rarely have to write your own implementation of **Executor** (or **ExecutorService**). Instead, use one of the static methods defined in the **Executors** class, a utility class.

```
public static ExecutorService newSingleThreadExecutor()

public static ExecutorService newCacheThreadPool()

public static ExecutorService newFixedThreadPool(int numOfThreads)
```

newSingleThreadExecutor returns an **Executor** that contains a single thread. You can submit multiple tasks to the **Executor**, but only one task will be executing at any given time.

newCacheThreadPool returns an **Executor** that will create more threads to cater for multiple tasks as more tasks are submitted. This is suitable for running short lived asynchronous jobs. However, use this with caution as you could run out of memory if the **Executor** attempts to create new threads while memory is already low.

newFixedThreadPool allows you to determine how many threads will be maintained in the returned **Executor**. If there are more tasks than the number of threads, the tasks that were not allocated threads will wait until the running threads finish their jobs.

Here is how you submit a **Runnable** task to an **Executor**.

```
Executor executor = Executors.newSingleThreadExecutor();
executor.execute(new Runnable() {
    @Override
    public void run() {
        // do something
    }
});
```

Constructing a **Runnable** task as an anonymous class like this is suitable for short tasks and if you don't need to pass arguments to the task. For longer tasks or if you need to pass an argument to the task, you need to implement **Runnable** in a class.

The example in Listing 28.2 illustrates the use of **Executor**. It is a Swing application with a button and a list that will search for JPG files when the button is clicked. The results will be shown in the list. We limit the results to 200 files or we run the risk of running out of memory.

Listing 28.2: The ImageSearcher class

```
package app28.imagesearcher;
import java.awt.BorderLayout;
import java.awt.event.ActionEvent;
import java.awt.event.ActionListener;
import java.nio.file.FileSystems;
import java.nio.file.Path;
import java.util.concurrent.Executor;
import java.util.concurrent.Executors;
import java.util.concurrent.atomic.AtomicInteger;
import javax.swing.DefaultListModel;
import javax.swing.JButton;
import javax.swing.JFrame;
import javax.swing.JList;
import javax.swing.JScrollPane;

public class ImageSearcher extends JFrame
        implements ActionListener {
    public static final int MAX_RESULT = 300;
    JButton searchButton = new JButton("Search");
    DefaultListModel listModel;
    JList imageList;
    Executor executor = Executors.newFixedThreadPool(10);
    AtomicInteger fileCounter = new AtomicInteger(1);

    public ImageSearcher(String title) {
        super(title);
        init();
    }

    private void init() {
        this.setDefaultCloseOperation(JFrame.EXIT_ON_CLOSE);
        this.setLayout(new BorderLayout());
        this.add(searchButton, BorderLayout.NORTH);
        listModel = new DefaultListModel();
```

```
        imageList = new JList(listModel);
        this.add(new JScrollPane(imageList), BorderLayout.CENTER);
        this.pack();
        this.setSize(800, 650);
        searchButton.addActionListener(this);
        this.setVisible(true);
        // center frame
        this.setLocationRelativeTo(null);
    }

    private static void constructGUI() {
        JFrame.setDefaultLookAndFeelDecorated(true);
        ImageSearcher frame = new ImageSearcher("Image Searcher");
    }

    public void actionPerformed(ActionEvent e) {
        Iterable<Path> roots =
                FileSystems.getDefault().getRootDirectories();
        for (Path root : roots) {
            executor.execute(new ImageSearchTask(root, executor,
                    listModel, fileCounter));
        }
    }

    public static void main(String[] args) {
        javax.swing.SwingUtilities.invokeLater(new Runnable() {
            public void run() {
                constructGUI();
            }
        });
    }
}
```

Look carefully at the **actionPerformed** method:

```
        Iterable<Path> roots =
                FileSystems.getDefault().getRootDirectories();
        for (Path root : roots) {
            executor.execute(new ImageSearchTask(root, executor,
                    listModel, fileCounter));
        }
```

The **FileSystem.getRootDirectories** method returns the roots of the file system. If you're on Windows, then it will return Drive C, Drive D, and so on. If you're using Linux or Mac, then it will return /. Notice how it creates an **ImageSearchTask** instance and pass it to the **Executor**? It passes a root directory, the **Executor**, a **DefaultListModel** object that the task can access, and an **AtomicInteger** that records how many files have been found.

The **ImageSearchTask** class in Listing 28.3 is an implementation of **Runnable** for searching JPG files in the given directory and its subdirectories. Note that for each subdirectory it spawns a new **ImageSearchTask** and submits it to the passed in **Executor**.

Listing 28.3: The ImageSearchTask class

```java
package app28.imagesearcher;

import java.io.IOException;
import java.nio.file.DirectoryStream;
import java.nio.file.Files;
import java.nio.file.Path;
import java.util.concurrent.Executor;
import java.util.concurrent.atomic.AtomicInteger;
import javax.swing.DefaultListModel;
import javax.swing.SwingUtilities;

public class ImageSearchTask implements Runnable {
    private Path searchDir;
    private Executor executor;
    private DefaultListModel listModel;
    private AtomicInteger fileCounter;

    public ImageSearchTask(Path searchDir, Executor executor,
      DefaultListModel listModel,
          AtomicInteger fileCounter) {
        this.searchDir = searchDir;
        this.executor = executor;
        this.listModel = listModel;
        this.fileCounter = fileCounter;
    }

    @Override
    public void run() {
        if (fileCounter.get() > ImageSearcher.MAX_RESULT) {
            return;
        }
        try (DirectoryStream<Path> children =
                Files.newDirectoryStream(searchDir)) {
            for (final Path child : children) {
                if (Files.isDirectory(child)) {
                    executor.execute(new ImageSearchTask(child,
                            executor, listModel, fileCounter));
                } else if (Files.isRegularFile(child)) {
                    String name = child.getFileName()
                            .toString().toLowerCase();
                    if (name.endsWith(".jpg")) {
                        final int fileNumber =
                                fileCounter.getAndIncrement();
                        if (fileNumber > ImageSearcher.MAX_RESULT){
                            break;
                        }

                        SwingUtilities.invokeLater(new Runnable() {
                            public void run() {
                                listModel.addElement(fileNumber +
                                        ": " + child);
```

```
                        }
                    });
                }
            }
        }
    } catch (IOException e) {
        System.out.println(e.getMessage());
    }
}
}
```

The **run** method inspects the directory passed to the task and checks its content. For each JPG file it increments the **fileCount** variable and for each subdirectory it spawns a new **ImageSearchTask** so that the search can be done more quickly.

Callable and Future

Callable is one of the most valuable members of the Concurrency Utilities. A **Callable** is a task that returns a value and may throw an exception. **Callable** is similar to **Runnable**, except that the latter cannot return a value or throw an exception.

Callable defines a method, **call**:

```
V call() throws java.lang.Exception
```

You can pass a **Callable** to an **ExecutorService**'s **submit** method:

```
Future<V> result = executorService.submit(callable);
```

The **submit** method returns a **Future** which can be used to cancel the task or retrieve the return value of the **Callable**. To cancel a task, call the **cancel** method on the **Future** object:

```
boolean cancel(boolean myInterruptIfRunning)
```

You pass **true** to **cancel** if you want to cancel the task even though it's being executed. Passing **false** allows an in-progress task to complete undisturbed. Note that **cancel** will fail if the task has been completed or previously cancelled or for some reason cannot be cancelled.

To get the result of a **Callable**, call the **get** method of the corresponding **Future**. The **get** method comes in two overloads:

```
V get()
```

```
V get(long timeout, TimeUnit unit)
```

The first overload blocks until the task is complete. The second one waits until a specified time lapses. The *timeout* argument specifies the maximum time to wait and the *unit* argument specifies the time unit for *timeout*.

To find out if a task has been cancelled or complete, call **Future**'s **isCancelled** or **isDone** method.

```
boolean isCancelled()
```

```
boolean isDone()
```

For example, the **FileCountTask** class in Listing 28.4 presents a **Callable** task for counting the number of files in a directory and its subdirectories.

Listing 28.4: The FileCountTask class

```
package app28.filecounter;
import java.io.IOException;
import java.nio.file.DirectoryStream;
import java.nio.file.Files;
import java.nio.file.Path;
import java.nio.file.Paths;
import java.util.ArrayList;
import java.util.List;
import java.util.concurrent.Callable;

public class FileCountTask implements Callable {
    Path dir;
    long fileCount = 0L;
    public FileCountTask(Path dir) {
        this.dir = dir;
    }

    private void doCount(Path parent) {
        if (Files.notExists(parent)) {
            return;
        }
        try (DirectoryStream<Path> children =
                    Files.newDirectoryStream(parent)) {
            for (Path child : children) {
                if (Files.isDirectory(child)) {
                    doCount(child);
                } else if (Files.isRegularFile(child)) {
                    fileCount++;
                }
            }
        } catch (IOException e) {
            e.printStackTrace();
        }
    }

    @Override
    public Long call() throws Exception {
        System.out.println("Start counting " + dir);
        doCount(dir);
        System.out.println("Finished counting " + dir);
        return fileCount;
    }
}
```

The **FileCounter** class in Listing 28.5 uses **FileCountTask** to count the number of files in two directories and prints the results. It specifies a **Path** array (**dirs**) that contains the paths to the directories which you want to count the number of files of. Replace the values of **dirs** with directory names in your file system.

Listing 28.5: The FileCounter class

```
package app28.filecounter;
import java.nio.file.Path;
import java.nio.file.Paths;
import java.util.concurrent.ExecutionException;
import java.util.concurrent.ExecutorService;
import java.util.concurrent.Executors;
import java.util.concurrent.Future;

public class FileCounter {
    public static void main(String[] args) {
        Path[] dirs = {
            Paths.get("C:/temp"),
            Paths.get("C:/temp/data")
        };

        ExecutorService executorService =
                Executors.newFixedThreadPool(dirs.length);

        Future<Long>[] results = new Future[dirs.length];
        for (int i = 0; i < dirs.length; i++) {
            Path dir = dirs[i];
            FileCountTask task = new FileCountTask(dir);
            results[i] = executorService.submit(task);
        }

        // print result
        for (int i = 0; i < dirs.length; i++) {
            long fileCount = 0L;
            try {
                fileCount = results[i].get();
            } catch (InterruptedException | ExecutionException ex){
                ex.printStackTrace();
            }
            System.out.println(dirs[i] + " contains "
                    + fileCount + " files.");
        }

        // it won't exit unless we shut down the ExecutorService
        executorService.shutdownNow();
    }
}
```

When run, the **FileCounter** class creates the same number of threads as the number of directories in **dirs** using the **newFixedThreadPool** method of **ExecutorService**. One thread for each directory.

```
        ExecutorService executorService =
                Executors.newFixedThreadPool(dirs.length);
```

It also defines an array of **Future**s for containing the results of executing the

FileCountTask tasks.

```
Future<Long>[] results = new Future[dirs.length];
```

It then creates a **FileCountTask** for each directory and submits it to the **ExecutorService**.

```
for (int i = 0; i < dirs.length; i++) {
    Path dir = dirs[i];
    FileCountTask task = new FileCountTask(dir);
    results[i] = executorService.submit(task);
}
```

Finally, it prints the results and shuts down the **ExecutorService**.

```
// print result
for (int i = 0; i < dirs.length; i++) {
    long fileCount = 0L;
    try {
        fileCount = results[i].get();
    } catch (InterruptedException | ExecutionException ex){
        ex.printStackTrace();
    }
    System.out.println(dirs[i] + " contains "
            + fileCount + " files.");
}
// it won't exit unless we shut down the ExecutorService
executorService.shutdownNow();
```

Swing Worker

In any Swing application, a single thread is responsible for painting the GUI and handling events. This thread is called the event-dispatching thread (EDT). The use of the same thread for both tasks guarantees that each event handler finishes executing before the next one executes and that GUI painting will not be interrupted by events. If an event handler must perform a lengthy task, the task needs to run in a separate thread, or else your application will become unresponsive during the execution of the event handler. On the other hand, Swing components should be accessed on the EDT only, and, unfortunately, communication between the EDT and another thread could be tricky. Therefore, if you need to access Swing components from another thread, you need to be extra-careful.

The **javax.swing.SwingWorker** abstract class is a utility class that helps you with time-consuming tasks in a Swing application. After you instantiate a subclass of **SwingWorker**, you can call its **execute** method to start the worker. Calling **execute** in turn invokes the **doInBackground** method on a different thread. You should write your code in this method. From within **doInBackground** you can call the **publish** method to publish intermediate data that will be received by the **process** method. **SwingWorker** invokes the **process** method each time the **publish** method is called on the EDT. Therefore, this is your chance to update any Swing component. For example, you can send intermediate results to the **publish** method from **doInBackground** and let **process** prints the results in a **JLabel**. Finally, when **doInBackground** finishes executing, **SwingWorker** will invoke the **done** method. In addition, there are also a **cancel** method to cancel a running **SwingWorker** and a **isCancelled** method that indicates if the worker has been cancelled.

The following example shows a Swing application with a **SwingWorker** subclass named **CounterTask**. The task takes 10 seconds to complete and during its execution all other Swing components must still be responsive. For example, you can click a **Cancel** button to cancel the task. During execution, it will also repeatedly send the status that will be displayed in a **JTextArea** in the application. The **CounterTask** class is given in Listing 28.6. The main Swing application that instantiates **CounterTask** and provides a handler to call the **CounterTask**'s **execute** method is named **SwingWorkerDemo** and is presented in Listing 28.7.

Listing 28.6: The CounterTask class

```java
package app28.swingworker;
import java.util.List;
import javax.swing.JTextArea;
import javax.swing.SwingWorker;

public class CounterTask extends SwingWorker<Integer, Integer> {
    private static final int DELAY = 1000;
    private JTextArea textArea;

    // A calling application must pass a JTextArea
    public CounterTask(JTextArea textArea) {
        this.textArea = textArea;
    }

    @Override
    protected Integer doInBackground() throws Exception {
        int i = 0;
        int count = 10;
        while (! isCancelled() && i < count) {
            i++;
            publish(new Integer[] {i});
            setProgress(count * i / count);
            Thread.sleep(DELAY);
        }

        return count;
    }

    @Override
    protected void process(List<Integer> chunks) {
        for (int i : chunks)
            textArea.append(i + "\n");
    }

    @Override
    protected void done() {
        if (isCancelled())
            textArea.append("Cancelled !");
        else
            textArea.append("Done !");
    }
```

```
}
```

Listing 28.7: The SwingWorkerDemo class

```java
package app28.swingworker;
import java.awt.LayoutManager;
import java.awt.event.ActionEvent;
import java.awt.event.ActionListener;
import java.beans.PropertyChangeEvent;
import java.beans.PropertyChangeListener;
import javax.swing.BoxLayout;
import javax.swing.JButton;
import javax.swing.JFrame;
import javax.swing.JPanel;
import javax.swing.JProgressBar;
import javax.swing.JScrollPane;
import javax.swing.JTextArea;
import javax.swing.SwingUtilities;

public class SwingWorkerDemo {
    private static void constructGUI() {
        // Text area that displays results
        JTextArea textArea = new JTextArea(10, 20);

        // Progress bar displaying the progress of the
        // time-consuming task
        final JProgressBar progressBar = new JProgressBar(0, 10);

        final CounterTask task = new CounterTask(textArea);
        task.addPropertyChangeListener(new PropertyChangeListener(){
            public void propertyChange(PropertyChangeEvent evt) {
                if ("progress".equals(evt.getPropertyName())) {
                    progressBar.setValue(
                            (Integer)evt.getNewValue());
                }
            }
        });

        // Start button
        JButton startButton = new JButton("Start");
        startButton.addActionListener(new ActionListener() {
            public void actionPerformed(ActionEvent e) {
                task.execute();
            }
        });

        // Cancel button
        JButton cancelButton = new JButton("Cancel");
        cancelButton.addActionListener(new ActionListener() {
            public void actionPerformed(ActionEvent e) {
                task.cancel(true);
            }
        });
```

```
        JPanel buttonPanel = new JPanel();
        buttonPanel.add(startButton);
        buttonPanel.add(cancelButton);

        JPanel cp = new JPanel();
        LayoutManager layout = new BoxLayout(cp, BoxLayout.Y_AXIS);
        cp.setLayout(layout);
        cp.add(buttonPanel);
        cp.add(new JScrollPane(textArea));
        cp.add(progressBar);

        JFrame frame = new JFrame("SwingWorker Demo");
        frame.setDefaultCloseOperation(JFrame.EXIT_ON_CLOSE);
        frame.setContentPane(cp);
        frame.pack();
        frame.setVisible(true);
    }

    public static void main(String[] args) {
        SwingUtilities.invokeLater(new Runnable() {
            public void run() {
                constructGUI();
            }
        });
    }
}
```

If you run the application, you can see a Swing application with two buttons like the one in Figure 28.1. Click the **Start** button to start the process. Notice that the **Cancel** button is still responsive during the **SwingWorker** execution and can be clicked to cancel the execution.

Figure 28.1: SwingWorker demo

Locks

In Chapter 27, "Java Threads" you have learned that you can lock a shared resource using the **synchronized** modifier. While **synchronized** is easy enough to use, such a locking mechanism is not without limitations. For instance, a thread attempting to acquire such a lock cannot back off and will block indefinitely if the lock cannot be acquired. Also, locking and unlocking are limited to methods and blocks; there's no way to lock a resource in a method and release it in another method.

Luckily, the Concurrency Utilities comes with much more advanced locks. The **Lock** interface, the only one discussed in this book, offers methods that overcome the limitations of Java's built-in locks. Lock comes with the **lock** method as well as the **unlock** method. This means, you can release a lock anywhere in the program as long as you retain a reference to the lock. In most circumstances, however, it is a good idea to call **unlock** in a finally clause following the invocation of **lock** to make sure unlock is always called.

```
aLock.lock();
try {
    // do something with the locked resource
} finally {
    aLock.unlock();
}
```

If a lock is not available, the **lock** method will block until it is. This behavior is similar to the implicit lock resulting from using **synchronized**.

In addition to **lock** and **unlock**, however, the **Lock** interface offers the **tryLock** methods:

```
boolean tryLock()
```

```
boolean tryLock(long time, TimeUnit timeUnit)
```

The first overload returns **true** only if the lock is available. Otherwise, it returns false. In the latter case, it does not block.

The second overload returns **true** immediately if the lock is available. Otherwise, it will wait until the specified time lapses and will return false if it fails to acquire the lock. The *time* argument specifies the maximum time it will wait and the *timeUnit* argument specifies the time unit for the first argument.

The code in Listing 28.8 shows the use of **ReentrantLock**, an implementation of **Lock**. This code is taken from a document management suite that allows users to upload and share files. Uploading a file with the same name as an existing file in the same server folder will make the existing file a history file and the new file the current file.

To improve performance, multiple users are allowed to upload files at the same time. Uploading files with different names or to different server folders poses no problem as they will be written to different physical files. Uploading files with the same name to the same server folder can be a problem if the users do it at the same time. To circumvent this issue, the system uses a **Lock** to ensure multiple threads attempting to write to the same physical file do not do so concurrently. In other words, only one thread can do the writing and other threads will have to wait until the first one is done.

In Listing 28.8, which in fact is real code taken from the document management package by Brainy Software, the system uses a **Lock** to protect access to a file and obtains locks from a thread-safe map that maps paths with locks. As such, it only prevents writing files with the same name. Writing files with different names can occur at the same time because different paths maps to different locks.

Listing 28.8: Using locks to prevent threads writing to the same file

```
ReentrantLock lock = fileLockMap.putIfAbsent(fullPath,
        new ReentrantLock());
lock.lock();
try {

    // index and copy the file, create history etc

} finally {
    lock.unlock();
    fileLockMap.remove(fullPath, lock);
}
```

The code block starts by attempting to obtain a lock from a thread-safe map. If a lock is found, it means another thread is accessing the file. If no lock is found, the current thread creates a new **ReentrantLock** and stores it in the map so that other threads will notice that it's currently accessing the file.

```
ReentrantLock lock = fileLockMap.putIfAbsent(fullPath,
        new ReentrantLock());
```

It then calls **lock**. If the current thread is the only thread trying to acquire the lock, the **lock** method will return. Otherwise, the current thread will wait until the lock holder releases the lock.

Once a thread successfully obtains a lock, it has exclusive access to the file and can do anything with it. Once it's finished, it calls **unlock** and the map's **remove** method. The **remove** method will only removes the lock if no thread is holding it.

Summary

The Concurrency Utilities are designed to make writing multi-threaded applications easier. The classes and interfaces in the API are meant to replace Java's lower-level threading mechanism such as the **Thread** class and the **synchronized** modifier. This chapter discussed the basics of the Concurrency Utilities, including atomic variables, executors, **Callable**, **Future**, and **SwingWorker**.

Quiz

1. What are atomic variables?
2. How do you obtain an **ExecutorService** instance?
3. What is a **Callable** and what is a **Future**?
4. Name one of the standard implementations of the **Lock** interface.

Chapter 29
Internationalization

In this era of globalization, it is now more compelling than ever to be able to write applications that can be deployed in different countries and regions that speak different languages. There are two terms you need to be familiar with in this regard. The first is internationalization, often abbreviated to i18n because the word starts with an i and ends with an n, and there are 18 characters between the first i and the last n. Internationalization is the technique for developing applications that support multiple languages and data formats without rewriting the programming logic. The second term in localization, which is the technique of adapting an internationalized application to support a specific locale. A locale is a specific geographical, political, or cultural region. An operation that takes a locale into consideration is said to be locale-sensitive. For example, displaying a date is locale-sensitive because the date must be in the format used by the country or region of the user. The fifteenth day of November 2016 is written 11/15/2016 in the US, but printed as 15/11/2016 in Australia. For the same reason internationalization is abbreviated i18n, localization is abbreviated l10n.

Java was designed with internationalization in mind, employing Unicode for characters and strings. Making internationalized applications in Java is therefore easy. How you internationalize your applications depends on how much static data needs to be presented in different languages. There are two approaches.

1. If a large amount of data is static, create a separate version of the resource for each locale. This approach normally applies to Web application with lots of static HTML pages. It is straightforward and will not be discussed in this chapter.
2. If the amount of static data that needs to be internationalized is limited, isolate textual elements such as component labels and error messages into text files. Each text file stores the translations of all textual elements for a locale. The application then retrieves each element dynamically. The advantage is clear. Each textual element can be edited easily without recompiling the application. This is the technique that will discussed in this chapter.

This chapter starts by explaining what a locale is. Next comes the technique for internationalizing your applications, followed by a Swing example.

Locales

The **java.util.Locale** class represents a locale. There are three main components of a **Locale** object: language, country, and variant. The language is obviously the most important part; however, sometimes the language itself is not sufficient to differentiate a locale. For example, the English language is spoken in countries such as the US and England. However, the English language spoken in the US is not exactly the same as the one used in the UK. Therefore, it is necessary to specify the country of the language. As another example, the Chinese language used in China is not exactly the same as the one used in Taiwan.

The variant argument is a vendor- or browser-specific code. For example, you use WIN for Windows, MAC for Macintosh, and POSIX for POSIX. Where there are two variants, separate them with an underscore, and put the most important one first. For example, a Traditional Spanish collation might construct a locale with parameters for language, country, and variant as es, ES, Traditional_WIN, respectively.

To construct a **Locale** object, use one of the **Locale** class's constructors.

```
public Locale(java.lang.String language)

public Locale(java.lang.String language, java.lang.String country)

public Locale(java.lang.String language, java.lang.String country,
        java.lang.String variant)
```

The language code is a valid ISO language code. Table 29.1 displays examples of language codes.

The country argument is a valid ISO country code, which is a two-letter, uppercase code specified in ISO 3166, which you can download from this site:

```
http://userpage.chemie.fu-berlin.de/diverse/doc/ISO_3166.html
```

Table 29.1 lists some of the country codes in ISO 3166.

Code	Language
de	German
el	Greek
en	English
es	Spanish
fr	French
hi	Hindi
it	Italian
ja	Japanese
nl	Dutch
pt	Portuguese
ru	Russian
zh	Chinese

Table 29.1: Examples of ISO 639 Language Codes

Country	Code
Australia	AU
Brazil	BR
Canada	CA
China	CN
Egypt	EG
France	FR
Germany	DE
India	IN
Mexico	MX
Switzerland	CH
Taiwan	TW
United Kingdom	GB
United States	US

Table 29.2: Examples of ISO 3166 Country Codes

For example, to construct a **Locale** object representing the English language used in Canada, write this.

```
Locale locale = new Locale("en", "CA");
```

In addition, the **Locale** class provides static final fields that return locales for specific countries or languages, such as **CANADA**, **CANADA_FRENCH**, **CHINA**, **CHINESE**, **ENGLISH**, **FRANCE**, **FRENCH**, **UK**, **US**, etc. Therefore, you can also construct a **Locale** object by calling its static field:

```
Locale locale = Locale.CANADA_FRENCH;
```

In addition, the static **getDefault** method returns the user computer's locale.

```
Locale locale = Locale.getDefault();
```

Internationalizing Applications

Internationalizing and localizing your applications require you to

1. isolate textual components into properties files
2. be able to select and read the correct properties file

This section elaborates the two steps and provides a simple example. The section "An Internationalized Swing Application" later in this chapter presents another example.

Isolating Textual Components into Properties Files

An internationalized application stores its textual elements in a separate properties file for each locale. Each file contains key/value pairs, and each key uniquely identifies a locale-specific object. Keys are always strings, and values can be strings or any other type of object. For example, to support American English, German, and Chinese you will have three properties files, all of which have the same keys.

The following is the English version of the properties file. Note that it has two keys:

greetings and **farewell**.

```
greetings = Hello
farewell = Goodbye
```

The German version would be as follows:

```
greetings = Hallo
farewell = Tschüß
```

And the properties file for the Chinese language is as follows:

```
greetings=\u4f60\u597d
farewell=\u518d\u89c1
```

Read the sidebar "Converting Chinese Characters to Unicode" on how we arrived at the previous properties file.

Converting Chinese Characters to Unicode

In the Chinese language, 你好 (meaning hello, represented by the Unicode codes 4f60 and 597d, respectively) and 再见 (meaning good bye and is represented by Unicode codes 518d and 89c1, respectively) are the most common expressions. Of course, no one remembers the Unicode code of each Chinese character. Therefore, you create the .properties file in two steps:

1. Using your favorite Chinese text editor, create a text file like this:

```
greetings=你好
farewell=再见
```

2. Convert the content of the text file into the Unicode representation. Normally, a Chinese text editor has the feature for converting Chinese characters into Unicode codes. You will get the end result:

```
greetings=\u4f60\u597d
farewell=\u518d\u89c1
```

Now, you need to master the **java.util.ResourceBundle** class. It enables you to easily choose and read the properties file specific to the user's locale and look up the values. **ResourceBundle** is an abstract class, but it provides static **getBundle** methods that return an instance of a concrete subclass.

A **ResourceBundle** has a base name, which can be any name. In order for a **ResourceBundle** to pick up a properties file, the filename must be composed of the **ResourceBundle** base name, followed by an underscore, followed by the language code, and optionally followed by another underscore and the country code. The format for the properties file name is as follows:

```
basename_languageCode_countryCode
```

For example, suppose the base name is **MyResources** and you define the following three locales:

- US-en
- DE-de
- CN-zh

Then you would have these three properties files:

- **MyResources_en_US.properties**
- **MyResources_de_DE.properties**
- **MyResources_zh_CN.properties**

Reading Properties Files using ResourceBundle

As mentioned previously, **ResourceBundle** is an abstract class. Nonetheless, you can obtain an instance of **ResourceBundle** by calling its static **getBundle** method. The signatures of its overloads are

```
public static ResourceBundle getBundle(java.lang.String baseName)
```

```
public static ResourceBundle getBundle(java.lang.String baseName,
        Locale locale)
```

For example:

```
ResourceBundle rb =
        ResourceBundle.getBundle("MyResources", Locale.US);
```

This will load the **ResourceBundle** with the values in the corresponding properties file.

If a suitable properties file is not found, the **ResourceBundle** object will fall back to the default properties file. The name of the default properties file will be the base name with a **properties** extension. In this case, the default file would be **MyResources.properties**. If this file is not found, a **java.util.MissingResourceException** will be thrown.

Then, to read a value, you use the **ResourceBundle** class's **getString** method, passing the key.

```
public java.lang.String getString(java.lang.String key)
```

If the entry with the specified key is not found, a **java.util.MissingResourceException** will be thrown.

An Internationalized Swing Application

The following example illustrates the effort to support internationalization with two languages: English and French. This example uses three properties files:

- **MyResources_en_US.properties**, given in Listing 29.1
- **MyResources_fr_CA.properties**, shown in Listing 29.2
- **MyResources.properties** (the default), presented in Listing 29.3

These files are placed in the directory specified in the class path.

Listing 29.1: The MyResources_en_US.properties File

```
userName=User Name
password=Password
login=Login
```

Listing 29.2: The MyResources_fr_CA.properties File

```
userName=Compte
password=Mot de passe
login=Ouvrir session
```

Listing 29.3: The MyResources.properties File

```
userName=User Name
password=Password
login=Login
```

Note

The properties file should be placed in the working directory, even if the class that uses the **ResourceBundle** class is part of a non-default package.

The **I18NDemo** class, shown in Listing 29.4, obtains the **ResourceBundle** object according to the locale of your computer and supplies localized messages for the **JLabel**s and **JButton**.

Listing 29.4: The I18NDemo class

```java
package app29;
import java.awt.GridLayout;
import java.util.Locale;
import java.util.ResourceBundle;
import javax.swing.JButton;
import javax.swing.JFrame;
import javax.swing.JLabel;
import javax.swing.JPasswordField;
import javax.swing.JTextField;
import javax.swing.SwingUtilities;

public class I18NDemo {
    private static void constructGUI() {
        Locale locale = Locale.getDefault();
        ResourceBundle rb =
                ResourceBundle.getBundle("MyResources", locale);
        JFrame.setDefaultLookAndFeelDecorated(true);
        JFrame frame = new JFrame("I18N Test");
        frame.setDefaultCloseOperation(JFrame.EXIT_ON_CLOSE);
        frame.setLayout(new GridLayout(3, 2));
        frame.add(new JLabel(rb.getString("userName")));
        frame.add(new JTextField());
        frame.add(new JLabel(rb.getString("password")));
        frame.add(new JPasswordField());
        frame.add(new JButton(rb.getString("login")));
        frame.pack();
        frame.setVisible(true);
    }

    public static void main(String[] args) {
        SwingUtilities.invokeLater(new Runnable() {
            public void run() {
                constructGUI();
            }
```

```
        });
    }
}
```

The English version of the application is shown in Figure 29.1.

Figure 29.1: The English version of the example

To test a different language, change your computer locale setting.

In practice, most internationalized applications will create localized contents that are based on different languages, rather than different locales. This is to say that if an application has provided textual elements in the German language for people from Germany, chances are slim that it will also provide another variant of German for people in Austria or Switzerland. Providing many variants of the same language is expensive and impractical. Any German speaking user should understand any variant of the German language, anyway.

Summary

This chapter explains how to develop an internationalized application. First it explained the **java.util.Locale** class and the **java.utilResourceBundle** class. It then continued with an example of an internationalized application.

Quiz

1. What is the approach to internationalizing applications with plenty of static contents?
2. How do you isolate textual elements of a Java application?
3. What are the two classes used in internationalization and localization?

Chapter 30
Java Networking

Computer networking is concerned with communication between computers. Nowadays, this form of interaction is ubiquitous. Whenever you surf the Internet, it is your machine exchanging messages with remote servers. When you transfer a file over an FTP channel, you are also using some kind of networking service. Java comes equipped with the **java.net** package that contains types that make network programming easy. We'll examine some of the types after an overview of networking. Towards the end of the chapter, some examples are presented for you to play with.

An Overview of Networking

A network is a collection of computers that can communicate with each other. Depending on how wide the coverage is, a network can be referred to as a local area network (LAN) or a wide area network (WAN). A LAN is normally confined to a limited geographic area, such as a building, and comprises from as few as three to as many as hundreds of computers. A WAN, by contrast, is a combination of multiple LANs that are geographically separate. The largest network of all is, of course, the Internet.

The communication medium within a network can be cables, telephone lines, high-speed fiber, satellites, and so on. As the wireless technology gets more and more mature and inexpensive, a wireless local area network (WLAN) is becoming more commonplace nowadays.

Just like two people use a common language to converse, two computers communicate by using a common 'language' both agreed on. In computer jargon, this 'language' is referred to as protocol. What's confusing is that there are several layers of protocols. This is because at the physical layer two computer communicate by exchanging bitstreams, which are collections of ones and zeroes. This is too hard to be understood by applications and humans. Therefore, there is another layer that translates bitstreams into something more tangible and vice versa.

The easiest protocols are those at the application layer. Writing applications require you to understand protocols in the application layer. There are several protocols in this layer: HTTP, FTP, telnet, etc.

Application layer protocols use the protocols in the transport layer. Two popular ones at the transport layer are TCP and UDP. In turn transport layer protocols utilize the protocols at the layer below it. The diagram in Figure 30.1 shows some of these layers.

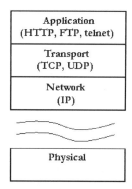

Figure 30.1: Layers of protocol in the computer network

Thanks to this strategy, you don't have to worry about protocols in other layers than the application layer. Java even goes the extra mile to provide classes that encapsulate application layer protocols. For example, with Java, you do not need to understand the HTTP to be able to send a message to an HTTP server. The HTTP, one of the most popular protocols, is covered in detail in this chapter for those who want to know more than the surface.

Another thing that you should know is that a network employs an addressing system to distinguish a computer from another, just like your house has an address so that the mailman can deliver your mail. The equivalent of the street address on the Internet is the IP address. Each computer is assigned a unique IP address.

The IP address is not the smallest unit in the network addressing system. The port is. The analogy is an apartment building that share the same street address but has many units, each with its own suite number.

The Hypertext Transfer Protocol (HTTP)

The HTTP is the protocol that allows web servers and browsers to send and receive data over the Internet. It is a request and response protocol. The client requests a file and the server responds to the request. HTTP uses reliable TCP connections—by default on TCP port 80. The first version of HTTP was HTTP/0.9, which was then overridden by HTTP/1.0. Replacing HTTP/1.0 is the current version of HTTP/1.1, which is defined in Request for Comments (RFC) 2616 and downloadable from http://www.w3.org/Protocols/HTTP/1.1/rfc2616.pdf.

In the HTTP, it is always the client who initiates a transaction by establishing a connection and sending an HTTP request. The web server is in no position to contact a client or make a callback connection to the client. Either the client or the server can prematurely terminate a connection. For example, when using a web browser you can click the Stop button on your browser to stop downloading a file, effectively closing the HTTP connection with the Web server.

HTTP Requests

An HTTP request consists of three components:

- Method—Uniform Resource Identifier (URI)—Protocol/Version
- Request headers
- Entity body

The following is an example of an HTTP request:

```
POST /examples/default.jsp HTTP/1.1
Accept: text/plain; text/html
Accept-Language: en-gb
Connection: Keep-Alive
Host: localhost
User-Agent: Mozilla/5.0 (Macintosh; U; Intel Mac OS X 10.5; en-US;
    rv:1.9.2.6) Gecko/20100625 Firefox/3.6.6
Content-Length: 33
Content-Type: application/x-www-form-urlencoded
Accept-Encoding: gzip, deflate

lastName=Franks&firstName=Michael
```

The method—URI—protocol version appears as the first line of the request.

```
POST /examples/default.jsp HTTP/1.1
```

where **POST** is the request method, **/examples/default.jsp** the URI and **HTTP/1.1** the Protocol/Version section.

Each HTTP request can use one of the many request methods as specified in the HTTP standards. The HTTP 1.1 supports seven types of request: GET, POST, HEAD, OPTIONS, PUT, DELETE, and TRACE. GET and POST are the most commonly used in Internet applications.

The URI specifies an Internet resource. It is usually interpreted as being relative to the server's root directory. Thus, it should always begin with a forward slash /. A Uniform Resource Locator (URL) is actually a type of URI (See http://www.ietf.org/rfc/rfc2396.txt). The protocol version represents the version of the HTTP protocol being used.

The request header contains useful information about the client environment and the entity body of the request. For example, it could contain the language the browser is set for, the length of the entity body, and so on. Each header is separated by a carriage return/linefeed (CRLF) sequence.

Between the headers and the entity body, there is a blank line (CRLF) that is important to the HTTP request format. The CRLF tells the HTTP server where the entity body begins. In some Internet programming books, this CRLF is considered the fourth component of an HTTP request.

In the previous HTTP request, the entity body is simply the following line:

```
lastName=Franks&firstName=Michael
```

The entity body can easily become much longer in a typical HTTP request.

HTTP Responses

Similar to an HTTP request, an HTTP response also consists of three parts:

- Protocol—Status code—Description
- Response headers
- Entity body

The following is an example of an HTTP response:

```
HTTP/1.1 200 OK
Server: Apache-Coyote/1.1
Date: Thu, 12 Aug 2010 13:13:33 GMT
Content-Type: text/html
Last-Modified: Thu, 5 Aug 2010 13:13:12 GMT
Content-Length: 112

<html>
<head>
<title>HTTP Response Example</title>
</head>
<body>
Welcome to Brainy Software
</body>
</html>
```

The first line of the response header is similar to the first line of a request header. The first line tells you that the protocol used is HTTP version 1.1, the request succeeded (200 is the success code), and that everything went okay.

The response headers contain useful information similar to the headers in the request. The entity body of the response is the HTML content of the response itself. The headers and the entity body are separated by a sequence of CRLFs.

---

java.net.URL

A URL is a unique address to an Internet resource. For example, every page on the Internet has a different URL. Here is a URL:

```
http://www.yahoo.com:80/en/index.html
```

A URL has several components. The first component denotes the protocol to use to retrieve the resource. In the preceding example, the protocol is HTTP. The second part, www.yahoo.com, is the host. It tells you where the resource resides. Number 80 after the host is the port number. The last part, /en/index.html, specifies the path of the URL. By default, the HTTP uses port 80.

The HTTP is the most common protocol used in a URL. However, it is not the only one. For example, this URL refers to a jpeg file in the local computer.

```
file://localhost/C:/data/MyPhoto.jpg
```

Detailed information about URLs can be found at this location:

```
http://www.ietf.org/rfc/rfc2396.txt
```

In Java, a URL is represented by a **java.net.URL** object. You construct a **URL** by invoking one of the **URL** class's constructors. Here are some easier constructors:

```
public URL(java.lang.String spec)

public URL(java.lang.String protocol, java.lang.String host,
        java.lang.String file)

public URL(java.lang.String protocol, java.lang.String host,
        int port, java.lang.String file)

public URL(URL context, String spec)
```

Here is an example.

```
URL myUrl = new URL("http://www.brainysoftware.com/");
```

Because no page is specified, the default page is assumed.

As another example, the following lines of code create identical URL objects.

```
URL yahoo1 = new URL("http://www.yahoo.com/index.html");
URL yahoo2 = new URL("http", "www.yahoo.com", "/index.html");
URL yahoo3 = new URL("http", "www.yahoo.com", 80, "/index.html");
```

Parsing a URL

You can retrieve the various components of a URL object by using these methods:

```
public java.lang.String getFile()

public java.lang.String getHost()

public java.lang.String getPath()

public int getPort()

public java.lang.String getProtocol()

public java.lang.String getQuery()
```

For example, the code in Listing 30.1 creates a URL and prints its various parts.

Listing 30.1: Parsing a URL
```
package app30;
import java.net.URL;

public class URLDemo1 {
    public static void main(String[] args) throws Exception {
        URL url = new URL(
          "http://www.yahoo.com:80/en/index.html?name=john#first");
        System.out.println("protocol:" + url.getProtocol());
        System.out.println("port:" + url.getPort());
```

```
            System.out.println("host:" + url.getHost());
            System.out.println("path:" + url.getPath());
            System.out.println("file:" + url.getFile());
            System.out.println("query:" + url.getQuery());
            System.out.println("ref:" + url.getRef());
        }
    }
}
```

The result of running the **URLTest1** class is as follows.

```
protocol:http
port:80
host:www.yahoo.com
path:/en/index.html
file:/en/index.html?name=john
query:name=john
ref:first
```

Reading A Web Resource

You can use the URL class's **openStream** method to read a web resource. Here is the signature of this method.

```
public final java.io.InputStream openStream()
        throws java.io.IOException
```

For example, the **URLDemo2** class in Listing 30.2 prints the content of http://www.google.com.

Listing 30.2: Opening a URL's stream

```
package app30;
import java.io.BufferedReader;
import java.io.IOException;
import java.io.InputStream;
import java.io.InputStreamReader;
import java.net.MalformedURLException;
import java.net.URL;

public class URLDemo2 {
    public static void main(String[] args) {
        try {
            URL url = new URL("http://www.google.com/");
            InputStream inputStream = url.openStream();
            BufferedReader bufferedReader = new BufferedReader(
                    new InputStreamReader(inputStream));
            String line = bufferedReader.readLine();
            while (line!= null) {
                System.out.println(line);
                line = bufferedReader.readLine();
            }
            bufferedReader.close();
        }
        catch (MalformedURLException e) {
```

```
            e.printStackTrace();
        }
        catch (IOException e) {
            e.printStackTrace();
        }
    }
}
```

Note
You can use a **URL** only to read a web resource. To write to a server, use a **java.net.URLConnection** object.

---

java.net.URLConnection

A **URLConnection** represents a connection to a remote machine. You use it to read a resource from and write to a remote machine. The **URLConnection** class does not have a public constructor, so you cannot construct a **URLConnection** using the **new** keyword. To obtain an instance of **URLConnection**, call the **openConnection** method on a **URL** object.

The **URLConnection** class has two **boolean** fields, **doInput** and **doOutput**, that indicate whether the **URLConnection** can be used for reading and writing, respectively. The default value of **doInput** is **true**, indicating you can always use a **URLConnection** to read a Web resource. The default value of **doOutput** is **false**, meaning a **URLConnection** is not for writing. To use a **URLConnection** object to write, you need to set the value of **doOutput** to **true**. Setting the values of **doInput** and **doOutput** can be done using the **setDoInput** and **setDoOutput** methods:

```
public void setDoInput(boolean value)
```

```
public void setDoOutput(boolean value)
```

You can use the following methods to get the values of **doInput** and **doOutput**:

```
public boolean getDoInput()
```

```
public boolean getDoOutput()
```

To read using a **URLConnection** object, call its **getInputStream** method. This method returns a **java.io.InputStream** object. This method is similar to the **openStream** method in the **URL** class. This is to say that

```
URL url = new URL("http://www.google.com/");
InputStream inputStream = url.openStream();
```

has the same effect as

```
URL url = new URL("http://www.google.com/");
URLConnection urlConnection = url.openConnection();
InputStream inputStream = urlConnection.getInputStream();
```

However, **URLConnection** is more powerful than **URL.openStream** because you can also read the response headers and write to the server. Here are some methods you can use to read the response headers:

```
public java.lang.String getHeaderField(int n)
```
Returns the value of the nth header.

```
public java.lang.String getHeaderField(java.lang.String headerName)
```
Returns the value of the named header.

```
public long getHeaderFieldDate(java.lang.String headerName,
        long default)
```
Returns the value of the named field as a date. The result is the number of milliseconds that has lapsed since January 1, 1970 GMT. If the field is missing, *default* is returned.

```
public java.util.Map getHeaderFields()
```
Returns a **java.util.Map** containing the response headers.

And, here are some other useful methods:

```
public java.lang.String getContentEncoding()
```
Returns the value of the **content-encoding** header

```
public int getContentLength()
```
Returns the value of the **content-length** header.

```
public java.lang.String getContentType()
```
Returns the value of the **content-type** header.

```
public long getDate()
```
Returns the value of the **date** header.

```
public long getExpiration()
```
Returns the value of the expires header.

Reading Web Resources

Listing 30.3 shows a class that reads from a server and displays the response headers.

Listing 30.3: Reading a web resource's headers and content

```java
package app30;
import java.io.BufferedReader;
import java.io.IOException;
import java.io.InputStream;
import java.io.InputStreamReader;
import java.net.MalformedURLException;
import java.net.URL;
import java.net.URLConnection;
import java.util.List;
import java.util.Map;
import java.util.Set;

public class URLConnectionDemo1 {
    public static void main(String[] args) {
        try {
            URL url = new URL("http://www.java.com/");
            URLConnection urlConnection = url.openConnection();
            Map<String, List<String>> headers =
                    urlConnection.getHeaderFields();
```

```
            Set<Map.Entry<String, List<String>>> entrySet =
                    headers.entrySet();
            for (Map.Entry<String, List<String>> entry : entrySet){
                String headerName = entry.getKey();
                System.out.println("Header Name:" + headerName);
                List<String> headerValues = entry.getValue();
                for (String value : headerValues) {
                    System.out.print("Header value:" + value);
                }
                System.out.println();
                System.out.println();
            }
            InputStream inputStream =
                    urlConnection.getInputStream();
            BufferedReader bufferedReader = new BufferedReader(
                    new InputStreamReader(inputStream));
            String line = bufferedReader.readLine();
            while (line != null) {
                System.out.println(line);
                line = bufferedReader.readLine();
            }
            bufferedReader.close();
        } catch (MalformedURLException e) {
            e.printStackTrace();
        } catch (IOException e) {
            e.printStackTrace();
        }
    }
}
```

The first few lines of the response are the headers: (you might get different ones)

```
Header Name:Connection
Header value:keep-alive

Header Name:Last-Modified
Header value:Sat, 24 Nov 2014 02:01:26 UTC

Header Name:Server
Header value:Oracle-Application-Server-11g

Header Name:Content-type
Header value:text/html; charset=UTF-8

Header Name:null
Header value:HTTP/1.1 200 OK
```

The headers are followed by the resource content (not displayed here to save space).

Writing to a web server

You can use a **URLConnection** to send an HTTP request. For example, the snippet here sends a form to http://www.mydomain.com/form.jsp page.

```
URL url = new URL("http://www.mydomain.com/form.jsp");
URLConnection connection = url.openConnection();
connection.setDoOutput(true);
PrintWriter out = new PrintWriter(connection.getOutputStream());
out.println("firstName=Joe");
out.println("lastName=Average");
out.close();
```

While you can use a **URLConnection** to post messages, you don't normally use it for this purpose. Instead, you use the more powerful **java.net.Socket** and **java.net.ServerSocket** classes discussed in the next sections.

java.net.Socket

A socket is an endpoint of a network connection. A socket enables an application to read from and write to the network. Two software applications residing on two different computers can communicate with each other by sending and receiving byte streams over a connection. To send a message from your application to another application, you need to know the IP address as well as the port number of the socket of the other application. In Java, a socket is represented by a **java.net.Socket** object.

To create a socket, you can use one of the many constructors of the **Socket** class. One of these constructors accepts the host name and the port number:

```
public Socket(java.lang.String host, int port)
```

where *host* is the remote machine name or IP address and *port* is the port number of the remote application. For example, to connect to yahoo.com at port 80, you would construct the following **Socket** object:

```
new Socket("yahoo.com", 80)
```

Once you create an instance of the **Socket** class successfully, you can use it to send and receive streams of bytes. To send byte streams, you must first call the **Socket** class's **getOutputStream** method to obtain a **java.io.OutputStream** object. To send text to a remote application, you often want to construct a **java.io.PrintWriter** object from the **OutputStream** object returned. To receive byte streams from the other end of the connection, you call the **Socket** class's **getInputStream** method that returns a **java.io.InputStream**.

The code in Listing 30.4 simulates an HTTP client using a socket. It sends an HTTP request to the host and displays the response from the server.

Listing 30.4: A simple HTTP client
```
package app30;
import java.io.BufferedReader;
```

```java
import java.io.IOException;
import java.io.InputStreamReader;
import java.io.OutputStream;
import java.io.PrintWriter;
import java.net.Socket;

public class SocketDemo1 {
    public static void main(String[] args) {
        String host = "books.brainysoftware.com";
        try {
            Socket socket = new Socket(host, 80);
            OutputStream os = socket.getOutputStream();
            boolean autoflush = true;
            PrintWriter out = new
                    PrintWriter(socket.getOutputStream(),
                    autoflush);
            BufferedReader in = new BufferedReader(
                    new InputStreamReader(socket.getInputStream()));

            // send an HTTP request to the web server
            out.println("GET / HTTP/1.1");
            out.println("Host: " + host + ":80");
            out.println("Connection: Close");
            out.println();

            // read the response
            boolean loop = true;
            StringBuilder sb = new StringBuilder(8096);
            while (loop) {
                if (in.ready()) {
                    int i = 0;
                    while (i != -1) {
                        i = in.read();
                        sb.append((char) i);
                    }
                    loop = false;
                }
            }

            // display the response to the out console
            System.out.println(sb.toString());
            socket.close();
        } catch (IOException e) {
            e.printStackTrace();
        }
    }
}
```

To get a proper response from the Web server, you need to send an HTTP request that complies with the HTTP protocol. If you have read the previous section, "The Hypertext Transfer Protocol (HTTP)," you should be able to understand the HTTP request in the code above.

Note
The HttpClient library from the Apache HTTP Components project (http://hc.apache.org) provides classes that can be used as a more sophisticated HTTP client.

java.net.ServerSocket

The **Socket** class represents a "client" socket, i.e. a socket that you construct whenever you want to connect to a remote server application. Now, if you want to implement a server application, such as an HTTP server or an FTP server, you need a different approach. Your server must stand by all the time as it does not know when a client application will try to connect to it. In order for your application to be able to do this, you need to use the **java.net.ServerSocket** class. **ServerSocket** is an implementation of a server socket.

ServerSocket is different from **Socket**. The role of a server socket is to wait for connection requests from clients. Once the server socket gets a connection request, it creates a **Socket** instance to handle the communication with the client.

To create a server socket, you need to use one of the four constructors the **ServerSocket** class provides. You need to specify the IP address and port number the server socket will be listening on. Typically, the IP address will be 127.0.0.1, meaning that the server socket will be listening on the local machine. The IP address the server socket is listening on is referred to as the binding address. Another important property of a server socket is its backlog, which is the maximum queue length of incoming connection requests before the server socket starts to refuse the incoming requests.

One of the constructors of the **ServerSocket** class has the following signature:

```
public ServerSocket(int port, int backLog,
        InetAddress bindingAddress);
```

Notice that for this constructor, the binding address must be an instance of **java.net.InetAddress**. An easy way to construct an **InetAddress** object is by calling its **getByName** static method, passing a **String** containing the host name, such as in the following code.

```
InetAddress.getByName("127.0.0.1");
```

The following line of code constructs a **ServerSocket** that listens on port 8080 of the local machine. The **ServerSocket** has a backlog of 1.

```
new ServerSocket(8080, 1, InetAddress.getByName("127.0.0.1"));
```

Once you have a **ServerSocket**, you can tell it to wait for an incoming connection request to the binding address at the port the server socket is listening on. You do this by calling the **ServerSocket** class's **accept** method. This method will only return when there is a connection request and its return value is an instance of the **Socket** class. This **Socket** object can then be used to send and receive byte streams from the client application, as explained in the previous section, "java.net.Socket." Practically, the **accept** method is the only method used in the application accompanying this chapter.

The web server application in the next section, "A Web Server Application" illustrates the use of **ServerSocket**.

A Web Server Application

This application illustrates the use of the **ServerSocket** and **Socket** classes to communicate with remote computers. The Web server application contains the following three classes that belong to the **app30.webserver** package:

- **HttpServer**
- **Request**
- **Response**

The entry point of this application is the **main** method in the **HttpServer** class. The method creates an instance of **HttpServer** and calls its **await** method. The **await** method, as the name implies, waits for HTTP requests on a designated port, processes them, and sends responses back to the clients. It keeps waiting until a shutdown command is received.

The application cannot do more than sending static resources, such as HTML files and image files, residing in a certain directory. It also displays the incoming HTTP request byte streams on the console. However, it does not send any header, such as dates or cookies, to the browser.

We will now look at the three classes in the following subsections.

The HttpServer Class

The **HttpServer** class represents a web server and is presented in Listing 30.5. Note that the **await** method is given in Listing 30.6 and is not included in Listing 30.5 to save space.

Listing 30.5: The HttpServer class

```
package app30.webserver;
import java.net.Socket;
import java.net.ServerSocket;
import java.net.InetAddress;
import java.io.InputStream;
import java.io.OutputStream;
import java.io.IOException;

public class HttpServer {

    // shutdown command
    private static final String SHUTDOWN_COMMAND = "/SHUTDOWN";

    // the shutdown command received
    private boolean shutdown = false;

    public static void main(String[] args) {
        HttpServer server = new HttpServer();
        server.await();
```

```java
        }

    public void await() {
        ServerSocket serverSocket = null;
        int port = 8080;
        try {
            serverSocket = new ServerSocket(port, 1, InetAddress
                    .getByName("127.0.0.1"));
        } catch (IOException e) {
            e.printStackTrace();
            System.exit(1);
        }
        // Loop waiting for a request
        while (!shutdown) {
            Socket socket = null;
            InputStream input = null;
            OutputStream output = null;
            try {
                socket = serverSocket.accept();
                input = socket.getInputStream();
                output = socket.getOutputStream();
                // create Request object and parse
                Request request = new Request(input);
                request.parse();

                // create Response object
                Response response = new Response(output);
                response.setRequest(request);
                response.sendStaticResource();

                // Close the socket
                socket.close();

                // check if the previous URI is a shutdown command
                shutdown =
                        request.getUri().equals(SHUTDOWN_COMMAND);
            } catch (Exception e) {
                e.printStackTrace();
                continue;
            }
        }
    }
}
```

The code listings include a directory called **webroot** that contains some static resources that you can use for testing this application. To request for a static resource, you type the following URL in your browser's Address or URL box:

```
http://machineName:port/staticResource
```

If you are sending a request from a different machine from the one running your application, *machineName* is the name or IP address of the computer running this application. If your browser is on the same machine, you can use **localhost** as the machine name. *port* is 8080 and *staticResource* is the name of the file requested and must reside in WEB_ROOT.

For instance, if you are using the same computer to test the application and you want to ask the **HttpServer** object to send the index.html file, you use the following URL:

```
http://localhost:8080/index.html
```

To stop the server, you send a shutdown command from a web browser by typing the pre-defined string in the browser's Address or URL box, after the **host:port** section of the URL. The shutdown command is defined by the SHUTDOWN static final variable in the **HttpServer** class:

```
private static final String SHUTDOWN_COMMAND = "/SHUTDOWN";
```

Therefore, to stop the server, you use the following URL:

```
http://localhost:8080/SHUTDOWN
```

Now, let's look at the **await** method printed in Listing 30.6.

Listing 30.6: The HttpServer class's await method

```java
public void await() {
    ServerSocket serverSocket = null;
    int port = 8080;
    try {
        serverSocket = new ServerSocket(port, 1, InetAddress
                .getByName("127.0.0.1"));
    } catch (IOException e) {
        e.printStackTrace();
        System.exit(1);
    }
    // Loop waiting for a request
    while (!shutdown) {
        Socket socket = null;
        InputStream input = null;
        OutputStream output = null;
        try {
            socket = serverSocket.accept();
            input = socket.getInputStream();
            output = socket.getOutputStream();
            // create Request object and parse
            Request request = new Request(input);
            request.parse();

            // create Response object
            Response response = new Response(output);
            response.setRequest(request);
            response.sendStaticResource();

            // Close the socket
            socket.close();

            // check if the previous URI is a shutdown command
            shutdown = request.getUri().equals(SHUTDOWN_COMMAND);
```

```
        } catch (Exception e) {
            e.printStackTrace();
            continue;
        }
    }
}
```

The method name **await** is used instead of **wait** because the latter is the name of an important method in **java.lang.Object** that is frequently used in multithreaded programming.

The **await** method starts by creating an instance of **ServerSocket** and then entering a **while** loop.

```
serverSocket =  new ServerSocket(port, 1,
        InetAddress.getByName("127.0.0.1"));
    ...
// Loop waiting for a request
while (!shutdown) {
    ...
}
```

The code inside the **while** loop stops at the **accept** method of **ServerSocket**, which blocks until an HTTP request is received on port 8080:

```
socket = serverSocket.accept();
```

Upon receiving a request, the **await** method obtains a **java.io.InputStream** and a **java.io.OutputStream** from the **Socket** returned by the **accept** method.

```
input = socket.getInputStream();
output = socket.getOutputStream();
```

The **await** method then creates a **Request** and calls its **parse** method to parse the HTTP request raw data.

```
// create Request object and parse
Request request = new Request(input);
request.parse();
```

Afterwards, the **await** method creates a **Response**, assigns the **Request** to it, and calls its **sendStaticResource** method.

```
// create Response object
Response response = new Response(output);
response.setRequest(request);
response.sendStaticResource();
```

Finally, the **await** method closes the **Socket** and calls the **getUri** method of **Request** to check if the URI of the HTTP request is a shutdown command. If it is, the **shutdown** variable is set to **true** and the program exits the **while** loop.

```
// Close the socket
socket.close();

//check if the previous URI is a shutdown command
```

```
shutdown = request.getUri().equals(SHUTDOWN_COMMAND);
```

The Request Class

The **Request** class represents an HTTP request. An instance of this class is constructed by passing the **java.io.InputStream** object obtained from the **Socket** object that handles communication with the client. You call one of the **read** methods on the **InputStream** object to obtain the HTTP request raw data.

The **Request** class is offered in Listing 30.7. It has two public methods, **parse** and **getUri**, which are given in Listings 30.8 and 30.9, respectively.

Listing 30.7: The Request class

```java
package app30.webserver;
import java.io.InputStream;
import java.io.IOException;

public class Request {
    private InputStream input;
    private String uri;

    public Request(InputStream input) {
        this.input = input;
    }

    public void parse() {
        ...
    }

    private String parseUri(String requestString) {
        ...
    }

    public String getUri() {
        return uri;
    }
}
```

The **parse** method parses the raw data in the HTTP request. Not much is done by this method. The only information it makes available is the URI of the HTTP request that it obtains by calling the private method **parseUri**. **parseUri** stores the URI in the **uri** variable. The public **getUri** method is invoked to return the URI of the HTTP request.

To understand how **parse** and **parseUri** work, you need to know the structure of an HTTP request, discussed in the previous section, "The Hypertext Transfer Protocol (HTTP)." In this section, we are only interested in the first part of the HTTP request, the request line. A request line begins with a method token, followed by the request URI and the protocol version, and ends with carriage-return linefeed (CRLF) characters. Elements in a request line are separated by a space character. For instance, the request line for a request for the index.html file using the GET method is as follows.

```
GET /index.html HTTP/1.1
```

The **parse** method reads the whole byte stream from the socket's **InputStream** that is passed to the **Request** and stores the byte array in a buffer. It then populates a **StringBuilder** called **request** using the bytes in the buffer byte array, and passes the string representation of the **StringBuilder** to the **parseUri** method.

The **parse** method is given in Listing 30.8.

Listing 30.8: The Request class's parse method

```java
public void parse() {
    // Read a set of characters from the socket
    StringBuilder request = new StringBuilder(2048);
    int i;
    byte[] buffer = new byte[2048];
    try {
        i = input.read(buffer);
    } catch (IOException e) {
        e.printStackTrace();
        i = -1;
    }
    for (int j = 0; j < i; j++) {
        request.append((char) buffer[j]);
    }
    System.out.print(request.toString());
    uri = parseUri(request.toString());
}
```

The **parseUri** method then obtains the URI from the request line. Listing 30.9 presents the **parseUri** method. This method searches for the first and the second spaces in the request and obtains the URI from it.

Listing 30.9: the Request class's parseUri method

```java
private String parseUri(String requestString) {
    int index1 = requestString.indexOf(' ');
    int index2;
    if (index1 != -1) {
        index2 = requestString.indexOf(' ', index1 + 1);
        if (index2 > index1) {
            return requestString.substring(index1 + 1, index2);
        }
    }
    return null;
}
```

The Response Class

The **Response** class represents an HTTP response and is given in Listing 30.10.

Listing 30.10: The Response class

```java
package app30.webserver;
import java.io.OutputStream;
import java.io.IOException;
import java.io.InputStream;
import java.nio.file.Files;
import java.nio.file.Path;
```

```java
import java.nio.file.Paths;

/*
 HTTP Response =
 Status-Line (( general-header | response-header | entity-header ) CRLF)
 CRLF
 [ message-body ]
 Status-Line = HTTP-Version SP Status-Code SP Reason-Phrase CRLF
 */

public class Response {

    private static final int BUFFER_SIZE = 1024;
    Request request;
    OutputStream output;

    public Response(OutputStream output) {
        this.output = output;
    }

    public void setRequest(Request request) {
        this.request = request;
    }

    public void sendStaticResource() throws IOException {
        byte[] bytes = new byte[BUFFER_SIZE];
        Path path = Paths.get(System.getProperty("user.dir"),
                "webroot", request.getUri());
        if (Files.exists(path)) {
            try (InputStream inputStream =
                        Files.newInputStream(path)) {
                int ch = inputStream.read(bytes, 0, BUFFER_SIZE);
                while (ch != -1) {
                    output.write(bytes, 0, ch);
                    ch = inputStream.read(bytes, 0, BUFFER_SIZE);
                }
            } catch (IOException e) {
                e.printStackTrace();
            }
        } else {
            // file not found
            String errorMessage = "HTTP/1.1 404 File Not Found\r\n"
                    + "Content-Type: text/html\r\n"
                    + "Content-Length: 23\r\n" + "\r\n"
                    + "<h1>File Not Found</h1>";
            output.write(errorMessage.getBytes());
        }
    }
}
```

First note that the **Response** class's constructor accepts a **java.io.OutputStream** object:

```
public Response(OutputStream output) {
    this.output = output;
}
```

A **Response** object is constructed by the **HttpServer** class's **await** method by passing the **OutputStream** object obtained from the socket.

The **Response** class has two public methods: **setRequest** and **sendStaticResource** method. The **setRequest** method is used to pass a **Request** object to the **Response** object.

sendStaticResource is used to send a static resource, such as an HTML file. It starts by creating a **Path** that points to a resource under the **webroot** directory under the user directory:

```
Path path = Paths.get(System.getProperty("user.dir"),
        "webroot", request.getUri());
```

It then tests if the resource exists. If it exists, **sendStaticResource** calls **Files.newInputStream** and gets an **InputStream** that connects to the resource file. Then, it invokes the **read** method of the **InputStream** and writes the byte array to the **OutputStream** output. Note that in this case the content of the static resource is sent to the browser as raw data.

```
if (Files.exists(path)) {
    try (InputStream inputStream =
            Files.newInputStream(path)) {
        int ch = inputStream.read(bytes, 0, BUFFER_SIZE);
        while (ch != -1) {
            output.write(bytes, 0, ch);
            ch = inputStream.read(bytes, 0, BUFFER_SIZE);
        }
    } catch (IOException e) {
        e.printStackTrace();
    }
}
```

If the resource does not exist, **sendStaticResource** sends an error message to the browser.

```
String errorMessage = "HTTP/1.1 404 File Not Found\r\n" +
    "Content-Type: text/html\r\n" +
    "Content-Length: 23\r\n" +
    "\r\n" +
    "<h1>File Not Found</h1>";
output.write(errorMessage.getBytes());
```

Running the Application

To run the application, from the working directory, type the following:

```
java app30.webserver.HttpServer
```

To test the application, open your browser and type the following in the URL or Address box:

```
http://localhost:8080/index.html
```

You will see the **index.html** page displayed in your browser, as in Figure 30.2.

On the console, you can see the HTTP request similar to the following:

```
GET /index.html HTTP/1.1
Accept: image/gif, image/x-xbitmap, image/jpeg, image/pjpeg,
        application/vnd.ms-excel, application/msword, application/vnd.ms-
        powerpoint, application/x-shockwave-flash, application/pdf, */*
Accept-Language: en-us
Accept-Encoding: gzip, deflate
User-Agent: Mozilla/5.0 (Macintosh; U; Intel Mac OS X 10.5; en-US;
        rv:1.9.2.6) Gecko/20100625 Firefox/3.6.6
Host: localhost:8080
Connection: Keep-Alive

GET /images/logo.gif HTTP/1.1
Accept: */*
Referer: http://localhost:8080/index.html
Accept-Language: en-us
Accept-Encoding: gzip, deflate
User-Agent: Mozilla/5.0 (Macintosh; U; Intel Mac OS X 10.5; en-US;
        rv:1.9.2.6) Gecko/20100625 Firefox/3.6.6
Host: localhost:8080
Connection: Keep-Alive
```

Figure 30.2: The output from the web server

Note
This simple web server application was taken from my other book, "How Tomcat Works: A Guide to Developing Your Own Java Servlet Container." Consult this book for more detailed discussion of how web servers and servlet containers work.

Summary

With the emergence of the Internet, computer networking has become an integral part of life today. Java, with its **java.net** package, makes network programming easy. This chapter discussed the more important types of the **java.net** package, including **URL**, **URLConnection**, **Socket**, and **ServerSocket**. The last section of the chapter presented a simple Web application that illustrates the use of **Socket** and **ServerSocket**.

Quiz

1. Why are there several layers of protocols in computer networking?
2. What are the components of a URL?
3. What is the class that represents URLs?
4. What is a socket?
5. What is the difference between a socket and a server socket?

Chapter 31
Security

Along with a bag of goodies, the Internet brings with it a box full of viruses, spyware and other malevolent programs. You've been warned too many times to always watch what you run on your PC or Mac. A malicious program, once run, can do anything, including send your confidential files over the Internet and mercilessly wipe your hard disk. If only all applications were written in Java, then you wouldn't need to worry so much.

Java was designed with security in mind and Java security was designed for:

- Java users, i.e. people running Java applications. With Java, at least, there is ease of mind. However, as you will see later, Java users need to understand Java's security feature in order to configure security settings.
- Java developers. You can use Java APIs to incorporate fine-grained security features into your applications, such as security checks and cryptography.

There are two main topics of Java security in this chapter:

- Restricting running Java applications. Unlike applets that by default run in a restricted environment, Java applications are unrestricted.
- Cryptography, namely encrypting and decrypting your message and Java code.

This chapter starts with an overview of the security feature in Java. This section explains how you can secure a Java application and how it works in general. Then, it discusses cryptography with emphasis on asymmetric cryptography, the type of cryptography used extensively over the Internet. The immediate and practical use of cryptography is to digitally sign your code, an example of which is also given in at the end of this chapter.

Java Security Overview

When people say that Java is secure, it does not mean security comes automatically. Generally, running a Java application is not secure because it runs in an unrestricted environment. This means, a malicious Java program can do anything to its environment, including making you cry when it deletes all your precious data. It can do anything because by default, when you run an application, you give it permissions to do anything.

To impose restrictions, you must run the application with the security manager, which is a Java component responsible for restricting access to system resources. When the security manager is on, all the permissions are revoked.

Web browsers install a security manager that imposes security restrictions on applets. This is why applets by default run in a restricted environment. Java applications, on the other hand, by default run with the security manager turned off.

The security model in Java is traditionally called the sandbox model. The idea of a sandbox is that you, the user of a Java application, may restrict the application you're running within a certain "playing ground." This means, you may dictate what the application can and cannot do, especially with regard to file reading/writing, network access, etc.

With the security manager on, a Java application is pretty limited because no access to system resources is allowed. For example, it cannot read from and write to a file, it cannot establish connections to a network, it cannot read system properties, etc. I mean, you can still write methods that do those things, however when your application is run with the security manager on, the application will be paralyzed.

Most applications cannot run properly in this very restricted situation, so you need to relax some of the restrictions by giving the application some permissions. For example, you might give an application the permission to read files but not to delete them. Or, you might grant an application access to the network but ban input/output operations. The way to tell the security manager what permissions are allowed is by passing a policy file. A policy file is a text file, so no programming is necessary to configure security settings for the security manager.

Using the Security Manager

The security manager is often used in a Java program that executes other Java classes written by other people. Here are some examples:

- An applet viewer. An applet viewer is a Java application that runs applets. Applets can be written by other parties and it is in the interest of the applet viewer to make sure those applets do not attack the host.
- A servlet container is a Java application that runs servlets. Servlets are like applets but run on the server side. A servlet container is normally written in Java, and when run, it can be set to restrict access of the servlets it is running. For example, if you are an ISP, you want to make sure the servlets you are hosting do not breach security.

To run a Java application with the security manager, invoke the **java** program with a **–D** flag.

```
java -Djava.security.manager MyClass arguments
```

Applications invoked this way will run under the scrutiny of the security manager and will have none of the permissions discussed in the previous section. In other words, the application will not have access to a file, will not be able to open a socket connection, and so on. In many cases, this is too restrictive.

You can give an application permissions to perform otherwise restricted operations by telling the security manager which permissions you are willing to relax. You do this by writing a policy file. It is a text file with the **policy** extension and lists all the permissions granted to the application.

Note
You can use a text editor to create or edit a policy file or you can use the Policy Tool, which is included in the JDK. The Policy Tool is discussed in the section "The Policy Tool."

Here is the syntax for passing a policy file to the **java** tool.

```
java -Djava.security.manager -Djava.security.policy=policyFile
     MyClass arguments
```

where *policyFile* is the path to a policy file, *MyClass* is the Java class to invoke, and *arguments* is the list of arguments for the Java class.

If the **java** program is invoked with **–Djava.security.manager** but no **-Djava.security.policy** is used, the default policy files is used. The default policy files are specified in the security properties file (**java.security** file) under the **${java.home}/lib/security** directory, where **${java.home}** is the installation directory of your JRE.

The security properties file specifies security-related settings, such as policy files, provider package names, whether or not property file expansion is allowed, etc.

To add a policy file into the security properties file, use the property name **policy.url.*n***, where *n* is a number. For instance, the following sets a policy file called **myApp.policy** located in **C:\user** directory (in Windows):

```
policy.url.3=file:/C:/user/myApp.policy
```

And, this one sets the policy file **myApp.policy** in **/home/userX** directory:

```
policy.url.3=file:/home/userX/myApp.policy
```

Policy Files

A policy configuration file, or a policy file for short, contains a list of entries. It can contain an optional **keystore** entry and any number of **grant** entries. Listing 31.1 shows the the content of the default policy file **java.policy** that can be found under **${java.home}/lib/security**. It has two **grant** entries and no **keystore** entry. Note that the line starting with // is a comment.

Listing 31.1: The default policy file
```
// Standard extensions get all permissions by default
grant codeBase "file:${{java.ext.dirs}}/*" {
        permission java.security.AllPermission;
};

// default permissions granted to all domains
grant {
    // Allows any thread to stop itself using the
    // java.lang.Thread.stop() method that takes no argument.
    // Note that this permission is granted by default only to
    // remain backwards compatible.
    // It is strongly recommended that you either remove this
```

```
        // permission from this policy file or further restrict it to
        // code sources that you specify, because Thread.stop() is
        // potentially unsafe.
        // See the API specification of java.lang.Thread.stop() for more
        // information.
        permission java.lang.RuntimePermission "stopThread";

        // allows anyone to listen on dynamic ports
        permission java.net.SocketPermission "localhost:0", "listen";

        // "standard" properies that can be read by anyone
        permission java.util.PropertyPermission "java.version", "read";
        permission java.util.PropertyPermission "java.vendor", "read";
        permission java.util.PropertyPermission "java.vendor.url",
            "read";
        permission java.util.PropertyPermission "java.class.version",
            "read";
        permission java.util.PropertyPermission "os.name", "read";
        permission java.util.PropertyPermission "os.version", "read";
        permission java.util.PropertyPermission "os.arch", "read";
        permission java.util.PropertyPermission "file.separator",
            "read";
        permission java.util.PropertyPermission "path.separator",
            "read";
        permission java.util.PropertyPermission "line.separator",
            "read";

        permission java.util.PropertyPermission
            "java.specification.version", "read";
        permission java.util.PropertyPermission
            "java.specification.vendor", "read";
        permission java.util.PropertyPermission
            "java.specification.name", "read";

        permission java.util.PropertyPermission
            "java.vm.specification.version", "read";
        permission java.util.PropertyPermission
            "java.vm.specification.vendor", "read";
        permission java.util.PropertyPermission
            "java.vm.specification.name", "read";
        permission java.util.PropertyPermission "java.vm.version",
            "read";
        permission java.util.PropertyPermission "java.vm.vendor",
            "read";
        permission java.util.PropertyPermission "java.vm.name", "read";
};
```

The default policy file lists the activities that are permitted when running the security manager using this file. For example, the last few lines specify the permission to read system properties. The **java.version**, and **java.vendor** system properties are allowed to be read. But, reading other system properties, such as **user.dir** is not allowed. Therefore, the default policy is very restricted. In most cases you want to write a policy file that gives the application more room to maneuver.

The rest of this section discusses **keystore** and **grant** entries. It teaches you how to write your own policy file.

Note
Policy file syntax can be found at
http://download.oracle.com/javase/8/docs/technotes/guides/security/ PolicyFiles.html.

keystore

This entry specifies a keystore that stores private keys and related certificates. Keystores are discussed in the section "Java Cryptography."

grant

A **grant** entry includes one or more permission entries, preceded by optional **codeBase**, **signedBy**, and **principal** name/value pairs that specify which code to be granted permissions. The syntax of the **grant** entry is as follows.

```
grant [signedBy "signerNames"], [codeBase "URL"],
  [ principal principal_class_name_1 "principal_name_1",
    principal principal_class_name_2 "principal_name_2",
    ...
    principal principal_class_name_n principal_name_n
  ]
{
  permission permission_class_name_1 "target_name_1", "action_1",
    signedBy "signer_name_1"
  permission permission_class_name_2 "target_name_2", "action_2",
    signedBy "signer_name_2"
  ...
  permission permission_class_name_n "target_name_n", "action_n",
    signedBy "signer_name_n"
}
```

The order of **signedBy**, **codeBase**, and **principal** values is not important.

A **codeBase** value indicates the URL of the source code you are granting permission(s) to. An empty **codeBase** means any code. For example, the following **grant** entry grants the permission associated with the **java.security.AllPermission** class to the directory denoted by the value of **java.ext.dirs** directory:

```
grant codeBase "file:${{java.ext.dirs}}/*" {
    permission java.security.AllPermission;
};
```

The **signedBy** entry indicates the alias for a certificate stored in the keystore. This explanation probably does not make sense unless you have read and understood the section on Java cryptography. Therefore, feel free to revisit this section after you read the whole chapter.

A **principal** value specifies a *className/principalName* pair which must be present within the executing threads principal set. Again, revisit this section after you've understood the concept of Java cryptography.

For now, note that a **grant** entry consists of one or more **permission** entry. Each entry specifies a permission type that the application is allowed to perform. For instance, the following permission entry specifies that the application may read the value of the **java.vm.name** system property.

```
permission java.util.PropertyPermission "java.vm.name", "read";
```

The permission entry is discussed in the next section "Permissions."

Permissions

A permission is represented by the **java.security.Permission** class, which is an abstract class. Its subclasses represent permissions to access different types of access to system resources. For example, the **java.io.FilePermission** class represents a permission to read and write to a file.

The permission entry in a policy file has the following syntax:

```
permission permissionClassName target action
```

The *permissionClassName* argument specifies a permission type that corresponds to a specific permission. For example, the **java.io.FilePermission** class refers to file manipulation operations.

The *target* argument specifies the target of the permission. Some permission types require a target, some don't.

The *action* argument specifies the type of action associated with this permission.

For example, consider the following **permission** entry.

```
permission java.util.PropertyPermission "os.name", "read";
```

The permission class **java.util.PropertyPermission** concerns with reading and writing system properties. The "os.name" target specifies the system property **os.name**, and "read" specifies the action. The permission entry says that the application is permitted to read the system property **os.name**.

The following subsections describe each of the standard permission classes in Java.

java.io.FilePermission

This class represents permissions for file reading, writing, deletion, and execution. The constructor of this class accept two arguments, a target and an action.

```
public FilePermission(java.lang.String path,
        java.lang.String actions)
```

The *target* argument contains the name of a file or a directory. There must be no white spaces in the string. You can use an asterisk to represent all files in a directory and a hyphen to represent the contents of a directory recursively. Table 31.1 lists some examples and their descriptions.

The *action* argument describe a possible action. Its value is one of the following:

read, **write**, **delete**, and **execute**. You can use the combination of the four. For example, "read,write" means that the permission concerns the reading and writing of the target file or directory.

Target	Description
myFile	the myFile file in the current directory
myDirectory	the myDirectory directory in the current directory
myDirectory/	the myDirectory directory in the current directory
myDirectory/*	all files in the myDirectory directory
myDirectory/-	all files under myDirectory and under direct and indirect subdirectories of myDirectory
*	all files in the current directory
-	all files under the current directory
<<ALL FILES>>	a special string that denotes all files in the system.

Table 31.1: Examples of targets of FilePermission

Note
Use \ as the directory separator in Windows. Therefore, **C:\\temp*** denotes all files under **C:\temp**. You need to escape the backslash character.

java.security.BasicPermission

The **BasicPermission** class is a subclass of **Permission**. It is used as the base class for "named" permissions, i.e. ones that contain no actions. Subclasses of this class include **java.lang.RuntimePermission**, **java.security.SecurityPermission**, **java.util.PropertyPermission**, and **java.net.NetPermission**.

java.util.PropertyPermission

The **PropertyPermission** class represents the permissions to read the specified system property (by using the **getProperty** method on **java.lang.System**) and to alter the value of the specified property (by invoking the **setProperty** method on **java.lang.System**). The targets for this permission are the names of Java properties, such as "java.home" and "user.dir". You can use an asterisk to denote any property or to substitute part of the name of a property. In other words, "user.*" denotes all properties whose names have the prefix "user.".

java.net.SocketPermission

This permission represents access to a network via sockets. The target for this permission has the following syntax.

```
hostName:portRange
```

where *hostname* can be expressed as a single host, an IP address, localhost, an empty string (the same as localhost), hostname.domain, hostname.subDomain.domain, *.domain (all hosts in the specified domain), *.subDomain.domain, and * (all hosts).

portRange can be expressed as a single port, **N-** (all ports numbered N and above), **-N** (all ports numbered N and below), and **N1-N2** (all ports between N1 and N2, inclusive). A port number must be between 0 and 65535 (inclusive).

The possible values for actions are **accept**, **connect**, **listen**, and **resolve**. Note that the first three values imply **resolve** as well.

java.security.UnresolvedPermission

This class represents permissions that were unresolved when the Policy was initialized, i.e. permissions whose classes do not yet exist at the time the policy is initialized.

java.lang.RuntimePermission

The **RuntimePermission** class represents a runtime permission. It is used without an action and the target can be one of the following (all self-explanatory)

```
createClassLoader
getClassLoader
setContextClassLoader
setSecurityManager
createSecurityManager
exitVM
setFactory
setIO
modifyThread
modifyThreadGroup
stopThread
getProtectionDomain
readFileDescriptor
writeFileDescriptor
loadLibrary.{libraryName}
accessClassInPackage.{packageName}
defineClassInPackage.{packageName}
accessDeclaredMembers.{className}
queuePrintJob
```

java.awt.AWTPermission

AWTPermission represents permissions related to the AWT package. It has no actions and its possible targets are

```
accessClipboard
accessEventQueue
listenToAllAWTEvents
showWindowWithoutWarningBanner
```

java.net.NetPermission

This permission is also used without actions, and its possible targets are

```
requestPasswordAuthentication
setDefaultAuthenticator
specifyStreamHandler
```

java.lang.reflect.ReflectPermission

This permission is related to reflective operations and has no actions. There is only one name defined: **suppressAccessChecks**, which is used to denote the permission to suppress the standard Java language access checks for public, default, protected, or private members.

java.io.SerializablePermission

This permission has no action and its target is one of the following.

```
enableSubclassImplementation
enableSubstitution
```

java.security.SecurityPermission

The **SecurityPermission** class represents a permission to access security-related objects, such as Identity, Policy, Provider, Security, and Signer. This permission is used with no actions and here are its possible targets.

```
setIdentityPublicKey
setIdentityInfo
printIdentity
addIdentityCertificate
removeIdentityCertificate
getPolicy
setPolicy
getProperty.{key}
setProperty.{key}
insertProvider.{providerName}
removeProvider.{providerName}
setSystemScope
clearProviderProperties.{providerName}
putProviderProperty.{providerName}
removeProviderProperty.{providerName}
getSignerPrivateKey
setSignerKeyPair
```

java.security.AllPermission

This permission is used as a shortcut to denote all permissions.

javax.security.auth.AuthPermission

This permission represents authentication permissions and authentication-related objects, such as **Configuration**, **LoginContext**, **Subject**, and **SubjectDomainCombiner**. This class is used without actions and can have one of the following as its target.

```
doAs
doAsPrivileged
getSubject
getSubjectFromDomainCombiner
setReadOnly
modifyPrincipals
modifyPublicCredentials
modifyPrivateCredentials
refreshCredential
destroyCredential
createLoginContext.{name}
getLoginConfiguration
setLoginConfiguration
refreshLoginConfiguration
```

Using the Policy Tool

Using a text editor to create and edit a policy file is error-prone. Besides, you will have to remember a number of things, including the permission classes and the syntax of each entry. Java comes with a tool named Policy Tool that you can invoke by typing **policytool**.

Figure 31.1 shows the Policy Tool window. When it opens it always attempts to open the **.java.policy** file (note, the filename starts with a .) in the user's home directory. If it cannot find one it will report it as an error.

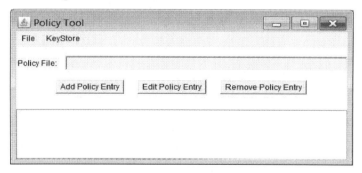

Figure 31.1: The Policy Tool window

If the default policy file is not found, you can create a new one by clicking **New** from the **File** menu or open an existing one by clicking **Open** from the File menu. The File menu also contains the **Save** menu item that you can click to save the policy file.

You can now proceed with adding a policy entry by clicking the **Add Policy Entry** button, that will open the Policy Entry window as shown in Figure 31.2.

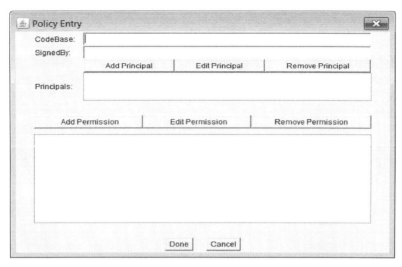

Figure 31.2: The Policy Entry window

You can add a permission by clicking the **Add Permission** button in the Policy Entry window. This will bring up the Permissions window, shown in Figure 31.3.

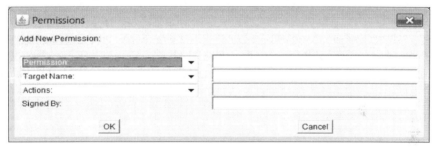

Figure 31.3: The Permission window

From the Permission window, you can select a permission class name, specify a target, and select an action. After you're finished, click the OK button, the new permission will be added to the lower box on the Policy Entry window. You can continue adding permissions and then save the policy file when you are done.

Applet Security

By default, web browsers run applets with the security manager on. In fact, an applet is very restricted because most of the time you run one written by someone else. Applets downloaded from the Net are untrusted applets and are prohibited from doing the following:

- Reading and writing to files in the client computer
- Making network connections other than the originating host.
- Defining native calls.

An applet can be made trusted by doing one of these.

- Installing the applet class on the local hard disk.
- Digitally sign the applet.

The first one is normally not an option because this means you cannot distribute your applet on the Internet. This leaves us with the second option, which is fortunately is easy enough to do using the JarSigner tool, one of the tools included in the JDK. In fact, the section "The JarSigner Tool" later in this chapter tells you how to sign an applet. However, digital signing requires you to understand cryptography, therefore you should read the section "Cryptography Overview" before starting to sign your code.

Note
More information on applet security can be found at
http://www.oracle.com/technetwork/java/javase/tech/index-jsp-136007.html.

Programming with Security

Your users may run your application with the security manager on. If nothing is done to check this in your code, your application could throw a security exception and exit unexpectedly.

To make your application security manager aware, watch out for methods that can throw a **java.lang.SecurityException**. For example, the **delete** method of the **java.nio.file.Files**, which you can use to delete a file, has the following signature:

```
public static void delete(Path path) throws java.io.IOException
```

However, if you read the description for the method in the Javadoc more carefully , you will see the following entry:

Throws:
```
SecurityException - In the case of the default provider, and a security
      manager is installed, the SecurityManager.checkDelete(String)
      method is invoked to check delete access to the file.
```

This indicates that the **File.delete** method can be restricted by a security manager. If the user runs your application that performs **Files.delete** with a security manager that does not allow this operation, your program will crash. To avoid such an abrupt exit, enclose your code with a **try** block that catches a **SecurityException**. For example:

```
try {
    Path file = Paths.get(filename);
    Files.delete(file);
} catch (IOException e) {
} catch (SecurityException e) {
    System.err.println("You do not have permission to " +
            "delete the file.");
}
```

Cryptography Overview

From time to time there has always been a need for secure communication channels, i.e. where messages are safe and other parties cannot understand and tamper with the messages even if they can get access to them.

Historically, cryptography was only concerned with encryption and decryption, where two parties exchanging messages can be rest assured that only they can read the messages. In the beginning, people encrypt and decrypt messages using symmetric cryptography. In symmetric cryptography, you use the same key to encrypt and decrypt messages. Here is a very simple encryption/decryption technique. Today, of course, encryption techniques are more advanced than the example.

Suppose, the encryption method uses a secret number to shift forward each character in the alphabet. Therefore, if the secret number is 2, the encrypted version of "ThisFriday" is "VjkuHtkfca". When you reach the end of the alphabet, you start from the beginning, therefore y becomes a. The receiver, knowing the key is 2, can easily decrypt the message.

However, symmetric cryptography requires both parties know in advance the key for encryption/decryption. Symmetric cryptography is not suitable for the Internet for the following reasons

- Two people exchanging messages often do not know each other. For example, when buying a book at Amazon.com you need to send your particulars and credit card details. If symmetric cryptography was to be used, you would have to call Amazon.com prior to the transaction to agree on a key.
- Each person wants to be able to communicate with many other parties. If symmetric cryptography was used, each person would have to maintain different unique keys, each for a different party.
- Since you do not know the entity you are going to communicate with, you need to be sure that they are really who they claim to be.
- Messages over the Internet pass through many different computers. It is fairly trivial to tap other people's messages. Symmetric cryptography does not guarantee that a third party may not tamper with the data.

Therefore, today secure communication over the Internet uses asymmetric cryptography that offers the following three features:

- encryption/decryption. Messages are encrypted to hide the messages from third parties. Only the intended receiver can decrypt them.
- authentication. Authentication verifies that an entity is who it claims to be.
- data integrity. Messages sent over the Internet pass many computers. It must be ensured that the data sent is unchanged and intact.

In asymmetric cryptography, public key encryption is used. With this type of encryption, data encryption and decryption is achieved through the use of a pair of asymmetric keys: a public key and a private key. A private key is private. The owner must keep it in a secure place and it must not fall into the possession of any other party. A public key is to be distributed to the public, usually downloadable by anyone who would like to communicate with the owner of the keys. You can use tools to generate pairs of public keys and private keys. These tools will be discussed later in this chapter.

The beauty of public key encryption is this: data encrypted using a public key can only be decrypted using the corresponding private key; at the same token data encrypted using a private key can only be decrypted using the corresponding public key. This elegant algorithm is based on very large prime numbers and was invented by Ron Rivest, Adi Shamir, and Len Adleman at Massachusetts Institute of Technology (MIT) in 1977. They simply called the algorithm RSA, based on the initials of their last names.

The RSA algorithm proves to be practical for use on the Internet, especially for e-commerce, because only a vendor is required to have one single pair of keys for communications with all its buyers and purchasers do not need to have a key at all.

An illustration of how public key encryption works normally use two figures called Bob and Alice, so we'll use them too here.

Encryption/Decryption

One of the two parties who want to exchange messages must have a pair of keys. Suppose Alice wants to communicate with Bob and Bob has a public key and a private key. Bob will send Alice his public key and Alice can use it to encrypt messages sent to Bob. Only Bob can decrypt them because he owns the corresponding private key. To send a message to Alice, Bob encrypts it using his private key and Alice can decrypt it using Bob's public key.

However, unless Bob can meet with Alice in person to hand over his public key, this method is far from perfect. Anybody with a pair of keys can claim to be Bob and there is no way Alice can find out. On the Internet, where two parties exchanging messages often live half a globe away, meeting in person is often not possible.

Authentication

In SSL authentication is addressed by introducing certificates. A certificate contains the following:

- a public key,
- information about the subject, i.e. the owner of the public key,
- the certificate issuer's name,
- some timestamp to make the certificate expire after a certain period of time.

The crucial thing about a certificate is that it must be digitally signed by a trusted certificate issuer, such as VeriSign or Thawte. To digitally sign an electronic file (a document, a Java jar file, etc) is to add your signature to your document/file. The original file is not encrypted, and the real purpose of signing is to guarantee that the document/file has not been tampered with. Signing a document involves creating the digest of the document and encrypted the digest using the signer's private key. To check if the document is still in its still original condition, you perform these two steps.

1. Decrypt the digest accompanying the document using the signer's public key. You will soon learn that the public key of a trusted certificate issuer is widely available.
2. Create a digest of the document.
3. Compare the result of Step 1 and the result of Step 2. If the two match, then the file is original.

Such authentication method works because only the holder of the private key can encrypt the document digest, and this digest can only be decrypted using the associated public key. Assuming you trust that you hold the original public key, then you know that the file has not been changed.

Note
Because certificates can be digitally signed by a trusted certificate issuer, people make their certificates publicly available, instead of their public keys.

There are a number of certificate issuers, including VeriSign and Thawte. A certificate issuer has a pair of public key and private key. To apply for a certificate, Bob has to generate a pair of keys and send his public key to a certificate issuer, who would later authenticate Bob by asking him to send a copy of his passport or other types of identification. Having verified Bob, a certificate issuer will sign the certificate using its private key. By 'signing' it means encrypting. Therefore, the certificate can only be read by using the certificate issuer's public key. The public key of a certificate issuer is normally distributed widely. For example, Internet Explorer, Netscape, FireFox and other browsers by default include several certificate issuers' public keys.

For example, in Chrome, click the Chrome menu on the browser toolbar --> Settings --> Show advanced settings --> Manage certificates. Then, click the Trusted Root Certification Authorities tab to see the list of certificates. (See Figure 31.4).

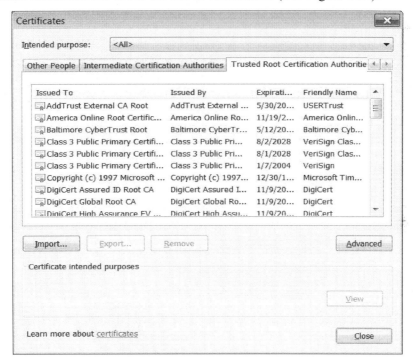

Figure 31.4: Certificate issuers whose public keys are embedded in Chrome

Now, having a certificate, Bob will distribute the certificate instead of his public key before exchanging messages with another party.

Here is how it works.

A->B   Hi Bob, I'd like to speak with you, but first of all I need to make sure that you're really Bob.

B->A   Understandable, here is my certificate

A->B   This is not sufficient, I need something else from you

B->A   Alice, it's really me + [message digest encrypted using Bob's private key]

In the last message from Bob to Alice, the message has been signed using Bob's private key, to convince Alice that the message is authentic. This is how authentication is proved. Alice contacts Bob and Bob sends his certificate. However, a certificate alone is not sufficient because anyone can get Bob's certificate. Remember that Bob sends his certificate to anyone who wants to exchange messages with him. Therefore, Bob sends her a message ("Alice, it's really me") and the digest of the same message encrypted using his private key.

Alice gets Bob's public key from the certificate. She can do it because the certificate is signed using the certificate issuer's private key and Alice has access to the certificate issuer's public key (her browser keeps a copy of it). Now, she also gets a message and the digest encrypted using Bob's private key. All Alice needs to do is digest the message and compare it with the decrypted digest Bob sent. Alice can decrypt it because it has been encrypted using Bob's private key, and Alice has Bob's public key. If the two match, Alice can be sure that the other party is really Bob.

The first thing Alice does after authenticating Bob is to send a secret key that will be used in subsequent message exchange. That's right, once a secure channel is established, SSL uses symmetric encryption because it is much faster than asymmetric encryption.

Now, there is still one thing missing from this picture. Messages over the Internet pass many computers. How do you make sure the integrity of those messages because anyone could intercept those messages on the way?

Data Integrity

Mallet, a malicious party, could be sitting between Alice and Bob, trying to decipher the messages being sent. Unfortunately, even though he could copy the messages, they are encrypted and Mallet does not know the key. However, Mallet could still destroy the messages or not relay some of them. To overcome this, SSL introduces a message authentication code (MAC). A MAC is a piece of data that is computed by using a secret key and some transmitted data. Because Mallet does not know the secret key, he cannot compute the right value for the digest. The message receiver can and therefore will discover if there is an attempt to tamper with the data, or if the data is not complete. If this happens, both parties can stop communicating.

One of such message digest algorithm is MD5. It is invented by RSA and is very secure. If 128-bit MAC values are employed, for example, the chance of a malicious party's of guessing the right value is about 1 in 18,446,744,073,709,551,616, or practically never.

How SSL Works

Now you know how SSL addresses the issues of encryption/decryption, authentication, and data integration, let's review how SSL works. This time, let's take Amazon as an example (in lieu of Bob) and a buyer (instead of Alice). Amazon.com, like any other bona fide e-commerce vendor has applied for a certificate from a trusted certificate issuer. The buyer is using Chrome, which embeds the public keys of trusted certificate issuers. The buyer does not really need to know about how SSL works and does not need to have a public key or a private key. One thing he needs to ensure is that when entering important details, such as a credit card number, the protocol being used is HTTPS, instead of HTTP. This has to appear on the URL box. Therefore, instead of http://www.amazon.com, it has to start with https, such as https://secure.amazon.com. Most browsers also display a secure icon on the status bar or the URL field. Figure 31.5 shows a secure sign in Chrome.

Figure 31.5: The secure sign in Chrome

When the buyer enters a secure page (when he finishes shopping), this is the sequence of events that happens in the background, between his browser and Amazon's server.

browser: Are you really Amazon.com?

server: Yes, here is my certificate.

The browser then checks the validity of the certificate using the certificate issuer's public key to decrypt it. If something is wrong, such as if the certificate has expired, the browser warns the user. If the user agrees to continue despite the certificate being expired, the browser will continue.

browser: A certificate alone is not sufficient, please send something else.

server: I'm really Amazon.com + [the digest of the same message encrypted using Amazon.com's private key].

The browser decrypts the digest using Amazon's public key and create a digest of "I'm Really Amazon.com". If the two match, authentication is successful. The browser will then generate a random key, encrypt it using Amazon's public key. This random key is to encrypt and decrypt subsequent messages. In other words, once Amazon is authenticated, symmetric encryption is used because it is faster then asymmetric cryptography. In addition to messages, both parties also send message digests for making sure that the messages are intact and unchanged.

Let's now examine how you can create a digital certificate of your own.

Creating Certificates

You can use a Java tool called Keytool, discussed in the section "The Keytool Program," to generate pairs of public and private keys. A public key is normally wrapped in a certificate since a certificate is a more trusted way of distributing a public key. The certificate is signed using the private key that corresponds to the public key contained in the certificate. It is called a self-signed certificate. In other words, a self-signed certificate is one for which the signer is the same as the subject described in the certificate.

A self-signed certificate is good enough for people to authenticate the sender of a signed document if those people already know the sender. For better acceptance, you need a certificate signed by a Certificate Authority, such as VeriSign and Thawte. You need to send them your self-signed certificate.

After a CA authenticates you, they will issue you a certificate that replaces the self-signed certificate. This new certificate may also be a chain of certificates. At the top of the chain is the 'root', which is the self-signed certificate. Next in the chain is the certificate from a CA that authenticates you. If the CA is not well known, they will send it to a bigger CA that will authenticate the first CA's public key. The last CA will also send the certificate, hence forming a chain of certificates. This bigger CA normally has their public keys widely distributed so people can easily authenticate certificates they sign.

Java provides a set of tools and APIs that can be used to work with asymmetric cryptography explained in the previous section. With them you can do the following:

- Generate pairs of public and private keys. You can then send the public key generated to a certificate issuer to obtain your own certificate. For a fee, of course.
- Store your private and public keys to a database called a keystore. A keystore has a name and is password protected.
- Store other people's certificates in the same keystore.
- Create your own certificate by signing it with your own private key. However, such certificates will have limited use. For practice, self-signed certificates are good enough.
- Digitally sign a file. This is particularly important because browsers will only allow applets access to resources if the applets are stored in a jar file that has been signed. Signed Java code guarantee the user that you are really the developer of the class. If they trust you they may have less doubt in running the Java class.

Let's now review the tools.

The KeyTool Program

The KeyTool program is a utility to create and maintain public and private keys and certificates. It comes with the JDK and is located in the **bin** directory of the JDK. Keytool is a command-line program. To check the correct syntax, simply type keytool at the command prompt. The following will provide examples of some important functions.

Generating Key Pairs

Before you start, there are a few things to notice with regard to key generation in Java.

1. Keytool will generate a pair of public key and private key and create a certificate signed using the private key (self-signed certificate). Among others, the certificate contains the public key and the identity of the entity whose key it is. Therefore, you need to supply your name and other information. This name is called a distinguished name and contains the following information:

   ```
   CN= common name, e.g. Joe Sample
   OU=organizational unit, e.g. Information Technology
   O=organization name, e.g. Brainy Software Corp
   L=locality name, e.g. Vancouver
   S=state name, e.g. BC
   C=country, (two letter country code) e.g. CA
   ```

2. Your keys will be stored in a database called a keystore. A keystore is file-based and password-protected so that no unauthorized persons can access the private keys stored in it.

3. If no keystore is specified when generating keys or when performing other functions, the default keystore is assumed. The default keystore is named **.keystore** in the user's home directory (i.e. in the directory defined by the

user.home system property. For example, for Windows XP the default keystore is located under C:\Documents and Settings*userName* directory in Windows.
4. There are two types of entries in a keystore:
    a. Key entries, each of which is a private key accompanies by the certificate chain of the corresponding public key.
    b. Trusted certificate entries, each of which contains the public key of an entity you trust. Each entry is also password-protected, therefore there are two types of passwords, the one that protects the keystore and one that protects an entry.
5. Each entry in a keystore is identified by a unique name or an alias. You must specify an alias when generating a key pair or doing other activities with kcytool.
6. If when generating a key pair you don't specify an alias, **mykey** is used as an alias.

The shortest command to generate a key pair is this.

```
keytool -genkeypair
```

Using this command, the default keystore will be used or one will be created if none exists in the user's home directory. The generated key will have the alias **mykey**. You will then be prompted to enter a password for the keystore and supply information for your distinguished name. Finally, you will be prompted for a password for the entry.

Invoking **keytool –genkeypair** again will result in an error because it will attempt to create a pair key and use the alias **mykey** again.

To specify an alias, use the –alias argument. For example, the following command creates a key pair identified using the keyword **email**.

```
keytool -genkeypair -alias email
```

Again, the default keystore is used.

To specify a keystore, use the **–keystore** argument. For example, this command generate a key pair and store it in the keystore named **myKeystore** in the C:\javakeys directory.

```
keytool -genkeypair -keystore C:\javakeys\myKeyStore
```

After you invoke the program, you will be asked to enter mission information.

A complete command for generating a key pair is one that uses the genkeypair, alias, keypass, storepass and dname arguments. For example.

```
keytool -genkeypair -alias email4 -keypass myPassword -dname
"CN=JoeSample, OU=IT, O=Brain Software Corp, L=Surrey, S=BC, C=CA"
-storepass myPassword
```

Getting Certified

While you can use Keytool to generate pairs of public and private keys and self-signed certificates, your certificates will only be trusted by people who already know you. To get more acceptance, you need your certificates signed by a certificate authority (CA), such as VeriSign, Entrust or Thawte.

If you intend to do this, you need to generate a Certificate Signing Request (CSR) by using the –certreq argument of Keytool. Here is the syntax:

```
keytool -certreg -alias alias -file certregFile
```

The input of this command is the certificate referenced by *alias* and the output is a CSR, which is the file whose path is specified by *certregFile*. Send the CSR to a CA and they will authenticate you offline, normally by asking you to provide valid identification details, such as a copy of your passport or driver's license.

If the CA is satisfied with your credentials, they will send you a new certificate or a certificate chain that contains your public key. This new certificate is used to replace the existing certificate chain you sent (which was self-signed). Once you receive the reply, you can import your new certificate into a keystore by using the **importcert** argument of Keytool.

Importing a Certificate into the Keystore

If you receive a signed document from a third party or a reply from a CA, you can store it in a keystore. You need to assign an alias you can easily remember to this certificate.

To import or store a certificate into a keystore, use the **importcert** argument. Here is the syntax.

```
keytool -importcert -alias anAlias -file filename
```

As an example, to import the certificate in the file joeCertificate.cer into the keystore and give it the alias brotherJoe, you use this:

```
keytool -importcert -alias brotherJoe -file joeCertificate.cer
```

The advantages of storing a certificate in a keystore is twofold. First, you have a centralized store that is password protected. Second, you can easily authenticate a signed document from a third party if you have imported their certificate in a keystore.

Exporting a Certificate from the Keystore

With your private key you can sign a document. When you sign the document, you make a digest of the document and then encrypt the digest with your private key. You then distribute the document as well as the encrypted digest.

For others to authenticate the document, they must have your public key. For security, your public key needs to be signed too. You can self-sign it or you can get a trusted certificate issuer to sign it.

The first thing to do is extract your certificate from a keystore and save it as a file. Then, you can easily distribute the file. To extract a certificate from a keystore, you need to use the **–exportcert** argument and pass the alias and the name of the file to contain your certificate. Here is the syntax:

```
keytool -exportcert -alias anAlias -file filename
```

A file containing a certificate is typically given the .cer extension. For example, to extract a certificate whose alias is Meredith and save it to the meredithcertificate.cer file, you use this command:

```
keytool -exportcert -alias Meredith -file meredithcertificate.cer
```

Listing Keystore Entries

Now that you have a keystore to store your private keys and the certificates of parties you trust, you can enquiry its content by listing it using the keytool program. You do it by using the **list** argument.

```
keytool -list -keystore myKeyStore -storepass myPassword
```

Again, the default keystore is assumed if the keystore argument is missing.

The JarSigner Tool

As you have seen, Keytool is a great tool for generating keys and maintaining them. To sign documents or Java classes, you need another tool: JarSigner. In addition to sign documents, JarSigner can also be used to verify the signatures and integrity of signed jar files from third parties.

Using JarSigner, you must first save your file(s) in a jar file. You can do this using the **jar** tool, which was explained in Appendix C, "jar." In addition to signing a jar file, JarSigner can also be used to verify the signature and integrity of a signed jar file. Let's review these two functions below.

Signing JAR Files

As the name implies, JarSigner can only be used to sign jar files, one at a time. Therefore, if you have a document you want to sign, you need to first package it using the **jar** tool (explained in Appendix C, "jar").

Here is the syntax for JarSigner.

```
jarsigner [options] -signedJar newJarFile jarFile alias
```

where *jarFile* is the path to the jar file to be signed, and *newJarFile* is the resulting output. The new jar file is exactly the same as the signed jar, except that it has two extra files under the META-INF directory. The two extra files are a signature file (with a .SF extension) and a signature block file (with a .DSA extension).

You can sign a jar file multiple times, each using a different alias.

Verifying Signed JAR Files

Verifying a signed jar file includes checking that the signature in the jar file is valid and the documents signed have not been tampered with. You use the **jarsigner** program with the –verify argument to verify a signed jar file. Its syntax is as follows:

```
jarsigner -verify [options] jarFile
```

where *jarFile* is the path to the jar file to be verified.

The **jarsigner** program verifies a jar file by examining the signature in the .SF file and the digest listed in each entry in the .SF file with each corresponding section in the manifest.

An Example: Signing an Applet

The following example shows how to use Java cryptography to sign an applet. The applet class (**MyApplet**) is given in Listing 31.2.

Listing 31.2: MyApplet.java

```java
package app31;
import java.applet.Applet;
import java.awt.Graphics;
import java.io.BufferedWriter;
import java.io.IOException;
import java.io.PrintWriter;
import java.nio.charset.Charset;
import java.nio.file.Files;
import java.nio.file.Path;
import java.nio.file.Paths;
import java.nio.file.StandardOpenOption;

public class MyApplet extends Applet {

    StringBuilder buffer = new StringBuilder();

    public void start() {
        buffer.append("Trying to create Test.txt "
                + "in the browser's installation directory.");
        Path file = Paths.get("Test.txt");
        Charset charset = Charset.forName("US-ASCII");
        try (BufferedWriter bufferedWriter = Files.newBufferedWriter(
                file, charset, StandardOpenOption.CREATE,
                StandardOpenOption.APPEND);
            PrintWriter pw = new PrintWriter(bufferedWriter)) {
            pw.write("Hello");
            pw.close();
            buffer.append(" Writing successful");
        } catch (IOException e) {
            buffer.append(e.toString());
        } catch (SecurityException e) {
            buffer.append(e.toString());
        }
        repaint();
    }

    public void paint(Graphics g) {
        //Draw a Rectangle around the applet's display area.
        g.drawRect(0, 0, getSize().width - 1,
                getSize().height - 1);
        g.drawString(buffer.toString(), 10, 20);
    }
}
```

The **MyApplet** applet attempts to write to a file and needless to say it will throw a **SecurityException** if run in a browser because the browser will impose a security restriction against access to the client's file system. Signing the applet would persuade the browser to relax its security restriction. The browser will check if the applet has been signed by a trusted party. If it has, the applet will be granted access. If the signer is not trusted, the browser will ask the user to either grant or reject permissions.

Before you can sign the applet, you must first package it in a jar file. This is very easy to achieve by using the jar program discussed in Appendix C, "jar." Basically, all you need is run this command in the directory that contains the **app31** subdirectory where the class file resides.

```
jar -cf MyJar.jar app31/MyApplet.class
```

You'll get a jar file named **MyJar.jar**.

Now, sign the jar file using jarsigner:

```
jarsigner -verbose -signedJar MySignedJar.jar MyJar.jar mykey
```

where **mykey** is a key in your keystore. you'll be prompted to enter the password for the keystore. The result will be the **MySignedJar.jar** file. We're ready to test it to run in a browser. The HTML file in Listing 31.3 is needed to call the applet.

Listing 31.3: The HTML that calls the applet

```
<html>
<head>
<title>Testing Signed Applet</title>
</head>
<body>
<applet code="app31.MyApplet.class" archive="MySignedJar.jar" width="600"
        height="50">
</applet>
</body>
</html>
```

Now, when you invoke the HTML page containing the applet, the browser will ask you the permission to run the applet, because the applet has not been signed by a trusted CA. Figure 31.6 shows the security warning.

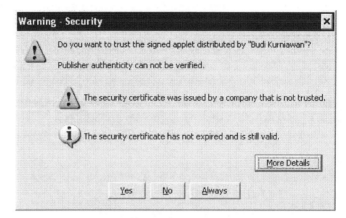

Figure 31.6: The security warning asking the user whether to grant permissions to an applet

The More Details button reveals the details of the signature in the signed applet. Figure 31.7 shows these details.

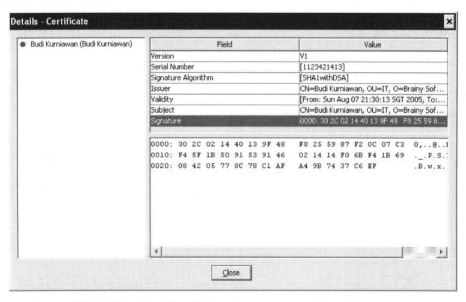

Figure 31.7: The details of the signature used to sign the applet

If you grant it access, the applet will have access to create a file and write to the file. You will see something like Figure 31.8.

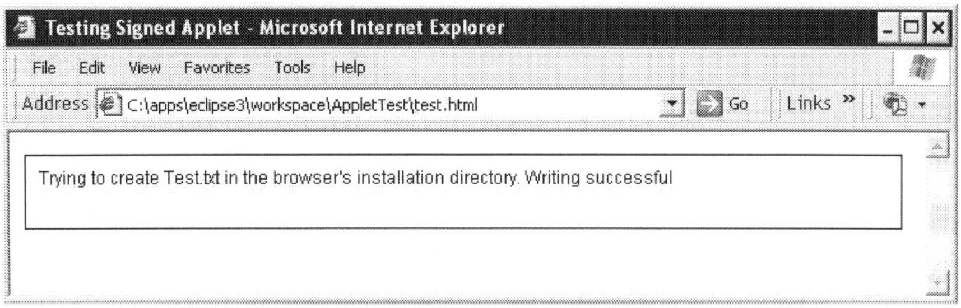

Figure 31.8: The applet has successfully access the file system

Note
The application that accompanies this chapter include the **MySignedJar.jar** file
that has been signed using my signature. Included for your convenience.

Java Cryptography API

For a beginner, it is sufficient if you understand the concept of public key encryption and
know how to generate key pairs and sign a jar file. Java offers more, however. You can do
what you can do with keytool programmatically by using the Java Cryptography API.
You are recommended to look into the **javax.crypto** package if you are interested in
knowing more about Java cryptography.

Summary

This chapter explained how the security manager restricts a Java application and how to
write a policy file to grant permissions to the application. It also discussed asymmetric
cryptography and how Java implements it. Towards the end of the chapter you have seen
how to digitally sign an applet so it could write to the user's file system.

Quiz

1. What is a policy file?
2. Why is symmetric cryptography not suitable for use on the Internet?
3. What is a keystore?
4. What are the steps to digitally sign an applet?

Chapter 32
Java Web Applications

There are three 'official' technologies for developing web applications in Java: Servlet, JavaServer Pages (JSP), and JavaServer Faces (JSF). They are not part of the Java Standard Edition (SE) but members of the Java Enterprise Edition (EE). However, considering that web applications are the most popular applications today, they are also covered in this book. Each technology is complex enough to require a book of its own, therefore I can only promise an introduction here. I recommend my own *Servlet & JSP: A Tutorial* (ISBN 978-0-9808396-2-3) if you're interested in learning more.

Of the three, Servlet is the core technology on which JSP and JSF are based. The emergence of JSP after servlets did not make Servlet obsolete. Rather, they are used together in modern Java web applications.

This chapter explores the Servlet 3.0 API and presents a few servlet applications as examples. Chapter 33, "JavaServer Pages" covers JSP.

Servlet Application Architecture

A servlet is basically a Java program. A servlet application consists of one or more servlets. A servlet application runs inside a servlet container and cannot run on its own. A servlet container, also known as a servlet engine, passes requests from the user to the servlet application and responses from the servlet application back to the user. Most servlet applications include at least several JSP pages. As such, it's more appropriate to use the term "servlet/JSP application" to refer to a Java web application than to leave JSP out.

Figure 32.1 shows the architecture of a servlet/JSP application. Web users use a web browser such as Internet Explorer, Mozilla Firefox or Google Chrome to access servlet applications. A web browser is referred to as a web client.

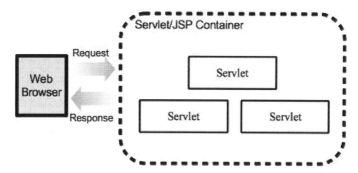

Figure 32.1: Servlet/JSP application architecture

In all web applications, the server and the client communicate using a language they both are fluent in: the Hypertext Transfer Protocol (HTTP). Because of this, a web server is also called an HTTP server. HTTP is covered in Chapter 30, "Java Networking."

A servlet/JSP container is a special web server that can process servlets as well as serve static contents. In the past, people were more comfortable running a servlet/JSP container as a module of an HTTP server such as the Apache HTTP Server because an HTTP server was considered more robust than a servlet/JSP container. In this scenario, the servlet/JSP container was tasked with generating dynamic contents and the HTTP server with serving static resources. Today servlet/JSP containers are considered mature and widely deployed without an HTTP server. Apache Tomcat and Jetty are the most popular servlet/JSP containers that are free and open-source. You can download them from http://tomcat.apache.org and http://jetty.codehaus.org, respectively.

Servlet and JSP are two of a multitude of technologies defined in the Java EE. Other Java EE technologies include Java Message Service (JMS), Enterprise JavaBeans (EJB), JavaServer Faces (JSF), and Java Persistence. The complete list of technologies in Java EE version 7 (the current version) can be found here.

```
http://www.oracle.com/technetwork/java/javaee/tech/index.html
```

To run a Java EE application, you need a Java EE container, such as GlassFish, WildFly, Apache TomEE, Oracle WebLogic or IBM WebSphere. You can deploy a servlet/JSP application in a Java EE container, but a servlet/JSP container is sufficient and is more light-weight than a Java EE container. Tomcat and Jetty are not Java EE containers, so they can't run EJB or JMS.

Servlet API Overview

The Servlet API comes in four packages

- **javax.servlet**. Contains classes and interfaces that define the contract between a servlet and a servlet container.
- **javax.servlet.http**. Contains classes and interfaces that define the contract between an HTTP servlet and a servlet container.
- **javax.servlet.annotation**. Contains annotations to annotate servlets, filters, and listeners. It also specifies the metadata for the annotated component.
- **javax.servlet.descriptor**. Contains types that provide programmatic access to a web application's configuration information.

This chapter focuses on some of the more important members of the **javax.servlet** and **javax.servlet.http** packages.

The javax.servlet Package

Figure 32.2 shows the main types in the **javax.servlet** package.

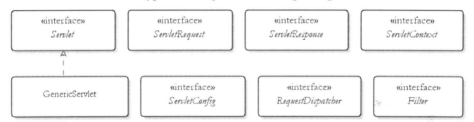

Figure 32.2: Prominent members of the javax.servlet package

At the center of Servlet technology is **Servlet,** an interface that all servlet classes must implement either directly or indirectly. This interface defines a contract between a servlet and the servlet container. The contract boils down to the promise by the servlet container to load the servlet class into memory and call specific methods on the servlet instance. There is only one instance for each servlet type, which is shared by all requests for the servlet. See the section "Servlet" for details.

A user request for a servlet causes the servlet container to call the servlet's **service** method, passing an instance of **ServletRequest** and an instance of **ServletResponse**. The **ServletRequest** object encapsulates the current HTTP request. The **ServletResponse** object represents the HTTP response for the current user and makes sending response to the user easy.

In addition, the servlet container creates an instance of **ServletContext** that encapsulates the environment all servlets in the same application are running on. For each servlet, there is also a **ServletConfig** object that encapsulates the servlet configuration.

Let's look at these interfaces in detail in the next sections.

Servlet

All servlets must implement **javax.servlet.Servlet**, either directly or indirectly. The **Servlet** interface defines five methods:

```
void init(ServletConfig config) throws ServletException

void service(ServletRequest req, ServletResponse res)
        throws ServletException, java.io.IOException

void destroy()

java.lang.String getServletInfo()

ServletConfig getServletConfig()
```

init, **service**, and **destroy** are life cycle methods. The servlet container invokes these three methods according to these rules.

- **init**. The servlet container invokes this method the first time the servlet is requested. This method is not called at subsequent requests. You use this method to write initialization code. When invoking this method, the servlet container passes a **ServletConfig**. Normally, you assign the **ServletConfig** to a class level variable so that this object can be used from other points in the servlet class.
- **service**. The servlet container invokes this method each time the servlet is requested. You write the code that the servlet is supposed to do here. The first time the servlet is requested, the servlet container calls the **init** method and, if the **init** method finishes successfully, the **service** method. For subsequent requests, only the **service** method is invoked. When invoking the **service** method, the servlet container passes two objects: a **ServletRequest** object and a **ServletResponse** object.
- **destroy**. The servlet container invokes this method when the servlet is about to be destroyed. A servlet container destroys a servlet when the application is unloaded or when the servlet container is being shut down. Normally, you write clean-up code in this method.

getServletInfo and **getServletConfig** are non-life cycle methods defined in **Servlet**.

- **getServletInfo**. This method returns the description of the servlet. You can return any string that might be useful or even **null**.
- **getServletConfig**. This method returns the **ServletConfig** object passed by the servlet container to the **init** method. However, for the **getServletConfig** method to be able to do so, you must have assigned the **ServletConfig** object to a class level variable in the **init** method. **ServletConfig** is explained in the section "ServletConfig" in this chapter.

A very important point to note is thread safety. The servlet container creates an instance of a servlet which is shared among all users, so class-level variables are not recommended, unless they are read-only or atomic variables.

The next section, "Writing a Basic Servlet Application," shows how to implement **Servlet** to write your first servlet. Implementing **Servlet** directly is not the easiest way to write a servlet. It would be easier to extend either **GenericServlet** or **HttpServlet**. However, working directly with **Servlet** will familiarize you with the most important member of the API.

Writing a Basic Servlet Application

Writing a servlet application is surprisingly easy. You just need to create a directory structure and place your servlet classes in a certain directory. In this section you learn how to write a simple servlet application named **app32a**. Initially it contains only one servlet, **MyServlet**, which sends a greeting to the client.

You need a servlet container to run your servlets. Tomcat, an open source servlet container, is available free of charge and runs on any platform where Java is available. You should now read the following section and install Tomcat if you haven't done so.

Installing Tomcat

You can download Tomcat from http://tomcat.apache.org. To run the examples in this chapter, you need Tomcat 7 or later. You should get the latest binary distribution in either zip or gz.

After you download a Tomcat binary, extract the file. You will see several directories under the installation directory. Of special interest are the **bin** and **webapps** directories. In the **bin** directory, you will find programs to start and stop Tomcat. The **webapps** directory is important because you store your servlet applications there.

After the extraction, set the **JAVA_HOME** environment variable to the JDK installation directory.

For Windows users, it is a good idea to download the Windows installer for easier installation.

Once you're finished, you can start Tomcat by running the **startup.bat** (in Windows) or the **startup.sh** file (in Unix/Linux). By default, Tomcat runs on port 8080, so you can test Tomcat by directing your Web browser to this address:

```
http://localhost:8080
```

Writing and Compiling the Servlet Class

After you install a servlet container on your local machine, the next step is to write and compile a servlet class. This servlet class must implement **javax.servlet.Servlet**. The servlet class for this example, **MyServlet**, is given in Listing 32.1. By convention, the names of servlet classes are suffixed with **Servlet**.

Listing 32.1: The MyServlet class

```
package app32a;
import java.io.IOException;
import java.io.PrintWriter;
import javax.servlet.Servlet;
import javax.servlet.ServletConfig;
import javax.servlet.ServletException;
import javax.servlet.ServletRequest;
import javax.servlet.ServletResponse;
import javax.servlet.annotation.WebServlet;

@WebServlet(name = "MyServlet", urlPatterns = { "/my" })
```

```java
public class MyServlet implements Servlet {

    private transient ServletConfig servletConfig;

    @Override
    public void init(ServletConfig servletConfig)
            throws ServletException {
        this.servletConfig = servletConfig;
    }

    @Override
    public ServletConfig getServletConfig() {
        return servletConfig;
    }

    @Override
    public String getServletInfo() {
        return "My Servlet";
    }

    @Override
    public void service(ServletRequest request,
            ServletResponse response) throws ServletException,
            IOException {
        String servletName = servletConfig.getServletName();
        response.setContentType("text/html");
        PrintWriter writer = response.getWriter();
        writer.print("<html><head></head>"
                + "<body>Hello from " + servletName
                + "</body></html>");
    }

    @Override
    public void destroy() {
    }
}
```

The first thing that springs to mind when looking at the source code in Listing 32.1 is this annotation.

```java
@WebServlet(name = "MyServlet", urlPatterns = { "/my" })
```

The **WebServlet** annotation type is used to declare a servlet. You can name the servlet as well as tell the container what URL invokes the servlet. The **name** attribute is optional and, when present, is ordinarily given the name of the servlet class. What's important is the **urlPatterns** attribute, which is also optional but almost always present. When present, **urlPatterns** specifies the URL pattern or patterns to invoke the servlet. In **MyServlet**, **urlPatterns** is used to tell the container that the pattern **/my** should invoke the servlet.

Note that a URL pattern must begin with a forward slash.

The **init** method in **MyServlet** assigns the private transient **servletConfig** variable to the **ServletConfig** object passed to the method.

```java
    private transient ServletConfig servletConfig;
```

```
@Override
public void init(ServletConfig servletConfig)
        throws ServletException {
    this.servletConfig = servletConfig;
}
```

You only have to assign the passed **ServletConfig** to a class variable if you intend to use it from inside your servlet.

The **service** method sends a String "Hello from MyServlet" to the browser. It is invoked for every incoming HTTP request that targets the servlet.

To compile the servlet, you must include the types in the Servlet API used in the class. Tomcat includes the **servlet-api.jar** file that packages members of the **javax.servlet** and **javax.servlet.http** packages. The jar file is located in the **lib** directory under Tomcat's installation directory.

Application Directory Structure

A servlet application must be deployed in a certain directory structure. Figure 32.3 shows the directory structure for this application.

> 📂 app32a
> ⬘ 📂 WEB-INF
>   ⬘ 📂 classes
>   ⬘ 📂 app32a
>   📄 MyServlet.class
>   📂 lib

Figure 32.3: The application directory structure

The **app32a** directory at the top of the hierarchy is the application directory. Under the application directory is the **WEB-INF** directory. It in turn has two subdirectories.

- **classes**. Your servlet classes and other Java classes must reside here. The directories under classes reflect the class package. In Figure 32.3 there is one class deployed, **app32a.MyServlet**.
- **lib**. Deploy jar files required by your servlet application here. The Servlet API jar file does not need to be deployed here because the servlet container already has a copy of it. In this application, the **lib** directory is empty. An empty **lib** directory may be deleted.

You should not include your source code with your application.

A servlet/JSP application normally has JSP pages, HTML files, image files, and other resources. These should go under the application directory and are often organized in subdirectories. For instance, all image files should go to an **image** directory, all JSPs to **jsp**, etc.

Now, deploy the application to Tomcat. There are a couple of ways of doing this. The easiest is to copy the application directory and its content to the **webapps** directory under Tomcat installation. Other servlet containers offer different ways of deploying applications.

Alternatively, you can deploy your application as a war file. A war file is a jar file with **war** extension. You can create a war file using the **jar** program that comes with the JDK or other tools like WinZip. After you create a war file, copy it to Tomcat's **webapps** directory, restart Tomcat, and Tomcat will extract the WAR file automatically when it starts.

Another way to deploy a Web application on Tomcat is by editing the **server.xml** file in Tomcat's **conf** directory or by deploying a special XML file.

Invoking the Servlet

Start or restart Tomcat and direct your browser to the following URL (assuming Tomcat is configured to listen on port 8080, its default port):

```
http://localhost:8080/app32a/my
```

The output should be similar to Figure 32.4.

Figure 32.4: Response from MyServlet

ServletRequest

For every HTTP request, the servlet container creates an instance of **ServletRequest**, which encapsulates the information about the request and passes the object to the servlet's **service** method.

These are some of the methods in the **ServletRequest** interface.

```
public int getContentLength()
```
Returns the number of bytes of the request body. If the length is not known, this method returns -1.

```
public java.lang.String getContentType()
```
Returns the MIME type of the body of the request, or null if the type is not known.

```
public java.lang.String getParameter(java.lang.String name)
```
Returns the value of the specified request parameter.

```
public java.lang.String getProtocol()
```
Returns the name and version of the protocol of this HTTP request.

The most important method is **getParameter**. A common use of this method is to return the value of an HTML form field. You'll learn how to retrieve form values in the section "HTTP Servlets" later in this chapter.

getParameter can also be used to get the value of a query string. For example, if a servlet is invoked using this URI

```
http://domain/context/servletName?id=123
```

you can retrieve the value of **id** from inside your servlet using this statement:

```
String id = request.getParameter("id");
```

getParameter returns null if the parameter does not exist.

In addition to **getParameter**, you can also use **getParameterNames**, **getParameterMap**, and **getParameterValues** to retrieve form field names and values as well as the values of query strings. See the section "Http Servlets" for examples on how to use these methods.

ServletResponse

The **javax.servlet.ServletResponse** interface represents a servlet response. Prior to invoking a servlet's **service** method, the servlet container creates a **ServletResponse** object and pass it as the second argument to the **service** method. The **ServletResponse** object hides the complexity of sending response to the client's browser.

The most important method of **ServletResponse** is the **getWriter** method, which returns a **java.io.PrintWriter** object for sending character text to the client. By default, the **PrintWriter** object uses ISO-8859-1 encoding.

When sending response to the client, you send it as HTML. Before sending any HTML tag, you also want to set the content type of the response by calling the **setContentType** method, passing "text/html" as the argument. This is how you tell the browser that the content type is HTML. Most browsers by default render a response as HTML in the absence of a content type. However, some browsers will display HTML tags as plain text if you don't set the response content type.

ServletConfig

You've seen that the servlet container passes a **ServletConfig** object to the servlet's **init** method when the servlet container initializes the servlet. The **ServletConfig** object encapsulates configuration information that you can pass to a servlet. This could be useful if you want to pass dynamic information that may be different from one deployment to another to the application.

Every piece of information for the **ServletConfig** object is called an initial parameter. An initial parameter has two components: key and value. You pass an initial parameter to a servlet by using an attribute in **@WebServlet** or by declaring it in a configuration file called the deployment descriptor. You'll learn more about the deployment descriptor later in this chapter.

To retrieve an initial parameter from inside a servlet, call the **getInitParameter** method on the **ServletConfig** passed by the servlet container to the servlet's **init** method. The signature of **getInitParameter** is as follows.

```
java.lang.String getInitParameter(java.lang.String name)
```

For example, to retrieve the value of the **contactName** parameter, you would write

```
String contactName = servletConfig.getInitParameter("contactName");
```

Another method, **getInitParameterNames**, returns an **Enumeration** of all initial parameter names:

```
java.util.Enumeration<java.lang.String> getInitParameterNames()
```

In addition to **getInitParameter** and **getInitParameterNames**, **ServletConfig** offers another useful method, **getServletContext**. Use this method to retrieve the **ServletContext** object from inside a servlet. See the section "ServletContext" later in this chapter for a discussion of this object.

As an example on how to use **ServletConfig**, let's add a servlet named **ServletConfigDemoServlet** to **app26a**. The new servlet is given in Listing 32.2.

Listing 32.2: The ServletConfigDemoServlet class

```java
package app32a;
import java.io.IOException;
import java.io.PrintWriter;
import javax.servlet.Servlet;
import javax.servlet.ServletConfig;
import javax.servlet.ServletException;
import javax.servlet.ServletRequest;
import javax.servlet.ServletResponse;
import javax.servlet.annotation.WebInitParam;
import javax.servlet.annotation.WebServlet;

@WebServlet(name = "ServletConfigDemoServlet",
    urlPatterns = { "/servletConfigDemo" },
    initParams = {
        @WebInitParam(name="admin", value="Harry Taciak"),
        @WebInitParam(name="email", value="admin@example.com")
    }
)
public class ServletConfigDemoServlet implements Servlet {
    private transient ServletConfig servletConfig;

    @Override
    public ServletConfig getServletConfig() {
        return servletConfig;
    }

    @Override
    public void init(ServletConfig servletConfig)
            throws ServletException {
        this.servletConfig = servletConfig;
    }
```

```
    @Override
    public void service(ServletRequest request,
            ServletResponse response)
            throws ServletException, IOException {
        ServletConfig servletConfig = getServletConfig();
        String admin = servletConfig.getInitParameter("admin");
        String email = servletConfig.getInitParameter("email");
        response.setContentType("text/html");
        PrintWriter writer = response.getWriter();
        writer.print("<html><head></head><body>" +
                "Admin:" + admin +
                "<br/>Email:" + email +
                "</body></html>");
    }

    @Override
    public String getServletInfo() {
        return "ServletConfig demo";
    }

    @Override
    public void destroy() {
    }
}
```

As you can see in Listing 32.2, you pass two initial parameters (admin and email) to the servlet in the **initParams** attribute in **@WebServlet**:

```
@WebServlet(name = "ServletConfigDemoServlet",
    urlPatterns = { "/servletConfigDemo" },
    initParams = {
        @WebInitParam(name="admin", value="Harry Taciak"),
        @WebInitParam(name="email", value="admin@example.com")
    }
)
```

You can invoke **ServletConfigDemoServlet** using this URL:

```
http://localhost:8080/app32a/servletConfigDemo
```

The result should be similar to that in Figure 32.5.

Figure 32.5: ServletConfigDemoServlet in action

Alternatively, you can pass initial parameters in the deployment descriptor. Utilizing the deployment descriptor for this purpose is easier since the deployment descriptor is a text file and you can edit it without recompiling the servlet class. On the other hand, passing initial parameters in a @WebServlet feels counter-intuitive since initial parameters were originally designed to be easily passable to a servlet, i.e. without recompiling the servlet class.

The deployment descriptor is discussed in the section "Using the Deployment Descriptor" later in this chapter.

ServletContext

The **ServletContext** object represents the servlet application. There is only one context per web application. In the case of distributed environment, where the same application is deployed simultaneously to multi containers, there is one **ServletContext** object per Java Virtual Machine.

You can obtain the **ServletContext** object by calling the **getServletContext** method on the **ServletConfig** object.

The main reason for the existence of **ServletContext** is to share common information among resources in the same application and to enable dynamic registration of web objects. The former is done by storing objects in an internal **Map** within the **ServletContext**. Objects stored in **ServletContext** are called attributes, and objects stored here can be accessed by any servlets in the application.

The following methods are defined in **ServletContext** to deal with attributes:

```
java.lang.Object getAttribute(java.lang.String name)

java.util.Enumeration<java.lang.String> getAttributeNames()

void setAttribute(java.lang.String name, java.lang.Object object)

void removeAttribute(java.lang.String name)
```

For example, this code snippet stores a **List** in the **ServletContext**:

```
List<String> countries = ...
servletContext.setAttribute("countries", countries);
```

GenericServlet

The preceding examples showed how you could write servlets by implementing the **Servlet** interface. However, did you notice that you had to provide implementations for all methods in **Servlet**, even though often some of the methods did not contain code? In addition, you needed to preserve the **ServletConfig** object into a class level variable.

Fortunately, there is the **GenericServlet** abstract class. To ease development, **GenericServlet** implements both **Servlet** and **ServletConfig** (as well as **java.io.Serializable**) and perform the following tasks:

- Assign the **ServletConfig** object in the **init** method to a class level variable so that it can be retrieved by calling **getServletConfig**.
- Provide default implementations of all methods in the **Servlet** interface.
- Provide methods that call the methods in the **ServletConfig** object.

GenericServlet preserves the **ServletConfig** object by assigning it to a class level variable **servletConfig**. However, if you override this method, the **init** method in your servlet will be called instead. To preserve the **ServletConfig** object, you must call **super.init(servletConfig)** before your initialization code. To save you from having to do so, **GenericServlet** provides a second **init** method that does not take arguments. This method is called by the first **init** method after **ServletConfig** is assigned to **servletConfig**:

```
public void init(ServletConfig servletConfig)
        throws ServletException {
    this.servletConfig = servletConfig;
    this.init();
}
```

This means, you can write initialization code by overriding the no-argument **init** method and the **ServletConfig** object will still be preserved by the **GenericServlet** instance.

The **GenericServletDemoServlet** class in Listing 32.3 is a rewrite of **ServletConfigDemoServlet** in Listing 32.2. Note that the new servlet extends **GenericServlet** instead of implementing **Servlet**.

Listing 32.3: The GenericServletDemoServlet class

```
package app32a;
import java.io.IOException;
import java.io.PrintWriter;
import javax.servlet.GenericServlet;
import javax.servlet.ServletConfig;
import javax.servlet.ServletException;
import javax.servlet.ServletRequest;
import javax.servlet.ServletResponse;
import javax.servlet.annotation.WebInitParam;
import javax.servlet.annotation.WebServlet;

@WebServlet(name = "GenericServletDemoServlet",
    urlPatterns = { "/generic" },
    initParams = {
        @WebInitParam(name="admin", value="Harry Taciak"),
        @WebInitParam(name="email", value="admin@example.com")
```

```
    }
)
public class GenericServletDemoServlet extends GenericServlet {

    private static final long serialVersionUID = 62500890L;

    @Override
    public void service(ServletRequest request,
            ServletResponse response)
            throws ServletException, IOException {
        ServletConfig servletConfig = getServletConfig();
        String admin = servletConfig.getInitParameter("admin");
        String email = servletConfig.getInitParameter("email");
        response.setContentType("text/html");
        PrintWriter writer = response.getWriter();
        writer.print("<html><head></head><body>" +
                "Admin:" + admin +
                "<br/>Email:" + email +
                "</body></html>");
    }
}
```

As you can see, by extending **GenericServlet** you do not need to override methods that you don't plan on changing. As a result, you have cleaner code. In Listing 32.3, the only method overridden is the **service** method. Also, there is no need to preserve the **ServletConfig** object yourself. If you need to access the **ServletConfig** object, you can simply call the **getServletConfig** method of **GenericServlet**.

Invoke the servlet using this URL and the result should be similar to that of **ServletConfigDemoServlet**.

```
http://localhost:8080/app32a/generic
```

Even though **GenericServlet** is a nice enhancement to Servlet, it is not something you use frequently, however, as it is not as advanced as **HttpServlet**. **HttpServlet** is in fact the real deal and used in real-world applications. This class is explained in the next section, "HTTP Servlets."

HTTP Servlets

Most, if not all, servlet applications you write will work with HTTP. The **javax.servlet.http** package contains classes and interfaces you can use to write HTTP servlet applications. Many of the members in **javax.servlet.http** override those in **javax.servlet**. Most of the time, you will use the members in **javax.servlet.http**.

Figure 32.6 shows the main types in **javax.servlet.http**.

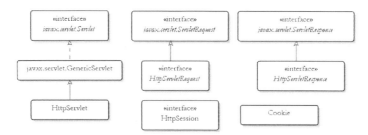

Figure 32.6: The main members of javax.servlet.http

HttpServlet

The **HttpServlet** class overrides **javax.servlet.GenericServlet**. When using **HttpServlet**, you will also work with the **HttpServletRequest** and **HttpServletResponse** objects that represent the servlet request and the servlet response, respectively. The **HttpServletRequest** interface extends **javax.servlet.ServletRequest** and **HttpServletResponse** extends **javax.servlet.ServletResponse**.

HttpServlet overrides the **service** method in **GenericServlet** and adds another **service** method with the following signature:

```
protected void service(HttpServletRequest request,
        HttpServletResponse response)
        throws ServletException, java.io.IOException
```

The difference between the new **service** method and the one in **javax.servlet.Servlet** is that the former accepts an **HttpServletRequest** and an **HttpServletResponse**, instead of a **ServletRequest** and a **ServletResponse**.

The servlet container, as usual, calls the original **service** method in **javax.servlet.Servlet**, which in **HttpServlet** is written as follows:

```
public void service(ServletRequest req, ServletResponse res)
        throws ServletException, IOException {
    HttpServletRequest request;
    HttpServletResponse response;
    try {
        request = (HttpServletRequest) req;
        response = (HttpServletResponse) res;
    } catch (ClassCastException e) {
        throw new ServletException("non-HTTP request or response");
    }
    service(request, response);
}
```

The original **service** method downcasts the request and response objects from the servlet container to **HttpServletRequest** and **HttpServletResponse**, respectively, and call the new **service** method. The **downcasting** is always successful because the servlet container always passes an **HttpServletRequest** and an **HttpServletResponse** objects when calling a servlet's **service** method, to anticipate the use of HTTP. Even if you are implementing **javax.servlet.Servlet** or extending **javax.servlet.GenericServlet**, you can downcast the servlet request and servlet response passed to the **service** method to **HttpServletRequest** and **HttpServletResponse**.

The new **service** method in **HttpServlet** then examines the HTTP method used to send the request (by calling **request.getMethod**) and call one of the following methods: **doGet**, **doPost**, **doHead**, **doPut**, **doTrace**, **doOptions**, and **doDelete**. Each of the seven methods represents an HTTP method. **doGet** and **doPost** are the most frequently used. In addition, you rarely override the **service** methods anymore. Instead, you override **doGet** or **doPost** or both **doGet** and **doPost**.

To summarize, there are two features in **HttpServlet** that you do not find in **GenericServlet**:

- Instead of the **service** method, you will override **doGet**, **doPost**, or both of them. In rare cases, you will also override any of these methods: **doHead**, **doPut**, **doTrace**, **doOptions**, **doDelete**.
- You will work with **HttpServletRequest** and **HttpServletResponse**, instead of **ServletRequest** and **ServletResponse**.

HttpServletRequest

HttpServletRequest represents the servlet request in the HTTP environment. It extends the **javax.servlet.ServletRequest** interface and adds several methods. Some of the methods are:

```
java.lang.String getContextPath()
```
Returns the portion of the request URI that indicates the context of the request.

```
Cookie[] getCookies()
```
Returns an array of Cookie objects.

```
java.lang.String getHeader(java.lang.String name)
```
Returns the value of the specified HTTP header.

```
java.lang.String getMethod()
```
Returns the name of the HTTP method with which this request was made.

```
java.lang.String getQueryString()
```
Returns the query string in the request URL.

```
HttpSession getSession()
```
Returns the session object associated with this request. If none is found, creates a new session object.

```
HttpSession getSession(boolean create)
```
Returns the current session object associated with this request. If none is found and the create argument is **true**, create a new session object.

HttpServletResponse

HttpServletResponse represents the servlet response in the HTTP environment. Here are some of the methods defined in it.

```
void addCookie(Cookie cookie)
```
Adds a cookie to this response object.

```
void addHeader(java.lang.String name, java.lang.String value)
```
Adds a header to this response object.

```
void sendRedirect(java.lang.String location)
```

Sends a response code that redirects the browser to the specified location.

Writing an Http Servlet

Extending **HttpServlet** is similar to subclassing **GenericServlet**. However, instead of overriding the **service** method, you override the **doGet** and **doPost** methods in a **HttpServlet** subclass.

The **app32b** application that accompanies this chapter features a servlet that renders an HTML form and process the form submission. The servlet is given in Listing 32.4.

Listing 32.4: The FormServlet class

```
package app32b;
import java.io.IOException;
import java.io.PrintWriter;
import java.util.Enumeration;
import javax.servlet.ServletException;
import javax.servlet.annotation.WebServlet;
import javax.servlet.http.HttpServlet;
import javax.servlet.http.HttpServletRequest;
import javax.servlet.http.HttpServletResponse;

@WebServlet(name = "FormServlet", urlPatterns = { "/form" })
public class FormServlet extends HttpServlet {
    private static final long serialVersionUID = 54L;
    private static final String TITLE = "Order Form";

    @Override
    public void doGet(HttpServletRequest request,
            HttpServletResponse response)
            throws ServletException, IOException {
        response.setContentType("text/html");
        PrintWriter writer = response.getWriter();
        writer.println("<html>");
        writer.println("<head>");
        writer.println("<title>" + TITLE + "</title></head>");
        writer.println("<body><h1>" + TITLE + "</h1>");
        writer.println("<form method='post'>");
        writer.println("<table>");
        writer.println("<tr>");
        writer.println("<td>Name:</td>");
        writer.println("<td><input name='name'/></td>");
        writer.println("</tr>");
        writer.println("<tr>");
        writer.println("<td>Address:</td>");
        writer.println("<td><textarea name='address' "
                + "cols='40' rows='5'></textarea></td>");
        writer.println("</tr>");
        writer.println("<tr>");
        writer.println("<td>Country:</td>");
        writer.println("<td><select name='country'>");
        writer.println("<option>United States</option>");
        writer.println("<option>Canada</option>");
```

```java
            writer.println("</select></td>");
            writer.println("</tr>");
            writer.println("<tr>");
            writer.println("<td>Delivery Method:</td>");
            writer.println("<td><input type='radio' " +
                      "name='deliveryMethod'"
                    + " value='First Class'/>First Class");
            writer.println("<input type='radio' " +
                      "name='deliveryMethod' "
                    + "value='Second Class'/>Second Class</td>");
            writer.println("</tr>");
            writer.println("<tr>");
            writer.println("<td>Shipping Instructions:</td>");
            writer.println("<td><textarea name='instruction' "
                    + "cols='40' rows='5'></textarea></td>");
            writer.println("</tr>");
            writer.println("<tr>");
            writer.println("<td> </td>");
            writer.println("<td><textarea name='instruction' "
                    + "cols='40' rows='5'></textarea></td>");
            writer.println("</tr>");
            writer.println("<tr>");
            writer.println("<td>Please send me the latest " +
                      "product catalog:</td>");
            writer.println("<td><input type='checkbox' " +
                      "name='catalogRequest'/></td>");
            writer.println("</tr>");
            writer.println("<tr>");
            writer.println("<td> </td>");
            writer.println("<td><input type='reset'/>" +
                      "<input type='submit'/></td>");
            writer.println("</tr>");
            writer.println("</table>");
            writer.println("</form>");
            writer.println("</body>");
            writer.println("</html>");
    }

    @Override
    public void doPost(HttpServletRequest request,
            HttpServletResponse response)
            throws ServletException, IOException {
        response.setContentType("text/html");
        PrintWriter writer = response.getWriter();
        writer.println("<html>");
        writer.println("<head>");
        writer.println("<title>" + TITLE + "</title></head>");
        writer.println("</head>");
        writer.println("<body><h1>" + TITLE + "</h1>");
        writer.println("<table>");
        writer.println("<tr>");
        writer.println("<td>Name:</td>");
        writer.println("<td>" + request.getParameter("name")
```

```
            + "</td>");
writer.println("</tr>");
writer.println("<tr>");
writer.println("<td>Address:</td>");
writer.println("<td>" + request.getParameter("address")
        + "</td>");
writer.println("</tr>");
writer.println("<tr>");
writer.println("<td>Country:</td>");
writer.println("<td>" + request.getParameter("country")
        + "</td>");
writer.println("</tr>");
writer.println("<tr>");
writer.println("<td>Shipping Instructions:</td>");
writer.println("<td>");
String[] instructions = request
        .getParameterValues("instruction");
if (instructions != null) {
    for (String instruction : instructions) {
        writer.println(instruction + "<br/>");
    }
}
writer.println("</td>");
writer.println("</tr>");
writer.println("<tr>");
writer.println("<td>Delivery Method:</td>");
writer.println("<td>"
        + request.getParameter("deliveryMethod")
        + "</td>");
writer.println("</tr>");
writer.println("<tr>");
writer.println("<td>Catalog Request:</td>");
writer.println("<td>");
if (request.getParameter("catalogRequest") == null) {
    writer.println("No");
} else {
    writer.println("Yes");
}
writer.println("</td>");
writer.println("</tr>");
writer.println("</table>");
writer.println("<div style='border:1px solid #ddd;" +
            "margin-top:40px;font-size:90%'>");

writer.println("Debug Info<br/>");
Enumeration<String> parameterNames = request
        .getParameterNames();
while (parameterNames.hasMoreElements()) {
    String paramName = parameterNames.nextElement();
    writer.println(paramName + ": ");
    String[] paramValues = request
            .getParameterValues(paramName);
    for (String paramValue : paramValues) {
```

```
                writer.println(paramValue + "<br/>");
            }
        }
        writer.println("</div>");
        writer.println("</body>");
        writer.println("</html>");
    }
}
```

You invoke the FormServlet using this URL:

```
http://localhost:8080/app32b/form
```

Typing the URL in your browser invokes the servlet's **doGet** method and you'll see an HTML form in your browser. The form is shown in Figure 32.7.

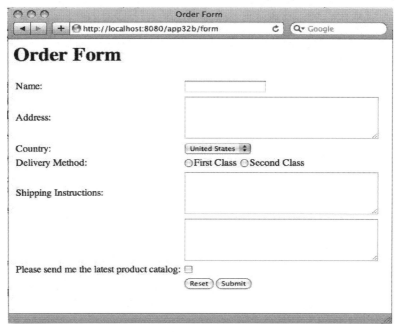

Figure 32.7: The empty Order form

If you look at the HTML source, you'll find a form with a post method like this:

```
<form method='post'>
```

Submitting the form will invoke the servlet's **doPost** method. As a result, you'll see in your browser the values that you entered to the form. Figure 32.8 shows the result of submitting the Order form.

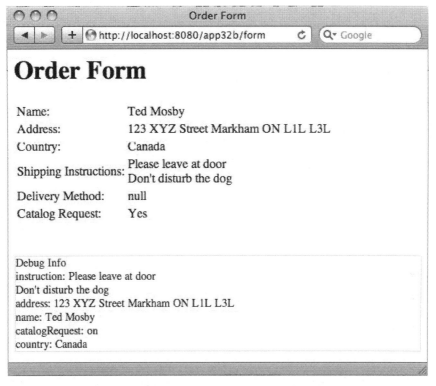

Figure 32.8: Result from submitting the Order form

Using the Deployment Descriptor

As you can see in the previous examples, writing and deploying a servlet application is easy. One aspect of deployment deals with mapping your servlet with a path. In the examples, you used the **WebServlet** annotation type to map a servlet with a path. There's another way of doing this, by using the deployment descriptor. In this section you'll learn how to configure your application using the deployment descriptor.

The **app26c** application contains two servlets, **SimpleServlet** and **WelcomeServlet** to demonstrate how you can use the deployment descriptor to map servlets. Listings 32.5 and 32.6 show **SimpleServlet** and **WelcomeServlet**, respectively. Note that the servlet classes are not annotated **@WebServlet**.

Listing 32.5: The SimpleServlet class

```
package app32c;
import java.io.IOException;
import java.io.PrintWriter;
import javax.servlet.ServletException;
import javax.servlet.http.HttpServlet;
import javax.servlet.http.HttpServletRequest;
import javax.servlet.http.HttpServletResponse;
```

```java
public class SimpleServlet extends HttpServlet {

    private static final long serialVersionUID = 8946L;

    @Override
    public void doGet(HttpServletRequest request,
            HttpServletResponse response)
            throws ServletException, IOException {
        response.setContentType("text/html");
        PrintWriter writer = response.getWriter();
        writer.print("<html><head></head>" +
                "<body>Simple Servlet</body></html");
    }
}
```

Listing 32.6: The WelcomeServlet class

```java
package app32c;
import java.io.IOException;
import java.io.PrintWriter;
import javax.servlet.ServletException;
import javax.servlet.http.HttpServlet;
import javax.servlet.http.HttpServletRequest;
import javax.servlet.http.HttpServletResponse;

public class WelcomeServlet extends HttpServlet {

    private static final long serialVersionUID = 27126L;

    @Override
    public void doGet(HttpServletRequest request,
            HttpServletResponse response)
            throws ServletException, IOException {
        response.setContentType("text/html");
        PrintWriter writer = response.getWriter();
        writer.print("<html><head></head>"
                + "<body>Welcome</body></html>");
    }
}
```

Listing 32.7 shows the deployment descriptor for **app26c** that includes mapping information for the two servlets. The deployment descriptor must be named **web.xml** and saved to the **WEB-INF** directory of the application.

Listing 32.7: The deployment descriptor

```xml
<?xml version="1.0" encoding="ISO-8859-1"?>
<web-app xmlns="http://java.sun.com/xml/ns/javaee"
    xmlns:xsi="http://www.w3.org/2001/XMLSchema-instance"
    xsi:schemaLocation="http://java.sun.com/xml/ns/javaee
        http://java.sun.com/xml/ns/javaee/web-app_3_0.xsd"
    version="3.0">
```

```
    <servlet>
        <servlet-name>SimpleServlet</servlet-name>
        <servlet-class>app32c.SimpleServlet</servlet-class>
        <load-on-startup>10</load-on-startup>
    </servlet>

    <servlet-mapping>
        <servlet-name>SimpleServlet</servlet-name>
        <url-pattern>/simple</url-pattern>
    </servlet-mapping>

    <servlet>
        <servlet-name>WelcomeServlet</servlet-name>
        <servlet-class>app32c.WelcomeServlet</servlet-class>
        <load-on-startup>20</load-on-startup>
    </servlet>

    <servlet-mapping>
        <servlet-name>WelcomeServlet</servlet-name>
        <url-pattern>/welcome</url-pattern>
    </servlet-mapping>
</web-app>
```

There are many advantages of using the deployment descriptor. For one, you can include elements that have no equivalent in **@WebServlet**, such as the **load-on-startup** element. This elements loads the servlet at the application start-up, rather than when the servlet is first called. Using **load-on-startup** means the first call to the servlet will not take longer than subsequent calls. This is especially useful if the **init** method of the servlet may take a while to complete.

Another advantage of using the deployment descriptor is that you don't need to recompile your servlet class if you need to change configuration values, such as a servlet path. In addition, you can pass initial parameters to a servlet and edit them without recompiling the servlet class.

The deployment descriptor also allows you to override values specified in a servlet annotation. A **WebServlet** annotation on a servlet that is also declared in the deployment descriptor will have no effect. However, annotating a servlet not in the deployment descriptor in an application with a deployment descriptor will still work. This means, you can have annotated servlets and declare servlets in the deployment descriptor in the same application.

Figure 32.9 shows the directory structure of **app26c**. The directory structure does not differ much from that of **app26a**. The only difference is that **app26c** has a **web.xml** file (the deployment descriptor) in the **WEB-INF** directory.

Figure 32.9: Directory structure of app32c with deployment descriptor

Now that **SimpleServlet** and **WelcomeServlet** are declared in the deployment descriptor, you can use these URLs to access them:

```
http://localhost:8080/app32c/simple
```

```
http://localhost:8080/app32c/welcome
```

Summary

Servlet technology is part of the Java EE. Servlets run in a servlet container, and the contract between the container and servlets takes the form of the **javax.servlet.Servlet** interface. The **javax.servlet** package also provides the **GenericServlet** abstract class, a convenient class that you can extend to write a servlet. However, most modern servlets will work in the HTTP environment and, as such, subclassing the **javax.servlet.http.HttpServlet** class is more convenient. The **HttpServlet** class itself is a subclass of **GenericServlet**.

Quiz

1. What are the three life cycle methods of the **javax.servlet.Servlet** interface?
2. What's the main difference between the **getWriter** method and the **getOutputStream** method in the **javax.servlet.ServletResponse** interface? Which one of the two do you use more often?
3. Name four interfaces in **javax.servlet** and three interfaces in **javax.servlet.http**.

Chapter 33
JavaServer Pages

As evidenced in Chapter 32, there are two drawbacks servlets are not capable of overcoming. First, when sending a response, all HTML tags must be enclosed in strings, making sending HTTP response a tedious effort. Second, all text and HTML tags are hardcoded, and, as a result, minor changes to an application presentation part, such as changing a page background color, requires recompilation.

JavaServer Pages (JSP) comes to the rescue and solves the two problems in servlets. JSP does not replace Servlet, however, but complements it. Modern Java Web applications use servlets and JSP pages at the same time. The latest version of JSP at the time of writing is 2.3.

A JSP Overview

A JSP page is essentially a servlet. However, working with JSP pages is easier than with servlets because of two reasons. First, you do not have to compile JSP pages. Second, JSP pages are basically text files with the **jsp** extension and you can use any text editor to write them.

JSP pages run on a JSP container. A servlet container is normally also a JSP container. Tomcat, for instance, is a servlet/JSP container. The first time a JSP page is requested, the JSP container does two things:

1. Translate the JSP page into a JSP page implementation class. This class must implement the javax.servlet.Servlet interface. The result of the translation is dependent on the JSP container. The class name is also JSP container-specific. You do not have to worry about this implementation class or its name because you never need to work with it directly. If there is a translation error, an error message will be sent to the client.
2. If the translation was successful, the JSP container compiles the implementation class, and then loads and instantiate it and perform the normal lifecycle operations it does for a servlet.

For subsequent requests for the same JSP page, the JSP container checks if the JSP page has been modified since the last time it was translated. If so, it was retranslated, recompiled, and executed. If not, the JSP servlet already in memory is executed. This way, the first invocation of a JSP page always takes longer than subsequent requests because it involves translation and compilation. To get around this problem, you can do one of the following:

- Configure the application so that all JSP pages will be called (so that they will be translated and compiled) when the application starts, rather than wait for the first

requests.
- Precompile the JSP pages and deploy them as servlets.

JSP comes with an API that comprises three packages. However, when working with JSP, you do not often work directly with this API. Instead, you will work with classes and interfaces in the Servlet API. In addition, you need to familiarize yourself with the syntax of a JSP page.

A JSP page can contain template data and syntactic elements. An element is something that has a special meaning to the JSP translator. For example, **<%** is an element because it denotes the start of a Java code block within a JSP page. **%>** is also an element because it ends a Java code block. Anything else that is not an element is template data. Template data is sent as is to the browser. For instance, HTML tags and text in a JSP page are template data.

Listing 33.1 presents a JSP page named **welcome.jsp** that sends "Welcome" to the client. Notice how simple it is compared to the servlet in Listing 32.1 that does the same thing?

Listing 33.1: The welcome.jsp page

```
<!DOCTYPE html>
<html>
<head><title>Welcome</title></head>
<body>
Welcome
</body>
</html>
```

In addition, JSP application deployment is simpler too. A JSP page is compiled into a servlet class, but a JSP does not need to be registered in the deployment descriptor or mapped. Every JSP page deployed in an application directory can be invoked by typing the name of the page. Figure 33.1 shows the directory structure of **app26**, the JSP application accompanying this chapter..

Figure 33.1: The app33 directory structure

With only a JSP page, the structure of the **app33** application is very simple. It only has the **WEB-INF** directory and the **welcome.jsp** page. The **WEB-INF** directory is empty. You don't even need a deployment descriptor.

You can invoke the **welcome.jsp** page using this URL:

```
http://localhost:8080/app33/welcome.jsp
```

Note
You do not need to restart Tomcat when adding a new JSP page.

Listing 33.2 shows how to use Java code to produce a dynamic page. The **todaysDate.jsp** page in Listing 33.2 shows today's date.

Listing 33.2: The todaysDate.jsp page

```
<%@page import="java.time.LocalDate"%>
```

```
<%@page import="java.time.format.DateTimeFormatter"%>
<%@page import="java.time.format.FormatStyle"%>
<!DOCTYPE html>
<html>
<head><title>Today's date</title></head>
<body>
<%
  LocalDate today = LocalDate.now();
  String s =
      today.format(DateTimeFormatter.ofLocalizedDate(FormatStyle.LONG));
  out.println("Today is " + s);
%>
</body>
</html>
```

The **todaysDate.jsp** page sends the string "Today is" followed by today's date (in the long format, such as August 30, 2015) to the browser.

There are two things to note. First, Java code can appear anywhere in a page and is enclosed by **<%** and **%>**. Second, to import a type to be used from Java code, you use the **import** attribute of the **page** directive. Both the **<% … %>** block and the **page** directive will be discussed much later in this chapter.

You can invoke the **todayDate.jsp** page using this URL:

```
http://localhost:8080/app33/todaysDate.jsp
```

jspInit, jspDestroy, and Other Methods

As mentioned before, a JSP is translated into a servlet source file and then compiled into a servlet class. A JSP page body more or less translates into the **service** method of **Servlet**. However, in a servlet you have the **init** and **destroy** methods for writing initialization and cleaning up code. How do you override these methods in a JSP page?

In a JSP page you have two similar methods:

- **jspInit**. This method is similar to the **init** method in **Servlet**. **jspInit** is invoked when the JSP page is initialized. One difference is **jspInit** does not take an argument. You can still obtain the **ServletConfig** object through the **config** implicit object. (See the next section, "Implicit Objects.")
- **jspDestroy**. This method is similar to the **destroy** method in **Servlet** and is invoked when the JSP page is about to be destroyed.

A method definition in a JSP page is enclosed with **<%!** and **%>**. Listing 33.3 presents the **lifeCycle.jsp** page that demonstrates how you can override **jspInit** and **jspDestroy**.

Listing 33.3: The lifeCycle.jsp page

```
<%!
    public void jspInit() {
        System.out.println("jspInit ...");
    }
    public void jspDestroy() {
        System.out.println("jspDestroy ...");
```

```
        }
%>
<!DOCTYPE html>
<html>
<head><title>jspInit and jspDestroy</title></head>
<body>
Overriding jspInit and jspDestroy
</body>
</html>
```

You can invoke the JSP page by using this URL:

```
http://localhost:8080/app27/lifeCycle.jsp
```

You will see "jspInit ..." on your console when you first invoke the JSP page, and "jspDestroy ..." when you shut down Tomcat.

A **<%! ... %>** block can appear anywhere in a JSP page, and there can be more than one **<%! ... %>** block in a single page.

You can also write other methods using the **<%! ... %>** block. These methods can be invoked from inside the JSP page.

Implicit Objects

With the **service** method in **javax.servlet.Servlet**, you get an **HttpServletRequest** and an **HttpServletResponse** objects. You also get a **ServletConfig** object (passed to the **init** method) and the **ServletContext** object. In addition, you can obtain an **HttpSession** object by calling the **getSession** method on the **HttpServletRequest** object.

In JSP, you retrieve those objects using JSP implicit objects. The implicit objects are listed in Table 33.1.

Object	Type
request	javax.servlet.http.HttpServletRequest
response	javax.servlet.http.HttpServletResponse
out	javax.servlet.jsp.JspWriter
session	javax.servlet.http.HttpSession
application	javax.servlet.ServletContext
config	javax.servlet.ServletConfig
pageContext	javax.servlet.jsp.PageContext
page	javax.servlet.jsp.HttpJspPage
exception	java.lang.Throwable

Table 33.1: JSP Implicit Objects

For example, the **request** implicit object represents the **HttpServletRequest** object passed by the servlet/JSP container to the servlet's **service** method. You can use **request** as if it was a variable reference to the **HttpServletRequest** object. For instance, the following code retrieves the **userName** parameter from the **HttpServletRequest** object.

```
<%
    String userName = request.getParameter("userName");

%>
```

The **out** implicit object references a **JspWriter** object, which is similar to the **java.io.PrintWriter** object you obtain from the **getWriter** method of the **HttpServletResponse** object. You can call its **print** method overloads just as you would a **PrintWriter** object, to send messages to the browser.

```
out.println("Welcome");
```

The **implicitObjects.jsp** page in Listing 33.4 demonstrates the use of some of the implicit objects.

Listing 33.4: The implicitObjects.jsp page

```
<%@page import="java.util.Enumeration"%>
<!DOCTYPE html>
<html>
<head><title>JSP Implicit Objects</title></head>
<body>
<b>Http headers:</b><br/>
<%
    for (Enumeration e = request.getHeaderNames();
            e.hasMoreElements(); ) {
        String header = (String) e.nextElement();
        out.println(header + ": " + request.getHeader(header) +
                "<br/>");
    }
%>
<hr/>
<%
    out.println("Buffer size: " + response.getBufferSize() +
        "<br/>");
    out.println("Session id: " + session.getId() + "<br/>");
    out.println("Servlet name: " + config.getServletName() +
        "<br/>");
    out.println("Server info: " + application.getServerInfo());
%>
</body>
</html>
```

Even though you can have retrieve the **HttpServletResponse** object through the **response** implicit object, you do not need to set the content type. By default, the JSP compiler sets the content type of every JSP to **text/html**.

The **page** implicit object represents the current JSP page and is not normally used by JSP page authors.

JSP Syntactic Elements

To write JSP pages, you need to be familiar with the JSP syntax, more than with the JSP API. There are three types of JSP syntactic elements: directives, scripting elements, and actions. Directives and scripting elements are discussed in this chapter.

Directives

Directives are instructions for the JSP translator on how a JSP page should be translated into a servlet implementation class. There are several directives defined in JSP 2.1, but only the two most important ones, **page** and **include**, are discussed in this chapter. The other directives that are not covered are **taglib**, **tag**, **attribute**, and **variable**.

The page Directive

You use the **page** directive to instruct the JSP translator on certain aspects of the current JSP page. For example, you can tell the JSP translator the size of the buffer that should be used for the **out** implicit object, what content type to use, what Java types to import, and so on.

You use the **page** directive using this syntax:

```
<%@ page attribute1="value1" attribute2="value2" ... %>
```

where the space between @ and **page** is optional and *attribute1*, *attribute2*, and so on are the **page** directive's attributes. There are 13 attributes of the **page** directive.

- **import**. Specifies the type that will be imported and useable by the Java code in this page. For example, specifying **import="java.util.ArrayList"** will import the **ArrayList** class. You can use the wildcard * to import the whole package, such as in **import="java.util.*"**. To import multiple types you can separate two types with a comma, such as in **import="java.util.ArrayList, java.nio.file.Files, java.io.PrintWriter"**. All types in the following packages are implicitly imported: **java.lang**, **javax.servlet**, **javax.servlet.http**, **javax.servlet.jsp**.
- **session**. A value of **true** indicates that this page participates in session management, and a value of **false** indicates otherwise. By default, the value is **true**, which means the invocation of this page will cause a **javax.servlet.http.HttpSession** instance to be created, if one does not yet exist.
- **buffer**. Specifies the buffer size of the **out JspWriter** object in kilobytes. The suffix **kb** is mandatory. The default buffer size is 8kb or more, depending on the JSP container. It is also possible to assign **none** to this attribute to indicate that no buffering should be used, which will cause all output is written directly through to the corresponding **PrintWriter** object.
- **autoFlush**. A value of **true**, the default value, indicates that the buffered output should be flushed automatically when the buffer becomes full. A value of **false** indicates that buffer is only flushed if the **flush** method of the response object is called. Consequently, an exception will be thrown in the case of buffer overflow.
- **isThreadSafe**. Indicates the level of thread safety implemented in the page. JSP authors are advised against using this attribute as it could result in the generated

servlet containing deprecated code.

- **info**. Specifies the return value of the **getServletInfo** method of the generated servlet.
- **errorPage**. Indicates the page that will handler errors in this page.
- **isErrorPage**. Indicates if this page is an error page handler.
- **contentType**. Specifies the content type of the response object of this page. By default, the value is **text/html**.
- **pageEncoding**. Specifies the character encoding for this page. By default, the value is **ISO-8859-1**.
- **isELIgnored**. Indicates whether EL expressions are ignored. EL, which is short for expression language, is not discussed in this chapter.
- **language**. Specifies the scripting language used in this page. By default, its value is **java** and this is the only valid value in JSP 2.0.
- **extends**. Specifies the superclass that this JSP page's implementation class must extend. This attribute is rarely used and should only be used with extra caution.

The **page** directive can appear anywhere in a page, except if it contains the **contentType** attribute or the **pageEncoding** attribute, because the content type and the character encoding must be set prior to sending any content.

The **page** directive can also appear multiple times. However, an attribute that appears in multiple **page** directives must have the same value. An exception to this is the **import** attribute. The effect of the **import** attribute appearing in multiple **page** directives is cumulative. For example, the following page directives import both **java.util.ArrayList** and **java.nio.file.Path**.

```
<%@page import="java.util.ArrayList"%>
<%@page import="java.nio.file.Path"%>
```

This is the same as

```
<%@page import="java.util.ArrayList, java.nio.file.Path"%>
```

As another example, here is another **page** directive:

```
<%@page session="false" buffer="16kb"%>
```

The include Directive

You use the **include** directive to include the content of another file in the current JSP page. You can use multiple **include** directives in a JSP page. Modularizing a particular content into an include file is useful if that content is used by different pages or used by a page in different places.

The syntax of the include directive is as follows:

```
<%@ include file="url"%>
```

where the space between **@** and **include** is optional and *url* represents the relative path to an include file. If *url* begins with a forward slash (/), it is interpreted as an absolute path on the server. If it does not, it is interpreted as relative to the current JSP page.

The JSP translator translates the **include** directive by replacing the directive with the content of the include file. In other words, if you have written the **copyright.html** file in Listing 33.5.

Listing 33.5: The copyright.html include file

```
<hr/>
&copy;2015 BrainySoftware
<hr/>
```

And, you have the **main.jsp** page in Listing 33.6.

Listing 33.6: The main.jsp page

```
<!DOCTYPE html>
<html>
<head><title>Including a file</title></head>
<body>
This is the included content: <hr/>
<%@ include file="copyright.html"%>
</body>
</html>
```

Using the **include** directive in the **main.jsp** page has the same effect as writing the following JSP page.

```
<!DOCTYPE html>
<html>
<head><title>Including a file</title></head>
<body>
This is the included content: <hr/>
<hr/>
&copy;2015 BrainySoftware
<hr/>
</body>
</html>
```

For the above **include** directive to work, the **copyright.html** file must reside in the same directory as the including page.

Scripting Elements

You use scripting elements to insert Java code into a JSP page. There are three types of scripting elements: scriptlets, declarations, and expressions. They are discussed in the following subsections.

Scriptlets

A scriptlet is a block of Java code. A scriptlet starts with the **<%** tag and ends with the **%>** tag. You have seen the use of scriplets throughout this chapter. As another example, consider the JSP page in Listing 33.7.

Listing 33.7: Using a scriplet

```
<%@page import="java.util.Enumeration"%>
<!DOCTYPE html>
<html>
<head><title>Scriptlet example</title></head>
<body>
```

```
<b>Http headers:</b><br/>
<%
    for (Enumeration e = request.getHeaderNames();
            e.hasMoreElements(); ) {
        String header = (String) e.nextElement();
        out.println(header + ": " + request.getHeader(header) +
                "<br/>");
    }
    String message = "Thank you.";
%>
<hr/>
<%
    out.println(message);
%>
</body>
</html>
```

There are two scriptlets in the JSP page in Listing 33.7. Note that variables defined in a scriptlet is visible to other scriptlets below it.

It is legal for the first line of code in a scriptlet to be in the same line as the <% tag and for the %> tag to be in the same line as the last line of code. However, this would result in a less readable page.

Expressions

An expression is evaluated and its result is fed to the **print** method of the **out** implicit object. An expression starts with **<%=** and ends with **%>**. For example, here is an expression:

```
Today is <%=java.time.LocalDate.now().toString()%>
```

Note that there is no semicolon after the expression. With this expression, the JSP container first evaluates **java.time.LocalDate.now().toString()**, and then passes the result to **out.print()**. This is the same as writing the following scriptlet:

```
Today is
<%
    out.print(java.time.LocalDate.now().toString());
%>
```

Declarations

You can declare variables and methods that can be used in a JSP page. You enclose a declaration with <%! and %>. For example, Listing 33.8 shows a JSP page that declares a method named **getTodayDate**.

Listing 33.8: Using a declaration

```
<%!
    public String getTodaysDate() {
        return java.time.LocalDate.now().toString();
    }
%>
```

```
<!DOCTYPE html>
<html>
<head><title>Declarations</title></head>
<body>
Today is <%=getTodaysDate()%>
</body>
</html>
```

Handling Errors

Error handling is well supported in JSP. Java code can be handled using the **try** statement, however you can also specify a page that will be displayed should any of the pages in the application encounter an uncaught exception. In such events, the user will see a well designed page that explains what happened, and not an error message that makes them frown.

You make a JSP page an error page by using the attribute **isErrorPage** attribute of the **page** directive. The value of the attribute must be **true**. Listing 33.9 shows such an error handler.

Listing 33.9: The errorHandler.jsp page

```
<%@page isErrorPage="true"%>
<html>
<head><title>Error</title></head>
<body>
An error has occurred. <br/>
Error message:
<%
  out.println(exception.toString());
%>
</body>
</html>
```

Other pages that need protection against uncaught exception will have to use the **errorPage** attribute of the **page** directive, citing the path to the error handling page as the value. For example, the **buggy.jsp** page in Listing 33.10 uses the error handler in Listing 33.9.

Listing 33.10: The buggy.jsp page

```
<%@page errorPage="errorHandler.jsp"%>
Deliberately throw an exception
<%
  Integer.parseInt("Throw me");
%>
```

If you run the **buggy.jsp** page, it will throw an exception. However, you will not see the error message produced by the servlet/JSP container. Instead, the content of the **errorHandler.jsp** page is displayed.

Summary

JSP is the second technology for building Web applications. JSP was invented after Servlet to complement it, not to replace it. Well designed Java Web applications use both servlets and JSP.

This chapter presented a brief introduction to JSP.

Quiz

1. What are the two problems in Servlet technology that JSP solves?
2. Why is it easier to program JSP than to write servlets?

Chapter 34
Javadoc

You already know how to write comments in your classes using the // and /* ... */ notations. These comments serve as documentation that is good mostly for the developer who is writing the class and developers who will continue work on the class. There is another type of documentation in Java. This type is suitable if you are writing API that will be used by other people. This chapter shows how to use the **javadoc** program to generate Java API documentation.

Overview

You use the **javadoc** program that comes with the JDK and can be found under the bin directory of your JDK installation. By default, **javadoc** generates HTML files that describe packages and types. Every single HTML file generated describes either a package or a type. Within a description of a type you can also describe methods and fields of the type, plus constructors of the type if the type is a class.

The input to **javadoc** is Java source files and **javadoc** is happy to overlook any compile errors in the source code. This means, you can generate documentation even before the project is complete. The output by default is a set of HTML files, however you can customize **javadoc** to format output differently.

The chapters provides two topics of discussions.

- How to write documentation in your Java class,
- How to use **javadoc** to generate HTML files.

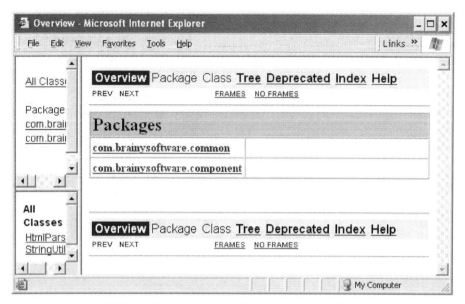

Figure 34.1: Java API documentation

Writing Documentation in Java Classes

This section teaches you how to embed documentation comments, or doc comments for short, in your source code. You can write doc comments for a class, an interface, a method, constructor, and a field.

A doc comment begins with a /* sequence and ends with a */. It can contains one or more lines of text, which is called the main description, and each line can be preceded by a *. When parsed, any leading * and tabs are ignored. A doc comment must appear right before the declaration of a class, an interface, a constructor, a method, or a field.

For example, here is a doc comment with a description "This is a comment".

```
/**
 * This is a comment
 */
```

Because by default doc comments will be generated as HTML files, be careful when part of the text in a comment contains what looks like an HTML tag, such as <b> or <i>. These will be interpreted by the browser as HTML tags. Therefore, a < has to be written as its entity code (<) and > as >, and ampersand & as **&**.

A doc comment can also contain tags, which are special keywords that can be processed. Tags must appear after the description of a doc comment. There can be multiple tags in a comment and it is possible to have tags and no description.

There are two types of tags:

- Block tags or standalone tags. Appear as **@tag**
- In-line tags. Appear within curly braces, as **{@tag}**.

To be processed, a tag must appear at the beginning of a line, ignoring leading asterisks, white spaces, and the separator (/**). A **@tag** that appears elsewhere will not be translated as a tag. If part of the description starts a line with @, you need to escape it using the HTML entity @.

For example, the following doc comment contains an **author** tag that specifies the name of the developer writing the class.

```
/**
 * This is a comment
 * @author Brian Softwood
 */
```

The following sections list tags that can be used in doc comments.

@author

You use the **author** tag to specify the author of the commented class or method. You can have multiple **author** tags in a doc comment, in which case two names will be separated by a comma in the resulting HTML.

You specify the **author** tag by using this syntax:

```
@author name
```

For example:

```
@author John Clueless
```

or

```
@author Keunho Lee; Cindy Choa
```

Note that the **author** tag will only be included in documentation if the **-author** option is used when using **javadoc**.

{@code}

You use the **code** tag to display text in code font, the same as using the HTML **code** tag. For example, the following doc comment results in **StringParser** printed in font code:

```
This method creates a {@code StringParser} object.
```

This is similar to:

```
This method creates a <code>StringParser</code> object.
```

The difference is HTML tags within a {@code} will be printed literally. For example, **{@code StringUtil}** will be printed as **StringUtil**, whereas **<code>StringUtil</code>** will be printed as **StringUtil** in bold face.

{@docRoot}

You use **{@docRoot}** to specify the generated document's root directory. This tag is useful when you need to include an external file in all generated pages. **{@docRoot}** can appear in any doc comment, including the text portion of another tag.

For example, the following **{@docRoot}** specifies the location of the **help.html** file.

```
Details can be found in <a href="{@docRoot}/help.html">here</a>
```

@deprecated

Use **@deprecated** to indicate that a type or a method is deprecated. See also the **Deprecated** annotation in Chapter 18, "Annotations."

@exception

You use **@exception** in a doc comment for a method or a constructor to indicate that the method or constructor may throw an exception. For example, the **openFile** method below may throw a **java.io.FileNotFoundException**.

```
/**
 * @throws java.io.FileNotFoundException. If the specified file is
 * not found.
 */
public void openFile(String filename) {
  // code
}
```

@exception and **@throws** are synonyms.

{@inheritDoc}

This tag explicitly inserts a description in a method main description or **@return**, **@param**, or **@throws** tag comment from the nearest superclass or implemented interface.

Note that if a main description, or **@return**, **@param**, or **@throws** tag is missing from a method comment, **javadoc** automatically copies the corresponding main description or tag comment from the method it overrides or implements.

{@link}

Inserts an HTML hyperlink that references the documentation for the specified package, class, or member name of a referenced class. The syntax of this tag is

```
{@link package.class#member label}
```

where *label* denotes the text that will appear as the link in code font. If one of the *package*, *class*, or *member* elements is missing, the same package or class as the documented type is assumed.

For example, if you have the **com.brainysoftware.common.StringUtil** class in your API, and it possesses the **convertString** method whose signature is as follows:

```
public java.lang.String convertString(java.lang.String s)
```

From another class you can reference the **convertString** method by using this **link** tag:

Use the {@link

```
  com.brainysoftware.common.StringUtil#toMixedCase(java.lang.String)
  StringUtil.toMixedCase} method.
```

The link will be translated into this HTML tag in the generated HTML document:

```
Use the
<A HREF="../../../com/brainysoftware/common/StringUtil.html#
toMixedCase(java.lang.String)"><CODE>StringUtil.toMixedCase</CODE>
</A> method.
```

{@linkplain}

This tag is very similar to **{@link}**, except that the label is not shown in code font.

{@literal}

You use this tag if you want to display text and escape all special characters in the text. This means, **<i>** does not mean italicizing the text. The syntax for this tag is

```
{@literal text}
```

@param

You use this tag to describe a parameter of a method or a constructor. The syntax of the **param** tag is as follows.

```
@param parameterName description
```

For example, the following method is described using the **param** tag.

```
/**
 * Convert the specified string according to Rule A
 * @param s the String to be converted
 */
public String convertString(String s) {
  // code
}
```

@return

Use this tag to describe the return value of a method. The syntax is

```
@return description
```

For example, the return value of the **convertString** method below is described.

```
/**
 * Convert the specified string according to Rule A.
 * @param s the String to be converted
 * @return A new String object converted according to Rule A.
 */
public String convertString(String s) {
```

```
    // code
}
```

@see

Use this tag to add a "See Also" section, which may be followed by a text entry or a link that references a resource. The syntax has three forms:

```
@see text
@see link
@see package.class#member label
```

The first form does not generate a hyperlink. For example:

```
@see "The Specification Guide"
```

The second form is followed by an HTML hyperlink. For instance:

```
@see <a href="guide.html">Specification Guide</a>
```

The third form is most common and is similar to a {@link}. For example:

```
* @see com.brainysoftware.common.StringUtil#toMixedCase(
java.lang.String) StringUtil.toMixedCase method
```

@serial

This tag is used to describe a default serializable field. Its syntax is

```
@serial fieldDescription | include | exclude
```

The optional *fieldDescription* argument explains the meaning of the field and list acceptable values. The *include* and *exclude* arguments indicate whether a class or package should be included or excluded from the serialized form page. The rule is as follows.

- A public or protected class that implements java.io.Serializable is included unless that class or its package is marked **@serial exclude**.
- A private or package-private class implementing **java.io.Serializable** is excluded unless that class or its package is marked **@serial include**.

@serialData

Describes the types and order of data in the serialized form.

@serialField

Describes an **ObjectStreamField** component of a **Serializable** class's **serialPersistentFields** member.

@since

Adds a "Since" heading with the specified argument. The syntax is

```
@since text
```

Normally, the text argument contains the software version since which a class or a class member became available. For example:

```
@since 1.7
```

@throws

This tag is a synonym for **@exception**.

{@value}

The syntax of **{@value}** has two forms:

```
{@value}
{@value package.class#field}
```

When used without an argument, this tag describes a static field and displays the value of that constant. For example:

```
/**
 * The default value is {@value}.
 */
public static final int FIELD_COUNT = 5;
```

When used with the argument *package.class#field*, this tag can be used to described any program element and displays the value of the specified constant. For example, the following value tag is used in a doc comment for a method.

```
/**
 * Insert {@value #FIELD_COUNT} columns.
 */
public void insertColumns() {
    // code
}
```

@version

Use this tag to add a "Version" subheading with the specified text argument. Its syntax is

```
@version text
```

This tag will only appear in the documentation if javadoc is invoked using the **–version** option.

Javadoc Syntax

The **javadoc** tool is an application to generate API documentation. It reads Java source files and generate output based on doc comments found in the source files. Javadoc formulates its output based on the standard doclet that generates HTML pages. Doclets are Java programs that use the Doclet API to specify the content and format of the output of the **javadoc** tool.

You can use **javadoc** to generate documentation for a single Java source file, multiple source files, or the whole package. Just like other Java tools, Javadoc can be used with options. Among others, there are options to specify the location of the source files and the location of generated output. The rule for specifying these locations are similar to that used by **java** and **javac**.

One way to generate documentation for a single source file is to run **javadoc** from the directory containing the source file. For example, to generate documentation for the **com.brainysoftware.component.HtmlParser.java** file, run javadoc from the directory containing the **com** folder.

```
javadoc com/brainysoftware/component/HtmlParser.java
```

To generate documentation from multiple sources, separate two filenames with a space. For example, the following javadoc command reads two sources:

```
javadoc com/domain/Parent.java com/domain/Child.java
```

To generate a documentation for a package, use the asterisk wild character:

```
javadoc com/domain/*.java
```

Of course, you can generate from multiple packages by separating two packages with a space:

```
javadoc packageA/*.java packageB/*.java packageC/*.java
```

However, it is also easy to generate documentation for a whole package and recursively traverse subpackages in it. For example, the following javadoc command documents the contents of the com package and all its subpackages:

```
javadoc -subpackages com
```

Or, you can specify multiple packages too, by separating two package names with a space or a colon:

```
javadoc -subpackages com:org
```

If you don't specify an output location, the generated documentation will be stored in the same folder as the source, using the same directory structure. However, often you want to separate source files from documentation, and for this purpose you can use the -d option provided by the standard doclet. For example, the following javadoc command saves the generated documents in the doc folder under the current directory:

```
javadoc -subpackages com -d ./doc
```

Alternatively, you can use an absolute path such as this:

```
javadoc -subpackages com -d C:/documents/java/doc
```

or

```
javadoc -subpackages com -d /home/user1/doco
```

Javadoc options are discussed in the subsection "Javadoc Options" and standard doclet options in the subsection "Standard Doclet Options." The last subsection "Generated Documents" discuss the types of documents that Javadoc and the standard doclet generates.

Javadoc Options

You can pass options to Javadoc. To use an option, you use a hyphen right before the option name. An option may take arguments. The syntax is as follows:

```
javadoc -optionA argumentA ... -optionN argumentN
```

Here are some of the more important options.

`-classpath classPathList`
> Specifies the paths where javadoc will look for referenced classes.

`-doclet class`
> Uses the specified doclet class in generating the documentation.

`-exclude packageName1:packageName2:...`
> Excludes the specified packages and their subpackages.

`-help`
> Displays the online help that lists all javadoc command line options.
> Instructs javadoc to obtain the text for the overview documentation from the file specified by *path/filename* and place it on the **overview-summary.html** file.

`-overview path/filename`
> Instructs javadoc to obtain the text for the overview documentation from the file specified by *path/filename* and place it on the overview-summary.htm file.

`-package`
> Documents only package, protected, and public classes and members.

`-private`
> Documents all classes and members.

`-protected`
> Documents only public and protected classes and members. This is the default.

`-public`
> Documents only public classes and members.

`-source javaVersion`
> Specifies the version of source code accepted. The default is **1.8**, which refers to JDK 1.8. Other possible values are **1.7, 1.6, 1.5, 1.4** and **1.3**.

`-sourcepath sourcePathList`
> Specifies the search paths for finding Java source files to be documented.

`-subpackages package1:package2:...`
> Indicates that javadoc should traverse the specified packages recursively.

Standard Doclet Options

Unless explicitly ordered otherwise, javadoc uses the standard doclet to generate HTML files that document an API. You can pass options to the standard doclet too, the same way as passing arguments to the javadoc. Also, options for the standard doclet can be interspersed with options for javadoc.

Here is the list of the more important options for the standard doclet.

-author
> Includes @author text in the generated documents.

-d *directory*
> Specifies the target directory to which generated HTML files will be saved.

-doctitle *title*
> Specifies the title for the overview summary file.

-footer *text*
> Specifies the footer that will be place in the end of every generated file.

-header *text*
> Specifies the header that will be placed at the beginning of every generated file.

-nodeprecated
> Excludes any deprecated API.

-nodeprecatedlist
> Indicates to the standard doclet to not generate the deprecated-list.html file.

-noindex
> Omits the index from the generated documents.

-nosince
> Ignore all @since tags.

-notree
> Omits the class/interface hierarchy pages from the generated documents.

-stylesheetfile *path/filename*
> Specifies the path of a stylesheet file other than the standard one.

-windowtitle *title*
> Specifies the value for the HTML title tag in the generated documents. The *title* argument should not contain any HTML tags.

Generated Documents

Javadoc generates an HTML file for each Java class. The location of this HTML file is in accordance with the package the class belonging in. If a Java class belongs to the **com.domain** package, the corresponding HTML file will be located in the **com/domain** directory.

In addition, there are three other HTML files generated for each package:

- **package-frame.html**. Lists the members of a package.
- **package-summary.html**. Provides a brief description of each package member.
- **package-tree.html**. Contains the package class hierarchy.

By default, there is no description in the **package-summary.html** file. You can provide a description by creating either a **package-info.java** file or a **package.html** file in the package directory. The **package-info.java** option is preferred. For example, here is a **package-info.java** file.

```
/**
 * The com.brainysoftware.common package contains classes
 * that are shared by all other packages.
 */
package com.brainysoftware.common;
```

Note that you must have the package declaration in the Java source.

On top of package-specific files, Javadoc creates files that summarize all packages in the document. These files are located at the root of the destination directory and are as follows.

- **allclasses-frame.html**. List all classes and interfaces. Interfaces are printed in italic. This file is to be one of the frames contained by the **index.html** file.
- **allclasses-noframe.html**. Similar to **allclasses-frame.html** but to be used when the user browser does not support frames.
- **constant-values.html**. List constant field values.
- **deprecated-list.html**. List all deprecated members.
- **help-doc.html**. A general file explaining the organization of the API document.
- **index.html**. The main page that conveniently acts as the entry point to the whole documentation. It contains framesets that reference the **overview-frame.html**, **allclasses-frame.html**, and **overview-summary.html** files. Figure 34.1 shows a typical **index.html** file.
- **index-all.html**. An index of all package names and package member names.
- **overview-frame.html**. Provides an overview of the document.
- **overview-summary.html**. Provides descriptions of all packages in the document. The descriptions are taken from the **package-info.java** or **package.html file** for each package.
- **overview-tree.html**. Contains the hierarchy of each package in the document.
- **package-list**. Lists all packages.
- **stylesheet.css**. The stylesheet for the generated HTML files.

Summary

One secret to successful API is the availability of documentation that explains how to safely use the members of the API and its class hierarchies. Java supports this by allowing you to provide comments for each package, type, and type member of your API. Each doc comment can contain a description and tags.

Javadoc is a tool that comes with the JDK to generate the document based on comments found in source files. Javadoc works by reading source files and generates document based on a doclet. The standard doclet in Javadoc generates HTML files.

Quiz

1. What is the difference between doc comments and Java comments in code?

Chapter 35
Application Deployment

After you finish developing and testing your application, you now need to think about deploying it to the end user. The technology for Java application deployment is Java Web Start (JWS). It is a tool that runs on the Java Network Launching Protocol (JNLP). This chapter starts with an overview of JWS and proceeds with JNLP. At the end of this chapter, an example is given.

JWS Overview

JWS is a sophisticated deployment tool for deploying Java applications over the Internet, a local network, or from a CD. The most common is through Internet deployment, however. You can also configure JWS to automatically download the correct version of JRE if the user's computer does not have the right JRE installed. Caching is also supported. If you decide to let JWS cache your application, JWS can run it even though the user computer is not connected to the Internet.

In short, to deploy your application you need to package it in a jar file and create a JNLP file that describes the jar file. The JNLP file can also give the user instructions on what to do to download and install the application. In addition, you may need to configure your web server to add a MIME type for the **jnlp** extension, if the MIME type has not been added. Optionally, you can create an HTML page that provides a link to the JNLP file and uses JavaScript to check the JDK versions in the user's computer.

Typically, here are what you tell JWS to do using a JNLP file.

1. If there is no JRE installed on the user's computer, Java Web Start can download the latest version of JRE and installs it.
2. If there is a JRE with the correct version, JWS simply runs the application.
3. If the JRE on the user's machine is older than that required to run the application, JWS installs the appropriate JRE and runs the application using the downloaded JRE. The new JRE is only used to run this application and will not affect the old JRE.

JWS is installed as part of the JDK. If the user computer does not have a JDK yet, then no JWS is available. Therefore, you need to detect if JWS is already installed and download it automatically if it has not.

If JWS is not installed, then you have two options:

1. Install it silently (only works if the user is using IE, in other words on Windows only)
2. Direct the user to a page that provides links to download a JRE (in Linux/Unix)

In the example that illustrates the use of JWS in this chapter, you can use a JavaScript script to detect if JWS is available and either installs it silently or redirects the user to a JRE download area.

JNLP File Syntax

You need a JNLP file that guides JWS to run your application smoothly. A JNLP is an XML document, and in it you can specify the following:

- What version of JWS can handle this JNLP file.
- What version of JRE is required to run the described application
- The name and the location of the jar file containing Java classes, icons, and other resources.
- The name of the main Java class to invoke.
- The permission the application requires.
- Whether or not the user will be allowed to run the application offline.
- Whether or not a shortcut should be created on the desktop that points to this application for the user to run it after the first time.

The root element of a JNLP file if **jnlp**. Nested within <jnlp> are the following:

- **information**
- **security**
- **resources**
- **application-desc**
- **applet-desc**

All the tags are discussed in these sections.

The jnlp Element

The **jnlp** element is the root element in a JNLP document. It can have three attributes:

- **spec**. Specifies the version of JWS required to handle this JNLP file. The default is "1.0+", which means all JWS can handle this. Another valid values are "1.6" or "1.6+", which means only JWS that comes with JRE 6 or later can handle it. In most cases, you may want to use the default value so users with older versions of JWS can still run your application.
- **codebase**. Specifies a base URL to which all URL specified in this JNLP file will be relative.
- **href**. The URL of this JNLP file. The value can be an absolute URL or a relative URL to the value of the **codebase** attribute.

For example, the following **jnlp** element specifies that this JNLP file can be handled by any version of JWS and that this JNLP file can be found at http://books.brainysoftware.com/java/deploy/myApp.jnlp.

```
<jnlp
    spec="1.0+"
    codebase="http://books.brainysoftware.com/java/deploy"
    href="myApp.jnlp">
```

The **jnlp** element also implies that the name of this JNLP file is **myApp.jnlp**.

Starting from JDK 7, the **codebase** attribute does not have to contain an absolute path. If no **codebase** attribute is specified, it is assumed that the codebase is relative to the web page from which the JWS application is launched. This is a significant change because it means now you can deploy your JNLP file in different environments without updating the **codebase** attribute.

The information Element

This element specifies informational details of the application. It can have the following subelements, some of which are required.

- **title**. The name of the application. This is a required element.
- **vendor**. Specifies the application vendor. This is a required element.
- **homepage**. You use its **href** attribute to point to a web site that provides more information about the application. The user can get this information from the Java Application Cache Viewer.
- **description**. A short description about the application. And, more than one **description** element can appear in the same JNLP file. Which one to use depends on the situation and on the value of the **kind** attribute. The value of the **kind** attribute is one of the following: **one-line**, **short** and **tooltip**. You use **one-line** if the application will display a description in a list or a table. You use **short** if the application will display a description in a paragraph and there is enough room for it. You use **tooltip** if the application will display a description as a tooltip. Only one description element of each kind can be specified.
- **icon**. Its **href** attribute specifies the URL of an image (in gif or jpeg) used to represent the application during the application launch, in the Java Application Cache Viewer, and as a desktop shortcut. For example:

```
<icon href="images/splash.gif"/>
```

If an **icon** element has a **kind="splash"** attribute, the icon specified will be used as a splash screen during the application launch.

- **offline-allowed**. If present, indicates that the application can be launched offline. If JWS launches an application offline, it will still check for updates but will not wait long. This means, if the user connection is slow the cached version of the application will be launched. If the connection is fast, there is a chance that the more up to date version will be downloaded and launched.
- **shortcut**. Creates a shortcut on the desktop. It may nest the **desktop** and **menu** subelements. For example, the following **shortcut** element causes a shortcut to the application is created both on the desktop and in the menu. The sub menu is My Swing Apps.

```
<shortcut online="false">
    <desktop/>
    <menu submenu="My Swing Apps"/>
</shortcut>
```

- **association**. Tells the client computer to register the application with the operating system as the primary handler of certain extensions and a certain mime-type. If present, the **association** element must have the extensions and mime-type attributes. For example, this **association** element begs the operating system to associate the extension SwingApp with the MIME type application-x/swing-app.

```
<association mime-type="application-x/swing-app"
    extensions="swingApp"/>
```

The security Element

By default, applications deployed using JWS will have restricted access which is effectively the same as an applet in the web browser. You can use the **security** element if you want to have unrestricted access. However, for unrestricted access your jar file must be signed. See Chapter 25, "Security" for information on how to digitally sign a jar file.

For example, the following **security** element requests unrestricted access for the application.

```
<security>
  <all-permissions/>
</security>
```

The resources Element

You use the resources element to specify the location of your resources, such as your jar file(s), system properties, and images. Here are some of the subelements that can reside inside the **resources** element.

- **jar**. Specifies a jar file that is part of the application's classpath.
- **nativelib**. Specifies a jar file containing native libraries.
- **j2se**. This element specifies what JRE version is required to run the application.
- **java**. This element also specifies what JRE version is required to run the application. It is a new addition to Java 6 and only works in JRE 6 or later and will one day replace the **j2se** element entirely.
- **property**. Defines a system property that will be available to the application. This property has two attributes, **name** and **value**, to specify the attribute key and value, respectively.

The application-desc Element

Use this element to describe the application, such as the main class to invoke through the **main-class** attribute. The presence of this element also indicates to JWS that the JNLP file is launching a Java application (and not an applet). You can pass arguments through the use of the **argument** subelement. For example, the following **application-desc** element specifies the Java class to launch and passes two arguments.

```
<application-desc
    main-class="app35.SwingApp">
    <argument>Simple App</argument>
    <argument>400</argument>
</application-desc>
```

The applet-desc Element

Use this element if the JNLP file is used to launch a Java applet. The applet itself must be contained in the jar file specified using the **resources** element. The **applet-desc** element has the following attributes:

- **documentBase**. The document base of the applet. This must be specified explicitly since applets launched using JWS are not embedded in an HTML page.
- **name**. The name of the applet
- **main-class**. Specifies the fully qualified name of the applet.
- **width**. The width of the applet.
- **height**. The height of the applet.

The **applet-desc** element can have the **param** subelement that has two attributes, **name** and **value**.

For example, the following **applet-desc** element launches the **AnimationApplet** applet.

```
<applet-desc documentBase="http://www.brainysoftware.com/applet/"
    name="Animation Applet Demo"
    main-class="app35.AnimationApplet"
    width="400"
    height="400">
    <param name="interval" value="100"/>
</applet-desc>
```

A Deployment Example

The following is an example of how to deploy a Java Swing application.

Configure the web server to use the Java Web Start MIME type

The browser needs to know what it needs to do when it downloads a jnlp file, just as it knows that it has to start Microsoft Word when the user clicks on a **doc** file. You need to configure your web server so that for the **jnlp** file extension, the content type **application/x-java-jnlp-file** will be used. How to configure depends on the type of the web server. You should consult the documentation provided by the web server.

For example, for the Apache web server you must add the following line to the **httpd.conf** configuration file:

```
application/x-java-jnlp-file JNLP
```

Create a jnlp file

The jnlp file for this example is given in Listing 35.1.

Listing 35.1: myApp.jnlp file

```
<?xml version="1.0" encoding="utf-8"?>
<jnlp
    spec="1.0+"
    codebase="http://books.brainysoftware.com/java/deploy"
    href="myApp.jnlp">
    <information>
```

```
        <title>A Demo Swing Application</title>
        <vendor>Crouching Panda Software, Inc.</vendor>
        <description>A little app that swings</description>
        <description kind="short">Swing JMenu</description>
        <icon kind="splash" href="images/splash.gif"/>
        <offline-allowed/>
        <shortcut online="false">
            <desktop/>
            <menu submenu="My Downloaded Apps"/>
        </shortcut>
    </information>
    <resources>
        <j2se version="1.6+"/>
        <jar href="MySwingApp.jar"/>
    </resources>
    <application-desc main-class="JMenuTest1"/>
</jnlp>
```

Create an HTML File

An optional HTML file named **download.html** (given in Listing 35.2) is provided. This HTML file uses JavaScript to detect the browser type (IE or Netscape) and whether or not JWS can be found, and act based on those situations.

Listing 35.2: The HTML file

```html
<script type="text/javascript">
  var jnlpUrl =
    "http://books.brainysoftware.com/java/deploy/myApp.jnlp";
  var isIE = (navigator.userAgent.indexOf("MSIE")!=-1);
  var jwsFound = false;
  if (isIE) {
    try {
      if (new ActiveXObject("JavaWebStart.isInstalled"))
        jwsFound = true;
    }
    catch(e) {}
  }
  else { // is not IE
    // a Netscape/FireFox
    if (navigator.mimeTypes && navigator.mimeTypes.length) {
      if (navigator.mimeTypes['application/x-java-jnlp-file'])
        jwsFound = true;
    }
  }


  if (jwsFound) {
    // redirect to JNLP file
    location=jnlpUrl;
  }
  else {
    if (isIE) {
```

```
    // use ActiveX component to automatically download
    document.write('<object codebase=' +
      '"http://java.sun.com/update/1.6.0/' +
      'jinstall-6-windows-i586.cab#Version=6,0,0,0" ' +
      'classid="clsid:5852F5ED-8BF4-11D4-A245-0080C6F74284" ' +
      'height="0" width="0">' +
      '<param name="app" value="' + jnlpUrl + '">' +
      '<param name="back" value="true">' +
      '<a href="http://java.sun.com/javase/downloads/ea.jsp">' +
      'Download Java Web Start</a>"' +
      '</object>');
  }
  else { //no JWS and not IE
    // provide a link to download
    document.write('You do not have a Java Runtime Environment ' +
      'to run the application. ' +
      'Please download JRE 6.0 from ' +
      '<a href="http://java.sun.com/javase/downloads/ea.jsp">' +
      'here</a>');
  }
}
</script>
```

Test the deployment

You can try this example by directing your browser to

`http://books.brainysoftware.com/java/deploy/download.html`

If the correct JRE can be found on the user computer, the user will see a dialog similar to the one in Figure 35.1.

Figure 35.1: A dialog that tells the user that the correct JRE was found

If you click Yes, you will see the JMenuTest1 application shown in Figure 35.2.

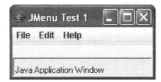

Figure 35.2: The deployed application

If the correct JRE cannot be found, the user will see a dialog like that in Figure 35.3.

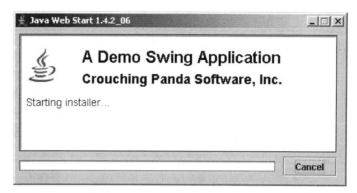

Figure 35.3: A dialog that tells the user that the correct JRE could not be found

In the case where the correct JRE cannot be found, JWS will offer to download the correct one. If you agree to download, it will show the license agreement that you must agree on. Once you accept, it will download the correct JRE.

Security Concerns

Chapter 31, "Security" explained the difference between an applet and an ordinary Java application in terms of security. Because applets may come from untrusted resources, the JRE impose security restrictions that cause applets not to be able to access the file system, etc. Unless the applets are signed.

Likewise, applications that are deployed over the Internet are more like applets and the JRE will impose the same restrictions as it does applets. If you are deploying your applications over the Internet and want to have access to resources, then you must deploy your applications in a jar file and sign it. See Chapter 31, "Security" on how to digitally sign a jar file.

Summary

In this chapter you have seen how you can deploy Java applications. JWS is the main tool for deployment and using it you can deploy applications over the Internet or a local network. Also, you can do it from a CD. JWS is also smart enough to detect if the user computer has the correct version of JRE and acts accordingly.

Quiz

1. What does JWS stand for?
2. What are the steps required to deploy a Java application via JNLP?
3. Why does the JRE restrict Java applications downloaded from the Internet?

Appendix A
javac

javac is a Java compiler for compiling Java programs to bytecode. Source files must have a **java** extension and be organized in a directory structure that reflects the package tree. The results are **class** files in a directory structure reflecting the package tree.

javac has the following syntax.

```
javac [options] [sourceFiles] [@argFiles]
```

where *options* are command-line options, *sourceFiles* one or more Java source files, and *@argFiles* one or more files that list options and source files.

You can pass source code file names to **javac** in one of two ways:

- List the file names on the command line. This method is suitable if the number of source files is small.
- List the file names in a file, separated by blanks or line breaks, then pass the path to the list file to the **javac** command line prefixed by an **@** character. This is appropriate for a large number of source files.

Options

Options are used to pass instructions to **javac**. For example, you can tell **javac** where to find classes referenced in the source files, where to put the generated class files, etc. There are two types of options, standard and nonstandard. Nonstandard options start with -X.

Here are the lists of standard and nonstandard options.

Standard Options

```
-classpath classpath
```
If in your source files you reference other Java types than those packaged in the Java standard libraries, you need to tell **javac** how to find these external types by using the **–classpath** option. The value should be the path to a directory containing referenced Java types or a jar file containing them. The path can be absolute or relative to the current directory. Two paths are separated by a semicolon in Windows and by a colon in Unix/Linux.

For example, the following Windows command line compiles **MyClass.java** that references the **primer.FileObject** class located in the **C:\program\classes** directory.

```
javac -classpath C:/program/classes/ MyClass.java
```

Note that the **FileObject** class is in the **primer** package, so you pass the directory containing the package.

The following Linux command line compiles **MyClass.java** that references the **primer.FileObject** class located in the **/home/user1/classes** directory.

```
javac -classpath /home/user1/classes/ MyClass.java
```

To reference class files packaged in a jar file, pass the full path to the jar file. For instance, here is how you compile **MyClass.java** that reference **primer.FileObject** in the **MyLib.jar** file located in **C:\temp** in a Windows system.

```
javac -classpath C:/temp/MyLib.jar MyClass.java
```

This example compiles **MyClass.java** that references classes located in the **/home/user1/lib** directory and packaged in the **Exercises.jar** file located in the **/home/jars** directory in Linux:

```
javac -classpath /home/user1/lib/:/home/user1/Exercises.jar
MyClass.java
```

If you are referencing a class whose root is the same as the class being compiled, you can pass **./** as the value for the classpath. For example, the following command line compiles **MyClass.java** that references both **C:\temp** and the current directory:

```
javac -classpath C:/temp/;./ MyClass.java
```

The alternative to the **classpath** option is to assign the value to the **CLASSPATH** environment variable. However, if the **classpath** option is present, the value of the **CLASSPATH** environment variable will be overridden.

If the **-sourcepath** option is not specified, the user class path is searched for both source files and class files.

```
-cp classpath
```
> The same as -classpath.

```
-Djava.endorsed.dirs=directories
```
> Override the location of endorsed standards path.

```
-d directory
```
> Specify the target directory for class files. The target directory must already exist. **javac** puts the class files in a directory structure that reflects the package name, creating directories as needed.
>
> By default, **javac** creates class files in the same directory as the source file.

```
-deprecation
```
> List each use or override of a deprecated member or class. Without this option, **javac** shows the names of source files that use or override deprecated members or classes. **-deprecation** is shorthand for **-Xlint:deprecation**.

```
-encoding encoding
```
> Specify the source file encoding name, such as UTF-8. By default, **javac** uses the platform default converter.

```
-g
```
> Print debug information, including local variables. By default, only line number and source file information is generated.

`-g:none`

Prevent **javac** from generating debug information.

`-g:{keyword list}`

Generate only some kinds of debug information, specified by a comma separated list of keywords. Valid keywords are:
- **source**. Source file debug information
- **lines**. Line number debug information
- **vars**. Local variable debug information

`-help`

Print a description of standard options.

`-nowarn`

Disable warning messages. This has the same effect as **-Xlint:none**.

`-source release`

Specifies the version of source code accepted. The values allowed are **1.3** to **1.8** and **6** to **8**.

`-sourcepath sourcePath`

Set the source code path to search for class or interface definitions. As with the user class path, source path entries are separated by semicolons (in Windows) or colons (in Linux/Unix) and can be directories, jar archives, or zip archives. If packages are used, the local path name within the directory or archive must reflect the package name.

Note: Classes found through the classpath are subject to automatic recompilation if their sources are found.

`-verbose`

Include information about each class loaded and each source file compiled.

`-X`

Display information about nonstandard options.

Nonstandard Options

`-Xbootclasspath/p:path`

Prepend to the bootstrap class path.

`-Xbootclasspath/a:path`

Append to the bootstrap class path.

`-Xbootclasspath/:path`

Override location of bootstrap class files.

`-Xlint`

Enable all recommended warnings.

`-Xlint:none`

Disable all warnings not mandated by the Java Language Specification.

`-Xlint:-xxx`

Disable warning *xxx*, where *xxx* is one of the warning names supported for **-Xlint:xxx**.

`Xlint:unchecked`

Provide more detail for unchecked conversion warnings that are mandated by the

Java Language Specification.

`-Xlint:`*path*
> Warn about nonexistent path directories specified in the **classpath**, **sourcepath**, or other option.

`-Xlint:serial`
> Warn about missing serialVersionUID definitions on serializable classes.

`-Xlint:finally`
> Warn about **finally** clauses that cannot complete normally.

`-Xlint:fallthrough`
> Check switch blocks for fall-through cases and provide a warning message for any that are found. Fall-through cases are cases in a **switch** block, other than the last case in the block, whose code does not include a **break** statement.

`-Xmaxerrors` *number*
> Specify the maximum number of errors that will be reported

`-Xmaxwarns` *number*
> Specify the maximum number of warnings to be reported.

`-Xstdout` *filename*
> Send compiler messages to the named file. By default, compiler messages go to System.err.

The -J Option

`-J`*option*
> Pass option to the java launcher called by javac. For example, **-J-Xms48m** sets the startup memory to 48 megabytes. Although it does not begin with **-X**, it is not a `standard option' of **javac**. It is a common convention for -J to pass options to the underlying VM executing applications written in Java.

Command Line Argument Files

If you have to pass long arguments to **javac** again and again, you will save a lot typing if you save those arguments in a file and pass the file to **javac** instead. An argument file can include both **javac** options and source filenames in any combination. Within an argument file, you can separate arguments using a space or separate them as new lines. The **javac** tool even allows multiple argument files.

For example, the following command line invokes **javac** and passes the file **MyArguments** to it:

```
javac @MyArguments
```

The following passes two argument files, **Args1** and **Args2**:

```
javac @Args1 @Args2
```

Appendix B
java

The **java** program is a tool for launching a Java program. Its syntax has two forms.

```
java [options] class [argument ...]
java [options] -jar jarFile [argument ...]
```

where *options* represents command-line options, *class* the name of the class to be invoked, *jarFile* the name of the jar file to be invoked, and *argument* the argument passed to the invoked class's **main** method

Options

There are two types of options you can pass to **java**, standard and nonstandard.

Standard Options

`-client`
> Select the Java HotSpot Client VM.

`-server`
> Select the Java HotSpot Server VM.

`-agentlib:libraryName[=options]`
> Load native agent library libraryName. Example values of *libraryName* are **hprof**, **jdwp=help**, and **hprof=help**.

`-agentpath:pathname[=options]`
> Load a native agent library by full pathname.

`-classpath classpath`
> The same as the **-cp** option.

`-cp classpath`
> Specify a list of directories, jar archives, and zip archives to search for class files. Two class paths are separated by a colon in Unix/Linux and by a semicolon in Windows. For examples on using -cp and –classpath, see the description of the **javac** tool's **classpath** option in Appendix A.

`-Dproperty=value`
> Set a system property value.

`-d32`
> See the description of the **–d64** option.

`-d64`

Specify whether the program is to be run in a 32-bit or a 64-bit environment if available. Currently only the Java HotSpot Server VM supports 64-bit operation, and the **-server** option is implicit with the use of -d64. This is subject to change in a future release. If neither **-d32** nor **-d64** is specified, the default is to run in a 32-bit environment, except for 64-bit only systems. This is subject to change in a future release.

`-enableassertions[:<package name>"..." | :<class name> ]`
See the description for the **–ea** option.

`-ea[:<package name>"..." | :<class name> ]`
Enable assertions. Assertions are disabled by default.

`-disableassertions[:<package name>"..." | :<class name> ]`
See the description for the **–da** option.

`-da[:<package name>"..." | :<class name> ]`
Disable assertions. This is the default.

`-enablesystemassertions`
See the description for the **–esa** option.

`-esa`

Enable asserts in all system classes (set the default assertion status for system classes to **true**).

`-disablesystemassertions`
See the description for the **–dsa** option.

`-dsa`

Disables asserts in all system classes.

`-jar`

Execute a Java class in a jar file. The first argument is the name of the jar file instead of a startup class name. To tell **java** the class to invoke, the manifest of the jar file must contain a line of the form **Main-Class: *classname***, where *classname* identifies the class having the public static void **main(String[] args)** method that serves as your application's starting point.

`-javaagent:jarpath[=options]`
Load a Java programming language agent.

`-verbose`
See the description for the **–verbose:class** option.

`-verbose:class`
Display information about each class loaded.

`-verbose:gc`
Report on each garbage collection event.

`-verbose:jni`
Report information about use of native methods and other Java Native Interface activity.

`-version`
Display the JRE version information and exit.

`-showversion`

Display the version information and continue.

`-?`

See the description for the **-help** option.

`-help`

Display usage information and exit.

`-X`

Display information about nonstandard options and exit.

Nonstandard Options

`-Xint`

Operate in interpreted-only mode. Compilation to native code is disabled, and all bytecodes are executed by the interpreter. You will not be able to enjoy the performance benefits offered by the Java HotSpot VMs' adaptive compiler.

`-Xbatch`

Disable background compilation so that compilation of all methods proceeds as a foreground task until it completes. Without this option, the VM will compile the method as a background task, running the method in interpreter mode until the background compilation is finished.

`-Xdebug`

Start with support for JVMDI enabled. JVMDI has been deprecated and is not used for debugging in Java SE 5 and later.

`-Xbootclasspath:`*bootclasspath*

Specify a list of directories, jar archives, and zip archives to search for boot class files. Entries are separated by colons (in Linux/Unix) or by semicolons (in Windows). These are used in place of the boot class files included in Java 5 and 6.

`-Xbootclasspath/a:`*path*

Specify a list of directories, jar archives, and zip archives to append to the default bootstrap class path. Entries are separated by colons (in Linux/Unix) or by semicolons (in Windows).

`-Xbootclasspath/p:`*path*

Specify a list of directories, jar archives, and zip archives to prepend in front of the default bootstrap class path. Entries are separated by colons (in Linux/Unix) or by semicolons (in Windows).

`-Xcheck:jni`

Perform additional checks for Java Native Interface (JNI) functions. Specifically, the Java Virtual Machine validates the parameters passed to the JNI function as well as the runtime environment data before processing the JNI request. Any invalid data encountered indicates a problem in the native code, and the JVM will terminate with a fatal error in such cases. Using this option imposes a performance penalty.

`-Xfuture`

Perform strict class-file format checks. For backwards compatibility, the default format checks performed by the Java 2 SDK's virtual machine are no stricter than the checks performed by 1.1.x versions of the JDK software. This flag turns on stricter class-file format checks that enforce closer conformance to the class-file format specification. Developers are encouraged to use this flag when developing new code because the stricter checks will become the default in future releases of the Java application launcher.

`-Xnoclassgc`

Disable class garbage collection.

`-Xincgc`

Enable the incremental garbage collector. The incremental garbage collector, which is off by default, will reduce the occasional long garbage-collection pauses during program execution. The incremental garbage collector will at times execute concurrently with the program and during such times will reduce the processor capacity available to the program.

`-Xloggc:`*file*

Report on each garbage collection event, as with **-verbose:gc**, but record this data to file. In addition to the information **-verbose:gc** gives, each reported event will be preceded by the time (in seconds) since the first garbage-collection event. Always use a local file system for storage of this file to avoid stalling the JVM due to network latency. The file may be truncated in the case of a full file system and logging will continue on the truncated file. This option overrides the **-verbose:gc** option if both are present.

`-Xms`*n*

Specify the initial size of the memory allocation pool in bytes. The value must be a multiple of 1024 greater than 1MB. Append the letter **k** or **K** to indicate kilobytes, or **m** or **M** to indicate megabytes. The default value is 2MB. For example:

```
-Xms6291456
-Xms6144k
-Xms6m
```

`-Xmx`*n*

Specify the maximum size of the memory allocation pool in bytes. The value must a multiple of 1024 greater than 2MB. Append **k** or **K** to indicate kilobytes, or **m** or **M** to indicate megabytes. The default value is 64MB. For instance:

```
-Xmx83880000
 -Xmx8192k
 -Xmx86M
```

`-Xprof`

Profile the running program and send profiling data to standard output. This option is provided as a utility that is useful in program development and should not be used in production.

`-Xrunhprof[:`*help*`][:<`*suboption*`>-<`*value*`>,...]`

Enable cpu, heap, or monitor profiling. This option is typically followed by a list of comma-separated "<suboption>=<value>" pairs. You can display the list of suboption and their default values by running the command **java -Xrunhprof:help**.

`-Xrs`

Reduce the use of operating-system signals by the Java virtual machine (JVM).

`-Xss`*n*

Set thread stack size.

`-XX:+UseAltSigs`

The JVM uses SIGUSR1 and SIGUSR2 by default, which can sometimes conflict with applications that signal-chain SIGUSR1 and SIGUSR2. This option will cause the JVM to use signals other than SIGUSR1 and SIGUSR2 as the default.

Appendix C
jar

jar, short for Java archive, is a tool for packaging Java class files and other related resources into a jar file. The **jar** tool is included in the JDK and initially the reason for its creation was so that an applet class and its related resources could be downloaded with a single HTTP request. Over time, **jar** became the preferred way of packaging any Java classes, not only applets.

The jar format is based on the zip format. As such, you can change the extension of a jar file to **.zip** and view it using a ZIP viewer, such as WinZip. A jar file can also include the META-INF directory for storing package and extension configuration data, including security, versioning, extension and services. jar is also the only format that allows you to digitally sign your code.

This appendix provides the syntax of the **jar** tool and examples of how to use it.

Syntax

You can use **jar** to create, update, extract, and list the content of a jar file. A **jar** command can be used with options, which are explained in the section "Options." Here is the syntax of the **jar** program commands.

To create a jar file, use this syntax.

```
jar c[v0M]f jarFile [-C dir] inputFiles [-Joption]
jar c[v0]mf manifest jarFile [-C dir] inputFiles [-Joption]
jar c[v0M] [-C dir] inputFiles [-Joption]
jar c[v0]m manifest [-C dir] inputFiles [-Joption]
```

To update a jar file, use this syntax.

```
jar u[v0M]f jarFile [-C dir] inputFiles [-Joption]
jar u[v0]mf manifest jarFile [-C dir] inputFiles [-Joption]
jar u[v0M] [-C dir] inputFiles [-Joption]
jar u[v0]m manifest [-C dir] inputFiles [-Joption]
```

To extract a jar file, use this.

```
jar x[v]f jarFile [inputFiles] [-Joption]
jar x[v] [inputFiles] [-Joption]
```

To list the contents of a jar file, use the following syntax.

```
jar t[v]f jarFile [inputFiles] [-Joption]
```

```
jar t[v] [inputFiles] [-Joption]
```

And, to add index to a jar file, use this syntax.

```
jar i jarFile [-Joption]
```

The arguments are as follows.

`cuxtiv0Mmf`
> Options that control the **jar** command. These will be detailed in the section "Options."

`jarFile`
> The jar file to be created, updated, extracted, have its contents viewed, or add index to. The absence of the **f** option and *jarFile* indicates that we are accepting input from the standard input (when extracting and viewing the contents) or sending output to the standard output (for creating and updating).

`inputFiles`
> Files or directories, separated by spaces, to be packaged into a jar file (when creating and updating), or to be extracted or listed from *jarFile*. All directories are processed recursively. The files are compressed unless option O (zero) is used.

`manifest`
> Pre-existing manifest file whose **name: value** pairs are to be included in **MANIFEST.MF** in the jar file. The options **m** and **f** must appear in the same order that manifest and jarFile appear.

`-C dir`
> Temporarily changes directories to dir while processing the following *inputFiles* argument. Multiple -C *dir inputFiles* sets are allowed.

`-Joption`
> Option to be passed into the Java runtime environment. (There must be no space between -J and *option*).

Options

The options that can be used in a jar command is as follows.

`c`
> Indicates that the **jar** command is invoked to create a new jar file.

`u`
> Indicates that the **jar** command is invoked to update the specified jar file.

`x`
> Indicates that the **jar** command is invoked to extract the specified jar file. If *inputFiles* is present, only those specified files and directories are extracted. Otherwise, all files and directories are extracted.

`t`
> Indicates that the **jar** command is invoked to list the contents of the specified jar file. If *inputFiles* is present, only those specified files and directories are listed. Otherwise, all files and directories are listed.

i

> Generate index information for the specified *jarFile* and its dependent jar files.

f

> Specifies the file *jarFile* to be created, updated, extracted, indexed, or viewed.

v

> Generates verbose output to standard output.

0

> This is a zero that indicates that files should be stored without being compressed.

M

> Indicates that a manifest file entry should not be created for creation and update. This option also instructs the **jar** tool to delete any manifest during update.

m

> Includes **name: value** attribute pairs from the specified manifest file manifest in the file at **META-INF/MANIFEST.MF**. A **name: value** pair is added unless one with the same name already exists, in which case its value is updated.

-C *dir*

> Temporarily changes directories (cd dir) during execution of the **jar** command while processing the following *inputFiles* argument.

-Joption

> Pass option to the Java runtime environment, where option is one of the options described on the reference page for the java application launcher. For example, **-J-Xmx32M** sets the maximum memory to 32 megabytes.

Examples

The following are examples of how to use **jar**.

Create

This **jar** command packages all directories and files in the current directory into a jar file named **MyJar.jar**.

```
jar cf MyJar.jar *
```

The following, with the **v** option, does the same but outputs all messages to the console:

```
jar cvf MyJar.jar *
```

The following packages all class files in the **com/brainysoftware/jdk/** directory into the **MyJar.jar** file.

```
jar cvf MyJar.jar com/brainysoftware/jdk/*.class
```

Update

This command adds **MathUtil.class** to **MyJar.jar**.

```
jar uf MyJar.jar MathUtil.class
```

This command updates the **MyJar.jar** manifest with the name: value pairs in manifest.

```
jar umf manifest MyJar.jar
```

The following command adds **MathUtil.class** in the **classes** directory to **MyJar.jar**.

```
jar uf MyJar.jar -C classes MathUtil.class
```

List

The following command lists the contents of **MyJar.jar**:

```
jar tf MyJar.jar
```

Extract

The following command extracts all files in **MyJar.jar** to the current directory.

```
jar xf MyJar.jar
```

Index

This command generates in **MyJar.jar** an **INDEX.LIST** file that contains location information for each package in **MyJar.jar** and all the jar files specified in the **Class-Path** attribute of **MyJar.jar**.

```
jar i MyJar.jar
```

Setting an Application Entry Point

The **java** tool, explained in Appendix B, allows you to invoke a class in a jar file. Here is the syntax:

```
java -jar jarFile
```

For **java** to be able to invoke the correct class, you need to include in the jar file a manifest that has the following entry:

```
Main-Class: className
```

Appendix D
NetBeans

Sun Microsystems launched the NetBeans open source project in 2000. The name NetBeans came from Netbeans Ceska Republika, a Czech company that Sun bought over. The new project was based on the code Sun acquired as the result of the purchase.

This appendix provides a quick tutorial to using NetBeans to build Java applications. NetBeans requires a JDK to work.

Download and Installation

You can download NetBeans free from http://netbeans.org. The latest version at the time of writing is 8.0. You need version 8 or later to enjoy the new features in Java 8. NetBeans is written in Java and, as such, can run on any platform where Java is available. Each distribution includes an installer for easy installation. Make sure you download the correct version for your operating system. The installer guides you through step-by-step instructions that are easy to follow. You will be prompted to agree on the terms and conditions of use, specify the installation directory, and select the JDK version to use if your computer has more than one.

Once installed, you can run the NetBeans IDE just like you would other applications.

Creating a Project

NetBeans organizes resources in projects. Therefore, before you can create a Java class, you must first create a project. To do so, follow these steps.

- Click **File**, **New Project**. The **New Project** dialog will be displayed (See Figure D.1).

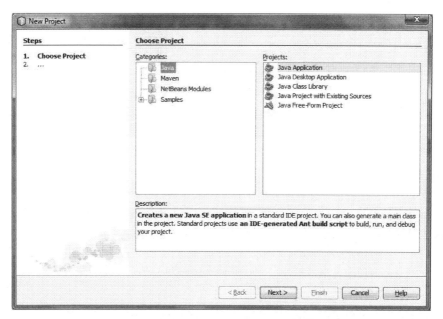

Figure D.1: The New Project dialog

- Click **Java** from the **Categories** box and **Java Application** from the **Projects** box. And then, click **Next**. The next screen will be displayed, as shown in Figure D.2.
- Enter a project name in the **Project Name** box and browse to the directory where you want to save the project's resources. Afterwards, click **Finish**.
  NetBeans will create a new project plus the first class in the project. This is depicted in Figure D.3.

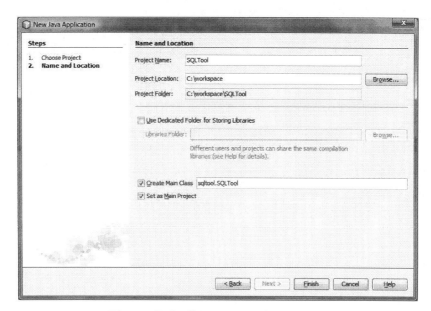

Figure D.2: Select a project name

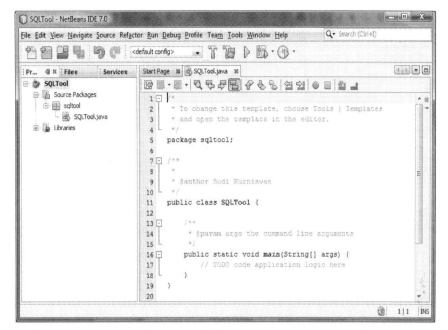

Figure D.3: A Java Project

Figure D.3 shows two windows, the **Projects** window on the left and the source file window on the right. You are ready to write your code.

Creating a Class

To create a class other than that created by default by NetBeans, right-click the project icon in the **Projects** window, then click **New**, **Java Class**. You will see the **New Java Class** dialog like that in Figure D.4.

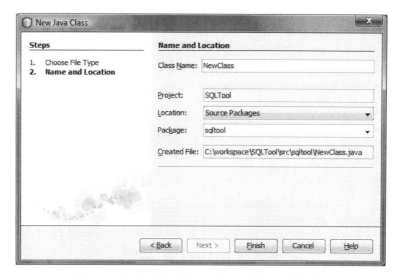

Figure D.4: The New Java Class dialog

Type in the class name and the package for this class, then click **Finish**. A new Java class will be created for you. You can see the new class listed on the **Projects** window.

You can now write your code. As you type, NetBeans will check and correct the syntax of your Java code. You can save your code by clicking **Ctrl+S** and NetBeans automatically compiles it as you save.

Running a Java Class

Once you are finished with a class, you can run it to test it. To run a class, click **Run**, **Run File**, then select the Java class you want to run. Any result will be displayed in the Console window. Another way to run a Java class is to right-click on the source code and click **Run File**.

Also, to run the last run class, press **Shift+F6**.

Adding Libraries

Oftentimes your classes or interfaces reference types in other projects or in a jar file. To compile these classes/interfaces, you need to tell NetBeans where to find the referenced library by adding a reference to it. You do this by right-clicking the **Libraries** icon in the **Projects** window, and then clicking **Add JAR/Folder**. A navigation window will then appear that lets you select your library file.

Debugging Code

A powerful feature offered by many IDE's is support for debugging. In NetBeans, you can step through a program line by line. The steps for debugging a program are as follows.

1. Add a breakpoint. You do this by clicking on the line on your code and click **Toggle Breakpoint**.
2. Execute the program by clicking **Run**, **Run File**, and then select the Java class to debug.

After selecting a class to debug in Step 2, these windows will open: **Watches**, **Call Stack**, and **Local Variables**. They allow you to monitor the progress of your code. The **Local Variables** window, for instance, allows you to inspect the value of a local variable.

To continue, click the **Run** menu and select whether to step into, step over, continue, or pause the program.

Appendix E
Eclipse

IBM launched Eclipse in 2001 after buying Object Technology International, a Canadian company. Including the purchase, IBM spent $40 million on the code that it finally released as an open source project. Written in Java, Eclipse ships with its own compiler, so it does not rely on Oracle's Java compiler. As a result, you don't need a JDK to run Eclipse, just a JRE. In fact, Eclipse comes with compilers for other languages as well, such as C, C++ and PHP because its developers have the ambition to make Eclipse the ultimate IDE.

Another thing to note, even though Eclipse is written in Java, it does not use the Swing technology. It uses its own graphics library called the Standard Widget Toolkit in order to make Eclipse look and feel more like a native application. You can still use Eclipse to write Swing applications, though.

This appendix provides a quick tutorial to using Eclipse to build Java applications.

Download and Installation

You can download Eclipse free from http://www.eclipse.org. Only version 4.4 (code-named Luna) and later support Java 8. Make sure you download the version that will run on your operating system. Currently Eclipse is available on Windows, Linux and Mac OS X. You can even download the source code.

Eclipse distributions are packaged in a zip or gz file. In addition, if you have slow Internet connection, you can download Eclipse in torrent format. The are many package solutions available. Make sure you choose **Eclipse IDE for Java Developers**.

Installation is a matter of extracting the distribution zip or gz file into a directory. No other steps are necessary. Once you have extracted the distribution file, you will find an executable file that you can double-click to launch Eclipse.

The first time you run Eclipse, you will see the Workspace Launcher dialog like that in Figure E1, prompting you to select a workspace folder. A workspace folder is the default directory for storing all the files in your Eclipse projects.

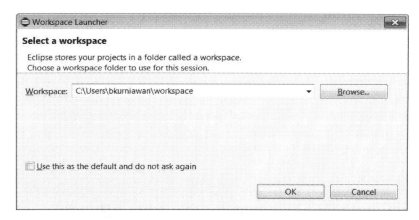

Figure E.1: The Workspace Launcher dialog

Even though you selected a workspace folder, you can choose a different directory than the workspace folder for your project files. You can even have multiple workspaces that each contains a different set of projects.

After you select a workspace, Eclipse will show its main window, shown in Figure E.2. If you instead see a Welcome page, just close the page.

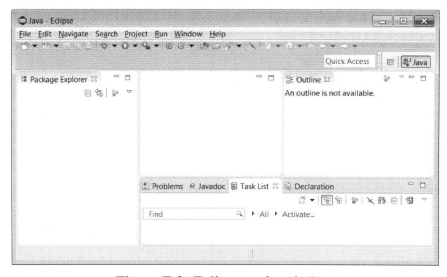

Figure E.2: Eclipse main window

Adding A JRE

Even though Eclipse ships with its own Java compiler, it still needs a JRE or a JDK to run Java programs. Make sure you have installed a JRE 1.8 or a JDK 1.8. Then, follow these steps to add the JRE/JDK so that you can use it in your Java projects.

- Click the Window menu on the Eclipse main window, and then select Preferences. The Preferences dialog will appear, as shown in Figure E.3.

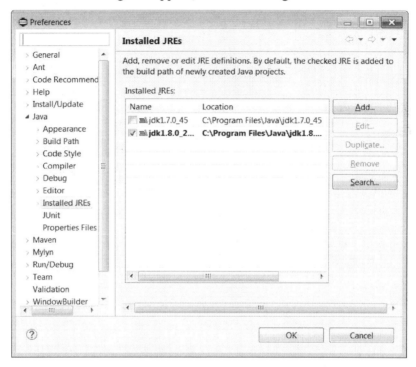

Figure E.3: Eclipse Preferences dialog

- On the left pane, click **Java** and select **Installed JREs**. If you don't see a JRE 1.8 or a JDK 1.8 on the center pane, click the Add button and browse to the installation directory of the JDK you have installed.
- Select the JRE 1.8 or JDK 1.8 as the default and click the **OK** button.

Creating a Java Project

Eclipse organizes resources in projects. Therefore, before you can create a Java class, you must first create a Java project. To do so, follow these steps.

- Click **File**, **New** and **Java Project**. Make sure you click **Java Project**, and not **Project**, after you click **New**. The New Java Project dialog will appear (See Figure E.4).
- Supply a name for your project. Once you type something in the **Project name** box, the **Next** and **Finish** buttons will become active. Note that by default your project will be created in the current workspace folder. However, you can choose a different location by unchecking the **Use default location** checkbox and browsing to a directory in your file system.
- Make sure **Java SE 1.8** is selected in the JRE panel. If you do not see **Java SE 1.8**, it means you have not added one and need to do so by following the instructions in the previous section. Next, click **Next** or **Finish**. Clicking **Finish** uses default settings to create the project, clicking **Next** allows you to select directories for your source and class files. For now, simply click **Finish**. A project will be created for you. Figure E.5 shows a project named **SQLTool**.

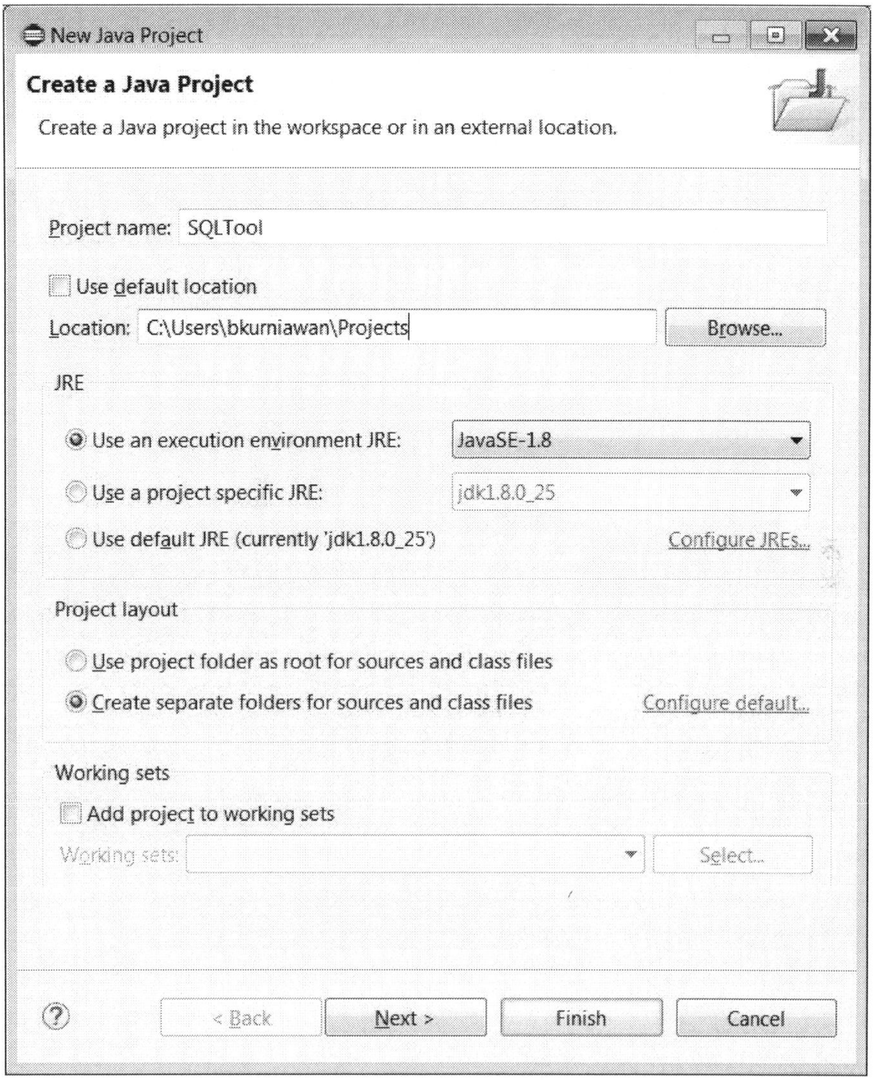

Figure E.4: Select a project name

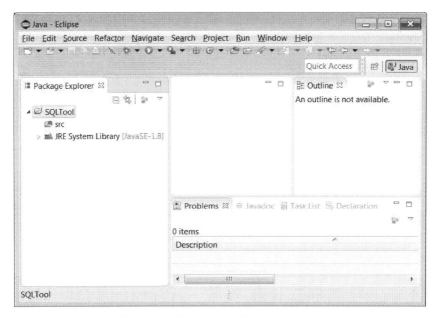

Figure E.5: A new Java project

What you see in Figure E.5 is called the Java perspective. A perspective is the combination of views that are suitable for performing a certain task. The Java perspective is used for writing Java code. It consists of the Package Explorer View on the left, the Outline view on the right, and the Problems view at the bottom. The location of each view is changeable by dragging the header of the view. Figure E.5 shows the default position of each view. There are many other views, all of which can be seen by clicking **Window**, **Show View**.

 Other perspectives include Java browsing and Debug. You can select a perspective by clicking **Window**, **Open Perspective**.

Creating a Class

To create a class, right-click the project icon in the Package Explorer view, then click **New**, **Class**. You will see the **New Java Class** dialog like the one in Figure E.6.

Figure E.6: The New Java Class dialog

Enter the package and the class name, then click **Finish** to create a class. The Java perspective displays the class code in a new pane, as shown in Figure E.7.

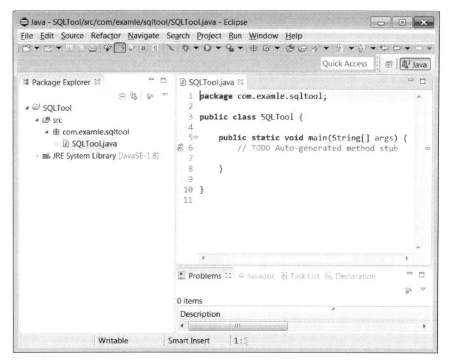

Figure E.7: Editing a Java class

You can now write your code. As you type, Eclipse checks and corrects the syntax of your Java code. You can save your work by clicking **Ctrl+S** and Eclipse automatically compiles it.

Running a Java Class

Once you are finished with a class, you can run it to test it. To run a class, click **Run**, **Run As**, **Java Application**. Any result will be displayed in the Console view. Another way to run a Java class is to right-click on the class pane and click **Run As**, **Java Application**.

Also, to run the last run class, press **Ctrl+F11**.

Adding Libraries

Oftentimes your classes or interfaces reference types in a jar file or in another project. To compile these classes/interfaces, you need to tell Eclipse where to find the library by adding a reference to it. You do this by clicking **Project**, **Properties**. The Properties window will appear.

Click **Java Build Path** on the right pane and then click the **Libraries** tab on the left. Then, click **Add External JARs** and navigate to select the jar file. If the referenced types are in another project, click the **Projects** tab and add the required project.

Debugging Code

A powerful feature offered by many IDE's is support for debugging. In Eclipse, you can step through a program line by line. The steps for debugging a program are as follows.

1. Add a breakpoint. You do this by clicking on the line on your code and click **Run**, **Toggle Line Breakpoint**.
2. Execute the program by clicking **Run**, **Debug As**, **Java Application**.

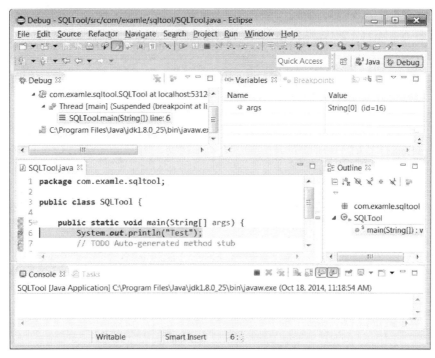

Figure E.8: The Debug Perspective

Debugging requires the Debug perspective be open. After clicking **Java Application** in Step 2, a window will appear that asks you if you want to switch to the Debug perspective. Click **Yes**, and you will see the Debug perspective like that in Figure E.8.

A useful view that appears is the **Variables** view. It displays the list of variables in your program and lets you inspect their values.

To continue, click the **Run** menu and select whether to step into, step over, resume, or terminate the program.

Useful Shortcuts

There are many useful shortcuts that can speed up development. In my opinion, the top six shortcuts are

1. Type **main** in a class definition and press **Ctrl+space** to create the **main** method.
2. Type **syso** in a method and press **Ctrl+space** to add **System.out.println()**.
3. Press **Ctrl+Shift+F** in a class definition to format the code.
4. Press **Ctrl+F11** to run a class.
5. Press **F11** to start debugging a class.
6. Press Ctrl+Shift+O to automatically import types and remove unused imports. For example, if you type **Scanner** in a method and press **Ctrl+Shift+O**, Eclipse will import the **java.util.Scanner** class to the class.

Answers

Chapter 1: Getting Started

1. What is a compiler?

A compiler is a computer program that converts program source code into an executable file or an intermediate format such as bytecode.

2. How is Java different from traditional programming?

In traditional programming, the source code is compiled into an executable file that is native to the target operating system. Therefore, the executable can only run on Windows or Linux. In Java, the source code is compiled into bytecode, which can only be run by a Java Virtual Machine (JVM). Since JVMs are available in many operating systems, the same bytecode can run on multiple operating systems, hence the term cross-platform or platform-independence.

3. What is bytecode?

Bytecode is a set of instructions that can run on a virtual machine. The concept of bytecode is used in Java and other programming frameworks such as Microsoft's .NET Framework.

4. What is the difference between the JRE and the JDK?

The JRE is needed to run a Java program. It contains the Java Virtual Machine and the Java core libraries. The JDK is required for developing Java programs. The JDK includes a compiler and other tools as well as the JRE.

5. If you had saved the code in Listing 1.1 using a different name, such as **whatever.java**, would it have compiled?

Yes, since it is not a public class. However, you should name your Java file the same as the class name.

6. If you had used a file extension other than java when saving the code in Listing 1.1, for example as **MyFirstProgram.txt**, would it have compiled?

No, a Java source file must have **java** extension.

7. Are these valid Java class names: **FirstJava**, **scientificCalculator**, **numberFormatter**?

They all are valid Java class names. However, by convention the first letter of a Java class name should be capitalized. In addition, if a class name consists of multiple words, the first letter of each word should be in upper case. Therefore, instead of **scientificCalculator**, you should call it **ScientificCalculator**. Instead of **numberFormatter**, it should be **NumberFormatter**.

8. How do you write to the console?

By using **System.out.print()** or **System.out.println()**. The latter adds an end-of-line character to the output.

9. Write a Java class named **HelloWorld** that will print "Hello World" when run.

Create a **HelloWorld.java** file with the following content.

```
class HelloWorld {

    public static void main(String[] args) {
        System.out.println("Hello World");
    }

}
```

Chapter 2: Language Fundamentals

1. What does ASCII stand for?

ASCII stands for American Standard Code for Information Interchange.

2. Does Java use ASCII characters or Unicode characters?

Java uses both ASCII characters and Unicode characters. It uses ASCII characters for almost all input elements, except comments, identifiers, and the contents of characters and strings. Java uses Unicode characters for comments, identifiers and the contents of characters and strings.

3. What is a reference type variable, and what is a primitive type variable?

A reference type variable holds the reference (address) of an object, a primitive type variable is used to store a primitive.

4. How are constants implemented in Java?

By using the **final** keyword.

5. What is an expression?

An expression is a legal combination of Java operators and operands that gets evaluated.

6. You need to assign the British pound symbol to a **char** but you do not have the £ key on your keyboard. How do you do this if you know the Unicode code for it is 00A3?

By escaping the Unicode code like so:

```
char britishPound = '\u00A3';
```

7. Name at least ten operators in Java.

- unary minus operator (-).
- increment operator (++)
- decrement operator (--)
- logical complement operator (!)
- bitwise complement operator (~)
- addition operator (+)
- subtraction operator (-)
- modulus operator (%)
- AND conditional operator (&&)
- OR conditional operator (||)
- left shift operator (<<)

8. What is the ternary operator in Java?

A ternary operator operates on three operands. The ? : operator is the only ternary operator in Java.

9. What is operator precedence?

The operator precedence indicates which operation is performed first in the presence of multiple operators in an expression.

10.Consider the following code. What are the values of result1 and result2? Why the difference?

```
int result1 = 1 + 2 * 3;
int result2 = (1 + 2) * 3;
```

1 + 2 * 3 = 7, because the * operator has higher precedence over the + operator so 2 * 3 is evaluated first and its result is added to 1.

(1 + 2) * 3 = 9, because the parentheses have the highest precedence so (1 + 2) is evaluated first.

11. Name two types of Java comments.

Traditional comments and end-of-line comments.

Chapter 3: Statements

1. What is the difference between an expression and a statement?

An expression is a legal combination of Java operators and operands that gets evaluated. A statement is an instruction to do something.

2. How do you escape from the following **while** loop?

```
while (true) {
    // statements
}
```

You can escape from a **while** loop using the **break** statement. For example:

```
while (true) {
    // statements
    if (expression) {
        break;
    }
}
```

3. Is there any difference between using the postfix increment operator and the prefix increment operator as the update statement of a **for** loop?

```
for (int x = 0; x < length; x++)

for (int x = 0; x < length; ++x)
```

No. Both **for** statements have the same effect.

4. What will be printed on the console if the code below is executed:

```
int i = 1;
switch (i) {
case 1 :
    System.out.println("One player is playing this game.");
case 2 :
    System.out.println("Two players are playing this game.");
    break;
default:
    System.out.println("You did not enter a valid value.");
}
```

This will be printed because there is no break after case 1.

```
One player is playing this game.
Two players are playing this game.
```

5. Write a class that uses **for** to print all even numbers from 1 to 9.

```
package app03;
public class ForDemo1 {

    public static void main(String[] args) {

        for (int i = 2; i < 9; i+=2) {

            System.out.println(i);

        }

    }

}
```

6. Write a class that uses **for** to print all even numbers between two integers, *a* and *b*, including *b* if *b* is an even number.

Since you do not know if *a* is even or odd, you do not know if you can use *a* to initialize the variable of the for statement. Therefore, you cannot use the same technique as in the previous assignment. However, you can inquiry if a number is even by checking the modulus after dividing the number by two. If the modulus is zero, then it is an even number.

```
package app03;
public class ForDemo2 {

    public static void main(String[] args) {

        int a = ...;
        int b = ...;
        for (int i = a; i <= b; i++) {
            if (i % 2 == 0) {
                System.out.println(i);
            }
        }
    }
}
```

7. Same as before, but print the numbers in descending order.

```
package app03;
public class ForDemo3 {

    public static void main(String[] args) {
        int a = 10;
        int b = 16;
        for (int i = b; i >= a; i--) {
            if (i % 2 == 0) {
                System.out.println(i);
            }
        }
    }
}
```

Chapter 4: Objects and Classes

1. Name at least three element types that a class can contain.

Constructors, methods and fields.

2. What are the differences between a method and a constructor?

A constructor is used to construct an object. A method is used to perform an action. A constructor does not have a return value, and, as you will see in Chapter 7, "Inheritance," methods are inherited but constructors are not.

3. Does a class in a class diagram display its constructors?

No.

4. What does **null** mean?

A null reference variable is not referencing any object.

5. What do you use the **this** keyword for?

To refer to the current object from a method or a constructor.

6. When you use the == operator to compare two object references, do you actually compare the contents of the objects? Why?

No. Applying the equal operator == to reference variables compare the addresses to objects, not the contents of the objects.

7. What is variable scope?

Variable scope refers to the accessibility of a variable.

8. What does "out of scope" mean?

Technically, a variable that has been destroyed or no longer accessible.

9. How does the garbage collector decide which objects to destroy?

By checking if the object is still being referenced.

10. What is method overloading?

Having more than one method with the same name in the same class.

11. Create a class whose fully-qualified name is **com.example.Tablet** to model an Android tablet. The class must have three private fields, **weight** (int), **screenSize** (float) and **wifiOnly** (boolean). Access to the fields must be through pairs of public **get** and **set** methods, i.e. **getWeight/setWeight**, **getScreenSize/setScreenSize** and **isWifiOnly/setWifiOnly**. The class must also have one constructor, a no-argument constructor.

Because the fully-qualified name is **com.example.Tablet**, the class name must be Tablet and the package name **com.example**. Here is the class definition.

```
package com.example;

public class Tablet {

    private int weight;
    private float screenSize;
    private boolean wifiOnly;

    public int getWeight() {
        return weight;
    }

    public void setWeight(int weight) {
        this.weight = weight;
    }
```

```
    public float getScreenSize() {
        return screenSize;
    }

    public void setScreenSize(float screenSize) {
        this.screenSize = screenSize;
    }

    public boolean isWifiOnly() {
        return wifiOnly;
    }

    public void setWifiOnly(boolean wifiOnly) {
        this.wifiOnly = wifiOnly;
    }
}
```

For a boolean field, the **get*XXX*** method is often named **is*XXX***. Note that since the class only has one constructor, which is the default constructor, the compiler will create one automatically in the absence of an explicit constructor.

12. Create a **TabletTest** class in the package **com.example.test** and instantiate the **Tablet** class. Print the value of the fields (by calling its get methods) right after instantiation. Then, set the field values and print them again.

Here is the **TabletTest** class. Since it is in a different package than **Tablet**, it must import the **Tablet** class.

```
package com.example.test;
import com.example.Tablet;

public class TabletTest {

    public static void main(String[] args) {
        Tablet tablet = new Tablet();
        System.out.println("Weight: " + tablet.getWeight());
        System.out.println("Screen Size: " + tablet.getScreenSize());
        System.out.println("Wifi Only: " + tablet.isWifiOnly());
        System.out.println("=== Setting tablet field values ...");

        tablet.setWeight(600);
        tablet.setScreenSize(8.9F);
        tablet.setWifiOnly(true);

        System.out.println("Weight: " + tablet.getWeight());
        System.out.println("Screen Size: " + tablet.getScreenSize());
        System.out.println("Wifi Only: " + tablet.isWifiOnly());
    }
}
```

Here is what you will see on the console when the class is run. Initially, all fields will have default values.

```
Weight: 0
```

```
Screen Size: 0.0
Wifi Only: false
=== Setting tablet field values ...
Weight: 600
Screen Size: 8.9
Wifi Only: true
```

Chapter 5: Core Classes

1. What does it mean when people say that **Strings** are immutable objects?

The state of an immutable object cannot change. **String** objects are immutable and manipulating a **String** object, such as calling its **trim** method, returns a new **String** instance.

2. How do you receive user input without **Scanner**? And, how do you do it with **Scanner**?

Prior to JDK 5, use **System.in.read()** as in the **getUserInput** method below

```
public String getUserInput() {
    StringBuilder sb = new StringBuilder();
    try {
        char c = (char) System.in.read();
        while (c != '\r' && c != '\n') {
            sb.append(c);
            c = (char) System.in.read();
        }
    } catch (IOException e) {
    }

    return sb.toString();
}
```

In Java 5 and later, use the **java.util.Scanner** class.

```
Scanner scanner = new Scanner(System.in);
String input = scanner.nextLine();
scanner.close();
```

3. What is varargs?

Varargs is a feature in Java 5 and later that allows methods to have a variable length of argument list.

4. Create a **com.example.Car** class that has these private fields: **year (int)**, **make (String)**, **model (String)**. Make **Car** immutable by providing only get methods. Fields are set by passing values to the constructor.

You can make a class immutable by making all its fields private and providing **get** methods without **set** methods.

```
package com.example;
```

```
public class Car {
    private int year;
    private String make;
    private String model;

    public Car(int year, String make, String model) {
        this.year = year;
        this.make = make;
        this.model = model;
    }

    public int getYear() {
        return year;
    }

    public String getMake() {
        return make;
    }

    public String getModel() {
        return model;
    }
}
```

5. Create a **com.example.test.CarTest** class to instantiate Car and print its field values by calling the get methods.

Here is the **CarTest** class.

```
package com.example.test;
import com.example.Car;

public class CarTest {

    public static void main(String[] args) {
        Car car = new Car(2015, "Ford", "Escape");
        System.out.println("Year: " + car.getYear());
        System.out.println("Make: " + car.getMake());
        System.out.println("Model: " + car.getModel());
    }

}
```

6. Create a utility/helper class named **StringUtil** in **com.example.util**. This class should have two static methods, **getFileName** and **getFileExtension**. Both methods receive a file path and returns a file name or file extension, respectively. Create a **com.example.test.StringUtilTest** class to test the methods.

Assume that a file path may contain \ or / that separates a directory from a file or a subdirectory. An extension is optional and is the substring after the last period. For instance, in the file path "C:\temp\document.txt", the file name will be document.txt and the extension will be txt.

Here is the **StringUtil** class.

```
package com.example.util;

public class StringUtil {

    public static String getFileName(String path) {
        int lastIndex1 = path.lastIndexOf("\\");
        int lastIndex2 = path.lastIndexOf("/");
        int index = lastIndex1 < lastIndex2? lastIndex2 : lastIndex1;
        if (index != -1) {
            return path.substring(index + 1);
        } else {
            return path;
        }
    }

    public static String getFileExtension(String path) {
        int lastIndex = path.lastIndexOf(".");
        if (lastIndex != -1) {
            return path.substring(lastIndex + 1);
        } else {
            return "";
        }
    }
}
```

Here is the **StringUtilTest** class.

```
package com.example.test;

import com.example.util.StringUtil;
public class StringUtilTest {

    public static void main(String[] args) {
        String path1 = "C:\\temp\\document.txt";
        String fileName = StringUtil.getFileName(path1);
        String extension = StringUtil.getFileExtension(path1);
        System.out.println("File Name: " + fileName);
        System.out.println("Extension: " + extension);

        String path2 = "/home/users/jayden/README";
        fileName = StringUtil.getFileName(path2);
        extension = StringUtil.getFileExtension(path2);
        System.out.println("File Name: " + fileName);
        System.out.println("Extension: " + extension);

        String path3 = "Help.html";
        fileName = StringUtil.getFileName(path3);
        extension = StringUtil.getFileExtension(path3);
        System.out.println("File Name: " + fileName);
        System.out.println("Extension: " + extension);

        String path4 = "setup";
        fileName = StringUtil.getFileName(path4);
        extension = StringUtil.getFileExtension(path4);
```

```
        System.out.println("File Name: " + fileName);
        System.out.println("Extension: " + extension);
    }

}
```

7. Show how you can use the **java.util.StringTokenizer** class to print the number of tokens in a **String** and each individual token.

     StringTokenizer is easy to use.

```
package app05;
import java.util.StringTokenizer;

public class StringTokenizerDemo {

    public static void main(String[] args) {
        String text = "Energy   efficient car";
        StringTokenizer tokenizer = new StringTokenizer(text);
        System.out.format("Number of tokens: %d\n",
                tokenizer.countTokens());
        System.out.println("Tokens:");
        while (tokenizer.hasMoreTokens()) {
            System.out.println("- " + tokenizer.nextToken());
        }
    }
}
```

Running the class prints this on the console.

```
Number of tokens: 3
Tokens:
- Energy
- efficient
- car
```

Chapter 6: Arrays

1. What is an array?

     A Java feature to group primitives or objects of the same type. An array has a fixed size.

2. How do you resize an array?

     You cannot resize an array, but you can create another array and copy the contents of the first array to the new one.

3. How do you create an array and pass it to a method without first assigning it to a variable?

     Use this syntax:

```
new type[] { elements }
```

For example:

```
method1(new int[] { 1, 2, 3, 10 });
```

4. Write a **com.example.app06a.ArrayUtil** class that contains two static methods, **min** and **max**. Both methods receive an array of **int**s and returns the smallest and largest element, respectively.

Below is the **ArrayUtil** class. It comes with a **main** method to test the **min** and **max** methods.

```
package com.example.app06;

public class ArrayUtil {
    public static int min(int[] numbers) {
        int smallest = Integer.MAX_VALUE;
        for (int i = 0; i < numbers.length; i++) {
            int element = numbers[i];
            if (element < smallest) {
                smallest = element;
            }
        }
        return smallest;
    }

    public static int max(int[] numbers) {
        int largest = Integer.MIN_VALUE;
        for (int element : numbers) {
            if (element > largest) {
                largest = element;
            }
        }
        return largest;
    }

    public static void main(String[] args) {
        int[] numbers = {-1, 9, -100, 1000, 255};
        System.out.printf("Min: %d\n", min(numbers));
        System.out.printf("Max: %d\n", max(numbers));
    }
}
```

Running the **ArrayUtil** class prints this on the console.

```
Min: -100
Max: 1000
```

Chapter 7: Inheritance

1. Does a subclass inherit its superclass's constructors?

No.

2. Why is it legal to assign an instance of a subclass to a superclass variable?

Because of the "is a" relationship between a subclass and a superclass. An instance of a subclass can therefore be assigned to a superclass variable.

3. What is the difference between method overriding and method overloading?

Method overloading is a feature in many OOP language that allows methods in the same class to have the same name. Method overriding is an OOP feature that enables you to change the behavior of a method in a subclass. In method overloading, the signatures of the methods must not be the same. In method overriding, the signatures of the methods must be identical.

4. Why is it necessary for an instance of a subclass to be accompanied by an instance of each parent?

So that you can call a method in the parent class and not overridden in the subclass.

5. Write a public **com.example.transport.Car** class that adds a public void method called **run** and overrides **toString()**. **run** prints the return value of **toString()**. Write another public class called **SUV** in the same package. **SUV** extends **Car** and overrides its **run** and **toString** methods. The **run** class of SUV should print the return value of the parent's **toString** method and its own **toString** method. Next, add a **main** method in **SUV** that creates an **SUV** object and calls its **run** method.

Here are the **Car** and **SUV** classes. Since they are public classes, the **Car** class must be saved in a **Car.java** file and **SUV** in a **SUV.java** file.

```
package com.example.transport;

public class Car {

    @Override
    public String toString() {
        return "I am a car.";
    }

    public void run() {
        System.out.println(toString());
    }
}


package com.example.transport;

public class SUV extends Car {
```

```
    @Override
    public String toString() {
        return "I can carry stuff.";
    }

    @Override
    public void run() {
        System.out.println(super.toString());
        System.out.println(toString());
    }

    public static void main(String[] args) {
        SUV suv = new SUV();
        suv.run();
    }
}
```

If you run the **SUV** class, you will see this printed on the console.

```
I am a car.
I can carry stuff.
```

Chapter 8: Error Handling

1. What is the advantage of the **try** statement?

The **try** statement provides an easy way to handle runtime errors. The alternative to this strategy is a series of if statements that tests each of the conditions that might lead to an error. Using the latter is harder and may make your code hard to read.

2. Can a **try** statement be used with **finally** and without **catch**?

Yes.

3. What is try-with-resources?

This is a feature added to JDK 7 to automatically close a resource after use. try-with-resource can be used with any resource whose class implements **java.lang.AutoCloseable**.

4. Write a utility class called **Util** (part of **com.example.app08**) that has a static method named **addArray** for adding two arrays of the same length. The signature of **addArray** is as follows.

```
public static long[] addArray(int[] array1, int[] array2)
        throws MismatchedArrayException,
        java.lang.NullPointerException
```

The method throws a **MismatchedArrayException** if the lengths of both arguments are not the same. The toString method of the exception class must return this value:

```
Mismatched array length. The first array's length is length1. The
second array's length is length2
```

where **length1** is the length of the first array and **length2** the length of the second array.

The method throws a **NullPointerException** if one of the arrays is null.

First, notice from the **addArray** method signature that **MismatchedArrayException** is written without package information, which means it is in the same package as the containing class. This is therefore a user-defined exception class. Second, the class must somehow have access to the lengths of both arrays, which means you have to pass the two arguments to **MismatchedArrayException**.

The **MismatchedArrayException** class is as follows.

```
package com.example.app08;

public class MismatchedArrayException extends Exception {

    private int[] array1;
    private int[] array2;

    public MismatchedArrayException(int[] array1, int[] array2) {
        this.array1 = array1;
        this.array2 = array2;
    }

    @Override
    public String toString() {
        return "Mismatched array length. "
                + "The first array's length is " + array1.length
                + ". The second array's length is "
                + array2.length;
    }
}
```

And here is the **Util** class.

```
package com.example.app08;

import java.util.Arrays;

public class Util {

    public static long[] addArrays(int[] array1, int[] array2)
            throws MismatchedArrayException,
            NullPointerException {

        if (array1 == null || array2 == null) {
            throw new NullPointerException(
                    "One of the arrays is null");
        }

        if (array1.length != array2.length) {
            throw new MismatchedArrayException(array1, array2);
```

```
        }
        int length = array1.length;
        long[] result = new long[length];
        for (int i = 0; i < length; i++) {
            result[i] = (long) array1[i] + array2[i];
        }
        return result;
    }

    public static void main(String[] args) {
        int[] array1 = {100, 1000, 10000, Integer.MAX_VALUE};
        int[] array2 = {10, 100, 1000, Integer.MAX_VALUE};
        int[] array3 = {1, 2};
        try {
            long[] result = addArrays(array1, array2);
            System.out.println(Arrays.toString(result));
        } catch (NullPointerException e) {
            System.out.println(e);
        } catch (MismatchedArrayException e) {
            System.out.println(e);
        }

        try {
            long[] result = addArrays(array1, array3);
            Arrays.toString(result);
        } catch (NullPointerException e) {
            System.out.println(e);
        } catch (MismatchedArrayException e) {
            System.out.println(e);
        }
    }
}
```

Running the **Util** class gives you the following message on the console.

```
[110, 1100, 11000, 4294967294]

Mismatched array length. The first array's length is 4. The second
array's length is 2
```

Chapter 9: Working with Numbers

1. What can you do with the **java.lang.Math** class's static methods?

   Simple and complex mathematical operations as well as random number generation.

2. Are wrapper classes still useful since boxing and unboxing happen automatically in Java?

   Yes. Some classes, such as those in the Collection framework, only deal with objects and not primitives. In addition, wrapper classes posses methods that can be used for parsing and formatting.

3. Explain why you should not use doubles or floats to perform monetary calculations. What should you use instead?

Due to bit representation of floats and doubles, they are not precise. You should use **java.math.BigDecimal**.

4. Write a class called **RangeRandomGenerator** that can generate random numbers between two integers that you specify when instantiating the class.

The class is printed below.

```
package com.example;

public class RangeRandomGenerator {

    private int from;
    private int to;
    private int range;
    /*
     * Returns a random number between 'from' and 'to' (inclusive)
     */

    public int generate() {
        double random = Math.random();
        return (int) (from + random * range);
    }

    public RangeRandomGenerator(int from, int to) {
        this.from = from;
        this.to = to;
        this.range = this.to - this.from + 1;
    }

    public static void main(String[] args) {
        RangeRandomGenerator generator =
                new RangeRandomGenerator(5, 20);
        for (int i = 0; i < 10; i++) {
            System.out.println(generator.generate());
        }
    }
}
```

Chapter 10: Interfaces and Abstract Classes

1. Why is it more appropriate to regard an interface as a contract than as a implementation-less class?

Because thinking of an interface as a class without implementation misses the big picture. An interface defines methods that both the service provider and its client must

Java: A Beginner's Tutorial (Fourth Edition)

agree on.

2. What is a base class?

A concrete class that provides default implementations of an interface.

3. What is an abstract class?

A class that provides partial implementation. An abstract cannot be instantiated and must be extended by another class.

4. Is a base class the same as an abstract class?

Base classes and abstract classes look similar but their reasons for existence are different, albeit similar.

5. Create an interface named **Calculator** in **com.example** with three methods, **add**, **subtract** and **multiply**. All methods take two **int** arguments and return a **long**.

Here is the interface.

```
package com.example;

public interface Calculator {

    long add(int a, int b);
    long subtract(int a, int b);
    long multiply(int a, int b);

}
```

6. Write an implementation of **Calculator** called **ScientificCalculator** and implement all the methods.

Here is the implementing class.

```
package com.example;

public class ScientificCalculator implements Calculator {

    @Override
    public long add(int a, int b) {
        return a + b;
    }

    @Override
    public long subtract(int a, int b) {
        return a - b;
    }

    @Override
    public long multiply(int a, int b) {
        return a * b;
    }
}
```

Chapter 11: Polymorphism

1. In your own words, describe polymorphism.

The ability of the JVM to invoke the correct method implementation when a superclass variable is assigned an instance of a subclass.

2. In what situations is polymorphism most useful?

When the type of object is not known at compile time.

Chapter 12: Enums

1. How do you write an enum?

You use the enum keyword to define an enum, which can be part of a class or it can stand alone. For the latter, you write it as you would a class.

2. Why are enums safer than static final fields?

Enums are safer than static final fields as enumerated values because they can restrict values. On the other hands, with static final fields you use **int**s and can assign any **int**.

3. Write an abstract **Car** class that has two fields, name (of type **String**) and **fuelEfficiency** (of type FuelEfficiency given in Listing 12.4) and methods for calculating the minimum and maximum gas usage for a given distance (in miles). Next, write three child classes, **EfficientCar**, **AcceptableCar** and **GasGuzzler**. The constructor of each of this suclasses takes a name and sets the **fuelEfficiency** field. Finally, write a class to test it.

All the classes are given below in a single file named **FuelEfficiencyTest**.

```
package com.example.test;

import com.example.FuelEfficiency;

abstract class Car {

    protected String name;
    protected FuelEfficiency fuelEfficiency;

    public double calculateMinGasUsage(int miles) {
        int mpg = fuelEfficiency.getMax();
        return (double) miles / mpg;
    }

    public double calculateMaxGasUsage(int miles) {
        int mpg = fuelEfficiency.getMin();
        return (double) miles / mpg;
    }
```

```
        public String getName() {
            return this.name;
        }

}

class EfficientCar extends Car {
    public EfficientCar(String name) {
        this.name = name;
        this.fuelEfficiency = FuelEfficiency.EFFICIENT;
    }
}

class AcceptableCar extends Car {
    public AcceptableCar(String name) {
        this.name = name;
        this.fuelEfficiency = FuelEfficiency.ACCEPTABLE;
    }
}

class GasGuzzler extends Car {
    public GasGuzzler(String name) {
        this.name = name;
        this.fuelEfficiency = FuelEfficiency.GAS_GUZZLER;
    }
}

public class FuelEfficiencyTest {

    public static void main(String[] args) {
        Car[] cars = new Car[3];
        cars[0] = new EfficientCar("2015 Jupiter CX");
        cars[1] = new AcceptableCar("2015 SoSo");
        cars[2] = new GasGuzzler("2015 Guzzly");
        int miles = 1000;

        for (Car car : cars) {
            System.out.printf("To drive %d miles in a \"%s\",%n"
                    + "you need between %.2f and %.2f gallons "
                    + "of gasoline.%n%n",
                    miles, car.name,
                    car.calculateMinGasUsage(miles),
                    car.calculateMaxGasUsage(miles));
        }
    }
}
```

Running the **FuelEfficiencyTest** class prints this on the console.

```
To drive 1000 miles in a "2015 Jupiter CX",
you need between 18.18 and 30.30 gallons of gasoline.

To drive 1000 miles in a "2015 SoSo",
```

```
you need between 31.25 and 50.00 gallons of gasoline.

To drive 1000 miles in a "2015 Guzzly",
you need between 52.63 and 1000.00 gallons of gasoline.
```

Chapter 13: Working with Dates and Times

1. What were the two core classes in the old Date-Time API?

   java.util.Date and **java.util.Calendar**.

2. Why is the old Date-Time API being phased out?

   The core classes are hard to use.

3. What are the new packages for the new Date-Time API?

   java.time, **java.time.chrono**, **java.time.format**, **java.time.temporal** and **java.time.zone**.

4. What are the main classes in the core package?

   Instant, LocalDate, LocalTime, LocalDateTime, ZonedDateTime, Period, Duration.

5. What are the two static methods for creating a **LocalDate, LocalDateTime** and **ZonedDateTime**?

   now and **of**.

6. What is the difference between **Period** and **Duration**?

   Period is date-based, **Duration** is time-based.

7. What is the easiest way to time an operation?

   By creating **Instant**s using the static method **now** right before and after the operation and calculate the **Duration** between the two.

8. How do you get a **Set** of all timezone identifiers?

   By calling the static method **getAvailableZoneIds** of the **ZoneId** class.

9. What is the date-time formatter class in the new Date and Time API?

   java.time.format.DateTimeFormatter.

Chapter 14: The Collections Framework

1. Name at least seven types in the Collections Framework.

   Collection, List, Set, Queue, ArrayList, Vector, Comparator, Map, HashMap, Hashtable.

2. What is the different between **ArrayList** and **Vector**?

ArrayList is unsynchronized, **Vector** is synchronized.

3. Why is **Comparator** more powerful than **Comparable**?

Comparator is more powerful than **Comparable** because with **Comparator** you can compare objects in more than one way.

4. Write a method to convert an array of **String**s to a resizable **List**.

The method is called **arrayToList** and written as a member of a **ListUtil** class.

```
package com.example;

import java.util.ArrayList;
import java.util.List;

public class ListUtil {

    public static List arrayToList(String[] array) {
        List list = new ArrayList();
        for (String s : array) {
            list.add(s);
        }
        return list;
    }

    public static void main(String[] args) {
        String[] names = {"Ariana", "April", "Sydney"};
        List list = ListUtil.arrayToList(names);
        list.add("Julie");
        for (Object name : list) {
            System.out.println(name);
        }
    }
}
```

Chapter 15: Generics

1. What are the main benefits of generics?

Generics impose stricter type checking at compile time and eliminates most type castings.

2. What is a parameterized type?

A parameterized type is a generic type.

3. What is type inference?

Type inference is a language feature that enables the compiler to determine the type parameter(s) for a generic method from the corresponding declaration.

Chapter 16: Input Output

1. What is an I/O stream?

   An I/O stream connects Java code to a data reservoir.

2. Name four abstract classes that represent streams in the **java.io** package.

   InputStream, **OutputStream**, **Reader**, **Writer**.

3. What is object serialization?

   Storing objects to persistent storage, such as a file.

4. What is the requirement for a class to be serializable?

   The class must implement **java.io.Serializable**.

Chapter 17: Annotations

1. What is an annotation type?

   An annotation type is a type of annotation objects. Technically, an annotation type is a special type of interface. Annotations are instances of annotation types.

2. What is a meta-annotation?

   An annotation type for annotation annotations.

3. What were the standard annotation types fist included in Java 5?

   Override, **Deprecated** and **SuppressWarnings**.

Chapter 18: Inner Classes

1. What is a nested class and what is an inner class?

   A nested class is a class declared within the body of another class or interface. An inner class is a type of nested class, a non-static one.

2. What can you use nested classes for?

   You can use nested classes to completely hide an implementation. Anonymous classes provide for a shorter way of writing event listeners.

3. What is an anonymous class?

   A class that has no name.

Chapter 19: Lambda Expressions

1. Why add lambda expressions to Java?

    They can make certain constructs shorter and more expressive.

2. What are lambda expressions also known as?

    Closures.

3. What is a function interface?

    An interface with exactly one abstract method that does not override a method of **java.lang.Object**.

4. What is a method reference?

    A reference to a method or constructor that can be passed to a method in lieu of a lambda expression.

5. What is the operator used in the method reference?

    The double colon operator (::).

6. What are the four classes in java.util for handling null pointer exceptions?

    Optional, **OptionalInt**, **OptionalLong** and **OptionalDouble**.

Chapter 20: Working with Streams

1. What is a Stream?

    A pipe for transferring data.

2. What are the four main types of streams?

    Stream, **IntStream**, **LongStream** and **DoubleStream**.

3. What are reduction operations?

    Operations that reduce the elements in a stream to a single value or element.

4. When do you use a parallel stream?

    When you have a resource-intensive task that can be split into different threads.

Chapter 21: Java Database Connectivity

1.Name the four steps to accessing a database and manipulating the data in it.

    Load the JDBC driver, create a **Connection** object, create a **Statement** or **PreparedStatement** object, and optionally obtain a **ResultSet** object.

2.Name the five most important types in the **java.sql** package.

    Driver, **DriverManager**, **Connection**, **Statement**, **ResultSet**.

3.What pattern can you use to hide the complexity of JDBC-related code?

    The Data Access Object (DAO) pattern.

Chapter 22: Swing Basics

1. Why is studying AWT still relevant today?

    Because Swing still rely on the AWT, among others for layout management and event handling. In addition, Swing components are descendants of AWT components and Swing application will often use AWT classes such as Font, Color, Dimension, etc.

2. What is the AWT class that represents a component?

    java.awt.Component.

3. What is the easiest way to construct a **Color** object?

    By invoking one of the java.awt.Color class's static final fields.

4. What is the only non-menu child component that can be added to a **Jframe**?

    javax.swing.JRootPane.

5. What is the significance of using **SwingUtilities.invokeLater** to construct Swing GUI?

    To make sure that Swing GUI will be constructed by the event-dispatching thread.

6. What are the three top-level Swing containers?

    JApplet, JFrame, JDialog.

Chapter 23: Swinging Higher

1. What is a layout manager?

    A layout manager is a component in a container that is responsible for resizing and positioning the child components of the container.

2. Name at least four types of layout managers.

    BorderLayout, FlowLayout, GridLayout, BoxLayout.

3. What is a source object in event-handling?

    An object that raises the event.

4. Name at least four Swing events.

    Action event, window event, mouse event, key event.

5. What is the advantage of writing your listener as an anonymous class?

An anonymous class does not need a name and its code is tightly integrated with the definition of the component that raises the event.

Chapter 24: Applets

1. What are the life cycle methods of an applet?

   init, **start**, **stop**, **destroy**.

2. How do you pass parameters to an applet?

   By using the param tag within the applet tag in the HTML file.

3. Is **JApplet** an applet or a **JFrame**?

   A **JApplet** is an applet because **JApplet** is a subclass of **java.applet.Applet**. However, **JApplet** is also a member of the Swing API that has similar functionality as **JFrame**.

Chapter 25: Introduction to JavaFX

1. What is the class that is a template for all JavaFX applications?

   javafx.application.Application.

2. What is the top-level container window in JavaFX?

   javafx.stage.Stage.

3. What is a node?

   Basically, a UI component.

4. What is the best way to style JavaFX UI components?

   By using CSS.

Chapter 26: JavaFX with FXML

1. What is FXML?

   FXML is an XML-based markup language for constructing JavaFX user interface (UI). Using FXML in JavaFX applications is a great way of separating the presentation layer and the business logic.

2. What is a controller class?

A controller is a Java class that implements **javafx.fxml.Initializable**. A controller contains event-handlers and bound fields.

Chapter 27: Java Threads

1. What is a thread?

The smallest unit of processing.

2. What does the **synchronized** modifier do?

Protecting a critical section so that only one thread at a time can access an object's critical sections.

3. What is a critical section?

A code segment that guarantees only one thread at a time have access to a shared resource.

4. Where do you write a scheduled task for a **java.util.Timer**?

In a subclass of **java.util.TimerTask**.

5. What is the difference between **java.util.Timer** and **javax.swing.Timer**.

java.util.Timer is a general purpose timer, **javax.swing.Timer** is a more precise timer that can only be used in Swing applications.

Chapter 28: Concurrency Utilities

1. What are atomic variables?

Classes in the **java.util.concurrent.atomic** package that can perform atomic operations.

2. How do you obtain an **ExecutorService** instance?

By calling one of these static methods in the **java.util.concurrent.Executors** class: **newSingleThreadExecutor, newCacheThreadPool, newFixedThreadPool**.

3. What is a **Callable** and what is a **Future**?

A **Callable** is a task that returns a value and may throw an exception. A **Future** represents the result of an asynchronous computation.

4. Name one of the standard implementations of the **Lock** interface.

java.util.concurrent.locks.ReentrantLock.

Chapter 29: Internationalization

1. What is the approach to internationalizing applications with plenty of static contents?

   Create different versions of the parts with static contents.

2. How do you isolate textual elements of a Java application?

   By creating a different properties file for every locale.

3. What are the two classes used in internationalization and localization?

   java.util.Locale and **java.util.ResourceBundle**.

Chapter 30: Java Networking

1. Why are there several layers of protocols in computer networking?

   Because it is very hard to deal with data streams directly at the hardware level.

2. What are the components of a URL?

   The protocol, the host, the port, and the path.

3. What is the class that represents URLs?

   java.net.URL.

4. What is a socket?

   A socket is an endpoint of a network connection. A socket enables an application to read from and write to the network. Two software applications residing on two different computers can communicate with each other by sending and receiving byte streams over a connection.

5. What is the difference between a socket and a server socket?

   A server socket is used in a server application and its primary task is to wait for connections. For each connection obtained, a server socket creates a socket to communicate with the remote computer making the connection.

Chapter 31: Security

1. What is a policy file?

   A policy file is a text file with the **policy** extension that lists all the permissions granted to the application that is run with the security manager turned on.

2. Why is symmetric cryptography not suitable for use on the Internet?

Symmetric cryptography is not suitable for the Internet for the following reasons

- Two people exchanging messages must first agree on a key. This is not practical since Internet users are scattered all around the world.
- Each person wants to be able to communicate with many other parties. If symmetric cryptography was used, each person would have to maintain different unique keys, each for a different party.
- Since you do not know the entity you are going to communicate with, you need to be sure that they are really who they claim to be.
- Messages over the Internet pass through many different computers. It is fairly trivial to tap other people's messages. Symmetric cryptography does not guarantee that a third party may not tamper with the data.

3. What is a keystore?

A keystore is a database to store your own public and private keys as well as certificates from third parties.

4. What are the steps to digitally sign an applet?

Steps to digitally signing an applet:

- Package the applet in a jar file using the **jar** tool.
- Sign the jar file using the **jarsigner** tool.

Chapter 32: Java Web Applications

1. What are the three life cycle methods of the **javax.servlet.Servlet** interface?

init, **service**, **destroy**.

2. What's the main difference between the **getWriter** method and the **getOutputStream** method in the **javax.servlet.ServletResponse** interface? Which one of the two do you use more often?

You use the **getWriter** method to obtain a **PrintWriter** for sending text. You call the **getOutputStream** method to get an **OutputStream** for sending binary data. Most of the time you will use **getWriter**.

3. Name four interfaces in **javax.servlet** and three interfaces in **javax.servlet.http**.

Four interfaces in **javax.servlet**: **Servlet, ServletRequest, ServletResponse, ServletConfig**. Three interfaces in **javax.servlet.http**: **HttpServletRequest, HttpServletResponse, HttpSession**.

Chapter 33: JavaServer Pages

1. What are the two problems in Servlet technology that JSP solves?

When sending a response in a servlet, all HTML tags must be enclosed in strings, making sending HTTP response a tedious effort. In addition, all text and HTML tags are hardcoded, causing minor changes to require recompilation.

2. Why is it easier to program JSP than to write servlets?

JSP pages are compiled automatically and reloaded every time they are modified.

Chapter 34: Javadoc

1. What is the difference between doc comments and Java comments in code?

Java comments are for Java programmers to maintain the code. Doc comments are for the users of the API.

Chapter 35: Application Deployment

1. What does JWS stand for?

Java Web Start.

2. What are the steps required to deploy a Java application via JNLP?

Package the application as a jar file and create a jnlp file that describes the jar file.

3. Why does the JRE restrict Java applications downloaded from the Internet?

Because they are untrusted resources.

Index

Made in the USA
Lexington, KY
14 September 2016